1001
Recipes

1001
Recipes
YOU'VE ALWAYS
WANTED TO COOK

COLLINS & BROWN

Published in the United Kingdom in 2015 by Collins & Brown
1 Gower Street
London
WC1E 6HD

An imprint of Pavilion Books Company Ltd

Copyright © Collins & Brown Ltd 2015

All rights reserved. No part of this publication may be copied,
displayed, extracted, reproduced, utilized, stored in a retrieval system
or transmitted in any form or by any means, electronic, mechanical
or otherwise including but not limited to photocopying, recording, or
scanning without the prior written permission of the publishers.

ISBN 978-1-910231-34-0

A CIP catalogue record for this book is available from the British
Library.

10 9 8 7 6 5 4 3 2 1

Reproduction by Rival Colour Ltd, UK
Printed and bound by 1010 Printing International Ltd, China

This book can be ordered direct from the publisher at
www.pavilionbooks.com

Compiled and edited by Heather Thomas

Photographers: Martin Brigdale (pages 131, 145, 147, 392); Nicki Dowey (pages 16, 22, 30, 44, 55, 61, 63, 67,
69, 119, 122, 155, 158, 163, 173, 189, 207, 219, 237, 308, 313, 336, 339, 357, 375, 376, 391, 402, 413, 438, 471,
474, 476, 489, 491, 495, 499, 509); Liz and Max Haarala Hamilton (back cover R and pages 265, 544, 547, 551,
553, 555, 557, 559, 561); William Lingwood (page 355); Craig Robertson (pages 203, 204, 254, 257, 359, 433,
449, 469, 472, 473, 481, 485); Lucinda Symons (back cover M and pages 6, 11, 38, 50, 58, 83, 95, 96, 103, 105,
181, 227, 231, 233, 239, 263, 267, 273, 279, 283, 295, 299, 319, 325, 345, 361, 365, 369, 373, 373, 379, 395,
401, 417, 427, 431, 434, 443, 466, 505, 515, 589); Karen Thomas (front cover image, back cover L and pages
89, 125, 170, 185, 388, 405, 407, 410, 440, 455, 520, 523, 525, 527, 529, 531, 533, 537, 566).

CONTENTS

Light meals	6
Easy suppers	58
Meals in minutes	122
One pot suppers	170
Family favourites	204
Entertaining	254
Party food & drinks	308
Barbecues, grills & al fresco	336
Chocolate treats	388
Home baking	410
Desserts	440
Eating lite	476
Food from the freezer	520
Gluten free	544
Basic recipes	564
Index	594

LIGHT MEALS

When you feel like something light and delicious, we've got the right dish for you, whether it's a warming vegetable soup, a healthy salad or a simple egg dish. In this chapter you will find great recipes for sandwiches, toasts, and filled wraps and pittas as well as burgers and pancakes – perfect for brunch, lunch or even a simple supper.

The soups can be made in advance, stored in the fridge and reheated for quick and easy meals during the week, or they can be frozen in individual portions. As well as the classic French onion soup and tomato soup, there are more unusual recipes for cream of Jerusalem artichoke soup and borscht. Some of the soups are so filling that they are a meal in a bowl by themselves – minestrone and smoked haddock chowder both fall into this category.

Eggs always make a nutritious and economical light meal when you're in a hurry, so try our delicious take on French toast, eggs Benedict or a colourful piperade from the Basque area. And if you really don't have time to cook, there's always mushrooms or beans on toast, or even a tangy Welsh rarebit. You'll never be short of ideas.

< American-style Pancakes (page 39)

CALABRESE AND GOAT'S CHEESE SOUP

50g/2oz/4 tbsp butter

2 onions, chopped

2 celery sticks, chopped

1 litre/1¾ pints/4 cups vegetable stock

700g/1½lb calabrese, broken into florets, stalks chopped

1 tbsp olive oil

175g/6oz chevre goat's cheese

salt and ground black pepper

croûtons to serve

1 Melt the butter over a low heat. Add the onions and celery, cover the pan and cook for 5 minutes until tender. Add half the stock and bring to the boil. Add the calabrese and bring back to the boil again. Cover the pan, reduce the heat and simmer for 15 minutes or until the calabrese is tender.

2 Let the soup cool a little, then add the goat's cheese and blitz in batches in a blender or food processor until smooth. Return to the pan and add the remaining stock. Reheat gently and season to taste with salt and pepper.

3 Ladle the soup into bowls, scatter with croûtons and serve immediately.

preparation 10 minutes   cooking time 20 minutes

Serves 6

SUMMER TOMATO SOUP WITH BASIL

1 large onion, thinly sliced

25g/1oz/2 tbsp butter

3 tbsp plain (all-purpose) flour

1 litre/1¾ pints/4 cups vegetable stock

1kg/2¼lb ripe tomatoes

2 tbsp tomato paste

a few fresh basil leaves, torn, plus extra to garnish

6 tbsp crème fraîche (optional)

salt and ground black pepper

1 Fry the onion in the butter until golden brown. Add the flour and cook gently for 1 minute, stirring. Remove the pan from the heat and gradually stir in the stock. Bring to the boil slowly and continue to cook, stirring, until thickened.

2 Halve the tomatoes, scoop out the seeds into a sieve placed over a bowl. Press the seeds to remove all the tomato pulp and juice; discard the seeds and put the juice aside.

3 Stir in the tomato purée, herbs, tomatoes and juice. Season to taste. Cover and simmer gently for 30 minutes.

4 Cool slightly, then blitz the soup in a blender. Strain through a sieve into a clean pan and reheat gently.

5 Ladle the soup into six soup bowls and swirl in the crème fraîche (optional). Garnish with basil and serve.

preparation 15 minutes   cooking time 40 minutes

Serves 6

BORSCHT

1kg/2¼lb raw beetroot (beets)
2 onions, chopped
1.2 litres/2 pints/5 cups vegetable stock
2 medium potatoes, diced
juice of 1 lemon
salt and ground black pepper
4 tbsp soured cream and chopped fresh dill to garnish

1 Peel the beetroot and grate them coarsely. Put them in a large pan with the onions, vegetable stock and seasoning. Bring to the boil, then reduce the heat, cover the pan and simmer gently for 30 minutes. Add the potatoes and continue simmering for 15 minutes
2 Strain, discarding the vegetables, then add the lemon juice to the soup. Check the seasoning. Leave to cool, then cover and chill in the fridge.
3 Serve the soup well chilled, garnished with a swirl of soured cream and some chopped dill.

preparation 10 minutes   cooking time 45 minutes plus chilling

Serves 4

LENTIL AND BACON SOUP

175g/6oz/1 cup red lentils
1.7 litres/3 pints/7½ cups vegetable stock
1 onion, chopped
2 carrots, diced
200g/7oz lean bacon rashers (slices), diced
1 x 200g/7oz can tomatoes
2 large potatoes, diced
salt and ground black pepper
6 tsp pesto
grated Cheddar cheese to garnish

1 Put the lentils in a large pan with the stock. Add the onion, carrots, bacon, tomatoes and seasoning.
2 Bring to the boil, then reduce the heat, cover the pan and simmer for 1 hour or until the lentils are soft.
3 Add the potatoes and cook for 20 minutes or until tender.
4 Leave the soup to cool slightly, then sieve or blitz in a blender or food processor until smooth.
5 Reheat the soup in the pan. Check the seasoning and serve in six soup bowls, topped with the pesto and sprinkled with grated Cheddar cheese.

preparation 10 minutes   cooking time 1 hour 40 minutes

Serves 6

FRENCH ONION SOUP

50g/2oz/4 tbsp butter
1 tbsp olive oil
1kg/2¼lb onions, sliced
1 tsp sugar
4 garlic cloves, crushed
2 tbsp plain (all-purpose) flour
200ml/7fl oz/¾ cup white wine
1.4 litres/2½ pints/6¼ cups hot vegetable stock
salt and ground black pepper
8–12 thick slices French bread (baguette)
50g/2oz Gruyère cheese, grated

1 Heat the butter and oil in a large pan. Add the onions and cook over a very low heat, stirring frequently, until really soft and golden brown – this takes at least 30 minutes. Add the sugar, garlic and flour and cook, stirring, for 1 minute.
2 Turn up the heat, add the wine and cook until reduced by half. Add the hot stock and seasoning. Bring to the boil, then reduce the heat and simmer gently, uncovered, for about 30 minutes.
3 Remove from the heat and allow to cool a little. Blitz half of the soup in a blender or food processor until smooth, then stir back into the remaining soup in the pan.
4 Preheat the grill (broiler). Lightly toast the bread slices on both sides. Reheat the soup and check the seasoning.
5 Pour the soup into four heatproof bowls. Place 2–3 slices of toasted bread on each portion and sprinkle with grated cheese. Pop the bowls under the hot grill until the cheese melts and turns golden brown. Serve immediately.

preparation 30 minutes   cooking time 1 hour

Serves 4

SMOKED HADDOCK CHOWDER

25g/1oz/2 tbsp butter
2 onions, finely chopped
125g/4oz smoked streaky bacon rashers (slices), chopped
3 garlic cloves, finely chopped
600ml/1 pint/2½ cups milk
450g/1lb potatoes, diced
2 celery sticks, thinly sliced
140g/5oz frozen sweetcorn kernels, drained
450g/1lb skinless smoked haddock fillet, roughly flaked
salt and ground black pepper

1 Heat the butter in a large, wide saucepan. Add the onions and cook for 5 minutes until tender. Add the bacon and garlic and cook for 5 minutes.
2 Add the milk and 600ml/1 pint/2½ cups boiling water. Season with salt and pepper, then add the potatoes, celery and sweetcorn and cook for 10–15 minutes until the vegetables have softened.
3 Stir in the flaked smoked haddock. Cover the pan and cook for 10 minutes or until the fish is just cooked.
4 Ladle the soup into four bowls and serve hot.

preparation 15 minutes   cooking time 35 minutes

Serves 4

PARSNIP SOUP WITH SPICY CHORIZO

50g/2oz/4 tbsp butter
1 onion, chopped
2 celery sticks, chopped
675g/1½lb parsnips, cubed
1 tsp paprika
1.1 litres/2 pints/5 cups vegetable stock
450ml/¾ pint/1¾ cups milk
125g/4oz chorizo sausage, diced
salt and ground black pepper
8 tsp natural yogurt
chopped fresh parsley to serve

1 Melt the butter in a large pan over a low heat. Add the onion and celery and cook for 5 minutes until tender. Add the parsnips and paprika and cook gently, stirring occasionally, for 15 minutes or until the vegetables begin to soften.
2 Add the stock and milk and bring to the boil, then reduce the heat and simmer for 25 minutes or until the vegetables are tender. Season to taste with salt and pepper.
3 Add most of the chorizo. Allow the soup to cool a little, then blitz in batches in a blender or food processor until smooth. Check the seasoning and return the soup to the pan.
4 Reheat gently and serve in eight bowls with a swirl of yogurt, sprinkled with the remaining chorizo and the parsley.

preparation 20 minutes   cooking time 1 hour

Serves 8

LEEK AND POTATO SOUP

2 tbsp vegetable oil
1 onion, finely chopped
1 garlic clove, crushed
450g/1lb leeks, chopped
225g/8oz potatoes, cubed
1.2 litres/2 pints/5 cups hot vegetable stock
150ml/¼ pint/scant ⅔ cup crème fraîche

1 Heat the oil in a pan over a gentle heat, then cook the onion for 10–15 minutes until soft. Add the garlic and cook for 1 minute. Add the leeks and cook for 5–10 minutes until softened. Stir in the potatoes.
2 Add the hot stock and bring to the boil. Reduce the heat and simmer for 20 minutes until the potatoes are tender.
3 Allow the soup to cool a little, then blitz in batches in a blender or food processor until smooth.
4 Return the soup to the pan and stir in the crème fraîche. Reheat gently and serve hot.

preparation 10 minutes   cooking time 45 minutes

Serves 4

SPICY SWEET POTATO SOUP

2 tbsp olive oil
1 large onion, finely chopped
2 garlic cloves, crushed
1 fresh red chilli, diced
450g/1lb butternut squash, peeled and chopped
3 sweet potatoes, peeled and chopped
225g/8oz tomatoes, diced
1.7 litres/3 pints/7½ cups hot vegetable stock
chopped fresh coriander (cilantro) to serve

1 Heat the oil in a large pan over a gentle heat and fry the onion for 10 minutes or until soft. Add the garlic and chilli and cook for 2 minutes.
2 Add the squash, sweet potatoes and tomatoes and cook for 5 minutes. Add the hot stock, then cover the pan and bring to the boil. Reduce the heat and simmer for 15 minutes or until the vegetables are soft.
3 Allow the soup to cool a little, then blitz in batches in a blender or food processor until smooth. Reheat gently and serve hot, sprinkled with coriander.

Serves 8

preparation 20 minutes   cooking time 35 minutes

CARROT AND CORIANDER SOUP

2 tbsp olive oil
1 large onion, chopped
675g/1½lb carrots, sliced
1 tsp ground coriander
1.1 litres/2 pints/5 cups vegetable stock
150ml/¼ pint/scant ⅔ cup half-fat crème fraîche
salt and ground black pepper
1 bunch fresh coriander (cilantro) , chopped

1 Heat the oil in a large pan. Add the onion and carrots, then cover the pan and cook gently for about 10 minutes until the vegetables begin to soften but not colour.
2 Stir in the ground coriander and cook for 1 minute. Add the stock and bring to the boil. Season with salt and pepper, then reduce the heat and simmer, covered, for 20 minutes, until the vegetables are tender.
3 Allow the soup to cool a little, then blitz in batches in a blender or food processor until smooth. Return to the pan and stir in the crème fraîche. Reheat gently without boiling.
4 Stir in the chopped coriander and serve immediately.

Serves 6

preparation 15 minutes   cooking time 30 minutes

COURGETTE AND LEEK SOUP

1 tbsp olive oil

2 large leeks, sliced

450g/1lb potatoes, diced

900g/2lb courgettes (zucchini), thinly sliced

1.6 litres/2¾ pints/6¾ cups hot vegetable stock

1 bunch spring onions (scallions), sliced

125g/4oz Cheddar cheese, grated

salt and ground black pepper

1 Heat the oil in a large pan. Add the leeks and potatoes and cook over a low heat for 10 minutes. Add the courgettes and cook, stirring occasionally, for 5 minutes until all the vegetables have softened.

2 Add the hot stock and spring onions and bring to the boil. Season with salt and pepper, reduce the heat and simmer gently for 20 minutes.

3 Allow the soup to cool a little, then blitz in batches in a blender or food processor until thick and smooth. Pour into a clean pan and reheat gently.

4 Serve the soup in warmed shallow soup bowls, sprinkled with the grated Cheddar cheese.

preparation 15 minutes **cooking time** 35–40 minutes

Serves 8

QUICK PEA SOUP

1 tbsp olive oil

1 small onion, chopped

450g/1lb frozen peas, thawed

600ml/1 pint/2½ cups vegetable stock

125ml/4fl oz/½ cup double (heavy) cream

salt and ground black pepper

1 Heat the olive oil in a pan and add the onion. Cook over a low heat for 10 minutes until softened but not browned. Add the peas and stock.

2 Pour the soup into a food processor or blender and blitz in batches until smooth.

3 Return to the pan and bring to the boil. Reduce the heat and simmer for 5 minutes. Stir in the cream and season with salt and pepper to taste. Serve immediately.

preparation 2 minutes plus thawing **cooking time** 20 minutes

Serves 4

JERUSALEM ARTICHOKE SOUP

450g/1lb Jerusalem artichokes
2 tbsp olive oil
1 small onion, diced
1 garlic clove, crushed
1 litre/1¾ pints/4 cups vegetable stock
125ml/4fl oz/½ cup white wine
4 tbsp single (light) cream
freshly grated nutmeg to taste
salt and ground black pepper
snipped fresh chives to garnish

1 Scrub the Jerusalem artichokes thoroughly, then pat dry with kitchen paper. Slice thinly.
2 Heat the oil in a large pan, add the onion and cook gently for 10 minutes until tender and golden.
3 Add the garlic and cook for 1 minute. Add the artichokes, stock and wine and stir well. Bring to the boil, then reduce the heat, cover the pan and simmer for 15 minutes or until the artichokes are cooked and tender.
4 Add the cream and nutmeg. Blitz the soup in batches in a blender or food processor until smooth, then pass through a sieve into a clean pan.
5 Reheat the soup gently. Season to taste before ladling into warmed bowls and sprinkling with chives.

preparation 15 minutes   cooking time 30 minutes

Serves 6

CURRIED PARSNIP SOUP

2 tbsp olive oil
1 onion, sliced
900g/2lb parsnips, diced
1 tsp curry powder
½ tsp ground turmeric
1.2 litres/2 pints/5 cups vegetable stock
150ml/¼ pint/scant ⅔ cup milk
salt and ground black pepper
chopped fresh coriander (cilantro) to garnish

1 Heat the oil in a large pan, add the onion and cook gently for 5 minutes or until starting to soften. Add the parsnips and cook for 3 minutes.
2 Stir in the curry powder and turmeric. Cook for 2 minutes.
3 Add the stock, season to taste with salt and pepper and bring to the boil. Reduce the heat, cover the pan and simmer for 30 minutes until the parsnips are tender.
4 Allow to cool a little, then blitz in batches in a blender or food processor until smooth. Return the soup to the pan and stir in the milk. Reheat gently without boiling.
5 Ladle the soup into warmed bowls, sprinkle with coriander and serve.

preparation 20 minutes   cooking time 45 minutes

Serves 6

MINESTRONE WITH PESTO

2 tbsp olive oil
1 onion, finely chopped
2 carrots, chopped
1 celery stick, chopped
2 garlic cloves, crushed
a few sprigs of fresh thyme
1 litre/1¾ pints/4 cups hot vegetable stock
1 x 400g/14oz can chopped tomatoes
1 x 400g/14oz can borlotti or cannellini beans, drained
125g/4oz/1 cup soup pasta
salt and ground black pepper
4 tsp fresh pesto
4 slices toasted bread

1 Heat the oil in a large pan and add the onion, carrots and celery. Cook for 10 minutes over a low heat until softened. Add the garlic and thyme and cook for 2–3 minutes.

2 Add the hot stock, tomatoes and beans to the pan and then bring to the boil. Reduce the heat and simmer gently for about 20 minutes.

3 Add the soup pasta and cook for a further 10 minutes until the vegetables are tender and the pasta is cooked. Check the seasoning and remove the thyme.

4 Serve the soup in four warmed bowls topped with a small spoonful of fresh pesto and slices of toasted bread.

preparation 10 minutes **cooking time** 50 minutes

Serves 4

PUMPKIN AND SQUASH SOUP

900g/2lb pumpkin, peeled and cubed

750g/1lb 10oz butternut squash, peeled and cubed

1 red onion, chopped

1 garlic clove, chopped

4 tbsp olive oil

600ml/1 pint/2½ cups vegetable stock

600ml/1 pint/2½ cups milk

salt and ground black pepper

a pinch each of ground nutmeg and cloves

crème fraîche to garnish

1　Preheat the oven to 220°C/425°F/Gas 7.
2　Put the pumpkin, squash, red onion and garlic in a roasting pan and drizzle with the oil. Season with salt and pepper and bake in the oven for 30 minutes until golden and tender.
3　Meanwhile, heat the stock in a large pan. Add the roasted vegetables and the milk. Heat through and season to taste.
4　Blitz the soup in batches in a blender or food processor until smooth. Reheat gently and stir in the ground spices.
5　Serve the soup immediately in warmed bowls, garnished with a swirl of crème fraîche.

preparation 20 minutes　cooking time 40 minutes

Serves 4

LEEK AND KALE SOUP

2 tbsp olive oil

450g/1lb leeks, sliced

4 streaky bacon rashers (slices), chopped

450g/1lb kale, chopped

1 litre/1¾ pints/4 cups chicken stock

2 tbsp cornflour (cornstarch)

150ml/¼ pint/scant ⅔ cup milk

salt and ground black pepper

2 tbsp chopped fresh parsley

1　Heat the oil in a pan, add the leeks and bacon and cook for 5 minutes. Remove from the pan and set aside. Add the kale to the pan and cook for 5 minutes.
2　Return the leeks and bacon to the pan with the stock and season to taste with salt and pepper. Cover the pan and bring to the boil, then reduce the heat and simmer gently for 30 minutes.
3　Allow the soup to cool a little, then blitz in batches in a blender or food processor until smooth.
4　Return the soup to a clean pan. Blend the cornflour to a smooth paste with the milk. Add to the pan and reheat gently, stirring all the time, until it thickens.
5　Ladle the soup into warmed bowls and serve, sprinkled with chopped parsley.

preparation 10 minutes　cooking time 50 minutes

Serves 6

MIXED VEGETABLE SOUP

2 tbsp olive oil
1 onion, diced
450g/1lb potatoes, diced
125g/4oz cooked ham, diced
1 garlic clove, chopped
100g/3½oz leek, chopped
leaves stripped from 2 fresh thyme sprigs
1.2 litres/2 pints/5 cups hot vegetable stock
125g/4oz spring greens (collards), shredded
salt and ground black pepper

1. Heat the oil in a large pan and add the onion, potatoes, ham, garlic, leek and thyme. Season to taste with salt and pepper. Cover the pan and cook gently over a low heat, stirring occasionally, for 15 minutes until the vegetables are tender.
2. Add the hot stock and bring to the boil, then reduce the heat and simmer and simmer for 20 minutes.
3. Blitz half the soup in a blender or food processor until smooth. Pour back into the pan with the remaining soup.
4. Reheat the soup gently, add the spring greens and simmer for 5 minutes. Ladle into warmed bowls and serve.

preparation 15 minutes   cooking time 45 minutes

Serves 4

WINTER LENTIL SOUP

2 tbsp olive oil
1 onion, finely chopped
2 garlic cloves, crushed
1 celery stick, chopped
225g/8oz swede (rutabaga), peeled and diced
2 carrots, diced
225g/8oz/1⅓ cups red lentils
1 x 400g/14oz can tomatoes
1 litre/1¾ pints/4 cups hot vegetable stock
bunch of fresh parsley, chopped
salt and ground black pepper

1. Heat the oil in a pan. Add the onion, garlic, celery, swede and carrots and cook gently over a low heat for 10–15 minutes until the vegetables have softened.
2. Stir in the lentils, tomatoes and hot stock. Season to taste with salt and pepper. Cover the pan and bring to the boil, then reduce the heat and cook, uncovered, for 25 minutes or until the lentils are soft, the vegetables are tender and the soup has thickened.
3. Stir in the parsley and ladle the soup into warmed bowls.

preparation 15 minutes   cooking time 45 minutes

Serves 6

QUICK SPICY BROTH WITH TOFU

1 tbsp Thai red curry paste

200ml/7fl oz/¾ cup reduced-fat coconut milk

600ml/1 pint/2½ cups hot vegetable stock

200g/7oz tofu, cubed

2 pak choi (bok choy), chopped

a handful of sugarsnap peas

4 spring onions (scallions), chopped

1 Heat the Thai red curry paste in a pan for 2 minutes. Add the coconut milk and hot stock and bring to the boil.
2 Add the tofu, pak choi, sugarsnap peas and spring onions. Reduce the heat and simmer, uncovered, for 2 minutes.
3 Ladle the soup into four warmed bowls and serve.

preparation 10 minutes   **cooking time** 6–8 minutes

Serves 4

CREAM OF PARSLEY SOUP

25g/1oz/2 tbsp butter

2 large bunches of fresh parsley, roughly chopped

2 onions, chopped

1 small fennel bulb, diced

2 tbsp plain (all-purpose) flour

2 litres/3½ pints/8 cups vegetable stock

150ml/¼ pint/scant ⅔ cup crème fraîche

salt and ground black pepper

fresh parsley sprigs to garnish

1 Melt the butter in a large pan and add the parsley, onions and fennel. Cover the pan and cook gently for 10 minutes or until the vegetables are soft, stirring occasionally.
2 Stir in the flour and then add the stock. Season to taste and bring to the boil, then reduce the heat, cover the pan and simmer for 30 minutes.
3 Allow the soup to cool a little, then blitz in batches in a blender or food processor until smooth. Set aside to cool completely, then chill.
4 Reheat the soup and stir in the crème fraîche. Serve in warmed bowls, garnished with sprigs of parsley.

preparation 15 minutes plus chilling   **cooking time** 45 minutes

Serves 8

MUSHROOM AND MISO SOUP

1 tbsp olive oil
1 onion, thinly sliced
175g/6oz shiitake mushrooms, thinly sliced
450g/1lb baby spinach leaves
1.2 litres/2 pints/5 cups vegetable stock
4 tbsp miso

1 Heat the oil in a large pan over a low heat. Add the onion and cook gently for 15 minutes or until soft.
2 Add the mushrooms and cook for 5 minutes, then stir in the spinach and hot stock. Heat gently for 3 minutes.
3 Stir in the miso but take care that the soup does not boil. Ladle the soup into warmed bowls and serve immediately.

preparation 5 minutes   **cooking time** 25 minutes

Serves 6

SPRING VEGETABLE SOUP

1 tbsp olive oil
1 onion, chopped
1 leek, chopped
5 small carrots, chopped
1.2 litres/2 pints/5 cups hot vegetable stock
2 courgettes (zucchini), chopped
1 bunch of asparagus, chopped
450g/1lb broad beans, shelled
salt and ground black pepper
fresh pesto to serve

1 Heat the oil in a large pan. Add the onion, leek and carrots and cook gently over a low heat for 5 minutes until the vegetables start to soften.
2 Add the hot stock, cover the pan and bring to the boil. Add the courgettes, asparagus and broad beans, then reduce the heat to a simmer and cook for 10 minutes until all the vegetables are tender. Season to taste.
3 Ladle the soup into warmed bowls and stir a little pesto into each bowl before serving.

preparation 10 minutes   **cooking time** 20 minutes

Serves 4

CREAMY CELERY SOUP

25g/1oz/2 tbsp butter
1 tbsp olive oil
1 onion, chopped
6 celery sticks, finely sliced
1 garlic clove, crushed
900ml/1½ pints/3¾ cups hot chicken stock
150ml/¼ pint/scant ⅔ cup crème fraîche
salt and ground black pepper

1 Melt the butter in a pan and add the oil. Add the onion and cook for 10 minutes or until tender. Add the celery and garlic and cook for 5 minutes.
2 Add the hot stock and milk. Season with salt and pepper, then cover the pan and bring to the boil. Reduce the heat and simmer for 10–15 minutes until the celery is tender.
3 Allow the soup to cool a little, then blitz in batches in a blender or food processor until smooth. Return to the pan and reheat gently. Stir in the crème fraîche.
4 Ladle the soup into warmed bowls and serve immediately.

preparation 10 minutes   cooking time 30–40 minutes

Serves 4

HERB AND PASTA SOUP

1.7 litres/3 pints/7½ cups chicken stock
150g/5oz dried vermicelli soup pasta
3 medium (US large) eggs
juice of 1 large lemon
6 tbsp chopped fresh parsley
1 bunch chopped fresh chives
salt and ground black pepper

1 Bring the stock to the boil in a large pan. Add the pasta and cook for 5 minutes or according to the pack instructions.
2 Beat the eggs in a bowl, then add the lemon juice and 1 tbsp cold water. Slowly stir in two ladlefuls of the hot stock. Add to the pan with the rest of the stock. Warm through gently over a very low heat for 3 minutes.
3 Add the chopped herbs and season with salt and pepper. Serve the soup immediately in warmed bowls.

preparation 10 minutes   cooking time 15 minutes

Serves 6

CREAM OF WATERCRESS SOUP

2 tbsp olive oil

1 onion, finely chopped

675g/1½lb potatoes, cubed

600ml/1 pint/2½ cups milk

900ml/1½ pints/3⅔ cups vegetable stock

2 large bunches watercress, trimmed and chopped

a pinch of grated nutmeg

salt and ground black pepper

watercress sprigs to garnish

cheesy croûtes to serve

1 Heat the oil in a large pan, add the onion and cook gently for 10 minutes or until soft. Add the potatoes and cook for 2 minutes. Add the milk and stock. Bring to the boil, then reduce the heat and simmer for 20 minutes or until tender.
2 Stir in the chopped watercress, then blitz in batches in a blender or food processor until smooth.
3 Pour the soup into a clean pan. Season with salt and pepper to taste and a pinch of nutmeg. Heat through gently.
4 Serve the soup in bowls, garnished with watercress sprigs and topped with a cheesy croûte.

preparation 15 minutes   cooking time 30 minutes

Serves 6

BUTTERNUT SQUASH SOUP

1 medium butternut squash

2 tbsp olive oil plus extra to brush

1 onion, finely chopped

1 carrot, diced

2 tsp curry powder

1 tbsp grated fresh root ginger

1.2 litres/2 pints/5 cups vegetable stock

leaves stripped from 1 fresh sprig rosemary

salt and ground black pepper

1 Peel the butternut squash, cut in half and remove the seeds. Cut into 1cm/¾in slices. Brush with oil and place in the grill (broiling) pan. Grill (broil) for 8–10 minutes until soft.

2 Meanwhile, heat the oil in a pan, add the onion and carrot and cook over a low heat for 10 minutes or until soft. Stir in the curry powder and ginger and cook for 2 minutes, then add the stock and rosemary. Bring to the boil, then reduce the heat, cover the pan and simmer gently for 15 minutes.

3 Allow to cool slightly, then pour the soup into a blender or food processor. Add the squash and blitz until smooth. Season to taste with salt and pepper.

4 Return the soup to the pan to reheat. Serve immediately in six warmed bowls.

Serves 6

preparation 15 minutes   cooking time 30 minutes

LETTUCE SOUP

25g/1oz/2 tbsp butter

450g/1lb butterhead (romaine) lettuce leaves, shredded

1 large bunch of spring onions (scallions), chopped

1 tbsp plain (all-purpose) flour

600ml/1 pint/2½ cups vegetable stock

150ml/¼ pint/scant ⅔ cup milk

salt and ground black pepper

1 Melt the butter in a pan, add the lettuce and spring onions and cook gently for 10 minutes until softened.

2 Stir in the flour and cook, stirring, for 1 minute. Add the stock and bring to the boil. Reduce the heat, cover the pan and simmer for 45 minutes.

3 Allow the soup to cool a little, then blitz in batches in a blender or food processor until smooth. Return to the pan and stir in the milk. Reheat and season to taste. Serve the soup in warmed bowls.

Serves 4

preparation 5 minutes   cooking time 1 hour 15 minutes

COURGETTE AND BEAN SOUP

2 tbsp olive oil

1 onion, finely chopped

2 garlic cloves, crushed

1 tsp mild curry powder

450g/1lb courgettes (zucchini), sliced

350g/12oz potatoes, diced

1 x 400g/14oz can butter (lima) beans, drained and rinsed

1 x 400g/14oz can borlotti beans, drained and rinsed

1.5 litres/2½ pints/6¼ cups vegetable stock

salt and ground black pepper

snipped fresh chives to garnish

1 Heat the oil in a pan. Add the onion and garlic and cook over a low heat for 5 minutes. Add the curry powder and cook, stirring, for 1 minute. Add the courgettes and potatoes and cook for 2 minutes.

2 Add the beans and stock and bring to the boil. Reduce the heat, cover the pan and then simmer gently for 25 minutes, stirring occasionally, until the potatoes are tender. Season to taste with salt and pepper.

3 Serve the soup in warmed bowls sprinkled with chives.

preparation 10 minutes   cooking time 30 minutes

Serves 6

HOT-AND-SOUR SOUP

1 tbsp vegetable oil

340g/12oz boneless, skinless chicken breast, cut into strips

5cm/2in piece fresh root ginger, peeled and grated

4 spring onions (scallions), diced

1 tbsp Thai red curry paste

75g/3oz/⅓ cup basmati rice

1.2 litres/2 pints/5 cups hot chicken stock

200g/7oz green beans, sliced

juice of 1 lime

4 tbsp chopped fresh coriander (cilantro) to garnish

1 Heat the oil in a deep pan over a medium heat. Add the chicken and cook for 5 minutes until browned. Add the ginger and spring onions and cook for 2 minutes. Stir in the Thai red curry paste and cook for 2 minutes.

2 Stir in the rice and cook for 1 minute. Add the hot stock and bring to the boil. Reduce the heat, cover the pan and simmer gently for 20 minutes.

3 Add the green beans and cook for 5 minutes or until the rice is tender. Add the lime juice and stir well.

4 Serve the soup in warmed bowls sprinkled with coriander.

preparation 20 minutes   cooking time 30–35 minutes

Serves 4

LENTIL AND COCONUT SOUP

4 tbsp coconut oil

350g/12oz potatoes, diced

1 large onion, chopped

2 carrots, cut into matchsticks

2 garlic cloves, crushed

1 tbsp green Thai curry paste

900ml/1½ pints/3¾ cups hot vegetable stock

300ml/½ pint/1¼ cups reduced-fat coconut milk

225g/8oz/1⅓ cups green lentils

grated zest and juice of 1 lime

salt and ground black pepper

fresh coriander (cilantro) sprigs to garnish

1 Heat the oil in a large pan. Add the potatoes and cook gently for 5 minutes, stirring occasionally, until golden. Remove with a slotted spoon and set aside.
2 Add the onion and carrots to the pan and cook gently over a low heat for 10 minutes until tender. Add the garlic and green Thai curry paste and cook for 2 minutes. Add the hot stock, coconut milk and lentils and bring to the boil.
3 Reduce the heat, cover the pan and simmer gently for 20 minutes or until the lentils are tender but not mushy.
4 Add the potatoes and the lime juice and zest and season to taste. Cook for 5 minutes until the potatoes are tender.
5 Serve the soup in warmed bowls, garnished with coriander.

preparation 20 minutes   cooking time 40 minutes

Serves 4

CHICKEN AND VEGETABLE BROTH

1 tbsp olive oil

450g/1lb boneless, skinless chicken breast, cubed

2 garlic cloves, crushed

1 red onion, finely chopped

1 litre/1¾ pints/4 cups hot chicken stock

225g/8oz each green beans, broccoli, sugarsnap peas and asparagus, chopped

dash of Tabasco or chilli sauce

1 Heat the oil in a large pan over a medium heat. Add the chicken, garlic and red onion and cook for 10 minutes or until the chicken is browned all over.
2 Add the hot stock and bring to the boil. Add the vegetables, reduce the heat and simmer gently for 5 minutes or until the chicken is cooked right through.
3 Season the broth with a dash of Tabasco or chilli sauce and serve immediately in warmed bowls.

preparation 10 minutes   cooking time 15 minutes

Serves 4

THAI CHICKEN NOODLE SOUP

1 tbsp olive oil

450g/1lb boneless skinless chicken breast, shredded

2 garlic cloves, roughly chopped

1 tbsp green Thai curry sauce

1 lemongrass stalk, finely sliced

1 tsp grated fresh root ginger

1 litre/1¾ pints/4 cups hot chicken stock

75g/3oz rice noodles

150g/5oz mangetout, halved

125g/4oz bean sprouts

bunch of spring onions (scallions), sliced

2 tbsp Thai fish sauce

grated zest and juice of 1 lime

chopped fresh coriander (cilantro) to garnish

1. Heat the oil in a large pan over a medium heat. Add the chicken, garlic, green Thai curry sauce, lemongrass and ginger and cook, stirring frequently, for 5 minutes until the chicken is turning golden brown.
2. Add the hot stock and bring to the boil. Simmer gently for 5 minutes or until the chicken is cooked through.
3. Add the rice noodles and cook for 1 minute, then add the mangetout and cook for 2 minutes.
4. Add the bean sprouts, spring onions, fish sauce and the lime zest and juice. Simmer gently until heated through.
5. Divide the soup among four warmed bowls. Garnish with the coriander and serve immediately.

preparation 20 minutes **cooking time** 20–25 minutes

Serves 4

CHESTNUT SOUP

2 tbsp olive oil

1 large onion, chopped

250g/9oz Brussels sprouts, trimmed

1 litre/1¾ pints/4 cups hot chicken or turkey stock

1 x 400g/14oz can whole chestnuts, drained

2 tbsp chopped fresh parsley plus extra to garnish

salt and ground black pepper

4 tbsp crème fraîche

1. Heat the oil in a large pan, add the onion and cook gently for 5 minutes until tender.
2. Add the sprouts to the pan, cover and cook for 5 minutes, shaking the pan frequently.
3. Pour in the hot stock and bring to the boil. Add the chestnuts and parsley. Reduce the heat, cover the pan and simmer for 30 minutes or until the vegetables are tender.
4. Allow the soup to cool a little, then blitz in batches in a blender or food processor until smooth. Return to the pan and stir in the crème fraîche. Reheat gently.
5. Season to taste and serve in warmed bowls, sprinkled with chopped parsley.

preparation 4 minutes **cooking time** 45 minutes

Serves 4

CREAMY CHICKEN SOUP

2 5g/1oz/2 tbsp butter
1 onion, choppped
2 tbsp plain (all-purpose) flour
150ml/¼ pint/scant ⅔ cup milk
1.2 litres/2 pints/5 cups hot
chicken stock
250g/9oz cooked chicken, diced
1 tsp lemon juice
4 tbsp single (light) cream
salt and ground black pepper

1 Melt the butter in a large pan and add the onion. Cook for 10 minutes over a low heat, stirring occasionally, until soft.
2 Stir in the flour and then add the hot stock, a little at a time, stirring after each addition. Simmer gently for 20 minutes.
3 Stir in the chicken and lemon juice, and season to taste with salt and pepper. Stir in the cream and cook gently over a low heat for 5 minutes.
4 Serve the soup immediately in warmed bowls.

preparation 10 minutes   cooking time 30 minutes

Serves 4

TURKEY AND HAM SOUP

250g/8oz/1⅓ cups green split peas, soaked overnight
2 tbsp olive oil
1 onion, chopped
400g/14oz carrots, cubed
2 garlic cloves, crushed
2 litres/3½ pints/8 cups ham or turkey stock
225g/8oz potatoes, cubed
125g/4oz each cooked turkey and ham, cut into chunks
250g/9oz spring greens (collards) or kale, shredded
salt and ground black pepper
grated Cheddar cheese to seve

1 Drain the split peas and put them in a pan. Cover with cold water and bring to the boil. Reduce the heat and simmer for 10 minutes. Drain well.
2 Heat the oil in a pan, add the onion and carrots and cook for 10 minutes. Add the garlic and cook for 1 minute.
3 Add the split peas and stock to the pan. Bring to the boil, then reduce the heat and simmer for 40 minutes or until the split peas are tender.
4 Add the potatoes and cook for 15 minutes. Season to taste with salt and black pepper.
5 Add the turkey, ham and spring greens or kale and bring to the boil. Reduce the heat and simmer for 3 minutes.
6 Ladle the soup into warmed bowls, sprinkle with grated Cheddar cheese and serve immediately.

preparation 20 minutes plus soaking   cooking time 1 hour 20 minutes

Serves 6

CHICKEN AND BULGUR SOUP

1 tbsp olive oil

1 onion, finely chopped

1 red (bell) pepper, seeded and diced

2 skinless, boneless chicken breasts, cut into strips

1 litre/1¾ pints/4 cups hot chicken stock

100g/3½oz/¼ cup bulgur wheat

2 x 400g/14oz cans cannellini beans, drained

1 x 400g/14oz can chopped tomatoes

2 courgettes (zucchini), chopped

2 tbsp chopped fresh basil

salt and ground black pepper

1 Heat the oil in a large pan. Add the onion and red pepper and cook over a low heat for 10 minutes or until softened. Add the chicken and stir-fry for 3 minutes or until golden.
2 Add the hot stock to the pan and bring to a simmer. Stir in the bulgur wheat and simmer for 15 minutes.
3 Stir in the cannellini beans, tomatoes and courgettes and simmer gently for 5 minutes. Stir in the chopped basil and season to taste with salt and pepper.
4 Divide the soup among four warmed bowls.

preparation 10 minutes cooking time 30 minutes

Serves 4

HOT-AND-SOUR TURKEY SOUP

1 tbsp vegetable oil

340g/12oz skinless turkey breast, cut into strips

1 tbsp grated fresh root ginger

1 red onion, finely chopped

1 tbsp Thai red curry paste

75g/3oz/⅓ cup basmati rice

1.2 litres/2 pints/5 cups hot chicken or turkey stock

200g/7oz mangetouts, sliced

juice of 1 lime

chopped coriander (cilantro) to garnish

1 Heat the oil in a deep pan. Add the turkey and cook over a medium heat for 5 minutes, stirring occasionally, until golden brown.
2 Add the ginger and red onion and cook for 2–3 minutes. Stir in the Thai red curry paste and cook for 1–2 minutes.
3 Add the rice and stir to coat in the curry paste. Pour the hot stock into the pan, stir once and bring to the boil. Reduce the heat and simmer gently, covered, for 20 minutes.
4 Add the mangetouts and simmer gently for 2 minutes, then stir in the lime juice. Serve in four warmed bowls scattered with chopped coriander.

preparation 15 minutes cooking time 40 minutes

Serves 4

SPINACH AND RICE SOUP

2 tbsp olive oil

1 red onion, finely chopped

2 sticks celery, diced

2 garlic cloves, crushed

1 tsp chopped fresh thyme

1 tsp chopped fresh rosemary

1 bay leaf

zest of 1 lemon

2 tsp grated nutmeg

a pinch of cayenne pepper

125g/4oz/½ cup risotto rice

1.2 litres/2 pints/5 cups vegetable stock

450g/1lb baby spinach leaves

4 heaped tsp pesto sauce

salt and ground black pepper

freshly grated Parmesan to serve

1 Heat the oil in a pan. Add the red onion, celery, garlic, herbs, lemon zest and spices, then cook gently, stirring occasionally, over a low heat for 5 minutes.

2 Add the rice and cook for 1 minute, stirring to coat all the rice grains until they are glistening with oil. Add the stock and bring to the boil, then reduce the heat and simmer gently for 20 minutes or until the rice is tender.

3 Stir in the spinach and cook gently for 2 minutes, then season to taste with salt and pepper. Remove and discard the lemon zest and bay leaf.

4 Ladle the soup into four warmed bowls and swirl in the pesto. Sprinkled over the grated Parmesan and serve.

preparation 10 minutes   cooking time 25–30 minutes

Serves 4

PIPERADE

3 tbsp olive oil

1 red onion, finely chopped

2 garlic cloves, crushed

1 red or green (bell) pepper, seeded and chopped

450g/1lb plum tomatoes, diced

dash of balsamic vinegar

8 medium (US large) eggs

4 thin slices proscuitto or Parma ham

salt and ground black pepper

chopped fresh parsley to garnish

1 Heat 2 tbsp oil in a large frying pan over a low heat. Add the onion and garlic and cook gently for 5 minutes. Add the red pepper and cook for 10 minutes until softened.
2 Add the tomatoes and balsamic vinegar, increase the heat and cook for 10 minutes or until they are reduced to a thick pulp. Season to taste with salt and pepper.
3 Lightly whisk the eggs and add to the pan. Stir gently with a wooden spoon until they start to set but are still creamy.
4 Heat the remaining oil in a clean pan and quickly fry the proscuitto or Parma ham until golden brown and crisp.
5 Serve the piperade sprinkled with parsley with the crispy ham on the side.

preparation 20 minutes   **cooking time** 20 minutes

Serves 4

EGGS BENEDICT

2 muffins
4 medium (US large) eggs
1 tsp vinegar
150ml/¼ pint/scant ⅔ cup hollandaise sauce (see page 572)
4 thin slices lean ham or crisp cooked bacon
fresh parsley sprigs to garnish

1 Split the muffins in half and toast lightly on both sides.
2 Poach the eggs by lowering them carefully into a pan of simmering water to which you have added a spoonful of vinegar. Cook gently until the whites are set but the yolks are still runny. Remove them carefully with a slotted spoon on to a sheet of kitchen paper to drain.
3 Gently warm the hollandaise sauce in a small pan.
4 Top each muffin half with a folded slice of ham or bacon, then with a poached egg. Spoon the hollandaise sauce over the top.
5 Garnish each egg with a sprig of parsley and serve.

preparation 15 minutes **cooking time** 10 minutes

Serves 4

EGGS MAYONNAISE

4 medium (US large) eggs, hard-boiled
a few lettuce leaves
150ml/¼ pint/scant ⅔ cup mayonnaise (see page 576)
chopped fresh parsley and cayenne pepper to garnish
baby plum tomatoes to serve

1 Shell the eggs and cut them in half lengthways.
2 Wash and drain the lettuce and arrange on a plate.
3 Place the eggs on the lettuce, cut-side down, and coat with the mayonnaise. Sprinkle with parsley, dust lightly with a little cayenne and serve with baby plum tomatoes.

preparation 10 minutes **cooking time** 10 minutes

Serves 2

BAKED EGGS WITH MUSHROOMS AND SPINACH

2 tbsp olive oil

175g/6oz mushrooms, chopped

250g/9oz fresh spinach, trimmed and roughly chopped

2 medium (US large) eggs

2 tbsp single (light) cream

salt and ground black pepper

a pinch of paprika

1 Preheat the oven to 200°C/400°C/Gas 6.
2 Heat the oil in a large frying pan, add the mushrooms and cook for 1 minute, stirring. Add the spinach and stir until wilted. Season to taste, then divide the mixture between 2 shallow individual ovenproof dishes.
3 Carefully break an egg into the centre of each dish, then spoon the cream over the top.
4 Cook in the oven for 12 minutes or until the eggs are just set – they will continue cooking once they're out of the oven. Dust lightly with paprika and serve.

preparation 10 minutes cooking time 15 minutes

Serves 2

WELSH RAREBIT

225g/8oz Cheddar cheese, grated

25g/1oz/2 tbsp butter

1 tsp English mustard

2 tsp Worcestershire sauce

4 tbsp Guinness or beer

freshly ground black pepper

4 slices bread, crusts removed

salt and ground black pepper

1 Put the cheese, butter, mustard, Worcestershire sauce, beer and black pepper in a pan and place over a low heat. Stir occasionally until the cheese melts and the mixture is smooth and creamy. Season to taste with salt and pepper.
2 Toast the bread under the grill (broiler) on one side only. Turn the slices over and spread the cheese mixture on the untoasted side.
3 Pop back under the grill for 1 minute or until golden brown and bubbling. Serve immediately.

preparation 5 minutes cooking time 6 minutes

Serves 4

FRENCH TOAST

2 medium (US large) eggs

150ml/¼ pint/scant ⅔ cup skimmed milk

a pinch of freshly grated nutmeg or ground cinnamon

4 slices white bread

50g/2oz/¼ cup butter

maple syrup and crisp cooked bacon slices or fresh strawberries to serve

1 Whisk together the eggs, milk and nutmeg or cinnamon in a shallow dish.
2 Dip the slices of bread into the beaten egg, coating them well and soaking up some of the mixture.
3 Heat half the butter in a frying pan over a low heat. When the butter is foaming, fry the egg-coated bread in batches, until golden brown on both sides. Drain on kitchen paper.
4 Serve immediately, drizzled with maple syrup, with crispy bacon or strawberries.

preparation 5 minutes cooking time 10 minutes

Serves 2

SCRAMBLED EGGS WITH SMOKED SALMON

6 large eggs

small bunch of fresh chives, snipped

25g/1oz/2 tbsp butter

100g/3½oz/½ cup soft cheese

125g/4oz smoked salmon, diced

6 slices bread, toasted and buttered

salt and ground black pepper

1 Beat the eggs together in a bowl and season with salt and pepper. Stir in the chives.
2 Melt the butter in a non-stick pan over a low heat. Add the eggs and stir constantly until the mixture thickens.
3 Stir in the soft cheese and cook for 1–2 minutes, until the mixture starts to set, then fold in the smoked salmon. Add a grinding of black pepper
4 Serve immediately with the buttered toast.

preparation 10 minutes cooking time 5 minutes

Serves 6

AVOCADO BLT

225g/8oz lean bacon slices
1 large ripe avocado, halved,
peeled and stoned
juice of ½ lemon
8 large slices bread
50g/2oz/4 tbsp butter, softened
4 tbsp mayonnaise
175g/6oz iceberg lettuce,
shredded
2 large tomatoes, thinly sliced
salt and ground black pepper

1 Grill (broil) the bacon for 3 minutes, turning once, until crisp.
   Transfer to a plate, cover and keep warm.
2 Cut the avocado into slices, across the length, squeeze over
   the lemon juice to prevent browning, cover and set aside.
3 Toast the slices of bread. Butter them and spread 4 slices
   with mayonnaise. Layer the bacon, lettuce, tomatoes and
   avocado on top. Season with salt and pepper and top with
   the remaining 4 slices of buttered toast.
4 Cut each sandwich in half, diagonally. Serve immediately.

preparation 10 minutes   cooking time 5 minutes

Serves 4

STEAK AND RED
ONION SANDWICHES

2 red onions, thinly sliced
3 tbsp olive oil
1 small ciabatta loaf
2 x 125g/4oz thin minute steaks
2 tsp Dijon mustard
a handful of rocket (arugula)
leaves
2 ripe tomatoes, sliced
salt and ground black pepper

1 Put the red onions in a bowl with half of the olive oil and toss
   together to coat.
2 Spread the onion over the base of a foil-lined grill (broiling)
   pan. Grill (broil) for 10 minutes, turning the onions
   occasionally until soft and starting to caramelize. Set aside.
3 Cut the ciabatta in half lengthways and brush the cut
   side with olive oil. Place the two halves under the hot grill
   (broiler) and cook for 3–4 minutes, until warm. Remove,
   wrap in kitchen foil and keep warm.
4 Brush the steaks with olive oil and season with salt and
   pepper. Cook under the hot grill for 3–4 minutes, turning
   once, until cooked to your liking.
5 Spread the two bottom halves of the bread with mustard.
   Add the rocket and tomatoes, then the steak. Pile the onions
   on top, cover with the remaining bread and serve warm.

preparation 5 minutes   cooking time 15–20 minutes

Serves 2

VEGETABLE PITTA POCKETS

4 tbsp olive oil

2 garlic cloves, crushed

salt and ground black pepper

2 courgettes (zucchini), sliced

1 red (bell) pepper, quartered and seeded

1 yellow (bell) pepper, quartered and seeded

1 small aubergine (eggplant), cut into small chunks

4 baby plum tomatoes, halved

4 pitta breads

4 tbsp hummus

a handful or rocket (arugula)

salt and ground black pepper

1 In a bowl, mix together the oil and garlic and season with salt and pepper. Add the courgettes, peppers and aubergine. Toss the vegetables in the oil mixture.
2 Grill (broil) the vegetables for 8–10 minutes, until soft. Transfer to a bowl and add the tomatoes. Season to taste with salt and pepper.
3 Split the pitta breads to form pockets. Spoon a tablespoon of hummus into each one, and divide the grilled vegetables between them. Add the rocket and serve immediately while the vegetables are warm.

preparation 10 minutes cooking time 10–12 minutes

Serves 4

QUICK STEAK AND ROCKET SANDWICHES

50g/2oz/4 tbsp butter, softened

2 tbsp barbecue sauce

1 tbsp wholegrain mustard

4 slices crusty white bread

1 tbsp olive oil

4 thin frying steaks

a large handful of rocket (arugula) or watercress

3 tomatoes, sliced

1 Mix the butter, barbecue sauce and mustard together in a bowl and set aside. Toast the bread.
2 Heat the oil in a large frying pan set over a high heat. When the pan is really hot, add the steaks and cook for 20 seconds–1 minute on each side, depending on how you like them.
3 Spread the toast with the barbecue butter. Add some rocket or watercress and tomato, place a steak on top and serve.

preparation 15 minutes cooking time 2 minutes

Serves 4

CHICKEN AVOCADO WRAPS

250g/9oz cooked skinless chicken breasts, cubed

1 avocado, chopped

a handful of rocket (arugula)

juice of ½ lemon

3 tbsp mayonnaise

4 flour tortillas

4 tbsp tomato salsa

salt and ground black pepper

1 Put the chicken, avocado and rocket in a bowl. Season to taste with plenty of salt and pepper and mix well.
2 In a separate bowl, blend the lemon juice with the mayonnaise. Spread over the tortillas.
3 Divide the chicken mixture among the tortillas. Top with a spoonful of salsa, then roll up or fold over and serve or wrap in clingfilm (plastic wrap) for a packed lunch.

preparation 10 minutes

Serves 4

HOMEMADE MIXED BEANS ON TOAST

1 tbsp olive oil

2 garlic cloves, finely sliced

1 x 400g/14oz can cannellini beans, drained and rinsed

1 x 400g/14oz can chickpeas, drained and rinsed

1 x 400g/14oz can chopped tomatoes

2 tbsp tomato ketchup

4 slices sourdough bread

4 tbsp grated Parmesan

1 Heat the oil in a pan over a low heat, add the garlic and cook for 1 minute, stirring gently.
2 Add the beans, chickpeas and tomatoes, and bring to the boil. Stir in the tomato ketchup, reduce the heat and simmer gently for 10 minutes until thickened.
3 Meanwhile, toast the bread on both sides.
4 Spoon the beans over the toast and sprinkle with grated Parmesan. Serve immediately.

preparation 5 minutes   cooking time 10 minutes

Serves 4

EGGS AND MUSHROOMS ON TOAST

4 large eggs

2 tbsp olive oil

1 red onion, finely diced

2 garlic cloves, crushed

600g/1lb 5oz mushrooms, diced

2 tbsp Marsala or sherry (optional)

4 tbsp chopped fresh parsley

4 slices sourdough bread, toasted

1 Crack the eggs into a wide pan of simmering water. Cook gently for 3–4 minutes until the whites are set and the yolks are still runny. Remove carefully with a slotted spoon and transfer to a shallow dish of warm water.
2 Heat the oil in a large frying pan and cook the red onion and garlic for 10 minutes. Increase the heat, add the mushrooms and cook for 5 minutes. Add the Marsala or sherry, if using, then stir in the parsley.
3 Top each piece of toast with a pile of mushrooms. Lift the eggs out of the water and pat with kitchen paper. Put an egg on each slice of toast and serve immediately.

preparation 20 minutes cooking time 20 minutes

Serves 4

BLT BAGELS WITH HOLLANDAISE SAUCE

3 large bagels, cut in half

25g/1oz/2 tbsp butter, softened

12 streaky bacon rashers (slices)

3 tomatoes, thickly sliced

150ml/¼ pint/scant ⅔ cup hollandaise sauce (see page 572)

a handful of crisp lettuce leaves

ground black pepper

1 Preheat the grill (broiler) to high, then grill (broil) the halved bagels until golden brown. Spread with the butter and cover with kitchen foil to keep warm.
2 Grill the bacon until crisp, then remove and keep warm.
3 Pop the tomatoes under the grill and cook for 1–2 minutes until lightly charred.
4 Put the hollandaise sauce in a small pan and heat gently.
5 Top the warm bagels with a few lettuce leaves, the tomatoes and bacon. Spoon the warm hollandaise sauce over the bacon and season with black pepper. Serve immediately.

preparation 15 minutes cooking time 8 minutes

Serves 6

STUFFED ROASTED PEPPERS

5 tbsp olive oil

4 Romano (bell) peppers, halved, with stalks on and seeded

3 tbsp olive oil

350g/12oz mushrooms, chopped

4 tbsp chopped fresh parsley

8 black olives, pitted and diced

100g/3½oz feta cheese

50g/2oz/1 cup fresh white breadcrumbs

salt and ground black pepper

1 Preheat the oven to 180°C/350°F/Gas 4. Use a little of the olive oil to grease a shallow ovenproof dish and put the peppers in it, side by side.

2 Heat 3 tbsp of the remaining oil in a pan. Add the mushrooms and fry until golden brown and there's no excess liquid left in the pan. Stir in the parsley and olives, then spoon the mixture into the pepper halves.

3 Crumble the feta cheese over the mushrooms. Sprinkle the breadcrumbs over the top, season with salt and pepper and drizzle with the remaining oil.

4 Cook in the oven for 45 minutes or until the peppers are tender and the filling is golden brown. Serve warm.

preparation 20 minutes   cooking time 45 minutes

Serves 8

AMERICAN-STYLE PANCAKES

175g/6oz/1½ cups self-raising (self-rising) flour

1 tsp baking powder

1 tsp bicarbonate of soda (baking soda)

a pinch of salt

50g/2oz/¼ cup caster superfine)sugar

2 medium (US large) eggs, beaten

300ml/½ pint/1¼ cups buttermilk

50g/2oz/4 tbsp butter, melted, plus extra for frying

milk (optional)

bacon and maple syrup to serve

1 In a bowl, sift together the flour, baking powder and bicarbonate of soda with a pinch of salt. Stir in the sugar.
2 Mix the eggs, buttermilk and melted butter and gradually whisk into the flour to make a smooth batter – if it's too thick, add a drop of milk. Leave to stand for 5 minutes.
3 Put a large frying pan over a medium heat. When hot, brush the surface with a little melted butter. Pour about 2 tbsp of the mixture into the pan to form a 10cm (4in) circle. Cook for 2 minutes or until small holes appear on the surface, then flip it over and cook the other side until golden and set.
4 Continue cooking the pancakes in this way in batches until you have used up all the batter.
5 Serve the pancakes warm with crisp bacon drizzled with maple syrup.

Makes 12

preparation 10 minutes cooking time 15 minutes

SKINNY BEAN TACOS

2 x 400g/14oz cans chopped tomatoes

1 x 400g/14oz can cannellini beans, drained and rinsed

1 x 400g/14oz can kidney beans, drained and rinsed

1 x 200g/7oz can sweetcorn, drained

dash of hot chilli sauce

salt and ground black pepper

8 corn taco shells

reduced-fat guacamole and soured cream to serve

1 Put the tomatoes in a pan over a high heat. Bring to the boil, then reduce the heat and simmer for 10 minutes or until thickened. Season with salt and pepper.
2 Add the beans and sweetcorn to the pan and heat through. Add some hot chilli sauce to taste.
3 Warm the taco shells according to the pack instructions.
4 Fill the warm tacos with the bean mixture and top with some guacamole and soured cream. Serve immediately.

Serves 4

preparation 15 minutes cooking time 10 minutes

CHICKPEA AND CORIANDER CAKES

2 x 400g/14oz cans chickpeas, rinsed and drained

2 garlic cloves, crushed

1 small red onion, finely chopped

1 chilli, seeded and diced

2 tbsp chopped fresh coriander (cilantro)

1 small egg, beaten

2 tbsp plain (all-purpose) flour plus extra to shape

salt and ground black pepper

natural yogurt to serve

chilli powder to dust

lemon wedges to garnish

1 Put the chickpeas in a food processor or blender and blitz until smooth. Add the garlic and red onion and blitz until well combined but still coarse.

2 Transfer the mixture to a bowl with the chilli, coriander, egg and flour. Mix well and season with salt and pepper. If the mixture is too soft, add more flour. Cover and chill in the refrigerator for 30 minutes.

3 With floured hands, shape the mixture into 12 cakes. If time allows, chill again for 1 hour.

4 Preheat the grill (broiler). Place the cakes in a foil-lined grill (broiling) pan and grill (broil) for 6–8 minutes, turning them over halfway through, until browned.

5 Serve hot with yogurt, dusted with chilli powder, with lemon wedges for squeezing.

preparation 15 minutes plus chilling **cooking time** 6–8 minutes

Serves 4

HALLOUMI STACKS

2 red (bell) peppers, quartered and seeded

4 tbsp olive oil

2 aubergines (eggplants)

340g/12oz halloumi cheese

salt and ground black pepper

Pesto vinaigrette:

4 baby plum tomatoes

2 spring onions (scallions), diced

6 tbsp olive oil

1 tbsp lemon juice

2 tbsp pesto

1 To make the pesto vinaigrette, cut the tomatoes in half and remove the seeds. Cut into small dice. Place in a bowl with the spring onions, olive oil, lemon juice and pesto, and season with salt and pepper. Set aside.

2 Brush the peppers with oil and cook under a hot grill (broiler) for 6–8 minutes, until slightly charred and soft. Set aside. Cut the aubergine and halloumi cheese into 8 slices each. Brush lightly with oil and season with salt and pepper. Grill (broil) them for 5 minutes, until golden brown.

3 Place an aubergine slice in the middle of a serving plate, lay a slice of halloumi on top and then some red pepper. Continue layering up with another slice of halloumi and a slice of aubergine. Repeat on three more plates.

4 Spoon the pesto dressing around the stacks and serve.

preparation 15 minutes **cooking time** 15 minutes

Serves 4

MOZZARELLA MUSHROOMS

8 large field mushrooms

8 slices marinated red, yellow or green (bell) peppers

8 fresh basil leaves

125g/4oz mozzarella cheese, cut into 8 slices

8 slices ciabatta bread

salt and ground black pepper

1 Preheat the oven to 200°C/400°C/Gas 6.
2 Lay the mushrooms, side by side, in a roasting tin and season with salt and pepper. Top each one with a slice of pepper and a basil leaf. Put a slice of mozzarella on top and grind over a little black pepper.
3 Bake in the oven for 15–20 minutes until the mushrooms are tender and the cheese has melted.
4 Meanwhile, toast the ciabatta until golden brown. Put a mozzarella mushroom on top of each slice and serve.

preparation 3 minutes   cooking time 20 minutes

Serves 4

SCOTCH BROTH

2 tbsp olive oil

340g/12oz lean lamb, cubed

1 swede (rutabaga), peeled and roughly chopped

2 carrots, roughly chopped

1 onion, finely chopped

2 sticks celery, diced

1 potato, finely diced

125g/4oz/½ cup pearl barley

1 litre/1¾ pints/4 cups beef or lamb stock

salt and ground black pepper

1 bunch of fresh parsley, finely chopped

1 Heat the oil in a large pan over a high heat. Add the lamb and cook for 5 minutes, stirring, until browned all over. Add the swede, carrots, onion, celery and potato and cook over a medium heat for 5 minutes.
2 Add the pearl barley and mix well. Pour in the stock and stir well with a wooden spoon, scraping any sticky bits from the bottom of the pan.
3 Bring to the boil, then reduce the heat, cover the pan and simmer gently for 40–50 minutes until the lamb is tender and all the vegetables are cooked. Season to taste with salt and pepper and stir in the parsley.
4 Ladle the soup into warmed bowls and serve immediately.

preparation 15 minutes   cooking time 1 hour

Serves 4

ORIENTAL CHICKEN WINGS

2 garlic cloves, crushed

2.5cm/1in piece fresh root ginger, peeled and grated

1 tbsp sweet chilli sauce

2 tbsp soy sauce

2 tbsp hoisin sauce

16 chicken wings

4 spring onions (scallions)

For the dipping sauce

6 tbsp plum sauce

2 tbsp sweet chilli sauce

1 tbsp soy sauce

1 garlic clove, crushed

1 Put the garlic, ginger, chilli sauce, soy sauce and hoisin sauce in a large shallow dish and mix together. Add the chicken wings and turn to coat thoroughly. Cover and leave to marinate overnight in the refrigerator.
2 To make the dipping sauce, put the plum sauce, chilli sauce, soy sauce and garlic in a bowl and mix together.
3 Remove the chicken wings from the marinade and pat dry on kitchen paper. Arrange them in a foil-lined grill (broiling) pan.
4 Cook under a hot grill (broiler) for 10–12 minutes, turning, until browned all over and cooked right through.
5 Cut the spring onions into shreds and scatter over the chicken wings. Serve hot with the dipping sauce.

preparation 10 minutes plus marinating **cooking time** 10–12 minutes

Serves 4

PIRI-PIRI CHICKEN PIECES

1 red (bell) pepper

3 red chillies, seeded and diced

6 tbsp olive oil

juice of 1 lemon

2 garlic cloves, crushed

a pinch of salt

1kg/2lb 4oz chicken thighs, skin on

For the pepper mayonnaise

1 roasted red (bell) pepper

150ml/¼ pint/scant ⅔ cup mayonnaise

2 tbsp chopped fresh coriander (cilantro)

1 Cut the pepper into quarters and remove the seeds. Cook under a hot grill (broiler) for 10 minutes until soft and charred. Place the chillies and red pepper in a food processor or blender. Add the olive oil, lemon juice, garlic and salt and blitz to a purée.
2 Pierce each chicken thigh in several places with a sharp knife. Place in a shallow dish and pour over the marinade. Turn the chicken to coat thoroughly. Cover and chill in the refrigerator overnight.
3 Make the pepper mayonnaise. Deseed the red pepper, chop finely and mix with the other ingredients. Set aside.
4 Remove the chicken from the marinade and pat dry with kitchen paper. Place in a foil-lined grill (broiling) pan and cook under a hot grill for 10 minutes, until browned and cooked through. Serve with the pepper mayonnaise.

preparation 15 minutes plus marinating **cooking time** 20 minutes

Serves 4

CHICKEN BURGERS

225g/8oz minced (ground) chicken

1 small onion, finely chopped

2 tbsp chopped fresh parsley

25g/1oz/½ cup fresh white breadcrumbs

1 large (US extra-large) egg yolk

olive oil to grease

salt and ground black pepper

toasted sesame burger buns, mayonnaise, salad leaves and sliced tomato to serve

1 Put the chicken in a bowl with the onion, parsley, breadcrumbs and egg yolk. Mix well together, then beat in 5 tbsp cold water and season with salt and pepper.
2 Lightly oil a foil-lined baking sheet. Divide the chicken mixture into two portions, shape into burgers and put on the foil. Cover and chill for 30 minutes.
3 Preheat the barbecue or grill (broiler). If cooking on the barbecue, lift the burgers straight on to the grill rack; if cooking under the grill, slide the baking sheet under the grill. Cook the burgers for 5–6 minutes each side until thoroughly cooked. Serve in toasted burger buns with mayonnaise, a few salad leaves and sliced tomato.

preparation 20 minutes plus chilling   **cooking time** 12 minutes

Serves 2

TANDOORI CHICKEN PITTAS

75g/3oz/6 tbsp low-fat yogurt, plus extra to serve (optional)

3 tbsp tandoori paste

4 skinless, boneless chicken breasts

olive oil to grease

salt and ground black pepper

4 wholemeal pitta breads

¼ iceberg lettuce, shredded

2 tomatoes, sliced

a large handful of fresh coriander (cilantro) leaves

1 lemon, cut into wedges

mango chutney to serve

1 In a large bowl, mix together the yogurt, tandoori paste and a little salt and pepper. Add the chicken and coat with the spicy yogurt mixture.
2 Heat an oiled griddle pan over a medium heat and cook the chicken for 15–20 minutes, turning once, until golden brown and cooked right through.
3 Meanwhile, toast the pittas and make a slit with a knife down one side of each one.
4 Slice the cooked chicken breasts diagonally.
5 Fill the pittas with the sliced chicken, lettuce, tomatoes and coriander. Serve with lemon wedges and mango chutney plus extra yogurt, if you like.

preparation 20 minutes   **cooking time** 15–20 minutes

Serves 4

CHICKEN CAESAR SALAD

2 tbsp olive oil

1 garlic clove, crushed

2 thick slices crusty bread, cubed

1 cos (romaine) lettuce, washed, chilled and cut into pieces

700g/1½lb cooked chicken breast, sliced

2 tbsp freshly grated Parmesan

For the dressing

4 tbsp mayonnaise

2 tbsp lemon juice

1 tsp Dijon mustard

6 tbsp freshly grated Parmesan

2 anchovy fillets, chopped

1 Preheat the oven to 180°C/350°F/Gas 4.
2 Put the oil, garlic and bread cubes in a bowl and toss well together. Spread them out on a baking sheet and bake in the oven for 10 minutes, turning halfway through, until crisp and golden brown.
3 Put all the ingredients for the dressing in a bowl, season with salt and pepper and blend well together.
4 Put the lettuce and sliced chicken in a serving bowl. Pour the dressing over the top and toss gently together.
5 Top with the cheese croûtons and Parmesan and serve with a grinding of black pepper.

preparation 15–20 minutes   cooking time 12 minutes

Serves 4

FALAFEL PITTAS

vegetable oil to shallow-fry

1 onion, chopped

2 garlic cloves, crushed

2 x 400g/14oz cans chickpeas (garbanzos), drained and rinsed

1 tsp ground cumin

½ tsp dried chilli flakes

a small handful of fresh parsley, finely chopped

75g/3oz/½ cup ready-to-eat dried apricots, finely chopped

1 large egg, lightly beaten

100g/3½oz/1 cup plain (all-purpose) flour

salt and ground black pepper

toasted pitta breads, hummus and salad to serve

For the mint and yogurt sauce
125g/4oz/½ cup natural yogurt
2 tbsp chopped fresh mint
finely grated zest of ½ lemon

1 Heat 1 tbsp oil in a large deep pan, add the onion and cook gently over a low heat for 10 minutes until softened. Add the garlic and cook for 1 minute.
2 Tip into a food processor with the chickpeas, cumin, chilli, parsley and seasoning. Blitz until fairly well combined but the mixture still retains some texture.
3 Transfer to a bowl and stir in the apricots, egg and flour.
4 Pour enough oil into a pan so that it comes 3cm/1¼in up the sides and set over a medium-high heat. Drop small spoonfuls of the chickpea mixture into the hot oil – it should sizzle. Turn the falafels when they are golden brown on one side and cook until golden on the other side.
5 Use a slotted spoon to lift the falafels out of the oil on to kitchen paper.
6 Meanwhile, make the sauce: stir all the ingredients together in a bowl and season to taste.
7 Serve the falafels drizzled with the sauce, with toasted pittas, hummus and salad.

preparation 20 minutes   **cooking time** 10 minutes

Serves 4

HONEY-MUSTARD CHICKEN SALAD

4 tbsp pinenuts (pignoli)
2 garlic cloves, crushed
3 tbsp runny honey
2 tbsp Dijon mustard
1 tbsp lemon juice
1 tbsp soy sauce
2 x 200g/7oz skinless chicken breasts, cut into strips
100g/3½oz rocket (arugula)

For the dressing
4 tbsp olive oil
1 tbsp balsamic vinegar
salt and ground black pepper

1 Put the pinenuts in a foil-lined grill (broiling) pan and cook under a hot grill (broiler) for 1–2 minutes, until browned.
2 To make the marinade, put the garlic, honey, mustard, lemon juice and soy sauce in a bowl and mix together.
3 Add the chicken strips to the marinade and toss to coat thoroughly. Cover and chill in the refrigerator for 1 hour.
4 To make the dressing, whisk together all the ingredients in a bowl.
5 Arrange the chicken strips in a foil-lined grill (broiling) pan and cook under a hot grill, turning occasionally, for 5 minutes or until cooked through and browned.
6 Put the rocket in a bowl and add enough of the dressing to barely coat the leaves. Arrange a pile of rocket on four serving plates and stack the chicken strips on top. Sprinkle over the pine nuts and serve.

preparation 15 minutes plus marinating **cooking time** 7 minutes

Serves 4

DUCK AND MANGO SALAD

2 x 175g/6oz duck breasts
2 tbsp runny honey
1 tsp Chinese five-spice paste
1 tsp soy sauce
125g/4oz green beans, halved
175g/6oz bag mixed salad leaves
1 mango, peeled and stoned

For the dressing
6 tbsp sunflower oil
1 tbsp lime juice
1 tbsp soy sauce
2 tsp grated fresh root ginger
2 tbsp chopped fresh coriander (cilantro)

1 Remove the skin from the duck. Mix together the honey, five-spice paste and soy sauce and brush over the duck.
2 Cook the duck under a hot grill (broiler), turning once, for 10 minutes or until cooked through. Set aside for 5 minutes.
3 Meanwhile, cook the beans in a pan of boiling salted water for 4 minutes. Drain and refresh with cold water. Set aside.
4 Put the dressing ingredients in a bowl and whisk together.
5 Toss the salad leaves with a little of the dressing and arrange on plates. Place the remaining dressing in a small pan and heat gently.
6 Cut the duck breasts into thin slices and arrange on top of the salad leaves. Slice the mango and add to the duck with the green beans. Drizzle over the warm dressing and serve.

preparation 15 minutes **cooking time** 10 minutes

Serves 4

WARM LENTIL AND CHICKEN SALAD

125g/4oz/¾ cup Puy lentils
225g/8oz mangetouts, chopped
1 garlic clove, crushed
1 tsp Dijon powder
2 tbsp balsamic vinegar
4 tbsp olive oil
1 red (bell) pepper, seeded and sliced into rings
340g/12oz cooked chicken breast, shredded
salt

1 Put the lentils in a pan and cover them with boiling water. Cook according to the pack instructions. Drain well.
2 Blanch the mangetouts in a pan of boiling water for 2 minutes. Drain, refresh under cold water and set aside.
3 In a bowl, with a wooden spoon, combine the garlic with a pinch of salt until creamy. Whisk in the mustard, balsamic vinegar and 3 tbsp oil. Set aside.
4 Heat the remaining oil in a frying pan, add the red pepper and cook for 5 minutes, stirring often, until tender.
5 Add the chicken and mangetouts to the pan and stir-fry for 2 minutes. Stir in the lentils and the dressing.
6 Serve the salad while it's still warm.

preparation 20 minutes   cooking time 25 minutes

Serves 4

WARM CHICKEN LIVER SALAD

25g/1oz/2 tbsp butter
450g/1lb chicken livers, trimmed of sinew and fat, and patted dry
3 oranges, peeled and cut into segments
300g/11oz cooked asparagus tips
125g/4oz wild rocket (arugula)

For the orange dressing
grated zest and juice of 2 oranges
150ml/¼ pint/scant ⅔ cup olive oil
4 tbsp red wine vinegar
2 tbsp clear honey
salt and ground black pepper

1 Make the dressing: whisk all the ingredients together and put in a small pan. Bring to the boil, remove from the heat and set aside to cool.
2 Heat the butter in a large pan and add the chicken livers. Cook over a high heat for 5 minutes or until well browned. Remove from the pan and keep warm.
3 Add a little of the dressing to the pan. Let it bubble away for 2–3 minutes, stirring and scraping the bottom of the pan to dissolve any sediment.
4 Divide the chicken livers, orange segments, asparagus tips and wild rocket among six plates. Drizzle with the dressing and serve warm.

preparation 10 minutes   cooking time 15–20 minutes

Serves 6

PARMA HAM, ROCKET AND PARMESAN SALAD

4 tbsp olive oil

1 tbsp balsamic vinegar

125g/4oz borettane onions in balsamic vinegar, drained

200g/7oz rocket (arugula)

12 thin slices Parma ham

50g2oz Parmesan

salt and ground black pepper

1 To make the dressing, whisk the oil, balsamic vinegar, salt and pepper in a bowl until well combined.
2 Put the borettane onions in a large bowl with the rocket, Parma ham and dressing. Gently toss everything together and divide among four serving plates.
3 Using a potato peeler, pare the Parmesan into large shavings and scatter them on top of the salad.

preparation 10 minutes

Serves 4

BACON AND ANCHOVY CAESAR SALAD

4 tbsp olive oil

75g/3oz white bread, cubed

a pinch of sea salt flakes

6 streaky bacon rashers (slices)

2 Little Gem (Bibb) lettuces, broken into leaves

4 tbsp grated Parmesan

25g/1oz watercress, trimmed

50g/2oz marinated fresh anchovies

½ quantity Caesar Dressing (see page 44)

1 Put half the oil in a frying pan and heat gently until a cube of bread sizzles. Add half the bread cubes and fry for 2–3 minutes, stirring, until golden brown and crisp. Remove with a slotted spoon and drain on kitchen paper. Repeat with the remaining oil and bread, then toss the croûtons in the salt and set aside to cool.
2 Grill (broil) the bacon for 3–4 minutes each side until golden and crisp. Drain on kitchen paper, then roughly chop.
3 Toss the lettuce and Parmesan with the croûtons, crispy bacon, watercress and anchovies in a bowl.
4 Just before serving, drizzle the dressing over the salad.

preparation 15 minutes plus cooling   cooking time 15 minutes

Serves 8

BACON AND AVOCADO SALAD

125g/4oz streaky bacon rashers (slices), cut into small pieces

½ red onion, finely chopped

125g/4oz mixed salad leaves

1 ripe avocado

50g/2oz/½ cup pinenuts (pignoli)

4 tbsp olive oil

4 tbsp red wine vinegar

1 tsp honey mustard

salt and ground black pepper

1 Cook the bacon in a frying pan over a medium heat for 1–2 minutes until the fat starts to run. Add the onion and cook gently for 5 minutes until tender and golden.
2 Divide the salad leaves among four serving plates. Halve, stone and peel the avocado, then slice the flesh. Arrange on top of the salad leaves.
3 Add the pinenuts, oil, vinegar and honey mustard to the pan and let it bubble for 1 minute. Season with salt and pepper.
4 Pour the contents of the pan over the salad and serve it immediately while still warm.

preparation 5 minutes   cooking time 7 minutes

Serves 4

CHICORY, HAM AND WALNUT SALAD

2 sweet dessert apples, cored and sliced

50g/2oz/½ cup shelled walnuts

340g/12oz cooked ham, cubed

2 chicory (Belgian endive) heads, divided into leaves

125g/4oz Roquefort, cubed

4 tbsp fresh chopped parsley

For the honey mustard dressing

1 tsp clear honey

1 tsp Dijon mustard

2 tbsp cider vinegar

9 tbsp olive oil

juice of 1 lemon

salt and ground black pepper

1 Make the dressing: whisk together the honey, mustard, vinegar and seasoning in a small bowl. Whisk in the oil until well combined and emulsified and stir in the lemon juice. Put aside while you prepare the salad.
2 Put the apples, walnuts, ham and chicory in a large serving bowl. Stir in the Roquefort cubes.
3 Toss the salad with the dressing and adjust the seasoning if necessary. Garnish with chopped parsley and serve.

preparation 15 minutes

Serves 6

SALADE NICOISE

450g/1lb fresh tuna steaks

2 tbsp olive oil plus extra to cook

2 small red (bell) peppers, halved and seeded

2 large (US extra large) eggs

220g/8oz podded broad (fava) beans

340g/12oz tomatoes, quartered

½ cucumber, seeded and cut into chunks

50g/2oz/½ cup small black olives, pitted

6 spring onions (scallions), chopped

1 x 50g/2oz can anchovy fillets, drained and chopped

50g/2oz rocket (arugula)

salt and ground black pepper

For the dressing

2 tbsp lemon juice

1 tbsp white wine vinegar

1 tsp Dijon mustard

6 tbsp extra virgin olive oil

1 Put the tuna steaks in a dish, spoon over 2 tbsp oil, then cover and leave to marinate in the fridge for at least 3 hours.
2 Cook the tuna on an oiled griddle pan set over a medium to high heat for a few minutes each side until cooked to your liking. Remove and set aside to cool.
3 Grill (broil) the peppers, skin-side up, under a hot grill (broiler) until charred. Place in a bowl, cover with clingfilm (plastic wrap) and leave until cool. Skin the peppers, cut into thick strips and set aside.
4 Bring a small pan of water to the boil, add the eggs and simmer for 8 minutes. Cool under cold running water, then shell and cut into quarters.
5 Boil the broad beans in a pan of water for 2 minutes. Drain and refresh in cold water. Slip off the skins.
6 Make the dressing: put all the ingredients in a screw-topped jar, season to taste and shake well.
7 Break the tuna into large flakes in a salad bowl. Add the grilled peppers, tomatoes, eggs, cucumber, olives, spring onions, anchovies and broad beans with some of the dressing. Toss gently and check the seasoning.
8 Gently stir in the rocket leaves, coating them with the remaining dressing.
9 Serve the salad immediately before the rocket starts to wilt.
.

preparation 40 minutes plus marinating   **cooking time** 30 minutes

Serves 4

SMOKED MACKEREL SALAD

250g/9oz cooked beetroot (beets), diced

1 tbsp olive oil

1 tsp balsamic vinegar

340g/12oz potato salad

juice of ½ lemon

4 smoked mackerel fillets, skinned and flaked

3 tbsp chopped fresh parsley plus extra to garnish

salt and ground black pepper

1 Put the beetroot in a bowl. Sprinkle with the oil and vinegar. Season with salt and pepper and toss together.
2 In a large bowl, mix the potato salad with the lemon juice. Season to taste with salt and pepper. Mix in the flaked smoked mackerel and parsley and toss together.
3 Just before serving, divide the mackerel mixture among four serving plates. Sprinkle the beetroot over the top of the salad and garnish with parsley.

Serves 4

preparation 15 minutes

FRESH TUNA SALAD NICOISE

340g/12oz new potatoes

125g/4oz green beans, halved

4 x 175g/6oz tuna steaks

175g/6oz mixed salad leaves

225g/8oz cherry tomatoes, halved

3 hard-boiled eggs, quartered

50g/2oz anchovy fillets in oil, drained

12 black olives

For the vinaigrette

½ tsp Dijon mustard

1 tbsp white wine vinegar

salt and ground black pepper

125ml/4fl oz/½ cup olive oil

1 tbsp chopped fresh chives

1 To make the vinaigrette, whisk together the mustard, vinegar, salt and pepper. Whisk in the oil, then stir in the chives. Set aside.
2 Cut the potatoes in half or quarters, depending on size. Cook in a pan of boiling salted water for 10 minutes or until tender. Drain and place in a large bowl. Add 1 tbsp of the vinaigrette, mix gently and leave to cool.
3 Cook the green beans in a pan of boiling salted water for 3–4 minutes until just tender. Drain, rinse under cold water and drain again. Add to the potatoes and mix together.
4 Brush the tuna steaks on both sides with vinaigrette. Cook under a hot grill (broiler) (or in a griddle pan) for 5–6 minutes, turning once, until just cooked through.
5 Meanwhile, place the salad leaves in a bowl and toss with half the remaining vinaigrette. Divide them among four serving plates. Arrange the potatoes, beans, tomatoes, eggs, anchovies and olives on top. Top with the tuna steaks and drizzle over the remaining vinaigrette.

Serves 4

preparation 15 minutes cooking time 15 minutes

SMOKED MACKEREL, AND GRAPEFRUIT SALAD

1 grapefruit

1 tbsp Dijon mustard

1 tbsp olive oil

175g/6oz smoked mackerel, skinned and flaked

1 large ripe avocado, stoned, peeled and cut into cubes

1 x 400g/14oz can lentils, drained and rinsed

seeds of 1 pomegranate

bunch of fresh chives, snipped

100g/3½oz mixed salad leaves

salt and ground black pepper

1 Slice the top and bottom off the grapefruit and sit it on a board. Use a small serrated knife to cut away the peel and pith. Holding the grapefruit over a small bowl, cut between the membranes to separate the segments. Squeeze the membranes into a separate small bowl to extract as much juice as possible.
2 Whisk the mustard, oil and plenty of seasoning into the grapefruit juice to make the dressing.
3 Put the smoked mackerel, avocado, lentils, pomegranate seeds, chives and salad leaves in a large bowl and toss together. Drizzle the dressing over the top and add the grapefruit segments. Serve immediately.

preparation 15 minutes

Serves 4

SMOKED MACKEREL AND GREEN BEAN SALAD

225g/8oz thin green beans

225g/8oz peppered smoked mackerel fillets

125g/4oz mixed watercress, spinach and rocket (arugula)

1 red onion, finely chopped

1 avocado

1 tbsp olive oil

1 tbsp chopped fresh coriander (cilantro)

grated zest and juice of 1 lemon

1 Trim the green beans and blanch in a pan of boiling water for 3 minutes until they are just tender. Drain, rinse under cold running water, drain well and set aside.
2 Preheat the grill (broiler) and cook the mackerel for 2 minutes or until warmed through. Flake into bite-sized pieces, discarding the skin, and put in a bowl with the green beans, salad leaves and red onion.
3 Halve, stone and peel the avocado, and cut the flesh into thin slices. Add to the bowl. Whisk together the oil, coriander, lemon zest and juice. Toss with the salad and serve.

preparation 10 minutes cooking time 5 minutes

Serves 6

HERRING, POTATO AND DILL SALAD

1kg/2¼lb new potatoes

8 gherkins (cornichons), thinly sliced

450g/1lb sweet cured herrings, drained and sliced

For the creamy dressing

4 tbsp natural yogurt

4 tbsp mayonnaise

4 tbsp chopped fresh dill

dash of lemon juice

1 Put the potatoes in a pan of cold water, bring to the boil and cook for 15–20 minutes until tender. Drain, then cut in half.
2 To make the dressing, mix the yogurt, mayonnaise, dill and lemon juice together in a bowl.
3 Put the potatoes, gherkins and herrings in a bowl with the dressing. Toss together lightly and serve. .

preparation 15 minutes cooking time 15–20 minutes

Serves 4

TUNA, BEAN AND ONION SALAD

2 x 400g/14oz cans cannellini beans, drained and rinsed

1 small red onion, thinly sliced

1 tbsp red wine vinegar

1 x 225g/8oz can tuna steak in oil

4 tbsp chopped fresh parsley

salt and ground black pepper

1 Put the beans, red onion and vinegar in a bowl. Season with a little salt and mix well. Add the tuna with its oil, breaking the fish into large flakes.
2 Add half the parsley and grind over plenty of black pepper. Toss the salad gently together, then scatter the remaining parsley over the top.

preparation 5 minutes

Serves 4

HALLOUMI AND AVOCADO SALAD

250g/9oz halloumi, cut into 8 slices

1 tbsp flour

2 tbsp olive oil

200g/7oz mixed salad leaves

1 bunch of fresh mint, chopped

2 avocados, halved, stoned, peeled and sliced

lemon halves to serve

For the dressing

grated zest and juice of 1 lemon

6 tbsp olive oil

3 tbsp chopped fresh parsley

salt and ground black pepper

1 Make the dressing: whisk together the lemon juice, oil and mint, then season with salt and pepper.
2 Dust the halloumi lightly with the flour. Heat the oil in a large frying pan and cook the cheese for 1 minute each side or until golden brown. Remove and keep warm.
3 In a large bowl, add half the dressing to the salad leaves, mint and avocado and toss together. Divide the mixture among four plates.
4 Arrange the slices of halloumi on top and drizzle with the remaining dressing. Serve immediately with lemon halves.

preparation 10 minutes cooking time 2 minutes

Serves 4

PEAR, BLUE CHEESE AND WALNUT CAESAR SALAD

50g/2oz/¼ cup walnut pieces

1 tbsp olive oil

15g/½oz/1 tbsp butter

4 pears, quartered, cored and thickly sliced

1 cos (romaine) lettuce

2 tbsp bread croûtons

100g/3½oz Roquefort, crumbled

½ quantity Caesar dressing (see page 44)

1 Dry-fry the walnuts in a non-stick frying pan over a medium heat for 1 minute until lightly toasted. Set aside.
2 Heat the oil and butter in the pan and add the pears. Cook for 2 minutes each side until golden. Remove from the pan with and set aside.
3 Separate the lettuce into leaves. Cut into biggish pieces and place in a large bowl. Add the walnuts, pears, croûtons and blue cheese. Toss lightly in the Caesar dressing and serve immediately.

preparation 15 minutes

Serves 6

FRUITY CHICKPEA AND BARLEY SALAD

250g/9oz/1 cup pearl barley

125g/4oz mangetouts, halved

2 ripe peaches or nectarines

½ cucumber, halved lengthways, seeded and diced

50g/2oz rocket (arugula)

1 x 400g/14oz can chickpeas (garbanzos), drained and rinsed

2 tbsp balsamic vinegar

1 tbsp extra virgin olive oil

juice of 1 small orange

salt and ground black pepper

1. Put the pearl barley in a large pan and cover with water. Add some salt and bring to the boil. Reduce the heat and simmer for 25 minutes until the barley is just tender. Add the mangetouts for the final 3 minutes. Drain and put aside.
2. Meanwhile, peel, stone and halve the peaches. Cut each peach half into 4 wedges and place them in a large serving bowl. Add the cucumber, rocket and chickpeas.
3. Add the balsamic vinegar, oil, orange juice and seasoning to the salad with the drained barley and mangetouts and lightly mix together. Check the seasoning and serve.

preparation 15 minutes   cooking time 30 minutes

Serves 4

GREEK PASTA SALAD

3 tbsp olive oil

juice of 1 lemon

175g/6oz/1½ cups cooked pasta shapes, cooled

75g/3oz feta, crumbled

2 tomatoes, roughly chopped

2 tbsp small pitted black olives

½ cucumber, roughly chopped

1 small red onion, thinly sliced

salt and ground black pepper

chopped fresh parsley and oregano to garnish

1. Mix the oil and lemon juice together in a salad bowl to make a dressing. Season with salt and pepper.
2. Add the cooked pasta, crumbled feta, tomatoes, black olives, cucumber and red onion. Season to taste with a little salt and pepper, then stir to mix.
3. Sprinkle with parsley, oregano and lemon zest and serve.

preparation 10 minutes   cooking time 20 minutes

Serves 2

MIXED BEAN SALAD WITH LEMON VINAIGRETTE

1 x 400g/14oz can red kidney beans, drained and rinsed

1 x 400g/14oz can chickpeas (garbanzos), drained and rinsed

1 bunch spring onions (scallions), thinly sliced

fresh parsley sprigs and lemon zest to garnish

For the lemon vinaigrette
grated zest and juice of 1 lemon
2 tsp honey mustard
125ml/4fl oz/½ cup olive oil
4 tbsp chopped fresh parsley
salt and ground black pepper

1 Put the beans, chickpeas and spring onions in a large bowl.
2 To make the lemon vinaigrette, whisk together the lemon zest and juice, honey mustard and seasoning. Gradually whisk in the oil and then add the parsley.
3 Pour the lemon vinaigrette over the bean mixture and toss together.
4 Serve the salad, garnished with the parsley sprigs and lemon zest.

preparation 15 minutes

Serves 6

WARM GOAT'S CHEESE SALAD

1 bunch of watercress

4 slices chèvre goat's cheese (with rind)

4 tsp red pesto

40g/1½oz walnut halves, toasted

For the dressing
1 tbsp walnut oil
2 tbsp rapeseed oil
a few drops of raspberry vinegar
salt and ground black pepper

1 Make the dressing: whisk all the ingredients together in a bowl, seasoning with salt and pepper to taste.
2 Trim the watercress and discard any thick stalks.
3 Lay the goat's cheese slices on a foil-lined grill (broiling) pan. Cook under a preheated hot grill (broiler), as close to the heat as possible, for 1–2 minutes until browned.
4 Toss the watercress leaves with the dressing and divide among four serving plates. Put a slice of goat's cheese on top with a spoonful of pesto.
5 Scatter the walnuts over the salad and serve immediately.

preparation 20 minutes cooking time 1–2 minutes

Serves 4

EASY SUPPERS

This chapter is packed with fuss-free dishes, such as simple frittatas or speedy stir-fries, to help you put meals on the table easily. When you come home from work and you're cooking from scratch, you want something quick and healthy.

If you're looking for something easy but delicious and filling, there are some great pasta dishes that can be cooked in minutes as well as substantial salads. You'll also find meals that require minimal preparation such as pasta bakes, so that you can enjoy hearty suppers without slaving away in the kitchen for hours. And if you fancy something really warming, there are soups, curries and spicy dishes that will do the trick.

There are meat-free options, too, for vegetarians or for those times when you don't feel like eating meat or fish. Many of the risotto and pasta dishes are flavoured with seasonal vegetables, and beans and lentils feature, too.

If you're being thrifty, you won't be disappointed. Many of the recipes in this section have economical ingredients and utilize store-cupboard items, such as dried pasta, rice, grains and pulses. A simple dish of pasta tossed in a sauce of canned chopped tomatoes, bottled olives and anchovies can be put together in minutes and – hey presto – supper is served!

< *Clams with Chilli Spaghetti (page 93)*

ITALIAN STUFFED CHICKEN BREASTS

olive oil to grease
8 slices mozzarella
4 x 125g/4oz boneless, skinless chicken breasts
4 fresh sage leaves
8 slices Parma ham
ground black pepper
cherry tomatoes on the vine

1 Preheat the oven to 200°C/400°F/Gas 6. Lightly oil a baking sheet.
2 Put 2 mozzarella slices on top of each chicken breast and then add a sage leaf. Wrap each chicken breast in 2 slices of Parma ham, covering the mozzarella. Season with pepper.
3 Place the chicken on the baking sheet and cook in the oven for 20 minutes or until the chicken is cooked through, the cheese has melted and the ham is golden brown.
4 Serve with grilled (broiled) cherry tomatoes.

preparation 5 minutes   cooking time 20 minutes

Serves 4

STUFFED CHICKEN THIGHS

100g/3½oz/2 cups fresh white breadcrumbs
4 tbsp freshly grated Parmesan
2 medium (US large) eggs, beaten
3 tbsp chopped fresh basil
finely grated zest of 1 lemon
8 boneless, skinless chicken thighs
8 streaky bacon rashers (slices)
salt and ground black pepper

1 Preheat the oven to 220°C/425°F/Gas 7.
2 Mix together the breadcrumbs, Parmesan, beaten eggs, basil, lemon zest and seasoning in a bowl.
3 Open out the chicken thighs, smooth-side down, and spoon half of the stuffing down the centre of each. Fold the chicken over the filling and wrap each fillet in bacon.
4 Place the wrapped thighs, seam-side down, on a non-stick baking tray. Cook in the oven for 25–30 minutes until golden brown and cooked through. Serve with green vegetables.

preparation 20 minutes   cooking time 30 minutes

Serves 4

CHICKEN AND ARTICHOKE PIE

340g/12oz boneless, skinless chicken breasts

150ml/¼ pint/scant ⅔ cup chicken stock

225g/8oz/1¼ cups reduced-fat soft cheese

1 x 400g/14oz can artichoke hearts, drained and quartered

6 sheets filo pastry

melted butter to brush

salt and ground black pepper

1 Preheat the oven to 200°C/400°F/Gas 6.
2 Put the chicken and stock in a pan and bring to the boil. Reduce the heat, cover and simmer for 10 minutes. Remove the chicken and set aside.
3 Add the soft cheese to the pan and mix with the stock until smooth. Bring to the boil, then simmer until thickened.
4 Cut the chicken into chunks and stir into the sauce with the artichoke hearts. Season to taste.
5 Spoon the mixture into a baking dish. Brush the filo pastry sheets with melted butter and use to cover the dish. Bake in the oven for 30–35 minutes until crisp and golden brown.

preparation 20 minutes   cooking time 45 minutes

Serves 4

CHICKEN AND VEGETABLE GRATIN

1 tbsp olive oil

1 onion, thinly sliced

450g/1lb pumpkin, peeled and cut into chunks

125g/4oz cherry tomatoes

3 boneless, skinless chicken breasts, cut into strips

50g/2oz/4 tbsp butter

50g/2oz/½ cup plain (all-purpose) flour

500ml/17fl oz/2 cups milk

100g/3½oz bread, made into breadcrumbs

3 tbsp grated Parmesan

salt and ground black pepper

1 Preheat the oven to 180°C/350°F/Gas 4.
2 Heat the oil in a pan and cook the onion, leek and pumpkin over a low heat for 15 minutes or until tender, stirring occasionally. Add the cherry tomatoes and set aside.
3 Meanwhile, put the chicken in a separate pan, cover with cold water and bring to the boil. Lower the heat and simmer for 5 minutes. Drain well and add to the vegetables.
4 Melt the butter in a pan and stir in the flour. Cook gently for 1 minute. Remove from the heat and gradually beat in the milk, with a wooden spoon, until you have a smooth sauce. Return to the heat and cook, stirring constantly, until the sauce thickens. Season to taste.
5 Stir the sauce into the vegetable and chicken mixture and transfer to an ovenproof dish. Scatter with the breadcrumbs and grated Parmesan.
6 Cook in the oven for 30 minutes until the top is golden brown and crisp and the filling is bubbling.

preparation 15 minutes   cooking time 50 minutes

Serves 4

CHICKEN CRISPBAKES

75g/3oz/¾ cup frozen peas

1kg /2¼lb potatoes

3 tbsp plain (all-purpose) flour

1 medium (US large) egg, beaten

4 spring onions (scallions), diced

2 skinless cooked chicken breasts, diced

100g/3½oz/1 cup grated Cheddar

2 tbsp olive oil

salt and ground black pepper

1 Preheat the oven to 200°C/400°F/Gas 6. Line a baking tray with parchment paper .

2 Fill and boil a kettle. Put the peas in a colander in the sink and pour the boiling water over them. Set aside.

3 Peel and coarsely grate the potatoes. Put the grated potato on a clean teatowel. Fold it over the potato and squeeze out as much moisture as you can. Put the squeezed potato in a large bowl, then mix in the remaining ingredients and some salt and pepper. With your hands, mould the mixture into eight patties and place on the prepared baking tray.

4 Cook the crispbakes in the oven for 30 minutes or until golden and cooked through.

preparation 20 minutes   cooking time 35 minutes

Serves 4

BUFFALO WINGS AND AVOCADO DIP

1.1kg/2½lb chicken wings

1 tsp olive oil

100g/3½oz/½ cup tomato ketchup

1 tbsp hot chilli sauce

15g/½oz/1 tbsp butter

juice of ½ lemon

2 tsp cornflour (cornstarch)

salt and ground black pepper

For the avocado dip

125g/4oz/½ cup natural yogurt

1 tbsp mayonnaise

1 avocado, peeled and stoned

1 Preheat the oven to 220°C/425°F/Gas 7.

2 Put the chicken wings in a roasting pan, drizzle over the oil and season well. Cook for 30 minutes or until golden brown.

3 In a small pan, heat the tomato ketchup, chilli sauce, butter and lemon juice until smooth.

4 Mix the cornflour with a little water, then stir into the tomato and chilli mixture to thicken it, stirring over a low heat for a few minutes. Pour the mixture over the chicken to coat it.

5 Put the chicken back in the oven and cook for 10–15 minutes until the sauce is sticky.

6 To make the dip, mix the yogurt and mayonnaise together in a small bowl. Mash the avocado flesh and stir into the yogurt mixture, then season to taste. Serve the wings with the dip.

preparation 20 minutes   cooking time 45 minutes

Makes 12 wings

SPICY CHICKEN WITH QUINOA

2 tbsp mango chutney

juice of ½ lemon

2 tbsp olive oil

1 tsp curry powder

340g/12oz chicken breast fillets, cut into thick strips

200g/7oz/1 cup quinoa

1 cucumber, roughly chopped

1 red onion, finely chopped

175g/6oz baby plum tomatoes, diced

4 tbsp chopped fresh mint

4 tbsp chopped fresh parsley

salt and ground black pepper

1 Put the chutney, lemon juice, half the oil and the curry powder in a large bowl and mix well. Add the chicken to the marinade and stir to coat.
2 Cook the quinoa in boiling water for 10 minutes until tender, or according to the pack instructions. Drain thoroughly.
3 Put the quinoa in a bowl with the cucumber, red onion, tomatoes, herbs and remaining oil. Stir and season to taste.
4 Meanwhile, put the chicken and marinade in a frying pan and cook over a high heat for 2–3 minutes. Stir in 150ml/ ¼ pint/scant ⅔ cup water and bring to the boil. Reduce the heat and simmer for 5 minutes or until the chicken is cooked.
5 Serve the chicken immediately with the quinoa.

preparation 15 minutes   cooking time 10–12 minutes

Serves 4

CHICKEN PILAU

2 tbsp olive oil

2 onions, thinly sliced

2 garlic cloves, crushed

1 tbsp medium curry powder

1 tsp ground turmeric

450g/1lb skinless, boneless cooked chicken, cut into strips

340g/12oz/1½ cups basmati rice

salt and ground black pepper

a pinch of saffron

50g/2oz/⅓ cup sultanas (golden raisins)

225g/8oz tomatoes, chopped

coriander (cilantro) to garnish

1 Heat the oil in a large heavy-based pan over a medium heat. Add the onions and garlic and cook for 5 minutes or until tender. Remove half the onion mixture and put aside.
2 Add the curry powder and turmeric and cook for 1 minute. Stir in the chicken and cook for 4 minutes or until browned.
3 Stir in the rice, then add 900ml/1½ pints/3⅔ cups boiling water, some salt and the saffron. Cover and bring to the boil. Reduce the heat to low and cook for 20 minutes or until the rice is tender and most of the liquid has been absorbed.
4 Stir in the reserved onion mixture, the sultanas and tomatoes. Cook gently for 5 minutes to warm through, then serve garnished with coriander.

preparation 15 minutes   cooking time 35–40 minutes

Serves 4

STICKY CHICKEN THIGHS

2 garlic cloves, crushed

1 tbsp clear honey

2 tbsp sweet chilli sauce

2 tbsp stem ginger in syrup, diced

4 chicken thighs

boiled rice or noodles to serve

1 Preheat the oven to 200°C/400°F/Gas 6.
2 Stir the garlic in a bowl with the honey, chilli sauce and stem ginger in syrup. Add the chicken thighs and toss to coat.
3 Put the chicken in a roasting pan and roast in the oven for 15–20 minutes until golden and cooked through – the juices should run clear when the thighs are pierced with a skewer.
4 Serve immediately with boiled rice or noodles.

preparation 5 minutes   cooking time 20 minutes

Serves 4

MOROCCAN CHICKEN WITH CHICKPEAS

2 tbsp olive oil

12 chicken thighs and drumsticks

1 large onion, sliced

2 garlic cloves, crushed

1 tbsp harissa paste

1 tsp ground cumin

1 cinnamon stick

600ml/1 pint/2½ cups hot chicken stock

75g/3oz/½ cup ready-to eat dried apricots, diced

2 x 400g/14oz cans chickpeas (garbanzos), drained and rinsed

1 Heat the oil in a large non-stick frying pan over a medium heat. Add the chicken pieces to the pan and fry, turning them occasionally, until browned all over. Add the onion and garlic and cook, stirring, for 5 minutes or until tender.
2 Add the harissa, cumin and cinnamon stick. Pour in the hot stock and bring to the boil. Reduce the heat, cover the pan and simmer gently for 25–30 minutes until the chicken is tender and cooked.
3 Add the apricots and chickpeas, and bring to the boil, then reduce the heat and simmer, uncovered, for 5–10 minutes.
4 Serve hot with some warm pitta bread or boiled rice.

preparation 10 minutes   cooking time 50 minutes

Serves 6

TANDOORI CHICKEN

3 tbsp olive oil
450g/1lb/2¼ cups natural yogurt
juice of 1 lemon
4 tbsp tandoori paste
600g/1lb 5oz boneless, skinless chicken breasts, cut into strips
½ cucumber, cut into thin strips with a vegetable peeler
1 green chilli, finely diced
1 bunch of fresh mint, chopped plus extra to garnish
salt and ground black pepper

1 Mix 1 tbsp oil, two-thirds of the yogurt and the lemon juice into the tandoori paste in a bowl. Add the chicken and stir well to coat. Cover the bowl and leave to marinate in the refrigerator for at least 4 hours.
2 Preheat the oven to 220°C/425°F/Gas 7. Brush a roasting pan with a little of the oil. Put the chicken in the pan, drizzle the remaining oil over the top and roast in the oven for about 15–20 minutes until cooked through.
3 Meanwhile, prepare the raita. Put the cucumber strips in a bowl and gently stir in the remaining yogurt with the chilli and mint. Season to taste and chill until ready to serve.
4 Serve the hot tandoori chicken, sprinkled with mint, with the chilled raita.

preparation 45 minutes plus marinating cooking time 20 minutes

Serves 4

CHICKEN, BEAN AND SPINACH CURRY

1 tbsp olive oil
340g/12oz boneless, skinless, chicken breasts, cut into strips
2 garlic cloves, crushed
1 x 300g/11oz jar curry sauce
1 x 400g/14oz can aduki beans, drained and rinsed
175g/6oz thin green beans, trimmed
150g/5oz/1¼ cups natural yogurt, plus extra to serve
175g/6oz baby spinach leaves
boiled rice to serve

1 Heat the oil in a large pan over a medium heat and fry the chicken strips with the garlic until golden.
2 Add the curry sauce and beans, then cover the pan and simmer gently for 15 minutes or until the chicken is cooked through and tender. Add the green beans and cook gently for a further 5 minutes
3 Over a low heat, stir in the yogurt and heat through without boiling. Stir in the spinach and cook for 1–2 minutes until it starts to wilt.
4 Serve immediately with extra yogurt and boiled rice.

preparation 10 minutes cooking time 20 minutes

Serves 4

CHICKEN NOODLE STIR-FRY

250g/9oz egg noodles
2 tbsp oil
2 garlic cloves, crushed
4 boneless, skinless chicken thighs, sliced
3 carrots, cut into thin strips
1 red (bell) pepper, seeded and cut into strips
1 bunch of spring onions (scallions), sliced
200g/7oz mangetouts, trimmed
150g/5oz black bean stir-fry sauce

1 Fill a large pan with water and bring to the boil. Add the noodles to the boiling water and cook according to the pack instructions.
2 Meanwhile, heat the oil in a wok or deep frying pan. Add the garlic and stir-fry for 1 minute. Add the chicken and stir-fry for 5 minutes, then stir in the carrot strips and stir-fry for a further 3 minutes.
3 Add the red pepper, spring onions, mangetouts and stir-fry sauce to the wok and stir-fry for 5 minutes.
4 Drain the cooked noodles thoroughly and add to the wok. Toss everything together and serve immediately.

preparation 20 minutes   cooking time 30 minutes

Serves 4

COCONUT CHICKEN NOODLES

1 tsp chilli powder
1 tsp ground ginger
675g/1½lb boneless, skinless chicken breasts, sliced
250g/9oz thin egg noodles
2 tbsp coconut oil
1 bunch of spring onions (scallions), sliced
1 tbsp Thai red curry paste
150g/5oz/1¼ cups salted roasted peanuts, finely chopped
6 tbsp coconut milk
fresh coriander (cilantro) leaves to garnish

1 Mix the chilli powder and ginger in a bowl. Add the chicken and coat well with the spicy mixture.
2 Cook the noodles in a pan of boiling water according to the pack instructions, then drain.
3 Heat the oil in a frying pan or wok. Add the chicken and stir-fry for 5 minutes or until cooked through. Remove, cover and keep warm. Add the spring onions to the pan and fry for 1 minute. Remove and keep warm.
4 Add the curry paste to the pan with half of the peanuts and fry for 1 minute. Add the noodles and stir-fry for 1 minute. Stir in the coconut milk and toss the noodles over a high heat for 30 seconds.
5 Divide the noodle mixture among six serving plates. Pile the chicken and spring onions on top. Scatter with the remaining peanuts and coriander and serve immediately.

preparation 15–20 minutes   cooking time 15 minutes

Serves 6

SPICY CHICKEN NOODLE SOUP

1 tbsp olive oil

340g/12oz boneless, skinless chicken breasts, cubed

3 garlic cloves, crushed

2 red chillies, seeded and diced

900ml/1½ pints/2¾ cups chicken stock

125g/4oz each asparagus, green beans, broccoli, sugarsnap peas and courgettes (zucchini), sliced

75g/3oz vermicelli or soup pasta

1 Heat the oil in a large pan over a low heat. Add the chicken, garlic and chillies and cook for 5–10 minutes, stirring occasionally, until the chicken is golden brown all over.
2 Add the stock and bring to the boil, then reduce the heat, add the vegetables and simmer gently for 10 minutes or until the chicken and vegetables are cooked.
3 Add the pasta to the soup and continue cooking for a further 8–10 minutes until it is tender.
4 Ladle the soup into warmed bowls and serve immediately.

preparation 30 minutes   **cooking time** 25 minutes

Serves 4

CHICKEN AND LEEK CHEESY PASTA BAKE

1 tbsp olive oil

450g/1lb boneless, skinless chicken breasts, chopped

3 large leeks, sliced

340g/12oz penne pasta

340g/12oz carton fresh ready-made cheese sauce

2 tsp Dijon mustard

3 tbsp chopped fresh parsley

3 tbsp grated Cheddar cheese

salt and ground black pepper

1 Heat the oil in a large frying pan. Add the chicken and cook for 8–10 minutes, stirring occasionally. Add the leeks and continue cooking for 4–5 minutes.
2 Meanwhile, cook the pasta in a large pan of lightly salted boiling water according to the pack instructions. Drain well and return to the pan.
3 Preheat the grill (broiler). Stir the cheese sauce into the pasta with the mustard, then add the chicken mixture and parsley. Mix well and transfer to a large ovenproof dish. Season to taste and sprinkle over the grated Cheddar.
4 Pop under the hot grill for 4–5 minutes until golden brown and bubbling. Serve immediately.

preparation 10 minutes   **cooking time** 20 minutes

Serves 4

ORANGE TARRAGON CHICKEN

125ml/4fl oz/½ cup orange juice

grated zest of 1 orange

2 tbsp chopped fresh tarragon

2 tbsp chopped fresh parsley

1 garlic clove, crushed

4 boneless, skinless chicken breasts

1 orange, thinly sliced

salt and ground black pepper

1 Preheat the oven to 200°C/400°F/Gas 6.
2 Whisk the orange juice, orange zest, herbs and garlic together in a large bowl. Season with salt and pepper.
3 Slash the chicken breasts several times with a sharp knife. Place them in a large ovenproof dish. Pour the orange marinade over them.
4 Cook the chicken in the oven for 20–30 minutes, basting occasionally, until cooked right through.
5 Serve the chicken topped with orange slices with boiled rice.

preparation 10 minutes   cooking time 20–30 minutes

Serves 4

THAI CHICKEN CURRY

2 garlic cloves, peeled

1 onion, quartered

1 lemongrass stalk, halved

2.5cm/1in piece fresh root ginger, peeled and halved

2 fresh red chillies

a few fresh coriander (cilantro) sprigs plus extra to garnish

grated zest and juice of 1 lime

2 tbsp coconut oil

6 skinless chicken breast fillets

3 tomatoes, chopped

2 tbsp Thai fish sauce

900ml/1½ pints/3⅔ cups coconut milk

salt and ground black pepper

1 Put the garlic, onion, lemongrass, ginger, chillies, coriander, and lime zest and juice in a food processor or blender and blitz to a thick aromatic paste.
2 Heat the oil in a wok or deep frying pan over a medium heat. Add the spice paste and cook for 3–4 minutes, stirring constantly to prevent the mixture burning.
3 Cut the chicken into large pieces and add them to the wok. Stir into the spice mixture and cook for 5 minutes, stirring occasionally.
4 Add the tomatoes, fish sauce and coconut milk. Reduce the heat, cover the pan and simmer gently for 20 minutes or until the chicken is cooked.
5 Season with salt and pepper, garnish with coriander sprigs and serve with boiled rice.

preparation 15 minutes   cooking time 35 minutes

Serves 6

INDONESIAN CHICKEN

4 boneless, skinless chicken breasts, cut into strips
2 garlic cloves, crushed
2 tbsp groundnut (peanut) oil
juice of ½ lime
Thai fragrant rice and chopped fresh coriander (cilantro) to serve

For the peanut sauce
1 tbsp groundnut (peanut) oil
2 tbsp hot curry paste
1 tbsp brown sugar
3 tbsp chunky peanut butter
200ml/7fl oz/¾ cup coconut milk

1 Mix the chicken in a bowl with the garlic, oil and lime juice. Cover and chill in the refrigerator for 15 minutes.
2 To make the peanut sauce, heat the oil in a pan, add the curry paste, sugar and peanut butter and fry for 1 minute. Add the coconut milk and bring to the boil, stirring all the time. Reduce the heat and simmer for 5 minutes.
3 Meanwhile, heat a wok or deep frying pan and, when hot, stir-fry the chicken in its marinade in batches for about 3–4 minutes until cooked.
4 Arrange the chicken on a mound of Thai fragrant rice. Pour the peanut sauce over the top and sprinkle with coriander.

preparation 10 minutes plus 15 minutes marinating cooking time 10 minutes

Serves 4

CARIBBEAN CHICKEN

8 skinless chicken pieces
1 tbsp paprika
1 fresh chilli, chopped
1 onion, chopped
4 garlic cloves, crushed
2 tbsp dark soy sauce
juice of 1 lemon
2 tbsp coconut oil
2 tbsp light muscovado sugar
340g/12oz/1½ cups basmati rice
2 x 300g/11oz cans red kidney beans, drained and rinsed
175g/6oz fresh pineapple, peeled and chopped
West Indian hot pepper sauce to serve

1 Mix the chicken, paprika, chilli, onion and garlic in a bowl. Stir in the soy sauce and lemon juice. Cover and chill in the refrigerator for at least 4 hours.
2 Heat a large pan over a medium heat. Add the oil and sugar and cook for 3 minutes. Add the chicken, cover the pan and cook for 10 minutes, turning the chicken halfway, until evenly browned. Add the marinade and cook for 10 minutes.
3 Add the rice and pour in 900ml/1½ pints/3⅔ cups cold water. Cover the pan and simmer, without lifting the lid, for 20 minutes or until the rice is tender and most of the liquid has been absorbed.
4 Stir in the beans and pineapple. Cover and cook gently for 5 minutes until the beans are warmed through and all the liquid has been absorbed. Check that the rice doesn't stick to the bottom of the pan.
5 Serve hot with a dash of hot pepper sauce.

preparation 40 minutes plus minimum 4 hours marinating cooking time 45–50 minutes

Serves 4

GRILLED CHICKEN WITH BULGUR WHEAT

3 garlic cloves, crushed
2 tbsp olive oil
4 boneless, skinless chicken breasts
225g/8oz/1 cup bulgur wheat
12 cherry tomatoes, chopped
½ cucumber, chopped
1 small red onion, chopped
50g/2oz/⅓ cup raisins
3 tbsp chopped fresh parsley
3 tbsp chopped fresh mint
juice of 1 large lemon
salt and ground black pepper

1 Put the garlic in a bowl with 1 tbsp oil. Slash the chicken breasts 3 or 4 times with a knife and add to the marinade. Stir well to coat the chicken. Cover and leave to marinate while you prepare the bulgur wheat.
2 Cook the bulgur wheat according to the pack instructions. Transfer to a bowl and stir in the tomatoes, cucumber, red onion, raisins and herbs. Season well with salt and pepper. Add the remaining oil and the lemon juice and stir well.
3 Preheat the grill (broiler) to high. Put the chicken on a grill (broiling) rack and cook for 10 minutes on each side or until cooked right through – the juices should run clear when the meat is pierced with a sharp knife.
4 Cut the chicken into slices and serve with the bulgur wheat.

preparation 20 minutes   cooking time 30 minutes

Serves 4

CREAMY CHICKEN PASTA

1 tbsp olive oil
1 onion, chopped
400g/14oz chicken breast fillets
125g/4oz mushrooms, sliced
50ml/2fl oz/¼ cup Marsala
125ml/4fl oz/½ cup hot chicken stock
300g/11oz pasta shapes
150ml/¼ pint/scant ⅔ cup crème fraîche
2 tsp Dijon mustard
2 tbsp chopped fresh parsley

1 Heat the oil in a large frying pan over a medium heat. Add the onion and fry gently, stirring, for 5 minutes.
2 Chop the chicken into chunks and add to the pan. Cook until browned all over, stirring occasionally. Add the mushrooms and cook for 2 minutes.
3 Pour in the Marsala and hot stock, reduce the heat and simmer for 12–15 minutes until the chicken is cooked.
4 Meanwhile, cook the pasta in a large pan of lightly salted boiling water according to the pack instructions.
5 Stir the crème fraîche, mustard and basil into the chicken mixture and heat through gently.
6 Drain the pasta and return to the pan. Add the chicken sauce, toss well together and serve sprinkled with parsley.

preparation 10 minutes   cooking time 25 minutes

Serves 4

SESAME BEEF

3 tbsp soy sauce

juice of ½ lime

2 garlic cloves, crushed

400g/14oz rump steak, sliced

1 tbsp sesame oil

3 small pak choi (bok choy), chopped

1 bunch of spring onions (scallions), thickly sliced

1 tbsp sesame seeds

450g/1lb cooked egg noodles

1 Put the soy sauce, lime juice and garlic in a bowl and mix well. Stir in the steak strips and toss to coat.

2 Heat the oil in a large wok or deep frying pan over a high heat. When it's hot, add the steak and stir-fry quickly until it is seared all over.

3 Add any leftover marinade from the bowl to the wok and heat for 1 minute. Add the pak choi and spring onions and stir-fry for 5 minutes. Add the sesame seeds and fry for 1 minute.

4 Add the cooked egg noodles to the wok. Toss together and serve immediately.

preparation 20 minutes **cooking time** 10 minutes

Serves 4

BEEF STROGANOV

4 tbsp olive oil

1 onion, thinly sliced

2 garlic cloves, crushed

340g/12oz mushrooms, sliced

700g/1½lb rump steak, sliced

3 tbsp brandy

1 tsp Dijon mustard

1 tsp tomato paste

100ml/3½fl oz/⅓ cup half-fat crème fraîche

100ml/3½fl oz/⅓ cup soured cream

4 tbsp chopped fresh parsley

salt and ground black pepper

1 Heat half the oil in a large frying pan over a low heat. Add the onion and garlic. Cook gently for 10 minutes or until soft and golden. Remove with a slotted spoon and set aside.

2 Add the mushrooms to the pan and cook, stirring, for 2–3 minutes until golden brown; remove and set aside.

3 Increase the heat and add the remaining oil. Quickly stir-fry the steak, in batches, until browned all over. Remove from the pan. Add the brandy to the pan and let it bubble for a few minutes to reduce.

4 Return the steak, onion and mushrooms to the pan. Reduce the heat and stir in the mustard, tomato paste, crème fraîche and soured cream. Heat through very gently. Stir in the parsley and season to taste.

5 Serve immediately with boiled rice or noodles.

preparation 10 minutes **cooking time** 20 minutes

Serves 4

SWEDISH MEATBALLS

500g/1lb 2oz/2¼ cups minced (ground) beef
1 tbsp Dijon mustard
1 large egg, beaten
75g/3oz/1½ cups fresh white breadcrumbs
4 tbsp finely chopped fresh dill
1 tbsp olive oil
300ml/½ pint/1¼ cups hot beef stock
150ml/¼ pint/scant ⅔ cup soured cream
salt and ground black pepper

1 Put the beef mince, mustard, beaten egg, breadcrumbs, half the dill and seasoning in a large bowl and mix well. Form the mixture into 20 small balls.
2 Heat the oil in a large frying pan over a medium heat. Fry the meatballs for 8–10 minutes, turning them occasionally, until cooked through and golden brown all over.
3 Pour in the stock and soured cream, bring to the boil, then reduce the heat and let it bubble away for a few minutes. Stir in the remaining dill and check the seasoning.
4 Serve the meatballs in the creamy sauce with boiled rice.

preparation 15 minutes cooking time 15 minutes

Serves 4

STIR-FRIED BEEF AND MUSHROOMS

225g/8oz rump steak, sliced
2 tbsp oyster sauce
2 tbsp light soy sauce
25g/1oz dried shiitake mushrooms
2 tbsp vegetable oil
1 small onion, thinly sliced
2.5cm/1in piece fresh root ginger, peeled and sliced
2 carrots, cut into matchsticks
1 green (bell) pepper, seeded and cut into thin strips
2 tsp cornflour (cornstarch)

1 Put the steak, oyster and soy sauces in a bowl. Stir well, then cover and marinate in the refrigerator for 30 minutes.
2 Meanwhile, soak the mushrooms in boiling water for about 30 minutes. Drain and reserve the soaking liquid. Squeeze the mushrooms dry.
3 Heat the oil in a wok or large frying pan over a medium heat. Add the onion and stir-fry for 2 minutes. Add the mushrooms, ginger, carrots and green pepper and stir-fry for 3 minutes until slightly softened. Remove and set aside.
4 Add the steak and marinade to the pan and stir-fry for 2–3 minutes, until tender. Mix the cornflour with 4 tbsp soaking water from the mushrooms and add to the pan with the vegetables. Stir until the sauce thickens. Serve.

preparation 15 minutes plus soaking and marinating cooking time 15 minutes

Serves 2

BEEF JAMBALAYA

3 tbsp oil

150g/5oz chorizo, cut into strips

2 red (bell) peppers, seeded and sliced

400g/14oz rump steak, sliced

1 large onion, roughly chopped

2 garlic cloves, crushed

275g/10oz/1¼ cups basmati rice

1 tbsp tomato paste

2 tsp Cajun seasoning

900ml/1½ pints/3⅔ cups hot beef stock

1 x 400g/14oz can chopped tomatoes

salt and ground black pepper

1 Heat the oil in a large frying pan and cook the chorizo until golden brown. Add the red peppers and cook for 3 minutes until beginning to soften. Remove from the pan and set aside. Add the steak and fry in batches, then put aside and keep warm.

2 Add the onion to the pan and cook gently for 5 minutes until tender. Add the garlic, rice, tomato paste and the Cajun seasoning. Cook for 2 minutes, then stir in the hot stock, season with salt and bring to the boil.

3 Reduce the heat, add the tomatoes, cover the pan and simmer for 20 minutes, stirring occasionally, until the rice is tender and most of the liquid has been absorbed.

4 Add the steak, chorizo and red peppers. Heat gently, stirring, until piping hot. Season to taste and serve with a salad.

preparation 10 minutes   cooking time 40 minutes

Serves 4

SZECHUAN BEEF

340g/12oz rump steak, sliced

1 tsp ground Szechuan powder

3 tbsp hoisin sauce

2 tbsp vegetable oil

1 red chilli, finely chopped

1 large onion, thinly sliced

2 garlic cloves, crushed

2 red (bell) peppers, seeded and cut into chunks

1 carrot, cut into matchsticks

225g/8oz baby corn, halved

1 tsp fresh root ginger, grated

1 spring onion (scallion), diced

1 Put the beef in a bowl, add the Szechuan powder and hoisin sauce and stir. Cover and leave to marinate for 30 minutes.

2 Heat the oil in a wok or large frying pan until smoking hot. Add the chilli, onion and garlic and stir-fry over a medium heat for 3–4 minutes until tender. Remove and set aside. Add the red peppers, carrot and baby corn, increase the heat and stir-fry for 1 minute. Remove and set aside.

3 Add the steak and marinade to the pan in batches. Stir-fry over a high heat for 1 minute.

4 Return the vegetables to the pan. Add the ginger and stir-fry for 1 minute or until heated through. Sprinkle with the spring onion and serve immediately.

preparation 15 minutes plus marinating   cooking time 5–10 minutes

Serves 4

VEAL SCHNITZEL

4 veal escalopes
flour to coat
1 medium (US large) egg
1 tbsp lemon juice
1 tbsp double (heavy) cream
50g/2oz/1 cup fresh white breadcrumbs
4 tbsp oil
salt and ground black pepper
lemon wedges to serve

1 Lay the veal escalopes between two pieces of greaseproof paper and beat with a rolling pin to flatten them.
2 Season the veal, then coat lightly with flour. Beat the egg, lemon juice and cream together and dip the escalopes into the mixture. Next dip them into the breadcrumbs to coat them all over.
3 Heat 1 tbsp oil in a large heavy-based frying pan, add one coated escalope and fry for 1–2 minutes on each side until golden brown. Transfer to a heatproof plate and keep warm while you cook the remaining veal in the same way, using fresh oil for each escalope.
4 Serve the veal immediately with lemon wedges.

preparation 30 minutes   **cooking time** 15 minutes

Serves 4

ROAST LAMB AND PASTA

1.1kg/2½lb half leg of lamb
150ml/¼ pint/scant ⅔ cup red wine
1 x 400g/14oz can chopped tomatoes
75g/3oz pasta shapes
12 sunblush tomatoes
dash of balsamic vinegar
a few sprigs of fresh basil, chopped
salt and ground black pepper

1 Preheat the oven to 200°C/400°F/Gas 6.
2 Put the lamb in a small deep roasting pan and fry on the hob for 5 minutes or until the lamb is brown all over.
3 Remove the lamb and put aside. Pour the wine into the pan and let it bubble away for a few minutes. Stir well, scraping the bottom to loosen any crusty bits, then leave to bubble until half the wine has evaporated.
4 Stir in 300ml/½ pint/1¼ cups water and add the chopped tomatoes, pasta and sunblush tomatoes.
5 Put the lamb on a rack over the roasting pan and cook, uncovered, in the oven for 35 minutes.
6 Stir the balsamic vinegar and basil into the pasta, season to taste and put everything back in the oven for 5 minutes or until the lamb is tender and the pasta is cooked.
7 Carve the lamb thickly and serve with the pasta..

preparation 10 minutes   **cooking time** 50 minutes

Serves 4

LAMB WITH FRIED POTATOES

2 tbsp mint sauce (see page 253)
8 small lamb chops
3 medium potatoes, cut into large chunks
3 tbsp olive oil
2 garlic cloves, crushed
salt and ground black pepper

1 Spread the mint sauce over the lamb chops and leave in a cool place to marinate.
2 Cook the potatoes in a pan of lightly salted boiling water for 10–15 minutes until just tender. Cool and dice.
3 Meanwhile, heat the olive oil in a large frying pan and fry the chops for 4–5 minutes on each side until just cooked. Remove and keep warm.
4 Add the potatoes to the pan. Fry over a medium heat, stirring occasionally, for 10 minutes until crisp and golden. Add the garlic and cook for 1 minute. Season to taste.
5 Serve the fried potatoes immediately with the chops..

preparation 10 minutes plus marinating cooking time 20 minutes

Serves 4

PARMESAN-CRUMBED LAMB CUTLETS

75g/3oz/1½ cups fresh breadcrumbs
3 tbsp freshly grated Parmesan
8 lamb cutlets, well trimmed
2 medium (US large) eggs, beaten
3 tbsp olive oil
2 unpeeled garlic cloves
salt and ground black pepper
new potatoes and peas to serve

1 Mix together the breadcrumbs and Parmesan. Spread out the mixture on a large plate and set aside.
2 Season the lamb with salt and pepper and brush lightly with beaten egg. Press the lamb into the breadcrumb mixture to coat evenly all over. Season with salt and pepper
3 Heat the oil in a large non-stick frying pan, add the garlic cloves and cook gently over a low heat until golden brown. Remove and discard the garlic.
4 Add the lamb to the pan and cook over a low heat for about 4–5 minutes on each side until crisp and golden brown.
5 Serve the lamb with new potatoes and peas.

preparation 10 minutes cooking time 10 minutes

Serves 4

PORK WITH BLACK BEAN SAUCE

2 tbsp vegetable oil
450g/1lb pork fillet, cubed
1 garlic clove, crushed
1 tsp diced fresh root ginger
4 spring onions (scallions), cut into 2.5cm/1in pieces
1 red (bell) pepper, seeded and cut into chunks
1 green (bell) pepper, seeded and cut into chunks
1 tbsp light soy sauce
150g/5oz black bean sauce

1 Heat the oil in a wok or large frying pan, add the pork and stir-fry for 3–4 minutes until crisp and golden brown.
2 Add the garlic, ginger, spring onions and red and green peppers to the pan and stir-fry for 2 minutes.
3 Add the soy sauce and black bean sauce and continue stir-frying for 1–2 minutes until heated through.
4 Serve immediately with cooked egg noodles or boiled rice.

preparation 12 minutes plus cooling   **cooking time** 40 minutes

Serves 4

PORK AND GARLIC RISOTTO

6 thin pork escalopes
4 tbsp plain (all-purpose) flour
50g/2oz/4 tbsp unsalted butter
2 tbsp olive oil
1 onion, finely chopped
2 garlic cloves, crushed
225g/8oz/1 cup Arborio rice
300ml/½ pint/1¼ cups white wine
600ml/1 pint/ ½ cups hot chicken or vegetable stock
3 tbsp pesto sauce
6 tbsp freshly grated Parmesan
4 tbsp chopped fresh parsley

1 Preheat the oven to 180°C/350°F/Gas 4.
2 Season the pork escalopes with salt and pepper and dip in the flour.
3 Melt a little of the butter in a deep ovenproof pan. Fry the escalopes in batches for 2–3 minutes on each side until golden, adding more butter as needed. Remove the escalopes, cover and keep warm.
4 Heat the remaining butter and oil in the pan and fry the onion over a low heat for 10 minutes or until tender. Stir in the garlic and rice. Add the wine and hot stock. Bring to the boil, then cook in the oven, uncovered, for 20 minutes.
5 Stir in the pesto and Parmesan. If the rice has not absorbed all the liquid return to the oven for a few more minutes.
6 Serve the escalopes with the risotto, sprinkled with parsley.

preparation 15 minutes   **cooking time** 50 minutes

Serves 6

LAMB AND COCONUT CURRY

2 tbsp coconut oil
1 onion, chopped
1 tbsp grated fresh root ginger
1kg/2lb 4oz lean lamb, diced
3 tbsp hot curry paste
1 tbsp Thai fish sauce
400ml/14fl oz/1¾ cups coconut milk
600ml/1 pint/2½ cups hot lamb or chicken stock
450g/1lb potatoes, cubed
225g/8oz mangetouts, trimmed
75g/3oz/1 cup chopped peanuts
1 bunch of fresh coriander (cilantro), finely chopped

1 Heat the oil in a large heavy-based pan. Add the onion and cook over a medium heat for 8–10 minutes until golden. Add the ginger and cook for 1 minute. Remove and set aside.
2 Add the lamb and fry in batches, stirring occasionally, until browned all over. Set aside.
3 Add the curry paste and fish sauce to the pan and cook for 2–3 minutes. Stir in the onion and ginger mixture, lamb, coconut milk and hot stock.
4 Bring to the boil, then cover the pan with a lid, reduce the heat and simmer gently for 1 hour. Add the potatoes, remove the lid and cook for 20 minutes, then add the mangetouts and cook for 15 minutes.
5 Sprinkle with the peanuts and chopped coriander and serve with boiled rice.

preparation 20 minutes   cooking time 2 hours

Serves 8

GINGER PORK WITH RICE

1 tsp grated fresh root ginger
1 tbsp sherry
2 tbsp soy sauce
4 pork steaks
225g/8oz/1 cup basmati rice
2 tbsp olive oil
1 red onion, chopped
1 red (bell) pepper, seeded and chopped
2 carrots, cut into matchsticks
salt and ground black pepper

1 Mix the ginger, sherry and soy sauce in a shallow dish. Add the pork steaks, turning them to coat with the marinade. Set aside in a cool place.
2 Cook the rice according to the instructions on the packet.
3 Meanwhile, heat half the oil in a wok. Add the onion, red pepper and carrots and stir-fry for 3–4 minutes.
4 Heat the remaining oil in a frying pan and fry the pork steaks for 4–5 minutes on each side. Season with salt and pepper.
5 Serve the pork steaks immediately with the boiled rice and stir-fried vegetables.

preparation 10 minutes plus marinating   cooking time 20–25 minutes

Serves 4

COD FILLETS WITH CHEESE CRUST

50g/2oz/1 cup fresh white breadcrumbs
4 tbsp grated Cheddar cheese
2 tbsp chopped fresh parsley
2 tbsp chopped fresh chives
4 x 175g/6oz skinless cod fillets
flour to coat
1 large egg, beaten
oil to grease
salt and ground black pepper

1 Mix the breadcrumbs with the grated Cheddar, herbs and seasoning.
2 Season the cod fillets with salt and pepper and toss in flour to coat. Dip the floured cod fillets into the beaten egg, then roll immediately in the breadcrumb mixture to coat them all over. Place on a baking sheet, cover lightly and then chill in the refrigerator for 1 hour.
3 Put the cod fillets in a lightly oiled grill (broiling) pan and cook under a medium-hot grill (broiler) for 12–14 minutes until thoroughly cooked, turning halfway through. Serve with peas and tomatoes.

preparation 30 minutes plus chilling   **cooking time** 15 minutes

Serves 4

COD WITH LENTILS AND BUTTERNUT SQUASH

olive oil to brush
450g/1lb butternut squash, peeled, seeded and diced
2 x 400g/14oz cans green lentils, rinsed and drained
4 tsp balsamic vinegar
2 garlic cloves, finely chopped
300g/11oz cherry tomatoes
2 red onions, cut into wedges
4 x 150g/5oz frozen cod fillets
2 tsp harissa paste
3 tbsp olive oil
salt and ground black pepper
chopped parsley to serve

1 Preheat the oven to 180°C/350°F/Gas 4.
2 Brush a roasting pan with a little oil, then add the butternut squash. Roast in the oven for 10 minutes.
3 Turn the squash and push it to the edges of the roasting pan. Add the lentils to the centre of the pan. Drizzle with balsamic vinegar and mix in the garlic and a little salt and pepper.
4 Arrange the cherry tomatoes and red onion around the edge. Put the cod fillets on top of the lentils. Mix the harissa paste and oil, and drizzle over the fish and vegetables.
5 Roast for 25 minutes or until the fish and squash are cooked. Serve in bowls, sprinkled with a little parsley.

preparation 10 minutes   **cooking time** 35 minutes

Serves 4

TUNA AND SESAME NOODLES

2 fresh tuna steaks

225g/8oz egg noodles

2 tsp sesame oil

1 pak choi (bok choy), sliced

6 spring onions (scallions), sliced

2 tbsp chopped fresh coriander (cilantro)

2 tsp sesame seeds

For the marinade

1 garlic clove, crushed

2 tsp grated fresh root ginger

3 tbsp teriyaki sauce

1 tbsp clear honey

1 Mix together the marinade ingredients and add the tuna steaks. Cover and leave to marinate in the refrigerator for 1 hour.
2 Cook the egg noodles according to the pack instructions. Drain and cool under running water.
3 Meanwhile, preheat the grill (broiler) to high. Put the tuna on a grill (broiling) rack and cook for 3–4 minutes each side, brushing occasionally with the marinade.
4 Heat the sesame oil in a pan and add the pak choi. Cook for 2 minutes, then add the cooked noodles, spring onions, coriander and sesame seeds. Cook for 1 minute.
5 To serve, divide the noodles and vegetables between two serving plates and serve with the grilled tuna steaks.

preparation 20 minutes plus marinating   cooking time 10 minutes

Serves 2

KERALA FISH CURRY

2 tbsp coconut oil

1 onion, thinly sliced

1 garlic clove, crushed

1 green chilli, diced

2 tsp grated fresh root ginger

1 tsp ground turmeric

2 tsp garam masala

400ml/14fl oz/2 cups coconut milk

juice of ½ lime

4 skinless sole fillets

1 Heat the oil in a frying pan over a medium heat and cook the onion, garlic, chilli and ginger for 8–10 minutes until the onion is tender. Add the spices and cook for 1 minute.
2 Add the coconut milk and bring to the boil. Reduce the heat and simmer gently, uncovered, for 10 minutes until reduced, then stir in the lime juice.
3 Place the sole fillets in the pan (roll them up if necessary to make them fit) and simmer very gently for 2 minutes or until just cooked.
4 Serve immediately on a bed of boiled rice.

preparation 10 minutes   cooking time 20 minutes

Serves 4

COD AND COCONUT PILAU

1 tbsp coconut oil
1 small onion, chopped
1 tbsp Thai green curry paste
225g/8oz/1 cup basmati rice
600ml/1 pint/2½ cups hot fish or vegetable stock
150ml/¼ pint/scant ⅔ cup half-fat coconut milk
340g/12oz skinless cod fillet
225g/8oz sugarsnap peas
125g/4oz thin green beans, halved
squeeze of lemon juice
salt and ground black pepper
4 tbsp chopped fresh coriander (cilantro) to garnish

1 Heat the oil in a frying pan, add the onion and cook over a medium heat for 5 minutes until golden brown. Stir in the curry paste and cook for 1–2 minutes.
2 Add the rice, hot stock and coconut milk. Bring to the boil, then reduce the heat and cover the pan. Simmer gently for 15–20 minutes until all the liquid has been absorbed.
3 Cut the cod into bite-sized pieces and add to the pan. Cook for 5 minutes over a low heat.
4 Add the sugarsnap peas, green beans and lemon juice and cook for 3–4 minutes until just tender. Season to taste with salt and pepper.
5 Serve immediately, garnished with coriander.

preparation 15 minutes   cooking time 30 minutes

Serves 4

STIR-FRIED SALMON

2 tsp oil
1 red (bell) pepper, seeded and thinly sliced
1 red chilli, seeded and sliced
1 garlic clove, crushed
125g/4oz green beans, halved
4 spring onions (scallions), sliced
225g/8oz salmon, cut into strips
1 tsp Thai fish sauce
2 tsp soy sauce
cooked rice noodles to serve

1 Heat the oil in a wok or large frying pan. Add the red pepper, chilli, garlic, green beans and spring onions and stir-fry over a high heat for 3–4 minutes.
2 Add the salmon to the pan with the fish sauce and soy sauce and stir-fry for 2 minutes.
3 Serve the salmon and vegetables immediately with some rice noodles.

preparation 10 minutes   cooking time 5–6 minutes

Serves 2

SMOKED SALMON PASTA

450g/1lb penne or pasta tubed
1 tbsp olive oil
1 shallot, finely diced
250g/9oz/1 cup thick Greek yogurt
225g/8oz smoked salmon, diced
4 tbsp chopped fresh parsley
2 tbsp chopped fresh tarragon
salt and ground black pepper

1 Cook the pasta in a large pan of lightly salted boiling water according to the pack instructions, then drain, reserving a couple of tablespoons of the cooking water.
2 Meanwhile, heat the oil in a large pan. Add the shallot and cook over a low heat for 5 minutes until golden. Gently stir in the yogurt, smoked salmon and herbs.
3 Cook very gently for 1–2 minutes until warmed through. Be careful not to let the sauce boil.
4 Toss the pasta in the sauce, season with salt and pepper and serve immediately.

preparation 2 minutes cooking time 10 minutes

Serves 4

SALMON LINGUINE

2 unpeeled garlic cloves
225g/8oz salmon fillet
sunflower oil to brush
salt and ground black pepper
500g/1lb 2oz linguine
200ml/7fl oz/¾ cup crème fraîche
200g/7oz/1¾ cups frozen peas, thawed
2 tbsp chopped fresh dill
salt and ground black pepper

1 Place the garlic in a grill (broiling) pan and cook under a hot grill (broiler) for 8–10 minutes, until soft.
2 Brush the salmon fillet with oil and season with salt and pepper. Grill (broil) for 5–6 minutes, turning halfway through, until cooked through. Allow to cool then break the flesh into large flakes. Cover and set aside.
3 Cook the linguine in a large pan of lightly salted boiling water according to the pack instructions, then drain well, reserving 2 tbsp of the cooking water.
4 Put the crème fraîche and peas in a saucepan. Squeeze the garlic pulp out of its skin and add it to the pan. Heat the mixture gently until warm. Add the salmon flakes and dill, season with salt and pepper and warm through. Stir the reserved pasta cooking water into the sauce.
5 Toss the linguine in the sauce and serve immediately.

preparation 5 minutes cooking time 20 minutes

Serves 4

SALMON AND POTATO SALAD

900g/2lb sweet potatoes
1 red onion, cut into wedges
1 courgette (zucchini), sliced
1 tbsp olive oil
200g/7oz baby plum tomatoes
4 x 125g/4oz salmon fillets
100g/3½oz watercress
salt and ground black pepper
fresh basil leaves to garnish

For the dressing
juice of 1 lemon
1 tbsp wholegrain mustard
1 tbsp runny honey
50ml/2fl oz/¼ cup olive oil

1 Preheat the oven to 220°C/425°F/Gas 7.
2 Peel the sweet potatoes and cut into wedges. Put them with the red onion wedges and courgette in a roasting pan. Drizzle over the oil and roast in the oven for 30 minutes or until just tender.
3 Remove from the oven, stir in the plum tomatoes and lay the salmon fillets on top. Season with salt and pepper and return to the oven for 12 minutes or until the fish is opaque and cooked through.
4 To make the dressing, whisk together the lemon juice, mustard, honey, oil and some salt and pepper in a small bowl until well combined.
5 Divide the watercress among four serving plates. Spoon the roasted vegetables and salmon on top. Pour the dressing over and serve.

Serves 4

preparation 15 minutes   cooking time 50 minutes

ROASTED SALMON, PEA AND TOMATO SALAD

4 x 150g/5oz salmon fillets

1 tbsp olive oil plus extra to drizzle

3 spring onions (scallions), chopped

3 tomatoes, seeded and chopped

200g/7oz/1½ cups frozen peas

2 Little Gem (or 1 Boston) lettuce, sliced

salt and ground black pepper

1 Preheat the oven to 180°C/350°F/Gas 4.
2 Arrange the salmon fillets in an oiled roasting pan, drizzle with oil and sprinkle with salt and pepper. Roast for 20 minutes or until the fish is just cooked and flakes easily.
3 Heat the oil in a frying pan, add the spring onions and tomatoes and cook for 1 minute or until just softened. Add the peas (there's no need to thaw them first) and cook gently for 3 minutes, stirring until thawed.
4 Add the lettuce to the peas and cook for 30 seconds, then spoon on to serving plates and top with the salmon.

preparation 10 minutes   cooking time 20–25 minutes

Serves 4

PRAWN PILAFF

225g/8oz/1 cup basmati rice

150g/5oz baby corn, halved

200g/7oz sugarsnap peas

1 red (bell) pepper, seeded and thinly sliced

400g/14oz cooked and peeled king prawns (jumbo shrimp)

chopped fresh coriander (cilantro) to garnish

For the dressing

1 tbsp oil

1 tsp grated fresh root ginger

grated zest and juice of 1 lime

2 tbsp light soy sauce

1 Put the rice in a large wide pan. Add 600ml/1 pint/2½ cups boiling water. Cover the pan and bring to the boil, then reduce the heat to low and cook the rice according to the pack instructions.
2 About 10 minutes before the end of the cooking time, stir in the broccoli, baby corn, sugarsnap peas and red pepper. Cover the pan and cook gently over a low heat until the vegetables and rice are just tender.
3 Meanwhile, put the prawns in a bowl. Mix all the dressing ingredients together and pour over the prawns.
4 Mix the prawns and dressing into the cooked vegetables and rice, and toss well. Scatter with chopped coriander and serve immediately.

preparation 10 minutes   cooking time 15–20 minutes

Serves 4

PRAWN AND PEANUT NOODLES

300g/11oz straight-to-wok noodles

340g/12oz pack stir-fry vegetables

1 tsp coconut oil

6 tbsp coconut cream

1 tbsp Thai green curry paste

juice of ½ lime

225g/8oz cooked and peeled king prawns (jumbo shrimp)

a small handful of chopped fresh coriander (cilantro)

3 tbsp chopped peanuts

1 Put the noodles in a large heatproof bowl and cover with boiling water. Cover with clingfilm (plastic wrap) and leave for 5 minutes.

2 Meanwhile, quickly stir-fry the vegetables in the oil in a wok for 3–4 minutes.

3 Mix the coconut cream with the curry paste and lime juice in a small bowl.

4 Drain the noodles and place in a large serving bowl with the stir-fried vegetables. Toss with the prawns, coriander and the coconut dressing. Sprinkle over the peanuts and serve.

preparation 10 minutes   **cooking time** 5 minutes

Serves 4

YELLOW BEAN NOODLES WITH PRAWNS

300g/11oz egg noodles

1 tbsp oil

1 garlic clove, sliced

1 tsp grated fresh root ginger

1 small onion, thinly sliced

225g/8oz mushrooms, sliced

250g/9oz raw peeled tiger prawns (shrimp)

200g/7oz pak choi (bok choy), leaves separated

1 x 150g/5oz jar Chinese yellow bean stir-fry sauce

1 Put the noodles in a large bowl and pour boiling water over them. Leave to soak for 5 minutes, then drain and set aside.

2 Heat the oil in a wok or large frying pan. Add the garlic, ginger and mushrooms and stir-fry for 30 seconds. Add the onion and prawns and stir-fry for 2 minutes.

3 Add the pak choi and yellow bean sauce together with a little boiling water to thin the sauce. Stir well to mix.

4 Add the drained noodles to the pan and cook for 1 minute, tossing occasionally. Serve immediately.

preparation 10 minutes plus soaking   **cooking time** 5 minutes

Serves 4

SEAFOOD GUMBO

2 tbsp olive oil

2 tbsp Cajun seasoning

1 onion, chopped

1 green (bell) pepper, seeded
and chopped

1 red (bell) pepper, seeded and
chopped

1 garlic clove, crushed

1 x 400g/14oz can chopped
tomatoes

125g/4oz/½ cup basmati rice

1.2 litres/2 pints/5 cups hot
vegetable stock

225g/8oz okra, sliced

¼ tsp cayenne pepper

juice of ½ lemon

340g/12oz raw prawns (shrimp)

225g/8oz squid, sliced

225g/8oz white crabmeat

1 bunch of spring onions
(scallions), finely chopped

1 small bunch of fresh parsley,
finely chopped

salt and ground black pepper

1 Heat the oil in a large pan over a low heat. Add the Cajun
   seasoning and cook, stirring, for 1–2 minutes until golden
   brown. Add the onion, green and red peppers and garlic and
   cook over a low heat for 10 minutes, stirring occasionally,
   until the vegetables are tender.
2 Add the tomatoes and rice to the pan and stir well until the
   grains are coated. Add the hot stock, okra, cayenne pepper
   and lemon juice. Season with salt and black pepper.
3 Bring to the boil, then reduce the heat and simmer gently,
   covered, for about 20 minutes or until the rice is tender and
   most of the liquid has been absorbed – the gumbo should be
   a bit soupy.
4 Add the prawns, squid and crabmeat to the pan and cook
   gently for 5 minutes until the prawns are pink.
5 Stir in the spring onions and parsley, and heat through for a
   few minutes. Divide the gumbo between four shallow bowls
   and serve immediately.

Serves 4

preparation 20 minutes   cooking time 40 minutes

SWEETCORN AND COD CHOWDER

125g/4oz streaky bacon rashers (slices), chopped

25g/1oz/2 tbsp butter

2 large leeks, thinly sliced

2 tbsp plain (all-purpose) flour

600ml/1 pint/2½ cups milk

700g/1½lb skinned cod fillet

1 x 400g/14oz can sweetcorn in water, drained

450g/1lb potatoes, cubed

150ml/¼ pint/scant ⅔ cup double (heavy) cream

1 bunch fresh parsley, chopped

a pinch of paprika

salt and ground black pepper

1 Fry the bacon in a large pan over a gentle heat until the fat runs out. Add the butter to the pan and when it melts add the leeks and cook gently for 5 minutes until softened.

2 Stir in the flour and cook for a few seconds, then pour in the milk and 300ml/½ pint/1¼ cups water. Cut the cod into pieces and add to the pan with the sweetcorn and potatoes.

3 Bring to the boil, then reduce the heat and simmer gently for 10–15 minutes until the potatoes are cooked.

4 Stir in the cream and parsley. Season to taste with salt and pepper and the paprika and cook for 5 minutes over a low heat to warm through.

5 Ladle the chowder into warmed shallow bowls and serve immediately.

preparation 5 minutes cooking time 30 minutes

Serves 6

TANDOORI KING PRAWNS

16 king prawns (jumbo shrimp)

2 garlic cloves, crushed

juice of 1 lemon

4 tbsp thick Greek yogurt

1 tbsp tandoori paste

1 tsp ground cumin seeds

2 tsp grated fresh root ginger

salt and ground black pepper

For the mint yogurt

300g/11oz/1¼ cups Greek yogurt

4 tbsp chopped fresh mint

1 Peel the prawns and cut along the back of each one to remove the dark vein. Rinse and pat dry with kitchen paper.

2 In a bowl, mix together the garlic and lemon juice with some salt and pepper. Add the prawns and mix to coat thoroughly. Cover and chill in the refrigerator for 20 minutes.

3 In a bowl, mix together the yogurt, tandoori paste, cumin seeds and ginger. Remove the prawns from the marinade and pat dry with kitchen paper. Stir into the yogurt mixture, then cover and chill in the refrigerator for 20 minutes.

4 To make the mint yogurt, stir together the yogurt and mint.

5 Thread the prawns onto skewers and cook under a hot grill (broiler) for 4–5 minutes, turning halfway through, until firm and pink. Serve with the yogurt.

preparation 10 minutes plus marinating cooking time 4–5 minutes

Serves 4

SEAFOOD AND PASTA SALAD

175g/6oz penne pasta

3 tbsp olive oil

1 tbsp white wine vinegar

juice of 2 limes

1 red chilli, seeded and diced

250g/9oz pack cooked mixed seafood or fruits de mer

225g/8oz baby plum tomatoes

1 avocado, peeled and stoned

1 red onion, diced

3 tbsp chopped fresh coriander (cilantro)

salt and ground black pepper

1 Bring a large pan of lightly salted water to the boil, add the pasta and cook according to the pack instructions. Drain well, then transfer to a serving dish.
2 To make the dressing, whisk the oil and wine vinegar together in a small bowl. Whisk in the lime juice and the chilli and season to taste with salt and pepper.
3 Stir the dressing into the warm pasta with the seafood and baby plum tomatoes. Cut the avocado into cubes and add to the pasta with the red onion and coriander.
4 Divide among four serving plates and serve warm.

preparation 15 minutes   **cooking time** 10–12 minutes

Serves 4

CLAMS WITH CHILLI SPAGHETTI

300g/11oz spaghetti

2 tbsp olive oil

1 garlic clove, crushed

1 red chilli, finely chopped

1 x 400g/14oz can tomatoes

900g/2lb clams in their shells, washed and scrubbed

150ml/¼ pint/scant ⅔ cup white wine

4 tbsp chopped fresh parsley

1 Cook the spaghetti in a large pan of salted boiling water according to the pack instructions.
2 Meanwhile, heat the oil in a large pan. Add the garlic, chilli and tomatoes and cook for 5 minutes, stirring gently.
3 Add the clams and wine. Cover the pan with a lid and cook over a high heat for 3–4 minutes until the clams open – discard any that remain closed.
4 Drain the pasta, return to the pan, then add the clams with the sauce and the parsley. Toss together gently and serve.

preparation 15 minutes   **cooking time** 10 minutes

Serves 4

SPAGHETTI WITH ANCHOVIES AND TOMATOES

1 x 50g/2oz can anchovy fillets in oil
1 onion, finely chopped
4 garlic cloves, crushed
1 tbsp tomato paste
1 x 400g/14oz can chopped tomatoes
500g/1lb 2oz spaghetti
125g/4oz black olives, pitted and chopped
4 tbsp chopped fresh parsley
salt and ground black pepper

1 Drain the oil from the anchovies into a large pan. Heat the oil, then add the onion and garlic and cook for 5 minutes. Add the anchovies and tomato paste and cook, stirring, for 1 minute. Add the tomatoes and bring to the boil. Season with salt and pepper and simmer for 10–15 minutes.
2 Meanwhile, cook the spaghetti in a large pan of lightly salted boiling water according to the pack instructions. Strain, reserving 4 tbsp of the cooking water.
3 Stir the olives into the tomato sauce and add to the cooked spaghetti with the chopped parsley. Toss well to coat the pasta. Serve immediately in shallow bowls.

preparation 15 minutes   cooking time 20–25 minutes

Serves 4

LINGUINE ALLE VONGOLE

2 tbsp olive oil
1 onion, diced
3 garlic cloves, crushed
1 red chilli, finely chopped
250ml/8fl oz/1 cup white wine
grated zest of 1 lemon
340g/12oz linguine
2 x 200g/7oz cans clams, drained
salt and ground black pepper
bunch of fresh parsley, chopped

1 Heat the oil in a very large pan and gently fry the onion for 5 minutes. Add the garlic and chilli and cook for 1 minute.
2 Add the wine and let it bubble until reduced by half. Stir in the lemon zest and season with salt and pepper.
3 Meanwhile, cook the linguine in a large pan of lightly salted boiling water according to the pack instructions.
4 Add the clams to the sauce and simmer gently for about 2–3 minutes to warm them through.
5 Drain the linguine and toss with the clam sauce and parsley. Divide among four shallow bowls and serve.

preparation 10 minutes   cooking time 15 minutes

Serves 4

PENNE AND TUNA

2 tbsp olive oil

1 red onion, finely sliced

2 garlic cloves, crushed

1 x 400g/14oz can chopped tomatoes

500g/1lb 2oz penne or pasta tubes

2 x 200g/7oz cans tuna steak in spring water

3 tbsp small capers

a few fresh basil leaves, torn

salt and ground black pepper

1 Heat the oil in a pan, then add the red onion and fry over a low heat for 10 minutes or until softened but not browned. Add the garlic and cook for 1 minute.
2 Add the tomatoes and stir well. Season to taste with salt and pepper and simmer over a medium heat for 10 minutes until the sauce reduces and thickens
3 Meanwhile, cook the pasta in a large pan of lightly salted boiling water according to the pack instructions.
4 Drain the tuna and cut into small chunks. Stir into the tomato sauce along with the capers and basil.
5 Drain the pasta, return to the pan and toss with the tuna sauce. Serve immediately in shallow bowls.

preparation 10 minutes cooking time 30 minutes

Serves 4

SARDINE AND OLIVE PASTA

450g/1lb penne or fusilli pasta

1 tbsp olive oil

1 onion, finely chopped

1 garlic clove, crushed

1 x 400g/14oz can chopped tomatoes

1 x 125g/4oz can boneless, skinless sardine fillets, drained

50g/2oz/½ cup pitted black and green olives

salt and ground black pepper

chopped fresh parsley to garnish

1 Bring a large pan of lightly salted water to the boil and cook the pasta according to the pack instructions. Strain well, reserving a cupful of the cooking water.
2 Meanwhile, heat the oil in a large pan and fry the onion and garlic over a low heat for 10 minutes or until softened but not coloured. Add the tomatoes, then bring to the boil. Reduce the heat and simmer for 15 minutes until thickened. Stir in the sardines and olives.
3 Add the pasta to the sauce and toss well to combine.
4 Serve immediately in shallow bowls, sprinkled with plenty of chopped parsley.

preparation 10 minutes cooking time 25 minutes

Serves 4

AUBERGINE LINGUINE

1 large aubergine (eggplant)
4 tbsp olive oil
salt and ground black pepper
1 onion, finely chopped
2 garlic cloves, crushed
1 tbsp capers, drained and
roughly chopped
3 tbsp chopped fresh parsley
1 x 400g/14oz can chopped
tomatoes
450g/1lb linguine
2 tbsp freshly grated Parmesan

1 Cut the aubergine lengthways into 1cm/½in thick slices, discarding the sides. Brush the slices with oil and season with salt and pepper.
2 Grill (broil) the aubergine for 6–7 minutes, until browned and soft. Set aside to cool, then cut into strips.
3 Heat the remaining oil in a frying pan. Add the onion and cook gently over a low heat for 10 minutes until soft. Add the garlic and capers and cook for 1 minute. Add the parsley, tomatoes, salt and pepper and simmer for 10 minutes. Remove from the heat and stir in the strips of aubergine.
4 Meanwhile, bring a pan of lightly salted water to the boil and cook the linguine according to the pack instructions. Drain and return to the pan. Add the aubergine mixture and toss well. Serve in warmed bowls, sprinkled with Parmesan.

preparation 10 minutes cooking time 30 minutes

Serves 4

SQUASH AND RED ONION PASTA

2 red onions, thinly sliced
3 tbsp sunflower oil
700g/1lb 9oz butternut squash
225g/8oz fusilli pasta
4 tbsp chopped fresh parsley
1 garlic clove, crushed
4 tbsp crème fraîche
salt and ground black pepper
¼ tsp freshly grated nutmeg
2 tbsp freshly grated Parmesan

1 Toss the onions in a bowl with half of the olive oil. Spread them out in a foil-lined grill (broiling) pan and cook under a hot grill (broiler) for 1–2 minutes, stirring occasionally, until soft and beginning to caramelize. Set aside.
2 Peel and seed the squash and cut into 1cm/½in slices. Brush with the remaining oil. Grill (broil) for 8 minutes, turning occasionally, until soft and starting to brown. Cut the squash into bite-sized pieces.
3 Meanwhile, cook the pasta in a large pan of lightly salted boiling water according to the instructions on the pack. Drain, reserving 4 tbsp of the cooking water, and return to the pan.
4 Add the parsley, garlic, crème fraîche, nutmeg and reserved cooking water. Season to taste and toss everything together. Serve on warmed plates, sprinkled with Parmesan.

preparation 10 minutes cooking time 15 minutes

Serves 4

SPICY KALE AND ANCHOVY PASTA

75g/3oz/1½ cups fresh breadcrumbs

450g/1lb orecchiette or fusilli

175g/6oz kale or spring greens (collards), shredded

2 tbsp olive oil

1 red chilli, seeded and chopped

1 x 125g/4oz can boneless, skinless sardine fillets, drained

1 Preheat the grill (broiler) to medium and toast the breadcrumbs.
2 Cook the pasta in a large pan of lightly salted boiling water according to the pack instructions. Add the kale or spring greens for the last 4 minutes of the cooking time.
3 Heat 1 tbsp oil in a frying pan and fry the chilli for 1 minute. Add the anchovies and heat through for 2–3 minutes.
4 Drain the pasta and kale, then tip back into the pan. Add the breadcrumbs and the anchovy mixture and toss together. Serve immediately in shallow bowls.

preparation 5 minutes   cooking time 15 minutes

Serves 4

PASTA SHELLS WITH LEEKS AND MUSHROOMS

450g/1lb pasta shells

2 tbsp olive oil

2 medium leeks, thickly sliced

225g/8oz mushrooms, sliced

1 garlic clove, crushed

150ml/¼ pint/scant ⅔ cup creme fraîche

salt and ground black pepper

chopped fresh parsley to garnish

1 Cook the pasta in a large pan of lightly salted boiling water according to the pack instructions.
2 Meanwhile, heat the oil in a frying pan and add the leeks, mushrooms and garlic. Cook over a medium heat for about 5–10 minutes until the leeks are tender.
3 Reduce the heat, stir in the creme fraîche and season to taste with salt and pepper. Let it bubble and reduce a little.
4 Drain the pasta, add to the sauce and toss well. Serve immediately, garnished with parsley.

preparation 5 minutes   cooking time 15–20 minutes

Serves 4

EASY BEEF PASTA BAKE

1 tbsp olive oil
1 large onion, finely chopped
2 garlic cloves, crushed
225g/8oz mushrooms, sliced
450g/1lb/2 cups minced (ground) beef
2 x 400g/14oz cans tomatoes
1 tsp fresh thyme
450g/1lb penne pasta
1 x 300g/11oz jar cheese sauce
75g/3oz/¾ cup freshly grated Parmesan
salt and ground black pepper

1 Heat the oil in a pan. Add the onion and garlic and cook over a medium heat for 5 minutes until soft. Add the mushrooms and cook for 3 minutes, stirring. Add the beef and cook, stirring, until it browns. Add the tomatoes and thyme, reduce the heat and simmer gently for 25 minutes. Season to taste with salt and pepper.
2 Meanwhile, cook the pasta in a large pan of lightly salted boiling water according to the pack instructions.
3 Drain, return to the pan and stir in the cheese sauce. Heat through for 3–4 minutes.
4 Preheat the grill (broiler). Put alternate layers of mince and pasta into a heatproof dish and sprinkle with the Parmesan.
5 Cook under the hot grill until bubbling and golden brown. Serve immediately with salad..

preparation 5 minutes   cooking time 45 minutes

Serves 4

PASTA SHELLS WITH SPINACH AND RICOTTA

450g/1lb fresh spinach, washed
175g/6oz/1 cup ricotta cheese
1 medium (US large) egg
a pinch of freshly grated nutmeg
50g/2oz/⅓ cup freshly grated Parmesan
225g/8oz large pasta shells
½ quantity tomato sauce (see page 575)
salt and ground black pepper

1 Preheat the oven to 200°C/400°F/Gas 6.
2 Put the spinach in a large pan. Cover and cook over a low to medium heat for 2–3 minutes until wilted. Drain, squeeze out the excess liquid and chop finely.
3 Put the spinach in a large bowl with the ricotta and beat in the egg. Stir in the nutmeg and half the grated Parmesan, and season to taste.
4 Meanwhile, cook the pasta in a large pan of lightly salted boiling water according to the pack instructions. Drain well.
5 Spread the tomato sauce in the bottom of an ovenproof dish. Fill the shells with the spinach mixture and arrange on top of the sauce. Sprinkle with the remaining Parmesan. Cook in the oven for 20–25 minutes until golden and serve hot.

preparation 10 minutes   cooking time 45 minutes

Serves 4

TOMATO, CHILLI AND MOZZARELLA PASTA SALAD

7 tbsp olive oil
juice of 1 lemon
1 garlic clove, crushed
450g/1lb penne pasta
225g/8oz mozzarella, cubed
450g/1lb tomatoes, chopped
1 red chilli, seeded and diced
1 avocado, peeled and stoned
a small bunch of parsley, finely chopped
salt and ground black pepper

1 Whisk together the oil, lemon juice and garlic. Season with salt and pepper and set aside.
2 Bring a large pan of lightly salted water to the boil, add the pasta and cook according to the pack instructions. Drain well, then tip into a large bowl and toss with a little of the dressing. Set aside to cool.
3 Add the mozzarella, tomatoes and chilli to the pasta. Cut the avocado into large dice and add to the pasta with the parsley.
4 Pour the remaining dressing over and toss lightly together. Serve immediately.

preparation 20 minutes plus cooling   **cooking time** 10–12 minutes

Serves 4

PASTRAMI PASTA VINAIGRETTE

450g/1lb pasta shapes
125g/4oz pastrami, diced
225g/8oz baby plum tomatoes, quartered
½ cucumber, chopped
1 red onion, finely chopped
wholegrain mustard to taste
125ml/4fl oz/½ cup vinaigrette (see page 592)
1 bunch of fresh chives, snipped
salt and ground black pepper

1 Bring a large pan of lightly salted water to the boil, add the pasta and cook according to the pack instructions. Drain well and set aside to cool.
2 In a large bowl, mix together the cooked pasta, pastrami, tomatoes, cucumber and red onion.
3 Blend the mustard with the vinaigrette and pour the dressing over the salad.
4 Stir in the chives and toss everything gently together. Season to taste and serve immediately.

preparation 15 minutes   **cooking time** 10–12 minutes

Serves 4

SPRING LAMB AND BEAN SALAD

500g/1lb 2oz lean lamb fillet

4 tbsp olive oil plus extra to fry

grated zest and juice of 1 lemon

1 garlic clove, crushed

a few sprigs of fresh mint, chopped

1 x 400g/14oz can cannellini beans, drained and rinsed

125g/4oz frisée lettuce or curly endive

225g/8oz baby plum tomatoes, halved

salt and ground black pepper

1 Season the lamb with salt and pepper. Heat some oil in a frying pan and fry the lamb over a medium heat for 5–7 minutes on each side for medium rare; 8–10 minutes for well done. Remove the lamb, cover and set aside.

2 To make the dressing, whisk together the oil, lemon zest and juice, the garlic and mint in a small bowl.

3 Put the beans, frisée or curly endive and the tomatoes in a bowl. Pour over the dressing and toss together lightly. Season to taste with salt and pepper.

4 Carve the lamb into slices and serve with the bean salad.

preparation 5 minutes **cooking time** 10–20 minutes plus resting

Serves 4

CHICKPEA SOUP WITH PASTA AND PESTO

3 tbsp olive oil

1 onion, chopped

2 sticks celery, chopped

2 garlic cloves, finely chopped

1 x 400g/14oz can chickpeas (garbanzos)

1.2 litres/2 pints/5 cups hot vegetable stock

1 x 400g/14oz can tomatoes

2 courgettes (zucchini), diced

75g/3oz small soup pasta

225g/8oz baby spinach leaves

salt and ground black pepper

6 tsp green pesto

grated Parmesan to serve

1 Heat the oil in a large pan set over a low heat. Add the onion, celery and garlic and cook gently for 5 minutes or until softened but not coloured.

2 Add the chickpeas with their liquid, the hot stock and tomatoes. Bring to the boil, then reduce the heat, cover the pan and simmer for 40 minutes.

3 Add the courgettes and peas. Bring to the boil, then reduce the heat and simmer gently for 10 minutes.

4 Add the pasta and simmer for about 8 minutes until the pasta is just tender but not mushy. Stir in the spinach. Season to taste with salt and pepper.

5 Ladle the hot soup into warmed serving bowls and top with a spoonful of pesto. Sprinkle with grated Parmesan and serve immediately.

preparation 25 minutes **cooking time** 1 hour

Serves 6

SIMPLE FOUR-CHEESE GNOCCHI

450g/1lb fresh gnocchi

1 red (bell) pepper, seeded and cut in half

1 x 300g/11oz tub fresh four-cheese sauce

175g/6oz sunblush tomatoes

4 tbsp freshly grated Parmesan

salt and ground black pepper

fresh basil leaves to garnish

1 Cook the gnocchi in a large pan of lightly salted boiling water according to the pack instructions. Drain well and transfer to a heatproof dish.

2 Preheat the grill (broiler). Grill (boil) the red pepper until it blisters and starts to char. Cool, then peel and dice.

3 Heat the four-cheese sauce and tomatoes in a small pan set over a low heat. Stir in the grilled red pepper and pour over the gnocchi. Season to taste with salt and pepper.

4 Sprinkle with Parmesan and cook under the hot grill for about 5 minutes until golden and bubbling. Garnish with basil leaves and serve.

preparation 3 minutes **cooking time** 10 minutes

Serves 4

SPANISH OMELETTE

6 tbsp olive oil

1 large onion, thinly sliced

675g/1½lb waxy potatoes, peeled and thickly sliced

6 medium (US large) eggs

3 tbsp chopped fresh parsley

4 streaky bacon rashers (slices)

salt and ground black pepper

1 Heat the oil in a non-stick frying pan. Add the onion and potatoes, partially cover the pan and cook gently over a low heat for 25 minutes, stirring occasionally, until the onions are really tender and the potatoes are cooked and golden.
2 Beat the eggs in a bowl and season with salt and pepper. Pour the beaten eggs into the pan over the potatoes and onion and cook over a very low heat for about 10 minutes until the omelette is set and golden brown underneath. Use a spatula to shape the omelette as it cooks.
3 Meanwhile, grill (broil) the bacon until golden brown and crisp, then break into pieces.
4 Pop the omelette under the hot grill (broiler) for 2–3 minutes until the top is just set and golden brown.
5 Sprinkle over the bacon and parsley and set aside for about 10 minutes to cool a little before cutting into wedges to serve. This Spanish omelette can be eaten warm or cold.

preparation 15 minutes   **cooking time** 30–45 minutes

Serves 4

OMELETTE ARNOLD BENNETT

200g/7oz smoked haddock

4 medium (US large) eggs, separated

125ml/4fl oz/½ cup single (light) cream

3 tbsp chopped fresh parsley

25g/1oz/2 tbsp butter

50g/2oz/½ cup grated Parmesan

salt and ground black pepper

1 Put the haddock in a pan and cover with water. Bring to the boil, then reduce the heat and simmer gently for 10 minutes. Drain and flake the fish, discarding the skin and bones.
2 Beat the egg yolks in a bowl with most of the cream and some salt and pepper. Stir in the haddock and parsley.
3 Whisk the egg whites in a clean bowl until they form stiff peaks. Gently fold them into the beaten yolk and haddock mixture, using a metal spoon in a figure-of-eight movement.
4 Melt the butter in an omelette pan. Add the egg mixture and cook over a low heat until set underneath.
5 Preheat the grill (broiler). Mix the Parmesan and remaining cream and spread it lightly over the top of the omelette.
6 Cook under the hot grill until brown and bubbling. Cut in half and serve immediately.

preparation 15 minutes   **cooking time** 20 minutes

Serves 2

GOAT'S CHEESE AND TOMATO TART

1 x 340g/12oz sheet ready-rolled puff pastry

175g/6oz soft goat's cheese

340g/12oz baby plum tomatoes, quartered

1 red onion, thinly sliced

1 tbsp extra virgin olive oil

1 tbsp balsamic vinegar

salt and ground black pepper

a small handful of rocket (arugula) to garnish

1 Preheat the oven to 220°C/425°F/Gas 7. Line a baking tray with parchment paper.
2 Unroll the puff pastry sheet on to the baking tray. Crumble or spread the cheese over the pastry, leaving a border around the edge. Scatter the tomatoes and red onion over the top. Season with salt and pepper and drizzle with oil.
3 Cook in the oven for 25–30 minutes or until the pastry is golden brown, crisp and well risen.
4 Remove from the oven and drizzle with balsamic vinegar. Serve the tart warm or cold, cut into slices and scattered with fresh rocket leaves.

preparation 10 minutes cooking time 25–30 minutes

Serves 4

MUSHROOM FRITTATA

1 tbsp olive oil

450g/1lb mushrooms, sliced

1 small bunch of fresh parsley, finely chopped

6 medium (US large) eggs,

salt and ground black pepper

salad and crusty bread to serve

1 Heat the oil in a large deep frying pan set over a medium heat. Add the onion and mushrooms and cook for 5 minutes until tender and golden. Stir in the parsley.
2 Preheat the grill (broiler). Beat the eggs and season with salt and pepper. Pour into the pan and stir into the mushroom mixture.
3 Cook over a low heat for about 8–10 minutes until the omelette is set and golden brown underneath.
4 Pop the frittata under the hot grill for 4–5 minutes until just set and browned on top.
5 Slide onto a plate, cut into wedges and serve hot or warm.

preparation 15 minutes cooking time 20 minutes

Serves 4

BAKED EGGS AND BEANS

1 tbsp oil
1 red onion, finely sliced
1 red chilli, diced
125g/4oz diced chorizo
2 x 400g/14oz cans chopped tomatoes
a pinch of sugar
1 x 400g/14oz can kidney beans, drained and rinsed
1 bunch of fresh coriander (cilantro), chopped
8 medium (US large) eggs
3 tbsp soured cream
salt and ground black pepper

1 Preheat the oven to 200°C/400°F/Gas 6.
2 Heat the oil in a large frying pan and gently cook the red onion over a low heat for 10 minutes until softened. Stir in the chilli and chorizo and cook for 2 minutes.
3 Add the tomatoes, sugar and kidney beans and simmer gently for 10 minutes. Stir in the coriander and season to taste with salt and pepper.
4 Transfer to a large shallow ovenproof dish. Make eight small indentations in the mixture at regular intervals and break an egg into each one. Drizzle over the soured cream.
5 Cook in the oven for 15–20 minutes until the eggs are set.
6 Divide among four serving plates and serve hot.

preparation 15 minutes   cooking time 40 minutes

Serves 4

SPICED EGG PILAU

225g/8oz/1 cup basmati rice
125g/4oz/1 cup frozen peas
1 tbsp coconut oil
1 onion, chopped
150g/5oz mushrooms, sliced
4 medium (US large) eggs
200ml/7fl oz coconut cream
1 tsp curry paste
a few sprigs of fresh coriander (cilantro), chopped
mango chutney to serve

1 Cook the rice according to the instructions on the pack. Add the peas for the last 5 minutes of cooking time.
2 Put the eggs in a large pan of boiling water and simmer for 6 minutes, then drain and shell when cool.
3 Meanwhile, heat the coconut oil in a pan and cook the onion and mushrooms over a low heat for 10 minutes or until tender and golden. Stir in the coconut cream and curry paste and heat through gently.
4 Drain the rice and stir into the curry mixture with the chopped coriander.
5 Divide the rice among four bowls. Cut the eggs in half and arrange on top. Serve hot with mango chutney.

preparation 5 minutes   cooking time 20 minutes

Serves 4

TOFU NOODLE CURRY

225g/8oz fresh tofu, cubed

1 tbsp Thai fish sauce

½ red chilli, chopped

1 tsp grated fresh root ginger

1 tbsp coconut oil

1 onion, finely sliced

2 tbsp Thai red curry paste

200ml/7fl oz/¾ cup coconut milk

900ml/1½ pints/3⅔ cups hot vegetable stock

200g/7oz green beans, halved

150g/5oz asparagus tips

250g/9oz rice noodles

salt and ground black pepper

chopped fresh coriander (cilantro) to garnish

1 Put the tofu in a shallow dish with the Thai fish sauce, chilli and ginger. Toss to coat, then cover and leave in a cool place to marinate for 30 minutes.
2 Heat the oil in a large pan over a medium heat, then add the onion and fry for 10 minutes, stirring, until golden and tender. Add the curry paste and cook for 2 minutes.
3 Add the tofu and marinade, the coconut milk and hot stock and season with salt and pepper. Bring to the boil, add the green beans and asparagus, then reduce the heat and simmer gently for 8–10 minutes.
4 Meanwhile, put the rice noodles in a large bowl, pour boiling water over them and soak for 30 seconds or cook according to the pack instructions. Drain, then stir into the curry.
5 Spoon into shallow serving bowls and serve immediately garnished with coriander.

preparation 15 minutes plus marinating   **cooking time** 25 minutes

Serves 4

CURRIED TOFU BURGERS

1 tbsp coconut oil plus extra to fry

2 carrots, finely grated

1 large onion, finely grated

1 garlic clove, crushed

1 tsp curry paste

a pinch of ground turmeric

1 tsp tomato paste

225g/8oz fresh tofu

25g/1oz/½ cup fresh breadcrumbs

3 tbsp chopped hazelnuts

flour to dust

salt and ground black pepper

1 Heat the oil in a large frying pan over a medium heat. Add the carrots and onion and cook for 5 minutes until softened, stirring all the time. Add the garlic, curry paste, turmeric and tomato paste.Turn up the heat and cook for about 2–3 minutes, stirring all the time. Set aside to cool.
2 Mash the tofu in a bowl and stir in the cooked vegetables, breadcrumbs and hazelnuts. Season with salt and pepper. Mix thoroughly until the mixture starts to stick together. Shape into eight burgers and dust lightly with flour.
3 Heat some oil in a frying pan and fry the burgers for 3–4 minutes each side until golden brown. Alternatively, brush lightly with oil and cook under a hot grill (broiler) for 3 minutes each side. Drain on kitchen paper and serve.

preparation 20 minutes   **cooking time** 6-8 minutes

Serves 4

PANEER CURRY

1 tbsp coconut oil
1 onion, finely sliced
1 green and 1 red (bell) pepper,
seeded and cut into strips
1 garlic clove, crushed
1 tsp grated fresh root ginger
1 tsp mustard seeds
2 tbsp curry paste
200ml/7fl oz/¾ cup coconut milk
150g/5oz paneer cheese, diced
2 tomatoes, cut into wedges
125g/4oz baby spinach leaves

1 Heat the oil in a large pan over a low heat. Add the onion and green and red peppers and cook gently for 10 minutes or until soft.
2 Add the garlic, ginger and mustard seeds and cook gently for 1 minute. Add the curry paste and cook for 1 minute.
3 Stir in the coconut milk. Bring to the boil, then reduce the heat and simmer gently for 5 minutes.
4 Add the paneer cheese, season to taste and heat through gently. Add the tomatoes and cook for 2–3 minutes.
5 Stir in the spinach and serve immediately with boiled rice.

preparation 15 minutes   cooking time 25 minutes

Serves 4

GULASCHSUPPE

700g/1½lb stewing steak
3 tbsp olive oil
2 onions, chopped
1 green (bell) pepper, seeded
and chopped
2 garlic cloves, crushed
1 x 400g/14oz can tomatoes
2 tbsp tomato paste
600ml/1 pint/2½ cups beef stock
2 tbsp paprika
450g/1lb potatoes, cubed
4 tbsp chopped fresh parsley
6 tbsp soured cream
salt and ground black pepper

1 Trim any fat from the stewing steak and cut the meat into small cubes. Season with salt and pepper.
2 Heat the oil in a large pan, add the onions and green pepper and cook gently over a low heat, stirring occasionally, for 10 minutes until soft. Add the garlic and cook for 1 minute.
3 Add the steak, tomatoes, tomato paste, stock and paprika. Stir well and bring to the boil, then reduce the heat, cover the pan and simmer for 2 hours, stirring occasionally.
4 Add the potatoes and parsley and cook for 30 minutes or until the meat is tender and the vegetables are cooked.
5 Ladle the soup into six warmed bowls, swirl in a spoonful of soured cream and serve.

preparation 20 minutes   cooking time 2 hours 15 minutes

Serves 6

RISOTTO MILANESE

50g/2oz/4 tbsp butter
1 tbsp olive oil
1 onion, finely chopped
4 tbsp dry white wine
300g/11oz/1⅓ cups Arborio rice
1 litre/1¾ pints/4 cups chicken stock
a large pinch of saffron
50g/2oz/⅓ cup freshly grated Parmesan
salt and ground black pepper

1 Melt half the butter in a large pan. Add the onion and cook over a low heat for 10 minutes until soft but not coloured.
2 Add the wine and boil rapidly until it evaporates. Stir in the rice and cook, stirring, until all the grains are glistening.
3 Meanwhile, bring the stock to the boil in a separate pan, then lower the heat and keep it on a simmer.
4 Add the saffron and a ladleful of the stock to the rice and simmer, stirring, until absorbed. Continue adding the stock, a ladleful at a time, until the rice is tender but still retains a very slight bite. This takes about 25 minutes.
5 Remove from the heat, add the remaining butter and season to taste. Cover and set aside for 5 minutes.
6 Serve the risotto sprinkled with grated Parmesan.

preparation 15 minutes cooking time 40 minutes

Serves 4

LEEK AND GORGONZOLA RISOTTO

6 baby leeks, trimmed
4 tbsp olive oil
340g/12oz/1½ cups Arborio rice
150ml/¼ pint/scant ⅔ cup white wine
1l/1¾ pints/4 cups hot vegetable stock
115g/4oz Gorgonzola cheese, diced
salt and ground black pepper

1 Brush the leeks with oil. Grill (broil) for 10 minutes, turning occasionally, until charred and softened. When cool enough to handle, slice crossways with a sharp knife into 2.5cm/1in lengths and set aside.
2 Heat the remaining oil in a large frying pan, add the rice and stir until coated with oil. Increase the heat and stir in the wine. Cook, stirring, until most of the wine has been absorbed, then add 2 ladles of hot stock.
3 Reduce the heat and cook gently, stirring frequently and adding more stock as the liquid is absorbed.
4 When all the stock has been added and the rice is tender but still retains a slight 'bite', stir in the cheese and leeks and season with salt and pepper. Set aside to stand for 1 minute before serving on warmed plates.

preparation 5 minutes cooking time 45 minutes

Serves 4

MUSHROOM, BACON AND LEEK RISOTTO

25g/1oz dried porcini mushrooms

225g/8oz smoked bacon lardons

2 large leeks, chopped

300g/11oz/1⅓ cups Arborio rice

600ml/1 pint/2½ cups hot vegetable stock

1 bunch of fresh chives, snipped

4 tbsp freshly grated Parmesan

salt and ground black pepper

1 Put the porcini mushrooms in a bowl and cover with plenty of boiling water. Leave to soak for 10 minutes.
2 Meanwhile, cook the bacon and leeks in the bacon fat in a large pan for 7–8 minutes until soft and golden.
3 Stir in the rice, cook for 1 minute, then add the mushrooms and their soaking liquid. Simmer gently until the liquid is absorbed and then add some hot stock. Continue adding the stock, a little at a time, until the rice is cooked and the liquid has been absorbed. Stir in the chives and Parmesan, then season with salt and pepper and serve.

preparation 10 minutes   cooking time 30 minutes

Serves 4

SQUASH AND PANCETTA RISOTTO

125g/4oz pancetta, chopped

1 small butternut squash, peeled and cubed

1 onion, finely chopped

300g/11oz/1⅓ cups Arborio rice

1l/1¾ pints/4 cups hot vegetable stock

4 tbsp chopped parsley

50g/2oz Parmesan, grated

salt and ground black pepper

1 Put the pancetta and the butternut squash in a large frying pan and cook over a medium heat for 8–10 minutes until golden and the squash has softened. Add the onion to the pan and cook for 5 minutes until softened.
2 Stir in the rice, cook for 1 minute, then start adding the hot stock, a little at a time, stirring occasionally to prevent the rice sticking, until the stock has been absorbed and the rice and squash are cooked and tender. Season to taste.
3 Stir in the parsley and Parmesan and serve hot.

preparation 10 minutes   cooking time 40 minutes

Serves 4

SEAFOOD PAELLA

3 tbsp olive oil
1 large onion, chopped
2 garlic cloves, crushed
1 red chilli, diced
2 red (bell) peppers, seeded and thinly sliced
400g/14oz tomatoes, chopped
340g/12oz/1½ cups paella rice
1 litre/1¾ pints/4 cups hot chicken stock
a good pinch of saffron
500g/1lb 2oz cooked mussels
200g/7oz cooked peeled tiger prawns (shrimp)
300g/11oz squid, sliced
juice of 1 lemon
salt and ground black pepper

1 Heat the oil in a frying pan and cook the onion for 5 minutes or until soft. Add the garlic and cook for 1 minute. Add the red peppers and tomatoes and stir in the rice.
2 Add some of the hot stock and bring to the boil. Season with salt and pepper and stir in the saffron. Reduce the heat to a simmer and cook, uncovered, stirring frequently, until most of the liquid has been absorbed.
3 Add the remaining stock, a little at a time, letting the rice absorb it before adding more – this takes about 25 minutes. The rice should be quite wet and will continue to absorb the liquid. Stir frequently to prevent it sticking to the pan.
4 Add the mussels, prawns, squid and lemon juice. Stir well and cook for 5 minutes to heat through. Season to taste.
5 Divide the paella between six shallow bowls and serve.

preparation 15 minutes plus infusing **cooking time** 50 minutes

Serves 6

ASPARAGUS RISOTTO

50g/2oz/4 tbsp butter
1 onion, finely chopped
2 garlic cloves, crushed
225g/8oz/1 cup Arborio rice
500ml/17fl oz/2 cups hot vegetable stock
450g/1lb asparagus, trimmed
3 tbsp double (heavy) cream
4 tbsp chopped fresh parsley
50g/2oz/⅓ cup freshly grated Parmesan
salt and ground black pepper

1 Melt the butter in a heavy-based pan, add the onion and garlic and cook over a low heat until soft.
2 Stir in the rice, cook for 1 minute, then add one-third of the hot stock. Bring to the boil, then reduce the heat and simmer until the liquid has been absorbed. Continue adding the stock, a little at a time, until almost all the stock has been absorbed and the rice is tender. Stir frequently.
3 Meanwhile, cook the asparagus in a pan of salted boiling water until just tender. Drain well in a colander.
4 Add the cream, parsley and half the grated Parmesan to the pan. Stir in the asparagus and season with salt and pepper.
5 Divide the risotto among four plates, sprinkle with the remaining Parmesan and serve.

preparation 10 minutes **cooking time** 25 minutes

Serves 4

OVEN-BAKED SPINACH RICE

3 tbsp coconut oil

1 large red onion, thinly sliced

1 red chilli, seeded and sliced

1 tsp black mustard seeds

1 tsp garam masala

340g/12oz basmati rice

a little oil to grease

a handful of fresh coriander (cilantro), roughly chopped

100g/3½oz baby spinach leaves

3 tbsp flaked almonds, toasted

salt and ground black pepper

1 Heat the oil in a frying pan and fry the onion for 10 minutes over a medium heat until golden and soft. Add the chilli, mustard seeds and garam masala. Cook for 1 minute, then cool, cover and chill in the refrigerator.
2 Meanwhile, cook the rice according to the pack instructions. When cooked, spread it out on a baking sheet and leave to cool, then cover and chill in the refrigerator.
3 Preheat the oven to 200°C/400°F/Gas 6. Tip the rice into a lightly greased shallow ovenproof dish. Stir in the onion mixture and season with salt and pepper.
4 Cook in the oven for 20 minutes until piping hot. Stir in the coriander, spinach and almonds and serve immediately.

preparation 15 minutes plus chilling   cooking time 40 minutes

Serves 8

CHERRY TOMATO RISOTTO

2 tbsp olive oil

1 small onion, finely chopped

2 garlic cloves, crushed

350g/12oz/1½ cups Arborio rice

5 tbsp dry white wine

750ml/1¼ pints/3 cups hot vegetable stock

300g/11oz cherry tomatoes, halved

4 tbsp chopped fresh parsley

salt and ground black pepper

grated Parmesan to serve

1 Heat the oil in a large pan. Add the onion and garlic and cook over a low heat for 10 minutes or until softened.
2 Add the rice and stir until glistening and well coated with oil. Pour in the wine and cook for 2–3 minutes until it evaporates. Stir in the tomatoes and parsley.
3 Start adding the hot stock, a little at a time. When it has been absorbed, stir in a little more. Continue in this way, stirring frequently to stop the rice sticking, until all the liquid has been absorbed and the rice is tender. Season to taste.
4 Serve immediately sprinkled with grated Parmesan.

preparation 10 minutes   cooking time 25–30 minutes

Serves 6

CURRIED COCONUT RICE

1 large aubergine (eggplant)

500g/1lb 2oz butternut squash, peeled and seeded

250g/9oz fine green beans

50g/2oz coconut oil

1 large onion, chopped

1 tbsp black mustard seeds

1 tsp cumin seeds

3 tbsp curry paste

340g/12oz/1½ cups basmati rice

400ml/14fl oz/1⅔ cups coconut milk

salt and ground black pepper

1 Cut the aubergine and butternut squash into cubes. Slice the green beans and cut into small pieces.
2 Heat the coconut oil in a large pan. Add the onion and cook for 5 minutes or until softened. Add the mustard seeds and cumin seeds and cook, stirring, until they begin to pop. Stir in the curry paste and cook for 1 minute.
3 Add the aubergine and cook, stirring, for 5 minutes. Add the butternut squash, beans, rice and some salt, mixing well. Pour in the coconut milk and add 600ml/1 pint/2½ cups water. Bring to the boil, cover and simmer for 15 minutes.
4 When the rice and vegetables are cooked, remove from the heat. Check the seasoning and serve hot.

preparation 15 minutes **cooking time** 30 minutes plus standing

Serves 6

VEGGIE FRIED RICE

200g/7oz/scant 1 cup rice

2 tbsp oil

2 garlic cloves, crushed

1 red (bell) pepper, seeded and diced

125g/4oz mushrooms, sliced

4 spring onions (scallions), sliced diagonally

125g/4oz bean sprouts

125g/4oz/1 cup frozen peas

2 tbsp soy sauce

3 medium (US large) eggs, beaten

1 tsp Chinese five-spice powder

a few drops of sweet chilli sauce

1 Cook the rice according to the pack instructions. Cool in the pan, then cover with clingfilm (plastic wrap) and chill in the refrigerator for 2 hours or overnight.
2 Heat the oil in a wok or large frying pan over a high heat. Add the garlic, red pepper, mushrooms, spring onions, bean sprouts and peas and stir-fry for 3 minutes. Add the soy sauce and stir-fry briskly.
3 Fork up the cold rice, stir it into the vegetables in the wok and stir-fry for 2–3 minutes. Pour in the eggs and stir-fry for 2–3 minutes until the eggs have scrambled and the rice is heated through.
4 Stir in the five-spice powder and serve the rice hot, sprinkled with sweet chilli sauce.

preparation 10 minutes plus soaking and chilling **cooking time** 30 minutes

Serves 4

VEGETABLE KORMA

2 tbsp oil

1 large onion, chopped

2 garlic cloves, crushed

1 red chilli, diced

1 tsp grated fresh root ginger

1 tbsp coriander seeds

1 tsp whole cloves

4 green cardamoms

900g/2lb carrots, green beans, aubergine (eggplant), potatoes and cauliflower, cubed

2 tsp ground turmeric

grated zest and juice of ½ lime

200ml/7fl oz/¾ cup full-fat natural yogurt

3 tbsp flaked almonds

1 Heat the oil in a large heavy-based pan. Add the onion, garlic, chilli and ginger and fry very gently over a low heat, stirring frequently, for 10 minutes or until softened.
2 Meanwhile, finely grind the whole spices in an electric grinder or a pestle and mortar.
3 Add the ground spices to the pan and cook for 2 minutes, stirring all the time. Increase the heat, add the vegetables and turmeric and cook, stirring, for 2 minutes.
4 Add the lime zest and juice and 300ml/½ pint/1¼ cups water. Cover the pan and simmer for 30–40 minutes until the vegetables are just tender.
5 Stir in the cream and cook gently over a very low heat until heated through. Do not boil or it will curdle.
6 Sprinkle with the almonds and serve immediately.

preparation 20 minutes   **cooking time** 50 minutes

Serves 6

VEGETABLE BIRYANI

340g/12oz/1½ cups basmati rice

50g/2oz ghee or oil

1 large onion, chopped

1 tsp grated fresh root ginger

1 tbsp black mustard seeds

2 garlic cloves, crushed

1 tbsp hot curry paste

2 carrots, thinly sliced

225g/8oz green beans, trimmed

225g/8oz cauliflower florets

125g/4oz shelled fresh peas

juice of 1 lemon

2 tbsp roasted cashew nuts

1 Cook the rice according to the pack instructions.
2 Meanwhile, heat the ghee or oil in a large pan and cook the onion, ginger, mustard seeds and garlic over a low heat for 5 minutes until softened. Add the curry paste and cook for 2 minutes, stirring constantly.
3 Add 600ml/1 pint/2½ cups water and season with salt and pepper. Stir well and bring to the boil. Add the carrots and beans, reduce the heat and simmer for 15 minutes.
4 Add the cauliflower and peas and simmer for 10 minutes. Fold in the rice gently and heat through.
5 Stir in the lemon juice and simmer gently for a few minutes. Serve immediately sprinkled with roasted cashew nuts.

preparation 20 minutes   **cooking time** 45 minutes

Serves 4

POTATO AND CHICKPEA CURRY

2 tbsp olive oil

1 onion, thinly sliced

450g/1lb new potatoes, cut into large dice

1 tbsp curry paste

1 x 400g/14oz can chickpeas (garbanzos), drained and rinsed

2 carrots, sliced

250ml/9fl oz/1 cup hot vegetable stock

salt and ground black pepper

2 tbsp hot mango chutney

4 tbsp Greek yogurt

1 Heat the oil in a large frying pan over a low heat. Add the onions and potatoes and fry gently for 10 minutes until the onion is softened and the potatoes are tender and golden brown. Stir in the curry paste and cook for 1 minute.
2 Add the chickpeas, carrots and hot stock. Season with salt and pepper, then cook gently for 15–20 minutes, until all the vegetables are tender. Season with salt and pepper.
3 Mix the mango chutney and yogurt in a bowl.
4 Serve the curry topped with the mango yogurt with some boiled rice.

preparation 20 minutes   **cooking time** 35–40 minutes

Serves 4

SWEET POTATO CURRY

2 tbsp vegetable oil

1 onion, thinly sliced

2 garlic cloves, crushed

1 tsp ground turmeric

1 tsp mild chilli powder

1 tbsp black mustard seeds

900g/2lb sweet potatoes, peeled and cut into large chunks

1 aubergine (eggplant), cubed

450g/1lb tomatoes, chopped

600ml/1 pint/2½ cups hot vegetable stock

225g/8oz green beans, trimmed

2 tsp garam masala

1 Heat the oil in a pan over a low heat and fry the onions for 10 minutes until golden. Add the garlic, turmeric, chilli and mustard seeds. Cook gently for 1–2 minutes until the aroma from the spices is released.
2 Add the sweet potatoes and stir them into the spice mixture. Cook for 5 minutes, stirring frequently, then stir in the aubergine and cook for 3 minutes. Add the tomatoes and hot stock. Bring to the boil, then reduce the heat and simmer gently for 20 minutes until the sweet potatoes are tender.
3 Add the green beans and cook for 5 minutes or until they beans are tender but still retain some bite.
4 Stir in the garam masala and serve in six warm bowls with boiled rice or poppadums.

preparation 20 minutes   **cooking time** 50 minutes

Serves 6

JAMBALAYA

2 tbsp olive oil

340g/12oz boneless, skinless chicken breasts, cubed

75g/3oz chorizo, chopped

2 celery sticks, chopped

1 large onion, finely chopped

1 red (bell) pepper, seeded and thinly sliced

225g/8oz/1 cup long-grain rice

1 tbsp tomato paste

1 tbsp Cajun seasoning

400ml/14fl oz/1⅔ cups hot chicken stock

1 x 400ml/14fl oz can tomatoes

salt and ground black pepper

1 Heat 1 tbsp oil in a large pan and fry the chicken and chorizo over a medium heat for 6–8 minutes, stirring often, until browned. Remove from the pan and set aside.
2 Add the remaining oil to the pan with the celery, onion and red pepper. Cook gently over a low heat for 15 minutes or until the vegetables are softened but not coloured.
3 Add the rice and stir for 1 minute to coat in the oil. Add the tomato paste and Cajun seasoning and cook for 2 minutes.
4 Pour in the hot stock and return the chicken and chorizo to the pan with the tomatoes. Simmer for 20–25 minutes until all the stock has been absorbed and the rice is cooked.
5 Season to taste and serve in shallow bowls.

preparation 15 minutes   cooking time 50 minutes plus standing

Serves 4

LENTIL CHILLI

2 tbsp oil

1 red onion, chopped

1 tsp each ground coriander and ground cumin

2 garlic cloves, crushed

a pinch of dried chilli flakes

400ml/14fl oz/1⅔ cups hot vegetable stock

2 x 400g/14oz cans brown or green lentils, drained and rinsed

1 x 400g/14oz can chopped tomatoes

salt and ground black pepper

4 tbsp chopped fresh parsley

4 tbsp natural yogurt

1 Heat the oil in a pan and cook the onion over a low heat, stirring often, for 5 minutes. Stir in the coriander and cumin.
2 Add the garlic, chilli flakes and hot stock. Cover the pan and simmer for 10 minutes. Remove the lid and continue simmering until the onions are very tender and most of the liquid has been absorbed.
3 Stir in the lentils and canned tomatoes and season with salt and pepper. Simmer, uncovered, for 15 minutes or until thickened. Remove from the heat.
4 Ladle into four warm shallow bowls. Sprinkle with parsley and top with a spoonful of natural yogurt.

preparation 10 minutes   cooking time 30 minutes

Serves 4

MOZZARELLA, PROSCIUTTO AND ROCKET PIZZA

flour to dust

1 x 300g/11oz pack pizza base mix

340g/12oz fresh tomato sauce

250g/9oz mozzarella cheese, drained and roughly chopped

8 thin slices Parma ham, cut into strips

a handful of rocket (arugula)

a little olive oil to drizzle

salt and ground black pepper

1 Preheat the oven to 200°C/400°F/Gas 6. Lightly flour 2 large baking sheets.
2 Mix the pizza base dough according to the instructions on the pack. Divide the dough into two and knead each ball on a lightly floured surface for 5 minutes, then roll out to make two 23cm/9in rounds. Place on the prepared baking sheets.
3 Divide the tomato sauce between the pizza bases and spread it out, leaving a small border around each edge. Scatter the mozzarella over the top, then add the Parma ham. Season with salt and pepper.
4 Bake the pizzas in the oven for 15–18 minutes until crisp and golden. Top with rocket and drizzle with oil.

preparation 10 minutes   cooking time 15–18 minutes

Serves 4

BEAN BURGERS

1 tbsp sunflower oil

1 carrot, finely chopped

1 onion, finely chopped

2 garlic cloves, crushed

1 x 400g/14oz can red kidney beans, drained and rinsed

2 tbsp chopped fresh parsley

50g/2oz/1 cup fresh breadcrumbs

1 medium (US large) egg, beaten

salt and ground black pepper

sunflower oil to brush

4 burger buns

1 tomato, sliced

1 Heat the oil in a pan. Add the carrot, onion and garlic and cook over a low heat for 10 minutes or until soft. Transfer to a bowl and set aside to cool.
2 Blitz the drained beans in a food processor or blender and stir into the cooled vegetables with the parsley, breadcrumbs, egg, salt and pepper. Divide the mixture into 4 portions and shape into burgers. Cover and chill in the refrigerator for 2 hours.
3 Brush the burgers lightly with oil and cook under a hot grill (broiler) for 6–8 minutes, turning halfway through, until browned and cooked through. Keep warm. Alternatively, cook on an oiled griddle pan.
4 Split the burger buns and toast lightly for 1 minute. Place a burger with some sliced tomato in each bun and serve.

preparation 10 minutes plus chilling   cooking time 20 minutes

Serves 4

TOP 10 BRUNCHES

FRUIT CROSTINI

1 ripe banana, peeled and thinly sliced
225g/8oz/2 cups blueberries
175g/6oz/1 cup soft cheese, e.g. quark
4 slices sourdough bread
1 tbsp runny honey

1 Mix the fruits and soft cheese in a bowl.
2 Toast the bread, spread with the blueberry mixture. Drizzle with honey and serve.

preparation 5 minutes
cooking time 5 minutes

Serves 4

ENERGY MUESLI

500g/1lb 2oz/6 cups porridge oats
100g/3½oz/1 cup chopped toasted almonds
2 tbsp pumpkin seeds
4 tbsp sunflower seeds
100g/3½oz/¾ cup chopped dried apricots,
milk or yogurt to serve

1 Mix the oats with the almonds, seeds and apricots. Store in a sealable container for up to one month. Serve with milk or yogurt.

cooking time 5 minutes

Serves 12

FRUIT PORRIDGE

200g/7oz/2 cups porridge oats
400ml/14fl oz/1⅔ cups milk
75g/3oz/½ cup chopped dried fruits

1 Put the ingredients and 400ml/14fl oz/ 1⅔ cups water in a pan. Heat gently, stirring until the porridge thickens. Serve hot.

preparation 5 minutes
cooking time 5 minutes

Serves 4

NUTTY YOGURT

500g/1lb 2oz/2¼ cups natural yogurt
50g/2oz/⅓ cup sultanas (golden raisins)
50g/2oz/⅓ cup mixed chopped nuts
2 apples, grated

1 Mix all the ingredients and chill overnight. Use as a topping for breakfast cereal.

preparation 5 minutes
    plus overnight chilling

Serves 4

KICKSTART

1 large ripe banana, peeled and sliced
150g/5oz mango, peeled, stoned and chopped
225g/8oz/2 cups strawberries, hulled
3 tbsp porridge oats
250ml/8fl oz/1 cup chilled milk

1 Put all the ingredients in a blender and blitz until smooth. Pour into two glasses.

preparation 10 minutes

Serves 2

APPLE COMPOTE

2 cooking (green) apples, peeled, cored and diced
juice of ½ lemon
1 tbsp runny honey
a pinch of ground cinnamon
2 tbsp each raisins and chopped nuts
2 tbsp natural yogurt

1 Put the apples in a pan with the lemon juice,
   honey and 2 tbsp cold water. Cook gently for
   5 minutes or until soft. Transfer to a bowl,
   sprinkle with cinnamon, then cool.
2 Chill in the refrigerator for up to three days.
3 Serve with the raisins, nuts and yogurt.

preparation 10 minutes plus chilling
cooking time: 5 minutes plus cooling   *Serves 2*

QUICK CROQUE

4 slices white bread
butter to spread, plus extra to fry
Dijon mustard, to taste
125g/4oz Gruyère cheese, sliced
4 slices ham

1 Butter both sides of each slice of bread.
   Spread one side of two slices with mustard.
   Divide the cheese and ham between them
   Top with the other slices and press down.
2 Butter a griddle and heat until hot. Fry the
   sandwiches for 2–3 minutes on each side
   until golden. Cut in half and serve.

preparation 5 minutes
cooking time 8 minutes

TOFU SMOOTHIE

125g/4oz silken tofu, well chilled
1 large ripe banana, peeled and sliced
175ml/6fl oz/⅔ cup soya milk, well chilled
2 tsp thick honey
125g/4oz/1 cup strawberries, hulled

1 Drain the tofu, mash lightly with a fork and
   put in a blender with the milk, banana,
   honey and strawberries. Blitz until thick and
   smooth. Pour into a large glass.

preparation 5 minutes
Makes 400ml (14fl oz)   *Serves 1*

BERRY FREEZE

100g/3½oz/1 cup frozen summer berries
150ml/¼ pint/scant ⅔ cup skimmed milk
1 tsp runny honey

1 Blitz the frozen fruits and milk in a blender
   until thick and smooth. Add cold water,
   if wished, to get the right consistency.
   Sweeten with honey and serve in a glass.

preparation 5 minutes

FRUIT SALAD

2 oranges, peeled and cut into segments
1 mango, peeled, stoned and chopped
450g/1lb fresh pineapple, peeled and diced
225g/8oz/2 cups blueberries
½ Charentais or Galia melon, cubed
grated zest and juice of 2 oranges

1 Put all the fruit in a bowl with the orange
   zest and juice. Mix together and serve.

preparation 5 minutes   *Serves 4*

MEALS IN MINUTES

Too busy to cook? Even when you're in a hurry, there's always time to whip up a meal from scratch. All the recipes in this chapter are simple to prepare and cook, so you can create a delicious lunch or supper in no time at all. And they're healthier and often more filling and economical than buying a ready meal from the supermarket or ordering in a takeaway.

When you're making real fast food, it's important to use the best-quality, freshest ingredients to maximize the nutritional goodness and flavour. Don't mess about with them – prepare, cook and serve them in the simplest way without any fuss.

Most of the meals can be prepared and cooked in less than 45 minutes from start to finish – and they taste delicious, too. In the following pages you will find mouthwatering recipes for curries, pasta dishes, stir-fries and substantial salads, plus lots of vegetarian options.

There's no need to slave away for hours in the kitchen over a hot stove – if you prefer to spend your time eating in a relaxed and enjoyable way rather than cooking complicated and time-consuming food, these are the dishes for you.

< Lemon Chicken (page 126)

CHICKEN AND SPINACH CURRY

1 tbsp sunflower oil

2–3 tbsp curry paste

340g/12oz potatoes, cubed

1 x 400ml/14fl oz can full-fat coconut milk

250ml/8fl oz/1 cup chicken stock

4 boneless, skinless chicken breasts, sliced

250g/9oz baby spinach leaves

a large handful of fresh coriander (cilantro)

a small handful of fresh mint

salt and ground black pepper

3 tbsp toasted flaked almonds

1 Heat the oil in a pan, add the curry paste and cook for 2 minutes, stirring. Add the potatoes and cook for 2–3 minutes, stirring, until they start to brown.

2 Add the coconut milk and 125ml/4fl oz/½ cup stock, season with salt and pepper and bring to the boil. Reduce the heat, cover the pan and simmer for 10 minutes. Stir the chicken into the sauce and cook, covered, for 10–15 minutes until the chicken and potatoes are cooked through.

3 Finely chop the spinach and coriander and stir into the sauce. Bring to the boil and cook for 2 minutes. Add the remaining stock, if needed, and simmer for 2–3 minutes.

4 Serve the curry in shallow bowls, garnished with toasted flaked almonds, with rice or warmed naan breads.

preparation 20 minutes cooking time 35 minutes

Serves 4

JERK CHICKEN

1 tbsp fresh thyme leaves

2 tsp grated fresh root ginger

1 tsp ground allspice

2 tbsp brown sugar

2 tbsp soy sauce

2 garlic cloves, crushed

1 Scotch bonnet chilli, chopped

2 tbsp vegetable oil

8 chicken thighs or drumsticks

1 Preheat the grill (broiler) to medium and set the grill (broiling) rack about 15cm/6in from the heat.

2 Use a blender or a pestle and mortar to make the jerk marinade. Combine the thyme, ginger, allspice, sugar, soy sauce, garlic, chilli and oil until smooth.

3 Put the chicken pieces on a foil-lined baking sheet and pour the jerk marinade over them. Rub it into the chicken. Grill (broil) for 15 minutes, turning the chicken occasionally, until golden brown and cooked through.

4 Serve the chicken with boiled rice and some salad.

preparation 10 minutes cooking time 15 minutes

Serves 4

LEMON CHICKEN

4 x 150g/5oz skinless, boneless chicken breasts
juice of 2 lemons
2 garlic cloves, crushed
2 tbsp olive oil
salt and ground black pepper
lemon wedges and watercress sprigs to serve

1 Put the chicken breasts in a shallow bowl and season with salt and pepper. Pour over the lemon juice, garlic and oil.
2 Preheat the grill (broiler) to medium. Place the chicken in a foil-lined grill (broiler) pan.
3 Grill (broil) for about 6–8 minutes, then turn the chicken over and grill the other side until it is golden and the meat is cooked right through.
4 Serve the chicken, sprinkled with more black pepper, with lemon wedges and watercress.

preparation 2 minutes cooking time 12–16 minutes

Serves 4

SALTIMBOCCA ALLA ROMANA

4 veal escalopes
4 fresh sage leaves
4 thin slices Fontina cheese
8 thin slices Parma ham
50g/2oz/4 tbsp butter
1 tbsp oil
2 tbsp Marsala
salt and ground black pepper
fried sage leaves to garnish

1 Place the veal escalopes between two sheets of greaseproof paper and pound with a rolling pin to flatten them. Season with salt and black pepper.
2 Place a sage leaf on top of each escalope and then a slice of cheese. Wrap each one in two slices of Parma ham. Secure with a wooden cocktail stick (toothpick).
3 Heat the butter and oil in a frying pan over a low to medium heat. Add the escalopes in batches and cook gently until golden brown on both sides. Stir in the Marsala, then cover the pan and simmer gently for 6–8 minutes.
4 Serve the escalopes with the pan juices poured over them, garnished with fried sage leaves.

preparation 10 minutes cooking time 10 minutes

Serves 4

CHICKEN TIKKA PITTAS

4 pitta breads
200g/7oz mixed salad leaves
450g/1lb cooked chicken tikka breast fillets
½ red onion, finely chopped
8 cherry tomatoes, halved
4 tbsp natural yogurt
¼ cucumber, diced
2 tbsp mango chutney

1 Split each pitta bread down one side to form a pocket. Fill each pocket with a handful of salad leaves.
2 Divide the chicken among the pitta breads and add the red onion and cherry tomatoes.
3 In a bowl, mix together the yogurt, cucumber and mango chutney. Drizzle over the chicken mixture, then fold over the pittas and serve immediately.

preparation 10 minutes

Serves 4

FIERY MANGO CHICKEN

2 tbsp mango chutney
2 tbsp sweet chilli sauce
grated zest and juice of 1 lime
4 tbsp natural yogurt
4 tbsp chopped fresh coriander (cilantro) plus extra to garnish
4 chicken breasts with skin on
1 large ripe mango, peeled, stoned and cut into 8 slices
oil to brush
salt and ground black pepper
boiled rice to serve

1 In a shallow dish, mix together the mango chutney, chilli sauce, lime zest and juice, yogurt and coriander. Season with salt and pepper.
2 Put the chicken breasts, skin-side down, on a board, cover with clingfilm (plastic wrap) and beat with a rolling pin to flatten them. Slice each one into three or four pieces and stir into the yogurt mixture. Cover and chill for 15 minutes.
3 Preheat the grill (broiler). Brush the mango lightly with oil and grill (broil) for 2 minutes on each side or until lightly charred but still firm. Set aside.
4 Arrange the chicken on a foil-lined grill pan and grill for 5 minutes on each side until cooked and golden brown.
5 Serve hot, sprinkled with coriander with the grilled mango and boiled rice.

preparation 10 minutes plus marinating **cooking time** 10 minutes

Serves 4

GRILLED SPICY CHICKEN

4 boneless, skinless chicken breasts
1 tsp ground cumin
1 tsp ground turmeric
1 tsp curry paste
1 garlic clove, crushed
250g/9oz/1 cup natural yogurt
3 tbsp chopped fresh coriander (cilantro) plus extra to garnish
salt and ground black pepper

1 Prick the chicken breasts with a fork, cover with clingfilm (plastic wrap) and beat with a rolling pin until flattened.
2 Mix the cumin, turmeric, curry paste, garlic and yogurt in a shallow dish. Season with a little salt and pepper and stir in the coriander.
3 Add the chicken and turn in the yogurt mixture.
4 Preheat the grill (broiler). Place the chicken on a foil-lined grill (broiler) pan and cook, turning occasionally, for about 20 minutes until brown outside and cooked through inside.
5 Serve immediately, garnished with coriander.

preparation 10 minutes cooking time 20 minutes

Serves 4

CHICKEN FAJITAS

700g/1½lb skinless chicken breasts, cut into strips
2 tbsp fajita seasoning
1 tbsp olive oil
1 red and 1 green (bell) pepper, seeded and sliced
2 red onions, thinly sliced
1 bunch of spring onions (scallions), halved
8 flour tortillas
150g/5oz tomato salsa
125g/4oz guacamole
8 tbsp soured cream

1 Put the chicken in a large shallow dish and toss with the fajita seasoning.
2 Heat the oil in a large frying pan, add the chicken and cook for 5 minutes, turning, until golden brown and tender.
3 Add the red and green peppers and red onions and cook for about 8–10 minutes until tender.
4 Meanwhile, warm the tortillas in a microwave on full power for 45 seconds, or wrap in foil and warm in a preheated oven at 180°C/350°F/Gas 4.
5 Divide the chicken and vegetables among the tortillas and place two on each serving plate. Add the tomato salsa, guacamole and soured cream and roll up or fold over.
6 Serve the tortillas immediately.

preparation 10 minutes cooking time 20 minutes

Serves 4

GRILLED CHICKEN WALDORF

125g/4oz/1 cup walnuts
olive oil to brush
4 skinless, boneless chicken breasts
125g/4oz mixed salad leaves
2 red apples, cored and cubed
4 celery sticks, diced
4 tbsp chopped fresh parsley
125g/4oz Roquefort cheese
125ml/4fl oz/½ cup mayonnaise
salt and ground black pepper

1 Put the walnuts in a frying pan and place over a high heat, shaking the pan frequently, for 2–3 minutes until toasted and golden brown. Set aside to cool.
2 Lightly brush a griddle pan with oil and place over a medium heat. Season the chicken with salt and pepper and cook for 8–10 minutes on each side until golden brown. Set aside.
3 In a large bowl, mix together the salad leaves, apples, celery, parsley and walnuts. Crumble the Roquefort into the mayonnaise and mix well. Stir into the salad.
4 Thickly slice the chicken and arrange on four serving plates with the salad.

preparation 10 minutes cooking time 16–20 minutes

Serves 4

CHICKEN WITH BLACK-EYED BEANS

4 whole unpeeled garlic cloves
4 tbsp olive oil
1 tbsp Jamaican jerk seasoning
4 boneless chicken breasts
1 x 400g/14oz can black-eyed beans, drained and rinsed
2 tbsp chipotle chilli sauce
salt and ground black pepper
lemon quarters to serve

1 Preheat the oven to 200°C/400°F/Gas 6. Put the unpeeled garlic in a small roasting pan and drizzle with 1 tbsp oil. Roast in the oven for 15–20 minutes or until softened.
2 Meanwhile, preheat the grill (broiler). Rub the jerk seasoning into the chicken. Cook under the grill for 15–20 minutes or until golden brown and cooked through, turning occasionally.
3 Mash the black-eyed beans and place in a pan. Squeeze the garlic out of the skins into the pan. Add the remaining oil and the chipotle chilli sauce. Cook gently for 15 minutes.
4 Beat the bean mixture and divide among four plates. Serve with the chicken and lemon quarters.

preparation 5 minutes cooking time 25 minutes

Serves 4

THAI GREEN CHICKEN CURRY

2 tsp coconut oil

1 onion, finely chopped

3 tsp grated fresh root ginger

1 lemongrass stalk, trimmed

225g/8oz button mushrooms

1 tbsp Thai green curry paste

300ml/½ pint/1¼ cups coconut milk

150ml/¼ pint/scant ⅔ cup hot chicken stock

1 tbsp Thai fish sauce

4 skinless chicken breasts

12 raw tiger prawns (shrimp)

chopped fresh coriander (cilantro) plus sprigs to garnish

1 Heat the oil in a wok or deep frying pan over a medium heat. Add the onion, ginger, lemongrass and mushrooms and stir-fry for 5 minutes or until the mushrooms turn golden.
2 Stir in the curry paste and cook for 1 minute.
3 Add the coconut milk, hot stock and fish sauce. Bring to the boil. Cut each chicken breast into several large chunks and add to the wok.
4 Reduce the heat and simmer for 10 minutes or until the chicken is cooked and the liquid has reduced.
5 Add the prawns and cook for 3–4 minutes, turning halfway through, until cooked and pink.
6 Stir in the chopped coriander and serve the curry with some boiled rice, garnished with coriander sprigs.

preparation 10 minutes cooking time 15 minutes

Serves 6

SPICED CHICKEN WITH BEANS

4 skinless chicken breasts

5 tbsp olive oil

1 tbsp sweet chilli sauce

100g/3½oz/½ cup couscous

1 garlic clove, sliced

1 x 400g/14oz can cannellini beans, drained and rinsed

juice of 1 lemon

1 small red onion, diced

175g/6oz baby plum tomatoes, seeded and chopped

1 ripe mango, peeled, stoned and diced

2 tbsp chopped fresh parsley

2 tbsp chopped fresh mint

salt and ground black pepper

1 Put the chicken on a board, cover with clingfilm and flatten with a rolling pin. Mix 2 tbsp olive oil in a shallow bowl with the chilli sauce. Add the chicken and turn to coat.
2 Heat a frying pan and cook the chicken for 6–8 minutes on each side until golden brown and thoroughly cooked.
3 Meanwhile, put the couscous in a large bowl and pour over 100ml/3½ oz/⅓ cup boiling water. Cover with clingfilm (plastic wrap) and set aside.
4 Put the remaining oil in a small pan with the garlic and beans and place over a low heat for 3–4 minutes. Stir in the lemon juice and season with salt and pepper.
5 Fluff up the couscous with a fork and add the warm beans. Stir in the red onion, tomatoes, mango, parsley and mint.
6 Slice each chicken breast and serve with the bean and mango couscous.

preparation 10 minutes cooking time 16 minutes

Serves 4

HEALTHY CHICKEN SALAD

1 bunch of kale

4 cooked chicken breasts, skinned and shredded

1 avocado, halved, stoned, peeled and sliced

125g /4oz mixed sprouts

1 x 400g/14oz can cannellini beans, drained and rinsed

1 large carrot, cut into ribbons

3 tbsp olive oil

1 tbsp cider vinegar

1 tsp honey mustard

3 tbsp sunflower seeds

2 tbsp pine nuts (pignoli)

salt and ground black pepper

1 Cut the hard stems off the kale and discard them. Finely shred the kale leaves and place them in a large bowl.
2 Add the chicken, avocado, mixed sprouts, cannellini beans and carrot and toss together gently.
3 To make the dressing, whisk together the oil, cider vinegar and honey mustard in a small bowl until well combined.
4 Toss the dressing gently through the salad, then sprinkle the sunflower seeds and pine nuts over the top and serve.

preparation 15 minutes

Serves 4

MEXICAN CHICKEN SALAD

2 cooked chicken breasts

225g/8oz/1¼ cups canned corn kernels

50g/2oz/½ cup grated Cheddar

25g/1oz jalapeño peppers, diced

1 x 400g/14oz can kidney beans, drained and rinsed

½ iceberg lettuce, shredded

1 small avocado

6 tbsp soured cream

juice of 1 lime

50g/2oz tortilla chips

salt and ground black pepper

1 Cut the chicken into bite-size chunks and place in a bowl with the corn kernels.
2 Add the grated Cheddar, jalapeño peppers, kidney beans and lettuce. Mix gently together and season with salt and pepper.
3 Peel and stone the avocado and mash the flesh. Add the soured cream and lime juice and stir together to make a chunky dressing.
4 Toss the salad with the dressing. Roughly crush the tortilla chips and scatter over the salad. Mix through gently and serve immediately.

preparation 15 minutes

Serves 4

CARIBBEAN CHICKEN SALAD

450g/1lb sweet potatoes
1 red (bell) pepper, seeded and cut into chunks
1 red onion, sliced
2 tbsp olive oil
4 chicken breast fillets, skin on
1 tbsp Jamaican jerk seasoning
225g/8oz baby spinach leaves
juice of ½ lime
salt and ground black pepper

1 Preheat the oven to 200°C/400°F/Gas 6. Peel the sweet potatoes and cut them into chunks. Place in a roasting pan with the red pepper and red onion, drizzle with the oil and season with salt and pepper. Roast in the oven for 25 minutes until tender and golden brown.
2 Season the chicken breasts and rub with jerk seasoning. Preheat the grill (broiler) to high. Grill (broil) the chicken for 8 minutes on each side or until cooked through. Set aside.
3 Mix the roasted vegetables with the spinach and sprinkle with lime juice. Check the seasoning.
4 Divide the roasted salad mixture between four serving plates. Cut the chicken into thick slices and arrange on top of the salad.

preparation 10 minutes cooking time 25 minutes

Serves 4

TURKEY SESAME STIR-FRY

450g/1lb turkey breast fillets, cut into strips
4 tbsp teriyaki sauce
450g/1lb fine egg noodles
1 tbsp sesame oil plus extra for the noodles
2 carrots, cut into matchsticks
225g/8oz mangetouts
225g/8oz baby corns
2 tbsp sesame seeds, toasted

1 Put the turkey strips in a large bowl with the teriyaki sauce and stir to coat. Set aside for 5 minutes.
2 Cook the noodles in boiling water according to the pack instructions. Drain well, then toss in a little sesame oil.
3 Heat the sesame oil in a wok or deep frying pan and add the turkey, reserving the marinade. Stir-fry over a high heat for 2–3 minutes until starting to brown. Add the vegetables and reserved marinade and cook over a high heat, stirring, until the vegetables start to soften.
4 Stir in with the sesame seeds and serve immediately on top of the noodles.

preparation 5 minutes plus marinating cooking time 10 minutes

Serves 4

STEAK AU POIVRE

3 tbsp black peppercorns

4 x 225g/8oz lean rump or sirloin steaks

25g/1oz/2 tbsp butter

2 tbsp olive oil

2 whole garlic cloves, peeled

250ml/8fl oz/1 cup red wine

salt

1 Crush the peppercorns coarsely using a pestle and mortar. Scatter them on a plate, place the steaks on top and press down hard so that they stick to the surface of the meat. Repeat on the other side.
2 Heat the butter and oil in a large frying pan and quickly fry the garlic. Remove and add the steaks. Sear them on both sides over a high heat. Lower the heat slightly and cook for a further 4–12 minutes, according to personal preference, turning them often. Season to taste with salt.
3 Just before the steaks are cooked, add the red wine and let it bubble away and reduce to a syrupy consistency.
4 Pour the sauce over the steaks to serve.

preparation 10 minutes cooking time 4–12 minutes

Serves 4

CALF'S LIVER WITH SAGE AND BALSAMIC

30g/1oz/2 tbsp butter

1 tbsp olive oil

12 sage leaves

4 thin slices calf's liver

2 tbsp good-quality balsamic vinegar

grilled polenta to serve

1 Preheat the oven to 110°C/225°F/Gas ¼.
2 Heat the butter and oil in a heavy-based frying pan over a medium heat. Add the sage leaves and cook them briefly for 1–2 minutes until crisp. Remove, arrange in a single layer in a shallow dish and keep warm in the oven.
3 Add two slices of calf's liver to the hot pan and cook for about 30 seconds on each side over a high heat. Remove and quickly cook the remaining two slices.
4 Return the first two slices to the pan, add the balsamic vinegar and cook for 2 minutes until syrupy.
5 Serve with the sage leaves and some grilled polenta.

preparation 5 minutes cooking time 5 minutes

Serves 4

STIR-FRIED GINGER BEEF

1 tbsp vegetable oil

450g/1lb lean steak strips

5cm/2in piece fresh root ginger, peeled and cut into matchsticks

2 carrots, cut into matchsticks

1 green (bell) pepper, seeded and cut into thin strips

3 tbsp light soy sauce

1 tbsp cornflour (cornstarch)

1 tbsp sesame seeds

salt and ground black pepper

1 Heat the oil in a wok or deep frying pan set over a high heat. Add the steak and stir-fry for 2 minutes.
2 Stir in the ginger, carrots and green pepper and stir-fry until the vegetables are just tender.
3 Blend the soy sauce and cornflour and stir into the steak and vegetables in the wok. Cook, stirring occasionally, for about 30 seconds, until thick and syrupy. Season to taste and sprinkle with the sesame seeds.
4 Serve immediately with boiled rice or egg noodles.

preparation 15 minutes cooking time 8 minutes

Serves 4

PASTA AND SALAMI SALAD

450g/1lb ready-made pasta salad of your choice

75g/3oz salami, cut into matchsticks

340g/12oz tomatoes, diced

4 tbsp chopped fresh parsley

ground black pepper

1 Put the pasta salad in a large bowl and add the salami, tomatoes and parsley.
2 Toss together and season to taste with salt and ground black pepper. This salad can be made in advance and kept in a cool place for a few hours until needed.

preparation 10 minutes

Serves 4

THAI BEEF NOODLE SALAD

150g/5oz rice noodles
125g/4oz sliced lean roast beef
125g/4oz beansprouts
2 carrots
chopped coriander (cilantro) to garnish

For the Thai dressing
juice of 1 lime
1 red chilli, seeded and chopped
2 tsp chopped fresh root ginger
2 garlic cloves, crushed
2 tbsp Thai fish sauce
1 tbsp brown sugar
1 tbsp sesame oil

1 Put the rice noodles in a large bowl and pour boiling water over them to cover. Set aside for 15 minutes.
2 To make the dressing, whisk together the lime juice, chilli, ginger, garlic, fish sauce, sugar and oil in a small bowl, until well combined.
3 Drain the noodles while they are still warm. Transfer them to a serving bowl and toss with the dressing. Leave to cool.
4 Just before serving, add the roast beef and beansprouts to the noodles.
5 Peel the carrots lengthways into long thin strips with a potato peeler. Add to the beef and noodle mixture and toss everything together gently.
6 Sprinkle with coriander, divide among four serving plates and serve.

preparation 15 minutes plus soaking and cooling

Serves 4

HORSERADISH BEEF SALAD

4 rump steaks, fat removed
1 tbsp olive oil
125ml/4 fl oz/½ cup crème fraîche
2 tbsp creamed horseradish
a squeeze of lemon juice
100g/3½oz rocket (arugula)
150g/5oz beetroot (beets), diced
225g/8oz warm cooked new potatoes, cut into chunks
salt and ground black pepper

1 Season the steaks with salt and pepper on both sides.
2 Heat a frying pan over a high heat. Add the oil and turn the heat down to medium. Fry the steaks for 1½ minutes each side for rare, or 2 minutes each side for medium, depending on their thickness. Cover and leave to rest for 5 minutes.
3 Mix the crème fraîche with the horseradish and lemon juice.
4 Cut the steaks into slices and set aside.
5 Divide the rocket, beetroot and potatoes among four plates. Drizzle with the horseradish sauce and arrange the sliced steak on top. Serve immediately while still warm..

preparation 10 minutes cooking time 4 minutes plus resting

Serves 4

PESTO STEAK SALAD

2 x 250g/9oz rump steaks, fat removed

5 tbsp olive oil

2 tbsp fresh pesto

125g/4oz mixed salad leaves

50g/2oz sunblush tomatoes

a few marinated grilled peppers, cut into strips

3 tbsp toasted pinenuts (pignoli)

25g/1oz Parmesan, shaved

salt and ground black pepper

1 Season the steaks on both sides with salt and pepper.
2 Heat 1 tbsp oil in a large frying pan over a high heat. Fry the steaks for 1½ minutes on each side for rare; 2–3 minutes for medium; 4–5 minutes for well done. Cover and leave to rest for 5 minutes.
3 Meanwhile, mix the pesto with the remaining oil in a small bowl to make a dressing.
4 Put the salad leaves, tomatoes and grilled peppers in a large bowl, then pour most of the pesto dressing over and toss everything together.
5 Slice the warm steaks into strips. Add to the salad and drizzle the remaining pesto dressing over the top.
6 Sprinkle the pinenuts and Parmesan shavings over the salad and serve warm.

preparation 10 minutes cooking time 3–10 minutes plus resting

Serves 4

KOFTAS WITH RAITA

500g/1lb 2oz minced (ground) lean steak

1 small onion, finely chopped

1 garlic clove, crushed

1 tbsp chopped fresh coriander (cilantro)

½ tsp ground cumin

a pinch of chilli powder

salt and ground black pepper

sunflower oil to brush

For the raita

½ cucumber

2 tsp chopped fresh mint

250g/9oz/1 cup natural yogurt

1 To make the raita, peel the cucumber, then cut in half lengthways and scoop out the seeds. Cut into small dice and place in a bowl. Add the mint, yogurt and some salt and pepper. Stir well and transfer to a serving bowl. Cover and chill in the refrigerator until required.
2 Put the minced steak, onion, garlic, coriander, cumin, chilli powder, salt and pepper in a bowl and mix thoroughly.
3 Divide the mixture into 8 portions and roll into sausage shapes. Press onto 8 skewers and brush lightly with oil.
4 Cook under a hot grill (broiler), turning occasionally, for 8 minutes, until browned and cooked through. Serve with the raita.

preparation 15 minutes cooking time 8 minutes

Serves 4

PORK WIENER SCHNITZEL

4 pork loin steaks, thinly cut

4 tbsp plain (all-purpose) flour

2 medium (US large) eggs, beaten

125g/4oz/2 cups fresh white breadcrumbs

50g/2oz/½ cup grated Parmesan

2 tbsp olive oil

salt and ground black pepper

1 lemon, cut into wedges

1 Put a pork steak on a board and cover with clingfilm. Using a rolling pin, flatten it out to 5mm/¼in thick. Repeat with the remaining steaks.
2 Coat each steak in flour, shaking off the excess, then dip it into the beaten eggs. Mix together the breadcrumbs, Parmesan and salt and pepper on a plate, and dip the pork steaks into this mixture to coat them on both sides..
3 Heat the oil in a large non-stick frying pan over a medium heat. Fry the pork steaks for 5 minutes, turning halfway through, until golden and cooked. Serve with lemon wedges.

preparation 15 minutes cooking time 5 minutes

Serves 4

SWEET-AND-SOUR PORK

2 tbsp oil

340g/12oz pork fillet, cubed

1 red onion, finely sliced

1 red and 1 yellow (bell) pepper, seeded and finely sliced

2 carrots, cut into thin strips

3 tbsp sweet chilli sauce

1 tbsp white wine vinegar

1 x 200g/7oz can pineapple slices, chopped, plus 4 tbsp juice

1 tbsp cornflour (cornstarch)

juice of 1 orange

salt and ground black pepper

chopped fresh coriander (cilantro) to garnish)

1 Heat the oil over a high heat in a wok or deep frying pan. When it's really hot, add the pork, red onion, red and yellow peppers and carrots and stir-fry for 4–5 minutes, until the pork is cooked and the vegetables are starting to soften.
2 Stir in the chilli sauce and vinegar. Blend the pineapple juice with the cornflour to a smooth paste. Stir into the pan with the orange juice and bring to the boil. Reduce the heat and stir in the pineapple. Stir-fry for 2 minutes.
3 Check the seasoning, adding salt and pepper if needed. Scatter the chopped coriander over the pork and vegetables.
4 Divide among four serving bowls and serve immediately with some plain boiled rice or noodles.

preparation 15 minutes cooking time 10 minutes

Serves 4

STIR-FRIED PORK WITH MANGO

340g/12oz medium egg noodles
1 tbsp oil
1 red chilli, seeded and diced
1 tsp grated fresh root ginger
450g/1lb pork stir-fry strips
225g/8oz mangetouts
3 tbsp light soy sauce
1 ripe mango, peeled and sliced

1 Bring a large pan of water to the boil and cook the noodles for 4 minutes or according to the pack instructions. Drain, then plunge into cold water. Set aside.
2 Meanwhile, heat the oil in a wok or deep frying pan until very hot. Add the chilli, ginger and pork and stir-fry for 4 minutes over a high heat. Add the mangetouts and soy sauce and stir-fry for 2–3 minutes. Stir in the mango.
3 Drain the noodles and add to the wok. Stir-fry for 2 minutes until heated through. Serve immediately.

Serves 4

preparation 5 minutes cooking time 10 minutes

MUSHROOM AND HAM FUSILLI

340g/12oz fusilli pasta
3 tbsp olive oil
1 large onion, chopped
1 garlic clove, finely chopped
340g/12oz button mushrooms
225g/8oz ham, diced
250ml/8fl oz/1 cup half-fat crème fraîche
4 tbsp snipped fresh chives
salt and ground black pepper
4 tbsp grated Parmesan

1 Bring a large pan of lightly salted water to the boil and cook the pasta according to the pack instructions. Strain, reserving a cupful of the cooking water.
2 Meanwhile, heat the oil in a large, deep frying pan and cook the onion over a low heat for 5 minutes. Add the garlic and mushrooms and cook for 8 minutes. Stir in the chopped ham and crème fraîche.
3 Stir the pasta into the sauce. Season to taste with salt and pepper and stir in the chives.
4 Divide among four serving plates, sprinkle with Parmesan and serve immediately.

Serves 4

preparation 10 minutes cooking time 15 minutes

WARM BACON SALAD

125g/4oz pancetta, cubed
2 thick slices ciabatta, diced
4 medium (US large) eggs
125g/4oz baby spinach leaves
1 small red onion, diced
25g/1oz Parmesan, shaved
a few drops of balsamic glaze

For the dressing
3 tbsp olive oil
1 tbsp cider vinegar
2 tsp honey mustard
salt and ground black pepper

1 Fry the pancetta in a non-stick frying pan until it begins to release its fat. Add the ciabatta and fry, stirring occasionally, until the pancetta and bread are golden and crisp.
2 Put the dressing ingredients in a bowl and whisk together.
3 Half-fill a small pan with water and bring to the boil. Turn the heat down to a bare simmer. Break the eggs into a cup, then tip them gently into the pan and cook for 3–4 minutes until the whites are set but the yolks are still runny. Remove them with a slotted spoon and drain on kitchen paper.
4 Put the salad leaves and red onion in a large bowl. Add the pancetta, fried bread and Parmesan. Pour the dressing over the top and toss lightly.
5 Divide the salad between four plates, top with the poached eggs and drizzle with balsamic glaze. Serve immediately.

preparation 10 minutes cooking time 10–15 minutes

Serves 4

SMOKED HAM AND MUSHROOM PASTA

340g/12oz pasta shapes
2 tbsp olive oil
200g/7oz button mushrooms
4 tbsp Marsala
3 tbsp double (heavy) cream)
125g/4oz smoked ham, chopped
1 bunch of fresh chives, snipped
salt and ground black pepper

1 Cook the pasta in a large pan of lightly salted boiling water according to the pack instructions.
2 Meanwhile, heat the oil in a pan and fry the mushrooms over a medium heat for 5 minutes until golden brown. Add the Marsala and bubble away until reduced. Stir in the cream.
3 Drain the pasta, return to the pan and add the creamy mushrooms. Stir in the ham and chives.
4 Toss everything together, season with salt and pepper and heat through to serve.

preparation 10 minutes cooking time 12 minutes

Serves 4

PASTA WITH SPICY SAUSAGEMEAT

8 thick pork sausages
450g/1lb fettuccine
125ml/4fl oz/½ cup white vermouth, e.g. Noilly Prat
grated zest and juice of 1 lemon
a large pinch of dried chilli flakes
300ml/½ pint/1¼ cups half-fat crème fraîche
2 tbsp chopped fresh parsley
1 tbsp chopped fresh sage
3 tbsp freshly grated Parmesan
salt and ground black pepper

1 Remove the skin from the sausages. Heat a non-stick frying pan over a medium heat. When it's hot, add the sausagemeat and fry for 5 minutes, stirring occasionally, until cooked and browned.
2 Meanwhile, cook the pasta in a large pan of lightly salted boiling water according to the pack instructions.
3 Add the vermouth to the sausagemeat, bring to the boil and let it bubble away, stirring, for 2–3 minutes until the liquid has reduced. Add the lemon zest and juice, chilli and crème fraîche. Season with salt and pepper. Cook over a low to medium heat for 5 minutes until reduced.
4 Drain the pasta and return to the pan. Stir the parsley and sage into the sauce and toss with the pasta.
5 Serve immediately, sprinkled with grated Parmesan.

preparation 10 minutes cooking time 12 minutes

Serves 4

BACON, CHILLI AND HERB PASTA

400g/14oz fusilli pasta
225g/8oz streaky bacon, chopped
2 tbsp olive oil
2 garlic cloves, crushed
½ red chilli, seeded and chopped
4 tbsp chopped fresh parsley
salt and ground black pepper

1 Cook the pasta in a large pan of lightly salted boiling water according to the pack instructions.
2 Heat a large frying pan and fry the bacon for 3 minutes.
3 Add the oil, garlic and chilli and cook for 1 minute. Stir in the parsley and cook, stirring, for 1 minute.
4 Drain the pasta and toss with the bacon mixture. Season to taste and serve.

preparation 5 minutes cooking time 10 minutes

Serves 4

SPAGHETTI ALLA CARBONARA

2 tbsp olive oil

170g/6oz pancetta cubes

1 garlic clove, crushed

2 medium (US large) eggs

2 tbsp dry white wine

50g/2oz/½ cup grated Parmesan plus extra to serve

400g/14oz spaghetti

4 tbsp chopped fresh parsley

salt and ground black pepper

1 Heat the oil in a pan. Add the pancetta and cook over a medium heat for 5 minutes until the pancetta is crisp and golden. Add the garlic and cook for 1 minute..

2 Meanwhile, beat the eggs with the wine and Parmesan. Season with salt and pepper.

3 Cook the spaghetti in a large pan of lightly salted boiling water according to the pack instructions. Drain thoroughly, then return to the warm pan.

4 Immediately add the beaten egg mixture, pancetta and parsley. Stir together lightly – the eggs will scramble slightly in the sauce. Season to taste.

5 Serve in shallow bowls, sprinkled with grated Parmesan.

preparation 10 minutes cooking time 10 minutes

Serves 4

PORK NOODLE SOUP

340g/12oz pork fillet

1 tbsp coconut oil

2 tsp chopped fresh root ginger

2 garlic cloves, thinly sliced

1 tbsp Thai red curry paste

1 red or yellow (bell) pepper, seeded and thinly sliced

1 x 400ml/14fl oz can coconut milk

600ml/1 pint/2½ cups hot chicken stock

175g/6oz rice noodles

a handful of fresh coriander (cilantro), roughly chopped

1 Cut the pork fillet into thin strips. Heat the coconut oil in a pan and cook the pork over a medium heat, stirring occasionally, for 4–5 minutes until golden brown all over.

2 Add the ginger, garlic, curry paste and red or yellow pepper and cook for 3 minutes.

3 Add the coconut milk and hot stock and simmer gently for 5 minutes. Stir in the noodles and cook for 4 minutes or until the pork is cooked and the noodles are tender.

4 Divide the soup among four warmed soup bowls. Scatter the coriander on top and serve immediately.

preparation 10 minutes cooking time 20 minutes

Serves 4

THAI CURRIED MUSSELS

1 tbsp coconut oil

1 red onion, finely chopped

2 tbsp Thai green curry paste

1 x 400ml/14fl oz can coconut milk

2kg/4½lb live mussels, scrubbed and beards removed

a small handful of fresh coriander (cilantro), chopped

1 Heat the oil in a large deep pan. Add the onion and curry paste and cook gently for 5 minutes, stirring frequently, until the onion starts to soften.

2 Stir in the coconut milk, cover the pan with a lid and bring to the boil. Add the mussels, cover the pan and shake gently. Cook over a medium heat for 5 minutes, shaking the pan occasionally, until the mussels open.

3 Check the mussels and discard any that are still closed. Stir in the chopped coriander and serve immediately.

preparation 15 minutes cooking time 12 minutes

Serves 4

CHILLI CRAB NOODLES

300g/11oz medium egg noodles

2 tbsp groundnut oil

2 garlic cloves, thinly sliced

2.5cm/1in piece fresh root ginger, diced

1 bunch of spring onions (scallions), sliced

340g/12oz fresh crabmeat

2 ripe tomatoes, diced

3 tbsp sweet chilli sauce

chopped fresh coriander (cilantro) leaves

1 Cook the noodles according to the pack instructions. Drain well and set aside.

2 Heat the oil in a large wok or deep frying pan and stir-fry the garlic, ginger and spring onions over a medium heat for 2–3 minutes.

3 Stir in the crabmeat, tomatoes and chilli sauce and stir-fry briskly for 2 minutes.

4 Stir in the cooked noodles and coriander and toss everything together. Serve immediately.

preparation 10 minutes cooking time 15 minutes

Serves 4

EASY PAD THAI

250g/9oz wide rice noodles
1 tbsp coconut oil
2 garlic cloves
1 red chilli, diced
1 tsp grated fresh root ginger
100g/3½oz beansprouts
125g/4oz mangetouts, sliced
300g/11oz cooked peeled large prawns (jumbo shrimp)
2 tbsp Thai fish sauce
1 tbsp brown sugar
2 medium (US large) eggs
3 tbsp chopped roasted peanuts
lime wedges to serve

1 Cook the noodles according to the pack instructions.
2 Heat a wok or large frying pan until hot and add the coconut oil, chilli and ginger. Stir-fry for 1 minute.
3 Add the beansprouts and mangetouts and stir-fry briskly for 2 minutes.
4 Add the prawns and drained cooked noodles and stir-fry for 2 minutes. Stir in the fish sauce and brown sugar and cook for 1 minute.
5 Beat the eggs in a bowl and stir into the noodle mixture. Keep stirring until they start to set.
6 Divide the pad Thai among four serving dishes, sprinkle with peanuts and serve with lime wedges.

preparation 12 minutes plus soaking **cooking time** 6 minutes

Serves 4

SALMON AND COCONUT CURRY

1 tbsp oil
1 red onion, thinly sliced
2 tbsp Thai green curry paste
4 x 125g/4oz salmon fillets
1 x 400ml/14fl oz can coconut milk
juice of 1 lime
a handful of fresh basil, torn
lime wedges to serve

1 Heat the oil in a pan. Add the red onion and cook over a medium heat for 10 minutes or until soft.
2 Stir in the curry paste and cook for 1 minute. Add the salmon fillets to the pan and cook for 2 minutes, turning them once to coat in the spicy mixture.
3 Pour in the coconut milk and bring to the boil, then reduce the heat and simmer gently for 5 minutes or until the salmon is cooked through. Squeeze the lime juice over it and sprinkle with basil.
4 Serve the curry with lime wedges.

preparation 2 minutes **cooking time** 18 minutes

Serves 4

THAI RED FISH CURRY

1 tbsp coconut oil

1 lemongrass stalk, chopped

2 tbsp Thai red curry paste

450g/1lb firm white fish fillets, cut into large chunks

1 x 400ml/14fl oz can half-fat coconut milk

juice of 1 lime

2 tbsp Thai fish sauce

1 tbsp brown sugar

175g/6oz mangetouts

340g/12oz raw peeled prawns (shrimp)

1 small bunch of fresh coriander (cilantro), chopped

shredded chilli to garnish

1 Heat the oil in a wok or deep non-stick frying pan over a medium heat. When it's hot, add the lemongrass and curry paste and cook for 1–2 minutes.
2 Stir in the fish and cook for 1 minute. Pour in the coconut milk, lime juice, fish sauce and brown sugar.
3 Bring to the boil, then reduce the heat, add the mangetouts and prawns and simmer gently for 5 minutes or until the mangetouts are tender and the fish is thoroughly cooked.
4 Stir in the coriander and serve sprinkled with chilli.

preparation 10 minutes **cooking time** 8–10 minutes

Serves 4

CAJUN FISH TORTILLAS

2 tbsp plain (all-purpose) flour

1 tbsp Cajun spice

450g/1lb white fish fillets, cut into strips

4 flour tortillas

1 avocado, peeled, stoned and diced

1 red or yellow (bell) pepper, seeded and diced

4 tbsp salsa

4 tbsp soured cream

salt and ground black pepper

lime wedges to serve

1 Preheat the grill (broiler) to high. In a bowl, mix together the flour, Cajun spice and a little salt and pepper. Add the fish strips and coat in the spicy mixture. Place the coated fish on a non-stick baking tray.
2 Grill (broil) the fish for 4–5 minutes, turning once, until cooked through and golden brown.
3 Warm the tortillas in a griddle pan or a low oven.
4 Divide the grilled fish, avocado and red or yellow pepper among them. Top each one with a spoonful each of salsa and soured cream and roll up.
5 Serve immediately with lime wedges.

preparation 15 minutes **cooking time** 5 minutes

Serves 4

STIR-FRIED SALMON AND BROCCOLI

4 salmon fillets, skinned and cut into strips

3 tbsp soy sauce

1 tbsp sesame oil

2 garlic cloves, thinly sliced

2.5cm/1in piece fresh root ginger, diced

225g/8oz broccoli florets, sliced

2 spring onions (scallions), sliced

1 tbsp sesame seeds

rice or egg noodles to serve

1 Put the salmon in a bowl with the soy sauce and stir gently until thoroughly coated.
2 Heat the oil in a wok or large frying pan and add the garlic, ginger, broccoli and spring onions. Stir-fry over a high heat for 3–4 minutes.
3 Add the salmon in its marinade and stir-fry for 2 minutes. Stir in the sesame seeds.
4 Serve hot with boiled rice or egg noodles.

preparation 10 minutes cooking time 6 minutes

Serves 4

TERIYAKI SALMON

450g/1lb salmon fillet, sliced

3 tbsp teriyaki sauce

340g/12oz soba noodles

1 tbsp sesame oil

2 heads pak choi (bok choy), leaves separated

2 tbsp light soy sauce

1 tsp grated fresh root ginger

2 garlic cloves, crushed

1 small bunch of fresh coriander (cilantro), chopped

1 Put the salmon and teriyaki sauce in a bowl and stir gently. Cover and chill in the refrigerator for 1 hour.
2 Cook the noodles in boiling water according to the pack instructions. Drain and set aside.
3 Heat the oil in a wok or deep frying pan. Remove the salmon from the marinade and add to the wok. Cook over a high heat for 2–3 minutes. Remove and set aside.
4 Add the noodles to the wok with the pak choi and stir-fry for 1–2 minutes. Stir in the soy sauce, ginger and garlic and cook for 2 minutes. Add the coriander and stir well.
5 Return the salmon to the wok and gently toss with the noodles.
6 Divide among four plates and serve.

preparation 10 minutes plus marinating cooking time 10 minutes

Serves 4

TUNA MELT PIZZA

2 large ready-made pizza bases

2 tbsp tomato paste

1 red (bell) pepper, seeded and diced

2 x 200g/7oz cans tuna, drained

1 x 200g/7oz can sweetcorn kernels, drained

125g/4oz/1 cup grated Cheddar

1 Preheat the oven to 220°C/425°F/Gas 7.
2 Spread each pizza base thinly with tomato paste. Top each one with the red pepper, tuna and sweetcorn. Sprinkle over the grated Cheddar.
3 Put each pizza on a baking sheet and cook in the oven for 10–12 minutes until the cheese has melted and is golden.
4 Cut the pizzas into wedges to serve.

preparation 5 minutes cooking time 10–12 minutes

Serves 4

TUNA STEAKS WITH PAK CHOI

4 x 125g/4oz tuna steaks

5cm/2in piece fresh root ginger, peeled and grated

1 garlic clove, crushed

1 tbsp olive oil

2 tbsp soy sauce

juice of 1 orange

2 tbsp chopped fresh parsley

300g/11oz pak choi (bok choy), leaves separated and base sliced

ground black pepper

boiled rice to serve

1 Put the tuna steaks in a shallow dish with the ginger, garlic, oil, soy sauce, orange juice and parsley. Add a grinding of black pepper. Turn the tuna over in the marinade.
2 Heat a ridged griddle pan until really hot. Add the tuna steaks and marinade and cook for 2–3 minutes on each side until just cooked. Remove the tuna and keep warm.
3 Add the pak choi to the pan and cook, turning occasionally, for 1–2 minutes until just wilted but still firm.
4 Serve the tuna and pak choi on four warmed serving plates with some boiled rice.

preparation 10 minutes cooking time 8 minutes

Serves 4

TUNA AND FETA SALAD

1 tbsp olive oil

4 x 125g/4oz tuna steaks

1 tbsp balsamic glaze

200g/7oz fine green beans

4 Little Gem (Bibb) lettuces, leaves separated

a small handful of fresh mint, roughly chopped

225g/8oz tomatoes, quartered

125g/4oz feta cheese

For the dressing

3 tbsp olive oil

grated zest and juice of 1 lemon

a few drops of balsamic vinegar

1 Heat the oil in a large griddle or frying pan over a high heat and cook the tuna for 6–8 minutes, turning the steaks halfway through. Drizzle with balsamic glaze, remove from the pan and slice thickly.
2 Meanwhile, cook the beans in a small pan of boiling water for 5 minutes or until just tender. Drain.
3 Whisk all the dressing ingredients together in a small bowl.
4 Put the tuna in a large serving bowl with the green beans, lettuce, mint and tomatoes. Crumble the feta over the top.
5 Toss everything together in the dressing and serve warm.

preparation 15 minutes   cooking time 8 minutes

Serves 4

WARM NOODLE SALAD

1 tbsp olive oil

2 tsp grated fresh root ginger

1 garlic clove, crushed

6 baby corns, finely sliced

300g/11oz straight-to-wok rice noodles

1 cucumber, peeled into ribbons

1 carrot, peeled into ribbons

2 tbsp soy sauce

300g/11oz cooked peeled prawns (shrimp)

salt and ground black pepper

1 bunch of fresh chives, snipped

sweet chilli sauce to serve

1 Heat the oil in a wok or deep frying pan. Add the ginger and garlic and stir-fry for 1 minute.
2 Stir in the baby corns and rice noodles and cook, stir-fry for 3 minutes or until the noodles are tender.
3 Add the cucumber, carrot, soy sauce and prawns to the wok. Stir well and heat through. Season to taste with salt and pepper. Remove from the heat and stir in the chives.
4 Divide the warm noodle salad among four serving plates and serve with sweet chilli sauce.

preparation 10 minutes   cooking time 5 minutes

Serves 4

SPICY ROLLMOP SALAD

5 tbsp extra light mayonnaise
5 tbsp half-fat crème fraîche
½ tbsp mild curry powder
grated zest and juice of 1 lemon
1 celery stick, diced
½ fennel bulb, diced
1 apple, cored and diced
1 small red onion, finely chopped
4 tbsp chopped fresh parsley
salt and ground black pepper
340g/12oz rollmop herrings
1 tbsp chopped fresh herb fennel

1 In a small bowl, mix together the mayonnaise, crème fraîche, curry powder and lemon zest and juice until well blended.
2 Put the celery, fennel, apple, onion and parsley in a bowl. Season to taste with salt and pepper and add the curry-flavoured mayonnaise. Toss everything together gently until well coated.
3 Divide the celery and fruit salad mixture among four serving plates, top with the rollmop herrings and serve sprinkled with herb fennel.

preparation 15 minutes

Serves 4

PRAWN NOODLE SALAD

340g/12oz rice noodles
juice of 2 limes
2 tbsp Thai fish sauce
1 tbsp crunchy peanut butter
1 tbsp light soft brown sugar
1 red chilli, diced
1 tsp grated fresh root ginger
2 carrots, peeled into ribbons
225g/8oz bean sprouts
175g/6oz sugarsnap peas, sliced
340g/12oz cooked king prawns (jumbo shrimp), peeled
a large handful of fresh mint leaves, chopped

1 Put the rice noodles in a large heatproof bowl and pour enough boiling water from a kettle over the top to cover them. Leave for 5 minutes to heat through. Drain well and return the noodles to the bowl.
2 In a small bowl, mix together the lime juice, fish sauce, peanut butter, chilli and ginger for the dressing.
3 Add the carrots, bean sprouts, sugarsnaps, prawns and mint to the drained noodles.
4 Pour the dressing over the noodles and vegetables and toss gently. Divide between four plates and serve warm.

preparation 15 minutes

Serves 4

THAI GREEN CURRY PRAWN SALAD

2 tbsp Thai green curry paste

4 tbsp coconut cream

450g/1lb raw king prawns (jumbo shrimp), peeled

juice of 1 lime

2 carrots, peeled into ribbons

1 cucumber, peeled into ribbons

100g/3½oz fresh coconut, cubed

a handful of fresh basil, chopped

1 Place a large wok or frying pan over a medium heat. When it's really hot, stir in the curry paste and coconut cream. Cook for 1 minute.

2 Add the prawns and cook for 2–3 minutes, turning them over halfway through, until pink and cooked through.

3 Transfer the cooked prawns to a serving dish and add the lime juice, carrots, cucumber, fresh coconut and basil.

4 Toss everything lightly to combine. Divide among four serving plates and serve warm.

preparation 10 minutes cooking time 5 minutes

Serves 4

CURRIED SMOKED HADDOCK SALAD

200g/7oz/2 cups couscous

125g/4oz cooked smoked haddock, flaked

8 cherry tomatoes, chopped

a good pinch of curry powder

4 spring onions (scallions), finely sliced

4 tbsp chopped fresh parsley

1 hard-boiled egg, chopped

3 tbsp olive oil

juice of 1 lime

salt and ground black pepper

1 Cook the couscous according to the pack instructions. Drain if necessary.

2 Gently mix the couscous with the haddock, cherry tomatoes, curry powder, spring onions, parsley and chopped egg.

3 Sprinkle with the oil and lime juice and stir gently together.

4 Season to taste with salt and pepper and serve while the salad is still warm.

preparation 15 minutes cooking time 10 minutes

Serves 4

SPICY PRAWN NOODLE SALAD

450g/1lb egg noodles

2 tbsp Thai fish sauce

2 tbsp lime juice

2 tbsp rice vinegar

1 tbsp brown sugar

1 red chilli, diced

1 bunch of spring onions (scallions), finely sliced

125g/4oz beansprouts

½ cucumber, finely diced

340g/12oz cooked peeled prawns (shrimp)

4 tbsp chopped fresh coriander (cilantro)

1 Cook the noodles according to the pack instructions.
2 To make the dressing, whisk the fish sauce, lime juice vinegar, sugar and chilli together in a small bowl.
3 Drain the noodles and, while they are still warm, pour the dressing over them. Toss together, then set aside to cool.
4 Stir the spring onions, beansprouts, cucumber, prawns and coriander into the noodles and divide between four bowls.
5 Serve immediately while warm or cover and chill in the refrigerator for 1 hour before serving.

preparation 15 minutes plus soaking and chilling

Serves 4

SPEEDY FISH SOUP

2 tbsp olive oil

1 onion, finely chopped

2 garlic cloves, crushed

2 celery sticks, finely chopped

2 carrots, diced

1 small fennel bulb, chopped

4 tbsp dry white wine

750g/1lb 11oz mixed fish and shellfish, e.g. white fish, prawns (shrimp) and mussels

4 tomatoes, chopped

3 tbsp chopped fresh parsley

salt and ground black pepper

1 Heat the oil in a large pan set over a medium heat. Add the onion, garlic, celery, carrots and fennel and cook for 5 minutes, stirring occasionally, until the vegetables are tender and starting to colour.
2 Stir in 1.2 litres/2 pints/5 cups boiling water and the wine. Bring to the boil, then reduce the heat, cover the pan and simmer gently for 10 minutes.
3 Cut the fish into large chunks and add to the soup with the tomatoes and parsley. Simmer gently for a few minutes until the fish turns opaque. Add the prawns, cook for 1 minute, and then add the mussels, if using.
4 When all the mussels have opened (discard any that remain closed), season to taste with salt and pepper.
5 Ladle the soup into warmed bowls and serve.

preparation 10 minutes **cooking time** 20 minutes

Serves 4

PENNE WITH CREAMY SMOKED SALMON

340g/12oz penne or macaroni

200ml/7fl oz/¾ cup half-fat crème fraîche

150g/5oz smoked salmon trimmings, roughly chopped

grated zest and juice of 1 lemon

small bunch of fresh dill, chopped

ground black pepper

1 Cook the pasta in a large pan of lightly salted boiling water according to the pack instructions. Drain well and return to the warm pan.
2 Meanwhile, put the crème fraîche in a large bowl with the smoked salmon, lemon zest and juice and the dill. Season to taste with black pepper and mix together.
3 Gently stir the creamy salmon mixture into the drained pasta and serve immediately.

preparation 5 minutes cooking time 10–15 minutes

Serves 4

TRADITIONAL KIPPERS

2 kippers

2 knobs of butter

chopped fresh parsley and buttered toast to serve

1 Grill (broil) the kippers under a hot grill (broiler) for about 5 minutes.
2 Remove and top with a knob of butter and sprinkle with chopped parsley.
3 Serve immediately with buttered toast.
4 Alternatively, put the kippers in a large jug of boiling water and leave in a warm place for 5–10 minutes.
5 Or wrap them in foil and cook them in a preheated oven at 190°C/375°F/Gas 5 for 10–15 minutes. Serve as above.

preparation 0 minutes cooking time 5–15 minutes

Serves 2

RICOTTA SPINACH NOODLES

340g/12oz pappardelle pasta

450g/1lb baby leaf spinach, roughly chopped

25g/1oz/2 tbsp butter, softened

175g/6oz/1 cup ricotta cheese

freshly grated nutmeg

salt and ground black pepper

1 Cook the pappardelle in a large pan of lightly salted boiling water according to the pack instructions.

2 Drain the pasta well, return to the pan and add the spinach, butter and ricotta. Toss everything together for a few seconds until the spinach wilts and the butter melts.

3 Season to taste with a little nutmeg, salt and pepper and serve immediately.

preparation 5 minutes cooking time 12 minutes

Serves 4

MUSHROOM SPAGHETTI

450g/1lb spaghetti

30g/1oz/2 tbsp butter

450g/1lb wild or chestnut mushrooms, sliced

100g/3½oz/½ cup mascarpone cheese

4 tbsp freshly grated Parmesan plus extra to garnish

4 tbsp single (light) cream

finely grated zest of 1 lemon

a handful of fresh parsley, chopped

salt and ground black pepper

1 Cook the spaghetti in a large pan of lightly salted boiling water according to the pack instructions. Drain well.

2 Meanwhile, heat the butter in a large frying pan over a high heat. Add the mushrooms and cook for 5 minutes..

3 Stir in the mascarpone, Parmesan, cream and lemon zest.

4 Add the chopped parsley and pasta, toss gently together and heat through. Season to taste with salt and pepper.

5 Serve the pasta in four warmed shallow bowls, sprinkled with grated Parmesan.

preparation 10 minutes cooking time 10 minutes

Serves 4

PEA, MINT AND RICOTTA PASTA

450g/1lb pasta shapes
175g/6oz/1½ cups frozen peas
175g/6oz/1 cup ricotta cheese
4 tbsp chopped fresh mint
4 tbsp single (light) cream
salt and ground black pepper

1 Cook the pasta in a large pan of lightly salted boiling water according to the pack instructions. Add the frozen peas for the last 5 minutes of cooking.
2 Strain the pasta and peas, then return to the pan. Stir in the ricotta and mint with the cream
3 Season to taste and serve immediately.

preparation 5 minutes **cooking time** 10 minutes

Serves 4

PASTA WITH PESTO, POTATOES AND BEANS

400g/14oz pasta shells
225g/8oz fine green beans, trimmed and halved
175g/6oz baby new potatoes, cut into chunks
125g/4oz/½ cup green pesto
ground black pepper
grated Parmesan to serve

1 Cook the pasta in a large pan of lightly salted boiling water according to the pack instructions. Drain well.
2 Cook the beans and potatoes in a pan of lightly salted boiling for 8 minutes until the potatoes are just tender. Drain well.
3 Put the pasta and vegetables in a serving bowl and stir in the pesto. Season with black pepper and serve sprinkled with grated Parmesan..

preparation 5 minutes **cooking time** 15 minutes

Serves 4

PASTA WITH TOMATOES, COURGETTES AND PESTO

400g/14oz pasta tubed
2 tbsp olive oil
1 small onion, diced
250g/9oz mushrooms, sliced
2 courgettes (zucchini), sliced
225g/8oz cherry tomatoes, halved
1 tbsp pinenuts (pignoli)
4 tbsp fresh green pesto
50g/2oz Parmesan, shaved
salt and ground black pepper
torn basil leave to garnish

1 Cook the pasta in a large pan of lightly salted boiling water according to the pack instructions.
2 Heat the oil in a pan and add the onion, mushrooms and courgettes. Cook over a low heat for 8–10 minutes until the vegetables are tender.
3 Add the cherry tomatoes and pinenuts and cook gently for a further 2–3 minutes.
4 Drain the pasta and stir into the vegetables with the pesto. Toss well together. Season to taste with salt and pepper.
5 Serve the pasta sprinkled with Parmesan and basil.

preparation 5 minutes cooking time 10 minutes

Serves 4

QUICK CREAMY GNOCCHI

2 tbsp olive oil
675g/1½lb fresh gnocchi
200g/7oz/1 cup soft cheese
175g/6oz/1½ cups frozen peas
2 tbsp chopped fresh parsley
a pinch of freshly grated nutmeg
5 tbsp milk
40g/1½oz/⅓ cup grated Cheddar cheese
40g/1½oz/¾ cup fresh white breadcrumbs
salt and ground black pepper
crisp green salad to serve

1 Preheat the grill (broiler) to medium. Heat the oil in a large deep frying pan over a high heat and add the gnocchi. Cook, stirring occasionally, for 10 minutes or until the gnocchi are golden and starting to soften.
2 Stir in the soft cheese, peas, parsley, nutmeg, milk and salt and pepper to taste and heat through gently.
3 Transfer to a heatproof serving dish and sprinkle the cheese and breadcrumbs over the top.
4 Place the dish under the grill (broiler) for 4–5 minutes until golden and bubbling. Serve with a crisp green salad.

preparation 10 minutes cooking time 15 minutes

Serves 4

PASTA AND AVOCADO SALAD

2 tbsp extra light mayonnaise
2 tbsp green pesto
2 ripe avocados, halved, stoned, peeled and cubed
4 sunblush tomatoes, sliced
340g/12oz cooked pasta shapes
salt and ground black pepper
fresh basil leaves to garnish

1 In a small bowl, mix the mayonnaise with the pesto, avocado cubes and tomatoes.
2 Put the pasta in a large bowl and stir in the mayonnaise mixture. Season to taste with salt and pepper.
3 Scatter the salad with basil and serve.

preparation 10 minutes

Serves 4

CHILLI TOFU STIR-FRY

225g/8oz firm tofu, drained and cubed

2 tbsp light soy sauce

2 tbsp sesame oil

2 carrots, cut into matchsticks

175g/6oz mangetouts, halved

175g/6oz small broccoli florets

1 red (bell) pepper, seeded and thinly sliced

125g/4oz beansprouts

2 tbsp sweet chilli sauce

1 tbsp sesame seeds

1 Place the tofu in a shallow dish with the soy sauce. Cover and set aside to marinate for 10 minutes.
2 Heat the sesame oil in a wok. Add the tofu and stir-fry for 5 minutes. Remove and set aside.
3 Add all the vegetables and stir-fry for 3–4 minutes until just tender. Stir in the tofu.
4 Stir in the sweet chilli sauce and soy sauce and cook for 1 minute until heated through.
5 Sprinkle with the sesame seeds and serve immediately.

preparation 5 minutes plus marinating cooking time 12 minutes

Serves 4

CHEESE AND CHILLI QUESADILLAS

200g/7oz mild Cheddar or Monterey Jack cheese

4 flour tortillas

1 red chilli, seeded and diced

2 spring onions (scallions)

2 tbsp chopped fresh coriander (cilantro) plus extra to garnish

sunflower oil to brush

1 Grate the cheese coarsely and place one-quarter in the centre of each tortilla.
2 Scatter the chilli over the cheese. Roughly chop the spring onions, divide among the tortillas and then scatter the coriander over.
3 Fold two sides of each tortilla into the middle, overlapping, then fold over the ends to make square parcels. Brush the parcels lightly with oil.
4 Cook under a hot grill (broiler) for 3 minutes until toasted and the cheese has melted. Serve sprinkled with coriander.

preparation 10 minutes cooking time 3 minutes

Serves 4

VEGETABLE CURRY

1 tbsp curry paste

150ml/¼ pint/scant ⅔ cup hot vegetable stock

1 x 200g/7oz can chopped tomatoes

400g/14oz vegetables, e.g. broccoli, courgettes (zucchini) and cauliflower, chopped

1 x 200g/7oz can chickpeas (garbanzos), drained and rinsed

rice and cucumber raita to serve

1 Cook the curry paste in a large heavy-based pan over a medium heat for 1 minute, stirring all the time.
2 Add the stock and tomatoes and bring to the boil, then reduce the heat to low and add the vegetables. Simmer gently for 10 minutes until the vegetables are just tender.
3 Stir in the chickpeas and cook for 5 minutes.
4 Divide the vegetable curry among four serving plates and serve with plain boiled rice and cucumber raita.

preparation 10 minutes cooking time 20 minutes

Serves 4

SPICY BEAN MASALA

1 tbsp ghee

1 onion, thinly sliced

2 garlic cloves, crushed

2 tsp garam masala

1 tsp cumin seeds

1 red chilli, seeded and diced

4 tomatoes, roughly chopped

2 x 400g/14oz cans cannellini beans, drained and rinsed

a handful of fresh coriander (cilantro), chopped

salt and ground black pepper

1 Heat the ghee in a pan over a low heat, add the onion and cook for 5 minutes.
2 Stir in the garlic, garam masala, cumin seeds and chilli and cook gently for 1 minute, then add the tomatoes and 200ml/7fl oz/¾ cup water. Simmer gently for 5 minutes, stirring occasionally.
3 Stir in the beans and heat through. Add the coriander and season to taste with salt and pepper. Serve immediately.

preparation 10 minutes cooking time 15 minutes

Serves 2

CHICKPEAS WITH SPINACH

2 tbsp olive oil

2 tsp grated fresh root ginger

2 garlic cloves, chopped

2 tsp each ground coriander and cumin

1 tsp garam masala

2 x 400g/14oz cans chickpeas (garbanzos), drained and rinsed

6 tomatoes, roughly chopped

450g/1lb baby spinach leaves

salt and ground black pepper

1 Heat the oil in a large heavy-based pan over a medium heat. Add the ginger, garlic and ground spices and cook for 2 minutes, stirring. Stir in the chickpeas.
2 Add the tomatoes to the pan and cook gently for 10 minutes. Season to taste with salt and pepper.
3 Stir in the spinach and cook for 2 minutes until it wilts.
4 Divide among four serving plates and serve immediately with boiled rice and carrot raita.

preparation 10 minutes cooking time 12–15 minutes

Serves 4

TEX-MEX VEGGIE BURGERS

2 x 400g/14oz cans kidney beans, drained and rinsed

1 x 200g/7oz can sweetcorn kernels, drained

2 tbsp sliced jalapeño peppers

a handful of fresh coriander (cilantro), plus extra to garnish

2 medium (US large) eggs, beaten

50g/2oz/1 cup fresh white breadcrumbs

1 tbsp olive oil

4 seeded burger buns, toasted

1 avocado, peeled and stoned

salt and ground black peppper

soured cream and tomato salsa to serve

1 Put the beans, sweetcorn, peppers and coriander in a food processor and pulse briefly until everything is well combined but still has a rough, chunky texture. Season with salt and pepper.
2 Transfer to a large bowl and stir in the beaten eggs and breadcrumbs. Form into four burger shapes.
3 Heat the oil in a frying pan over a low to medium heat and gently fry the burgers for 8–10 minutes, carefully turning them once, until crisp and golden brown.
4 Serve the burgers in toasted buns. Cut the avocado into thin slices and place on top of the burgers. Add some soured cream and tomato salsa.

preparation 20 minutes cooking time 10 minutes

Serves 4

EASY FRIED RICE

225g/8oz/1 cup long-grain rice

2 tbsp oil

3 medium (US large) eggs, lightly beaten

225g/8oz/1 cup frozen peas

300g/11oz cooked peeled prawns (shrimp)

3 tbsp chopped fresh parsley

soy sauce to sprinkle

1 Cook the rice in a pan of boiling water for 10 minutes or according to the pack instructions. Drain well.
2 Heat 1 tsp oil in a large non-stick frying pan. Pour in half the beaten eggs and cook until set, stirring and tilting the pan. Slide the omelette out on to a warm plate. Repeat with the remaining beaten egg to make another omelette.
3 Add the remaining oil to the pan and stir in the cooked rice and peas. Stir-fry for 2–3 minutes until the peas are cooked. Add the prawns and parsley.
4 Roll up the omelettes and slice into thin strips. Add to the pan and cook for 2 minutes until heated through.
5 Divide the rice mixture among four serving bowls and serve immediately sprinkled with soy sauce.

preparation 5 minutes cooking time 20 minutes

Serves 4

STIR-FRIED PEPPERS WITH BEANSPROUTS

2 tbsp oil

2 garlic cloves, chopped

2 tsp chopped fresh root ginger

8 spring onions (scallions), sliced

2 red or yellow (bell) peppers, seeded and thinly sliced

340g/12oz beansprouts

2 tbsp soy sauce

1 tbsp sugar

boiled rice, sweet chilli sauce and chopped fresh coriander (cilantro) to serve

1 Heat the oil in a wok or large frying pan. Add the garlic, ginger, spring onions, red or yellow peppers and beansprouts and stir-fry over a medium heat for 3 minutes.
2 Add the soy sauce and sugar and stir-fry for 1 minute.
3 Divide among four serving bowls and serve with boiled rice, sweet chilli sauce and some chopped coriander.

preparation 10 minutes cooking time 4 minutes

Serves 4

LAST-MINUTE STIR-FRY

1 tbsp sesame oil

1 tsp puréed ginger

175g/6oz raw peeled tiger prawns (shrimp)

2–3 tbsp sweet chilli sauce

300g/11oz ready-prepared mixed stir-fry vegetables, e.g. sliced courgettes (zucchini), broccoli and green beans

1 Heat the oil in a large wok or deep frying pan over a medium heat. Add the ginger, prawns and sweet chilli sauce, and stir-fry for 2 minutes.
2 Add the mixed vegetables and stir-fry for 2–3 minutes until the prawns are cooked and the vegetables are heated through. Serve immediately.

Serves 2

preparation 2 minutes **cooking time** 5 minutes

QUICK CURRY

1 tbsp sunflower oil

1 onion, finely sliced

1 small aubergine (eggplant), cubed

1 garlic clove, crushed

1 red chilli, seeded and sliced

1 tsp ground garam masala

150ml/¼ pint/scant ⅔ cup coconut cream

2 x 400g/14fl oz cans chickpeas (garbanzos), drained and rinsed

250g/9oz baby spinach leaves

salt and ground black pepper

boiled rice to serve

1 Heat the oil in a large pan over a low heat and gently fry the onion and aubergine for 5 minutes or until softened.
2 Add the garlic and chilli and cook for 2 minutes. Stir in the garam masala and cook for 1 minute.
3 Add the coconut cream, chickpeas and 200ml/7fl oz/¾ cup water and heat through.
4 Stir in the spinach and cook for 1 minute until the leaves wilt. Season to taste with salt and pepper.
5 Serve the curry immediately with boiled rice.

Serves 4

preparation 10 minutes **cooking time** 10 minutes

ARTICHOKE AND MOZZARELLA SALAD

2 tsp sun-dried tomato paste
4 tbsp olive oil
1 tbsp white wine vinegar
juice of 1 lemon
225g/8oz artichoke hearts in oil, drained and sliced
250g/9oz cherry tomatoes, quartered
225g/8oz mozzarella, drained and cubed
100g/3½oz rocket (arugula)
salt and ground black pepper
balsamic vinegar to drizzle

1 Mix the sun-dried tomato paste, olive oil and wine vinegar in a small bowl to make the dressing.
2 Stir in the artichoke hearts and mix well.
3 Put the artichoke hearts in a salad bowl with the tomatoes, rocket and mozzarella. Toss everything together gently and season to taste with salt and pepper.
4 Divide the salad among four serving plates. Drizzle with balsamic vinegar and serve.

preparation 10 minutes cooking time 5 minutes

Serves 4

PORTOBELLO BURGERS

4 large Portobello mushrooms
4 tbsp olive oil
salt and ground black pepper
2 beefsteak tomatoes, sliced
4 slices halloumi cheese
4 burger buns
1 small red onion, thinly sliced

For the tarragon butter
50g/2oz/4 tbsp butter, softened
1 garlic clove, crushed
2 tbsp chopped fresh tarragon

1 To make the tarragon butter, place the butter, garlic and tarragon in a bowl, season with salt and pepper and blend.
2 Brush the mushrooms with olive oil and season with salt and pepper. Grill (broil) for 5 minutes, until softened. Remove and keep warm. Place the tomato slices under the grill (broiler) and cook for 1 minute to warm them through.
3 Cook the halloumi on a hot griddle pan for 2 minutes each side, until golden and softened.
4 Split the burger buns and spread thickly with the tarragon butter. Layer the red onion rings, mushrooms, tomatoes and halloumi on the bottom half of each bun. Cover with the top halves and serve.

preparation 10 minutes cooking time 6 minutes

Serves 4

CLASSIC OMELETTE

2 medium (US large) eggs
1 tbsp milk or water
25g/1oz/2 tbsp unsalted butter
salt and ground black pepper

1 Lightly whisk the eggs in a bowl and season with salt and pepper. Whisk in the milk or water.
2 Heat the butter in a non-stick omelette pan or 18cm/7in non-stick frying pan until it is foaming but not coloured. Add the eggs and stir gently with a wooden spoon, drawing the mixture in from the sides to the centre as it sets.
3 When set, stop stirring and cook for 30 seconds or until set and golden brown underneath and still creamy on top.
4 Fold over one-third of the omelette to the centre, then fold over the opposite third.
5 Slide out of the pan on to a warmed plate and serve.

preparation 5 minutes cooking time 5 minutes

Serves 1

MUSHROOM AND HALLOUMI KEBABS

340g/12oz halloumi cheese
1 red (bell) pepper
1 green (bell) pepper
2 small red onions
16 button mushrooms

For the marinade:
juice of ½ lemon
4 tbsp olive oil
1 garlic clove, crushed
1 tbsp chopped fresh oregano
salt and ground black pepper

1 Cut the halloumi into 2.5cm/1in squares. Cut the red and green peppers in half, remove the seeds and ribs and cut into 2.5cm/1in squares. Cut the red onions into quarters.
2 To make the marinade, put the lemon juice, oil, garlic, oregano, salt and pepper in a bowl and whisk together. Add the cheese, peppers and mushrooms to the marinade and stir to coat thoroughly.
3 Thread the cheese and the vegetables alternately onto thin skewers. Place under a hot grill (broiler) and cook for 8–10 minutes, turning frequently, until lightly charred. Serve immediately.

preparation 15 minutes cooking time 8—10 minutes

Serves 4

TOP 10 DIPS

BLUE CHEESE DIP

150ml/¼ pint/scant ⅔ cup soured cream
1 garlic clove, crushed
175g/6oz blue cheese
juice of 1 lemon
salt and ground black pepper

1   Put all the ingredients in a blender and blitz
    until smooth. Transfer to a serving dish and
    chill in the refrigerator until required.

preparation 5 minutes

Serves 6

AVOCADO DIP

175g/6oz/⅔ cup virtually fat-free fromage frais
1 ripe avocado, peeled, stoned and mashed
juice of 1 lemon
2 tbsp chopped fresh coriander (cilantro)

1   Mix all the ingredients together in a bowl
    until blended. Transfer to a serving dish
    and chill in the refrigerator until required.

preparation 5 minutes

Serves 6

YOGURT RAITA

250g/8oz/1 cup natural yogurt
a handful of fresh coriander (cilantro) leaves
1 red chilli, seeded and diced
¼ cucumber, grated

1   Blitz the yogurt and coriander in a blender,
    then mix with the chilli and cucumber. Place
    in a dish and chill in the refrigerator.

preparation 10 minutes

Serves 4

TAPENADE

3 tbsp capers, rinsed and drained
75g/3oz/½ cup pitted black olives
1 x 50g/2oz can anchovy fillets in oil, drained
2–3 tbsp extra virgin olive oil

1   Put the capers in a blender with the olives
    and anchovies. Blitz briefly to chop.
2   With the motor running, add the olive oil in
    a steady stream – enough to form a thick
    paste. Transfer to a serving bowl.

preparation 5 minutes

Serves 4

GUACAMOLE

2 ripe avocados, peeled, stoned and mashed
2 small tomatoes, seeded and chopped
juice of 2 limes
2 tbsp chopped fresh coriander (cilantro)
salt and ground black pepper

1 In a bowl, mix together the mashed
   avocado, tomatoes, lime juice and coriander.
   Season to taste. Chill in the refrigerator.

preparation 10 minutes   *Serves 6*

HUMMUS

1 x 400g/14oz can chickpeas, drained and rinsed
juice of 1 lemon
4 tbsp tahini
1 garlic clove, crushed
5 tbsp extra virgin olive oil

1 Put all the ingredients in a blender and blitz
   to a paste. Transfer to a bowl and chill in the
   refrigerator until required.

preparation 5 minutes   *Serves 6*

PESTO DIP

250g/8oz/1 cup virtually fat-free fromage frais
3 tbsp green pesto sauce
20 fresh basil leaves, chopped
2 ripe tomatoes, skinned, seeded and chopped

1 In a bowl, mix the fromage frais, pesto
   sauce, basil and tomatoes. Transfer to a
   bowl and chill in the refrigerator.

preparation 10 minutes   *Serves 6*

RED PEPPER DIP

1 x 300g/11oz jar roasted red peppers, drained
200g/7oz feta cheese, crumbled
1 small garlic clove
1 tbsp natural yogurt

1 Put all the ingredients in a blender and blitz
   until smooth. Chill in the refrigerator.

preparation 5 minutes   *Serves 6*

TZATZIKI

½ cucumber, seeded and diced
340g/12oz/1½ cups Greek yogurt
4 tbsp chopped fresh mint
juice of ½ lemon
salt and ground black pepper

1 Mix all the ingredients together in a bowl.
   Chill in the refrigerator until required.

preparation 10 minutes   *Serves 8*

TARAMASALATA

100g/3½oz white bread, crusts removed
75g/3oz smoked cod roe
2 tbsp lemon juice
100ml/3½fl oz/⅓ cup olive oil

1 Soak the bread in water for 10 minutes.
   Drain and squeeze out the water. Soak the
   roe in cold water for 10 minutes, then drain
   and skin. Blitz them in a blender with the
   lemon juice and oil. Chill in the refrigerator.

preparation 5 minutes plus soaking   *Serves 6*

ONE-POT SUPPERS

Cooking in one pot is a really easy and stress-free way to create a meal. Either you can prepare everything in advance and then leave it to cook away slowly in the pot while you relax, or you can cook a meal in minutes by briskly stir-frying fresh high-quality ingredients in a wok. Whether you're using a slow cooker, saucepan, casserole, sauté pan or wok, there's something very satisfying about this type of cookery. And there's no mess and hardly any washing up afterwards!

Many of these meals involve you only in assembling and preparing the ingredients and everything is cooked together in one pot. However, other dishes need the addition of bread, rice or potatoes to complete the meal.

It's also the perfect cooking method for cheaper cuts of meat, many of which require slow cooking in stews, braises and casseroles until they acquire a melting and succulent tenderness. Many one-pot recipes are particularly suited to autumnal and winter meals when the weather is colder and you want to fill up with something warming.

The recipes in this chapter are ideal for family weeknight suppers and some are smart enough to serve to your guests at an elegant dinner party. Dinner doesn't get easier than this!

< Simple Bouillabaisse (page 194]

COQ AU VIN

6 chicken joints
2 tbsp flour
125g/4oz/½ cup butter
125g/4oz lean bacon cubes
1 onion, chopped
2 carrots, sliced
600ml/1 pint/2½ cups red wine
2 garlic cloves, crushed
1 bouquet garni
2 tbsp olive oil
450g/1lb button onions
a pinch of sugar
340g/12oz button mushrooms
salt and ground black pepper

1 Dust the chicken with 1 tbsp flour. Melt a knob of butter in a flameproof casserole and fry the chicken until brown all over. Add the bacon, onion and carrot and cook until tender.
2 Pour in the wine and stir well. Add the garlic and bouquet garni and bring to the boil. Reduce the heat, cover and simmer for 1½ hours until the chicken is cooked through.
3 Melt 2 tbsp butter with 1 tsp oil in a pan. Fry the button onions until they start to brown. Add the sugar, then cover and cook gently for 10–15 minutes, stirring occasionally.
4 Melt 2 tbsp butter with 2 tsp oil in a pan. Fry the mushrooms and cook for a few minutes. Keep warm.
5 Remove the chicken and keep warm. Discard the bouquet garni. Boil the liquid for 5 minutes to reduce it.
6 Blend the remaining butter and flour to make a paste and add small pieces to the cooking liquid. Stir until smooth and cook until thickened. Return the chicken, onions and mushrooms to the casserole, season to taste and serve.

preparation 15 minutes cooking time 2 hours

Serves 6

CHICKEN IN A POT

2 tbsp olive oil
1 red onion, cut into wedges
1 x 1.6kg/3½lb chicken
6 carrots
2 parsnips, cut into wedges
1 garlic clove, crushed
1 bouquet garni
1 thin slice orange peel
600ml/1 pint/2½ cups hot chicken stock
100ml/3½ fl oz/⅓ cup dry white wine
12 button mushrooms
2 tbsp chopped fresh parsley
salt and ground black pepper

1 Heat the oil in a flameproof casserole. Fry the onion gently for 5 minutes or until golden. Remove and set aside.
2 Add the chicken to the casserole and fry for 10 minutes, turning to brown it all over. Remove and set aside.
3 Preheat the oven to 200°C/400°F/Gas 6. Add the carrots, parsnips and garlic to the casserole and cook for 5 minutes, then add the onion wedges.
4 Add the whole chicken with the bouquet garni, orange peel, hot stock and wine and season with salt and pepper. Bring to a simmer, then cover and cook in the oven for 30 minutes.
5 Remove the casserole from the oven and stir in the button mushrooms. Baste the chicken, then cover with a lid and cook in the oven for 50 minutes.
6 Lift out the chicken, then stir the parsley into the cooking liquid. Discard the bouquet garni and orange peel.
7 Carve the chicken and serve immediately with the vegetables and cooking liquid.

preparation 20 minutes cooking time 1 hour 40 minutes

Serves 6

CHICKEN CASSEROLE

1 x 1.4kg/3lb chicken
1 red onion, cut into wedges
2 carrots, sliced
2 leeks, thickly sliced
2 celery sticks, sliced
450g/1lb new potatoes
2 fresh thyme sprigs
1 fresh rosemary sprig
900ml/1½ pints/3⅔ cups hot chicken stock
4 tbsp chopped fresh parsley
salt and ground black pepper

1 Preheat the oven to 180°C/350°F/Gas 4.
2 Put the chicken in a large, flameproof casserole. Add the onion, carrots, leeks, celery, potatoes, herbs, hot stock and seasoning.
3 Bring to the boil, then cover the casserole and cook in the oven for 45 minutes or until the chicken is cooked through. The chicken is ready when you can pierce the thickest part of the leg with a knife and the juices run clear.
4 Add the parsley to the sauce. Remove the chicken and spoon the vegetables into six dishes.
5 Carve the chicken and divide among the dishes, then ladle the cooking liquid over the top.

preparation 15 minutes cooking time 50 minutes

Serves 6

ROAST CHICKEN WITH FRUIT AND COUSCOUS

3 large carrots, cut into chunks
2 red onions, cut into wedges
1 tbsp cumin seeds
1 tbsp olive oil
zest and juice of 1 lemon
8 boneless, skinless chicken thigh fillets
50g/2oz/⅓ cup dates, chopped
50g/2oz/⅓ cup dried apricots, chopped
salt and ground black pepper
couscous to serve

1 Preheat the oven to 200°C/400°F/Gas 6.
2 Put the carrots, red onions, cumin seeds, oil, lemon zest and juice and seasoning in a roasting pan and toss together.
3 Roast in the oven for 15 minutes until the carrots are beginning to soften.
4 Add the chicken, dates and apricots to the pan and cook for a further 25 minutes, basting the chicken in the pan juices, until it is cooked through and the vegetables are tender.
5 Serve the roast chicken and vegetables in the pan juices with some couscous.

preparation 15 minutes cooking time 40 minutes

Serves 4

TARRAGON CHICKEN

4 x 125g/4oz boneless chicken breasts, cut into chunks

2 tbsp olive oil

225g/8oz mushrooms, thinly sliced

150ml/¼ pint/scant ⅔ cup white vermouth, e.g. Noilly Prat

300ml/½ pint/1¼ cups crème fraîche

1 tsp Dijon mustard

2 tbsp chopped fresh tarragon plus extra to garnish

salt and ground black pepper

1 Sprinkle the chicken with some seasoning. Heat half the oil in a large frying pan over a medium heat. Cook the chicken for 5 minutes, turning occasionally, until golden brown on both sides. Remove and set aside.
2 Add the remaining oil to the pan and fry the mushrooms for 4–5 minutes until tender. Put the chicken back in the pan. Add the vermouth and simmer for 2 minutes, then stir in the crème fraîche, mustard and tarragon.
3 Bring to the boil, reduce the heat and simmer for 10 minutes or until the chicken is cooked through.
4 Season to taste. Sprinkle with the remaining tarragon and serve with new potatoes.

preparation 15 minutes cooking time 20 minutes

Serves 4

CHICKEN TAGINE

2 tbsp olive oil

8 chicken pieces

½ tsp each ground cumin, coriander and cinnamon

75g/3oz/½ cup ready-to-eat dried prunes, finely chopped

4 tbsp raisins

1 x 400g/14oz can chopped tomatoes

100g/3½oz/½ cup couscous

salt and ground black pepper

a handful of fresh coriander (cilantro), chopped, to garnish

1 Heat the oil in a large flameproof casserole over a medium heat and brown the chicken all over. Stir in the spices and cook for 1 minute.
2 Add the prunes, raisins, tomatoes, 400ml/14fl oz/1⅔ cups water and salt and pepper to taste. Bring to the boil, reduce the heat and simmer for 10 minutes.
3 Stir in the couscous and simmer for 5 minutes or until the couscous is tender and the chicken is cooked through.
4 Sprinkle with chopped coriander and serve immediately.

preparation 15 minutes cooking time 25 minutes

Serves 4

CHICKEN WITH BEANS AND TOMATOES

8 chicken thighs

1 red onion, sliced

1 x 400g/14oz can chopped tomatoes

1 x 400g/14oz can mixed beans, drained and rinsed

1 tbsp balsamic vinegar

4 tbsp chopped fresh parsley

1 Heat a non-stick pan over a medium heat and fry the chicken thighs, turning occasionally, until golden brown.
2 Add the onion and cook for 5 minutes. Add the tomatoes, mixed beans and balsamic vinegar. Cover the pan and simmer for 10–12 minutes until piping hot.
3 Garnish with parsley and serve immediately.

preparation 6 minutes **cooking time** 20–25 minutes

Serves 4

THAI RED CHICKEN CURRY

1 tbsp coconut oil

2 tbsp Thai red curry paste

4 boneless, skinless chicken breasts, sliced

1 x 400ml/14fl oz can coconut milk

300ml/½ pint/1¼ cups hot chicken stock

juice of 1 lime

200g/7oz pack baby corns

175g/6oz mangetouts, halved

225g/8oz straight to wok noodles

2 tbsp chopped fresh coriander (cilantro), plus sprigs to garnish

1 Heat the oil in a wok or deep frying pan over a low heat. Add the curry paste and cook for 2 minutes.
2 Add the sliced chicken and fry gently for 10 minutes, stirring occasionally, or until browned all over.
3 Add the coconut milk, hot stock, lime juice and baby corns to the pan and bring to the boil. Add the mangetouts, then reduce the heat and simmer for 4–5 minutes until the chicken is cooked.
4 Add the noodles to the wok and heat through gently, stirring once or twice, for 2–3 minutes
5 Stir in the chopped coriander and serve the curry, garnished with coriander sprigs.

preparation 5 minutes **cooking time** 20 minutes

Serves 4

SPANISH CHORIZO CHICKEN

12 boneless, skinless chicken thighs

12 thin slices chorizo

2 tbsp olive oil

1 onion, finely chopped

2 red (bell) peppers, seeded and thinly sliced

3 garlic cloves, crushed

1 x 400g/14oz can chopped tomatoes

4 tbsp sherry or red wine

12 pitted large green olives

salt and ground black pepper

1 Put the chicken thighs on a board, season with salt and pepper, roll up and wrap each one in a slice of chorizo. Secure each thigh with two wooden cocktail sticks (toothpicks) and set aside.

2 Heat the oil in a pan over a medium heat and cook the onion and red peppers for 10 minutes. Add the garlic and cook for 1 minute. Add the chicken and brown all over, turning occasionally, for 10–15 minutes.

3 Add the tomatoes and sherry or wine and bring to the boil. Reduce the heat and simmer gently for 5 minutes or until the juices run clear when the chicken is pierced with a skewer. Add the olives and warm through. Season to taste.

4 Remove the cocktail sticks from the chicken and serve.

preparation 15 minutes cooking time 30 minutes

Serves 6

CHICKEN CACCIATORE

2 tbsp olive oil

8 boneless, skinless chicken thighs

1 onion, chopped

2 garlic cloves, crushed

leaves from 2 fresh thyme sprigs

150ml/¼ pint/scant ⅔ cup white wine

1 x 400g/14oz can chopped tomatoes

12 pitted black olives

2 tbsp chopped fresh parsley

salt and ground black pepper

1 Heat the oil in a flameproof casserole over a high heat. Add the chicken and brown all over. Reduce the heat and add the onion, garlic, thyme and wine. Stir for 1 minute, then add the tomatoes and season with salt and pepper.

2 Bring to the boil, then reduce the heat, cover the casserole and simmer for 20 minutes or until the chicken is tender.

3 Remove the chicken and keep warm. Let the sauce bubble away for 5 minutes until reduced. Add the olives and parsley, stir well and cook for 3 minutes.

4 Serve the chicken in the sauce with rice and peas.

preparation 5 minutes cooking time 40 minutes

Serves 4

CHICKEN PROVENCAL

3 tbsp olive oil

4 boneless chicken breasts

1 red and 1 green (bell) pepper, seeded and sliced

1 onion, chopped

2 garlic cloves, crushed

1 x 400g/14oz can tomatoes

125ml/4fl oz/½ cup white wine

150ml/¼ pint/scant ⅔ cup chicken stock

2 tbsp chopped fresh basil

salt and ground black pepper

boiled rice to serve

1 Heat the oil in a shallow pan and cook the chicken over a medium heat for 5 minutes, turning occasionally, until golden brown on both sides. Remove and set aside.

2 Add the red and green peppers, onion and garlic to the pan and cook for 5 minutes, turning frequently, until lightly coloured and softened.

3 Stir in the tomatoes and wine and cook for 5 minutes until it starts to reduce and thicken. Add the stock and chicken breasts and basil. Season with salt and pepper, and cook gently for 20 minutes until the chicken is cooked through and the vegetables are tender.

4 Serve immediately with plain boiled rice.

preparation 10 minutes cooking time 35 minutes

Serves 4

CHICKEN NOODLE STIR-FRY

1 tbsp coconut oil

340g/12oz boneless, skinless chicken breasts, sliced

4 spring onions (scallions), chopped

225g/8oz rice noodles

125g/4oz mangetouts

175g/6oz baby asparagus

125g/4oz baby corns

2 tbsp sweet chilli sauce

fresh coriander (cilantro) leaves to garnish

1 Heat the oil in a wok or deep frying pan. Add the chicken and spring onions and stir-fry briskly over a high heat for 5–6 minutes until the chicken is golden brown.

2 Meanwhile, soak the rice noodles in some boiling water for 4 minutes or according to the pack instructions.

3 Add the mangetouts, asparagus, baby corns and chilli sauce to the chicken. Stir-fry for 3–4 minutes.

4 Drain the noodles, then add to the wok and toss everything together gently.

5 Scatter the coriander over the top and serve immediately.

preparation 10 minutes cooking time 12 minutes

Serves 4

SPANISH CHICKEN

2 tbsp olive oil
12 chicken pieces
175g/6oz chorizo sausage, cubed
1 onion, finely chopped
2 large garlic cloves, crushed
a pinch of dried chilli flakes
1 tbsp Spanish paprika
3 yellow (bell) peppers, seeded and chopped
400g/14oz/2 cups passata
2 tbsp tomato paste
5 tbsp red wine
300ml/½ pint/1¼ cups chicken stock
340g/12oz new potatoes, halved
a few fresh thyme sprigs

1 Preheat the oven to 190°C/375°F/Gas 5.
2 Heat the oil in a large flameproof casserole over a high heat and brown the chicken all over. Remove from the pan and set aside. Add the chorizo to the casserole and fry for 2–3 minutes until its oil starts to run.
3 Add the onion, garlic and chilli flakes and cook over a low heat for 5 minutes or until soft. Stir in the paprika.
4 Add the yellow peppers and cook for 2–3 minutes until soft. Stir in the passata, tomato paste, red wine, stock, potatoes and thyme. Cover and simmer for 10 minutes.
5 Return the chicken to the casserole. Cover and cook in the oven for 30–35 minutes. If the sauce is not thick enough, put the casserole on the hob over a medium heat and simmer briskly until it reduces and thickens.
6 Remove the thyme and serve immediately.

preparation 10 minutes cooking time 1 hour 10 minutes

Serves 6

QUICK CHICKEN AND VEGETABLE HOTPOT

4 x 125g/4oz chicken breasts
2 large parsnips, chopped
2 large carrots, chopped
2 sticks celery, chopped
300ml/½ pint/1¼ cups ready-made gravy
4 tomatoes, roughly chopped
salt and ground black pepper

1 Heat a non-stick frying pan or flameproof casserole until hot. Add the chicken breasts, skin-side down, and cook for 5 minutes until browned. Turn them over and add the parsnips, carrots and celery. Cook for 8–10 minutes.
2 Pour the gravy over the chicken and vegetables, then cover the pan and cook gently for 10 minutes.
3 Season with salt and pepper and stir in the tomatoes. Cover and cook for 5 minutes until the chicken is cooked and the vegetables are tender. Serve hot.

preparation 5 minutes cooking time 30 minutes

Serves 4

BOEUF BOURGUIGNON

2 tbsp oil

125g/4oz bacon lardons

1kg/2¼lb topside, rump or lean
braising steak, cut into cubes

1 garlic clove, crushed

2 tbsp plain (all-purpose) flour

1 bouquet garni

150ml/¼ pint/ scant ⅔ cup beef stock

300ml/½ pint/1¼ cups Burgundy
or other full-bodied red wine

50g/2oz/4 tbsp butter

12 baby onions, peeled

225g/8oz button mushrooms

salt and ground black pepper

2 tbsp chopped fresh parsley

1 Preheat the oven to 170°C/325°F/Gas 3.

2 Heat the oil in a large flameproof casserole over a medium
heat. Add the bacon and brown quickly all over, then remove
and set aside.

3 Add the steak in batches and cook, stirring, until browned.
Return the bacon to the casserole and add the garlic. Stir in
the flour and add the bouquet garni, stock and wine. Bring
to the boil, stirring. Season with salt and pepper, cover and
cook in the oven for 2½ hours.

4 Meanwhile, heat the butter in a frying pan and fry the onions
until tender and golden brown. Remove and set aside. Add
the mushrooms and fry for 2–3 minutes.

5 Add the mushrooms and onions to the casserole and cook
in the oven for 30 minutes. Discard the bouquet garni and
serve sprinkled with parsley.

preparation 30 minutes cooking time 3 hours

Serves 6

QUICK GOULASH

1 tbsp olive oil

1 onion, thinly sliced

450g/1lb lean beef, cubed

4 tbsp red wine

1 tbsp paprika

1 tbsp plain (all-purpose) flour

2 tbsp tomato paste

2 x 400g/14oz cans chopped
tomatoes

2 green (bell) peppers, seeded
and thinly sliced

salt and ground black pepper

4 tbsp chopped fresh parsley

soured cream and rice to serve

1 Heat the oil in a large pan over a low heat. Add the onion and
cook for 10 minutes until softened and lightly coloured.

2 Add the pork and cook for 5 minutes, stirring occasionally,
until browned all over. Pour in the wine, then stir in the
paprika, flour and tomato paste and cook for 1 minute.

3 Add the tomatoes, green peppers and some salt and pepper.
Simmer, stirring occasionally, for 10 minutes.

4 Check the seasoning and divide the goulash among four
serving plates. Sprinkle with parsley and top each portion
with a spoonful of soured cream. Serve with rice.

preparation 20 minutes cooking time 20 minutes

Serves 4

PAPRIKA BEEF STEW

450g/1lb lean braising steak
1 tbsp olive oil
2 tbsp flour
1 red onion, chopped
2 carrots, diced
2 red (bell) peppers, seeded and thinly sliced
1 tbsp paprika
4 tbsp tomato paste
500ml/17fl oz/2¼ cups beef stock
1 x 400g/14oz can tomatoes
salt and ground black pepper
fresh parsley to garnish

1 Trim the fat off the steak and cut the meat into cubes.
2 Heat the oil in a large pan over a medium heat. Dust the beef with the flour and then add to the pan. Cook, stirring, for a few minutes until well browned all over.
3 Add the onion, carrots, red peppers, paprika, tomato paste and tomatoes and cook for 5 minutes. Pour in the stock, bring to the boil, then reduce the heat, cover the pan and simmer for 1 hour or until the beef is tender and the liquid has reduced.
4 Season with salt and pepper to taste and sprinkle with the parsley. Serve with mashed potatoes.

preparation 20 minutes cooking time 1 hour 15 minutes

Serves 4

SPICY BEEF MINCE

1 tbsp olive oil
1 large onion, chopped
1 garlic clove, crushed
1 red chilli, finely diced
2 red (bell) peppers, seeded and chopped
400g/14oz minced (ground) beef
1 x 400g/14oz can tomatoes
2 x 400g/14oz cans mixed beans, drained and rinsed
2 tbsp chopped fresh coriander (cilantro)
salsa, soured cream and flour tortillas to serve

1 Heat the oil in a large heavy-based frying pan over a medium heat. Add the onion and cook for 10 minutes, stirring occasionally, until tender and golden.
2 Add the garlic and chilli and cook for 1–2 minutes. Add the red peppers and cook for 5 minutes.
3 Add the minced beef to the pan and cook, stirring, until browned all over. Add the tomatoes and mixed beans, then simmer for 20 minutes.
4 Divide among four serving plates and sprinkle the coriander over the top. Serve immediately with some salsa, soured cream and warmed tortillas.

preparation 10 minutes cooking time 40 minutes

Serves 4

BEEF PILAFF

1 tbsp olive oil
1 onion, thinly sliced
450g/1lb stewing beef, cubed
2 tbsp garam masala
225g/8oz/1 cup basmati rice
475ml/16fl oz/2 cups beef stock
200g/7oz fine green beans
75g/3oz/6 tbsp chopped ready-
to-eat dried apricots
4 tbsp mango chutney
salt and ground black pepper
3 tbsp chopped fresh parsley

1 Heat the oil in a large pan over a low heat. Add the onion and cook for 8 minutes, stirring occasionally, or until softened. Add the beef and cook, stirring, for 8 minutes until browned all over. Stir in the garam masala and rice and cook for 1 minute.
2 Pour in the stock and bring to the boil, then reduce the heat, cover the pan and simmer for 10 minutes.
3 Stir in the green beans and apricots and cook, covered, for 10 minutes or until the stock is absorbed and the rice is tender. Fold in the chutney and season to taste.
4 Sprinkle with chopped parsley and serve.

preparation 10 minutes cooking time 40 minutes

Serves 4

BEEF GOULASH

3 tbsp olive oil
1.1kg/2½lb stewing steak, diced
16 button onions
1 red chilli, seeded and chopped
3 garlic cloves, crushed
2 tbsp plain (all-purpose) flour
2 tbsp smoked paprika
700g/1½lb/2¾ cups passata
100ml/3½fl oz/⅓ cup beef stock
salt and ground black pepper
red cabbage and noodles
to serve

1 Preheat the oven to 170°C/325°F/Gas 3.
2 Heat the oil in a large flameproof casserole until very hot. Cook the beef, in batches, over a high heat, stirring until it is browned all over. Remove and set aside.
3 Reduce the heat and add the onions, chilli and garlic. Cook for 10 minutes, stirring often, or until the onions are golden brown. Return the meat to the casserole and stir in the flour and paprika. Cook, stirring, for 2 minutes, then add the passata and season to taste.
4 Cover the casserole and cook in the oven for 2½ hours or until the beef is really tender. Check after an hour – if the beef looks dry, add the hot beef stock.
5 Serve the hot goulash with red cabbage and noodles.

preparation 20 minutes cooking time 3 hours

Serves 8

BEEF AND MUSTARD HOTPOT

2 tbsp olive oil
1.1kg/2½lb stewing steak, diced
2 onions, finely chopped
4 tbsp plain (all-purpose) flour
1 litre/1¾ pints/4 cups beef stock
4 tbsp wholegrain mustard
2 tbsp light brown sugar
3 bay leaves
500g/1lb 2oz baby carrots, quartered
350g/12oz swede (rutabaga), cut into cubes
2 leeks, sliced
675g/1½lb potatoes, thinly sliced
2 tbsp melted butter
salt and ground black pepper

1 Preheat the oven to 170°C/325°F/Gas 3.
2 Heat 1 tbsp oil in a large frying pan, add the beef in batches, and cook, stirring, until browned all over. Transfer to a large flameproof casserole.
3 Add the onions to the pan and cook for 5 minutes or until softened and just beginning to brown. Sprinkle with flour and gradually stir in the stock. Bring to the boil and add half the mustard, the sugar, bay leaves and salt and pepper.
4 Pour over the beef, cover and cook in the oven for 1¼ hours.
5 Stir the carrots, swede and leek into the casserole and return to the oven for 45 minutes or until tender.
6 Cook the potatoes in boiling water for 5 minutes. Drain and arrange the slices, overlapping, on top of the casserole. Brush with melted butter and the rest of the mustard and return to the oven for 45 minutes, until the potatoes are golden brown and crisp.

preparation 30 minutes **cooking time** 3 hours 15 minutes

Serves 4

BEEF MADRAS CURRY

4 tbsp ghee or vegetable oil
2 onions, chopped
2 garlic cloves, crushed
1 tsp chilli powder
2 tsp ground coriander
2 tsp ground turmeric
¼ tsp ground black pepper
900g/2lb stewing beef, cubed
600ml/1 pint/2½ cups beef stock
300ml/½ pint/1¼ cups coconut milk
4 tbsp chopped fresh coriander (cilantro)

1 Heat the ghee or oil in a large heavy-based pan, add the onions and garlic and cook gently for 5 minutes or until soft and lightly coloured. Add the chilli powder and ground spices and cook, stirring constantly, for 3–4 minutes.
2 Add the beef and cook gently, stirring, for 2–3 minutes. Add the stock to the pan and bring slowly to the boil. Reduce the heat, cover and simmer gently for 1½ hours or until the beef is cooked and tender.
3 Add the coconut milk and bring to the boil. Reduce the heat and simmer for 8–10 minutes until slightly thickened. Stir in the chopped coriander.
4 Serve the curry immediately with boiled rice.

preparation 10 minutes **cooking time** 2 hours 45 minutes

Serves 6

OSSO BUCO

4 tbsp olive oil

1 onion, finely chopped

4 large veal shins, sawn into short lengths

2 tbsp seasoned flour

300ml/½ pint/1¼ cups white wine

300ml/½ pint/1¼ cups hot veal or beef stock

finely grated zest of 1 lemon

1 garlic clove, crushed

4 tbsp chopped fresh parsley

1 Heat the oil in a flameproof casserole, add the onion and fry gently over a low heat for 5 minutes or until tender.
2 Coat the veal in the flour, add to the casserole and cook for 10 minutes, stirring occasionally, until browned.
3 Add the wine, increase the heat and boil rapidly for 5 minutes, then add the hot stock and reduce the heat. Cover and simmer for 1½–2 hours, stirring occasionally.
4 Transfer the veal to a warmed serving dish, cover and keep warm. If necessary, boil the sauce rapidly to thicken it, then pour it over the meat.
5 Mix together the lemon zest, garlic and parsley and sprinkle over the top. Serve with risotto Milanese (see page 110).

preparation 15 minutes cooking time 1 hour 50 minutes–2 hours 20 minutes

Serves 4

BEAN CASSOULET

1 tbsp olive oil

225g/8oz bacon lardons

1 onion, chopped

2 red (bell) peppers, seeded and chopped

1 x 400g/14oz can chopped tomatoes

a pinch of dried chilli flakes

2 x 400g/14oz cans mixed beans, drained and rinsed

4 tbsp chopped fresh parsley

salt and ground black pepper

1 Heat the oil in a large pan over a medium heat and cook the lardons for 5 minutes until golden brown. Remove from the pan and set aside.
2 Add the onion and red peppers to the pan and cook gently for 10 minutes or until softened. Stir in the cooked lardons, the tomatoes, chilli flakes and 200ml/7fl oz/¾ cup water. Bring to the boil, then reduce the heat, cover the pan and simmer for 20 minutes, stirring occasionally.
3 Uncover the pan, add the beans and cook for 10 minutes. Stir in the chopped parsley and season to taste.
4 Divide among four serving dishes and serve immediately.

preparation 15 minutes cooking time 50 minutes

Serves 4

STIR-FRIED CHILLI BEEF

1 tbsp sesame oil
1 tsp grated fresh root ginger
2 tbsp soy sauce
1 green chilli, finely chopped
450g/1lb steak, cut into strips
1 red and 1 yellow (bell) pepper, seeded and roughly chopped
1 carrot, cut into thin strips
250g/9oz baby corn
200g/7oz mangetouts, halved
300g/11oz beansprouts
300g/11oz rice noodles
sweet chilli sauce to drizzle

1 Put the oil in a large bowl. Add the ginger, soy sauce, chilli and steak strips. Mix well and leave in a cool place to marinate for 10 minutes.
2 Heat a wok or large frying pan until hot. Add the beef to the pan. Stir-fry over a high heat for 5 minutes.
3 Add the red and yellow peppers, carrot, baby sweetcorn, mangetouts, beansprouts and remaining marinade and stir-fry for 2–3 minutes until the beef is cooked.
4 Meanwhile, soak the noodles for 4 minutes or according to the pack instructions. Drain the noodles, add to the pan and toss well. Serve immediately, drizzled with chilli sauce.

preparation 15 minutes plus marinating cooking time 8 minutes

Serves 4

PORK WITH CHEESE AND CIDER

4 pork loin chops
1 tbsp olive oil
400g/14oz new potatoes, halved lengthways
2 apples, cored and sliced
6 tbsp dry cider
6 tbsp hot vegetable stock
1 tbsp chopped fresh sage leaves
50g/2oz Roquefort cheese
3 tbsp double (heavy) cream
salt and ground black pepper
3 tbsp chopped fresh parsley

1 Preheat the oven to 230°C/450°F/Gas 8.
2 Snip the fat on the pork chops at regular intervals with a pair of scissors to stop them curling as they cook.
3 Heat the oil in a flameproof roasting pan set over a medium heat and brown the chops on both sides. Remove.
4 Add the potatoes to the roasting pan and turn them in the oil. Roast in the oven for 15 minutes.
5 Tuck the chops and apples in among the potatoes, then pour in the cider and hot stock. Add the sage and return to the oven for 15 minutes or until the pork is cooked through.
6 Crumble in the cheese and stir in the cream and return to the oven for 5 minutes until melted.
7 Season to taste and serve sprinkled with parsley.

preparation 10 minutes cooking time 40 minutes

Serves 4

SAUSAGE TRAYBAKE

8 pork sausages

2 red onions, cut into wedges

2 tbsp chopped fresh rosemary plus extra to garnish

4 unpeeled garlic cloves

4 large potatoes, peeled and cut into wedges

4 tbsp olive oil

salt and ground black pepper

balsamic vinegar to drizzle

1 Preheat the oven to 200°C/400°F/Gas 6.
2 Put the sausages in a large roasting pan with the onion wedges, rosemary, garlic, potatoes and oil. Season with salt and pepper and toss everything together.
3 Roast in the oven for 30-40 minutes, turning everything once or twice in the oil.
4 Squeeze the garlic out of the skins and mix with the vegetables.
5 Drizzle the vegetables with balsamic vinegar and serve garnished with sprigs of fresh rosemary.

preparation 15 minutes cooking time about 40 minutes

Serves 4

PORK VINDALOO

2 tbsp ghee or vegetable oil

1 large onion, thinly sliced

4 whole dried red chillies

1 tsp each cumin seeds and coriander seeds

1 tsp black peppercorns

2 tsp black mustard seeds

3 whole cloves

2 tsp grated fresh root ginger

½ tsp ground cinnamon

1 tsp ground turmeric

5 garlic cloves

4 tbsp white wine vinegar

2 tbsp tomato paste

900g/2lb pork shoulder, cubed

1 Heat half the ghee or oil in a large heavy-based frying pan or flameproof casserole. Add the onion and fry over a medium heat until it starts to turn brown.
2 Put the onion in a blender or food processor with the dried chillies, all the spices, garlic, vinegar and tomato paste. Blitz until smooth.
3 Heat the remaining ghee or oil in the pan, add the pork and fry over a medium heat, stirring, until browned on all sides.
4 Add the onion and spice mixture and cook for a few minutes over a high heat, stirring all the time.
5 Reduce the heat, cover the pan and simmer for 1½ hours or until the pork is tender and the sauce has reduced.
6 Serve hot with boiled rice or potatoes.

preparation 15 minutes cooking time 2 hours

Serves 4

LAMB AND LENTIL CURRY

450g/1lb lean stewing lamb, cut into large chunks
1 tsp ground turmeric
1 tsp garam masala
2 garlic cloves, crushed
1 red chilli, seeded and diced
1 tsp grated fresh root ginger
2 tbsp vegetable oil
1 onion, chopped
1 x 400g/14oz can tomatoes
225g/8oz red lentils, rinsed
salt and ground black pepper
4 tbsp natural yogurt
fresh coriander to garnish

1 Put the lamb in a shallow sealable container with the spices, garlic, chilli, ginger, salt and pepper. Stir well to mix, cover and put in the refrigerator for at least 30 minutes.
2 Heat the oil in a large flameproof casserole, add the onion and cook over a low heat for 5 minutes. Add the lamb and spice mixture and cook for 10 minutes, turning regularly, until the meat is evenly browned.
3 Add the tomatoes, 475ml/16fl oz/2 cups boiling water and the lentils and bring to the boil. Reduce the heat, cover the casserole and simmer for 1 hour.
4 Remove the lid and cook uncovered for 30 minutes, stirring occasionally, until the sauce is thick and the lamb is tender.
5 Serve the curry topped with yogurt and garnished with coriander sprigs.

preparation 15 minutes plus marinating cooking time 1 hour 50 minutes

Serves 4

THAI RED LAMB CURRY

2 tbsp coconut oil
1 onion, chopped
2 garlic cloves, crushed
450g/1lb lean lamb, cubed
2 tbsp Thai red curry paste
150ml/¼ pint/scant ⅔ cup hot lamb or beef stock
2 tbsp Thai fish sauce
2 tsp soft brown sugar
1 red (bell) pepper, seeded and sliced
125g/4oz thin green beans, halved
2 tbsp chopped fresh basil

1 Heat the oil in a wok or deep frying pan. Add the onion and garlic and fry over a medium heat for 5 minutes or until softened and starting to colour.
2 Add the lamb and curry paste and stir-fry for 5 minutes. Add the hot stock, fish sauce and sugar. Bring to the boil, then reduce the heat, cover and simmer gently for 20 minutes.
3 Stir the red pepper and green beans into the curry and cook, uncovered, for 10 minutes.
4 Sprinkle with basil and serve immediately with boiled rice.

preparation 10 minutes cooking time 45 minutes

Serves 4

STIFADO

500g/1lb 2oz lean lamb, cubed
4 tbsp olive oil
2 onions, thinly sliced
2 garlic cloves, crushed
1 x 400g/14oz can tomatoes
2 tbsp red wine vinegar
300ml/½ pint/1¼ cups red wine
1 tsp chopped fresh oregano
2 fresh rosemary sprigs
450g/1lb potatoes
salt and ground black pepper

1 Cook the lamb in the oil in a pan set over a medium heat, stirring occasionally, until browned all over. Remove from the pan and keep warm.
2 Add the onions and garlic to the pan and cook for 5 minutes, stirring occasionally, until tender. Stir in the tomatoes, vinegar, wine and herbs.
3 Return the lamb to the pan, then reduce the heat and simmer for 1 hour 20 minutes or until the lamb is tender and the sauce has thickened. Season to taste with salt and pepper.
4 Meanwhile, cut the potatoes into large pieces and cook in a pan of lightly salted boiling water until tender. Drain well.
5 Serve the stifado with the boiled potatoes.

preparation 10 minutes cooking time 1 hour 30 minutes

Serves 8

LAMB PASANDA

2 tbsp ghee or vegetable oil
2 onions, thinly sliced
2 garlic cloves
1 tsp chilli powder
1 tsp ground ginger
2 tsp ground coriander
½ tsp each ground turmeric, cardamom and cloves
1 cinnamon stick
700g/1½lb lean lamb, cubed
300ml/½ pint/1¼ cups coconut milk
2 tbsp lemon juice
boiled rice and yogurt cucumber raita to serve

1 Heat the ghee or oil in a large pan over a high heat, add the onions and garlic and cook for 5 minutes until starting to soften and brown.
2 Add the ground spices and cinnamon stick to the pan and cook, stirring, for 2 minutes. Add the lamb and cook over a high heat, stirring all the time, until browned all over.
3 Add the coconut milk and 150ml/¼ pint/ scant ⅔ cup water. Stir in the lemon juice and bring to the boil. Reduce the heat and simmer gently for 1½ hours or until the lamb is tender.
4 Serve with boiled rice and yogurt cucumber raita.

preparation 20 minutes cooking time 2 hours

Serves 4

BRAISED LAMB SHANKS

3 tbsp olive oil
6 lamb shanks
1 large onion, cut into wedges
2 large carrots, sliced
3 celery sticks, sliced
1 x 400g/14oz can chopped tomatoes
150ml/5fl oz/scant ⅔ cup red wine
3 tbsp balsamic vinegar
2 x 400g/14oz cans cannellini beans, drained and rinsed
salt and ground black pepper

1 Preheat the oven to 170°C/325°F/Gas 3.
2 Heat the oil in a large flameproof casserole and brown the lamb shanks all over. Remove and set aside.
3 Add the onion, carrots and garlic to the casserole and cook gently until softened and just beginning to colour. Add the lamb, tomatoes, red wine and balsamic vinegar and stir well. Season with salt and pepper.
4 Cover and cook in the oven for 2 hours, then add the beans plus some water or stock if it needs more liquid. Cover and return to the oven for 30 minutes.
5 Serve with potatoes and green vegetables.

preparation 15 minutes cooking time 2 hours 45 minutes

Serves 6

LIVER STROGANOV

1 tbsp olive oil
2 onions, thinly sliced
125g/4oz shiitake mushrooms, sliced
125g/4oz chestnut mushrooms, sliced
340g/12oz calf's liver, sliced
5 tbsp dry white wine
1 tbsp wholegrain mustard
150g/5oz/scant ⅔ cup half-fat crème fraîche
150g/5oz/scant ⅔ cup 2% fat Greek yogurt
salt and ground black pepper
3 tbsp chopped fresh parsley

1 Heat the oil in a large frying pan over a low heat. Add the onions and cook gently for 5 minutes until softened.
2 Increase the heat to medium and add the mushrooms. Cook, stirring, for 5 minutes or until tender.
3 Add the liver to the pan. Cook over a medium heat, stirring occasionally, for 5 minutes.
4 Stir in the wine, mustard, crème fraîche and yogurt and heat through gently for 2–3 minutes without boiling.
5 Season with salt and pepper to taste and sprinkle with parsley. Serve immediately with boiled rice.

preparation 15 minutes cooking time 20 minutes

Serves 4

SIMPLE BOUILLABAISSE

2 tbsp olive oil
1 onion, finely chopped
2 celery sticks, finely chopped
2 garlic cloves, crushed
500g/1lb 2oz tomatoes, chopped
250ml/9fl oz/1 cup white wine
250ml/9fl oz/1 cup fish stock
1 tbsp tomato paste
2 fresh thyme sprigs
500g/1lb 2oz white fish fillets
340g/12oz frozen mixed seafood
2 tbsp chopped flat-leaf parsley
1 small baguette, sliced
salt and ground black pepper
rouille to serve (see page 574)

1 Heat the oil in a pan over a low heat, add the onion and celery and cook gently for 10 minutes, stirring occasionally, until softened and golden. Stir in the garlic and tomatoes and cook for 2–3 minutes.
2 Stir in the wine, stock, tomato paste and thyme and season with salt and pepper. Bring to the boil, then reduce the heat, cover the pan and simmer for 15 minutes.
3 Add the fish fillets in a single layer and cook gently, covered, for 10 minutes or until the fish is just cooked. Lift the fillets out on to a plate and remove any skin and bones. Break into large flakes and return to the soup.
4 Add the thawed mixed seafood to the soup and reheat for 5 minutes. Sprinkle with chopped parsley.
5 Toast the baguette. Ladle the soup into shallow bowls and top with the toasted baguette and a spoonful of rouille.

preparation 20 minutes **cooking time** 40 minutes

Serves 4

PAELLA

1 tbsp olive oil
1 large onion, thinly sliced
4 chicken breast fillets
2 garlic cloves, crushed
a pinch of saffron
a pinch of paprika
1 red or green (bell) pepper, seeded and thinly sliced
340g/12oz/1½ cups paella rice
1.2 litres/2 pints/5 cups hot chicken stock
225g/8oz raw prawns (shrimp)
4 tbsp chopped fresh parsley
salt and ground black pepper

1 Heat the oil in a large paella pan or frying pan. Add the onion and cook for 5 minutes over a medium heat.
2 Cut the chicken into chunks, add to the pan and cook for 3 minutes, stirring, until starting to brown.
3 Stir in the garlic, saffron and paprika and cook for 1 minute to release the flavours.
4 Stir in the red or green pepper and the rice and cook for 1 minute until all the grains of rice are glistening. Pour in the hot stock and leave to simmer gently for 20 minutes, stirring occasionally, or until the rice is tender and cooked.
5 Stir in the prawns and parsley and check the seasoning. Cook for 3–4 minutes until the prawns turn pink.
6 Serve immediately with a crisp salad.

preparation 15 minutes **cooking time** 30 minutes

Serves 4

CITRUS COD AND BROCCOLI

125g/4oz Tenderstem broccoli, halved lengthways

225g/8oz asparagus, trimmed

4 x 125g/4oz boneless, skinless, cod fillets

juice of 1 orange

1 orange, cut into 8 wedges

2 tbsp olive oil

salt and ground black pepper

boiled rice or new potatoes to serve

1 Preheat the oven to 220°C/425°F/Gas 7.
2 Spread the broccoli and asparagus in an even layer in a roasting pan. Arrange the cod fillets on top and pour the orange juice over. Tuck the orange wedges around the fish. Drizzle with the oil and season with salt and pepper.
3 Cook in the oven for 10–12 minutes until the cod is cooked and the vegetables are just tender but still a little firm.
4 Serve immediately with boiled rice or new potatoes.

Serves 4

preparation 10 minutes cooking time 12 minutes

SPANISH FISH CASSEROLE

2 tbsp olive oil

1 onion, finely chopped

1 leek, thinly sliced

400g/14oz potatoes, cubed

150ml/¼ pint/scant ⅔ cup dry white wine

2 x 400g/14oz cans chopped tomatoes

a pinch of sugar

4 x 125g/4oz white fish fillets, skinned and boned

salt and ground black pepper

a handful of fresh basil, torn

1 Heat half the oil in a large pan over a low heat. Add the onion and leek and cook for 6–8 minutes until softened. Add the potatoes and pour in the wine. Cook for 2–3 minutes.
2 Stir in the tomatoes, sugar, some salt and pepper and 150ml/¼ pint/scant ⅔ cup water. Simmer for 35 minutes, stirring occasionally, until the potatoes are tender.
3 Season the fish fillets and add them to the pan. Cover and simmer gently for 5 minutes until the fish is cooked through. Stir gently to roughly flake the fish.
4 Sprinkle with basil and serve immediately.

Serves 4

preparation 15 minutes cooking time 55 minutes

SALMON PILAU

1 tbsp olive oil
1 onion, chopped
175g/6oz/1¾ cups bulgur wheat
450ml/¾ pint/1¾ cups fish stock
400g/14oz cooked salmon fillets, skinned and flaked
125g/4oz/1 cup frozen peas
3 tomatoes, roughly chopped
juice of 1 lemon
salt and ground black pepper

1 Heat the oil in a large pan. Add the onion and cook over a low heat until softened. Stir in the bulgur wheat to coat in the oil, then add the stock and bring to the boil.
2 Cover the pan, reduce the heat and simmer gently for 10–15 minutes until the stock has been fully absorbed.
3 Stir in the salmon, peas, tomatoes and lemon juice and cook until the peas are tender. Season to taste and serve.

preparation 5 minutes **cooking time** 20 minutes

Serves 4

PRAWN GUMBO

1 tbsp groundnut oil
1 onion, finely chopped
2 celery sticks, chopped
2 green peppers, seeded and roughly chopped
1 red chilli, diced
2 garlic cloves, crushed
1 x 400g/14oz can tomatoes
200g/7oz okra, roughly chopped
900ml/1½ pints/3¾ cups fish or vegetable stock
125g/4oz/½ cup basmati rice
300g/11oz cooked, peeled king prawns (jumbo shrimp)
salt and ground black pepper
4 tbsp chopped fresh parsley

1 Heat the oil in a large pan. Add the onion, celery and green peppers and cook over a low heat for 5 minutes until they start to soften.
2 Stir in the chilli, garlic, tomatoes, okra and stock. Bring to the boil, then reduce the heat and simmer for 20 minutes.
3 Stir in the rice, reduce the heat and simmer for 20 minutes, stirring occasionally, until the rice is cooked and the liquid has been absorbed.
4 Stir in the prawns and heat through. Season to taste with salt and pepper.
5 Spoon the gumbo into four serving bowls, garnish with chopped parsley and serve.

preparation 20 minutes **cooking time** 45 minutes

Serves 4

THAI GREEN SEAFOOD CURRY

1 tbsp coconut oil

3 tbsp Thai green curry paste

340g/12oz skinless cod fillets

340g/12oz large raw peeled prawns (jumbo shrimp)

1 x 400ml/14fl oz can coconut milk

200ml/7fl oz/¾ cup fish stock

juice of 1 lime

2 tbsp Thai fish sauce

125g/4oz fine green beans

3 tbsp fresh basil, torn

salt and ground black pepper

1 Heat the oil in a wok or deep frying pan. Add the curry paste and cook over a medium heat, stirring, for 1–2 minutes.
2 Cut the cod into chunks and add to the wok with the prawns. Stir well to coat them in the curry paste. Stir in the coconut milk, stock, lime juice and fish sauce and bring to the boil.
3 Add the green beans, reduce the heat and simmer gently for 5 minutes or until the beans and cod are tender. Stir in the basil and season to taste with salt and pepper.
4 Ladle the curry into bowls and serve with rice.

preparation 15 minutes cooking time 10 minutes

Serves 4

THAI RED SEAFOOD CURRY

1 tbsp coconut oil

1 lemongrass stalk, chopped

1 green chilli, chopped

4 tbsp chopped fresh coriander (cilantro) plus extra to serve

2 kaffir lime leaves, chopped

1–2 tbsp Thai red curry paste

1 x 400ml/14fl oz can coconut milk

450ml/¾ pint/1¾ cups fish stock

250g/9oz queen scallops

450g/1lb raw peeled tiger prawns (shrimp)

salt and ground black pepper

1 Heat the oil in a wok or deep frying pan over a medium heat. Add the lemongrass, chilli, coriander and lime leaves and stir-fry for 30 seconds. Add the curry paste and stir-fry for 1 minute.
2 Add the coconut milk and stock and bring to the boil. Reduce the heat and simmer for 5–10 minutes until slightly reduced. Season to taste with salt and pepper.
3 Add the scallops and prawns, bring to the boil, then reduce the heat and simmer for 2–3 minutes until cooked.
4 Divide the curry among six serving bowls and sprinkle with coriander. Serve immediately with rice.

preparation 10 minutes cooking time 15 minutes

Serves 6

STIR-FRIED SCALLOPS

500g/1lb 2oz large scallops

2 tbsp oil

1 bunch of spring onions (scallions), sliced diagonally

1 red (bell) pepper, seeded and thinly sliced

2 tsp grated fresh root ginger

2 garlic cloves, sliced

2 tbsp lime juice

3 tbsp chopped fresh coriander (cilantro)

sweet chilli sauce and boiled rice to serve

1 Cut the scallops into thick slices. Heat the oil in a wok or large frying pan. Add the scallops, spring onions, red pepper, ginger and garlic and stir-fry over a high heat for 2–3 minutes or until the vegetables are just tender.

2 Add the lime juice and cook for 1 minute. Stir in half the chopped coriander.

3 Serve the scallops immediately, sprinkled with the remaining chopped coriander, on a bed of boiled rice with some chilli sauce.

preparation 15 minutes **cooking time** 3 minutes

Serves 4

STIR-FRIED PRAWNS

2 tbsp coconut oil

2 garlic cloves, thinly sliced

1 lemongrass stalk, halved

1 small onion, thinly sliced

1 red chilli, seeded and sliced

2.5cm/1in piece fresh root ginger, peeled and shredded

450g/1lb large raw peeled prawns (jumbo shrimp)

340g/12oz pak choi (bok choy), shredded

2 tbsp Thai fish sauce

juice of 1 lime

1 Heat the oil in a wok or deep frying pan. Add the garlic, lemongrass, onion, chilli and ginger and stir-fry briskly over a high heat for 2 minutes.

2 Add the prawns and pak choi and stir-fry for 2–3 minutes until the pak choi is slightly tender but still crisp and the prawns are pink and succulent.

3 Add the fish sauce and lime juice and cook for 1 minute. Discard the lemongrass and serve immediately with boiled rice or noodles.

preparation 30 minutes **cooking time** 7 minutes

Serves 4

HUEVOS RANCHEROS

1 tbsp olive oil

1 red onion, finely sliced

1 yellow and 1 red (bell) pepper, seeded and thinly sliced

1 red chilli, diced

75g/3oz chorizo, cubed (optional)

2 x 400g/14oz cans chopped tomatoes

4 large eggs

salt and ground black pepper

3 tbsp chopped fresh parsley

1 Heat the oil in a large frying pan over a high heat. Add the onion, yellow and red peppers, chilli and chorizo (if using) and cook for 5 minutes, stirring, until softened.
2 Reduce the heat, add the tomatoes, season with salt and pepper and simmer for 5 minutes.
3 Use a wooden spoon to make 4 hollows in the tomato mixture and break an egg into each one.
4 Cover the pan and simmer gently for 5 minutes or until the egg whites are just set but the yolks are still runny.
5 Sprinkle with parsley and serve.

preparation 10 minutes cooking time 15 minutes

Serves 4

EGG FU YUNG

3 tbsp groundnut oil

8 spring onions (scallions), finely sliced, plus extra to garnish

125g/4oz shiitake or oyster mushrooms, sliced

1 red (bell) pepper, seeded and finely chopped

125g/4oz/1 cup frozen peas

75g/3oz smoked bacon, diced

6 medium (US large) eggs, beaten

a good pinch of chilli powder

dash of light soy sauce

salt and ground black pepper

1 Heat the oil in a wok or deep frying pan over a high heat. Add the spring onions, mushrooms, red pepper, peas and bacon and stir-fry for 2–3 minutes.
2 Season the beaten eggs with salt and chilli powder. Pour the eggs into the pan and cook, stirring all the time, until the egg mixture sets. Add a grinding of pepper.
3 Sprinkle the soy sauce over and stir well. Serve immediately, garnished with spring onions.

preparation 10 minutes cooking time 5 minutes

Serves 4

SUMMER VEGETABLE STEW

3 tbsp olive oil

3 aubergines (eggplants), cubed

1 onion, chopped

1 red and 1 yellow (bell) pepper, seeded and roughly chopped

340g/12oz new potatoes, sliced

1 x 400g/14oz can tomatoes

1 x 400g/14oz can flageolet beans, rinsed and drained

4 tbsp chopped fresh parsley

salt and ground black pepper

1 tbsp balsamic vinegar

1 Heat the oil in a large pan and cook the aubergines over a medium heat for 10 minutes or until golden brown and softened.
2 Add the onion, red and yellow peppers and new potatoes and cook for 5 minutes.
3 Add the tomatoes and beans, reduce the heat and simmer for 10 minutes or until the aubergine is completely tender.
4 Stir in the parsley. Season to taste with salt and pepper and remove from the heat.
5 Serve warm or at room temperature sprinkled with a little balsamic vinegar.

preparation 25 minutes cooking time 30 minutes

Serves 4

LENTIL BAKE

2 tbsp olive oil

2 onions, chopped

4 carrots, chopped

3 leeks, thinly sliced

450g/1lb button mushrooms

2 garlic cloves, crushed

225g/8oz/1⅓ cups red lentils

750ml/1¼ pints/3 cups hot vegetable stock

4 tomatoes, roughly chopped

4 tbsp chopped fresh parsley

salt and ground black pepper

1 Preheat the oven to 180°C/350°F/Gas 4.
2 Heat the oil in a flameproof casserole over a low heat. Add the onions, carrots and leeks and cook, stirring occasionally, for 5 minutes. Add the mushrooms and garlic and cook gently for 2–3 minutes.
3 Rinse and drain the lentils, then stir into the casserole with the hot stock and tomatoes. Season with salt and pepper and bring back to the boil.
4 Cover the casserole and cook in the oven for 45 minutes until the vegetables and lentils are cooked and tender. Stir in the parsley and serve.

preparation 20 minutes cooking time 1 hour

Serves 6

THAI VEGGIE CURRY

2 tbsp Thai green curry paste

1 tsp diced fresh root ginger

6 spring onions (scallions), diced

1 x 400ml/14fl oz can coconut milk

3 carrots, cut into matchsticks

1 broccoli head, cut into florets

a few fresh coriander (cilantro) sprigs, chopped

juice of 1 lime

1 Heat a large pan, add the curry paste, ginger and spring onions and stir-fry over a medium heat for 2–3 minutes.
2 Add the coconut milk, cover the pan and bring to the boil. Reduce the heat and add the carrots. Simmer for 5 minutes.
3 Add the broccoli florets and simmer for 5 minutes or until just tender but retaining a little bite.
4 Stir in the coriander and lime juice, then serve immediately with boiled rice.

preparation 10 minutes cooking time 15 minutes

Serves 4

VEGGIE BOURGUIGNONNE

2 tbsp olive oil

450g/1lb button onions

25g/1oz/2 tbsp butter

450g/1lb button mushrooms

3 large field mushrooms, sliced

2 garlic cloves, crushed

1 tbsp plain (all-purpose) flour

175ml/6fl oz/¾ cup red wine

250ml/9fl oz/1 cup hot vegetable stock

1 tbsp tomato paste

50g/2oz/½ cup walnut halves

1 bouquet garni

salt and ground black pepper

1 Preheat the oven to 170°C/325°F/Gas 3.
2 Heat 1 tbsp oil in a large frying pan, add the button onions and cook for 5 minutes, stirring, until golden brown. Remove and transfer to a casserole.
3 Add the remaining oil and the butter to the pan, then add the mushrooms and cook for 3 minutes, until starting to brown. Add the garlic and cook for 2 minutes.
4 Stir in the flour and then add the wine, hot stock, tomato paste and walnuts. Stir well and add the bouquet garni. Bring to the boil and then transfer to the casserole.
5 Cover the casserole and cook in the oven for 1 hour. Season to taste with salt and pepper.
6 Serve in shallow bowls with mashed potato.

preparation 25 minutes cooking time 1 hour 10 minutes

Serves 4

BEAN HOTPOT

2 tbsp olive oil

700g/1½lb mushrooms, sliced

1 large onion, finely chopped

2 garlic cloves, crushed

2 tbsp plain (all-purpose) flour

150ml/¼ pint/scant ⅔ cup white wine

1 x 400g/14oz can chopped tomatoes

2 tbsp tomato paste

2 x 400g/14oz cans mixed beans, drained and rinsed

3 tbsp tomato salsa

4 tbsp chopped fresh mint

1　Heat the oil in a large pan over a low heat, then add the mushrooms, onion and garlic and cook for 6–8 minutes until the onion is tender and golden.

2　Add the flour and cook, stirring, for 2 minutes.

3　Add the wine, tomatoes, tomato paste and beans. Bring to the boil, then reduce the heat and simmer gently for 30 minutes or until most of the liquid has reduced.

4　Just before serving, stir in the tomato salsa. Divide among six serving bowls and strew with the mint.

preparation 15 minutes **cooking time** 45 minutes

Serves 6

LENTIL AND HALLOUMI BAKE

2 red (bell) peppers, seeded and roughly chopped

200g/7oz mushrooms, sliced

2 large sweet potatoes, cubed

1 courgette (zucchini), cubed

8 cherry tomatoes

2 tbsp olive oil

150g/5oz/1 cup red lentils

1 litre/1¾ pints/4 cups hot vegetable stock

4 thick slices halloumi

4 tbsp chopped fresh parsley

1　Preheat the oven to 200°C/400°F/Gas 6.

2　Put all the vegetables in a large roasting pan, drizzle the oil over and season well with salt and pepper. Turn the vegetables to coat in the oil.

3　Roast in the oven for 25 minutes or until the vegetables are nearly tender. Sprinkle in the lentils and pour in the hot stock. Roast for 15 minutes until the lentils and vegetables are cooked through.

4　Preheat the grill (broiler) to high. Arrange the halloumi on top of the vegetables and grill (broil) for 2–3 minutes until golden brown.

5　Sprinkle the parsley over and serve in warmed bowls.

preparation 20 minutes **cooking time** 45 minutes

Serves 4

FAMILY FAVOURITES

You can serve up lots of tasty family-friendly meals if you experiment with the recipes in the following pages. You'll find something for everyone, from traditional roasts, hearty soups, hotpots and casseroles to time-honoured favourites, including roast chicken and spaghetti Bolognese. And there are quick and easy versions of many classic dishes, including cottage pie, meat loaf, pasties and chilli con carne. They will appeal to children and adults alike – no need to cook one dish for you and another for the kids.

Many of the recipes utilize store-cupboard staples and basic ingredients to create thrifty meals when you are cooking on a budget. In addition, there's a wide range of vegetable accompaniments and salads to add variety, nutrients and flavour as well as colour and texture.

There's no need to order a takeaway when you can make a healthier version yourself at home for a fraction of the cost. There are delicious recipes for fish and chips, hamburgers, chicken chow mein and chicken tikka masala.

Some recipes are perfect for everyday suppers while others work well for special occasions and family gatherings. There's nothing fussy or complicated – this is honest home-cooked food at its comforting best.

< Roast Rib of Beef (page 218)

FRIED CHICKEN

4 chicken pieces
3 tbsp flour
a good pinch of cayenne pepper
50g/2oz/4 tbsp clarified butter
salt and ground black pepper
green salad to serve

1 Wipe the chicken joints and pat dry with kitchen paper. Season with salt and pepper. Toss the chicken in the flour and cayenne until completely coated.
2 Heat the butter in a large frying pan over a high heat. Add the chicken and cook, turning occasionally, until golden brown on both sides.
3 Reduce the heat and cook for 30–40 minutes until tender. Drain on kitchen paper and serve.

preparation 5 minutes   cooking time 45 minutes

Serves 4

PESTO ROAST CHICKEN

20g/¾oz fresh basil, chopped
3 tbsp freshly grated Parmesan
50g/2oz/⅓ cup pinenuts (pignoli)
4 tbsp olive oil
1 x 1.4kg/3lb chicken
salt and ground black pepper
roast potatoes and green vegetables to serve

1 Preheat the oven to 200°C/400°F/Gas 6. To make the pesto, put the basil, Parmesan, pinenuts and oil in a food processor and mix to a rough paste. (Alternatively, grind the ingredients using a mortar and pestle.) Season to taste.
2 Put the chicken in a roasting pan. Ease your fingers under the skin of the neck end to separate the breast skin from the flesh, then push about three-quarters of the pesto under the skin, using your hands to spread it evenly. Smear the remainder over the chicken legs.
3 Season with pepper and roast for 1 hour 25 minutes or until the chicken is cooked and the juices run clear when the thickest part of the thigh is pierced with a skewer.
4 Cover the chicken loosely with foil and leave to rest for 15 minutes. Carve and serve with roast potatoes and green vegetables or salad.

preparation 20 minutes   cooking time 1 hour 25 minutes plus resting

Serves 4

COCK-A-LEEKIE SOUP

1 x 1.4kg/3lb chicken
2 onions, roughly chopped
2 carrots, roughly chopped
2 celery sticks, chopped
1 bay leaf
25g/1oz/2 tbsp butter
4 large leeks, sliced
125g/4oz/¾ cup ready-to-eat stoned prunes, sliced
salt and ground black pepper
chopped fresh parsley to serve

1 Put the chicken in a large pan with the chopped vegetables, bay leaf and chicken giblets (if available). Add 1.7 litres/ 3 pints/7½ cups water and bring to the boil, then reduce the heat, cover the pan and simmer gently for 1 hour.
2 Meanwhile, melt the butter in a pan over a low heat, add the leeks and cook gently for 10 minutes or until softened.
3 Remove the chicken from the pan. Strain the stock and set aside. Strip the chicken from the bones and shred roughly. Add to the stock with the prunes and softened leeks.
4 Pour everything back into the pan and bring to the boil. Reduce the heat and season to taste. Cover the pan and simmer for 15–20 minutes.
5 Serve the soup sprinkled with chopped parsley.

preparation 15 minutes   cooking time 1 hour 20 minutes

Serves 8

TARRAGON CHICKEN BURGER

2 tbsp sunflower oil plus extra to brush
1 onion, finely chopped
2 garlic cloves, crushed
675g/1½lb/3 cups minced (ground) chicken
2 tbsp chopped fresh tarragon
salt and ground black pepper
4 streaky bacon rashers (slices)
4 crusty wholemeal rolls
4 tbsp mayonnaise
salad leaves to serve

1 Heat the oil in a pan and cook the onion and garlic over a low heat for 6–8 minutes until soft. Set aside to cool, then place in a bowl with the chicken, tarragon, salt and pepper. Mix well to combine.
2 Divide the mixture into 4 equal portions and shape them into patties. Brush lightly with oil.
3 Cook the patties under a hot grill (broiler) for 4–6 minutes each side, until cooked through. Remove from the grill and keep warm.
4 Grill (broil) the bacon for 2–3 minutes, until cooked.
5 Split the rolls and arrange the salad leaves on the bottom half of each one. Top with a chicken burger, a spoonful of mayonnaise and a bacon rasher. Place the other half of the roll on top and serve.

preparation 15 minutes   cooking time 16–18 minutes

Serves 4

ROAST CHICKEN TRAYBAKE

2 garlic cloves

small bunch of fresh basil

small bunch of fresh mint

4 tbsp olive oil

4 chicken joints

1 aubergine (eggplant), chopped

3 sweet potatoes, peeled and cut into wedges

200g/7oz cherry tomatoes

2 yellow (bell) peppers, seeded and chopped

2 courgettes (zucchini), sliced

salt and ground black pepper

1 Blitz the garlic, basil and mint in a food processor or blender. Add 2 tbsp oil gradually through the feed tube until you have a thick aromatic paste.
2 Rub the paste over the chicken joints and place in a bowl. Cover and chill in the refrigerator for at least 30 minutes.
3 Preheat the oven to 200°C/400°F/Gas 6.
4 Put the aubergine, sweet potatoes, tomatoes, peppers and courgettes in a large roasting pan with the remaining oil and season with salt and pepper. Add the marinated chicken.
5 Roast in the oven for 35–40 minutes until the vegetables are tender and the chicken is cooked through.
6 Serve with a crisp salad.

preparation 15 minutes plus at least 30 minutes marinating   cooking time 40 minutes

Serves 4

CHICKEN BROTH

4 skinless chicken breasts

3 tbsp pesto

1.2 litres/2 pints/5 cups chicken stock

150g/5oz mushrooms, sliced

1 red chilli, seeded and halved

75g/3oz small soup pasta

2 tbsp soy sauce

a small handful of chopped flat-leaf parsley

1 Preheat the oven to 200°C/400°F/Gas 6.
2 Make a few slashes in the chicken breasts and rub the pesto over the chicken, pushing it into the cuts. Place the chicken in a roasting pan and roast in the oven for 20 minutes.
3 Meanwhile, put the stock in a pan and bring to the boil. Reduce the heat and add the mushrooms, chilli and pasta. Cover the pan and simmer gently for 5 minutes until the pasta is cooked. Stir in the soy sauce.
4 Slice the chicken and add to the broth with the parsley.
5 Ladle into warmed bowls and serve immediately.

preparation 20 minutes   cooking time 20 minutes

Serves 4

CHICKEN AND MUSHROOM PIES

2 tbsp olive oil

2 leeks, finely sliced

2 garlic cloves, crushed

340g/12oz boneless, skinless chicken thighs, cubed

300g/11oz mushrooms, sliced

1 tbsp plain (all-purpose) flour plus extra to dust

150ml/¼ pint/scant ⅔ cup double (heavy) cream

4 tbsp chopped fresh parsley

500g/1lb 2oz puff pastry

1 medium (US large) egg, beaten

salt and ground black pepper

1 Heat the oil in a pan, add the leeks and fry over a medium heat for 5 minutes. Add the garlic and cook for 1 minute. Add the chicken and cook for 10 minutes, stirring. Add the mushrooms and cook for 5 minutes. Stir in the flour.
2 Add the cream and bring to the boil. Cook for 5 minutes to make a thick sauce. Add the parsley and season with salt and pepper. Remove from the heat and leave to cool.
3 Roll out the pastry on a floured surface to a large square. Cut into four squares and brush the edges with water. Spoon the chicken mixture into the centre of each square. Bring each corner of the square up to the middle to make a parcel, leaving a small hole in the top. Brush with beaten egg and put on a baking sheet.
4 Preheat the oven to 200°C/400°F/Gas 6. Cook the pies in the oven for 30–40 minutes until golden brown.

preparation 20 minutes   cooking time 1 hour

Serves 4

CHICKEN AND HAM PIE

4 cooked chicken breasts, cut into cubes

225g/8oz cooked ham, cubed

150ml/¼ pint/scant ⅔ cup double (heavy) cream

4 tbsp chopped fresh parsley

1 tsp cornflour (cornstarch)

1 tsp Dijon mustard

300g/11oz puff pastry sheet

1 medium (US large) egg, beaten

salt and ground black pepper

1 Preheat the oven to 200°C/400°F/Gas 6.
2 Put the chicken in a large bowl with the ham, cream, parsley, cornflour and mustard. Season with salt and pepper, stir well and spoon into a shallow baking dish.
3 Unroll the puff pastry sheet and drape it over the top of the dish. Trim the edges to fit, then press them down lightly around the rim. Brush the pastry with beaten egg.
4 Cook in the oven for 30–35 minutes until the pastry is golden brown and well risen. Serve hot with vegetables.

preparation 15 minutes   cooking time 30–35 minutes

Serves 6

CHICKEN AND LEEK PIE

6 large potatoes, peeled and cut into chunks

200g/7oz/¾ cup crème fraîche

3 x 125g/4oz chicken breasts

3 large leeks, thickly sliced

2 garlic cloves, crushed

1 small bunch of fresh parsley, finely chopped

a pinch of freshly grated nutmeg

4 tbsp grated Cheddar cheese

salt and ground black pepper

1　Preheat the oven to 200°C/400°F/Gas 6.
2　Cook the potatoes in a pan of lightly salted boiling water until tender. Drain and put them back in the pan. Add 1 tbsp crème fraîche and some salt and pepper, then mash well.
3　Meanwhile, cook the chicken in a frying pan over a low heat for 15 minutes, turning occasionally, until cooked through. Remove the chicken from the pan and place on a board.
4　Add the leeks and garlic to the pan and cook over a low heat for 5 minutes or until softened.
5　Cut the cooled chicken into large chunks. Return to the pan, stir in the remaining crème fraîche and cook for 2–3 minutes until bubbling. Stir in the parsley and nutmeg, season to taste and transfer to an ovenproof dish.
6　Spread the mashed potato over the top, roughing it up with a fork Sprinkle over the grated Cheddar and cook in the oven for 20 minutes or until golden brown. Serve immediately.

preparation 15 minutes　cooking time 40 minutes

Serves 4

CHICKEN RAREBIT

4 large cooked chicken breasts

15g/½oz/1 tbsp butter

1 tbsp plain (all-purpose) flour

125ml/4fl oz/1 cup milk

175g/6oz/1½ cups grated Cheddar or Gruyère

25g/1oz/½ cup fresh white breadcrumbs

1 tsp wholegrain mustard

1 medium (US large) egg yolk

4 x cherry tomatoes on the vine

1　Melt the butter in a pan over a low heat, then stir in the flour and cook for 1 minute. Gradually add the milk, stirring until the mixture thickens to a smooth sauce.
2　Add the cheese, breadcrumbs and mustard to the sauce and cook for 1 minute. Cool a little, then beat in the egg yolk. Preheat the grill (broiler) to medium-high.
3　Preheat the grill (broiler). Spread the paste evenly over each chicken breast and place them in a flameproof dish, then grill (broil) for 2–3 minutes until golden brown.
4　Meanwhile, grill the cherry tomatoes until starting to soften and char. Serve with the hot chicken rarebits.

preparation 5 minutes　cooking time 25 minutes

Serves 4

CHICKEN WITH MANGO COUSCOUS

125g/4oz/⅔ cup couscous
125g/4oz tomato salsa
juice of 2 lemons
2 tbsp chopped fresh coriander (cilantro), plus extra to garnish
1 ripe mango, peeled, stoned and diced
200g/7oz cooked chicken fillets
8 tbsp virtually fat-free fromage frais
4 tsp sweet chilli sauce
salt and ground black pepper

1 Put the couscous in a bowl and pour over 300ml/½ pint/1¼ cups boiling water. Season well with salt and pepper, and leave to stand for 15 minutes.
2 Fluff up the couscous grains with a fork, then stir in the tomato salsa, lemon juice, coriander and mango.
3 Divide the couscous among four serving plates and arrange the chicken on top.
4 Sprinkle with chopped coriander and serve with some fromage frais topped with chilli sauce.

preparation 15 minutes plus soaking

Serves 4

CHICKEN AND PEPPERS

1 red and 1 yellow (bell) pepper, seeded and chopped
1 tbsp chopped fresh oregano
2 tbsp chopped fresh rosemary
2 tbsp olive oil
4 boneless, skinless chicken breasts
salt and ground black pepper

1 Preheat the oven to 200°C/400°F/Gas 6.
2 Put the red and yellow peppers in a bowl with the oregano, rosemary and oil. Season with salt and pepper and mix well.
3 Put the chicken in an ovenproof dish and spoon the peppers over the top. Cook in the oven for 20 minutes until the chicken is cooked through and the peppers are tender.
4 Serve with boiled rice or noodles.

preparation 5 minutes   cooking time 20 minutes

Serves 4

LEMON ROAST CHICKEN

1 x 1.4kg/3lb chicken
2 lemons
1 onion, cut into wedges
fresh sage and rosemary sprigs
2 bay leaves
50g/2oz/4 tbsp butter, cubed
450g/1lb potatoes, cut into large chunks
salt and ground black pepper
salad to serve

1 Preheat the oven to 190°C/375°F/Gas 5.
2 Put the chicken in a roasting pan. Cut 1 lemon into slices and squeeze the juice of the other. Put the onion, some of the herb sprigs and bay leaves inside the chicken. Season with salt and pepper and dot with butter and lemon slices. Arrange the potatoes around the chicken and pour the lemon juice over the top. Scatter with the remaining herbs.
3 Roast in the oven for 1¼ hours, basting halfway through, until the chicken is cooked and the juices run clear when the thickest part of the thigh is pierced with a skewer. Check the potatoes regularly and remove and keep warm when they are golden brown and tender.
4 Rest the chicken for 5 minutes. Carve the chicken and serve with the roast potatoes and a crisp salad.

preparation 30 minutes   cooking time 1 hour 20 minutes plus resting

Serves 5

GRIDDLED CHICKEN WITH RED PESTO

4 x 125g/4oz skinless chicken breasts
8 thin slices pancetta
2 tbsp olive oil plus extra to oil
1 red onion, thinly sliced
2 tbsp red pesto
salt and ground black pepper
torn fresh basil leaves to garnish
boiled rice or pasta to serve

1 Heat an oiled griddle. Season the chicken with salt and pepper and wrap the pancetta around them.
2 Cook on the griddle, skin-side down, over a medium heat for about 20 minutes, turning after 10 minutes, until golden brown and cooked through.
3 Meanwhile, heat the remaining oil in a frying pan and cook the red onion until it is tender and starting to caramelize.
4 Stir in the red pesto and serve sprinkled with basil with some boiled rice or pasta.

preparation 5 minutes   cooking time 20 minutes

Serves 4

CHICKEN AND PAPAYA SALSA

1 tbsp olive oil

4 x 125g/4oz chicken breasts

salt and ground black pepper

rocket (arugula) to serve

balsamic glaze to drizzle

For the papaya salsa

1 papaya, peeled, seeded and diced

3 juicy tomatoes, chopped

1 red chilli, seeded and diced

1 tbsp balsamic vinegar

juice of 1 lime

4 tbsp chopped fresh mint

1 Heat the oil in a frying pan. Season the chicken with salt and pepper and cook in the pan, skin-side down, over a medium heat for 10 minutes. Turn over and cook the other side for 10 minutes until well browned and cooked through.
2 Mix all the salsa ingredients together in a small bowl and season to taste with salt and pepper.
3 Serve the chicken with the salsa on a bed of rocket, drizzled with balsamic glaze..

preparation 10 minutes cooking time 20 minutes

Serves 4

CHICKEN CHOW MEIN

340g/12oz egg noodles

1 tbsp toasted sesame oil

2 boneless, skinless chicken breasts, cut into thin strips

1 bunch of spring onions (scallions), sliced diagonally

150g/5oz sugarsnap peas, sliced

125g/4oz beansprouts

1 red (bell) pepper, seeded and thinly sliced

125g/4oz sachet chow mein stir-fry sauce

1 Cook the noodles in boiling water for 4 minutes or according to the pack instructions. Drain, rinse thoroughly in cold water, then drain again and set aside.
2 Meanwhile, heat a wok or large frying pan until hot, then add the oil. Add the chicken and stir-fry over a high heat for 3–4 minutes until browned all over. Add the spring onions and sugarsnap peas and stir-fry for 2 minutes. Stir in the beansprouts and red pepper and stir-fry for 2 minutes.
3 Add the drained noodles, then pour in the chow mein sauce and toss together to coat. Stir-fry for 2 minutes and serve.

preparation 10 minutes cooking time 10 minutes

Serves 4

TANDOORI CHICKEN WITH CARROT RAITA

4 tbsp tandoori paste

340g/12oz/1½ cups natural yogurt

juice of ½ lemon

4 boneless, skinless chicken breasts, cut into slices

1 tbsp oil plus extra to grease

boiled riced to serve

For the carrot raita

1 tsp ghee or oil

1 tsp ground cumin

1 tbsp black mustard seeds

2 large carrots, grated

250g/9oz/1 cup natural yogurt

1 In a bowl, mix the tandoori paste with the yogurt and lemon juice. Add the chicken and stir well to coat. Cover the bowl and leave to marinate in a cool place for at least 4 hours.

2 Preheat the oven to 220°C/425°F/Gas 7.

3 Lightly oil a roasting pan and put the chicken pieces in it in their marinade. Drizzle the remaining oil over the chicken and roast in the oven for 20 minutes or until cooked through.

4 Meanwhile, make the raita. Heat the ghee or oil in a small pan and cook the cumin and mustrd seeds for 2 minutes. Put the carrots in a bowl and pour over some boiling water. Leave to soften for 5 minutes, then drain and refresh in cold water. Drain and squeeze out any excess liquid. Mix with the spices and yogurt in a bowl.

5 Serve the tandoori chicken with the carrot raita and some plain boiled rice.

preparation 45 minutes plus marinating   cooking time 20 minutes

Serves 4

CHICKEN TIKKA MASALA

2 tbsp vegetable oil or ghee

1 onion, thinly sliced

2 garlic cloves, crushed

6 boneless, skinless chicken thighs, cut into strips

2 tbsp tikka masala paste

1 x 400g/14oz can tomatoes

450ml/¾ pint/1¾ cups hot vegetable stock

225g/8oz/1 cup natural yogurt

2 tbsp mango chutney

boiled rice to serve

1 Heat the oil or ghee in a large pan. Add the onion and cook over a medium heat for 8 minutes until tender and golden. Add the garlic and chicken strips and cook, stirring occasionally, for 5 minutes or until golden brown.

2 Stir in the tikka masala paste, then add the tomatoes and hot stock. Bring to the boil, then reduce the heat, cover the pan and simmer over a low heat for 15 minutes or until the chicken is cooked through.

3 Stir in the yogurt and mango chutney and heat through very gently without boiling.

4 Serve hot on a bed of boiled rice.

preparation 15 minutes   cooking time 30 minutes

Serves 4

GRIDDLED CHILLI CHICKEN

450g/1lb boneless, skinless
chicken breasts, cut into strips
grated zest and juice of 2 lemons
2 tbsp olive oil
2 tbsp sweet chilli sauce
salt and ground black pepper
boiled rice and salad to serve

1 Put the chicken in a large bowl and season with salt and pepper. Add the lemon zest and juice, oil and chilli sauce and stir well to coat the pieces of chicken.
2 Heat a griddle over a medium heat. Add the chicken to the hot griddle and cook for 3–4 minutes until golden and sticky, then turn it over and cook the other side.
3 Divide the chicken among four serving plates and serve with rice and salad.

preparation 2 minutes **cooking time** 6–8 minutes

Serves 4

CHICKEN WITH OYSTER SAUCE AND MUSHROOMS

6 tbsp vegetable oil
450g/1lb skinless, boneless
chicken breasts, cut into chunks
3 tbsp oyster sauce
1 tbsp light soy sauce
100ml/3½fl oz/⅓ cup hot chicken
stock
1 garlic clove, thinly sliced
225g/8oz oyster or shiitake
mushrooms, sliced
125g/4oz sugarsnap peas
1 tsp cornflour (cornstarch)
salt and ground black pepper
boiled rice to serve

1 Heat 3 tbsp vegetable oil in a wok or deep frying pan. Add the chicken and stir-fry over a high heat, stirring continuously, for 2–3 minutes until lightly browned all over. Remove from the wok, drain on kitchen paper and set aside.
2 In a bowl, blend the oyster sauce with the soy sauce and hot chicken stock. Add the chicken and mix thoroughly.
3 Heat the remaining oil in the pan over a high heat and stir-fry the garlic for 30 seconds; add the mushrooms and cook for 1 minute. Add the chicken mixture, cover the wok and simmer for 5 minutes.
4 Stir in the sugarsnaps and cook for 2–3 minutes. Blend the cornflour with 1 tbsp water. Remove the wok from the heat and stir in the cornflour mixture. Return to the heat and stir until the sauce thickens.
5 Season with salt and pepper and serve with boiled rice.

preparation 10 minutes **cooking time** 18 minutes

Serves 4

EASY TURKEY CURRY

2 tbsp oil

1 large onion, chopped

2 garlic cloves, crushed

1 tsp ground turmeric

a good pinch of chilli powder

1 tsp each ground cumin and ground coriander

1 x 400g/14oz can tomatoes

600g/1lb 5oz cooked turkey

1 tsp garam masala

150g/5oz/scant ⅔ cup natural yogurt

fresh coriander (cilantro) to garnish

boiled rice and mango chutney to serve

1 Heat the oil in a heavy-based pan, add the onion and garlic and cook gently over a low heat until softened and golden. Add the turmeric, chilli powder, ground cumin and coriander and cook, stirring, for 1 minute.
2 Add the tomatoes and bring to the boil. Reduce the heat, cover the pan and simmer for 20 minutes.
3 Remove any skin from the turkey, then cut into chunks. Add to the pan with the garam masala and 4 tbsp yogurt. Cover and cook for 10 minutes, then stir in the remaining yogurt.
4 Garnish with chopped coriander and serve with boiled rice and mango chutney.

preparation 15 minutes **cooking time** 35 minutes

Serves 4

CHICKEN QUESADILLAS

1 x 200g/7oz can refried beans

8 flour tortillas

250g/9oz cooked chicken, shredded

4 tbsp hot tomato salsa

2 tbsp chopped fresh coriander (cilantro)

225g/8oz/2 cups grated Cheddar cheese

soured cream and guacamole to serve

1 Preheat the oven to 180°C/350°F/Gas 4.
2 Heat the refried beans in a small pan over a low heat for 2–3 minutes. Spread over four tortillas. Mix the chicken, salsa and coriander together and arrange on top of the refried beans. Sprinkle the cheese over and cover with the remaining tortillas.
3 Place the quesadillas on two baking sheets and cook in the oven for 3–4 minutes each side. Alternatively, microwave for long enough to warm them through and melt the cheese.
4 Serve the hot quesadillas cut into wedges with some soured cream and guacamole.

preparation 10 minutes **cooking time** 12 minutes

Serves 4

CHEESEBURGERS

1kg/2¼lb extra-lean minced (ground) beef
1 tbsp tomato ketchup
6 burger buns, halved
sunflower oil to brush
6 thin-cut slices havarti or raclette cheese
6 tbsp mayonnaise
6 lettuce leaves
3 large tomatoes, thickly sliced
6 cocktail gherkins, sliced
1 onion, thinly sliced
salt and ground black pepper

1 Put the minced beef and tomato ketchup in a large bowl and add some salt and plenty of pepper. Mix everything together.
2 Shape into six patties. Cover with clingfilm (plastic wrap) and chill in the refrigerator for at least 1 hour.
3 Heat a large griddle pan until it's really hot. Put the burger buns, cut-side down, on the griddle and toast.
4 Lightly oil the griddle and cook the burgers over a medium heat for 3–4 minutes, then turn the burgers over. Put a slice of cheese on top and cook for 3 minutes.
5 Spread the mayonnaise on the burger buns. Add the lettuce, tomatoes, gherkins and onion rings. Add the cooked burgers and sandwich with the top of each bun.

preparation 20 minutes plus chilling   cooking time 10 minutes

Serves 6

ROAST RIB OF BEEF

2.5kg/5½lb rib of beef
1 tbsp plain (all-purpose) flour
1 tbsp mustard powder
150ml/¼ pint/scant ⅔ cup red wine
600m/1 pint/2½ cups beef stock
600m/1 pint/2½ cups boiling water (or vegetable water)
1 tbsp redcurrant jelly, apple jelly or cranberry sauce
salt and ground black pepper
roast potatoes and vegetables to serve
mustard or horseradish sauce to serve

1 Preheat the oven to 230°C/450°F/Gas 8.
2 Put the beef, fat-side up, in a roasting pan. Mix the flour, mustard, salt and pepper and rub over the beef.
3 Roast in the centre of the oven for 30 minutes. Reduce the temperature to 220°C/425°F/Gas 7 and cook for 1–2 hours (depending on how well cooked you like your beef), basting occasionally with the fat.
4 Put the beef on a carving dish, cover loosely with foil and leave to rest while you make the gravy.
5 Skim off most of the fat from the roasting pan and place on the hob. Add the wine and boil until very syrupy. Pour in the stock and boil until syrupy. Add the water and fruit jelly or sauce and boil until syrupy. Check the seasoning.
6 Carve the beef. Serve with gravy, roast potatoes and vegetables with mustard or horseradish sauce.

preparation 5 minutes   cooking time 2 hours 30 minutes plus resting

Serves 6

COTTAGE PIE

1 tbsp olive oil
1 onion, chopped
2 carrots, diced
450g/1lb/2 cups minced (ground) beef
1 tbsp plain (all-purpose) flour
450ml/¾ pint/1¾ cups hot beef stock
3 tbsp tomato paste
2 tbsp Worcestershire sauce
125g/4oz/1 cup frozen peas
1kg/2¼lb potatoes, chopped
25g/1oz/2 tbsp butter
4–5 tbsp milk
salt and ground black pepper

1 Preheat the oven to 200°C/400°F/Gas 6.
2 Heat the oil in a large pan, add the onion and carrot and cook over a low heat for 15 minutes until softened.
3 Add the beef and cook, stirring, for 4–5 minutes until brown. Stir in the flour and then the hot stock and tomato paste and bring to the boil. Add the Worcestershire sauce, carrots and peas and season with salt and pepper. Reduce the heat, cover the pan and cook for 15 minutes.
4 Meanwhile, cook the potatoes in a large pan of salted water for 20 minutes or until soft. Drain and mash until smooth. Beat in the butter and milk and season to taste.
5 Spoon the meat mixture into a large ovenproof dish and cover with the mashed potato. Use a fork to rough up the top. Cook in the oven for 20–25 minutes until the topping is golden brown. Serve immediately.

preparation 15 minutes   cooking time 1 hour

Serves 4

MEAT LOAF

2 tbsp oil
1 onion, finely chopped
1 garlic clove, crushed
450g/1lb/2 cups minced (ground) beef
50g/2oz/1 cup fresh breadcrumbs
2 tbsp grated Parmesam
1 tbsp chopped fresh parsley
3 tbsp tomato paste
1 tsp mustard
1 medium (US large) egg, beaten
salt and ground black pepper

1 Preheat the oven to 180°C/350°F/Gas 4. Grease and base line a 450g/1lb loaf tin.
2 Heat the oil in a frying pan, add the onion and cook over a low heat for 10 minutes until softened. Add the paprika and cook for 1 minute. Turn the mixture into a large bowl.
3 Add the minced beef, breadcrumbs, Parmesan, parsley, tomato paste, mustard, beaten egg and seasoning. Stir until evenly mixed. Spoon the mixture into the prepared loaf tin, level the surface and cover tightly with foil.
4 Stand the loaf tin in a roasting pan and pour in water around it to a depth of 2.5cm/1in. Cook in the oven for 1½ hours.
5 Turn out, cut into slices and serve hot or cold.

preparation 10 minutes   cooking time 1 hour 40 minutes

Serves 4

CHILLI CON CARNE

2 tbsp olive oil

450g/1lb/2 cups minced (ground) beef

1 large onion, finely chopped

1 tsp hot chilli powder

3 tbsp tomato paste

300ml/½ pint/1¼ cups hot beef stock

1 x 400g/14oz can chopped tomatoes

1 x 400g/14oz can red kidney beans, drained and rinsed

1 bunch of fresh coriander (cilantro), chopped

salt and ground black pepper

1 Heat 1 tbsp oil in a large non-stick pan and cook the minced beef for 10 minutes over a medium heat until well browned, stirring. Remove and set aside.
2 Add the remaining oil to the pan and cook the onion for 10 minutes or until softened. Add the chilli powder and cook for 1 minute, then return the minced beef to the pan. Add the tomato paste, hot stock and tomatoes. Bring to the boil, then reduce the heat and simmer, uncovered, for 35–40 minutes until the sauce is well reduced.
3 Stir in the kidney beans and coriander, season with salt and pepper and simmer for 5 minutes.
4 Serve with boiled rice or tortilla chips and salsa, soured cream and grated Cheddar or Monterey Jack cheese.

preparation 5 minutes   cooking time 1 hour 5 minutes

Serves 4

CHILLI STEAK STIR-FRY

1 red chilli, finely chopped

1 garlic clove, chopped

2 tbsp soy sauce

2 tbsp sweet chilli sauce

340g/12oz lean rump steaks, cut into thin slices

1 tbsp oil

300g/11oz cooked egg noodles

1 onion, thinly sliced

1 green (bell) pepper, seeded and sliced

2 carrots, cut into matchsticks

225g/8oz beansprouts

1 Put the chilli, garlic, soy and chilli sauces in a shallow bowl and mix well. Add the steak and turn to coat.
2 Heat the oil in a wok or deep frying pan over a high heat. Remove the steaks from the marinade, reserving it, and cook for 1–2 minutes each side.
3 Add the noodles, onion, green pepper and carrots to the wok and stir-fry over a high heat for 2–3 minutes. Add the beansprouts and the marinade and stir-fry for 2 minutes.
4 Toss everything together and serve immediately.

preparation 15 minutes   cooking time 10 minutes

Serves 4

SWEET CHILLI BEEF STIR-FRY

2 tbsp soy sauce
1 tsp grated fresh root ginger
1 garlic clove, crushed
1 red chilli, seeded and chopped
400g/14oz steak, cut into strips
1 tbsp chilli oil
1 broccoli head, cut into small pieces
200g/7oz sugarsnap peas
1 yellow (bell) pepper, seeded and cut into strips

1 Put the soy sauce, ginger, garlic and chilli in a shallow dish and stir well. Add the steak and stir to coat.
2 Heat the oil in a wok or deep frying pan over a high heat until it is very hot. Remove the strips of beef from the marinade and stir-fry for 2–3 minutes until tender.
3 Add the broccoli, sugarsnap peas, yellow pepper and the reserved marinade to the wok. Stir-fry for 5 minutes until the vegetables start to soften.
4 Serve immediately with boiled rice.

preparation 10 minutes cooking time 10–11 minutes

Serves 4

SPICY BOLOGNESE

1 tbsp olive oil
1 large onion, finely chopped
1 red chilli, seeded and diced
450g/1lb/2 cups minced (ground) beef
125g/4oz smoked bacon, diced
1 green (bell) pepper, seeded and finely chopped
1 x 400g/14oz can tomatoes
125ml/4fl oz/½ cup red wine
a pinch of sugar
300g/11oz spaghetti
5 tbsp grated Cheddar cheese
2 tbsp chopped fresh parsley
salt and ground black pepper

1 Heat the oil in a large pan over a medium heat. Add the onion and chilli and fry for 10 minutes until softened. Add the minced beef and bacon and cook, stirring occasionally, for 5 minutes until well browned.
2 Stir in the green pepper, tomatoes, wine and sugar. Season with salt and pepper and bring to the boil, then reduce the heat and simmer gently for 30 minutes.
3 Meanwhile, cook the pasta in a large pan of lightly salted boiling water according to the pack instructions. Drain well.
4 Just before serving, stir the grated Cheddar and parsley into the sauce. Toss with the cooked spaghetti.

preparation 15 minutes cooking time 55 minutes

Serves 4

SPAGHETTI BOLOGNESE

2 tbsp olive oil

1 onion, finely chopped

2 carrots, diced

3 celery sticks, diced

2 garlic cloves, crushed

450g/1lb/2 cups minced (ground) beef

2 tbsp tomato paste

300ml/½ pint/1¼ cups red wine

1 x 400g/14oz can chopped tomatoes

a few fresh thyme sprigs

salt and ground black pepper

450g/1lb spaghetti

4 tbsp freshly grated Parmesan

1 To make the Bolognese sauce, heat the oil in a large pan, add the onion, carrots and celery and fry over a medium heat for 10 minutes or until tender. Add the garlic and cook for 1 minute.
2 Add the minced beef and cook, stirring occasionally, until browned. Stir in the tomato paste and wine and bring to the boil. Add the tomatoes and thyme, and season with salt and pepper. Bring back to the boil, then reduce the heat and simmer gently for 20 minutes.
3 Cook the spaghetti in a large pan of lightly salted boiling water according to the pack instructions. Drain well, then return to the pan.
4 Add the Bolognese sauce and toss together. Divide among four shallow bowls and sprinkle with Parmesan.

Serves 4

preparation 15 minutes   cooking time 40 minutes

CLASSIC LASAGNE

1 quantity Bolognese sauce (see above)

butter to grease and dot

12 fresh lasagne sheets

1 quantity of béchamel sauce (see page 572)

4 tbsp freshly grated Parmesan

1 Preheat the oven to 180°C/350°F/Gas 4.
2 Spoon one-third of the Bolognese sauce over the bottom of a greased 2.3 litre/4 pint ovenproof dish. Cover with a layer of 4 lasagne sheets, then a layer of béchamel sauce. Repeat these layers twice more, finishing with a layer of béchamel to cover the lasagne.
3 Sprinkle the Parmesan over the top and dot with butter. Stand the dish on a baking sheet and cook in the oven for 45 minutes or until golden brown and bubbling.

Serves 6

preparation 40 minutes   cooking time 45 minutes (without the Bolognese sauce)

ROAST LEG OF LAMB

2.5kg/5½lb leg of lamb
4 fresh rosemary sprigs
4 garlic cloves, cut into slivers
1 large onion, thickly sliced
2 lemons, cut into quartered
salt and ground black pepper
vegetables to serve

1 Take the lamb out of the refrigerator 1 hour before roasting. Pat dry with kitchen paper.
2 Preheat the oven to 220°C/425°F/Gas 7. Cut the rosemary into smaller sprigs. Make small, deep slits all over the meat and insert the garlic slivers and rosemary sprigs into them. Season with salt and pepper.
3 Put the onion in the bottom of a roasting pan. Place the lamb, fat-side up, on top of the onion. Tuck the lemon quarters into the gaps around the meat.
4 Reduce the oven temperature to 190°C/375°F/Gas 5. Roast the lamb for 15 minutes per 450g/1lb for pink meat, or for longer if you like it well cooked.
5 Remove the lamb and cover loosely with foil. Rest for 20 minutes before carving into thin slices.

preparation 15 minutes   **cooking time** 1 hour 45 minutes plus resting

Serves 8

LANCASHIRE HOTPOT

12 lamb cutlets
2 onions, sliced
2 large carrots, sliced
leaves from 2 fresh thyme sprigs
750ml/1¼ pints/3 cups hot lamb or beef stock
450g/1lb potatoes, sliced
25g/1oz/2 tbsp butter
salt and ground black pepper

1 Preheat the oven to 180°C/350°F/Gas 4.
2 Put a layer of lamb cutlets in a large casserole. Cover with a layer of onions and carrots and a sprinkling of thyme. Season with salt and pepper. Layer the remaining lamb, onions, carrots and thyme in the same way.
3 Pour in enough hot stock to almost cover the meat. Top with an overlapping layer of potatoes. Season, cover the casserole and cook in the oven for 2 hours.
4 Increase the oven temperature to 230°C/450°F/Gas 8. Remove the lid and dot the top of the casserole with butter. Cook for 30 minutes, uncovered, until the potatoes are crisp and golden brown.

preparation 20 minutes   **cooking time** 2 hours 30 minutes

Serves 4

IRISH STEW

700g/1½lb middle neck lamb cutlets, fat trimmed
2 onions, thinly sliced
450g/1lb potatoes, thinly sliced
2 tbsp chopped fresh parsley
1 tbsp dried thyme
300ml/½ pint/1¼ cups meat stock
salt and ground black pepper

1 Preheat the oven to 170°C/325°F/Gas 3.
2 Layer the meat, onions and potatoes in a deep casserole, sprinkling herbs and seasoning between the layers. Finish with a layer of potato, overlapping the slices.
3 Pour the stock over the potatoes. Cover with greaseproof paper and a lid. Cook in the oven for 2 hours.
4 Preheat the grill (broiler). Remove the lid and paper from the casserole and brown the top of the potatoes under the grill.
5 Serve immediately.

preparation 15 minutes   cooking time 2 hours

Serves 4

CORNISH PASTIES

450g/1lb stewing steak or beef skirt, diced
300g/11oz potatoes, diced
300g/11oz swede (rutabaga), peeled and diced
1 onion, finely chopped
1 tbsp chopped fresh parsley
500g/1lb 2oz shortcrust pastry, (see page 582)
flour to dust
1 medium (US large) egg, beaten
salt and ground black pepper

1 Preheat the oven to 220°C/425°F/Gas 7.
2 Put the steak in a bowl with the potato, swede and onion. Add the chopped parsley and seasoning, then mix well.
3 Divide the pastry into six and roll out each piece on a lightly floured surface to a 20cm/8in round. Spoon the filling on to one half of each round.
4 Brush the edges of the pastry with water, then fold the uncovered side over to make pasties. Press the edges firmly together to seal and crimp them. Put on a baking sheet.
5 Brush the pasties with beaten egg to glaze and bake in the oven for 15 minutes. Reduce the oven temperature to 170°C/325°F/Gas 3 and bake for 1 hour.
6 Serve the pasties warm or cold.

preparation 30 minutes   cooking time 1 hour 15 minutes

Serves 6

STUFFED PORK TENDERLOINS

4 tbsp olive oil
1 onion, finely chopped
1 tbsp chopped fresh thyme
6 dried apricots, diced
50g/2oz/1 cup fresh white breadcrumbs
2 pork fillets (tenderloins)
200ml/7fl oz/¾ cup hot chicken stock
50ml/2fl oz/¼ cup red wine
1 tbsp redcurrant jelly
salt and ground black pepper
mashed potato and carrots to serve

1 Heat 2 tbsp oil in a pan over a medium heat, add the onion and cook for 5 minutes until softened. Add the thyme and cook for 1 minute. Stir in the apricots and breadcrumbs. Season with salt and pepper and set aside to cool.
2 Preheat the oven to 190°C/375°F, Gas 5.
3 Cut each pork fillet lengthways down the middle, almost but not quite through. Open out and spoon half the breadcrumb mixture along each fillet. Bring the sides over to enclose the filling and tie with string at intervals to secure.
4 Heat the remaining oil in a roasting pan on the hob, add the pork and brown all over. Cook in the oven for 40–45 minutes.
5 Remove the pork, cover loosely with foil and set aside to rest. Add the hot stock and red wine to the roasting pan and bring to the boil, stirring. Add the redcurrant jelly and season to taste. Simmer for 5 minutes until syrupy.
6 Cut the pork into slices and serve with the sauce, mashed potato and carrots.

preparation 25 minutes plus cooling   **cooking time** 1 hour plus resting

Serves 6

LIVER AND ONIONS

25g/1oz/2 tbsp butter
3 large onions, thinly sliced
1 tsp chopped fresh sage
450g/1lb calf's or lamb's liver, cut into thin strips
salt and ground black pepper

1 Melt the butter in a frying pan, add the onions and fry gently over a low heat until they start to colour. Add the sage and season to taste. Cover the pan and simmer very gently for 10 minutes or until the onions are really tender.
2 Add the liver to the onions, increase the heat slightly and cook for 5 minutes, stirring all the time, until the liver is just cooked. Serve immediately with the onions.

preparation 10 minutes   **cooking time** 20 minutes

Serves 4

PEA AND HAM SOUP

450g/1lb dried yellow or green split peas, soaked overnight

2 tbsp olive oil

1 large onion, finely chopped

1 garlic clove, crushed

1.7 litres/3 pints/7½ cups ham or vegetable stock

1 bouquet garni

leaves stripped from 2 fresh thyme sprigs

340g/12oz cooked ham, diced

salt and ground black pepper

1 Drain the soaked split peas. Heat the oil in a large pan, add the onion and garlic and cook over a low heat for 10 minutes or until the onion is soft.
2 Add the drained split peas to the pan with the stock. Bring to the boil and skim the surface. Add the bouquet garni and thyme, then reduce the heat, cover the pan and simmer for 1 hour or until the peas are very soft.
3 Stir in the ham and season to taste with salt and pepper. Discard the bouquet garni.
4 Ladle the soup into warmed bowls and serve.

preparation 15 minutes plus soaking cooking time 1 hour 15 minutes

Serves 6

SPICED PORK CHOPS WITH APPLE MASH

5 large potatoes, chopped

4 lean pork chops

25g/1oz/2 tbsp butter plus a knob

2 apples, peeled, cored and diced

4 tbsp chopped fresh parsley

1 tsp wholegrain mustard

salt and ground black pepper

1 Boil the potatoes in a pan of lightly salted water for 15 minutes or until tender. Drain and mash.
2 Heat the butter in a pan. Add the chops and fry for 5 minutes on each side. Remove and keep warm.
3 Melt a knob of butter in another pan. Add the apples and cook, stirring, for 2–3 minutes until starting to soften. Beat into the mashed potato with the parsley, mustard and seasoning and serve with the pork chops.

preparation 5 minutes cooking time 15 minutes

Serves 4

ROAST PORK WITH APPLE SAUCE

1.6kg/3½lb boned rolled loin of pork

olive oil to rub

1kg/2¼lb cooking (green) apples, peeled, cored and chopped

2 tbsp sugar

ground cinnamon to dust

1 tbsp plain (all-purpose) flour

300ml/½ pint/1¼ cups hot chicken stock

300ml/½ pint/1¼ cups cider

salt and ground black pepper

roast potatoes and vegetables to serve

1 Score the pork skin, sprinkle with plenty of salt and leave at room temperature for 1 hour.
2 Preheat the oven to 220°C/425°F/Gas 7.
3 Wipe the salt off the pork skin, rub with oil and sprinkle with more salt. Place the pork in a roasting pan, skin-side up, and roast in the oven for 30 minutes. Reduce the oven temperature to 190°C/375°F/Gas 5 and roast for 1½ hours or until cooked.
4 Meanwhile, put the apples in a pan with the sugar and 2 tbsp water. Cover with a tight-fitting lid and cook over a low heat until just soft. Dust with cinnamon and set aside.
5 Remove the pork from the pan and set aside to rest. Skim off most of the fat, leaving about 1 tbsp and stir in the flour and then the hot stock and cider. Bring to the boil and boil hard for 2–3 minutes. Season and pour the gravy into a jug.
6 Carve the pork and serve with the apple sauce, gravy, some roast potatoes and vegetables.

preparation 30 minutes plus standing **cooking time** 2 hours plus resting

Serves 6

TOAD IN THE HOLE

125g/4oz/1 cup plain (all-purpose) flour, sifted

2 large eggs, lightly beaten

150ml/¼ pint/scant ⅔ cup milk

2 tbsp oil

4 pork sausages

salt and ground black pepper

broccoli to serve

1 Preheat the oven to 220°C/425°F/Gas 7.
2 Put the flour in a bowl, make a well in the centre and pour in the eggs and milk. Beat vigorously and season well with salt and pepper. Let the batter stand for 10 minutes.
3 Put the oil and sausages in a 600ml/1 pint shallow ovenproof dish and cook in the oven for about 10 minutes, turning the sausages once or twice.
4 Pour in the batter and return to the oven for 15–20 minutes until the batter is well risen, crisp and golden brown all over. Serve immediately with broccoli.

preparation 10 minutes cooking time 25–30 minutes

Serves 2

VENISON SAUSAGES

12 venison sausages

6 tsp redcurrant jelly

mashed potatoes to serve

For the red onion marmalade

450g/1lb red onions, chopped

2 tbsp olive oil

4 tbsp red wine vinegar

2 tbsp brown sugar

salt and ground black pepper

1 Preheat the oven to 220°C/425°F/Gas 7.
2 Put the sausages in a small roasting pan. Roast in the oven for 25 minutes, turning once or twice. Spoon the redcurrant jelly over them and return to the oven for 10 minutes.
3 Meanwhile, make the red onion marmalade. Gently cook the red onions in the oil over a very low heat for 20 minutes. Add the vinegar, sugar and seasoning. Simmer for 5 minutes or until the onions are very tender.
4 Serve the sausages with the red onion marmalade and some mashed potatoes.

preparation 15 minutes cooking time 35 minutes

Serves 6

SMOKED HADDOCK KEDGEREE

175g/6oz/¾ cup long-grain rice

450g/1lb smoked haddock fillets

2 medium (US large) eggs, hard-boiled and shelled

50g/2oz/4 tbsp butter

salt and cayenne pepper

chopped fresh parsley to garnish

1 Cook the rice according to the pack instructions.
2 Meanwhile, put the haddock in a large frying pan with just enough water to cover. Simmer very gently for about 10–15 minutes until tender. Drain, skin and flake the fish, discarding any bones.
3 Chop one egg and slice the other. Melt the butter in a pan, add the cooked rice, haddock, chopped egg and seasoning to taste. Stir over a low heat for 5 minutes.
4 Serve garnished with parsley and the sliced egg.

preparation 10 minutes   cooking time 20 minutes

Serves 4

QUICK FISH AND CHIPS

sunflower oil for deep-frying

50g/2oz/½ cup self-raising (self-rising) flour plus extra to coat

50g/2oz/½ cup cornflour (cornstarch)

1 medium (US large) egg white

125ml/4fl oz/½ cup cold sparkling water

4 x 150g/4oz cod or haddock fillets

900g/2lb potatoes, cut into chips

salt and ground black pepper

salt and vinegar to serve

1 Heat the oil in a deep-fryer to 190°C/375°F.
2 To make the batter, mix the flour, cornflour and salt and pepper in a large bowl. Whisk the egg white until frothy. Whisk the water into the flour, a little at a time, and then whisk in the egg white.
3 Coat two fish fillets lightly with flour and then dip into the batter, allowing some to drip off.
4 Put half the chips into the deep-fryer, then add the battered fish. Fry for 6 minutes or until just cooked, then remove and drain on kitchen paper. Keep warm.
5 Dip the remaining fish fillets into the flour and batter, then deep-fry with the remaining chips.
6 Serve immediately with salt and vinegar.

preparation 15 minutes   cooking time 12 minutes

Serves 4

CAULIFLOWER CHEESE

1 cauliflower
1 quantity béchamel sauce (see page 572)
2 tsp Dijon mustard
125g/4oz/1 cup grated Cheddar cheese, plus extra to sprinkle
salt and ground black pepper
a good pinch of cayenne pepper

1 Remove the outer leaves from the cauliflower and cut into four pieces or smaller florets.
2 Cook the cauliflower in a pan of lightly salted boiling water for 10–15 minutes until tender but not mushy. Drain well and place in an ovenproof dish. Preheat the grill (broiler) to hot.
3 Stir the mustard and grated Cheddar into the hot béchamel sauce until it melts. Pour over the cauliflower. Sprinkle with a little grated cheese, black pepper and cayenne.
4 Grill (broil) for 2–3 minutes until golden brown and bubbling.

preparation 5 minutes   cooking time 20 minutes

Serves 2

SPICED SAAG ALOO

2 tbsp vegetable oil
1 onion, thinly sliced
2 garlic cloves, crushed
1 tbsp black mustard seeds
1 tsp each cumin seeds, ground turmeric and garam masala
900g/2lb potatoes, cubed
salt and ground black pepper
450g/1lb baby spinach leaves

1 Heat the oil in a pan and fry the onion over a medium heat for 10 minutes or until golden, stirring occasionally.
2 Add the garlic, mustard and cumin seeds, garam masala and turmeric and cook for 1 minute. Add the potatoes, salt and pepper and 150ml/¼ pint/scant ⅔ cup water.
3 Cover the pan, bring to the boil, then reduce the heat and cook gently for 30 minutes until tender and most of the liquid has been absorbed.
4 Stir in the spinach and cook until it starts to wilt. Serve immediately with curry or boiled rice.

preparation 15 minutes   cooking time 55 minutes

Serves 4

MACARONI CHEESE

340g/12oz macaroni

1 quantity béchamel sauce (see page 572)

½ tsp grated nutmeg

225g/8oz/2 cups grated Cheddar cheese

3 tbsp fresh white breadcrumbs

salt and ground black pepper

1 Cook the pasta in a large pan of lightly salted boiling water according to the pack instructions. Drain well.
2 Make the béchamel sauce and stir in the grated nutmeg with the pasta and most of the cheese. Mix well, then transfer to an ovenproof dish.
3 Preheat the grill (broiler) to high. Sprinkle the breadcrumbs and remaining cheese over the top and pop under the grill for 4–5 minutes until golden brown and bubbling. Serve hot.

preparation 10 minutes   cooking time 15 minutes

Serves 4

QUICHE LORRAINE

225g/8oz shortcrust pastry (see page 582)

flour to dust

For the filling

25g/1oz/2 tbsp butter

1 small onion, finely chopped

225g/8oz unsmoked streaky bacon, chopped

4 large eggs, beaten

400ml/14fl oz/1⅔ cups crème fraîche

100g/4oz/1 cup grated Gruyère or Cheddar cheese

salt and ground black pepper

1 Preheat the oven to 200°C/400°F/Gas 6.
2 Roll out the pastry on a lightly floured surface and use to line a 23cm/9in deep, loose-based tart tin. Line with parchment paper and baking beans and bake in the oven for 15 minutes. Remove the paper and return to the oven for a further 5 minutes. Reduce the oven temperature to 190°C/375°F/Gas 5.
3 Melt the butter in a frying pan, add the onion and cook for 5 minutes over a medium heat. Add the bacon and cook, stirring, until golden brown.
4 Mix the eggs with the crème fraîche and grated cheese, and season with salt and pepper. Put the bacon mixture in the pastry case and pour over the egg mixture to fill the case.
5 Cook in the oven for 30–35 minutes until golden brown and just set. Serve lukewarm or cold, cut into wedges.

preparation 35 minutes   cooking time 1 hour plus cooling

Serves 8

CHICKPEA AND SPINACH PILAFF

2 tbsp olive oil

1 large onion, finely chopped

2 garlic cloves, crushed

25g/1oz/2 tbsp butter

1 tsp cumin seeds

175g/6oz/¾ cup long-grain rice

600ml/1 pint/2½ cups hot vegetable stock

1 x 400g/14oz can chickpeas (garbanzos), drained and rinsed

340g/12oz baby spinach leaves

salt and ground black pepper

natural yogurt to serve

1 Heat the oil in a large pan over a low heat. Add the onion and garlic and cook for 10 minutes, stirring, until tender.
2 Add the butter, then stir in the cumin seeds and rice. Cook for 2 minutes, then add the hot stock. Bring to the boil, then reduce the heat and simmer for 10–12 minutes until most of the liquid has been absorbed and the rice is tender.
3 Remove the pan from the heat and stir in the chickpeas and spinach. Cover with a lid and leave to stand for 5 minutes until the spinach has wilted and the chickpeas are heated through. Season to taste with salt and pepper.
4 Fluff up the rice grains with a fork and serve immediately with some natural yogurt.

preparation 10 minutes cooking time 25 minutes plus standing

Serves 4

FETTUCCINE CARBONARA

340g/12oz fettuccine

175g/6oz smoked bacon, diced

1 tbsp olive oil

2 large egg yolks

150ml/¼ pint/scant ⅔ cup double (heavy) cream

50g/2oz Parmesan, grated

4 tbsp chopped fresh parsley

salt and ground black pepper

1 Cook the pasta in a large pan of lightly salted boiling water according to the pack instructions. Drain.
2 Meanwhile, fry the bacon in the oil until golden brown and crisp. Add to the drained pasta and keep hot.
3 Beat the egg yolks and cream together in a bowl.
4 Stir into the pasta with the Parmesan and parsley, mixing well. Season to taste and serve immediately.

preparation 5 minutes cooking time 10 minutes

Serves 4

SPICY RICE BAKE

3 tbsp olive oil
1 large red onion, thinly sliced
1 red chilli, seeded and sliced
juice of 1 lime
1 tbsp brown sugar
340g/12oz/1½ cups basmati rice
1 bunch of fresh mint, chopped
a few fresh basil leaves, torn
3 tbsp toasted flaked almonds
salt and ground black pepper

1 Heat the oil in a frying pan and fry the onion for 10 minutes over a medium heat until golden and tender. Add the chilli, lime juice and sugar. Cool, then cover and chill.
2 Meanwhile, cook the rice according to the pack instructions. Spread on a baking sheet and leave to cool, then chill.
3 Preheat the oven to 200°C/400°F/Gas 6.
4 Put the rice in a shallow ovenproof dish. Stir in the onion mixture and season with salt and pepper.
5 Bake in the oven for 20 minutes until piping hot. Stir in the mint, basil and almonds and serve immediately.

preparation 15 minutes plus chilling cooking time 40 minutes

Serves 8

SPINACH AND RICOTTA CANNELLONI

1 tbsp olive oil
1 onion, finely chopped
2 garlic cloves, crushed
1 x 400g/14oz can tomatoes
2 tsp balsamic vinegar
450g/1lb spinach
500g/1lb 2oz/3 cups ricotta cheese
1 large (US extra-large) egg, beaten
4 tbsp freshly grated Parmesan
freshly grated nutmeg
12 cannelloni tubes
125g/4oz mozzarella, cubed
salt and ground black pepper

1 Heat the oil in a pan and gently cook the onion over a low heat for 10 minutes or until softened. Add the garlic and cook for 1 minute. Pour in the tomatoes and bring to the boil. Reduce the heat and simmer for 20 minutes or until slightly thickened. Add the balsamic vinegar.
2 Meanwhile, wash the spinach, discarding any tough stalks, and put in a large pan over a low heat. Cover the pan and cook for 2 minutes, shaking, until it wilts. Drain well in a colander, pressing down with a saucer, and roughly chop.
3 Preheat the oven to 180°C/350°F/Gas 4 and lightly oil a baking dish. Mix together the ricotta, egg, Parmesan and nutmeg with the spinach. Season with salt and pepper.
4 Use the spinach mixture to fill the cannelloni tubes and put in the baking dish in a single layer. Pour the tomato sauce over and dot with the mozzarella.
5 Bake in the oven for 30 minutes or until golden brown.

preparation 25 minutes   cooking time 1 hour

Serves 4

SQUID AND TOMATO PASTA

450g/1lb spaghetti
2 tbsp olive oil
2 garlic cloves, chopped
a pinch of dried chilli flakes
12 cherry tomatoes, chopped
2 squid, cleaned and sliced
salt and ground black pepper
lemon wedges to serve

1 Cook the pasta in a large pan of lightly salted boiling water according to the pack instructions.
2 Heat the oil in a pan and add the garlic. Cook for 1 minute, then add the chilli flakes and cook for 1 minute.
3 Stir in the tomatoes and squid and cook for 5 minutes until the squid is tender. Season with salt and black pepper.
4 Drain the pasta, return to the pan and add the sauce. Toss together and serve with lemon wedges.

preparation 5 minutes   cooking time 15 minutes

Serves 4

BOULANGERE POTATOES

butter to grease
1kg/2¼lb potatoes, peeled
1 tbsp fresh thyme leaves
475ml/16fl oz/scant 2 cups hot vegetable stock
salt and ground black pepper

1 Preheat the oven to 200°C/400°F/Gas 6. Butter a large ovenproof dish.
2 Slice the potatoes very thinly, preferably with a mandolin. Arrange half the slices in a layer in the buttered dish. Sprinkle with some of the thyme and salt and pepper and cover with the rest of the potatoes.
3 Pour the hot stock over the top and place a sheet of buttered parchment paper on top of the potatoes.
4 Cook in the oven for 30 minutes, then remove the parchment paper and cook uncovered for 1 hour until the potatoes are cooked and crisp and golden brown on top. Serve hot.

preparation 15 minutes   cooking time 1 hour 30 minutes

Serves 6

SPICED POTATO WEDGES

4 large sweet potatoes
3 large baking potatoes
4 tbsp olive oil
a pinch of dried chilli flakes
salt and ground black pepper

1 Preheat the oven to 200°C/400°F/Gas 6.
2 Cut the sweet potatoes and baking potatoes into wedges and place in a bowl. Pour the oil over, then sprinkle over the chilli flakes and season with salt and pepper.
3 Arrange the potato wedges in a large roasting pan and cook in the oven for 40–45 minutes, turning occasionally, until tender and golden brown. Serve immediately.

preparation 10 minutes   cooking time 45 minutes

Serves 8

ROAST POTATOES

1.5kg/3lb 5oz potatoes, cut into large chunks
4 tbsp duck fat or olive oil
sea salt

1 Put the potatoes in a large pan of salted water. Cover and bring to the boil. Boil for 6–7 minutes, then drain well.
2 Return the potatoes to the warm pan and shake them roughly, so they become fluffy around the edges.
3 Preheat the oven to 220°C/425°F/Gas 7.
4 Heat the fat or oil in a large roasting pan on the hob. When it sizzles, add the potatoes. Baste the potatoes, taking care as the fat will splutter.
5 Roast the potatoes in the oven for 1 hour, then reduce the oven temperature to 200°C/400°F/Gas 6 and roast for 40 minutes. Turn the potatoes only once during cooking to crisp and brown them.
6 Season with a little salt just before serving.

preparation 20 minutes   cooking time 1 hour 50 minutes

Serves 6

OVEN CHIPS

900g/2lb potatoes
3 tbsp olive oil
sea salt flakes

1 Preheat the oven to 240°C/475°F/Gas 9.
2 Peel the potatoes and cut into chips. Add to a pan of lightly salted boiling water, cover and bring back to the boil, then boil for 2 minutes. Drain well and pat dry with kitchen paper.
3 Transfer the potatoes to a large roasting pan. Toss with olive oil and season lightly with sea salt.
4 Bake for 35–40 minutes or until golden brown and cooked, turning occasionally. Drain on kitchen paper and serve.

preparation 10 minutes   cooking time 40 minutes

Serves 4

BUBBLE AND SQUEAK

900g/2lb potatoes, cut into chunks
50g/2oz/4 tbsp butter
1 large onion, chopped
2 large leeks, shredded
225g/8oz green cabbage, shredded
flour to dust
2 tbsp oil
salt and ground black pepper

1 Cook the potatoes in a large pan of lightly salted boiling water until tender, then drain and mash.
2 Heat half the butter in a large non-stick frying pan and cook the onion, leeks and cabbage over a low heat for 10 minutes, stirring, or until tender and starting to colour.
3 Mix the cooked vegetables with the mashed potatoes and season with salt and pepper. Leave to cool, then mould into 12 patties and dust with flour.
4 Heat the oil and remaining butter in a non-stick frying pan and cook the patties for 4 minutes on each side or until they are golden brown. Serve immediately.

preparation 15 minutes plus cooling **cooking time** 45 minutes

Serves 12

ROAST PARSNIPS

4 tbsp duck fat or sunflower oil
8 thick parsnips, quartered lengthways
3 tbsp semolina (farina)

1 Preheat the oven to 200°C/400°F/Gas 6.
2 Put the fat or oil in a large roasting pan and pop it in the oven to get spitting hot.
3 bring the parsnips to the boil in a pan of cold salted water. Boil for 5 minutes, then drain and leave in the colander for a few minutes. Put the semolina on a plate and use to coat the parsnips, shaking off any excess.
4 Put the parsnips in the roasting pan, tossing to coat in the hot fat. Roast in the oven for 35–40 minutes, turning twice, until they are crisp and golden brown. Serve immediately.

preparation 10 minutes **cooking time** 45 minutes

Serves 8

COLCANNON

900g/2lb potatoes, cut into chunks
50g/2oz/4 tbsp butter
1 small Savoy cabbage, shredded
75g/3oz lean bacon, chopped
100ml/3½fl oz/⅓ cup double (heavy) cream
salt and ground black pepper

1 Put the potatoes in a pan of cold salted water and bring to the boil. Reduce the heat and simmer for 15–20 minutes until tender. Drain well and keep warm.
2 Meanwhile, melt the butter in a large frying pan. Add the cabbage and bacon and cook briskly over a medium heat for 3–4 minutes.
3 Mash the potatoes with the cream until smooth. Add the cabbage and bacon and mix together. Season with salt and pepper and serve.

preparation 10 minutes   cooking time 20 minutes

Serves 4

NEEPS AND TATTIES

340g/12oz swede (rutabaga), peeled and cut into chunks
450g/1lb potatoes, cut into chunks
50g/2oz/4 tbsp butter
2 tbsp double (heavy) cream
freshly grated nutmeg
salt and ground black pepper
haggis to serve (optional)

1 Bring a pan of lightly salted water to the boil, add the swede and cook for 20 minutes or until tender. Drain well.
2 Meanwhile, boil the potatoes in another pan of lightly salted water and cook for 15 minutes until tender. Drain well.
3 Mash the potatoes and swede separately with half the butter and cream each. Season with nutmeg, salt and pepper and serve with haggis, if wished.

preparation 15 minutes   cooking time 20 minutes

Serves 4

BRAISED RED CABBAGE

1 tbsp olive oil

1 red onion, chopped

2 cooking (green) apples, peeled, cored and diced

1kg/2¼lb red cabbage, shredded

2 tbsp light brown sugar

2 tbsp red wine vinegar

½ tsp each ground allspice and cinnamon

300ml/½ pint/1¼ cups hot vegetable stock

salt and ground black pepper

1 Heat the oil in a large pan, add the onion and cook over a low heat for 5 minutes. Add all the remaining ingredients and season with salt and pepper.
2 Bring to the boil, then reduce the heat, cover the pan and simmer gently for 45 minutes until nearly all the liquid has evaporated and the cabbage is really tender. Serve hot.

preparation 15 minutes   **cooking time** 50 minutes

Serves 6

BAKED BEETROOT

1kg /2¼lb beetroot (beets)

15g/½oz/1 tbsp butter

salt and ground black pepper

chopped fresh parsley to garnish

balsamic vinegar to drizzle

1 Preheat the oven to 200°C/400°F/Gas 6.
2 Trim the beetroot and rinse in cold water.
3 Rub the butter over a large piece of foil. Place the beetroot on the buttered foil and season with salt and pepper. Bring the edges of the foil up to the centre over the beetroot and seal to make a parcel. Put on a baking sheet.
4 Bake in the oven for 1½ hours until the beetroot are tender and the skin peels away easily.
5 Set aside until cool enough to handle, then rub off the skins and cut the beetroot into cubes.
6 Scatter the chopped parsley or chives over the top and serve, if wished, drizzled with some balsamic vinegar.

preparation 15 minutes   **cooking time** 1 hour 30 minutes

Serves 6

WINTER ROAST ROOT VEGETABLES

1 large potato, cut into large chunks

1 large sweet potato, cut into large chunks

3 carrots, cut into large chunks

4 small parsnips, halved

1 small swede (rutabaga), cut into large chunks

5 tbsp olive oil

2 fresh rosemary and 2 fresh thyme sprigs

salt and ground black pepper

1 Preheat the oven to 200°C/400°F/Gas 6.
2 Put all the prepared vegetables in a large roasting pan and drizzle the oil over them.
3 Slip the herb sprigs between the vegetables, then season with salt and pepper and toss everything together.
4 Roast in the oven for 1 hour or until tender. Keep checking after 45 minutes to see if they are cooked and to turn the vegetables. Remove the herbs if they are charred and serve.

preparation 15 minutes   cooking time 1 hour

Serves 4

SPICED RED CABBAGE

1 tbsp olive oil

15g/½oz/1 tbsp butter

1 tsp each ground ginger and coriander

a pinch of freshly grated nutmeg

450g/1lb red cabbage, shredded

2 tbsp balsamic vinegar

1 tbsp caster (superfine) sugar

a large handful of fresh parsley, roughly chopped

salt and ground black pepper

1 Heat the oil and butter in a large pan over a high heat. Stir in the spices and cook for 1 minute. Add the red cabbage and cook for 10–15 minutes, stirring often, until just softened.
2 Add the balsamic vinegar and sugar and cook for 3 minutes, stirring occasionally.
3 Stir in the parsley and season to taste. Serve immediately.

preparation 10 minutes   cooking time 15–20 minutes

Serves 6

BRUSSELS SPROUTS WITH CHESTNUTS

900g/2lb Brussels sprouts, trimmed

1 tbsp olive oil

6 rashers (slices) streaky bacon, chopped

1 x 200g/7oz pack peeled cooked chestnuts

30g/1oz/2 tbsp butter

salt and ground black pepper

1 Add the sprouts to a large pan of lightly salted boiling water, return to the boil and blanch for 2 minutes. Drain well and refresh with cold water.
2 Heat the oil in a frying pan. Add the bacon and fry over a low heat for 5 minutes until crisp. Remove and set aside.
3 Add the butter and chestnuts and cook for 5 minutes to heat through gently.
4 Add the sprouts and cook for 5 minutes until just tender. Return the bacon and chestnuts to the pan, season to taste with salt and pepper and serve.

preparation 15 minutes cooking time 12 minutes

Serves 8

CREAMY LEEKS

900g/2lb leeks, thinly sliced

25g/1oz/2 tbsp butter

150ml/¼ pint/scant ⅔ cup crème fraîche

a pinch of freshly grated nutmeg

salt and ground black pepper

1 Cook the leeks in a pan of lightly salted boiling water for 8–10 minutes until just tender. Drain and plunge into a bowl of icy cold water. Drain and pat dry with kitchen paper.
2 Melt the butter in a frying pan, add the leeks and stir over a medium heat for 2–3 minutes. Stir in the crème fraîche and season with salt and pepper.
3 Cook for a few minutes until heated through and bubbling. Sprinkle with grated nutmeg and serve.

preparation 15 minutes plus cooling cooking time 20 minutes

Serves 8

THYME TOMATOES

1kg/2¼lb cherry tomatoes, on the vine
1 tbsp olive oil
3 fresh thyme sprigs, chopped
salt and ground black pepper

1 Preheat the oven to 220°C/425°F/Gas 7.
2 Cut the tomatoes into small bunches and place in a roasting pan. Drizzle the oil over and sprinkle over the thyme. Season with salt and pepper.
3 Roast in the oven for 10–12 minutes until the tomatoes are tender and starting to char. Serve hot.

preparation 3 minutes   cooking time 12 minutes

Serves 6

STIR-FRIED GREEN BEANS AND TOMATOES

450g/1lb green beans, trimmed
1 tbsp olive oil
2 garlic cloves, crushed
225g/8oz baby plum tomatoes, halved
2 tbsp chopped fresh parsley
salt and ground black pepper

1 Cook the beans in a pan of lightly salted boiling water for 4–5 minutes, then drain well.
2 Heat the oil in a wok or deep frying pan over a high heat. Briskly stir-fry the beans with the garlic and tomatoes for 2–3 minutes until the beans are tender and the tomatoes are starting to soften without losing their shape.
3 Season with salt and pepper, stir in the parsley and serve.

preparation 10 minutes   cooking time 8 minutes

Serves 6

CLASSIC COLESLAW

½ each green and white cabbage, finely shredded
2 carrots, grated
1 small onion, grated
1 bunch fresh parsley, chopped

For the dressing
8 tbsp natural yogurt
2 tbsp mayonnaise
1 tsp Dijon mustard
salt and ground black pepper

1 To make the dressing, put the yogurt, mayonnaise and mustard in a bowl. Season with salt and pepper and mix well together.
2 Put the cabbage, carrots and onion in a large bowl and mix together. Stir in the parsley.
3 Pour the dressing over the cabbage mixture and toss well.

preparation 15 minutes

Serves 8

MIXED GREEN SALAD

2 round lettuce hearts, leaves separated
125g/4oz watercress or rocket (arugula)
2 ripe avocados, peeled, stoned and roughly chopped
1 box salad cress, chopped
100g/3½oz mangetouts, sliced

For the vinaigrette dressing
4 tbsp olive oil
1 tbsp cider vinegar
1 tsp Dijon mustard
salt and ground black pepper

1 Put the lettuce hearts in a large bowl with the watercress or rocket, avocados, salad cress and mangetouts. Mix everything together.
2 To make the vinaigrette dressing, put all the ingredients in a screw-topped jar, secure the lid tightly and shake vigorously to mix. Or whisk together in a bowl.
3 Pour the dressing over the salad and toss gently together to mix. Serve immediately.

preparation 10 minutes

Serves 8

MUSTARDY POTATO SALAD

1.5kg/3lb 2oz new potatoes, cut into chunks
100ml/3½fl oz/⅓ cup olive oil
1 tbsp white wine vinegar
2 tbsp wholegrain mustard
juice of 1 lemon
1 bunch of spring onions (scallions), thinly sliced
salt and ground black pepper

1 Cook the potatoes in a pan of lightly salted boiling water for 15 minutes or until just tender but not breaking apart.
2 Meanwhile, whisk together the oil, vinegar, mustard, lemon juice and salt and pepper to taste.
3 Drain the potatoes, then return them to the pan. Pour the dressing over and stir in the spring onions. Mix gently so as not to break up the potatoes.
4 Transfer to a serving dish and serve warm or cold.

preparation 15 minutes cooking time 20 minutes

Serves 12

SWEET CHILLI RIBBON SALAD

3 large carrots, trimmed
1 cucumber, trimmed
2 courgettes (zucchini), trimmed
2 tbsp sweet chilli sauce
1 tbsp white wine vinegar
ground black pepper

1 Use a vegetable peeler to make carrot ribbons and place them in a large bowl. Peel the cucumber and courgette into ribbons and place in the bowl with the carrots.
2 Blend the sweet chilli sauce with the vinegar and drizzle over the vegetable ribbons. Grind over some black pepper. Toss together and serve.

preparation 10 minutes

Serves 6

PEA AND ROCKET SALAD

450g/1lb fresh or frozen peas
3 tbsp olive oil
2 tsp wholegrain mustard
grated zest and juice of 1 lemon
a small bunch of fresh mint, chopped
75g/3oz rocket (arugula), torn
salt and ground black pepper

1 Bring a large pan of water to the boil, add the peas, then bring back to the boil and cook for 1 minute. Drain, then plunge the peas into a bowl of iced water to cool. Drain well
2 Put the oil, mustard and lemon zest and juice in a small bowl with some seasoning and whisk to combine.
3 Put the mint, rocket and peas in a large bowl, pour over the dressing and toss gently together. Serve immediately.

preparation 10 minutes   cooking time 5 minutes

Serves 6

GRATED CARROT AND BEETROOT SALAD

3 large carrots, coarsely grated
500g/1lb 2oz raw beetroot (beets), coarsely grated
3 tbsp olive oil
1 tbsp cider vinegar
finely grated zest and juice of 1 large orange
4 tbsp chopped walnuts
a small handful of fresh parsley, roughly chopped
salt and ground black pepper

1 Put the carrots and beetroot in a serving bowl.
2 Mix the oil, vinegar, orange zest and juice and some salt and pepper together in a small bowl to make a dressing.
3 Scatter the walnuts and parsley over the grated vegetables. Pour over the dressing, toss lightly and serve.

preparation 15 minutes

Serves 6

BEETROOT AND RED CABBAGE SALAD

½ red cabbage, shredded

500g/1lb 2oz cooked beetroot (beets)

3 red apples, cored and diced

For the dressing

6 tbsp fruity olive oil

2 tbsp cider vinegar

juice of 1 lemon

a small handful of fresh parsley, chopped

salt and ground black pepper

preparation 15 minutes

1 Put the red cabbage in a large bowl. Cut the beetroot into thin matchstick strips and add to the cabbage with the apples. Toss well to mix.
2 To make the dressing, put the oil, cider vinegar, lemon juice and parsley in a bowl. Season with salt and pepper and whisk together until blended.
3 Pour the dressing over the salad and toss everything together. Serve immediately..

Serves 8

WALDORF SALAD

450g/1lb dessert apples

juice of 1 lemon

175g/6oz small red seedless grapes

6 celery sticks, sliced

4 tbsp chopped walnuts

150ml/¼ pint/scant ⅔ cup mayonnaise

1 cos (romaine) lettuce

salt and ground black pepper

preparation 15 minutes

1 Peel and core the apples and cut into dice. Sprinkle with lemon juice to prevent them discolouring.
2 Put the apples in a bowl with the grapes, celery and walnuts and gently stir in the mayonnaise. Season with salt and black pepper to taste.
3 Line a salad bowl with cos lettuce leaves. Pile the apple and celery mixture in the centre and serve.

Serves 4

TOP 10 SAUCES

CURRY SAUCE

50g/2oz/4 tbsp butter
1 small onion, finely chopped
1 tbsp curry powder
3 tbsp flour
450ml/¾ pint/1¾ cups milk
2 tbsp mango chutney

1 Melt the butter in a pan and fry the onion until golden. Stir in the curry powder and cook for 3–4 minutes. Add the flour and cook gently for 2–3 minutes.
2 Off the heat, stir in the milk. Bring to the boil slowly and cook, stirring, until the sauce thickens. Add the chutney and serve.

preparation 5 minutes
cooking time 20 minutes

Serves 4

BREAD SAUCE

1 onion, quartered and studded with 6 cloves
2 bay leaves
450ml/¾ pint/1¾ cups milk
125g/4oz/2 cups fresh white breadcrumbs
a good pinch of freshly grated nutmeg
50g/2oz/4 tbsp butter
200ml/7fl oz/¾ cup double (heavy) cream
salt and ground black pepper

1 Put the onion, bay leaves and milk in a pan. Heat very gently for 15 minutes.
2 Remove the onion and bay leaves. Stir in the breadcrumbs, nutmeg and butter. Add the cream and seasoning. Serve warm.

preparation 10 minutes
cooking time 15 minutes

Serves 8

BEURRE BLANC

3 tbsp white wine vinegar
3 tbsp white wine
2 shallots, finely chopped
225g/8oz/1 cup butter, chilled and diced
salt and ground black pepper

1 Put the vinegar, wine and shallots in a pan. Bring to the boil and reduce to 1 tbsp.
2 Over a low heat, whisk in the butter, a piece at a time, until the sauce thickens. Season with salt and pepper to taste.

preparation 5 minutes
cooking time 5 minutes

Serves 4

APPLE SAUCE

450g/1lb cooking (green) apples, peeled, cored and sliced
2 tbsp sugar
25g/1oz/2 tbsp butter

1 Put the apples in a pan with 2 tbsp water. Cook gently for 10 minutes, until soft.
2 Beat until smooth, then stir in sugar to taste and the butter. Serve warm.

preparation 10 minutes
cooking time 10 minutes

Serves 4

BBQ SAUCE

50g/2oz/4 tbsp butter
1 large onion, chopped
2 tbsp tomato ketchup
2 tbsp wine vinegar
2 tbsp Worcestershire sauce
2 tsp mustard powder

1 Fry the onion in the butter for 10 minutes.
   Add the tomato ketchup; cook for 2 minutes.
2 Mix the remaining ingredients with 150ml/
   ¼ pint/scant ⅔ cup water. Add to the pan,
   bring to the boil and cook for 10 minutes.

preparation 5 minutes
cooking time 25 minutes

Serves 4

HORSERADISH

2 tbsp grated fresh horseradish
juice of ½ lemon
2 tsp sugar
150ml/¼ pint/scant ⅔ cup double (heavy) cream

1 Mix the horseradish, lemon juice and sugar.
2 Whip the cream to soft peaks, then fold in
   the horseradish mixture.

preparation 5 minutes

Serves 4

MELBA SAUCE

225g/8oz/2 cups raspberries
juice of ½ lemon
2 tbsp icing (confectioner's) sugar

1 Put the raspberries, lemon juice and icing
   sugar in a blender and blitz until smooth.
   Press through a sieve to discard the seeds.

preparation 5 minutes

Serves 4

TARTARE SAUCE

150ml/¼ pint/scant ⅔ cup mayonnaise
1 tbsp snipped fresh chives
2 tbsp chopped fresh parsley
2 tsp each chopped capers and gherkins
1 tbsp lemon juice

1 Mix all the ingredients in a bowl. Set aside
   for 1 hour before serving.

preparation 5 minutes
plus standing

Serves 6

MINT SAUCE

1 small bunch of mint, finely chopped
2 tsp caster (superfine) sugar
2 tbsp white wine vinegar

1 Put the mint and sugar in a bowl. Add
   1 tbsp boiling water and leave for 5 minutes.
2 Stir in the wine vinegar. Set aside for 1 hour
   before serving.

preparation 10 minutes
plus standing

Serves 4

TOFFEE SAUCE

75g/3oz/6 tbsp butter
75g/3oz/⅓ cup soft brown sugar
400ml/14fl oz/1⅔ cups condensed milk

1 Melt the butter in a pan with the sugar. Mix
   in the condensed milk and cook over a low
   heat, stirring, for 3–4 minutes, until the
   sauce smells of toffee. Serve warm or cold.

preparation 2 minutes
cooking time 3-4 minutes

Serves 6

ENTERTAINING

Whatever the occasion, we've got great food for when you're entertaining your family and friends. Whether it's a stylish dinner party, a buffet lunch on a hot summer's day, or an informal supper, you will find some delicious recipes that are perfect for your special meal.

We have selected a fabulous array of dishes from around the world, including Chinese crispy duck, Malay peanut chicken and Vietnamese rice salad from Asia; a classic bouillabaisse and moules marinières from France; Italian fritto misto and Greek roast chicken from the Mediterranean; and ceviche from the New World. And for traditionalists, there's boeuf en croûte, retro-style seafood cocktail, lobster Thermidor and trout with almonds.

All the dishes are simple to prepare and cook, which takes all the hard work out of entertaining. Many can be made in advance and then served cold or reheated at the last minute, giving you more time to relax with your guests. Yet they are special enough to impress with their elegant appearance and sophisticated flavours. You will soon get accustomed to being complimented on your food and will acquire a reputation for being an impressive host and cook.

< *Moules Marinières (page 276)*

GREEK ROAST CHICKEN

1 x 1.4kg/3lb chicken
salt and ground black pepper
fresh oregano and thyme sprigs
500g/1lb 2oz new potatoes, halved or quartered
juice of 1 lemon
8 unpeeled garlic cloves
2 lemons
4 tbsp olive oil
4 tbsp water

1 Preheat the oven to 200°C/400°F/Gas 6.
2 Put the chicken in a large roasting pan. Season well and put a few herbs inside the cavity. Arrange the potatoes around it in the pan and tuck in the garlic. Squeeze 1 lemon over the chicken and potatoes. Put the squeezed halves inside the chicken. Cut the other lemon into wedges and place in the gaps. Strip the leaves off the remaining herbs and scatter over the top. Sprinkle with oil. Pour the water into the pan.
3 Roast in the oven for 1½ hours, basting occasionally with the pan juices, and turning the potatoes over as they brown.
4 Remove from the oven, cover with foil and set aside to rest for 10 minutes before carving the chicken. Serve with salad.

preparation 10 minutes cooking time 1 hour 30 minutes

Serves 4

ROAST CHICKEN WITH HERBS

900g/2lb floury potatoes, cut into chunks
125g/4oz/½ cup butter, softened
5 tbsp chopped fresh sage leaves, plus extra leaves
5 tbsp chopped fresh thyme, plus extra sprigs
1 x 1.4kg/3lb chicken
juice of 1 lemon, halves reserved
2 fennel bulbs, cut into wedges
1 red onion, cut into wedges
4 whole garlic cloves in their skins
salt and ground black pepper

1 Preheat the oven to 190°C/375°F/ Gas 5.
2 Put the potatoes in a large pan of lightly salted water and bring to the boil. Cook for 5 minutes. Drain and shake in the colander to roughen the edges.
3 Meanwhile, blend the butter and herbs. Season well.
4 Push the lemon halves inside the chicken. Ease your fingers under the skin of the neck end to separate the skin from the flesh. Gently push the herb butter up under the skin, reserving a little.
5 Put the chicken in a large roasting pan, pour the lemon juice over and top with the reserved butter. Tuck the potatoes, fennel, red onion and garlic cloves around the chicken.
6 Roast in the oven for 1 hour 20 minutes or until the juices run clear when the thickest part of the thigh is pierced with a skewer. Carve the chicken and serve with the vegetables.

preparation 40 minutes cooking time 1 hour 30 minutes

Serves 4

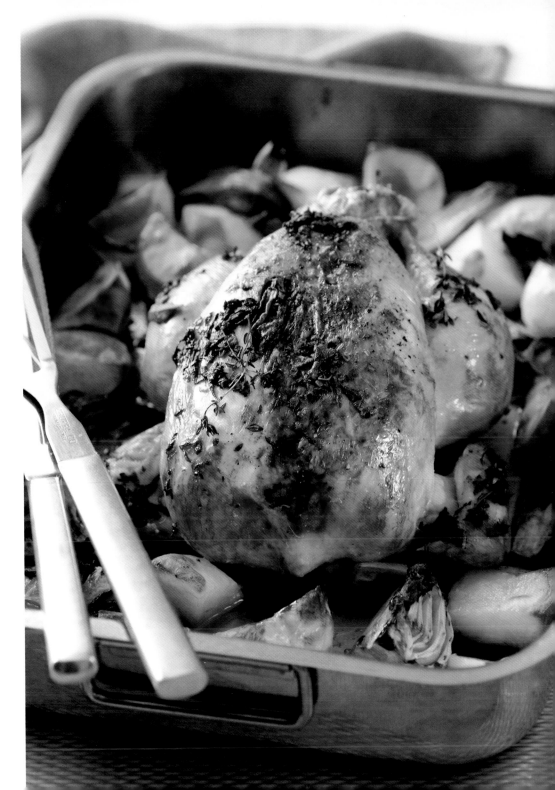

SLOW-COOKED SPANISH RICE

a pinch of saffron strands

1.1 litres/2 pints/5 cups hot chicken stock

2 tbsp olive oil

4 boneless, skinless chicken thighs, roughly diced

1 onion, chopped

1 red (bell) pepper, seeded and sliced

75g/3oz chorizo sausage, diced

2 garlic cloves, crushed

a pinch of chilli powder

300g/11oz/1⅓ cups rice

salt and ground black pepper

4 tbsp chopped fresh parsley

1 Stir the saffron into the hot stock. Set aside for 5 minutes. Meanwhile, heat the oil in a large frying pan over a medium heat. Add the chicken and cook for 10 minutes, turning often, until golden brown, then transfer to a slow cooker.
2 Add the onion to the pan and cook for 5 minutes until softened. Add the red pepper and chorizo and cook for 5 minutes, then add the garlic and cook for 1 minute. Stir in the chilli powder.
3 Stir in the rice and then add the stock and seasoning. Transfer to the slow cooker and stir well. Cover and cook on Low for 1–2 hours until the rice is tender and the chicken is cooked through.
4 Sprinkle with parsley and serve with rice or potatoes.

preparation 25 minutes plus infusing   cooking time 20 minutes in pan then 1–2 hours on Low

Serves 4

CHICKEN CONSOMME

340g/12oz skinless chicken breast, minced (ground)

1 large leek, thinly sliced

2 celery sticks, thinly sliced

1 large carrot, thinly sliced

1 small onion, chopped

2 medium (US large) egg whites, beaten, and their shells, crushed

1.7 litres/3 pints/7½ cups hot chicken stock

a dash of sherry or Madeira

salt and ground black pepper

1 Put the chicken and vegetables in a large pan and mix in the beaten egg whites and egg shells.
2 Gradually whisk in the hot stock, then bring to the boil, still whisking. As soon as it starts to boil, stop whisking, reduce the heat and simmer very gently for 1 hour.
3 Make a hole in the surface crust and ladle the clear stock underneath out into a muslin (cheesecloth)-lined sieve placed over a large bowl.
4 Leave the stock to drain through slowly. Pour into a clean pan and reheat gently. Season to taste and flavour with a little sherry or Madeira.

preparation 30 minutes   cooking time 1 hour 15 minutes

Serves 6

WARM CHICKEN SALAD

1 tbsp olive oil

3 x 125g/4oz chicken breasts

175g/6oz asparagus tips, trimmed

175g/6oz green beans, trimmed

1 ripe avocado, stoned, peeled and cubed

100g/3½oz mixed salad leaves

salt and ground black pepper

For the blue cheese dressing

50g/2oz creamy blue cheese, e.g. Cambazola or Danish Blue

125g/4oz/½ cup virtually fat-free fromage frais

milk to thin (optional)

1 Heat a griddle until hot and brush with the oil. Flatten the chicken with a rolling pin and cook on the hot griddle for 8–10 minutes on each side until cooked through and golden brown. Keep warm.
2 Cook the asparagus in a pan of lightly salted boiling water for 2–3 minutes until tender. Drain and keep warm.
3 Cook the green beans in a pan of lightly salted boiling water for 6 minutes until tender. Drain and keep warm.
4 To make the dressing, mash the blue cheese with a fork in a bowl and stir in the fromage frais, mixing to a creamy consistency. Thin with a little milk, if necessary.
5 Cut the chicken into slices. Toss in a bowl with the warm asparagus and beans. Mix in the avocado and salad leaves.
6 Divide between four serving plates and drizzle over the blue cheese dressing. Serve warm.

preparation 15 minutes **cooking time** 20 minutes

Serves 4

LEBANESE CHICKEN

450g/1lb new potatoes, halved

450g/1lb boneless, skinless chicken breasts, cubed

4 garlic cloves, crushed

juice of 2 lemons

1 lemon, cut into wedges

4 tbsp olive oil

a large pinch of paprika

3 tbsp chopped fresh parsley

salt and ground black pepper

harissa paste to serve

1 Preheat the oven to 190°C/375°F/Gas 5.
2 Put the potatoes and chicken in a shallow ovenproof dish. Sprinkle the garlic, lemon juice and seasoning over. Tuck in the unpeeled garlic cloves and lemon wedges. Sprinkle with olive oil and stir gently until everything is coated. Dust with paprika and cover the dish with kitchen foil.
3 Bake in the oven for 30 minutes before removing the foil. Return to the oven and cook for 15 minutes until the chicken is cooked through and the potatoes are tender. Sprinkle the parsley over the top.
4 Divide among four plates and serve with a little harissa.

preparation 10 minutes **cooking time** 45 minutes

Serves 4

CHICKEN STROGANOV

2 tbsp olive oil

1 onion, thinly sliced

2 garlic cloves, crushed

4 x 125g/4oz chicken breasts, cut into strips

340g/12oz mushrooms, sliced

125ml/4fl oz/½ cup hot chicken stock

150ml/¼ pint/scant ⅔ cup soured cream

4 tbsp chopped fresh parsley

salt and ground black pepper

boiled rice to serve

1 Heat 1 tbsp oil in a frying pan. Add the onion and garlic and cook gently over a low heat for 10–15 minutes until soft. Remove from the pan and set aside.
2 Add the remaining oil and fry the chicken over a medium heat, turning occasionally, until golden all over. Add the mushrooms and cook for 5 minutes.
3 Return the onion mixture to the chicken pan and gradually stir in the hot stock, then add the cream and 2 tbsp parsley. Simmer gently for 5 minutes, then season to taste.
4 Divide the chicken mixture between four plates. Sprinkle with the rest of the parsley and serve with boiled rice.

preparation 20 minutes   cooking time 30 minutes

Serves 4

MALAY PEANUT CHICKEN

4 skinless chicken breasts

2 garlic cloves, crushed

3 tbsp groundnut (peanut) oil

chopped fresh coriander (cilantro) to garnish

For the peanut sauce

1 tbsp groundnut (peanut) oil

1 tbsp curry paste

1 tbsp brown sugar

3 tbsp smooth peanut butter

250ml/9fl oz/1 cup coconut milk

1 Cut the chicken into strips, then mix in a bowl with the garlic and oil. Cover the bowl and leave to marinate in the refrigerator for 15 minutes.
2 To make the peanut sauce, heat the oil in a pan, then stir in the curry paste, sugar and peanut butter. Cook for 1 minute. Add the coconut milk and bring to the boil, stirring all the time, then reduce the heat and simmer for 5 minutes.
3 Meanwhile, heat a wok or deep frying pan and stir-fry the chicken and its marinade in batches over a medium to high heat for 4 minutes until cooked and golden brown.
4 Arrange the chicken on a bed of boiled rice or noodles, and pour the peanut sauce over. Scatter with coriander and serve immediately

preparation 10 minutes plus 15 minutes marinating   **cooking time** 10 minutes

Serves 4

CHICKEN WITH WINE AND CAPERS

1 tbsp olive oil
25g/1oz/2 tbsp butter
4 small boneless, skinless, chicken breasts
125ml/4fl oz/½ cup white wine
2 tbsp capers
grated zest and juice of 1 lemon
2 tbsp chopped fresh tarragon
salt and ground black pepper
cooked noodles to serve

1 Heat the oil and 1 tbsp butter in a frying pan set over a medium heat. Add the chicken breasts and then cook for 8–10 minutes on each side until cooked through. Transfer to a warmed plate, then cover and keep warm.
2 Add the wine and capers to the pan. Bring to the boil, then reduce the heat and simmer gently for 5 minutes until the wine is reduced by half. Add the lemon zest and juice and the remaining butter and stir in the tarragon. Season to taste with salt and pepper.
3 Divide the chicken among four warmed plates, pour the sauce over the top and serve immediately with noodles.

preparation 5 minutes   cooking time 20 minutes

Serves 4

SWEET-AND-SOUR DUCK

3 tbsp light soy sauce
1 tbsp dry sherry
2 tsp sesame oil
340g/12oz duck breast fillets, sliced
2 tsp cornflour (cornstarch)
2 tbsp white wine vinegar
1 tbsp tomato paste
juice of 1 orange
2 tbsp oil
1 red onion, cut into small wedges
1 garlic clove, crushed
1 carrot, cut into matchsticks
125g/4oz sugarsnap peas
½ small pineapple, peeled, cored and cubed

1 Mix 1 tbsp soy sauce with the sherry and sesame oil. Pour over the duck, then cover and leave to marinate in the refrigerator for at least 30 minutes.
2 Blend together the cornflour, vinegar, tomato paste, orange juice and remaining soy sauce. Set aside for the sauce.
3 Heat the oil in a wok or deep frying pan. Remove the duck from the marinade, reserving the marinade, and cook over a high heat for 3–4 minutes until golden brown and the fat is crisp. Remove and set aside.
4 Stir-fry the onion, garlic and carrot for 2–3 minutes, then add the sugarsnap peas and stir-fry for 1–2 minutes.
5 Add the pineapple, duck, cornflour mixture and the reserved marinade. Bring to the boil, stirring all the time, then reduce the heat and cook for 2–3 minutes until slightly thickened.
6 Serve immediately with boiled rice.

preparation 15 minutes plus marinating   cooking time 15 minutes

Serves 4

PEKING DUCK

2kg/4½lb duck
1 tbsp runny honey
2 tbsp dark soy sauce
a pinch of five-spice powder

To serve
12 ready-made Chinese pancakes
8 tbsp plum sauce
1 bunch of spring onions (scallions), cut into thin strips
½ cucumber, cut into thin strips

1 Put the duck in a large bowl. Pour a kettleful of boiling water over it. Remove the duck and dry inside and out with kitchen paper. Prick the skin all over with a fork, taking care not to pierce the flesh. Leave it somewhere cool and airy to dry overnight, with a bowl underneath to catch any drips.
2 Heat the oven to 190°C/375°F/Gas 5. Mix the honey and soy sauce with the five-spice powder and rub over the duck. Set aside to dry for 10 minutes. Put the duck on a wire rack over a roasting pan and roast in the oven for 1 hour.
3 Heat the pancakes according to the pack instructions.
4 Strip the skin and meat from the duck and place on a warmed plate.
5 Each person spreads a spoonful of plum sauce on to a pancake, adds some strips of spring onion and cucumber and pieces of duck, then rolls it up tightly.

preparation 10 minutes cooking time 1 hour

Serves 4

CRISPY DUCK

12 small duck legs
2 pieces star anise
4 garlic cloves, chopped
1 tbsp diced fresh root ginger
1 small bunch of fresh coriander (cilantro)
oil for deep-frying
frisée (curly endive) to serve

For the dip
2 tbsp sesame oil
2 tbsp soy sauce
3 tbsp tomato ketchup
1 tsp runny honey
juice of 1 small orange

1 Prick the duck legs all over with a skewer or fork. Put them in a large pan with the spices and coriander, cover with cold water and bring to the boil. Reduce the heat and simmer gently for 45 minutes.
2 Meanwhile, make the dip by whisking all the ingredients together in a bowl.
3 Drain the duck legs and remove the meat and skin from the bones. Cut into slices.
4 Heat the oil in a large heavy-based pan or deep-fat fryer to 180°C/350°F. Add the duck and fry in batches until crisp and golden brown. Drain on kitchen paper.
5 Serve the duck immediately with the dip and some frisée.

preparation 10 minutes cooking time 1 hour

Serves 4

BOEUF EN CROUTE

800g/1lb 12oz beef fillet
25g/1oz/2 tbsp unsalted butter
1 tbsp olive oil
175g/6oz shallots, finely chopped
250g/9oz mushrooms, diced
3 tbsp brandy
1 small bunch of fresh parsley, chopped
2 medium (US large) egg yolks
400g/14oz puff pastry
2 eggs, beaten
salt and ground black pepper

1 Sprinkle the beef with salt and pepper. Heat the butter and oil in a frying pan, add the beef and cook over a high heat, turning, until evenly browned: 6–7 minutes for rare; 9–10 minutes for medium; or 12–14 minutes for well done. Remove from the pan and set aside to cool.
2 Add the shallots to the pan and cook over a medium heat until softened and starting to brown. Add the mushrooms and cook for 3–4 minutes, stirring occasionally. Add the brandy and when it starts bubbling, set alight. When the flames subside, stir in the parsley and cook for 1 minute. Transfer the mixture to a bowl, mix with the egg yolks and set aside.
3 Preheat the oven to 200°C/400°F/Gas 6.
4 Roll out the pastry on a lightly floured board to form a large rectangle. Spread half the mushroom stuffing in a strip about the same size as the beef down the centre of the pastry. Place the beef on top and spread the remaining mushroom mixture over the beef.
5 Brush the edges of the pastry with beaten egg, then bring two sides up and over the long edges of the beef. Press together to seal well. Trim a little of the excess pastry from the ends, then fold up over the beef to make a parcel.
6 Roll out the pastry trimmings and cut out leaf shapes. Brush the parcel with beaten egg, arrange the pastry leaves over the pastry joins and brush with more egg.
7 Slide the beef on to a baking sheet and bake in the oven for 30 minutes, then reduce the oven temperature to 180°C/350°F/Gas 4 and cook for 10–15 minutes until the pastry is golden brown and puffed up.
8 Leave to stand for 10 minutes, then cut into thick slices and serve with salad or vegetables.

preparation 1 hour plus chilling cooking time 55 minutes

Serves 6

GLAZED HAM

4.5kg/10lb smoked gammon joint, on the bone
2 celery sticks, roughly chopped
1 onion, quartered
1 carrot, roughly chopped
1 tsp black peppercorns
2 tbsp cloves

For the glaze
3 tbsp Dijon mustard
4 tbsp Demerara sugar
juice of 1 orange

1 Put the gammon in a large pan with the celery, onion, carrot and peppercorns. Cover with cold water and then bring to the boil. Reduce the heat, cover the pan and simmer gently for 3½ hours, or allow 15–20 minutes per 450g/1lb plus 15 minutes. Lift out the gammon on to a board.
2 Preheat the oven to 200°C/400°F/Gas 6.
3 Remove the gammon rind and score the fat in a diamond pattern. Place the gammon in a roasting pan, then stud each diamond of fat with a clove.
4 Gently spread the mustard over the fat and lightly press the sugar into it with your hands. Pour over the orange juice.
5 Roast in the oven for 430 minutes, basting occasionally with the pan juices, until golden brown.
6 Serve the gammon hot or cold, carved into thin slices.

preparation 30 minutes   cooking time 4 hours

Serves 16

MELON, MINT AND CRISPY HAM

150g/5oz sliced Parma ham
1 large ripe Charentais melons
75g/3oz rocket (arugula)
3 spring onions (scallions), finely sliced and soaked in iced water
50g/2oz Parmesan, shaved

For the mint dressing
6 tbsp olive oil
2 tbsp white wine vinegar
a pinch of sugar
4 tbsp chopped fresh mint

1 To make the mint dressing, whisk together the oil, vinegar, sugar and mint in a bowl. Set aside.
2 Preheat the grill (broiler). Place the ham on the grill rack and grill (broil) for 1–2 minutes until crisp and golden brown. Break into large pieces.
3 Remove the skin and seeds from the melon and cut the flesh into chunks.
4 Divide the rocket among six serving plates and top with the melon and crispy ham.
5 Drizzle the mint dressing over the top and garnish with the spring onions. Sprinkle with Parmesan shavings and serve.

preparation 20 minutes   cooking time 4 minutes

Serves 6

MELON AND PRAWN SALAD

1 ripe Charentais melon
1 ripe Galia melon
grated zest and juice of 1 lime
125g/4oz/½ cup light mayonnaise
125g/4oz/½ cup fromage frais
340g/12oz large cooked peeled prawns (jumbo shrimp)
salt and ground black pepper
chopped fresh coriander (cilantro) to garnish

1 Cut the melons in half and scoop out the seeds. Strain them, reserving the juice. Remove the skin and cut the flesh into chunks. Cover and chill in the refrigerator.
2 Stir the lime zest and juice together with any melon juice into the mayonnaise and fromage frais. Mix together and season to taste with salt and pepper. Stir in the prawns.
3 Arrange the chilled melon and the prawns in mayonnaise on eight serving plates. Sprinkle with coriander and serve.

preparation 25 minutes plus chilling

Serves 8

FIG AND PROSCIUTTO SALAD

225g/8oz green beans, trimmed
4 tbsp olive oil
4 slices ciabatta, cubed
4 Little Gem (or 2 Boston) lettuces, separated into leaves
75g/3oz thinly sliced prosciutto (dry cured ham), torn into strips
4 figs, quartered
1 tsp Dijon mustard
1 tbsp red wine vinegar
salt and ground black pepper
Parmesan shavings to serve

1 Bring a small pan of water to the boil and cook the beans for 5 minutes or until just tender. Drain well.
2 Heat 1 tbsp oil in a frying pan and fry the ciabatta cubes, turning them frequently, until golden and crisp all over. Drain on kitchen paper and set aside to cool.
3 Put the lettuce in a bowl with the prosciutto, green beans, figs and fried ciabatta. Season lightly with salt and pepper.
4 In a small bowl, mix together the remaining oil with the mustard and vinegar.
5 Drizzle the dressing over the salad and divide among four serving plates. Scatter with Parmesan shavings and serve.

preparation 15 minutes   cooking time 5 minutes

Serves 4

MELON AND CHORIZO SALAD

1 cantaloupe melon
5 tbsp balsamic glaze
1 tsp runny honey
1 tsp olive oil
75g/3oz chorizo, diced
rocket (arugula) or watercress leaves to serve
1 small bunch of fresh chives, snipped

1 Halve the melon and discard the seeds. Cut each half into three wedges, remove the skin, then cover and chill.
2 Put the balsamic glaze and honey in a small pan and simmer gently for 5 minutes until syrupy. Leave to cool.
3 Heat the oil in a small frying pan over a medium heat and add the chorizo. Fry for 3–4 minutes, turning occasionally, until golden. Strain the oil into a bowl and put aside.
4 Put a melon wedge and some rocket or watercress on each serving plate and sprinkle with some chorizo. Drizzle with the warm chorizo oil and the balsamic glaze. Scatter with chives and serve immediately.

preparation 10 minutes plus chilling   cooking time 8 minutes

Serves 6

BEAN AND SALMON SALAD

340g/12oz new potatoes, sliced
175g/6oz fine green beans, trimmed and halved
100g/3½oz mixed salad leaves
bunch of spring onions (scallions), sliced
8 baby plum tomatoes, halved
250g/9oz cooked salmon, skinned, boned and flaked

For the dressing
3 tbsp sweet chilli sauce
1 tbsp light soy sauce
2 tbsp olive oil

1 Cook the potatoes and beans in a pan of boiling water for 6–8 minutes or until just tender. Drain and set aside.
2 Put the salad leaves, spring onions, baby plum tomatoes and salmon in a bowl.
3 In a small bowl, mix together the dressing ingredients.
4 Add the potatoes and beans to the salad bowl with the dressing and toss together gently.
5 Divide the salad mixture among four plates and serve.

preparation 15 minutes   cooking time 8 minutes

Serves 4

POTTED PRAWN PATE

225g/8oz peeled cooked prawns (shrimp)
125g/4oz/8 tbsp butter, softened
grated zest of 1 small lemon
a pinch of cayenne pepper
salt and ground black pepper
sliced baguette or Melba toasts to serve

1 Finely chop the prawns and place them in a bowl with half the butter, the lemon zest, cayenne and seasoning. Mix everything together well.
2 Spoon the prawn mixture into four ramekin dishes. Melt the remaining butter and pour over the top.
3 Chill in the refrigerator for at least 1 hour. Serve the pâté with sliced baguette or Melba toasts.

preparation 15 minutes plus chilling

Serves 4

TROUT WITH APPLE AND BEETROOT SALAD

4 x 150g/5oz trout fillets
1 tbsp olive oil plus extra to grease
2 apples, cored and cubed
4 cooked beetroot (not in vinegar), cubed
1 bunch of watercress
salt and ground black pepper
whole chives to garnish

For the dressing
3 tbsp olive oil
juice of 1 lemon
1 tsp Dijon mustard
a pinch of sugar

1 Preheat the oven to 200°C/400°F/Gas 6.
2 Put each trout fillet on a square of lightly oiled kitchen foil. Brush the fish with oil and season lightly with salt and pepper. Fold the foil around the fish to make a parcel. Press the edges together to seal, then bake in the oven for 15–20 minutes until the fish is cooked and tender.
3 Mix all the dressing ingredients together in a small bowl.
4 Put the apples, beetroot and watercress in a bowl. Add the dressing and mix together lightly.
5 Divide the salad among four serving plates. Add the trout fillets and garnish with chives.

preparation 15 minutes   cooking time 15–20 minutes

Serves 4

SMOKED TROUT AND TOMATO TOASTS

7 tbsp crème fraiche
2 tbsp horseradish cream
grated zest and juice of ½ lemon
300g/11oz smoked trout fillets, skinned and flaked
4 ripe tomatoes, sliced
olive oil to drizzle
4 thick slices bread
2 tbsp chopped fresh dill
a handful of mixed salad leaves
1 tbsp balsamic vinegar
salt and ground black pepper

1. Put the crème fraîche and horseradish cream, lemon zest and juice in a bowl and whisk together. Add the smoked trout and stir gently through the mixture.
2. Preheat the grill (broiler). Arrange the sliced tomatoes on a foil-lined grill pan and drizzle lightly with oil. Grill (broil) for 3–4 minutes until softened.
3. Toast the bread lightly on both sides.
4. Place a slice of toast on each serving plate. Arrange the warm sliced tomatoes on top and season with salt and pepper. Spoon the trout mixture over the tomatoes and sprinkle with dill.
5. Arrange a few salad leaves on the side of each plate. Drizzle with balsamic vinegar and serve.

preparation 20 minutes   cooking time 5 minutes

Serves 4

SMOKED MACKEREL PATE

300g/11oz smoked mackerel
125g/4oz/½ cup cream cheese
3 tbsp horseradish cream
grated zest of 1 lemon
ground black pepper
crusty bread to serve

1. Skin the mackerel and pick out any bones. Mash the flesh with a fork in a bowl.
2. Mix the mackerel with the cream cheese, horseradish cream and lemon zest. You can do this in a blender or food processor. Season with pepper.
3. Spoon into a serving dish and level the top. Cover and chill in the refrigerator, preferably overnight.
4. Serve the pâté with crusty bread.

preparation 10 minutes plus chilling

Serves 6

BOUILLABAISSE

2 tbsp olive oil
1 onion, chopped
1 fennel bulb, chopped
2 celery sticks, sliced
2 garlic cloves, crushed
450g/1lb tomatoes, chopped
1 tsp tomato paste
1 strip of orange zest
1.2 litres/2 pints/5 cups hot fish stock
a pinch of saffron
1kg/2¼lb cubed fish fillets and shellfish, e.g. red mullet, white fish, live mussels, prawns (shrimp) and crabmeat
4 tbsp chopped fresh parsley
salt and ground black pepper

1　Heat the oil in a large pan, add the onion, fennel, celery and garlic and cook over a low heat for 10 minutes or until softened. Add the tomatoes, tomato paste and orange zest, fish stock and saffron.
2　Season with salt and pepper and bring to the boil. Reduce the heat and simmer gently for 30 minutes.
3　Add the fish pieces and shellfish and cook for 5 minutes or until the fish is tender and just cooked and the mussels have opened – discard any mussels that stay closed.
4　Remove and discard the strip of orange peeel. Stir in the parsley and serve in four warmed bowls.

preparation 15 minutes　cooking time 50 minutes

Serves 4

SEAFOOD COCKTAIL

½ iceberg lettuce, shredded
340g/12oz cooked peeled prawns (shrimps) and white crabmeat
snipped fresh chives to garnish

For the dressing
5 tbsp mayonnaise
2 tbsp tomato chutney
dash of Tabasco
squeeze of lemon juice
salt and ground black pepper

1　Line four small glasses with shredded lettuce.
2　To make the dressing, put the mayonnaise in a bowl and mix with the tomato chutney, Tabasco and lemon juice. Season with salt and pepper to taste.
3　Mix the prawns and crabmeat into the dressing and spoon the mixture into the glasses.
4　Sprinkle with chives and serve.

preparation 15 minutes

Serves 4

CEVICHE

450g/1lb white fish fillets, skinned and cut into thin strips

1 red onion, thinly sliced

juice of 6 limes

2 tbsp olive oil

a pinch of sugar

4 tomatoes, seeded and roughly chopped

1 red chilli, diced

1 ripe avocado, peeled, stoned and diced

2 tbsp chopped fresh coriander (cilantro) plus extra to garnish

salt and ground black pepper

tortilla chips to serve

1 Put the fish strips in a bowl with the red onion. Pour over the lime juice and sprinkle lightly with salt. Cover and chill in the refrigerator for 24 hours, turning the fish occasionally.
2 Drain the fish and red onion from the marinade and mix with the oil, sugar, tomatoes, chilli, avocado and coriander. Season to taste with salt and pepper.
3 Divide among four serving plates, sprinkle with coriander and serve with tortilla chips.

preparation 20 minutes plus overnight chilling **cooking time** 7 minutes plus cooling and chilling   *Serves 4*

SPANISH FRIED SQUID

½ tbsp olive oil

340g/12oz baby squid, sliced

1 garlic clove, crushed

75g/3oz chorizo, cubed

75g/3oz rocket (arugula)

2 lemons, halved

sea salt and ground black pepper

1 Heat the oil in a frying pan and cook the squid and garlic for 1 minute over a medium heat or until the squid is cooked. Drain on kitchen paper and then transfer to a warmed serving dish. Sprinkle with sea salt and a good grinding of black pepper.
2 Cook the chorizo for 3–4 minutes until they turn golden and the fat runs.
3 Divide the rocket among four serving plates. Top with the chorizo and squid and serve with the lemons for people to squeeze over the top.

preparation 5 minutes **cooking time** 5 minutes   *Serves 4*

BALSAMIC-GLAZED SCALLOPS

175g/6oz pancetta cubes

18 scallops (with or without the corals), cleaned

1 tbsp olive oil

squeeze of lemon juice

salt and ground black pepper

a few drops of balsamic glaze

whole chives to garnish

1 Fry the pancetta in a large frying pan over a medium heat, turning occasionally, for 6–8 minutes or until golden brown. Remove from the pan and set aside.
2 Pat the scallops dry with kitchen paper and season with salt and pepper. Heat the oil in the pancetta pan and cook the scallops over a high heat for 3–4 minutes, turning halfway, until lightly golden and tender. Do not overcook.
3 Divide the scallops among six plates and spoon the pancetta mixture and any remaining oil around them. Add a squeeze of lemon juice. Dot the plates with balsamic glaze and serve immediately, garnished with whole chives.

preparation 15 minutes cooking time 15 minutes

Serves 6

SCALLOPS WITH ROCKET PESTO

16 scallops

olive oil to brush

salt and ground black pepper

lemon wedges to serve

For the rocket pesto

75g/3oz rocket

25g/1oz/¼ cup pinenuts (pignoli)

2 garlic cloves, crushed

50g/2oz/⅓ cup freshly grated Parmesan

juice of ½ lemon

150ml/¼ pint/scant ⅔ cup olive oil

1 To make the pesto, put the rocket, pinenuts, garlic, Parmesan and lemon juice in a food processor or blender. Blitz until well blended. With the motor running, gradually pour in the olive oil until thoroughly combined. Season with salt and pepper. Transfer to a serving bowl and set aside.
2 Pat the scallops dry with kitchen paper. Brush with a little oil and season with salt and pepper.
3 Grill (broil) the scallops for 2 minutes, turning once, until browned and just cooked through. Take care not to overcook them. Garnish with lemon wedges and serve with pesto.

preparation 15 minutes cooking time 2 minutes

Serves 4

MOULES MARINIERE

2kg/4½lb live mussels, scrubbed and beards removed

25g/1oz/2 tbsp butter

1 small onion, finely chopped

1 garlic clove, crushed

125ml/4fl oz/½ cup medium white wine

125ml/4fl oz/½ cup double (heavy) cream

4 tbsp chopped fresh parsley

salt and ground black pepper

1 Discard any mussels that are open or have broken shells. Heat the butter in a large pan and cook the onion and garlic over a medium heat for 10 minutes or until softened.

2 Add the wine to the pan and bring to the boil. Tip in the mussels and reduce the heat. Cover the pan and cook for 5 minutes, shaking the pan occasionally, until all the shells have opened – discard any mussels that fail to open.

3 Remove the mussels with a slotted spoon and put into serving bowls.

4 Add the cream and parsley to the pan, season with salt and pepper and cook for 1–2 minutes.

5 Pour the sauce over the mussels and serve immediately.

preparation 15 minutes   cooking time 20 minutes

Serves 4

LOBSTER THERMIDOR

25g/1oz/2 tbsp butter

1 shallot, finely chopped

4 tbsp white wine

300ml/½ pint/1¼ cups béchamel sauce (see page 572)

4 x 450g/1lb prepared cooked lobsters

2 tbsp chopped fresh parsley

1 tsp Dijon mustard

juice of ½ lemon

4 tbsp freshly grated Parmesan

a pinch of paprika

salt and ground black pepper

1 Melt the butter in a pan, add the shallot and cook gently over a low heat for 5 minutes or until softened. Add the wine and let it bubble away until reduced by half. Add the béchamel sauce and simmer until reduced.

2 Add the lobster meat to the sauce with the parsley, mustard, lemon juice and salt and pepper to taste.

3 Preheat the grill (broiler). Spoon the mixture into the lobster shells and sprinkle with the Parmesan.

4 Pop under the hot grill until browned and bubbling. Serve immediately, dusted with paprika.

preparation 30 minutes   cooking time 15 minutes

Serves 4

SCAMPI PROVENCALE

3 tbsp olive oil

1 onion, finely chopped

3 garlic cloves, crushed

1 tbsp tomato paste

150ml/¼ pint/scant ⅔ cup white wine

675g/1½lb tomatoes, skinned, seeded and roughly chopped

675g/1½lb peeled raw scampi or tiger prawns (jumbo shrimp)

salt and ground black pepper

3 tbsp chopped fresh parsley

1 Heat the oil in a large frying pan, add the onion and cook over a medium heat for 5 minutes. Add the garlic and cook for 1 minute, then stir in the tomato paste and cook for 1 minute. Pour in the wine, bring to the boil and let it bubble away for 10 minutes or until well reduced.

2 Add the chopped tomatoes and season with salt and pepper to taste. Bring to the boil, then reduce the heat and simmer gently for 5 minutes or until pulpy.

3 Add the scampi or tiger prawns to the hot sauce and simmer gently, stirring, for 2–3 minutes until they turn pink.

4 Scatter with parsley and serve immediately with rice.

preparation 25 minutes **cooking time** 20 minutes

Serves 4

SHELLFISH CURRY

1 tbsp coconut oil

1 lemongrass stalk, chopped

1 red chilli, diced

a handful of fresh coriander (cilantro), chopped

2 kaffir lime leaves, chopped

1 tbsp Thai green or red curry paste

1 x 400ml/14fl oz can coconut milk

475ml/16fl oz/2 cups fish stock

400g/14oz scallops

250g/9oz peeled raw tiger prawns (shrimp)

1 Heat the oil in a wok or deep frying pan over a high heat. Add the lemongrass, chilli, most of the coriander and the lime leaves and stir-fry for 1 minute. Add the curry paste and fry for 1 minute.

2 Add the coconut milk and stock and bring to the boil. Reduce the heat and simmer for 5–10 minutes until slightly reduced.

3 Add the scallops and prawns and bring back to the boil, then reduce the heat and simmer gently for 2–3 minutes until the scallops are cooked and the prawns turn pink.

4 Serve the curry, sprinkled with the remaining chopped coriander, with some boiled rice or noodles.

preparation 10 minutes **cooking time** 10–15 minutes

Serves 6

DRESSED CRAB

900g/2lb prepared crabs in their shells
1 tbsp lemon juice
2 tbsp fresh white breadcrumbs
1 hard-boiled egg
2 tbsp finely chopped fresh parsley
salt and ground black pepper
cayenne pepper to dust
mixed salad leaves and thinly sliced brown bread and butter to serve

1 Flake the white crab meat into a bowl, removing any pieces of shell, then add 1 tsp lemon juice and season to taste.
2 Put the brown crab meat in another bowl and stir in the breadcrumbs and remaining lemon juice. Season with salt and pepper to taste.
3 Put the white crab meat into the crab shells, arranging it down either side. Spoon the brown meat into the centre.
4 Finely chop the egg white and press the yolk through a sieve.
5 Arrange neat lines of chopped parsley, sieved egg yolk and chopped egg white between the white and brown crab meat.
6 Dust lightly with some cayenne pepper. Serve with salad leaves with some brown bread and butter.

preparation 30 minutes

Serves 2

CRABCAKES WITH CHILLI MAYO

250g/9oz/1 cup white crab meat
2 spring onions (scallions), chopped
1 red chilli, finely chopped
2 tsp grated fresh root ginger
1 tbsp Thai fish sauce
1 tbsp mayonnaise
2 tbsp chopped fresh coriander (cilantro)
50g/2oz/1 cup white breadcrumbs
plain flour to dust
1 tbsp oil

For the chilli mayo
150ml/¼ pint/scant ⅔ cup mayonnaise
1 garlic clove, crushed
2 tbsp Thai sweet chilli sauce

1 To make the crabcakes, put the crab meat, spring onions, chilli, ginger, fish sauce, mayonnaise and coriander in a blender or food processor and blitz until combined.
2 Add the breadcrumbs and blitz briefly. Form the mixture into 12 small patties and dust them lightly with flour. Cover and chill in the refrigerator for 1 hour.
3 To make the chilli mayo, mix together the mayonnaise, garlic and sweet chilli sauce in a bowl. Set aside.
4 Heat the oil in a frying pan over a medium heat and add the crabcakes. Cook for 2–3 minutes on each side or until crisp and golden brown.
5 Serve the hot crabcakes with the chilli mayo.

preparation 15 minutes plus chilling cooking time 6 minutes

Serves 4

SEAFOOD FRITTO MISTO

450g/1lb squid, cleaned

340g/12oz whitebait

450g/1lb firm white fish fillets, e.g. cod or haddock, skinned, and cut into thin strips

12 large raw prawns (shrimp), peeled with tails intact

4 tbsp seasoned flour

vegetable oil for deep-frying

salt and ground black pepper

lemon wedges and fresh parsley sprigs to garnish

1 Slice the body of the squid into rings and the tentacles into pieces. Toss all the fish and shellfish in seasoned flour.
2 Heat the oil in a deep-fat fryer to 190°C/375°F – test by frying a small cube of bread; it should brown in 20 seconds. Fry the fish and shellfish, in batches, until crisp and golden. Drain on kitchen paper and keep warm while frying the rest.
3 Divide the fish and shellfish among six warmed plates. Season with salt and pepper and serve immediately with sprigs of parsley and lemon wedges.

preparation 20 minutes   **cooking time** 10 minutes

Serves 6

FRIED DOVER SOLE

2 x 275g/10oz Dover soles, gutted and descaled

3 tbsp plain (all-purpose) flour

2 tbsp olive oil

25g/1oz/2 tbsp unsalted butter

3 tbsp chopped fresh parsley

juice of ½ lemon

salt and ground black pepper

lemon wedges to serve

1 Pat the Dover soles dry with kitchen paper. Put the flour on a large plate and season with salt and pepper. Dip the fish into the seasoned flour to coat both sides evenly.
2 Heat 1 tbsp oil in a large frying pan and fry one Dover sole for 4–5 minutes on each side until golden. Transfer to a plate and keep warm.
3 Add the remaining oil to the pan and cook the other sole in the same way, then remove and keep warm.
4 Melt the butter to the pan and remove from the heat. Add the parsley and lemon juice and season to taste with salt and pepper.
5 Pour over the fish and serve with lemon wedges.

preparation 5 minutes   **cooking time** 20 minutes

Serves 2

SEA BASS WITH ORANGE SAUCE

6 x 125g/4oz sea bass fillets
4 tbsp olive oil
salt and ground black pepper
finely chopped parsley to garnish
new potatoes or rice to serve

For the orange sauce
1 tsp cornflour (cornstarch)
300ml/½ pint/1¼ cups double (heavy) cream
finely grated zest and juice of 2 oranges
salt and ground black pepper

1 Score the skin of the sea bass 3 or 4 times with a knife. Season lightly with salt and pepper.
2 Heat the oil in a large frying pan over a medium heat. Add the sea bass, skin-side down, and press down with a spatula to flatten the fish. Cook for 3–4 minutes until the skin is crisp and golden, the turn the fish over and cook the other side for 2 minutes. Remove and keep warm.
3 Blend the cornflour with a little cold water in a small pan, then stir in the cream and orange zest and juice. Cook over a low heat, stirring, until slightly thickened. Simmer gently for 2–3 minutes and season to taste.
4 Divide the sea bass among six serving plates. Pour a little sauce around the fish and sprinkle with parsley. Serve with new potatoes or boiled rice.

preparation 25 minutes   cooking time 40 minutes

Serves 6

CRAB SALAD

50g/2oz mixed baby salad leaves
2 small dressed crabs
snipped chives to garnish
crusty bread to serve

For the orange vinaigrette
3 tbsp olive oil
grated zest and juice of 1 orange
1 tbsp cider vinegar
1 tsp Dijon mustard
salt and ground black pepper

1 To make the orange vinaigrette, whisk all the ingredients together in a bowl until thoroughly combined.
2 Toss the salad leaves in the orange vinaigrette.
3 Divide the dressed leaves between two serving plates. Add the dressed crabs, sprinkle with chives and serve with some crusty bread.

preparation 20 minutes

Serves 2

TROUT WITH ALMONDS

4 trout, cleaned and gutted
2 tbsp plain (all-purpose) flour
75g/3oz/5 tbsp butter
50g/2oz/¼ cup flaked almonds
juice of ½ lemon
4 tbsp chopped fresh parsley
salt and ground black pepper

1 Rinse the trout and pat dry with kitchen paper. Put the flour on a plate and season with salt and pepper. Dust the fish with the seasoned flour to coat lightly.
2 Melt most of the butter in a large frying pan over a medium heat. Fry the trout, two at a time, for 6–7 minutes on each side, turning once, until golden brown, crisp and cooked.
3 Remove from the pan, drain on kitchen paper and keep warm. Wipe out the pan.
4 Melt the remaining butter in the pan and fry the almonds until lightly browned. Add the lemon juice and parsley and spoon over the trout. Serve immediately.

preparation 5 minutes   cooking time 10–15 minutes

Serves 4

SALMON LAKSA

1 tbsp coconut oil
1 onion, thinly sliced
1–2 tbsp Thai red curry paste
200ml/7fl oz/¾ cup coconut milk
900ml/1½ pints/3⅔ cups hot fish or chicken stock
200g/7oz baby corn
500g/1lb 2oz skinless salmon fillet, cut into thick slices
225g/8oz beansprouts
300g/11oz rice noodles
salt and ground black pepper
bunch of spring onions (scallions), sliced
small bunch of fresh coriander (cilantro), chopped

1 Heat the oil in a wok or deep frying pan, then add the onion and fry over a medium heat for 10 minutes, stirring, until golden. Add the curry paste and cook for 2 minutes.
2 Add the coconut milk, hot stock and baby corn and season with salt and pepper. Bring to the boil, then reduce the heat and simmer for 5 minutes.
3 Add the salmon and beansprouts. Cook over a low heat, stirring occasionally, for 4 minutes or until the fish is cooked and opaque all the way through.
4 Meanwhile, put the noodles in a large heatproof bowl, pour boiling water over to cover and soak for 30 seconds, or cook according to the pack instructions. Drain well, then stir them into the curry with the spring onions and coriander.
5 Pour into four warmed serving bowls and serve immediately.

preparation 10 minutes   cooking time 20 minutes

Serves 4

GRILLED SARDINES

900g/2lb sardines, gutted
6 tbsp olive oil
3 tbsp lemon juice
2 tsp grated lemon zest
4 tbsp chopped fresh parsley
salt and ground black pepper
crusty bread to serve

1 Preheat the grill (broiler). Rinse the sardines and pat dry with kitchen paper. Remove the bones if wished.
2 In a bowl, mix together the oil, lemon juice, lemon zest, parsley and seasoning.
3 Place the sardines on a grill (broiling) rack, drizzle the dressing over them and grill (broil) under a medium-high heat for 5–7 minutes each side, basting frequently with the dressing. Serve hot with crusty bread.

preparation 10–30 minutes   **cooking time** 10 minutes

Serves 4

SWISS CHEESE FONDUE

1 large garlic clove, halved
200ml/7fl oz/¾ cup white wine
1 tbsp lemon juice
175g/6oz Gruyère cheese, grated
175g/6oz Emmental cheese, grated
ground black pepper
cubed crusty bread to serve

1 Rub the halved garlic clove around the inside of a fondue pan or heavy-based pan.
2 Put the wine, lemon juice and cheeses in the pan with the cheeses and gradually bring to the boil over a very low heat, stirring all the time.
3 Simmer gently for 3–4 minutes, stirring frequently. Season with black pepper.
4 Set the pan over the fondue burner (or over a heated serving tray) at the table. Serve with cubed crusty bread for dipping into the fondue.

preparation 10 minutes   cooking time 10 minutes

Serves 4

BROCCOLI AND GOAT'S CHEESE SOUP

2 tbsp olive oil
2 onions, chopped
2 celery sticks, diced
1 litre/1¾ pints/4 cups hot vegetable stock
900g/2lb broccoli, broken into florets, stalks chopped
125g/4oz goat's cheese
salt and ground black pepper
6 tbsp soured cream

1 Heat the oil in a pan over a low heat. Add the onions and celery, cover the pan and cook for 10 minutes or until tender. Add the stock and bring to the boil.
2 Add the broccoli and return to the boil, then cover the pan, reduce the heat and simmer gently for 15–20 minutes until the broccoli is tender.
3 Leave the soup to cool a little, then add the goat's cheese and blitz in batches in a blender or food processor until smooth. Return to the pan and reheat gently. Season to taste with salt and pepper.
4 Ladle the soup into warmed bowls and serve immediately with a swirl of cream.

preparation 10 minutes   cooking time 25–30 minutes

Serves 6

CREAMY CELERIAC SOUP

2 tbsp olive oil

1 large onion, chopped

450g/1lb celeriac , chopped

450g/1lb potatoes, chopped

1.2 litres/2 pints/5 cups hot
vegetable stock

300ml/½ pint/1¼ cups milk

300ml/½ pint/1¼ cups double
(heavy) cream

4 tbsp chopped fresh parsley

salt and ground black pepper

cheesy croûtons to serve

1 Heat the oil in a large pan, then add the onion and cook over a low heat for 10 minutes or until golden.
2 Add the celeriac, potatoes and hot stock and bring to the boil. Reduce the heat and simmer gently for 20–25 minutes until the celeriac and potatoes are tender.
3 Leave the soup to cool a little, then blitz in batches in a blender or food processor until smooth. Pour into a clean pan and stir in the milk, cream and parsley. Season with salt and pepper and simmer for 10 minutes.
4 Ladle the soup into warmed bowls and serve topped with cheesy croûtons.

preparation 10 minutes **cooking time** 35 minutes

Serves 8

CAMEMBERT MELT

1 x 250g/9oz wooden-boxed
Camembert

leaves stripped from 2 fresh
thyme sprigs

ground black pepper

2 tbsp cranberry sauce

crusty bread to serve

1 Preheat the oven to 200°C/400°F/Gas 6.
2 Take the cheese out of the box and unwrap, leaving it on the waxed paper. Slice off the top rind and discard. Return the cheese (on its paper), cut-side up, to the bottom half of the box and place on a baking sheet.
3 Sprinkle with thyme and season with black pepper. Cook in the oven for 15–20 minutes until the cheese is golden on top and melted inside.
4 Transfer the box to a board and serve with cranberry sauce and crusty bread.

preparation 5 minutes **cooking time** 20 minutes

Serves 2

WILD MUSHROOM RISOTTO

2 tbsp olive oil
25g/1oz/2 tbsp butter
1 onion, finely chopped
2 garlic cloves, crushed
450g/1lb wild mushrooms, sliced
350g/12oz/1½ cups Arborio rice
150ml/¼ pint/scant ⅔ cup white wine
900ml/1½ pints/3⅔ cups hot vegetable stock
4 tbsp creme fraîche
1 tbsp chopped fresh parsley
salt and ground black pepper
grated Parmesan to serve

1 Heat the oil and butter in a heavy-based pan. Add the onion and garlic and cook gently over a low heat for 5 minutes or until the onion has softened.
2 Add the mushrooms and cook gently for about 5 minutes until golden brown and tender. Stir in the rice and cook for 1 minute until the grains are coated with oil.
3 Stir in the wine, bring to the boil and let it bubble away until almost totally evaporated.
4 Gradually add the hot stock, a little at a time, stirring after each addition. When it has been absorbed, add some more. Continue adding the stock slowly until the rice is tender and all the liquid has been absorbed.
5 Season to taste with salt and pepper and stir in the creme fraîche and parsley. Heat through gently.
6 Serve sprinkled with grated Parmesan.

preparation 10 minutes   cooking time 30 minutes

Serves 6

PESTO RISOTTO WITH MUSSELS

50g/2oz/4 tbsp butter
1 large onion, finely chopped
3 garlic cloves, crushed
225g/8oz/1 cup Arborio rice
450ml/¾ pint/1¾ cups white wine
450ml/¾ pint/1¾ cups hot fish or vegetable stock
2 tbsp green pesto
50g/2oz Parmesan, grated
4 tbsp chopped fresh parsley
1.4kg/3lb live mussels, scrubbed and beards removed

1 Heat 2 tbsp butter in a large pan. Add the onion and cook over a low heat for 5 minutes until soft but not coloured. Stir in the garlic and rice and cook for 1 minute.
2 Add 300ml/½ pint/1¼ cups wine and the hot stock, a little at a time, letting the rice absorb the liquid after each addition before adding more.
3 Add the pesto, Parmesan and parsley and take off the heat.
4 Put the mussels in a large pan with the remaining butter, garlic and wine. Cover and cook for 5 minutes, shaking the pan frequently. Discard any mussels that do not open.
5 Divide the risotto among four serving plates. Add the mussels in their cooking juices and serve.

preparation 10 minutes   cooking time 35 minutes

Serves 4

SPECIAL FRIED RICE

225g/8oz/1 cup long-grain rice

2 tbsp oil

1 green (bell) pepper, seeded and chopped

200g/7oz kale, shredded

250g/9oz cooked peeled prawns (shrimp)

2 tbsp soy sauce

1 tbsp sunflower oil

2 medium (US large) eggs, beaten

2 spring onions (scallions), diced

1 Cook the rice according to the pack instructions.
2 Heat 1 tbsp oil in a wok or deep frying pan and stir-fry the green pepper and kale for 2 minutes. Stir in the prawns, then add the cooked rice and soy sauce and cook for about 5 minutes, stirring occasionally.
3 Heat the remaining oil in a non-stick frying pan and add the beaten eggs. Swirl around to cover the bottom of the pan and cook for 2–3 minutes until set and golden.
4 Roll up the omelette and cut it into strips. Serve the rice scattered with omelette strips and spring onions.

preparation 5 minutes **cooking time** 10–15 minutes

Serves 4

BAKED STUFFED PUMPKIN

1 x 1.4kg/3lb pumpkin

2 tbsp olive oil

1 red onion, chopped

2 garlic cloves, crushed

1 tsp paprika

125g/4oz/½ cup cooked long-grain rice

225g/8oz tomatoes, diced

125g/4oz/1 cup grated mature Cheddar cheese

salt and ground black pepper

1 Sliced the top off the pumpkin and set aside for the lid. Scoop out and discard the seeds. Cut out most of the pumpkin flesh, leaving a thin shell. Cut the pumpkin flesh into small cubes.
2 Heat the oil in a large pan over a low heat and cook the red onion, garlic and paprika for 10 minutes. Add the pumpkin and cook for 10 minutes or until tender and golden, stirring frequently. Transfer to a bowl.
3 Preheat the oven to 180°C/350°F/Gas 4.
4 Mix the pumpkin mixture with the cooked rice and tomatoes, and stir in the cheese. Season with salt and pepper.
5 Spoon the mixture into the pumpkin shell, cover with the lid and bake in the oven for 1¼ –1½ hours until the pumpkin is tender and the skin is browned.
6 Remove from the oven and serve immediately.

preparation 40 minutes **cooking time** 1¼ hours–1 hour 50 minutes plus 10 minutes resting

Serves 4

RED ONION BOULANGERE POTATOES

2kg/4½lb potatoes
2 red onions
butter for greasing
3 garlic cloves, crushed
leaves stripped from 4 fresh thyme sprigs
400ml/14fl oz/1⅔ cups hot vegetable stock
salt and ground black pepper

1 Preheat the oven to 200°C/400°F/Gas 6.
2 Peel the potatoes and cut them into very thin slices. This is best done with a mandolin if you have one.
3 Thinly slice the red onions. Lightly butter a large ovenproof serving dish.
4 Arrange a layer of sliced potatoes across the bottom of the dish and cover with a layer of red onions. Sprinkle with the garlic and thyme and season with salt and pepper. Continue layering the vegetables in this way, finishing with a layer of potatoes. Pour the hot stock over.
5 Cook in the oven for 1 hour. Uncover and cook for 30 minutes or until the potatoes are tender and golden.

preparation 25 minutes   cooking time 1½ hours plus resting

Serves 8

VIETNAMESE RICE SALAD

225g/8oz/1 cup basmati rice
2 tbsp light muscovado sugar
juice of 2 limes
4 tbsp Thai fish sauce
2 tbsp sesame oil
1 red chilli, seeded and diced
1 large carrot
1 large courgette (zucchini)
1 bunch of spring onions (scallions), thinly sliced
2 cooked chicken breasts, shredded
a handful of fresh coriander (cilantro) , chopped

1 Cook the rice according to the pack instructions. Put the drained cooked rice on a plastic tray, spread it out and set aside to cool, then transfer to a bowl.
2 Meanwhile, make the dressing. Put the sugar in a small pan with the lime juice and fish sauce. Stir over a low heat to dissolve the sugar. Remove from the heat and add the oil and chilli. Stir the dressing into the rice.
3 Peel the carrot and courgette into long thin ribbons and add to the rice with the spring onions and chicken.
4 Sprinkle the rice salad with the coriander. Cover and chill in the refrigerator before serving.

preparation 10 minutes   cooking time 20 minutes plus chilling

Serves 6

BROCCOLI AND BLUE CHEESE QUICHE

340g/12oz shortcrust pastry

flour to dust

1 large head broccoli, cut into small florets

125g/4oz blue cheese, e.g. Danish blue, crumbled

2 medium (US large) eggs plus 1 egg yolk

300ml/½ pint/1¼ cups double (heavy) cream

salt and ground black pepper

1 Preheat the oven to 200°C/400°F/Gas 6.
2 Roll out the pastry on a lightly floured surface and use to line a 23cm/9in deep fluted tart tin. Prick the base all over and chill for 15 minutes.
3 Fill with parchment paper and baking beans and cook in the oven for 20 minutes. Remove the paper and beans and reduce the oven temperature to 170°C/335°F/Gas 3.
4 Cook the broccoli in a pan of boiling water for 3 minutes, then drain. Arrange the broccoli in the pastry shell and sprinkle with the blue cheese. Whisk the eggs and egg yolk, cream and seasoning together and pour over the broccoli.
5 Cook in the oven for 40 minutes or until the filling is set and golden brown. Serve cut into slices..

preparation 15 minutes plus chilling **cooking time** 1 hour

Serves 6

GREEN BEANS AND ALMONDS

300g/11oz fine green beans, trimmed

15g/½oz/1 tbsp butter

4 tbsp flaked almonds

juice of ½ lemon

salt and ground black pepper

1 Bring a large pan of water to the boil. Add the green beans and cook for 4–5 minutes. Drain.
2 Meanwhile, melt the butter in a large frying pan. Add the almonds and cook for 1–2 minutes until golden. Remove from the heat, add the drained beans and toss.
3 Season and add the lemon juice, then serve.

preparation 5 minutes   **cooking time** 5–7 minutes

Serves 4

PASTA WITH COURGETTES

450g/1lb pasta ribbons

2 large courgettes (zucchini), coarsely grated

1 red chilli, diced

1 garlic clove, crushed

16 pitted black olives, roughly chopped

3 tbsp olive oil

small bunch of fresh parsley, chopped

4 tbsp freshly grated Parmesan

salt and ground black pepper

1 Cook the pasta in a large pan of lightly salted boiling water according to the pack instructions. About 1 minute before the end of the cooking time, add the courgettes, then simmer until the pasta is just cooked.

2 Meanwhile, cook the chilli, garlic and olives in the oil in a small pan over a low heat for 2–3 minutes.

3 Drain the pasta and courgettes and return to the pan. Stir in the hot chilli mixture and toss with the parsley. Season to taste with salt and pepper.

4 Divide among four shallow serving dishes and serve sprinkled with Parmesan.

preparation 5 minutes   cooking time 8–10 minutes

Serves 4

PASTA SHELLS WITH CHEESE AND TOMATOES

450g/1lb pasta shells

2 tbsp olive oil

1 red and 1 yellow (bell) pepper, seeded and chopped

1 tbsp tomato paste

75g/3oz sunblush tomatoes

125g/4oz soft goat's cheese

4 tbsp chopped fresh parsley

salt and ground black pepper

1 Cook the pasta in a large pan of lightly salted boiling water according to the pack instructions.

2 Meanwhile, heat the oil in a pan and cook the red and yellow peppers over a low heat for 6–7 minutes until softened and just beginning to brown. Add the tomato paste and cook for 1 minute. Add a ladleful of pasta cooking water to the pan and simmer for 2–3 minutes.

3 Drain the pasta and return to the pan. Pour the sauce over the top, and stir in the tomatoes, goat's cheese and parsley

4 Toss together, season to taste and serve.

preparation 5 minutes   cooking time 10 minutes

Serves 4

BRAISED CHICORY

50g/2oz/4 tbsp butter
6 chicory (Belgian endive), heads, trimmed
125ml/4fl oz/½ cup white wine
salt and ground black pepper
chopped fresh chives to serve

1 Preheat the oven to 190°C/375°F/Gas 5.
2 Grease a large ovenproof dish with 15g/½oz/1 tbsp butter and place the chicory in the dish.
3 Season with salt and pepper, add the wine and dot the remaining butter over the top. Cover with foil and cook in the oven for 1 hour or until soft. Sprinkle with chives and serve.

preparation 5 minutes   cooking time 1 hour

Serves 6

HONEY-GLAZED SHALLOTS

450g/1lb shallots, halved
25g/1oz/2 tbsp butter
1 tbsp runny honey
2 tbsp balsamic vinegar
salt and ground black pepper

1 Put the shallots in a wide pan with just enough cold water to cover them. Bring to the boil, then reduce the heat and simmer for 5 minutes. Drain well and return to the pan.
2 Add the remaining ingredients and stir until the shallots are coated with the glaze.
3 Cover the pan and cook gently, stirring occasionally, until the shallots are tender.
4 Remove the lid and let it bubble away for 2–3 minutes until the liquid is reduced and syrupy. Serve hot.

preparation 15 minutes plus soaking   cooking time 25 minutes

Serves 4

CREAMED SPINACH

900g/2lb spinach leaves, stalks removed and washed
6 tbsp crème fraîche
salt and ground black pepper
a pinch of freshly grated nutmeg

1 Cook the spinach with just the water clinging to the leaves in a covered large pan for 3–4 minutes until just wilted.
2 Stir in the crème fraîche and season with salt and pepper to taste and some nutmeg. Serve immediately.

preparation 15 minutes   **cooking time** 5 minutes

Serves 6

GREEN CABBAGE WITH CREME FRAICHE

1 x 900g/2lb Savoy cabbage
25g/1oz/2 tbsp butter
200ml/7fl oz/¾ cup crème fraîche
a pinch of grated nutmeg
salt and ground black pepper

1 Cut the Savoy cabbage into large wedges. Bring a pan of salted water to the boil, add the cabbage and return to the boil. Boil for 2 minutes, then drain thoroughly.
2 Heat the butter in a large frying pan, add the cabbage and stir-fry for 3–4 minutes.
3 Stir in the crème fraîche and nutmeg, toss briefly and season with pepper to taste. Serve immediately.

preparation 8 minutes   **cooking time** 5 minutes

Serves 6

PETITS POIS A LA FRANCAISE

1 round lettuce
50g/2oz/4 tbsp butter
900g/2lb fresh peas, shelled
12 spring onions (scallions), sliced
1 tsp sugar
150ml/¼ pint/scant ⅔ cup chicken stock

1 Remove and discard the outer leaves of the lettuce and cut the heart into quarters.
2 Melt the butter in a large pan, add the peas, spring onions, lettuce quarters, sugar and stock.
3 Bring to the boil, then reduce the heat, cover and simmer for 15–20 minutes. Serve immediately.

preparation 5 minutes **cooking time** 15 minutes

Serves 4

ROAST NEW POTATOES

1kg/2lb 2oz baby new potatoes
4 tbsp olive oil
salt and ground black pepper

1 Preheat the oven to 220°C/425°F/Gas 7.
2 Put the potatoes in a roasting pan and drizzle over the oil. Season well and toss gently to mix everything together.
3 Roast the potatoes for 30–35 minutes, turning occasionally, until tender and golden brown. Serve immediately.

preparation 3 minutes **cooking time** 35 minutes

Serves 6

POTATO CROQUETTES

900g/2lb potatoes, scrubbed

150g/5oz/2½ cups fresh white breadcrumbs

50g/2oz/4 tbsp butter, softened, plus extra to grease

75g/3oz/½ cup freshly grated Parmesan

4 tbsp chopped fresh parsley

2 eggs, beaten

olive oil to drizzle

salt and ground black pepper

1 Bring the potatoes to the boil in a pan of cold salted water. Reduce the heat and simmer for 20 minutes or until tender. Preheat the oven to 230°C/450°F/Gas 8.

2 Meanwhile, spread the breadcrumbs out on a baking sheet and bake for 15 minutes or until golden. Transfer to a plate.

3 Drain the potatoes and leave to cool for 5 minutes, then peel and mash until smooth with the butter, Parmesan and parsley. Season with salt and pepper and mix well.

4 Put the beaten eggs in a shallow bowl. Take about 2 tbsp of the potato mixture and shape into a small cylinder. Roll first in the beaten egg and then in the breadcrumbs to coat. Repeat with the remaining potato mixture.

5 Put the croquettes in two buttered roasting pans. Cover and chill for 30 minutes.

6 Drizzle with a little oil and bake in the oven for 25 minutes or until golden brown. Serve immediately.

preparation 30 minutes plus chilling cooking time 45 minutes

Serves 6

GRATIN DAUPHINOIS

900g/2lb potatoes, thinly sliced

1 onion, finely chopped

2 garlic cloves, crushed

125g/4oz Gruyère cheese, grated

150ml/¼ pint/ scant ⅔ cup single (light) cream

150ml/¼ pint/scant ⅔ cup milk

salt and ground black pepper

1 Preheat the oven to 180°C/350°F/Gas 4.

2 Layer the potatoes, onion, garlic and most of the cheese in a greased ovenproof dish. Season with salt and pepper and pour over the cream and milk.

3 Sprinkle with the remaining cheese, cover and cook in the oven for 45 minutes or until the potatoes are tender.

4 Uncover the dish and brown under a hot grill (broiler).

preparation 10 minutes cooking time 50 minutes

Serves 4-6

NEW POTATOES WITH MINT AND PETITS POIS

3 tbsp olive oil
900g/2lb new potatoes, scrubbed and thickly sliced
225g/8oz frozen petits pois
4 tbsp chopped fresh mint
salt and ground black pepper

1 Heat the oil in a large frying pan, add half the potatoes and cook over a medium heat for 5 minutes, turning, until browned on both sides. Remove with a slotted spoon and set aside. Add the rest of the potatoes to the pan and cook in the same way. Return the cooked potatoes to the pan and cook for 10–15 minutes.
2 Meanwhile, cook the petits pois in a pan of boiling water for 2 minutes, then drain well.
3 Add to the potatoes and cook gently for 2–3 minutes.
4 Stir in the mint and salt and pepper to taste, then serve.

preparation 15 minutes   cooking time 30 minutes

Serves 6

FENNEL AU GRATIN

3 fennel bulbs, trimmed
300ml/½ pint/1¼ cups hot vegetable stock
25g/1oz/2 tbsp butter
1 garlic clove, crushed
1 bunch of spring onions (scallions), finely chopped
300ml/½ pint/1¼ cups double (heavy) cream
50g/2oz/½ cup freshly grated Parmesan
salt and ground black pepper

1 Cut the fennel into slices and place in a large shallow pan with the hot stock. Bring to the boil, then reduce the heat, cover the pan and simmer gently for about 10–15 minutes until tender. Strain well, reserving the cooking liquid, and transfer to a gratin dish.
2 Meanwhile, melt the butter in a pan, add the garlic and spring onions and cook gently over a low heat for 5 minutes or until softened.
3 Add 150ml/¼ pint/scant ⅔ cup of the fennel cooking liquid to the pan, pour in the cream and bring to the boil. Reduce the heat and simmer for 1 minute. Remove from the heat and stir in the Parmesan. Season to taste.
4 Pour the sauce over the fennel and cook under a hot grill (broiler) for 1–2 minutes until bubbling and golden.

preparation 10 minutes   cooking time 15–20 minutes

Serves 6

CARAMELIZED CARROTS

700g/1½lb baby carrots
50g/2oz/4 tbsp butter
2 tbsp muscovado sugar
300ml/½ pint/1¼ cups hot
vegetable stock
2 tbsp balsamic vinegar
2 tbsp chopped fresh parsley
salt and ground black pepper

1 Scrape the carrots and cut them in half lengthways.
2 Place them in a pan with the butter, sugar and hot stock. Season with salt and pepper, cover the pan and bring to the boil. Reduce the heat and simmer for 5 minutes.
3 Add the balsamic vinegar, uncover the pan and cook for 5–10 minutes until the carrots are tender and the liquid has reduced to form a sticky glaze.
4 Sprinkle with chopped parsley and serve.

preparation 15 minutes   cooking time 10–15 minutes

Serves 8

SPICED OKRA

1 tbsp diced fresh root ginger
1 onion, quartered
2 garlic cloves, roughly chopped
2 tsp ground coriander
1 tsp turmeric
a pinch of chilli powder
2 tbsp coconut oil
1 x 400g/14oz can chopped
tomatoes
450g/1lb okra, trimmed
4 tbsp Greek yogurt
small bunch of fresh coriander
(cilantro), chopped
salt and ground black pepper

1 Blitz the ginger, onion, garlic and spices in a blender or food processor until smooth.
2 Heat the oil in a large frying pan, add the spice paste and cook over a medium heat for 5 minutes.
3 Add the tomatoes and season with salt and pepper. Cook for 5 minutes or until the tomatoes have reduced, then stir in the okra. Cover the pan and simmer gently for 5 minutes or until the okra is just tender.
4 Stir in the yogurt and coriander and heat through gently without boiling. Serve immediately.

preparation 20 minutes   cooking time 25 minutes

Serves 4

PESTO GOAT'S CHEESE SALAD

100g/3½oz watercress or rocket (arugula)

4 slices goat's cheese log

4 tsp green pesto

8 tbsp walnut halves, toasted

For the dressing

3 tbsp olive oil

1 tbsp cider vinegar

1 tsp honey mustard

salt and ground black pepper

1 To make the dressing, whisk the ingredients together in a bowl, seasoning with salt and pepper to taste.
2 Trim the watercress, if using, and discard the coarse stalks.
3 Place the goat's cheese slices on a foil-lined baking sheet. Cook under a hot grill (broiler) for 2 minutes until starting to melt and turn golden brown.
4 Toss the watercress and/or rocket leaves with the dressing and divide among four serving plates. Put a slice of goat's cheese on top with a spoonful of pesto.
5 Scatter the walnuts over the salad and serve immediately.

preparation 20 minutes **cooking time** 1–2 minutes

Serves 4

ASPARAGUS AND QUAIL'S EGG SALAD

100g/3½oz rocket (arugula)

18 quail's eggs

18 asparagus spears, trimmed

5 tbsp olive oil

1 tbsp white wine vinegar

1 tsp wasabi

1 tsp honey mustard

salt and ground black pepper

1 Add the quail's eggs to a pan of boiling water and cook for 2 minutes, then drain and plunge into cold water.
2 Cook the asparagus in a pan of lightly salted boiling water for 3–4 minutes or until just tender. Drain, plunge into cold water and leave to cool.
3 Whisk together the oil, vinegar, wasabi and honey mustard. Season to taste with salt and pepper.
4 Peel the quail's eggs and cut in half. Put in a large bowl with the asparagus and rocket.
5 Pour the dressing over and lightly toss all the ingredients together. Check the seasoning and serve.

preparation 30 minutes **cooking time** 2 minutes

Serves 6

CHICORY, FENNEL AND ORANGE SALAD

1 small fennel bulb

2 chicory (Belgian endive) heads, separated into leaves

2 oranges, peeled and cut into rounds, plus juice of ½ orange

2 tbsp chopped toasted walnuts

2 tbsp olive oil

1 tbsp balsamic vinegar

salt and ground black pepper

1 Finely slice the fennel bulb and put in a bowl with the chicory, orange slices and toasted walnuts.
2 Put the orange juice, oil and balsamic vinegar in a small bowl, season with salt and pepper and mix thoroughly.
3 Pour the dressing over the salad and toss everything gently together. Serve immediately.

preparation 15 minutes cooking time 2–3 minutes

Serves 4

ASPARAGUS AND MINTY RICE SALAD

175g/6oz/¾ cup basmati rice

1 red onion, finely diced

grated zest and juice of 2 lemons

2 tbsp olive oil

small bunch of fresh mint, roughly chopped

225g/8oz baby asparagus

salt and ground black pepper

1 Cook the rice according to the pack instructions. When cooked, spread the rice out on a baking sheet to cool quickly. When cool, transfer to a large bowl.
2 Stir the red onion, lemon zest and juice, oil and mint into the rice with a fork separating the grains.
3 Bring a large pan of lightly salted water to the boil. Add the asparagus and cook for 3–4 minutes until tender. Drain and refresh in a bowl of cold water.
4 Drain and stir into the rice, then serve immediately.

preparation 10 minutes cooking time 20 minutes

Serves 6

GOAT'S CHEESE AND RADICCHIO SALAD

2 heads radicchio, shredded
125g/4oz rocket (arugula)
1 red onion, finely chopped
150g/5oz walnut pieces
200g/7oz soft goat's cheese
salt and ground black pepper

For the dressing
8 tbsp olive oil
2 tbsp red wine vinegar
1 tsp runny honey

1 Whisk all the ingredients for the dressing together in a small bowl and set aside.
2 Put the radicchio, rocket and red onion in a large bowl. Pour the dressing over and toss well. Season to taste.
3 Divide the salad among six serving plates and sprinkle the walnuts over. Crumble the goat's cheese on top and serve.

preparation 10 minutes

Serves 6

WARM QUORN AND RASPBERRY SALAD

2 tbsp olive oil
1 onion, sliced
250g/9oz Quorn pieces
2 tbsp raspberry vinegar
150g/5oz/1 cup raspberries
175g/6oz mixed salad leaves
salt and ground black pepper

1 Heat the oil in a frying pan, add the onion and cook over a medium heat for 5 minutes or until soft and golden. Increase the heat and add the Quorn pieces. Cook, stirring frequently, for 5 minutes or until golden brown. Season with salt and pepper, then place in a large bowl and set aside.
2 Add the vinegar and 75ml/3fl oz/5 tbsp water to the pan. Bring to the boil and bubble for 1–2 minutes until it reaches a syrupy consistency. Add the raspberries.
3 Toss the Quorn, raspberry mixture and salad leaves gently together. Serve immediately.

preparation 5 minutes cooking time 12 minutes

Serves 4

AVOCADO, CLEMENTINE AND CHICORY SALAD

4 chicory (Belgian endive) heads, leaves separated

3 clementines, peeled and thinly sliced into rounds

2 ripe avocados, peeled, stoned and sliced

2 tbsp pinenuts (pignoli), toasted

For the dressing
juice of 3 clementines
4 tbsp olive oil
4 tbsp chopped fresh parsley
1 red chilli, diced

1 To make the dressing, put the orange juice in a small bowl with the oil and chilli. Whisk everything together.
2 Mix the chicory leaves with the clementines and avocado slices and divide among six serving plates.
3 Sprinkle the pinenuts over and spoon the dressing over the salad. Serve immediately.

preparation 10 minutes

Serves 6

BLUE CHEESE AND REDCURRANT SALAD

100g/3½oz mixed curly endive, radicchio and chicory (Belgian endive)

175g/6oz Gorgonzola or Danish blue, crumbled

125g/4oz fresh redcurrants

For the dressing
2 tbsp redcurrant jelly
3 tbsp olive oil
1 tbsp cider vinegar
1 tsp Dijon mustard
salt and ground black pepper

1 To make the dressing, put the redcurrant jelly, vinegar, mustard and oil in a small bowl and whisk together. Season to taste with salt and pepper.
2 Arrange the mixed salad leaves on a large plate and crumble the blue cheese over the top.
3 Spoon the dressing over the salad, sprinkle with redcurrants and serve.

preparation 10 minutes

Serves 4

FRUITY PARMESAN SALAD

2 large ripe pears, peeled, cored
and thickly sliced
125g/4oz rocket (arugula)
1 head radicchio, sliced
125g/4oz Parmesan, shaved
4 tbsp chopped walnuts
seeds of 1 pomegranate

For the dressing
3 tbsp olive oil
juice of 1 lemon
1 tbsp cider vinegar
1 tsp Dijon mustard
salt and ground black pepper

1 Whisk all the dressing ingredients together in a small bowl
   and season with salt and pepper.
2 Put the pears in a bowl. Pour the dressing over and toss
   together. Set aside to marinate for 15 minutes.
3 Put the rocket and radicchio in a large bowl. Add the pears
   and dressing and toss with the Parmesan shavings.
4 Divide the salad among four serving plates and top with the
   walnuts and pomegranate seeds. Serve immediately.

preparation 15 minutes plus marinating

Serves 4

WARM TOFU AND BEAN SALAD

2 tbsp olive oil
1 red onion, thinly sliced
1 tbsp balsamic vinegar
1 x 400g/14oz can red kidney
beans, drained and rinsed
4 tbsp chopped fresh parsley
juice of 1 lemon
225g/8oz smoked tofu, sliced
salt and ground black pepper

1 Heat the oil in a large frying pan. Add the onion and cook
   over a medium heat for 5–10 minutes. Stir in the vinegar and
   cook gently for 2 minutes.
2 Stir in the beans and parsley. Season with salt and pepper,
   then remove and place in a bowl with the lemon juice.
3 Add the tofu to the pan and cook for 2 minutes on each side
   or until golden.
4 Divide the bean mixture among four serving plates, top with
   the tofu and serve.

preparation 10 minutes   **cooking time** 15 minutes

Serves 4

BEAN AND SUNBLUSH TOMATO SALAD

1 red onion, diced

a small handful of fresh flat-leaf parsley, chopped

2 x 400g/14oz cans butter (lima) beans, drained and rinsed

75g/3oz sunblush tomatoes

For the dressing

1 ripe large avocado

4 tbsp olive oil

2 tbsp red wine vinegar

1 garlic clove, crushed

preparation 5 minutes plus marinating

1 To make the dressing, cut the avocado in half and remove the stone and peel. Scoop out the flesh and mash in a bowl. Add the oil, vinegar and garlic and mix together well until smooth and creamy.
2 Put the red onion, parsley, beans and sunblush tomatoes in a large bowl. Mix together and pour over the dressing. Toss gently until everything is lightly coated.
3 Divide the salad among six serving plates and serve.

Serves 6

FETA AND AVOCADO SALAD

24 baby plum tomatoes, halved

bunch of spring onions (scallions), sliced

6 tbsp chopped fresh coriander (cilantro)

2 ripe avocados

juice of 1 lime

200g/7oz feta cheese, crumbled

olive oil and balsamic vinegar to drizzle

salt and ground black pepper

tortilla chips to garnish

preparation 15 minutes   **cooking time** 20 minutes

1 Divide the baby plum tomatoes among six serving plates, then scatter the spring onions and coriander over the top.
2 Peel, stone and slice the avocados, sprinkle with lime juice and add to the plates. Crumble over the feta cheese.
3 Drizzle with olive oil and balsamic vinegar and season with salt and pepper.
4 Roughly crush the tortilla chips and sprinkle over the top of the salad and serve immediately.

Serves 6

WINTER SALAD

75g/3oz watercress

1 radicchio head

2 chicory (Belgian endive) heads

75g/3oz/¾ cup roughly chopped walnuts, toasted

3 red apples

For the dressing

4 tbsp olive oil

juice of 1 lemon

2 tbsp white wine vinegar

1 To make the dressing, mix the oil, lemon and vinegar together in a small bowl or jug.
2 Remove the woody stems from the watercress and put in a large bowl. Separate the radicchio and chicory into leaves and add to the bowl with the walnuts.
3 Core the apples and cut into small chunks. Mix with the salad leaves and nuts.
4 Toss the salad in the dressing and serve.

preparation 10 minutes   **cooking time** 2 minutes

Serves 6

PINK GRAPEFRUIT AND AVOCADO SALAD

225g/8oz green beans, trimmed

1 avocado, halved, stoned, peeled and sliced

1 pink grapefruit, segmented

75g/3oz rocket (arugula)

6 tbsp vinaigrette (see page 592)

1 Blanch the green beans in a pan of lightly salted boiling water for 2 minutes. Drain, refresh and drain again.
2 Cut the beans in half and mix with the avocado, grapefruit and rocket. Toss lightly in the vinaigrette and serve.

preparation 10 minutes   **cooking time** 1 minute

Serves 4

TOP 10 DRINKS

LEMONADE

4 lemons
175g/6oz/¾ cup sugar

1 Remove the lemon zest thinly with a potato peeler. Put the zest and sugar in a jug and pour on 900ml/1½ pints/3⅔ cups boiling water. Leave to cool, stirring occasionally.
2 Add the juice of the lemons and strain the lemonade. Serve chilled.

preparation 10 minutes

Serves 6

HEALTHY CRUSH

175g/6oz/1½ cups raspberries
100ml/3½fl oz/⅓ cup fresh orange juice
100ml/3½fl oz/⅓ cup almond milk, chilled
100g/3½ oz/⅓ cup low-fat natural yogurt, chilled
40g/1½oz/½ cup fine oatmeal
1 tsp wheat bran

1 Put all the ingredients in a blender and blitz until smooth. Pour into two glasses.

preparation 5 minutes

Serves 2

GINGER SODA

225g/8oz unpeeled fresh root ginger, finely sliced
175g/6oz/¾ cup caster (superfine) sugar
zest and juice of 2 lemons
1 litre/1¾ pints/4 cups soda water

1 Heat the ginger, sugar, lemon zest and juice in a pan with 600ml/1 pint/2½ cups cold water. Stir well and simmer for 10 minutes.
2 Strain through a fine sieve into a jug. When cool, top up with soda water.

preparation 5 minutes
cooking time 10–15 minutes,
    plus cooling

Serves 6

VITAMIN C TONIC

1 large orange, peeled
1 lemon, peeled
1 lime, peeled
½ pink grapefruit, peeled
1 tsp runny honey

1 Chop the flesh of all the fruits, discarding any pips, and put in a blender with honey to taste. Blitz until smooth and pour over crushed ice in a glass.

preparation 10 minutes

Serves 1

IRISH COFFEE

2 tbsp Irish whiskey
1 tsp brown sugar
125ml/4fl oz/½ cup hot strong coffee
2 tbsp double (heavy) cream, chilled

1 Put the whiskey and sugar in a glass. Add the black coffee and stir well. Fill to the brim with cream, poured over the back of a spoon, and stand for a few minutes.

preparation 5 minutes plus standing *Serves 1*

BLOODY MARY

1 tbsp Worcestershire sauce
dash of Tabasco sauce
2 tbsp vodka, chilled
150ml/¼ pint/scant ⅔ cup tomato juice, chilled
lemon juice and celery salt to taste

1 Pour the sauces, vodka and tomato juice into a tall glass and stir. Add ice cubes and the lemon juice and celery salt to taste.

preparation 2 minutes *Serves 1*

EGG NOG

1 medium (US large) egg
1 tsp sugar
50ml/2fl oz/¼ cup sherry
300ml/½ pint/1¼ cups milk

1 Beat the egg and sugar and add the sherry. Heat the milk and pour over the egg mixture. Stir well and serve hot in a glass.

preparation 5 minutes
cooking time 3 minutes   *Serves 1*

KIR

2 tbsp crème de cassis
150ml/¼ pint/scant ⅔ cup white wine

1 Pour the crème di cassis and white wine into a glass and serve.

preparation 2 minutes   *Serves 1*

DETOXER

200g/7oz cooked, peeled beetroot
2 tsp chopped fresh root ginger
juice of 1 lemon
150ml/¼ pint/scant ⅔ cup pressed carrot juice
150ml/¼ pint/scant ⅔ cup pressed orange juice

1 Roughly chop the beetroot and put in a blender with the other ingredients. Blitz until smooth and pour into two glasses.

preparation 10 minutes   *Serves 2*

HOT TOMATO

200g (7oz) canned pimientos
juice of 1½ lemons
1 onion, chopped
2 tbsp horseradish sauce
1 litre/1¾ pints/4 cups tomato juice
2 tsp Worcestershire sauce
a few drops of Tabasco sauce

1 Blitz the pimientos, lemon juice, onion and horseradish sauce in a blender. Pour into a jug and stir in the tomato juice. Season with the sauces and pepper. Chill well.

preparation 10 minutes
plus chilling *Serves 6*

PARTY FOOD & DRINKS

Make your party go with a swing with our wide-ranging selection of savoury canapés and finger foods, and punches, cocktails and non-alcoholic drinks. Whether it's a smart summer soirée or a Christmas drinks party, we've got the right nibbles and tipples for you.

To make the whole business of cooking for crowds easier, nearly all the recipes can be prepared or cooked in advance and frozen or chilled until you need to serve them. There are homely sausage rolls and traditional party food such as poached salmon and devils on horseback, as well as more contemporary ideas, such as jelly shots. And if you like spicy flavours, we have chicken satay bites, prawn poppadoms and even upmarket oysters with chilli sauce.

At the heart of a really good party are the drinks, and you can go adventurously beyond the usual bottles of red and white into more exotic flavours with our fruit cups, sherbets, fizzes, sparkles and juleps as well as the old favourites – sangria for warm summer evenings and mulled wine for festive fun.

< Chicken Crostini (page 315)

PARMESAN PUFFS

125g/4oz streaky bacon rashers (slices)

75g/3oz/6 tbsp unsalted butter

75ml/3fl oz/5 tbsp each milk and water

75g/3oz/¾ cup plain (all-purpose) flour

2 medium (US large) eggs, beaten

4 tbsp freshly grated Parmesan plus extra to sprinkle

salt and ground black pepper

cayenne pepper to dust

1 Cook the bacon in a frying pan until crisp and set aside.
2 In a large pan, heat the butter, milk and water. Bring to the boil, then remove from the heat and beat in the flour until the mixture comes away from the sides of the pan. Transfer to a bowl and set aside to cool.
3 Preheat the oven to 200°C/400°F/Gas 6. Gradually beat most of the beaten eggs into the flour mixture to give a dropping consistency. Set aside any leftover egg in a bowl.
4 Stir the Parmesan into the mixture and crumble in the bacon. Drop teaspoonfuls onto baking sheets, spacing them well apart. Brush with the leftover beaten egg and sprinkle lightly with Parmesan.
5 Bake in the oven for 10–12 minutes until golden and puffy. Serve immediately, sprinkled with a little salt and pepper and dusted with cayenne.

preparation 20 minutes cooking time 20 minutes

Makes 24

DEVILS ON HORSEBACK

2 tbsp mango chutney

8 ready-to-eat prunes, stoned

4 thin streaky bacon rashers (slices)

8 rounds of bread

50g/2oz/4 tbsp butter

salt and ground black pepper

1 Preheat the grill (broiler). Push a little mango chutney inside each prune.
2 Stretch the bacon rashers with the back of a knife and cut each one in half. Roll the bacon around the prunes and secure with a wooden cocktail stick (toothpick).
3 Cook under a medium grill, turning once, for a few minutes until the bacon is crisp and golden brown.
4 Meanwhile, cut the bread into 5cm/2in rounds with a pastry cutter. Fry the bread in the butter for 3–4 minutes, stirring, until golden brown on both sides.
5 Serve the bacon-wrapped prunes on the fried bread.

preparation 10 minutes cooking time 15 minutes

Makes 8

PROSCIUTTO MELONE

900g/2lb cantaloupe or
Charentais melon, chilled

8 thin slices Parma ham

ground black pepper

1 Cut the melon in half lengthways and scoop out and discard
the seeds. Cut each half into four wedges.
2 With a sharp knife, cut away the melon flesh from the skin.
Arrange the melon slices on four serving plates.
3 Drape the Parma ham slices over the melon and grind a
little black pepper over. Serve immediately.

preparation 10 minutes

Serves 4

SAUSAGE ROLLS

450g/1lb puff pastry
(see page 583)

flour to dust

450g/1lb pork sausagemeat

1 small onion, grated

a few fresh sage leaves, finely
chopped

milk to brush

beaten egg to glaze

salt and ground black pepper

1 Preheat the oven to 220°C/425°F/Gas 7.
2 Roll out half the puff pastry on a lightly floured surface to a
40 × 20cm/16 × 8in rectangle. Cut lengthways into two strips.
3 Mix the sausagemeat with the onion, sage and seasoning.
Divide into two portions and dust lightly with flour.
4 Shape the portions into long rolls, the length of the pastry,
and lay one along each pastry strip. Lightly brush the edges
with milk. Fold one side of the pastry over the sausagemeat
and press the long edges together to seal. Repeat with the
remaining pastry and sausagemeat. Trim the ends.
5 Brush the pastry with beaten egg and cut each roll into
5cm/2in lengths. Make two slits in the top of each one.
6 Place the sausage rolls on a baking sheet and cook in
the oven for 15 minutes. Reduce the oven temperature to
180°C/350°F/Gas 4 and cook for 10 minutes until golden
brown and puffed up. Serve hot or cold.

preparation 25 minutes   cooking time 30 minutes

Makes 28

CHICKEN SATAY BITES

1 tsp ground turmeric

3 garlic cloves, roughly chopped

grated zest and juice of 1 lime

1 hot chilli

1 tbsp vegetable oil

4 boneless, skinless chicken breasts, cut into long strips

cucumber strips to serve

For the satay sauce

200g/7oz/1⅓ cups salted peanuts

2 tbsp peanut butter

2 tbsp dark soy sauce

juice of 1 lime

1 x 200ml/7floz can coconut cream

1 Put the turmeric, garlic, lime zest and juice, chilli and oil in a blender or food processor. Blitz to a paste.

2 Transfer to a shallow dish and stir in the chicken strips to coat them. Cover and chill in the refrigerator for at least 30 minutes.

3 To make the satay sauce, put all the ingredients in a food processor and blitz until thick. Put in a serving dish, cover and chill until required.

4 Preheat the grill (broiler) until hot. Soak 24 bamboo skewers in some water for 20 minutes. Thread the marinated chicken strips on to the skewers.

5 Cook the chicken under the hot grill for 4–5 minutes on each side until it is cooked through and golden brown.

6 Serve with the satay sauce and some cucumber strips.

preparation 30 minutes plus chilling and soaking   cooking time 8–10 minutes

Makes 24

FRUITY CHICKEN SKEWERS

4 boneless, skinless chicken breasts, cut into chunks

4 tbsp fruity chutney

1 tsp vegetable oil

grated zest and juice of 2 limes

150g/5oz/scant ⅔ cup natural yogurt

¼ cucumber, grated

a small handful of fresh coriander (cilantro), chopped

salt and ground black pepper

1 Put the chicken in a bowl with the fruity chutney, oil and half each of the lime zest and juice. Season with salt and pepper and thread onto 24 bamboo skewers that have been soaked in water for 20 minutes.

2 Place a griddle pan over a high heat and cook the chicken for 6–8 minutes, turning occasionally, until cooked through and golden brown.

3 Meanwhile, stir together the yogurt, cucumber, remaining lime zest and juice and the coriander. Season well.

4 Serve the cooked chicken skewers with the yogurt mixture.

preparation 15 minutes   cooking time 10 minutes

Makes 24

TEX-MEX WRAPS

2 cooked chicken breasts, cut into bite-size pieces
1 carrot, grated
1 avocado, peeled, stoned and diced
a small handful of shredded lettuce
4 flour tortillas
4 tbsp fresh tomato salsa
4 tbsp soured cream
salt and ground black pepper

1 Put the chicken, carrot, avocado and lettuce in a large bowl. Season with salt and pepper and mix together.
2 Divide the chicken mixture among the tortillas. Top each one with a spoonful of salsa and another of soured cream.
3 Roll the tortillas up tightly or fold them over and serve.

preparation 10 minutes

Serves 4

CHILLI CHICKEN GOUJONS

340g/12oz boneless, skinless chicken thighs
50g/2oz/1 cup fresh white breadcrumbs
50g/2oz/½ cup plain (all-purpose) flour
1 tsp dried chilli flakes
grated zest of 1 lemon
1 medium (US large) egg, beaten
2 tbsp oil

For the dip
6 tbsp natural yogurt
6 tbsp light mayonnaise
¼ cucumber, seeded and diced
4 tbsp chopped fresh mint
a few drops of lemon juice

1 To make the dip, put the yogurt, mayonnaise, cucumber, mint and lemon juice in a bowl. Season with salt and pepper and mix well together. Cover and chill in the refrigerator until you are ready to serve.
2 Cut the chicken into strips. Put the breadcrumbs in a bowl with the flour, chilli flakes, lemon zest and salt. Mix well together.
3 Put the beaten egg on a plate and dip the chicken strips into it, then coat in the breadcrumb mixture.
4 Heat the oil in a frying pan over a medium heat. Fry the coated chicken, in batches, for 7–10 minutes until golden brown and cooked through.
5 Transfer them to a serving plate and serve with the dip.

preparation 15 minutes cooking time 20 minutes

Serves 4

CHICKEN CROSTINI

1 small ciabatta loaf
2 tbsp olive oil
175g/6oz cooked chicken breast
125g/4oz sunblush tomatoes
2 tbsp chopped fresh parsley

For the green sauce
3 tbsp each chopped fresh dill,
mint, chives and parsley
1 garlic clove, chopped
1 tbsp wholegrain mustard
4 anchovy fillets
2 tbsp capers
2 tbsp toasted pinenuts (pignoli)
12 green olives, pitted
grated zest and juice of 1 lemon

1 Put all the green sauce ingredients in a food processor or blender and blitz until smooth. Transfer to a bowl, cover and chill in the refrigerator.
2 Preheat the grill (broiler) to high. Cut the ciabatta into thick slices, then cut each slice in half. Arrange them on a foil-lined grill (broiler) pan and brush lightly with oil.
3 Grill (broil) for 1 minute on each side or until lightly toasted.
4 Cut the chicken into slices and place a slice on each toasted ciabatta slice. Top with a spoonful of green sauce.
5 Cut each sunblush tomato into 4 slices. Place a slice on top of each crostini and serve.

preparation 20 minutes plus chilling **cooking time** 2 minutes

Serves 16

PARTY ROLLS

10 slices smoked salmon
100g/3½oz/¾ cup soft cheese
1 tbsp chopped fresh dill
1 large courgette (zucchini)
2 tsp red chilli pesto
200g/7oz Parma ham
2 tbsp tomato chutney
1 bunch of fresh chives, chopped
ground black pepper

1 Arrange the smoked salmon on a board. Spread thinly with some of the soft cheese, sprinkle with dill and roll up.
2 Use a vegetable peeler to peel the courgette into long, wafer-thin ribbons. Spread with some of the soft cheese and dot with pesto, then roll up.
3 Lay the Parma ham on a board. Spread thinly with the remaining soft cheese, then tomato chutney and roll up.
4 Cover the rolls and chill in the refrigerator for up to 8 hours.
5 A few minutes before serving, sprinkle the rolls with chives and grind over some black pepper.

preparation 20 minutes plus chilling

Serves 10

MOZZARELLA BITES

250g/9oz small mozzarella balls, drained
75g/3oz thinly sliced Parma ham, cut into strips
15 stuffed olives, halved
30 small borettane onions in balsamic, drained
125g/4oz roasted (bell) peppers, cut into small pieces

1 Wrap each mozzarella ball in a strip of Parma ham.
2 Thread a halved olive on to a cocktail stick (toothpick), then add an onion, a pepper chunk and a mozzarella ball.
3 Repeat until all the ingredients are used up.
4 Serve the mozzarella bites immediately or cover and chill in the refrigerator until required.

preparation 15 minutes

Makes 30

PARTY EGGS BENEDICT

oil to grease
16 quail's eggs
4 slices white bread
3 tbsp ready-made hollandaise sauce
4 thin slices ham
16 small sprigs of dill

1 Half-fill a pan with water and bring to a simmer. Break the quail's eggs into the simmering water, a few at a time, and poach for 2–3 minutes until the whites are set and the yolks are still runny.
2 Remove them carefully, one at a time, with a slotted spoon and kitchen paper to absorb the water.
3 Meanwhile, lightly toast the bread on both sides. Cut out 16 circles of toast with a round cutter. Spread each one with a little hollandaise sauce. Cut out 16 ham circles and place on top of the hollandaise.
4 Use the cutter to stamp neatly around the yolks and lift them with a palette knife onto the toasts.
5 Serve warm garnished with sprigs of dill.

preparation 20 minutes   **cooking time** 5 minutes

Makes 16

SPICY TORTILLA CHIPS

2 ripe avocados
½ red onion, finely chopped
1 tomato, seeded and chopped
grated zest and juice of 1 lime
1 red chilli, finely diced
a small handful of fresh coriander (cilantro), chopped, plus extra to garnish
1 x 200g/7oz bag lightly salted tortilla chips
salt and ground black pepper

1 Halve, stone and peel the avocados. Finely dice the flesh and place in a bowl.
2 Add the red onion, tomato, lime zest and juice, chilli and chopped coriander to the bowl. Season to taste with salt and pepper. Mix everything together.
3 Spoon a little of the mixture on to the tortilla chips. Sprinkle with chopped coriander and serve.

preparation 15 minutes

Makes 30

SMOKED SALMON BLINIS

24 cocktail blinis
8 tbsp half-fat crème fraîche
125g/4oz thinly sliced smoked salmon
juice of 1 lemon
4 tbsp snipped fresh chives

1 Top the blinis with the crème fraîche. Cut the salmon into smaller pieces and place on top. Sprinkle with lemon juice.
2 Sprinkle the salmon blinis with some chopped chives and serve immediately.

preparation 5 minutes

Makes 24

BRUSCHETTA

1 long thin baguette
2 garlic cloves, halved
1 x 400g/14oz can cannellini beans, drained and rinsed
2 tbsp chopped fresh flat-leaf parsley
zest and juice of ½ lemon
2 tbsp olive oil
2 tbsp pomegranate seeds
2 courgettes (zucchini)
8 small mozzarella balls
2 tbsp fresh green pesto
3 marinated or grilled (broiled) red (bell) peppers, chopped
4 tbsp black olive tapenade
salt and ground black pepper
basil leaves to garnish

1 Cut the baguette into 24 thin slices and toast them lightly. Rub one side of each toasted slice with a cut clove of garlic. Discard the garlic.
2 In a bowl, mash together the beans, parsley, lemon zest and juice and oil. Season to taste with salt and pepper. Spoon on to eight toasts and top with pomegranate seeds.
3 Peel the courgettes into long ribbons and wind each one around a mozzarella ball. Place on eight toasts and drizzle with the pesto.
4 Top the remaining eight toasts with the red peppers and tapenade.
5 Arrange the bruschetta on a platter. Season lightly with salt and pepper and sprinkle with basil leaves.

preparation 25 minutes

Makes 24

SWEET CHILLI PRAWNS

30 cooked peeled large prawns
(jumbo shrimp)

125ml/4fl oz/½ cup sweet chilli
sauce

grated zest and juice of 1 lime

4 tbsp chopped fresh coriander
(cilantro)

3 courgettes (zucchini), trimmed

30 baby cherry tomatoes

1 Put the prawns, 2 tbsp chilli sauce, the lime zest and juice
   and the coriander in a bowl. Mix together to coat the prawns,
   then cover the bowl and chill in the refrigerator overnight.
2 Use a potato peeler to pare along the length of the
   courgettes to make 30 long thin strips.
3 Thread each courgette strip on to a cocktail stick (toothpick)
   in a concertina shape, then add a prawn and a cherry
   tomato. Cover and chill in the refrigerator until required.
4 Put the remaining chilli sauce in a small bowl. Arrange the
   prawn skewers on a serving plate and serve with the chilli
   sauce for dipping.

preparation 20 minutes plus overnight marinating

Makes 30

FISH GOUJONS

450g/1lb firm white fish fillets,
skinned and boned

1 medium (US large) egg, beaten

50g/2oz/1 cup fresh white
breadcrumbs

vegetable oil for deep-frying

tartare sauce to serve
(see page 253)

1 Cut the fish fillets into 20 pieces. Dip them in the beaten egg
   and then in to the breadcrumbs.
2 Heat the oil in a deep-fat fryer to 180°C/350°F. If you don't
   have a cooking thermometer, test it by frying a small cube
   of bread – it should brown in 40 seconds. Add the fish to the
   hot oil and fry until golden. Drain on kitchen paper.
3 Serve the goujons on cocktail sticks (toothpicks) with the
   tartare sauce.

preparation 15 minutes   cooking time 10 minutes

Makes 20

PRAWN POPPADOMS

1 tbsp sesame oil

24 raw peeled tiger prawns (shrimp)

4 tbsp sweet chilli sauce

150ml/¼ pint/scant ⅔ cup thick Greek yogurt

24 mini poppadoms

24 tiny sprigs of fresh basil or dill

1 Heat the oil in a frying pan over a medium heat. Add the prawns and cook for 3–4 minutes, turning halfway through, until they turn pink. Stir in 2 tbsp sweet chilli sauce.
2 Blend the remaining sweet chilli sauce with the yogurt and spoon on to the mini poppadoms.
3 Top each one with a prawn and a herb sprig. Serve hot.

preparation 10 minutes   cooking time 3 minutes

Makes 24

PESTO PEPPER CROUTES

1 long thin baguette

olive oil to brush

12 tsp fresh red pesto

24 small fresh basil leaves

4 grilled yellow (bell) pepper pieces, each sliced into 4 strips

1 Preheat the oven to 200°C/400°F/Gas 6.
2 Cut the baguette into 24 slices and lightly brush both sides of each slice with oil.
3 Place the bread on a baking sheet and bake in the oven for 15 minutes.
4 Spread ½ tsp pesto on each croûte and top with a basil leaf. Cover with a pepper strip and serve.

preparation 20 minutes   cooking time 15 minutes

Makes 24

CRAB CROUSTADES

125g/4oz fresh or canned white crabmeat

2 tsp Thai fish sauce

3 tbsp light mayonnaise

1 tbsp sweet chilli sauce

a small handful of fresh coriander (cilantro), chopped

16 mini croustade cases

ground black pepper

1 Put the crabmeat, fish sauce, mayonnaise, chilli sauce and coriander in a bowl. Mix together and season with pepper.
2 Fill each mini croustade case with a little of the crabmeat mixture and serve.

preparation 15 minutes

Makes 16

POACHED SALMON

1 x 2.5kg/5½lb whole salmon, cleaned and gutted

4 tbsp white wine

1 bay leaf

salt and ground black pepper

cucumber slices to garnish

lemon quarters to serve

mayonnaise (see page 576) or hollandaise sauce (see page 572) to serve

1 Fill a fish kettle or large shallow pan with water and add the white wine, bay leaf and some seasoning. Bring to the boil, then lower the salmon into the kettle or pan.
2 Bring back to the boil and cook for 5 minutes, then turn off the heat.
3 Cover the kettle or pan and leave the salmon to cool in the poaching liquid until it is completely cold.
4 Lift the salmon out of the liquid and carefully remove the skin and bones.
5 Place on a serving platter and garnish with cucumber slices and lemon quarters. If wished, arrange the cucumber along the length of the fish, overlapping like scales.
6 Serve cold with mayonnaise or hollandaise sauce.

preparation 15 minutes   cooking time 10 minutes plus cooling

Serves 8

FRESH OYSTERS

You can eat oysters with lemon juice and a dash of Tabasco, or try one of the following sauces. Allow 4–6 oysters per person, and always make sure they are really fresh. You can shuck them yourself or ask your fishmonger to do it for you. Serve the oysters on crushed ice or rock salt.

SHALLOT VINEGAR

2 shallots, finely chopped
8 tbsp red wine vinegar
a pinch of sugar

1 In a small bowl, mix together the shallots, red wine vinegar and sugar to taste. Stir and set aside to infuse for 1 hour.
2 Serve with the oysters.

preparation 5 minutes plus infusing

Dresses 24 oysters

LIME CHILLI SAUCE

1 red chilli, diced
grated zest and juice of 1 lime
2 tsp grated fresh root ginger
5 tbsp rice wine vinegar
fresh coriander (cilantro) sprigs
1 tsp sugar

1 In a small bowl, stir together the chilli, lime zest and juice, ginger, wine vinegar and sugar. Chop a few sprigs of coriander and add to the dip.
2 Serve with the oysters.

preparation 5 minutes plus infusing

Dresses 24 oysters

ASIAN SAUCE

2 tbsp sesame oil
4 tbsp soy sauce
1 tsp grated fresh root ginger
juice of ½ lemon
1 garlic clove, crushed
2 spring onions (scallions), diced

1 In a small bowl, stir together the oil, soy sauce, ginger, lemon juice, garlic and spring onions.
2 Serve with the oysters.

preparation 5 minutes plus infusing

Dresses 24 oysters

ELDERFLOWER CORDIAL

2kg/4½lb/9 cups sugar

75g/3oz citric acid

2 unwaxed lemons, sliced

20 fresh elderflower heads, shaken and stalks trimmed

1 Put the sugar and 1.2 litres/2 pints/5 cups water in a pan. Heat gently without boiling, stirring until the sugar dissolves.
2 Bring to the boil and then remove from the heat.
3 Stir in the citric acid, lemon slices and elderflowers. Cover the pan and leave to infuse overnight or for up to 24 hours.
4 Pass the liquid through a sieve lined with muslin (cheesecloth) into a bowl. Pour into sterilized bottles and store in the fridge

preparation 5 minutes **cooking time** 10 minutes plus infusing

Serves 30

FRESH FRUIT PUNCH

250ml/8fl oz/1 cup orange juice

250ml/8fl oz/1 cup pineapple juice

150ml/¼ pint/scant ⅔ cup peach juice

juice of 5 lemons

750ml/1¼ pints/3 cups sparkling water or tonic water

ice cubes

225g/8oz fresh strawberries, hulled and sliced

1 orange, cut into slices, then quartered

1 Put the orange, pineapple, lemon and peach juices and the blackcurrant cordial in a large punch bowl.
2 Stir well, then add the sparkling water or tonic water and plenty of ice.
3 Divide the strawberries and orange slices between eight tall glasses and top up with the fresh fruit punch. Serve the punch immediately.

preparation 5 minutes

Serves 8

CLEMENTINE JELLY SHOTS

5 gelatine leaves
16 clementines
125g/4oz/½ cup caster (superfine) sugar
4 tbsp vodka (optional)

1 Put the gelatine in a bowl and cover with cold water. Set aside to soak for 5 minutes.
2 Zest 2 clementines and put the zest in a large pan. Squeeze the juice from the zested and whole clementines and add to the pan with the sugar and the vodka (if using).
3 Lift the softened gelatine out of the soaking liquid and add to the pan. Heat gently, stirring until the sugar dissolves. Strain into a large jug with a pouring spout and make up to 1 litre/1¾ pints/4 cups with cold water. Pour into 12 small shot glasses and chill in the refrigerator for at least 5 hours.
4 Take the jellies out of the refrigerator 5 minutes before serving to allow them to soften slightly.

preparation 10 minutes plus chilling   **cooking time** 5 minutes

Makes 12

GINGER FIZZ

½ cantaloupe melon
1 lemon
2 pieces stem ginger in syrup
a few ice cubes
300ml/½ pint/1¼ cups dry ginger ale, chilled

1 Cut the melon into slices and remove the skin. Discard the seeds and roughly chop the flesh.
2 Peel the lemon, removing the white pith. Chop the lemon roughly, discarding any pips.
3 Chop the ginger and put in a blender with the melon and lemon. Blitz until smooth.
4 Pour into two tall glasses and add some ice cubes. Top up with dry ginger ale and serve.

preparation 10 minutes

Serves 2

FRUITY MINT JULEP

12 fresh mint leaves plus sprigs to garnish
2 tsp icing (confectioner's) sugar
75ml/3fl oz/5 tbsp bourbon
250g/9oz crushed pineapple
275g/10oz crushed ice

1 Put the mint leaves in a jug. Add the icing sugar and crush the leaves.
2 Add the bourbon and crushed pineapple and stir well.
3 Add the crushed ice and divide between two tall glasses. Serve garnished with mint sprigs.

preparation 10 minutes

Serves 2

ELDERFLOWER FIZZ

20 tbsp chilled elderflower cordial

3 bottles sparkling wine, e.g. cava or Prosecco, chilled

1 Pour 2 tbsp elderflower cordial into each of ten champagne flute glasses.
2 Top up each glass with sparkling wine and serve.

preparation 10 minutes plus chilling

Serves 10

CRANBERRY COOLER

ice cubes

150ml/¼ pint/scant ⅔ cup cranberry juice

lemonade

1 Half-fill two tall glasses with ice. Divide the cranberry juice between them.
2 Top up with lemonade, stir well and serve.

preparation 2 minutes

Serves 2

PIMM'S AND LEMONADE

ice cubes

200ml/7fl oz/¾ cup Pimm's No 1

600ml/1 pint/2½ cups chilled lemonade

¼ cucumber, thinly sliced

1 orange, thinly sliced

6 strawberries, hulled and sliced

a few fresh mint leaves

1 Put some ice cubes in a large jug (pitcher) and pour in the Pimm's and lemonade.
2 Add the cucumber, orange, strawberries and mint and stir well.
3 Serve immediately in four tall glasses.

preparation 10 minutes

Serves 4

FRUIT PUNCH

250g/9oz fresh pineapple
1 ripe papaya
1 large ripe mango
2 ripe guavas
2 passion fruit
a few ice cubes
300ml/½ pint/1¼ cups lemonade
300ml/½ pint/1¼ cups orange juice

1 Peel and core the pineapple, then roughly chop the flesh.
2 Peel the papaya and scoop out the black seeds. Roughly chop the flesh.
3 Slice the flesh off the central stone of the mango, then peel and chop the flesh.
4 Peel the guavas and discard the seeds. Chop roughly.
5 Halve the passion fruit and scoop out the seeds and pulp.
6 Put all the fruit in a blender and blitz until thick and smooth.
7 Transfer to a large jug and stir in some ice. Top up with lemonade and orange juice and serve.

preparation 10 minutes

Serves 4

SUMMER BERRY SHERBET

150g/5oz strawberries
150g/5oz raspberries
2 tbsp strawberry or raspberry syrup
1 egg white
4 ice cubes

1 Hull the strawberries. Wash all the fruit and pat dry with kitchen paper. Put them in a blender.
2 Add the fruit syrup and blitz briefly until smooth.
3 In a bowl, whisk the egg white until thick and foamy but not stiff. Add to the blender with the ice cubes.
4 Blitz for a few seconds until slushy. Pour into two glasses and serve.

preparation 10 minutes

Serves 2

SUMMER FRUIT CUP

340g/12oz ripe melon
340g/12oz raspberries
1.2 litres/2 pints/5 cups chilled lemonade
450ml/¾ pint/1¾ cups Pimm's
ice cubes
fresh mint sprigs to decorate

1 Quarter the melon and discard the peel and seeds.
2 Put the flesh in a blender and blitz until smooth. Sieve into a large serving jug.
3 Wash the raspberries and pat dry with kitchen paper. Add to the jug and top up with lemonade and Pimm's.
4 Add lots of ice and stir together. Serve in six glasses, decorated with sprigs of mint.

preparation 10 minutes

Serves 6

VEGGIE COCKTAIL

225g/8oz canned pimientos
juice of 2 lemons
1 onion, chopped
2 tbsp horseradish sauce
1 litre/1¾ pints/4 cups tomato juice
2 tsp Worcestershire sauce
dash of Tabasco sauce
finely chopped spring onions (scallions) to garnish

1 Put the pimientos in a blender with the lemon juice, onion and horseradish sauce. Blitz until smooth.
2 Transfer to a jug and gradually stir in the tomato juice. Season to taste with the Worcestershire sauce and Tabasco.
3 Chill in the refrigerator. Serve in six tall glasses, garnished with spring onions.

preparation 10 minutes plus chilling

Serves 6

CHAMPAGNE COCKTAIL

125ml/4fl oz/½ cup Grand Marnier or orange liqueur

4 tbsp grenadine

1 large orange, cut into 8 slices

8 sugar cubes

1 bottle champagne, cava or Prosecco, chilled

1 Divide the Grand Marnier and grenadine among eight champagne glasses.
2 Add an orange slice and a sugar cube to each glass.
3 Top up the glasses with the champagne, cava or Prosecco and serve immediately.

preparation 5 minutes

Serves 8

MULLED WINE

2 oranges

6 cloves

1 bottle fruity red wine

50ml/2fl oz/¼ cup brandy

1 cinnamon stick, broken, plus extra to garnish

a pinch of mixed spice

2 tbsp granulated sugar

1 Cut one of the oranges into six wedges and stud each one with a clove. Squeeze the juice from the other orange.
2 Put the clove-studded orange wedges in a stainless steel pan with the orange juice, red wine, brandy, cinnamon stick, mixed spice and sugar.
3 Warm gently over a low heat for 10–15 minutes, then remove from the heat and set aside for 10 minutes.
4 Strain into a serving jug and serve in heatproof glasses.

preparation 10 minutes plus infusing **cooking time** 10–15 minutes

Serves 6

SANGRIA

2 lemons, sliced
2 oranges, sliced
1 bottle red wine
50ml/2fl oz/¼ cup brandy
750ml/1¼ pints/3 cups lemonade
ice to serve

1 Put the lemon and orange slices in a large jug.
2 Add the red wine, brandy and lemonade to the jug and stir together to mix well.
3 Serve the sangria in tall glasses with plenty of ice.

preparation 5 minutes

Serves 8

ORANGE SODA

4 medium oranges
1 lemon
2 tbsp sugar syrup
a few ice cubes
soda water, chilled

1 Cut off the peel from the oranges and lemon, removing as much white pith as possible. Chop the flesh roughly, discarding any pips, and put in a blender and blitz until smooth. Sweeten with sugar syrup to taste.
2 Divide between two glasses and add a few cubes of ice. Top up with soda water and serve immediately.

preparation 5 minutes

Serves 2

PLANTER'S TEA PUNCH

2 tsp Indian tea leaves
5cm/2in piece cinnamon stick
2 tsp caster (superfine) sugar
1 large ripe mango
juice of 3 oranges
a few ice cubes
2 cinnamon sticks to serve

1 Put the tea leaves in a heatproof jug with the cinnamon and sugar. Pour in 225ml/8fl oz/1 cup boiling water and set aside to infuse for 5 minutes.
2 Strain through a fine sieve and set aside to cool.
3 Peel and stone the mango and chop the flesh. Blitz in a blender with the orange juice and cold tea.
4 Serve in two glasses with ice and cinnamon sticks.

preparation 10 minutes plus infusing and cooling

Serves 2

VIRGIN MARY

8 ripe tomatoes
a pinch of celery salt
dash of Worcestershire sauce
dash of Tabasco sauce
150g/5oz/scant ⅔ cup low-fat natural yogurt, well chilled
4 ice cubes, crushed
2 small celery sticks to serve

1 Quarter the tomatoes and put them in a blender.
2 Season with celery salt, Worcestershire sauce and Tabasco sauce. Add the yogurt and blitz until smooth.
3 Fill two large glasses with crushed ice, pour the tomato mixture over the top and serve with the celery sticks.

preparation 5 minutes

Serves 2

GIN SLING

2 lemons

3 tbsp caster (superfine) sugar

150ml/¼ pint/scant ⅔ cup freshly squeezed lemon juice

150ml/¼ pint/scant ⅔ cup freshly squeezed lime juice

150ml/¼ pint/scant ⅔ cup gin

ice cubes

soda water

1 Rub half a lemon around the rim of each of six glasses. Put 1 tbsp sugar on a saucer and press the rim of each glass into the sugar.
2 Put the lemon and lime juices in a cocktail shaker or screw-topped jar with the remaining sugar and the gin and shake vigorously.
3 Cut the remaining lemon into six slices.
4 Serve the gin sling over ice, topped up with soda water.

preparation 10 minutes

Serves 6

ICED COFFEE

150ml/¼ pint/scant ⅔ cup cold espresso or strong black coffee, chilled

3 tbsp coffee-flavoured liqueur

125ml/4fl oz/½ cup single (light) cream, chilled

1 tbsp sugar syrup to taste

crushed ice

1 Stir the coffee and coffee liqueur together in a jug. Cover and leave to chill in the refrigerator for at least 30 minutes or until ready to serve.
2 Stir in the cream and sweeten to taste with sugar syrup.
3 Put some crushed ice in two tall glasses and pour the coffee over. Serve immediately.

preparation 5 minutes plus chilling

Serves 2

TOP 10 COCKTAILS

PINK GIN

2–3 drops Angostura bitters
25ml/1fl oz/2 tbsp gin

1 Put the bitters in a glass and turn it until the sides are well coated. Add the gin and top up with iced water to taste.

preparation 2 minutes

Serves 1

WHISKY SOUR

juice of ½ lemon
1 tsp sugar
25ml/1fl oz/2 tbsp rye whisky

1 Mix the lemon juice, sugar and whisky, and shake well with some ice.

preparation 2 minutes

Serves 1

RUBY CRUSH

1 bottle sparkling wine
300ml/½ pint/1¼ cups Calvados
1l/1¾ pints/4 cups cranberry juice, chilled
450ml/¾ pint/1¾ cups sparkling water, chilled

1 Pour the sparkling wine, Calvados and cranberry juice into a glass serving bowl.
2 Add the sparkling water and some ice.

preparation 5 minutes

Serves 10

BRANDY ALEXANDER

25ml/1fl oz/2 tbsp brandy
25ml/1fl oz/2 tbsp crème de cacao
25ml/1fl oz/2 tbsp double (heavy) cream
a pinch of freshly grated nutmeg

1 Mix together the brandy, crème de cacao and cream. Shake well. Dust with nutmeg.

preparation 2 minutes

Serves 1

DRY MARTINI

50ml/2fl oz/¼ cup French vermouth
25ml/1fl oz/2 tbsp dry gin
1 stuffed olive

1 Shake the vermouth and gin together with some crushed ice. Pour into a glass and float an olive on top

preparation 2 minutes

Serves 1

DAIQUIRI

juice of ½ lime or ¼ lemon
1 tsp sugar
25ml/1fl oz/2 tbsp white rum

1 Shake the fruit juice, sugar and rum with some crushed ice. Pour into a frosted glass.

preparation 2 minutes

PINA COLADA

75ml/3fl oz/5 tbsp white rum
125ml/4fl oz/½ cup pineapple juice
50ml/2fl oz/¼ cup coconut cream

1 Blend the rum, pineapple juice and coconut cream with some crushed ice. Pour into a glass or a hollowed-out pineapple half.

preparation 2 minutes

Serves 1

WHISKY REFRESHER

100ml/3½fl oz/⅓ cup whisky or bourbon
500ml/17fl oz/2 cups lemonade

1 Fill four tumblers with crushed ice. Pour in the whisky and lemonade.

preparation 2 minutes

Serves 4

MARGARITA

1 tsp lemon juice plus extra to dip
salt
125ml/4fl oz/½ cup tequila
25ml/1fl oz/2 tbsp curaçao

1 Dip a chilled glass into lemon juice and then salt. Shake the tequila, curaçao and lemon juice and strain into the glass.

preparation 2 minutes

BUCK'S FIZZ

juice of 1 small orange
150ml/¼ pint/scant ⅔ cup champagne

1 Put the orange juice in a champagne flute and top up with chilled champagne.

preparation 2 minutes

Serves 1

BARBECUES, GRILLS & AL FRESCO

Everyone loves grilled food simply cooked on the barbecue and it doesn't have to be a burnt offering if you try the delicious dishes in the following pages. We have recipes for traditional grilled chicken, meat and kebabs flavoured with spicy and piquant marinades as well as barbecued seafood and vegetables. And there are even ideas for barbecued fruit.

And your al fresco eating doesn't end there – we have chilled delicately flavoured soups to start your meal, and exciting salads and griddled vegetables to accompany it. Whether it's a relaxed family gathering in the garden with barbecued pork and lamb steaks or sizzling sausages, or a more sophisticated affair with grilled swordfish and shrimp, there's something special about barbecued food that touches our deepest culinary instincts and fires up our taste buds. And you can enjoy these dishes all the year round – not just on warm summer evenings – as most of the recipes can be cooked indoors on a griddle pan or under an overhead grill, too.

And no barbecue or al fresco dining experience would be complete without some refreshing drinks. At the end of this section, you will find some fabulous fruity concoctions to cool you down and add the finishing touches to a perfect day.

< Chicken Brochettes (page 346)

RATATOUILLE

5 tbsp olive oil

2 onions, thinly sliced

3 garlic cloves, crushed

1 aubergine (eggplant), cubed

450g/1lb courgettes (zucchini), thinly sliced

450g/1lb tomatoes, peeled and roughly chopped

1 green and 1 red (bell) pepper, seeded and sliced

4 tbsp chopped fresh basil

2 tbsp tomato paste

salt and ground black pepper

chopped fresh parsley to garnish

1 Heat the oil in a large pan over a low heat, add the onions and garlic and fry gently for 10 minutes or until softened.
2 Add the aubergine, courgettes, tomatoes, green and red peppers, basil, parsley and tomato paste. Season with salt and pepper. Cook, stirring occasionally, for 5 minutes.
3 Simmer for 30 minutes or until all the vegetables are just tender. If the sauce is still quite liquid, simmer for longer, so the liquid evaporates and the sauce thickens.
4 Sprinkle with parsley, and serve the ratatouille hot, at room temperature or cold.

preparation 20 minutes   cooking time 45 minutes

Serves 4

GAZPACHO

1 medium cucumber, chopped

675g/1½lb ripe tomatoes, skinned and chopped

1 green (bell) pepper, seeded and chopped

1 red onion, chopped

2 garlic cloves, crushed

4 tbsp olive oil

2 tbsp sherry vinegar

450ml/¾ pint/1¾ cups tomato juice

2 tbsp tomato paste

salt and ground black pepper

ice cubes and diced red (bell) pepper to serve

1 In a large bowl, mix together the cucumber, tomatoes, green pepper, onion, garlic, oil, vinegar, tomato juice and tomato paste. Season with salt and pepper.
2 Blitz the mixture, in batches, in a blender or food processor until smooth.
3 Return the soup to the bowl, cover and then chill in the refrigerator for at least 2 hours.
4 Just before serving, add some ice cubes to the soup. Serve in shallow bowls topped with diced red pepper.

preparation 20 minutes plus chilling

Serves 6

ICED RED PEPPER SOUP

3 red (bell) peppers, seeded and chopped
1 red onion, chopped
340g/12oz tomatoes, sliced
1 tsp tomato paste
900ml/1½ pints/3⅔ cups vegetable stock
150ml/¼ pint/scant ⅔ cup milk
salt and ground black pepper
chopped coriander (cilantro) to serve

1 Put the red peppers, red onion, tomatoes, tomato paste and stock in a large pan. Bring to the boil, then reduce the heat, cover the pan and simmer gently for 15 minutes or until the vegetables are tender. Strain, reserving the liquid.
2 Blitz the vegetables in a blender or food processor until smooth. Push through a sieve to remove the tomato seeds.
3 Mix the reserved liquid, vegetable purée and milk in a bowl. Season with salt and pepper. Cool and then chill for at least 2 hours before serving.
4 Serve in chilled bowls sprinkled with coriander.

preparation 5 minutes plus chilling   cooking time 20 minutes

Serves 4

CHILLED CUCUMBER AND MINT SOUP

1 cucumber, coarsely grated
500g/1lb 2oz/2 cups Greek yogurt
a handful of fresh mint leaves, chopped
1 garlic clove, crushed
150ml/¼ pint/scant ⅔ cup vegetable or chicken stock
salt and ground black pepper
ice cubes to serve

1 Set aside a little of the grated cucumber for the garnish. Put the rest in a large bowl with the yogurt, mint, garlic and stock. Mix together and season to taste with salt and pepper.
2 Cover the bowl with some clingfilm (plastic wrap) and chill the soup in the refrigerator until ready to serve.
3 Just before serving, give the soup a stir and ladle it into six bowls. Add an ice cube and some of the reserved grated cucumber to each bowl.

preparation 15 minutes plus chilling

Serves 6

CHILLED VICHYSSOISE

50g/2oz/4 tbsp butter
2 onions, roughly chopped
900g/2lb leeks, chopped
1.2 litres/2 pints/5 cups vegetable stock
150ml/¼ pint/scant ⅔ cup double (heavy) cream
225g/8oz potatoes, cubed
salt and ground black pepper

1 Melt the butter in a large pan over a low heat. Cook the onions and leeks, stirring occasionally, for 10 minutes or until softened.
2 Stir in the stock, cream and potatoes and bring to the boil. Reduce the heat, cover the pan and simmer gently for 30–40 minutes until the vegetables are tender.
3 Blitz the soup in batches in a blender or food processor until smooth. Season to taste with salt and pepper.
4 Transfer the soup to a large bowl, cover and chill in the refrigerator for 6 hours or overnight.
5 Ladle the soup into chilled bowls and serve.

preparation 20 minutes plus chilling   cooking time 40 minutes

Serves 4

CHILLED TOMATO SOUP

675g/1½lb tomatoes, chopped
1 small onion, chopped
1 tbsp tomato paste
1 x 400g/14oz can chicken consommé
4 tbsp chopped fresh basil
150ml/¼ pint/scant ⅔ cup soured cream
salt and ground black pepper
2 spring onions (scallions), diced
fresh basil leaves to garnish

1 Blitz the tomatoes, onion, tomato paste, chicken consommé and basil in a blender or food processor until smooth.
2 Push the mixture through a nylon sieve into a pan. Heat gently over a low heat and season to taste.
3 Transfer to a large serving bowl, then cover and chill in the refrigerator for at least 2 hours.
4 Ladle the chilled soup into bowls and swirl in the soured cream. Garnish with spring onions and basil and serve.

preparation 20 minutes plus chilling

Serves 4

CHILLED ASPARAGUS SOUP

1kg/2¼lb asparagus, trimmed

3 tbsp olive oil

1 large onion, finely chopped

2 large leeks, finely chopped

900ml/1½ pints/3⅔ cups vegetable stock

salt and ground black pepper

snipped fresh chives to serve

1 Cut the tips off the asparagus and set aside. Cut the stalks into short lengths.
2 Heat the oil in a large pan over a low heat, add the onion and cook gently for 2–3 minutes. Add the leeks and cook, stirring occasionally, for 10 minutes or until they are soft.
3 Add the asparagus stalks and stock and season to taste with salt and pepper. Bring to the boil, then reduce the heat and simmer gently, uncovered, for 10 minutes or until the asparagus is tender.
4 Cool a little, then blitz in a blender or food processor until smooth. Pour the soup into a bowl and set aside to cool.
5 Add the asparagus tips to a pan of lightly salted boiling water and cook for 2–3 minutes until tender. Drain and refresh under cold running water.
6 Stir the asparagus tips into the soup, cover and chill in the refrigerator for several hours.
7 To serve, stir enough iced water into the soup to get the right consistency. Season with salt and pepper. Ladle into chilled bowls, sprinkle with chives and serve.

preparation 5 minutes plus chilling   **cooking time** 25 minutes

Serves 6

CHEESE AND COURGETTE SOUP

50g/2oz/4 tbsp butter

450g/1lb courgettes (zucchini), chopped

2 medium potatoes, diced

750ml/1¼ pints/3 cups vegetable stock

125g/4oz creamy blue cheese, diced

salt and ground black pepper

1 Melt the butter in a large pan over a low heat. Add the courgettes and potato, cover the pan and cook gently, shaking frequently, for 10 minutes or until softened.
2 Add the stock and bring to the boil, then reduce the heat and simmer gently for 20 minutes or until the vegetables are cooked and tender.
3 Put the soup and blue cheese in a blender or food processor and blitz until smooth. Transfer to a bowl, cover and leave until cold. Chill in the refrigerator overnight.
4 Ladle the soup into four chilled bowls and serve.

preparation 40 minutes plus chilling

Serves 4

ROASTED VEGETABLE SOUP

1kg/2¼lb ripe tomatoes, halved

2 onions, quartered

1 fennel bulb, sliced

4 garlic cloves

3 carrots, thickly sliced

3 red or yellow (bell) peppers, seeded and cut into chunks

4 tbsp olive oil

750ml/1¼ pints/3 cups passata

1 tsp sugar

grated zest and juice of 1 lime

salt and ground black pepper

1 Preheat the oven to 200°C/400°F/Gas 6.
2 Put the tomatoes, onions, fennel, whole garlic cloves, carrots and red or yellow peppers in two roasting pans. Drizzle the oil over and roast in the oven for 1 hour, turning occasionally, until the vegetables are tender and the skins are charred.
3 Blitz the roasted vegetables and passata in a blender or food processor until smooth. Season to taste with salt and pepper and stir in the sugar, lime zest and juice. Cover and chill in the refrigerator.
4 Ladle the soup into chilled bowls and serve immediately.

preparation 15 minutes plus chilling   cooking time 1 hour

Serves 8

CHILLED BEETROOT AND APPLE SOUP

340g/12oz cooked, peeled beetroot (beets), cut into chunks

grated zest and juice of 1 lemon

600ml/1 pint/2½ cups unsweetened apple juice, chilled

200g/7oz/¾ cup Greek yogurt

10cm/4in piece cucumber

1 tbsp chopped fresh mint

salt and ground black pepper

cayenne pepper to dust

1 Put the beetroot in a food processor with the lemon juice, half the apple juice and half the yogurt. Blitz for 1–2 minutes until smooth, then press through a sieve into a bowl.
2 Stir in the remaining apple juice, season to taste with salt and pepper and chill in the refrigerator.
3 Just before serving, grate the cucumber into the remaining yogurt and stir in the mint.
4 Ladle the soup into four bowls and stir some cucumber yogurt into the middle of each. Dust with cayenne and serve.

preparation 10 minutes plus chilling

Serves 4

SUMMER COUSCOUS WITH FETA

2 red onions, sliced

2 courgettes (zucchini), chopped

1 aubergine (eggplant), chopped

2 red (bell) peppers, seeded and chopped

2 garlic cloves, crushed

4 tbsp olive oil

340g/12oz tomatoes, quartered

225g/8oz/1⅓ cups couscous

300ml/½ pint/1¼ cups hot vegetable stock

4 tbsp chopped fresh parsley

2 tbsp balsamic vinegar

200g/7oz feta cheese, cubed

salt and ground black pepper

1 Preheat the oven to 200°C/400°F/Gas 6.
2 Put the red onions, courgettes, aubergine, red peppers and garlic in a roasting pan and drizzle with the oil. Season with salt and pepper, then roast in the oven for 30 minutes.
3 Add the tomatoes and toss together. Return to the oven and roast for 30 minutes.
4 Meanwhile, put the couscous in a large bowl and pour the hot stock over. Stir, cover and set aside for 10 minutes.
5 Fluff up the couscous with a fork. Stir in the parsley and roasted vegetables and sprinkle the balsamic over the top.
6 Toss everything together gently, then spoon into warmed shallow bowls, scatter the feta over and serve.

preparation 20 minutes plus soaking **cooking time** 1 hour

Serves 4

CHILLED SORREL SOUP

25g/1oz/2 tbsp butter

1 onion, finely chopped

175g/6oz fresh sorrel, shredded

340g/12oz potatoes, diced

750ml/1¼ pints/3 cups vegetable stock

juice of 1 lemon

150ml/¼ pint/scant ⅔ cup soured cream

salt and ground black pepper

1 Melt the butter in a large pan over a low heat and cook the onion for 5 minutes or until softened.
2 Add the sorrel and cook gently for 2–3 minutes until tender. Add the potatoes, stock and lemon juice. Season to taste with salt and pepper. Bring to the boil, then reduce the heat, cover the pan and simmer gently for 20 minutes.
3 Blitz the soup in batches in a blender or food processor until smooth. Stir in the soured cream and transfer to a bowl. Cover and chill in the refrigerator.
4 Ladle into chilled bowls to serve.

preparation 5 minutes plus chilling **cooking time** 30 minutes

Serves 4

CHICKEN BROCHETTES

2 tbsp balsamic vinegar
2 tbsp olive oil
grated zest and juice of 1 lemon
4 boneless, skinless chicken breasts, cut into chunks
lime wedges to serve

For the tabbouleh
75g/3oz/½ cup bulgur wheat
½ cucumber, diced
4 plum tomatoes, diced
1 small red onion, finely chopped
small bunch each chopped fresh mint and parsley
4 tbsp olive oil
juice of 1 lemon
salt and ground black pepper

1 In a large bowl, whisk together the balsamic vinegar, oil and lemon zest and juice. Stir in the chicken, then cover and chill in the refrigerator for at least 2 hours.
2 To make the tabbouleh, put the bulgur wheat in a bowl and pour double its volume of boiling water over. Set aside to soak for 15 minutes. Drain the bulgur wheat, squeeze out any excess liquid and return to the bowl.
3 Stir in the cucumber, tomatoes, red onion and herbs. Season with salt and pepper. Mix together the oil and lemon juice in a small bowl and stir gently into the bulgur wheat. Cover the bowl and chill in the refrigerator.
4 Meanwhile, preheat the barbecue, grill (broiler) or griddle. Soak eight wooden skewers in water for 20 minutes.
5 Remove the chicken from the marinade and thread on to the skewers. Cook for 10–12 minutes, turning occasionally, until cooked through and browned all over.
6 Serve the brochettes with the tabbouleh and lime wedges.

preparation 35 minutes plus marinating
cooking time 10–12 minutes plus soaking

Serves 4

STICKY BUFFALO WINGS

4 tbsp runny honey
4 tbsp wholegrain mustard
2 tbsp dark soy sauce
12 large chicken wings
salt and ground black pepper
grilled corn on the cob to serve

1 Put the honey, mustard and soy sauce in a large bowl and mix together. Add the chicken wings and turn to coat. Season with salt and pepper. Cover and leave to marinate in the refrigerator for 2 hours.
2 Preheat the barbecue or grill (broiler). Remove the chicken from the marinade and cook for 8–10 minutes on each side until cooked through. Serve hot with grilled corn on the cob.

preparation 10 minutes plus marinating   **cooking time** 20–45 minutes

Serves 6

GARLIC CHICKEN THIGHS

2 garlic cloves, crushed
2 tbsp chopped fresh oregano
grated zest and juice of 1 lemon
2 tbsp olive oil
4 chicken thighs
salt and ground black pepper

1 Preheat the barbecue or grill (broiler). Mix the garlic, herbs, lemon zest and juice, oil and seasoning in a bowl..
2 Make two or three slits in each chicken thigh and add to the bowl. Stir to coat with the garlic and herb mixture.
3 Grill for 6–7 minutes on each side until golden and cooked.

Serves 4

preparation 10 minutes   cooking time 10–15 minutes

SPICED CHICKEN KEBABS

2 tbsp olive oil
5 tbsp chopped fresh parsley
1 garlic clove
a good pinch of paprika
1 tsp ground cumin
grated zest and juice of 1 lemon
4 boneless, skinless chicken breasts, cut into chunks
rice or couscous to serve

1 Put the oil, parsley, garlic, paprika, cumin, lemon zest and juice in a blender and blitz to a paste.
2 Put the chicken in a shallow dish and add the spice paste. Rub in well and marinate in a cool place for 20 minutes.
3 Preheat the barbecue or grill (broiler). Soak four wooden skewers in water for 20 minutes.
4 Thread the chicken on to the skewers and cook for 10–12 minutes, turning occasionally, until cooked through.
5 Serve with rice or couscous.

Serves 4

preparation 10 minutes plus marinating   cooking time 10–12 minutes

BASIL AND LEMON CHICKEN

125g/4oz bacon rashers (slices)
450g/1lb cold roast chicken
125g/4oz rocket (arugula)

For the dressing
grated zest and juice of 1 lemon
1 tsp caster sugar
2 tsp Dijon mustard
8 tbsp olive oil
4 tbsp chopped fresh basil
salt and ground black pepper

1 To make the dressing, put the lemon zest and juice, sugar, mustard and oil in a bowl. Season with salt and pepper and beat together. Stir in the basil.
2 Cook the bacon under a hot grill (broiler) until crisp and browned. Crumble into small pieces.
3 Remove any bones from the roast chicken and cut into thick slices. Arrange on a dish and pour some of the dressing over. Cover and chill in the refrigerator for 15 minutes.
4 Put the rocket in a large bowl, pour the remaining dressing over and toss together. Arrange the chicken on top and sprinkle with the crispy bacon. Serve immediately.

preparation 15 minutes plus marinating   cooking time 3–4 minutes

Serves 4

CAJUN CHICKEN SALAD

4 skinless chicken breast fillets
1 tbsp Cajun seasoning
2 tbsp groundnut (peanut) oil plus extra to grease
salt and ground black pepper
sweet chilli sauce to drizzle

For the salad
2 carrots, cut into matchsticks
½ cucumber, cut into matchsticks
6 spring onions (scallions), cut into matchsticks
10 radishes, sliced
50g/2oz beansprouts
50g/2oz/½ cup peanuts, chopped
1 large red chilli, diced
2 tsp sesame oil

1 Preheat the grill (broiler) or barbecue.
2 Sprinkle the chicken breasts with the Cajun seasoning. Season with salt and pepper and brush with oil.
3 Place the chicken in a foil-lined grill (broiler pan) and cook under a hot grill (broiler) for 8 minutes on each side until cooked through. Alternatively, cook on a barbecue.
4 Place the carrots, cucumber, spring onions, radishes, beansprouts, peanuts and chilli in a bowl. Toss with the oil and season to taste with salt and pepper.
5 Divide the salad among four serving plates. Slice the warm chicken and arrange on top of the salad. Drizzle with the chilli sauce and serve.

preparation 15 minutes   cooking time 16 minutes

Serves 4

GRIDDLED LAMB STEAKS

1 small bunch of fresh mint, roughly chopped

2 garlic cloves, crushed

1 tbsp wholegrain mustard

grated zest and juice of 2 lemons

4 tbsp olive oil

4 lean lamb leg steaks

baked potatoes to serve

1 Put the mint, garlic, mustard, lemon zest and juice and oil in a small bowl. Mix together well.

2 Put the lamb in a bowl and spoon the herb mixture over. Cover and chill in the refrigerator for at least 10 minutes.

3 Preheat the barbecue or a griddle. Cook the lamb steaks for 4 minutes on each side for medium (or 5–6 minutes if you prefer them well done) until golden brown.

4 Serve the lamb with baked potatoes.

preparation 15 minutes plus marinating   **cooking time** 8–12 minutes

Serves 4

CHICKEN AND CHICORY SALAD

3 cooked skinless chicken breasts, cut into strips

2 oranges

2 large red chicory (Belgian endive) heads, sliced

4 tbsp chopped toasted walnuts

whole chives to garnish

For the dressing

5 tbsp olive oil

grated zest and juice of 2 oranges

1 tbsp cider vinegar

a pinch of sugar

3 tbsp chopped fresh tarragon

salt and ground black pepper

1 To make the dressing, whisk all the ingredients together in a small bowl or shake vigorously in a screw-topped jar until they are well combined.

2 Put the chicken strips in a bowl and spoon the dressing over. Cover and chill in the refrigerator for at least 1 hour.

3 Remove the peel and pith from the oranges, then cut them horizontally into slices.

4 Arrange a layer of chicory in a shallow salad bowl. Place the chicken and dressing on top.

5 Add the orange slices, scatter with the walnuts and serve garnished with chives.

preparation 15 minutes plus chilling

Serves 4

BAJAN SPICED GRILLED STEAKS

2 garlic cloves, crushed
1 red chilli, finely chopped
1 tsp ground allspice
1 tsp ground cumin
2 tbsp tomato ketchup
4 x 175g/6oz lean rump steaks
50g/2oz/4 tbsp butter, softened
2 spring onions (scallions), diced
4 corn cobs
salt and ground black pepper

1 Mix together the garlic, chilli, allspice, cumin and tomato ketchup. Brush over the steaks, cover and chill in the refrigerator for at least 30 minutes or overnight.
2 Blend the butter with the spring onions and some black pepper and set aside. Preheat the barbecue or grill (broiler).
3 Cook the corn cobs in a large pan of boiling water for 2 minutes. Drain well, then barbecue or grill (broil), turning occasionally, for 5 minutes or until cooked and tender.
4 Barbecue or grill the steaks for 5 minutes on each side until cooked through.
5 Serve with the corn, topped with the spring onion butter.

preparation 20 minutes plus marinating cooking time 10 minutes

Serves 4

BBQ SAUSAGES WITH MUSTARD DIP

12 pork sausages
12 extra thin streaky bacon rashers (slices)
4 tbsp honey mustard
2 tbsp Dijon mayonnaise
4 tbsp virtually fat-free fromage frais
225g/8oz cherry tomatoes
salt and ground black pepper

1 Wrap each sausage in a streaky bacon rasher and secure with a soaked wooden cocktail stick (toothpick).
2 Mix together the mustard, mayonnaise and fromage frais and season to taste with salt and pepper.
3 Preheat the barbecue or grill (broiler). Cook the sausages for 8 minutes, turning occasionally, or until cooked right through and well browned all over.
4 Barbecue or grill (broil) the tomatoes for 1 minute or until the skins begin to blister and burst.
5 Serve the sausages with the mustard dip and tomatoes.

preparation 10 minutes cooking time 11 minutes

Serves 4

PORK WITH TAPENADE

6 tbsp olive oil
4 tbsp tapenade
2 garlic cloves, crushed
4 lean pork steaks
ground black pepper
grilled sliced fennel and courgettes (zucchini) and boiled rice to serve

1 In a bowl, mix together the oil, tapenade and the garlic. Rub into the pork steaks and season with pepper. Cover and leave to marinate in the refrigerator for at least 30 minutes.
2 Preheat the barbecue or a griddle pan. Cook the pork steaks for 4–5 minutes on each side until cooked through.
3 Serve immediately with grilled fennel and courgettes and some boiled rice.

preparation 5 minutes plus marinating   cooking time 8-10 minutes

Serves 4

PARMESAN POTATO AND SAUSAGE KEBABS

36 new potatoes
6 tbsp olive oil, plus extra to brush
12 pork and leek sausages
50g/2oz/⅓ cup freshly grated Parmesan
salt and ground black pepper
salad or roasted vegetables to serve

1 Preheat the barbecue or grill (broiler). Soak twelve wooden skewers in water for 20 minutes.
2 Boil the potatoes in a pan of salted water for 10 minutes or until almost tender. Drain well and toss with the oil. Season with salt and pepper.
3 Cut each sausage into three pieces and thread on to the skewers alternately with the potatoes. Brush with oil and barbecue or grill (broil) for 8–10 minutes, turning occasionally, until the sausages are cooked through and the potatoes start to char on the edges.
4 Put the skewers on serving plates and sprinkle with the Parmesan. Serve with salad or roasted vegetables

preparation 15 minutes   cooking time 30 minutes

Serves 6

LEMON TUNA KEBABS

900g/2lb fresh tuna, cut into thick strips
1 lemon, cut into 8 wedges
3 tbsp chopped fresh parsley
ground black pepper
boiled rice or couscous to serve

For the lemon marinade
zest and juice of 2 lemons
2 garlic cloves, crushed
8 tbsp olive oil
salt and ground black pepper

1 Mix together the lemon marinade ingredients in a bowl.
2 Place the tuna in a shallow dish and pour the lemon marinade over them. Turn the tuna in the mixture to coat. Cover and chill in the refrigerator for at least 30 minutes.
3 Preheat the barbecue or grill (broiler) until hot. Soak eight bamboo skewers in water for 20 minutes.
4 Thread the tuna on to the skewers with the lemon wedges. Sprinkle over any remaining marinade and the parsley. Grind plenty of black pepepr over the top.
5 Cook the tuna kebabs on the barbecue or in a foil-lined grill (broiler) pan under the grill for 2–3 minutes on each side. Serve immediately with rice or couscous and salad.

preparation 15–20 minutes plus marinating   **cooking time** 4–6 minutes

Serves 8

MEXICAN SWORDFISH

1 tsp dried chilli flakes
4 tbsp olive oil
grated zest and juice of 1 lime
1 garlic clove, crushed
4 x 175g/6oz swordfish steaks
oil to brush
salt and ground black pepper
1 lime, sliced

1 Put the chilli flakes, oil, lime zest and juice and garlic in a shallow bowl and mix together. Add the swordfish and turn several times to coat completely. Cover and marinate in the refrigerator for 30 minutes.
2 Preheat the barbecue or an oiled griddle pan until hot.
3 Lift the swordfish out of the marinade and season with salt and pepper. Cook the steaks for 2 minutes on each side. Top with slices of lime and cook for 1 more minute or until the fish is cooked right through. Serve immediately.

preparation 10 minutes plus marinating   **cooking time** 10 minutes

Serves 4

BBQ SPARE RIBS

4 tsp Dijon mustard
4 tbsp soy sauce
2 garlic cloves, crushed
3 tbsp tomato ketchup
3 tbsp wine vinegar
2 tbsp Demerara sugar
dash of Tabasco sauce
3 tbsp runny honey
1kg/2¼lb pork spare ribs

1 Preheat the barbecue or grill (broiler) to hot.
2 In a bowl, mix together the mustard, soy sauce, garlic, tomato ketchup, vinegar, sugar, Tabasco and honey.
3 Add the spare ribs and turn to coat in the marinade. Cover and chill in the refrigerator for at least 30 minutes.
4 Cook the spare ribs on the barbecue or under the grill for 20–30 minutes, turning them frequently and basting with the marinade until cooked, charred, glossy and sticky.
5 Serve the hot ribs with couscous or rice and a crisp salad.

preparation 10 minutes plus marinating   **cooking time** 20–30 minutes

Serves 4

WARM CHORIZO SALAD

5 tbsp olive oil
175g/6oz chorizo, diced
1 red onion, chopped
1 large yellow (bell) pepper, seeded and chopped
2 garlic cloves, crushed
2 x 400g/14oz cans butter (lima) beans, drained and rinsed
4 tbsp chopped fresh coriander (cilantro)
juice of 1 lemon
salt and ground black pepper

1 Heat 1 tbsp oil in a frying pan over a medium heat and cook the chorizo for 1–2 minutes until lightly browned. Remove from the pan and set aside.
2 Add the red onion to the pan and cook for 10 minutes or until softened and starting to brown.
3 Add the yellow pepper, garlic and butter beans and cook for 5 minutes, stirring occasionally to prevent the vegetables sticking. Remove from the heat and stir in the chorizo.
4 Add the chopped coriander, lemon juice and remaining oil. Season to taste with salt and pepper and serve immediately on a bed of mixed salad leaves.

preparation 15 minutes   **cooking time** 17 minutes

Serves 4

PISSALADIERE

4 tbsp olive oil

4 large onions, thinly sliced

1 garlic clove, crushed

1 x 340g/12oz ready-rolled sheet puff pastry

125g/4oz roasted red (bell) peppers in oil, drained and sliced

1 x 50g/2oz can anchovies in olive oil, drained

12 pitted black olives, halved

salt and ground black pepper

1 Preheat the oven to 220°C/425°F/Gas 7.
2 Heat the oil in a deep frying pan over a low heat. Add the onions and garlic and cook gently for 30 minutes, stirring occasionally, until the onions are really soft and golden.
3 Meanwhile, cut the pastry into six equal rectangles and place on two small baking sheets.
4 Divide the cooked onion among the pastry bases, spreading it out evenly and leaving a 1cm/½in gap around the edges. Arrange the red peppers in a diamond-shaped lattice pattern over the top.
5 Cut the anchovies in half lengthways and arrange on top of the onions. Dot with the olives and sprinkle with thyme.
6 Cook in the oven for 20–25 minutes until golden and crisp.

preparation 10 minutes   cooking time 1 hour 5 minutes

Serves 6

GRIDDLED SARDINES AND VEGETABLES

3 tbsp olive oil

2 red onions, cut into wedges

2 garlic cloves, crushed

2 red (bell) peppers, seeded and cut into chunks

1 aubergine (eggplant), cubed

225g/8oz courgettes (zucchini), cut into chunks

900g/2lb fresh sardines, cleaned

salt and ground black pepper

olive oil and lemon juice to drizzle

1 Heat the oil in a large griddle pan over a medium heat. Add the onions and cook for 5 minutes or until almost soft. Add the garlic and red peppers and cook for 5 minutes, stirring occasionally. Stir in the courgettes and aubergine and cook for 4–5 minutes until almost soft. Remove from the griddle and keep warm.
2 Season the sardines with salt and pepper and cook on the griddle for 3–4 minutes on each side until cooked right through to the centre.
3 Drizzle the sardines with a little oil and lemon juice and serve with the hot griddled vegetables.

preparation 15 minutes   cooking time 20 minutes

Serves 6

CHILLI PRAWNS

6 tbsp groundnut (peanut) oil

6 tbsp coconut cream

1 tsp curry paste

3 garlic cloves, finely chopped

30 large peeled raw prawns (jumbo shrimp), with tail left on

salt and ground black pepper

For the chilli sauce

1 tbsp olive oil

2 garlic cloves, crushed

1 tbsp tomato paste

450g/1lb tomatoes, chopped

3 red chillies, seeded and diced

125g/4oz/½ cup molasses (dark brown) sugar

2 tbsp Thai fish sauce

1. In a large bowl, mix together the groundnut oil, coconut cream, curry paste, garlic and some salt and pepper. Add the prawns, turning to coat evenly. Cover and marinate in the refrigerator for at least 2 hours.
2. Meanwhile, make the chilli sauce. Heat the olive oil in a pan over a medium heat. Add the garlic and tomato paste and cook for 30 seconds. Stir in the tomatoes, chillies, sugar and fish sauce and bring to the boil. Reduce the heat and let it bubble away for 30 minutes or until reduced and pulpy.
3. Preheat the barbecue or grill (broiler). Soak six wooden skewers in water for 20 minutes. Thread five prawns on to each skewer and barbecue or grill (broil) for 3–4 minutes on each side, basting with the marinade.
4. Serve with rice and the chilli sauce for dipping.

preparation 30 minutes plus soaking   **cooking time** 50 minutes

Serves 6

SPICY LIME PRAWNS

grated zest and juice of 1 lime

1 garlic clove, crushed

2 small red chillies, seeded and finely chopped

5 tbsp olive oil

32 peeled raw tiger prawns (shrimp)

pitta bread to serve

1. Put the lime zest and juice, garlic, chillies and oil in a screw-topped jar. Close the lid tightly and shake well.
2. Put the prawns in a shallow dish and add the lime marinade. Cover and marinate in the refrigerator for at least 1 hour.
3. Preheat the barbecue or grill (broiler). Soak eight bamboo skewers in water for 20 minutes.
4. Thread four prawns on to each skewer. Cook the skewers on the barbecue or grill (broil) for 3–4 minutes on each side until they turn pink.
5. Serve immediately with warm pitta bread.

preparation 10 minutes plus marinating   **cooking time** 4 minutes

Serves 8

SPANAKOPITA PIE

1 tbsp olive oil
1 onion, finely chopped
1 garlic clove, crushed
450g/1lb baby spinach leaves
1kg/2¼lb potatoes, boiled in their skins, peeled and sliced
340g/12oz feta cheese, crumbled
bunch of spring onions (scallions), chopped
2 medium (US large) eggs, beaten
75g/3oz/6 tbsp butter, melted, plus extra to grease
375g/13oz pack filo pastry
salt and ground black pepper
Greek yogurt to serve

1 Heat the oil in a pan over a low heat and cook the onion gently for 10 minutes or until soft. Add the garlic and cook for 1–2 minutes. Add the spinach, cover the pan and cook for 1–2 minutes until it wilts.
2 Transfer to a bowl and set aside to cool. Add the potatoes, feta, spring onions and beaten eggs. Season and mix.
3 Preheat the oven to 200°C/400°F/Gas 6. Lightly butter a 30cm/12in tart tin.
4 Lay a sheet of filo pastry in the tin, overhanging the edge. Brush with melted butter and lay another sheet on top. Use half the sheets in this way, brushing each one with butter.
5 Add the spinach and feta filling and spread it out evenly, leaving a pastry border. Cover with the remaining pastry sheets, brushing with butter as before.
6 Fold the overhanging pastry over the top and roll up the edges to seal them. Brush with the remaining melted butter.
7 Bake in the oven for 35–45 minutes or until the pastry is crisp and golden. Cool a little before cutting into slices. Serve with Greek yogurt.

preparation 40 minutes plus cooling cooking time 45 minutes

Serves 10

SEAFOOD KEBABS

4 long fresh rosemary stalks
4 tbsp olive oil
grated zest and juice of 1 lime
340g/12oz cod, cut into chunks
225g/8oz large peeled raw prawns (jumbo shrimp)
340g/12oz tzatziki (see page 169)
boiled rice and lime wedges to serve

1 Preheat the barbecue or grill (broiler) to hot.
2 Strip almost all the leaves from the rosemary, apart from the top sprig. Chop the stripped leaves and mix with the oil, lime zest and juice. Stir in the cod and prawns.
3 Cut the tip of each rosemary stalk to a sharp point and skewer the cod and prawns. .
4 Preheat a grill (broiler). Arrange the kebabs on a grill (broiler) rack and cook for 4–5 minutes on each side or until the fish is opaque and the prawns are pink and cooked.
5 Serve immediately with tzatziki and boiled rice with lime wedges to squeeze over the kebabs.

preparation 25 minutes cooking time 10 minutes

Serves 4

PEPERONATA

3 red (bell) peppers
3 yellow (bell) peppers
1 green (bell) pepper
100ml/3½fl oz/⅓ cup olive oil
2 garlic cloves, crushed
6 plum tomatoes
2 tbsp capers
18 black olives
2 tbsp chopped fresh parsley
salt and ground black pepper

1 Halve the peppers and discard the ribs and seeds, leaving the stalks intact. Heat the oil in a large pan over a medium heat, add the garlic and tomatoes and cook for 2 minutes.
2 Add the peppers and turn to coat them in the oil. Cover the pan and cook gently over a low heat for 45 minutes or until the peppers are really tender.
3 Stir in the capers, olives and parsley and season to taste with salt and pepper.
4 Serve immediately or set aside to cool, then cover and chill in the refrigerator until required. .

preparation 15 minutes   cooking time 45 minutes

Serves 6

CHARGRILLED VEGETABLES

6 garlic cloves
1 red and 1 yellow (bell) pepper, seeded and cut into strips
2 courgettes (zucchini), sliced
1 aubergine (eggplant), cubed
1 sweet potato, peeled and cut into wedges
2 red onions, cut into wedges
6 tbsp olive oil
salt and ground black pepper

1 Put all the vegetables in a shallow dish and pour the oil over. Season with salt and pepper and stir well to coat. Cover and chill in the refrigerator for at least two hours.
2 Preheat the barbecue, a griddle or grill (broiler) to hot.
3 Lay the vegetables in a single layer on the grill rack or griddle and cook for 10–15 minutes, turning occasionally, or until they are tender and stating to char.
4 Serve the vegetables hot or cold.

preparation 10 minutes plus chilling   cooking time 15 minutes

Serves 4

CORN WITH CHILLI BUTTER

125g/4oz/½ cup unsalted butter, slightly softened
2 tbsp sweet chilli sauce
4 corn cobs
salt and ground black pepper

1 To make the chilli butter, mix the butter with the chilli sauce in a bowl. Season with salt and pepper. Cover with clingfilm (plastic wrap), then roll into a log and wrap it up. Put in the refrigerator to chill and firm up.
2 Strip the outer husks from the corn cobs and trim the bases. Bring a large pan of water to the boil, add the corn cobs and cook for 6–8 minutes until tender.
3 Drain the corn cobs and serve immediately, topped with slices of chilli butter.

preparation 15 minutes plus chilling cooking time 6–8 minutes

Serves 4

ROASTED TOMATO BULGUR SALAD

175g/6oz/1 cup bulgur wheat
700g/1½lb baby plum tomatoes
8 tbsp olive oil
a handful each of fresh mint and basil, roughly chopped
3 tbsp balsamic vinegar
juice of 2 lemons
1 red onion, diced
salt and ground black pepper
sprigs of fresh basil to garnish

1 Put the bulgur wheat in a bowl and cover with boiling water. Set aside to soak for 30 minutes.
2 Preheat the oven to 220°C/425°F/Gas 7.
3 Put the tomatoes in a roasting pan and drizzle with half the oil. Season with salt and pepper and roast in the oven for 10–15 minutes or until starting to soften.
4 Put the remaining oil, the balsamic vinegar and lemon juice in a large bowl. Add the warm pan juices from the tomatoes and the soaked bulgur wheat and stir gently.
5 Stir in the herbs and red onion. Add the tomatoes and mix well together. Season to taste.
6 Serve warm, garnished with basil sprigs.

preparation 10 minutes plus soaking and standing cooking time 10–15 minutes

Serves 4

GRILLED MUSHROOMS

125g/4oz/½ cup butter, softened
2 garlic cloves, crushed
4 tbsp chopped fresh parsley
12 large mushrooms, trimmed
1 tbsp olive oil
salt and ground black pepper

1 Preheat the grill (broiler) to hot. Blend the butter, garlic, parsley and a little salt and pepper in a bowl. Cover and chill in the refrigerator for at least 30 minutes.
2 Brush the mushrooms with oil and place them, gill-side down, on a foil-lined grill (broiling) pan. Cook for 5 minutes.
3 Meanwhile, cut the herb and garlic butter into pieces.
4 Turn the mushrooms over, dot with the butter and grill (broil) for 4–5 minutes until tender.
5 Serve immediately with meat, chicken or vegetables.

preparation 10 minutes plus chilling   **cooking time** 10 minutes

Serves 4

BBQ SQUASH

4 small butternut squash, quartered and seeded
coarse sea salt to sprinkle
75g/3oz/6 tbsp butter, melted
ground black pepper
cayenne pepper to dust

1 Preheat the barbecue to medium-hot.
2 Sprinkle the squash with sea salt, brush with melted butter and grind some black pepper over.
3 Cook the squash for 20 minutes until tender, turning occasionally. Serve hot, dusted lightly with cayenne.

preparation 10 minutes   **cooking time** 20 minutes

Serves 8

SLOW-COOKED TOMATOES

12 large ripe tomatoes, halved
2 garlic cloves, chopped
2 tbsp chopped fresh thyme
a pinch of sugar
4 tbsp olive oil
salt and ground black pepper
fresh basil leaves to garnish

1 Preheat the oven to 150°C/300°F/Gas 2.
2 Take the tomato halves and scoop out most of the seeds.
   Put the tomatoes in an ovenproof dish and sprinkle with
   the garlic, thyme and sugar. Drizzle the oil over the top and
   season with salt and pepper.
3 Roast in the oven for 2½ hours until the tomatoes are
   shrivelled. Set aside to cool.
4 Scatter with basil and serve hot or cold.

preparation 10 minutes   **cooking time** 2½ hours

Serves 6

BBQ RED ONIONS

3 large red onions, each cut
into 8 wedges
6 tbsp olive oil
2 tbsp balsamic vinegar
squeeze of lemon juice
1 tbsp chopped fresh oregano
salt and ground black pepper

1 Preheat the barbecue. Soak eight wooden skewers in water
   for 20 minutes.
2 Thread the red onion wedges on to the skewers. Brush with
   3 tbsp oil and season with salt and pepper.
3 Cook the kebabs for 30 minutes, turning them occasionally
   and brushing with oil, until tender and slightly charred.
4 Mix together the remaining oil, the balsamic vinegar, lemon
   juice and oregano to make a dressing.
5 Drizzle over the cooked onions and serve hot or cold.

preparation 20 minutes   **cooking time** 30 minutes

Serves 8

GREEK BEAN AND FETA SALAD

450g/1lb broad (fava) beans, podded
175g/6oz feta cheese, diced
6 tbsp chopped fresh mint
3 tbsp olive oil
juice of 1 lemon
salt and ground black pepper

1 Cook the beans in a pan of boiling water for 4–5 minutes until tender. Drain and set aside. When cool enough to handle, slip the beans out of their skins.

2 Put the warm beans in a bowl with the feta, mint, oil and lemon juice. Season to taste with salt and pepper and mix gently together. Serve warm.

preparation 10 minutes   **cooking time** 5 minutes

Serves 4

WARM LENTIL SALAD

2 medium eggs
1 tbsp olive oil
2 large leeks, chopped
1 red (bell) pepper, seeded and chopped
1 x 400g/14oz can lentils, drained
150ml/¼ pint/scant ⅔ cup vegetable stock
4 tbsp chopped fresh parsley
salt and ground black pepper

1 Bring a small pan of water to the boil and lower the eggs into the pan. Reduce the heat and simmer gently for 7 minutes. Remove the eggs and set aside to cool.
2 Meanwhile, heat the oil in a large pan and cook the leeks and red pepper over a low heat for 10 minutes, stirring occasionally, until softened.
3 Stir in the lentils and stock and bring to the boil. Reduce the heat and simmer gently for 3 minutes. Season to taste with salt and pepper and stir in the parsley.
4 Shell the eggs and cut them in quarters.
5 Divide the lentil mixture between two shallow serving bowls and top with the eggs.

preparation 10 minutes   cooking time 15 minutes

Serves 2

GRILLED SWEET POTATOES

2 x 225g/8oz sweet potatoes, peeled and cut into wedges
olive oil to brush
sea salt crystals and ground black pepper
paprika or cayenne pepper to sprinkle
sweet chilli sauce to serve

1 Preheat the barbecue or griddle.
2 Add the sweet potatoes to a pan of boiling water, bring back to the boil, then reduce the heat and simmer for 3 minutes. Drain and dry on kitchen paper.
3 Brush the sweet potatoes lightly with oil and season with sea salt and pepper. Cook on the hot barbecue or griddle, turning occasionally, for 10–15 minutes until browned on the outside and tender inside.
4 Sprinkle the sweet potato wedges with some paprika or cayenne and serve wth chilli sauce.

preparation 15 minutes   cooking time 15–20 minutes

Serves 4

INSALATA CAPRESE

3 x 150g/5oz balls mozzarella, drained

1kg/2¼lb juicy ripe tomatoes

olive oil to drizzle

a small handful of fresh basil leaves, roughly shredded

balsamic vinegar to drizzle

salt and ground black pepper

1 Slice the mozzarella balls into rounds and arrange them on a large serving plate.

2 Slice the tomatoes into rounds and place on top of the mozzarella in an attractive overlapping pattern.

3 Drizzle with the oil and season with salt and pepper. Scatter the basil over the top and serve immediately, drizzled with balsamic vinegar, if wished.

preparation 10 minutes

Serves 4

MIXED BEAN SALAD

1 x 400g/14oz can mixed beans, drained and rinsed

1 x 400g/14oz can chickpeas (garbanzos), drained and rinsed

1 red onion, diced

balsamic vinegar to drizzle

For the vinaigrette

6 tbsp olive oil

juice of 1 lemon

1 tsp honey mustard

6 tbsp chopped fresh parsley

salt and ground black pepper

1 Put the beans, chickpeas and red onion in a large bowl and mix gently together.

2 To make the vinaigrette, whisk together the oil, lemon juice, mustard and parsley until well combined. Season to taste with a little salt and pepper.

3 Pour the vinaigrette over the bean mixture and toss well, so that all the beans are glistening with dressing.

4 Serve immediately, drizzled with balsamic vinegar, or cover and chill in the refrigerator for up to two days.

preparation 15 minutes

Serves 4

POTATO SALAD

900g/2lb waxy new potatoes, scrubbed and sliced

6 tbsp olive oil

1 garlic clove, crushed

grated zest and juice of 1 lemon

1 tbsp white wine vinegar

1 bunch of fresh mint, chopped

4 spring onions (scallions), finely chopped

salt and ground black pepper

1 Cook the potatoes in a pan of lightly salted boiling water for 12–15 minutes until just tender.
2 Meanwhile, heat 1 tbsp oil in a large frying pan over a low heat. Cook the garlic and lemon zest for 5 minutes or until soft but not coloured.
3 In a bowl, whisk the remaining oil with the vinegar, lemon juice, mint and seasoning.
4 Drain the potatoes and tip them into a bowl. Immediately stir in the garlic and lemon mixture, the spring onions and the dressing. Toss lightly together and check the seasoning.
5 Set aside to cool. Serve at room temperature.

preparation 10 minutes   **cooking time** 15 minutes plus cooling

Serves 4

MELON AND MANGO SALAD

½ cucumber

1 Charentais melon

1 mango, peeled and stoned

chopped fresh coriander (cilantro) to serve

For the dressing

2 tbsp light soy sauce

juice of 1 lime

1 tsp runny honey

½ red chilli, seeded and diced

1 Cut the cucumber in half lengthways, remove the seeds and slice the flesh.
2 Cut the melon in half, scoop out the seeds and cut into wedges. Remove the skin and cut the flesh into cubes.
3 Cut the mango flesh into cubes, reserving any juice, and mix with the cucumber and melon in a bowl.
4 Whisk all the ingredients for the dressing in a small bowl, adding any melon and mango juice.
5 Pour the dressing over the salad and toss gently. Sprinkle with coriander and serve immediately.

preparation 15 minutes plus chilling

Serves 6

ROASTED PEPPERS WITH BALSAMIC SALSA

4 red and green (bell) peppers, seeded and cut into chunks

1 small red onion, chopped

4 tbsp olive oil

2 tbsp balsamic vinegar

175g/6oz tomatoes, chopped

4 tbsp chopped fresh parsley

a few dried chilli flakes

100g/3½oz rocket (arugula) or watercress and baby spinach leaves

salt and ground black pepper

1 Preheat the oven to 220°C/425°F/Gas 7.
2 Put the red and green peppers and red onion in a roasting pan and drizzle with half the oil. Roast in the oven for 30 minutes or until tender and slightly charred..
3 To make the balsamic salsa, put the roasted onion in a bowl with the pan juices, the rest of the oil and the balsamic vinegar. Add the tomatoes, parsley and dried chilli flakes. Season with salt and pepper to taste and mix well together.
4 Arrange the roasted peppers on four serving plates with rocket or watercress and baby spinach leaves and drizzle with the balsamic salsa..

preparation 15 minutes   cooking time 30 minutes

Serves 4

MIXED LEAF SALAD

3 round lettuce hearts, roughly shredded

100g/3½oz mixed baby salad leaves

2 ripe avocados

1 box salad cress, chopped

4 tbsp French dressing (see page 574)

Parmesan shavings to serve

1 Put the lettuce hearts in a bowl with the salad leaves.
2 Cut the avocados in half and remove the stones and peel. Cut the flesh into cubes and add to the salad leaves with the salad cress.
3 Pour the dressing over the salad and toss to mix. Serve sprinkled with Parmesan shavings.

preparation 10 minutes

Serves 8

TOMATO AND ONION SALAD

450g/1lb baby plum tomatoes, halved

450g/1lb plum tomatoes, sliced

4 beef tomatoes, sliced

1 bunch of spring onions (scallions), sliced

a handful of fresh basil leaves, torn, plus sprigs to garnish

a good pinch of sugar

4 tbsp pinenuts (pignoli), toasted

salt and ground black pepper

balsamic vinegar to drizzle

For the dressing
6 tbsp olive oil
3 tbsp red wine vinegar
1 tsp Dijon mustard

preparation 15 minutes plus standing

1 To make the dressing, whisk the oil, vinegar and mustard together in a bowl. Season with salt and pepper.
2 Put all the tomatoes, the spring onions, basil, sugar and pinenuts in a shallow serving bowl and season to taste with salt and pepper.
3 Pour the dressing over the salad and toss gently. Set aside for 1 hour.
4 Garnish with basil sprigs and serve with balsamic vinegar for drizzling.

Serves 8

GOAT'S CHEESE PLATTER

4 ripe peaches, halved, stoned and sliced

2 goat's cheese logs, sliced

4 grilled or marinated red and yellow (bell) peppers, sliced

125g/4oz marinated artichoke hearts in oil, drained

12 balsamic pickled small onions

50g/2oz rocket (arugula)

olive oil to drizzle

ground black pepper

preparation 15 minutes

1 On a large serving platter, arrange the peaches, goat's cheese, red and yellow peppers, artichoke hearts and balsamic onions.
2 Garnish with rocket and drizzle with oil.
3 Serve immediately with crusty bread, foccacia or crackers.

Serves 6

ROASTED VEGETABLES WITH MUSTARD MAYONNAISE

1kg/2¼lb fennel bulbs, baby new potatoes and red onion mix

2 unpeeled garlic cloves

5 fresh rosemary sprigs

4 tbsp olive oil

1 tbsp balsamic vinegar

salt and ground black pepper

For the mustard mayonnaise

150ml/¼ pint/scant ⅔ cup mayonnaise

2 tbsp Dijon mustard

1 Preheat the oven to 220°C/425°F/Gas 7.
2 Quarter the fennel bulbs, slice the new potatoes thickly and cut the red onions into wedges.
3 Put the vegetables, garlic and rosemary in a roasting pan Toss in the oil and season with salt and pepper.
4 Cook in the oven for 30–40 minutes or until tender and starting to char. Sprinkle with balsamic vinegar.
5 Meanwhile, make the mustard mayonnaise. Blend together the mayonnaise and mustard in a bowl.
6 Transfer the roasted vegetables to a serving dish and serve hot or cold with the mustard mayonnaise.

preparation 15 minutes cooking time 40 minutes

Serves 4

SUMMER VEGETABLE SALAD

900g/2lb mixed green beans, peas, trimmed asparagus, podded broad (fava) beans, sliced courgettes (zucchini), sliced runner beans

4 tbsp chopped fresh parsley

For the dressing

3 tbsp olive oil

1 tbsp cider vinegar

1 tsp Dijon mustard

salt and ground black pepper

1 Cook the green beans in a large pan of lightly salted boiling water for 3 minutes, then add all the other vegetables. Bring back to the boil and cook for 3–4 minutes. Drain and plunge immediately into a bowl of ice-cold water. Drain well.
2 Whisk all the dressing ingredients together in a small bowl and season with salt and pepper.
3 Toss the vegetables gently in the dressing with the parsley. Transfer to a large shallow bowl and serve.

preparation 10 minutes cooking time 6–7 minutes

Serves 4

SUMMER SALAD

2 Romaine lettuces

1 papaya

1 pink grapefruit

1 large ripe avocado

1 bunch of spring onions (scallions), chopped

a small bunch of fresh chives, snipped, plus whole chives to garnish

For the dressing

3 tbsp olive oil

juice of 1 lemon

1 tbsp sweet chilli sauce

1 Separate the lettuces into leaves and tear them into bite-size pieces. Put in a large bowl.
2 Peel and seed the papaya and dice the flesh. Peel the grapefruit, cutting away the white pith, and separate the segments. Cut the avocado in half and remove the stone and peel. Cut the flesh into dice.
3 Put the lettuce, fruit, avocado and spring onions in a bowl.
4 To make the dressing, mix together the oil, lemon juice and chilli sauce in a bowl.
5 Pour the dressing over the salad and toss well together. Season with salt and pepper.
6 Divide the salad among four serving plates. Scatter with the snipped chives and garnish with some whole ones .

preparation 30 minutes

Serves 4

MOROCCAN CARROT SALAD

1kg/2¼lb carrots

2 oranges, peeled and sliced

juice of 1 large lemon

juice of 1 orange

2 tbsp olive oil

salt and ground black pepper

a pinch of ground cinnamon

chopped fresh coriander
(cilantro) to serve

preparation 10 minutes

1 Peel the carrots and cut them into thin matchstick strips.
   Place in a large bowl with the oranges.
2 Mix together the lemon juice, orange juice, oil, salt and
   pepper and cinnamon, and stir into the carrot mixture.
3 Sprinkle with chopped coriander and serve.

Serves 4

TOMATO, PESTO AND MOZZARELLA SALAD

450g/1lb baby plum tomatoes,
halved

300g/11oz baby mozzarella
balls, drained

4 tbsp red pepper pesto

12 pitted black olives

100g/3½oz mixed salad leaves

ground black pepper

fresh basil sprigs to garnish

preparation 10 minutes

1 Put the plum tomatoes, mozzarella, red pepper pesto and
   olives in a large bowl and toss together. Season with black
   pepper. Cover the bowl and set aside.
2 Just before serving, toss the mixed leaves with the tomato
   and mozzarella mixture and garnish with basil sprigs.

Serves 4

HORIATIKI

1 red onion, thinly sliced

½ cucumber, halved and sliced

1 green (bell) pepper, seeded and thinly sliced

3 beef tomatoes, sliced

10 Kalamata olives, drained

200g/7oz feta cheese, chopped

juice of ½ lemon

4 tbsp extra virgin olive oil

salt and ground black pepper

1 Put the red onion, cucumber, green pepper, tomatoes, olives and feta in a large bowl and toss to mix. Season lightly with salt and grind over plenty of black pepper.
2 Drizzle the lemon juice and oil over the salad and toss everything together lightly. Set aside for 10 minutes before serving.

preparation 15 minutes plus standing

Serves 4

CHICKEN SALAD BASKETS

olive oil to brush

4 x 25g/1oz soft tortillas

2 tbsp vinaigrette (see page 592)

juice and grated zest of 1 orange

1 red chilli, seeded and diced

8 cherry tomatoes, halved

1 red (bell) pepper, seeded and chopped

½ red onion, finely chopped

50g/2oz baby salad leaves

225g/8oz cooked chicken breast, diced

4 tbsp guacamole

3 tbsp chopped fresh coriander (cilantro)

1 Preheat the oven to 200°C/400°F/Gas 6. Brush four Yorkshire-pudding moulds with oil.
2 Press the tortillas down into the moulds to make a basket shape. Cook in the oven for 8–10 minutes until crisp and golden. Remove from the oven and cool.
3 Mix together the vinaigrette, orange zest and juice and chilli for the dressing.
4 Mix together the tomatoes, red pepper, onion, salad leaves and chicken. Add the dressing and toss gently.
5 Divide between the tortilla baskets and top each one with the guacamole. Sprinkle with coriander.

preparation 15 minutes **cooking time** 8–10 minutes

Serves 4

BARBECUED FIGS WITH HONEY

12 large ripe figs
melted butter to brush
4 tbsp runny Greek honey
grated zest and juice of
2 oranges
Greek yogurt or vanilla ice cream
to serve

1 Heat a barbecue. Make a slit in each fig. Take two large sheets of foil and lay one sheet on top of the other. Brush lightly with melted butter.
2 Put the figs in the centre of the foil. Bring the sides of the foil up together and pour in the honey and orange zest and juice. Seal the edges of the foil together to loosely enclose the figs in a 'parcel'.
3 Put the foil parcel on the hot barbecue and leave to cook for 10–15 minutes.
4 Open up the foil slightly at the top and cook for a further 2–3 minutes until the juices become syrupy.
5 Serve the hot figs in their juices with some Greek yogurt or a scoop of vanilla ice cream.

preparation 10 minutes   **cooking time** 20 minutes

Serves 4

BARBECUE BANOFFEE

4 bananas, peeled
125g/4oz fudge, roughly chopped
butter to grease
4 tbsp rum or brandy
Greek yogurt or ice cream to
serve

1 Make a long slit in each banana. Divide the fudge among the bananas, then place the bananas on four large squares of buttered foil. Spoon 1 tbsp rum or brandy over each banana and scrunch the edges of the foil together to make loose parcels.
2 Put the foil parcels on the barbecue or under a hot grill (broiler) and cook for 4–5 minutes. Serve hot, with Greek yogurt or vanilla ice cream.

preparation 5 minutes   **cooking time** 4–5 minutes

Serves 4

WARM PLUM TOASTS WITH MASCARPONE

12 plums or greengages, halved and stoned

butter to grease

2 tbsp caster (superfine) sugar

grated zest and juice of 1 orange

grilled brioche and mascarpone cheese to serve

1 Heat the barbecue to hot. Place the plums on a large piece of buttered foil. Sprinkle the sugar over and add the orange zest and juice. Pull up the edges of the foil to enclose the plums and seal the edges to make a loose parcel.

2 Put the foil parcel on the barbecue and cook for 10 minutes.

3 Remove the vanilla pod and serve the hot plums on lightly grilled brioche slices spread with mascarpone cheese.

preparation 10 minutes   cooking time 10 minutes

Serves 8

BROWNIE AND STRAWBERRY KEBABS

4 chocolate brownies

16 large strawberries

whipped cream to serve

1 Cut the chocolate brownies into large chunks, and hull the strawberries.

2 Thread the brownie chunks and fruit alternately onto long kebab skewers.

3 Barbecue or grill (broil) for 3 minutes, turning occasionally.

4 Serve hot with whipped cream.

preparation 5 minutes   cooking time 3 minutes

Serves 4

RASPBERRY RIPPLE

300g/11oz raspberries
250ml/8fl oz/1 cup skimmed milk, chilled
250g/9oz/1 cup natural yogurt, chilled
2 scoops raspberry-flavoured frozen yogurt

1 Remove the hulls from the raspberries, then wash and pat them dry with kitchen paper.
2 Put the raspberries in a blender with the milk and natural yogurt. Blitz until thick and creamy.
3 Pour into two tall glasses and top each one with a scoop of frozen yogurt and serve.

preparation 5 minutes

Serves 2

TICKLED PINK

500g/1lb 2oz watermelon
125g/4oz fresh strawberries
2 scoops peach sorbet
crushed ice
300ml/½ pint/1¼ cups Prosecco, pink champagne or pink lemonade

1 Remove the peel and seeds from the watermelon. Discard them and roughly chop the flesh. Put in a blender.
2 Hull the strawberries, then wash and pat dry with kitchen paper. Add to the blender with the peach sorbet and blitz for a few seconds until smooth.
3 Put some crushed ice in two tall glasses and pour in the watermelon and strawberry mixture. Top up with Prosecco, pink champagne or lemonade.

preparation 10 minutes

Serves 2

ELDERFLOWER COOLER

225g/8oz strawberries
2 tbsp elderflower cordial
300ml/½ pint/1¼ cups Prosecco cava or champagne, chilled
a few ice cubes
mint sprigs to serve

1 Hull the strawberries, then wash and pat dry with kitchen paper. Put in a blender with the elderflower cordial and blitz briefly until smooth.
2 Pour into two large glasses and top up with Prosecco, cava or champagne.
3 Add a few ice cubes and serve garnished with mint sprigs.

preparation 5 minutes

Serves 2

HOMEMADE LEMONADE

6 large unwaxed lemons
1.2 litres/2 pints/5 cups boiling water
1–2 tbsp sugar
ice cubes
sparkling water to serve

1 Remove the zest in thin strips from 3 lemons. Place in a large jug with the squeezed juice of all 6 lemons. Add the boiling water and sugar and set aside to cool.
2 When completely cool, cover the jug and chill in the refrigerator overnight.
3 Strain the lemonade through a sieve or some muslin (cheesecloth) and store in corked bottles in the refrigerator. Serve over ice diluted with sparkling water.

preparation 15 minutes plus chilling

Serves 6–8

ICED CITRUS TEA

5 strong tea bags
1.2 litres/2 pints/5 cups boiling water
1–2 tbsp sugar
a few fresh mint sprigs
juice of 2 lemons
juice of 1 orange
ice cubes

1 Put the tea bags in a large teapot or jug and pour the boiling water over. Sweeten with sugar and add some mint.
2 Cover and set aside to infuse for 20 minutes. Discard the tea bags and, when the tea is cold, remove the mint.
3 Pour the cold tea into a large jug and stir in the lemon and orange juice.
4 Add some ice and sprigs of mint. Serve in six tall glasses.

preparation 15 minutes plus infusing and cooling

Serves 6

VIRGIN PINA COLADA

crushed ice
225g/8oz creamed coconut
900ml/1½ pints/3⅔ cups chilled unsweetened pineapple juice
fresh pineapple wedges and maraschino cherries to serve

1 Put the crushed ice, creamed coconut and pineapple juice in a blender.
2 Blitz briefly until smooth.
3 Serve in four tall glasses decorated with wedges of fresh pineapple and cherries.

preparation 10 minutes

Serves 4

WATERMELON AND GINGER COOLER

450g/1lb watermelon
2.5cm/1in piece fresh root ginger
juice of 3 limes
1–2 tbsp sugar
chilled sparkling water

1 Peel the watermelon and remove the seeds. Roughly chop the flesh and place in a blender.
2 Peel and chop the ginger. Add to the blender with the lime juice and blitz until smooth. Sweeten with sugar to taste.
3 Pour into two large glasses and top up with sparkling water.

preparation 5 minutes

Serves 2

MELON COOLER

450g/1lb Galia or Charentais melon
300g/11oz honeydew melon
150ml/¼ pint/scant ⅔ cup peach juice
a few ice cubes
sliced strawberries to serve

1 Cut the melons into slices and remove the skin. Discard the seeds and chop the flesh roughly. Place in a blender.
2 Pour in the peach juice and blitz for a few seconds until smooth.
3 Pour into two glasses over ice cubes and serve with sliced strawberries.

preparation 10 minutes

Serves 2

APRICOT AND CARROT SMOOTHIE

1 large carrot, peeled
5 ready-to-eat dried apricots
1 medium banana, cut into chunks
juice of 2 oranges
2 ice cubes

1 Put the carrot in a juicer and juice it.
2 Put the carrot juice in a blender with the apricots, banana, orange juice and ice cubes and blitz briefly.
3 Pour into a tall glass and serve.

preparation 10 minutes

Serves 1

SUMMER SMOOTHIE

½ pink grapefruit, peeled
½ melon
1 small, ripe banana
225g/8oz/1 cup natural yogurt
2 tsp thick honey
a few ice cubes

1 Chop the grapefruit flesh roughly, discarding any pips, and place in a blender.
2 Remove the melon seeds and skin. Chop the flesh roughly and add to the blender with the banana. Add the yogurt and honey and blitz briefly until smooth.
3 Pour over ice in two glasses and serve.

preparation 10 minutes

Serves 2

VIRGIN SEA BREEZE

600ml/1 pint/2½ cups chilled cranberry juice drink
600ml/1 pint/2½ cups chilled unsweetened grapefruit juice
ice cubes

1 Mix together the cranberry juice drink and grapefruit juice in a large jug, stirring well.
2 Put plenty of ice in six tall glasses and pour the cranberry and grapefruit mixture over the top. Serve immediately.

preparation 5 minutes

Serves 6

MIMOSA

1 bottle champagne or sparkling dry white wine, e.g. Prosecco
900ml/1½ pints/3⅔ cups unsweetened orange juice

1 Chill the champagne and orange juice in the refrigerator.
2 When thoroughly chilled, mix them together in a large jug and pour into 12 fluted champagne glasses. Serve.

preparation 5 minutes plus chilling

Serves 12

TOP 10 MARINADES

SPICY TOMATO

8 tbsp tomato ketchup
2 tbsp soy sauce
1 tbsp sweet chilli sauce
juice of 1 lemon
2 tsp Cajun seasoning

1   Mix all the ingredients together. Use for
    pork and sausages.

preparation 5 minutes   *Serves 6*

PINEAPPLE

grated zest and juice of 1 lime
¼ pineapple, peeled and chopped
200ml/7fl oz/¾ cup coconut milk
a dash of Tabasco sauce

1   Blend the lime zest and juice with the
    pineapple. Add the coconut milk and
    Tabasco sauce. Use for chicken or pork.

preparation 5 minutes   *Serves 8*

HERBY LEMON

grated zest and juice of 1 lemon
2 tbsp roughly chopped rosemary or thyme
6 tbsp olive oil

1   Mix together all the ingredients. Use for
    vegetables, fish, chicken or lamb.

preparation 3 minutes   *Serves 6*

MUSTARD

4 tbsp wholegrain mustard
150ml/¼ pint/scant ⅔ cup beer

1   Blend the beer and mustard together. Use
    for beef steaks or pork.

preparation 3 minutes   *Serves 6*

TERIYAKI

2 garlic cloves, crushed
2.5cm/1in piece fresh root ginger, peeled and
    grated
3 tbsp Teriyaki sauce
1 tbsp runny honey
1 tsp oil

1   Mix together the ingredients in a non-
    metallic dish. Use for chicken and fish.

preparation 3 minutes   *Serves 4*

HOT AND SPICY

1 garlic clove, crushed
2 tsp each ground coriander and cumin
1 tbsp paprika
a pinch of cayenne pepper
1 red chilli, seeded and chopped
juice of ½ lemon
2 tbsp dark soy sauce

1 Mix all the ingredients together. Use for
   pork, lamb and chicken.

preparation 5 minutes   *Serves 6*

TAMARIND

3 tbsp tamarind paste
2 tbsp runny honey
1 tbsp soy sauce

1 Mix all the ingredients together. Use as
   a marinade and glaze for pork chops
   or steaks.

preparation 3 minutes   *Serves 6*

HARISSA

3 tbsp harissa paste
1 tbsp tomato paste
3 tbsp olive oil
5 tbsp chopped fresh coriander (cilantro)

1 Mix together the harissa paste, tomato
   paste, olive oil and herbs. Use for chicken.

preparation 5 minutes   *Serves 4*

QUICK AND EASY

4 tbsp olive oil
juice of 1 lemon
2 garlic cloves, crushed

1 Mix everything together. Use for chicken or
   meat, vegetables, fish or shellfish, and chill
   in the refrigerator for at least 1 hour.

preparation 5 minutes   *Serves 8*

CHINESE

6 tbsp plum sauce
1 tbsp sesame seeds
juice of ½ orange

1 Mix all the ingredients together. Use for
   pork and chicken.

preparation 3 minutes   *Serves 8*

CHOCOLATE TREATS

Even if you're not a committed chocaholic, you will love the sumptuous recipes featured in this chapter, which is dedicated exclusively to chocolate. There are everyday treats, including moist muffins and crisp chocolate chip cookies, as well as cakes and desserts for special occasions.

Your family will enjoy the occasional chocolate indulgence, especially the children. For them, we have old-fashioned fudge, fashionable cupcakes and a no-cook refrigerator cake, which will last for days if you have enough self-control not to keep cutting 'just one more slice'. And no chocolate selection would be complete without at least one recipe for brownies – everyone's perennial favourite.

A classic Sachertorte adds a touch of sophistication and there are chocolate pots, roulade and a tart to add the finishing touches to an elegant dinner, plus hot puddings that ooze chocolate sauce when you cut into them. And to serve with coffee at the end of the meal, we have recipes for chocolate truffles and biscotti. There are even some fabulous richly flavoured chocolate drinks for when you need a pick-me-up.

< Chocolate Roulade (page 398)

STICKY CHOCOLATE BROWNIES

butter to grease

175g/6oz plain (semisweet) chocolate, broken into pieces

50g/2oz ready-to-eat prunes

2 tbsp Armagnac or brandy

200g/7oz/scant 1 cup Demerara (brown) sugar

4 medium (US large) egg whites

75g/3oz/¾ cup self-raising (self-rising) flour, sifted

4 tbsp chopped hazelnuts

icing (confectioner's) sugar to dust

1 Preheat the oven to 180°C/350°F/Gas 4. Butter a 15cm/6in square shallow baking tin and line the base with parchment paper.
2 Melt the chocolate in a bowl set over a pan of simmering water. Remove from the heat and set aside to cool slightly.
3 Put the prunes and Armagnac or brandy in a blender and blitz to a purée. Add the Demerara sugar and blitz.
4 Whisk the egg whites until they form soft peaks.
5 Gently fold the prune mixture, flour, nuts and egg whites into the melted chocolate. Pour into the prepared tin and bake in the oven for 1 hour or until firm to the touch.
6 Leave to cool in the tin. Turn out, cut into 12 squares and dust with icing sugar.

preparation 20 minutes cooking time 1 hour plus cooling

Makes 12

NUTTY WHITE CHOCOLATE BROWNIES

75g/3oz/6 tbsp butter plus extra to grease

450g/1lb white chocolate, chopped

4 medium (US large) eggs

175g/6oz/¾ cup golden caster (superfine) sugar

175g/6oz/1½ cups self-raising (self-rising) flour, sifted

175g/6oz/1 cup roughly chopped almonds

1 Preheat the oven to 190°C/375°F/Gas 5. Butter a 25 x 20cm/ 10 x 8in baking tin and line the base with parchment paper.
2 Melt 125g/4oz chocolate with the butter in a bowl set over a pan of gently simmering water. Remove and cool slightly.
3 Whisk the eggs and sugar in a large bowl until smooth, then gradually beat in the melted chocolate mixture.
4 Gently fold in the sifted flour with the almonds and the rest of the chocolate. Spoon into the tin and level the surface.
5 Bake in the oven for 30 minutes or until the centre is just firm to the touch. Set aside to cool in the tin.
6 Turn out and cut into 12 squares.

preparation 20 minutes cooking time 30 minutes plus cooling

Makes 12

CHEESECAKE BROWNIES

200g/7oz/scant 1 cup butter plus extra to grease

175g/6oz plain (semisweet) chocolate (minimum 70% cocoa solids), chopped

3 medium (US large) eggs

150g/5oz/⅔ cup golden caster (superfine) sugar

125g/4oz/1 cup self-raising (self-rising) flour, sifted

For the cheesecake mixture

125g/4oz/⅔ cup cream cheese

1 medium (US large) egg

2 tbsp caster (superfine) sugar

1 Preheat the oven to 200°C/400°F/Gas 6. Grease a 23cm/9in square baking tin and line with parchment paper.
2 Melt the chocolate and butter in a bowl set over a pan of gently simmering water and stir to combine. Remove from the heat and set aside to cool.
3 Put the eggs and sugar in a bowl and whisk until thick. Fold in the cooled chocolate mixture and the flour and pour into the prepared tin.
4 Beat the cream cheese, egg and sugar in a bowl.
5 Drop heaped teaspoonfuls over the surface of the brownie mixture, then use a skewer to swirl the two mixtures together in a marble pattern.
6 Bake in the oven for 25–30 minutes. Leave to cool in the tin for 10 minutes before turning out on to a wire rack. Set aside to cool completely. Cut into 9 brownies.

preparation 20 minutes   cooking time 25–30 minutes plus cooling

Makes 9

SACHERTORTE

175g/6oz/¾ cup butter plus extra to grease

225g/8oz plain (semisweet) chocolate (minimum 70% cocoa solids), chopped

175g/6oz/¾ cup caster (superfine) sugar

5 medium (US large) eggs, beaten

125g/4oz/1 cup self-raising (self-rising) flour

50g/2oz/½ cup ground almonds

1 x quantity warm chocolate ganache (see page 588)

sugared almonds to decorate

1 Preheat the oven to 190°C/375°F/Gas 5. Butter a 20cm/8in springform baking tin and line with parchment paper.
2 Melt the chocolate in a heatproof bowl set over a pan of gently simmering water. Remove from the heat and cool.
3 Cream the butter and sugar until pale and fluffy. Gradually beat in two-thirds of the beaten eggs. Sift in a little of the flour, then gradually beat in the remaining eggs. Fold in the remaining flour and the ground almonds. Fold in the melted chocolate and pour into the prepared tin.
4 Bake in the oven for 45 minutes or until a skewer inserted into the centre of the cake comes out clean. Cool in the tin for 30 minutes, then turn out on to a wire rack to cool.
5 Place the wire rack over a tray. Spoon the chocolate ganache over the top of the cake, letting it trickle down the sides. Use a palette knife to spread it evenly over the top and sides. Set aside for 1 hour to set. Decorate with sugared almonds.

preparation 35 minutes   **cooking time** 45–55 minutes plus cooling and setting

Makes 12 slices

CHOCOLATE MUFFINS

125g/4oz/½ cup butter

100g/3½oz plain (semisweet) chocolate, chopped

250g/9oz/2½ cups plain (all-purpose) flour

1 tsp bicarbonate of soda (baking soda)

2 tbsp cocoa powder

175g/6oz/¾ cup caster (superfine) sugar

2 medium (US large) eggs

200ml/7fl oz/¾ cup milk

125g/4oz/½ cup natural yogurt

a few drops of vanilla extract

1 Preheat the oven to 190°C/375°F/Gas 5. Line a 12-hole muffin pan with paper muffin cases.
2 Melt the butter and plain chocolate in a bowl set over a pan of gently simmering water. Mix together, then remove from the heat and set aside to cool a little.
3 Sift the flour, bicarbonate of soda and cocoa into a bowl. Add the sugar and stir well.
4 Break the eggs into a bowl and beat in the milk, yogurt and vanilla extract.
5 Pour the egg and the chocolate mixtures on to the dry ingredients and fold in gently – do not over-mix.
6 Divide the mixture among the paper cases. Bake in the oven for 20–25 minutes until well risen and springy to the touch. Cool the muffins on a wire rack.

preparation 20 minutes   **cooking time** 25 minutes plus cooling

Makes 12

CHOCOLATE CUPCAKES

125g/4oz/½ cup butter, softened

125g/4oz/½ cup caster (superfine) sugar

2 medium (US large) eggs, beaten

2 tbsp cocoa powder

125g/4oz/1 cup self-raising (self-rising) flour

175g/6oz plain (semisweet) chocolate (minimum 70% cocoa solids), roughly chopped

125ml/4fl oz/½ cup double (heavy) cream

1 Preheat the oven to 190°C/375°F/Gas 5. Line a 12-hole and a 6-hole muffin pan with paper muffin cases.
2 Beat the butter and sugar until light and fluffy. Gradually beat in the eggs. Sift the cocoa powder and flour and fold into the mixture with half the chopped chocolate.
3 Divide the mixture among the paper cases and bake in the oven for 20 minutes. Cool the cupcakes in their paper cases on a wire rack.
4 Put the cream and the remaining chocolate in a pan over a low heat and stir gently until melted. Set aside to cool and thicken slightly.
5 Spoon the topping on to the cupcakes and set aside for 30 minutes to set.

preparation 15 minutes   **cooking time** 20 minutes plus cooling and setting

Makes 18

CHOCOLATE ALMOND REFRIGERATOR CAKE

a little oil to grease

175g/6oz plain (semisweet) chocolate, chopped

175g/6oz milk chocolate, chopped

150g/5oz/⅔ cup butter

75g/3oz/¼ cup golden (corn) syrup

340g/12oz digestive biscuits (graham crackers), roughly crushed

50g/2oz/½ cup chopped pecans

75g/3oz/½ cup dried cherries

50g/2oz white chocolate, chopped

1 Lightly oil a deep 23cm/9in square baking tin and line the base and sides with parchment paper.
2 Melt the plain and milk chocolate, butter and syrup in a bowl set over a pan of gently simmering water. When melted, stir to combine. Set aside to cool slightly.
3 Put the biscuits in a bowl with the pecans and cherries. Pour the chocolate mixture over the top and stir well. Spoon into the prepared tin and level the surface.
4 Melt the white chocolate in a small bowl set over a pan of gently simmering water. Drizzle over the top of the chocolate mixture. Use a skewer to swirl the white chocolate in an attractive pattern. Cover with clingfilm (plastic wrap) or foil, making sure it doesn't touch the chocolate.
5 Chill in the refrigerator for at least 4 hours or overnight. Cut into squares to serve.

preparation 15 minutes cooking time 10 minutes plus chilling

Makes 24

WHITE CHOCOLATE CRUNCH

225g/8oz digestive biscuits (graham crackers), crushed

125g/4oz/½ cup butter, melted

675g/1½ lb white chocolate

600ml/1 pint/2½ cups double (heavy) cream

50g/2oz plain (semisweet) chocolate, coarsely grated

1 Line a 20 x 6.5cm/8 x 2½in springform tin with parchment paper. Stir the biscuit crumbs into the melted butter. Spread over the base of the tin and press down. Chill until set.
2 Chop the white chocolate and melt with half the cream in a bowl set over a pan of barely simmering water. Remove from the heat and stir until smooth. Set aside for 15 minutes or until starting to thicken but still a little warm.
3 In another bowl, whip the remaining cream until it stands in soft peaks. Gently fold into the chocolate mixture. Pour over the biscuit base and chill in the refrigerator for 3 hours.
4 Sprinkle the grated chocolate over the top, then remove from the tin and serve.

preparation 50 minutes plus chilling and freezing cooking time 2 minutes plus cooling

Serves 16

CHOC CHIP COOKIES

125g/4oz/½ cup butter, softened, plus extra to grease

125g/4oz/½ cup caster (superfine) sugar

1 medium (US large) egg

1 tsp vanilla essence

225g/8oz/2¼ cups plain (all-purpose) flour

½ tsp baking powder

125g/4oz plain (semisweet) chocolate (minimum 70% cocoa solids), cut into chunks

125g/4oz milk chocolate, cut into chunks

1 Preheat the oven to 180°C/350°F/Gas 4. Lightly butter two baking sheets.

2 Beat the butter and sugar in a bowl until pale and creamy. Beat in the egg and vanilla essence. Sift in the flour and baking powder and mix well. Stir in the chocolate chunks.

3 Drop dessert spoonfuls of the mixture on to the prepared baking sheets. Space them out to allow room for them to spread. Flatten slightly with the back of a fork.

4 Bake in the oven for 12–15 minutes until risen and golden brown, but still quite soft.

5 Leave on the baking sheets for 5 minutes, then transfer to wire rack and set aside until cool. Store in an airtight tin.

preparation 15 minutes cooking time 12–15 minutes plus cooling

Makes 18

CHOC CHIP BISCOTTI

225g/8oz/2¼ cups plain (all-purpose) flour plus extra to dust

75g/3oz/scant ⅓ cup caster (superfine) sugar

½ tsp baking powder

a pinch of salt

2 medium (US large) eggs, beaten

1 tbsp milk

grated zest of 1 orange

25g/1oz/¼ cup hazelnuts

4 tbsp plain (semisweet) chocolate chips

1 Preheat the oven to 200°C/400°F/Gas 6.

2 Sift the flour into a large bowl. Stir in the sugar, baking powder and salt. Make a well in the centre and stir in the beaten eggs, milk, orange zest, nuts and chocolate chips.

3 Turn out the dough on to a lightly floured surface and knead into a ball. Roll out into a 25cm/10in long cylinder and place on a non-stick baking sheet. Flatten slightly.

4 Bake in the oven for 20–25 minutes until pale golden. Reduce the oven temperature to 150°C/300°F, Gas 2 and place the biscotti cylinder on a board. Cut into 20 slices.

5 Place the slices on the baking sheet and return to the oven for 15 minutes or until golden brown and dry.

6 Transfer to a wire rack and set aside to cool completely.

preparation 10 minutes cooking time 35–40 minutes plus cooling

Makes 20

VIENNESE FINGERS

125g/4oz/½ cup butter, softened, plus extra to grease

25g/1oz/¼ cup icing (confectioner's) sugar

125g/4oz/1 cup plain (all-purpose) flour, sifted

1 tsp cornflour (cornstarch)

¼ tsp baking powder

1 tsp vanilla extract

50g/2oz plain (semisweet) chocolate

1 Preheat the oven to 190°C/375°F/Gas 5 and butter two baking sheets.
2 Beat the butter until smooth, then beat in the icing sugar until pale and fluffy. Beat in the flour, cornflour and baking powder. Stir in the vanilla extract.
3 Put the mixture in a piping (decorator's) bag fitted with a medium star nozzle. Pipe 20 finger shapes, about 7.5cm/3in long, on to the baking sheets, spacing them well apart.
4 Bake in the oven for 15 minutes. Cool on a wire rack.
5 Melt the chocolate in a bowl set over a pan of gently simmering water. Dip the ends of the Viennese Fingers into the melted chocolate and leave to set.

preparation 15 minutes **cooking time** 15 minutes plus cooling

Makes 20

FLORENTINES

75g/3oz/6 tbsp butter plus extra to grease

50g/2oz/¼ cup caster (superfine) sugar

2 tbsp double (heavy) cream

25g/1oz/¼ cup chopped mixed candied peel

4 tbsp mixed glacé (candied) cherries, roughly chopped

6 tbsp flaked almonds

2 tbsp plain (all-purpose) flour

200g/7oz plain (semisweet) chocolate (minimum 70% cocoa solids), broken into pieces

1 Preheat the oven to 180°C/350°F/Gas 4. Lightly butter two large baking sheets.
2 Melt the butter in a small pan over a low heat, then add the sugar, stirring until dissolved. Bring to the boil and remove from the heat. Stir in the cream, candied peel, cherries, almonds and flour. Mix well.
3 Drop heaped teaspoonfuls of the mixture on to the prepared baking sheets, spacing them well apart.
4 Bake in the oven for 8–10 minutes until spread out and golden brown. Leave on the baking sheet for 2 minutes, then transfer to a wire rack and set aside until cold.
5 Melt the chocolate in a bowl set over a pan of gently simmering water. Spread over the underside of each Florentine and use a fork to make wavy lines.
6 Arrange them, chocolate-side up, on parchment paper and set aside until the chocolate sets.

preparation 15 minutes **cooking time** 16–20 minutes plus cooling

Makes 18

SOFT CHOC CHIP COOKIES

225g/8oz/1 cup butter, softened

150g/5oz/⅔ cup caster (superfine) sugar

150g/5oz/⅔ cup light muscovado (brown) sugar

2 tbsp golden (corn) syrup

3 medium (US large) eggs

340g/12oz/3¼ cups plain (all-purpose) flour

1 tsp bicarbonate of soda (baking soda)

a pinch of salt

340g/12oz mixed milk and white chocolate, cut into chunks

1 Preheat the oven to 200°C/400°F/Gas 6. Line three baking sheets with parchment paper.
2 Put the butter, both sugars and golden syrup in a bowl and beat for 5 minutes or until pale and fluffy.
3 Beat the eggs, then gradually beat them into the butter mixture, adding 2 tbsp flour. Sift in the remaining flour, the bicarbonate of soda and salt and beat in quickly. Gently fold in the chocolate chunks.
4 Place heaped teaspoonfuls of the mixture on the prepared baking sheets, spacing them well apart. Don't flatten them – they will spread during cooking.
5 Bake in the oven for 10 minutes or until pale golden brown. Transfer to wire racks and set aside to cool.

preparation 15 minutes   cooking time 12 minutes

Makes 25

CHOCOLATE ROULADE

200g/7oz dark chocolate, broken into pieces

5 medium (US large) eggs, separated

175g/6oz/¾ cup caster (superfine) sugar plus extra to sprinkle

1l/1¾ pints/4 cups soft-scoop vanilla ice-cream

hot chocolate sauce to serve (see page 580)

1 Preheat the oven to 180°C/350°F/Gas 4. Line a 35 x 23cm/ 14 x 9in deep roasting pan with parchment paper.
2 Melt the chocolate in a bowl set over a pan of simmering water. Whisk the egg whites in a large bowl until stiff. Whisk in one-third of the sugar, a little at a time, until thick. In a separate bowl, whisk the yolks with the remaining sugar until pale and thick. Fold in the melted chocolate, then fold in the egg whites gently but thoroughly.
3 Pour the mixture into the prepared tin and bake in the oven for 15 minutes or until just set. Set aside for several hours.
4 Sprinkle a sheet of parchment paper with sugar. Turn the chocolate sponge out on to the paper and peel away the backing parchment. Spoon the ice-cream evenly over it and roll up the sponge in the paper, starting with the short edge.
5 Overwrap the paper with foil, twist the ends to seal, then freeze for 4 hours, or overnight.
6 Serve the frozen roulade cut into slices with the hot chocolate sauce.

preparation 45 minutes plus cooling   cooking time 15 minutes

Serves 8

CHOCOLATE BRIOCHE PUDDING

225g/8oz brioche

125g/4oz white chocolate, chopped

500ml/17fl oz/2¼ cups fresh custard

150ml/¼ pint/scant ⅔ cup milk

1 large (US extra-large) egg, beaten

butter to grease

1 tbsp icing (confectioner's) sugar

4 tbsp chopped nuts

3 tbsp chocolate buttons

1 Roughly chop the brioche and place in a large bowl.
2 Put the chocolate in a pan with the custard and milk. Stir over a low heat until the chocolate melts. Beat in the egg.
3 Pour the chocolate custard over the brioche. Cover the bowl and chill in the refrigerator for at least 4 hours.
4 Preheat the oven to 180°C/350°F/Gas 4. Butter a large, deep ovenproof dish.
5 Put the chocolate brioche mixture in the dish and bake in the oven for 30 minutes.
6 Sprinkle with sugar, nuts and chocolate buttons. Return to the oven for 20–30 minutes until lightly set. Serve warm.

preparation 20 minutes plus chilling **cooking time** 50 minutes–1 hour

Serves 6

MINI CHOCOLATE PUDDINGS

125g/4oz/½ cup butter plus extra to grease

125g/4oz/½ cup caster (superfine) sugar plus extra to dust

100g/3½oz plain (semisweet) chocolate (minimum 70% cocoa solids), broken into pieces

2 large (US extra-large) eggs

1 tsp vanilla extract

4 tbsp plain (all-purpose) flour

1 tsp icing (confectioner's) sugar

1 Preheat the oven to 200°C/400°F/Gas 6. Butter four 200ml/7fl oz/¾ cup ramekins and dust with sugar.
2 Melt the chocolate and butter in a bowl set over a pan of gently simmering water. Remove from the heat and set aside to cool for 5 minutes.
3 In a bowl, whisk the eggs, caster sugar, vanilla extract and flour together until smooth. Fold in the chocolate mixture and pour into the ramekins.
4 Stand them on a baking sheet and bake in the oven for 12–15 minutes until puffed and set on the outside, but still runny inside.
5 Turn out, dust with icing sugar and serve immediately.

preparation 15 minutes **cooking time** 12–15 minutes

Serves 4

CHOCA MOCHA MOUSSE

340g/12oz plain (semisweet) chocolate (minimum 70% cocoa solids), broken into pieces

6 tbsp espresso coffee

6 large (US extra-large) eggs, separated

chocolate shavings to decorate

1 Put the chocolate with the espresso coffee in a bowl set over a pan of gently simmering water. Leave to melt, stirring occasionally. Remove from the heat and set aside to cool for 3–4 minutes, stirring frequently.
2 Beat the egg yolks with 2 tbsp water and then beat into the chocolate mixture until well amalgamated.
3 Whisk the egg whites in a clean bowl until they form firm peaks. Fold gently into the chocolate mixture.
4 Pour into a 1.7 litre/3 pint/7½ cup soufflé dish or divide among eight ramekins. Chill for at least 4 hours, or overnight, until set. Just before serving, decorate with chocolate shavings.

preparation 20 minutes plus chilling

Serves 8

CHOCOLATE FONDANTS

150g/5oz/⅔ cup butter plus extra to grease

3 medium (US large) eggs plus 3 egg yolks

75g/3oz/scant ⅓ cup caster (superfine) sugar

150g/5oz plain (semisweet) chocolate (minimum 70% cocoa solids), broken into pieces

50g/2oz/½ cup plain (all-purpose) flour, sifted

6 chocolate truffles

1 Preheat the oven to 200°C/400°F/Gas 6. Lightly butter six 200ml/7fl oz/¾ cup ramekins.
2 Put the whole eggs, egg yolks and sugar in a large bowl and whisk for 8–10 minutes until pale and fluffy.
3 Meanwhile, melt the chocolate and butter in a bowl set over a pan of gently simmering water, stirring occasionally.
4 Stir a spoonful of the melted chocolate into the egg mixture, then gently fold in the remaining chocolate mixture followed by the flour. Use a figure-of-eight motion.
5 Put a large spoonful into each ramekin and then place a chocolate truffle in the middle of each. Spoon the rest of the mixture over the truffles.
6 Bake in the oven for 10–12 minutes until firm on top and starting to rise. Serve warm.

preparation 25 minutes cooking time 10–12 minutes

Serves 6

CHOCOLATE TART

sweet pastry (see page 583), flour to dust
icing (confectioner's) sugar to dust

For the filling
175g/6oz plain (semisweet) chocolate (minimum 50% cocoa solids), chopped
175ml/6fl oz/⅔ cup double (heavy) cream
75g/3oz/⅓ cup caster (superfine) sugar
2 medium (US large) eggs
grated rind and juice of ½ orange

1 Roll out the pastry on a lightly floured surface and use to line a 20cm/8in loose-based tart tin. Prick the base all over with a fork, put the tin on a baking sheet and chill for 30 minutes. Preheat the oven to 190°C/375°F/Gas 5.
2 Line the pastry case (pie crust) with parchment paper and fill with baking beans. Bake in the oven for 15 minutes, then remove the beans and paper. Set aside. Reduce the oven temperature to 170°C/325°F/Gas 3.
3 To make the filling, melt the chocolate in a bowl set over a pan of gently simmering water. Take off the heat and set aside to cool for 10 minutes.
4 Mix together the cream, sugar, eggs, orange rind and juice in a bowl. Gradually stir in the chocolate. Pour into the pastry case (pie crust) and bake in the oven for 20 minutes or until just set.
5 Serve warm or cold, dusted with icing sugar.

preparation 30 minutes plus chilling   **cooking time** 1 hour plus cooling

Serves 8

QUICK CHOCOLATE POTS

300g/11oz plain (semisweet) chocolate (minimum 70% cocoa solids), cut into chunks

300ml/½ pint/1¼ cups double (heavy) cream

250g/9oz/1½ cups mascarpone cheese

2 tbsp hot espresso coffee

6 tbsp crème fraîche

coffee beans to decorate

1 Melt the chocolate in a heatproof bowl set over a pan of gently simmering water. Remove from the heat and stir in the cream, mascarpone and espresso. Mix well until the chocolate blends with the cream and mascarpone.
2 Divide the chocolate mixture among six glasses or ramekins and chill in the refrigerator for 20 minutes.
3 Just before serving, spoon some crème fraîche on top and decorate with coffee beans.

preparation 10 minutes plus chilling cooking time 10 minutes

Serves 6

MALLOW MELTS

16 large strawberries

16 marshmallows

For the chocolate sauce

125g/4oz plain (semisweet) chocolate (minimum 70% cocoa solids), cut into chunks

150ml/¼ pint/scant ⅔ cup single (light) cream

8 marshmallows

1 tsp hazelnut chocolate spread

1 Put the chocolate, cream, marshmallows and hazelnut chocolate spread in a heatproof bowl over a pan of gently simmering water. Stir continuously until melted and then whisk until smooth.
2 Preheat the grill (broiler).
3 Thread the strawberries and marshmallows onto small wooden skewers that have been soaked in water for 20 minutes.
4 Grill (broil) for 30 seconds, until just warmed through. Serve drizzled with the chocolate sauce.

preparation 10 minutes cooking time 5 minutes

Serves 4

CHOCOLATE FUDGE

50g/2oz/4 tbsp butter plus extra to grease

225g/8oz/1 cup granulated sugar

1 x 400ml/14fl oz can sweetened condensed milk

100g/3½oz plain (semisweet) chocolate (minimum 70% cocoa solids), grated

6 tbsp shelled pistachios (optional)

1 Grease a 20cm/8in square baking tin and line the base and 2.5cm/1in up the sides with parchment paper.
2 Put the sugar in a pan with the butter and condensed milk. Stir over a low heat until the sugar dissolves. Bring to the boil, stirring, and boil for 6–8 minutes, stirring frequently. The mixture is ready when it reaches 115°C/240°F on a sugar thermometer. Or drop a little into cold water – if it forms a soft ball when squashed between your forefinger and thumb it's ready.
3 Remove from the heat and beat in the chocolate and nuts (if using) until smooth and glossy. Pour into the prepared tin and set aside for 2 hours or until set.
4 Remove the fudge from the tin and peel away the lining paper. Cut into squares and store in an airtight container.

preparation 15 minutes cooking time 6–8 minutes plus cooling

Makes 675g/1lb 7oz

CHOCOLATE TRUFFLES

200g/7oz plain (semisweet) chocolate (minimum 50% cocoa solids), broken into pieces

25g/1oz/2 tbsp butter

150ml/¼ pint/scant ⅔ cup double (heavy) cream

3 tbsp cocoa powder, sifted

100g/3½oz/⅔ cup finely chopped hazelnuts

1 Melt the chocolate in a heatproof bowl set over a pan of gently simmering water, then remove from the heat.
2 In another pan, melt the butter and cream. Bring to the boil, then remove from the heat and stir into the chocolate mixture.
3 Whisk until cool and thick, then chill in the refrigerator for 1–2 hours.
4 Put the cocoa powder in a shallow dish. Scoop out teaspoonfuls of the chilled chocolate mixture and roll in the cocoa powder or chopped nuts.
5 Chill the truffles in the refrigerator until ready to serve. Or put them in pretty boxes and use as edible gifts.

preparation 20 minutes cooking time 12 minutes plus chilling

Makes 30

BERRIES WITH WHITE CHOCOLATE SAUCE

340g/12oz frozen mixed summer berries

125ml/4fl oz/½ cup double (heavy) cream

1 tbsp runny honey

4 tbsp dry white wine

125g/4oz white chocolate, broken into pieces

1 Partly thaw the frozen summer berries in the microwave for 2 minutes on full power, then set aside to stand while you make the white chocolate sauce.
2 Pour the cream into a small pan and add the honey and white wine. Bring just to the boil, stirring. Reduce the heat, add the white chocolate and stir gently over a very low heat until it melts.
3 Divide the berries among four shallow glass dishes and pour the hot chocolate sauce over the top – the heat will finish thawing the fruit. Serve immediately.

preparation 10 minutes cooking time 4–5 minutes

Serves 4

GIFT CHOCOLATES

50g/2oz white chocolate, chopped

50g/2oz milk chocolate, chopped

50g/2oz plain (semisweet) chocolate, chopped

edible gold leaf to decorate

1 Put each chocolate in a separate small, microwave-safe bowl. Place the bowls in the microwave and heat on full power for 1 minute. Continue heating for 10-second bursts until the chocolates are melted and smooth.
2 Meanwhile, line two baking sheets with parchment paper. Drop teaspoonfuls of melted chocolate on to the prepared sheets, spacing them a little apart. Press down gently with the back of a teaspoon to smooth into rounds.
3 Decorate the chocolates with edible gold leaf. Put in the freezer for 10 minutes to set, then place in gift boxes.

preparation 10 minutes plus freezing cooking time 1 minute

Makes 36

COCO CHOCO FRAPPE

50g/2oz fresh coconut plus extra to decorate
175ml/6fl oz/⅔ cup coconut milk
4 tbsp chocolate syrup
2 scoops chocolate ice cream
200g/7oz crushed ice
1 tbsp plain chocolate shavings

1 Chop the coconut and put in a blender with the coconut milk, chocolate syrup, ice cream and crushed ice.
2 Blitz until smooth and creamy.
3 Pour into two glasses and serve immediately, decorated with coconut and chocolate shavings.

preparation 5 minutes

Serves 2

CHOCOLATE MARBLE

2 tbsp chocolate syrup
225ml/8fl oz/1 cup chocolate-flavoured milk, chilled
100ml/3½fl oz/⅓ cup single (light) cream, chilled
2 scoops coffee ice cream
2 tbsp dark chocolate sauce

1 Put the chocolate syrup in a blender with the chocolate milk and cream. Add the ice cream and blitz until smooth.
2 Divide between two tall glasses and swirl in the chocolate sauce to create a marbled effect.
3 Top up with ice and serve immediately.

preparation 5 minutes

Serves 2

DULCE DE LECHE SMOOTHIE

50g/2oz milk chocolate, coarsely grated
250ml/8fl oz/1 cup milk
4 scoops chocolate ice cream
150g/5oz crushed ice
2 tbsp dulce de leche
2 tsp dark chocolate sauce

1 Put the grated chocolate in a blender with the milk, ice cream, crushed ice and dulce de leche.
2 Blitz until thick, creamy and smooth.
3 Pour into two chilled glasses and drizzle with chocolate sauce. Serve immediately.

preparation 5 minutes

Serves 2

CHOCOLATE BERRY SMOOTHIE

300g/11oz strawberries
250ml/8fl oz/1 cup milk, chilled
250g/9oz/1 cup natural yogurt, chilled
2 scoops strawberry frozen yogurt
2 tsp chocolate sauce

1 Hull the strawberries, then wash and pat dry with kitchen paper.
2 Put the strawberries in a blender with the milk and yogurt. Blend until thick and creamy.
3 Pour into two glasses and top with a scoop of frozen yogurt. Drizzle with chocolate sauce and serve immediately.

preparation 5 minutes

Serves 2

HOME BAKING

In recent times, baking has undergone a renaissance as more of us embrace the pleasures of good old-fashioned home cooking and bake our own cakes and bread. In an age of austerity, we are becoming more thrifty and focused on creating great bakes with simple honest ingredients.

In the following pages you will find homely traditional cakes, including Victoria sponge, rock buns, fairy cakes and fruit cake, plus some modern fruity traybakes – a great way to enjoy seasonal fresh stone fruits and berries. There are also crisp cookies and sticky flapjacks in a range of flavours – perfect with a cup of tea or coffee when you're feeling peckish.

Muffins are popular at any time of day – for breakfast, brunch or teatime. As well as the ubiquitous blueberry ones, we have a version made with yogurt and even savoury ones flavoured with tangy cheese and flecked with spinach. Or why not try some scones, drop scones or potato farls? They are all so easy to make and cook in no time at all.

Finally, for the more adventurous, there are some basic bread recipes. Nothing beats the fragrance of freshly baked loaves wafting through your kitchen – and they taste delicious, too.

< *Herby Potato Farls (page 428)*

BLUEBERRY MUFFINS

2 medium (US large) eggs, beaten

250ml/9fl oz/1 cup milk

225g/8oz/1 cup caster (superfine) sugar

a pinch of grated nutmeg

340g/12oz/3¼ cups plain (all-purpose) flour

4 tsp baking powder

225g/8oz fresh blueberries

1 Preheat the oven to 200°C/400°F/Gas 6. Line a 12-cup muffin tin with paper muffin cases.
2 Mix the beaten eggs, milk, sugar and grated nutmeg together in a bowl.
3 In another bowl, sift the flour and baking powder together, then add the blueberries. Mix together and then make a well in the centre.
4 Add the egg mixture and mix in gently. Divide the mixture among the paper cases.
5 Bake in the oven for 20–25 minutes until risen and firm on top. Cool the muffins on a wire rack.

preparation 10 minutes   cooking time 20–25 minutes plus cooling

Makes 12

LEMON SUGAR MUFFINS

150g/5oz/1¼ cups plain (all-purpose) flour

2 tsp baking powder

a pinch of salt

1 medium (US large) egg, beaten

4 tbsp caster (superfine) sugar

50g/2oz/4 tbsp butter, melted

100ml/3½fl oz/⅓ cup milk

finely grated zest of 3 lemons

6 tsp lemon curd

3 brown sugar cubes, coarsely crushed

1 Preheat the oven to 200°C/400°F/Gas 6. Line a 6-hole muffin tin with paper muffin cases.
2 Sift the flour, baking powder and salt together.
3 Put the beaten egg, caster sugar, melted butter and milk in a large bowl and mix well. Gently fold in the sifted flour and the lemon zest.
4 Spoon the mixture into the paper cases and bake in the oven for 30–35 minutes until golden and risen. Cool the muffins on a wire rack.
5 Spread the lemon curd over the top of the muffins and sprinkle with the brown sugar.

preparation 10 minutes   cooking time 30–35 minutes plus cooling

Makes 6

ECCLES CAKES

225g/8oz puff pastry
flour to dust
25g/1oz/2 tbsp butter, softened, plus extra to grease
2 tbsp dark brown soft sugar
25g/1oz/¼ cup finely chopped candied peel
75g/3oz/½ cup currants
grated zest of 1 orange
½ tsp ground nutmeg
½ tsp ground ginger
½ tsp ground cinnamon
2 tbsp caster (superfine) sugar

1　Roll out the puff pastry on a lightly floured surface and cut into 9cm/3½in rounds.
2　In a bowl, mix together the butter, brown sugar, candied peel, currants, orange zest and the ground spices.
3　Place a spoonful of the spicy fruit and butter mixture in the middle of each pastry round. Draw up the pastry edges to enclose the filling, then brush the edges with water and pinch together to seal. Turn each round over and roll lightly until the currants just show through. Prick the top with a fork. Set aside to rest for 10 minutes in a cool place.
4　Preheat the oven to 230°C/450°F/Gas 8.
5　Place the pastry rounds on a buttered baking sheet and bake in the oven for 15 minutes or until golden.
6　Cool on a wire rack and sprinkle with sugar while still warm.

preparation 10 minutes plus resting　cooking time 15 minutes plus cooling

Makes 8

SAVOURY MUFFINS

150g/5oz/1¼ cups self-raising (self-rising) flour
1 tsp baking powder
75g/3oz/¾ cup grated Cheddar or Parmesan cheese
25g/1oz/2 tbsp butter, melted
100ml/3½fl oz/⅓ cup milk
2 medium (US large) eggs
1 tbsp whole-grain mustard
4 tbsp chopped fresh parsley
125g/4oz baby spinach leaves, chopped
salt and ground black pepper

1　Preheat the oven to 200°C/400°F/Gas 6. Line a 6-hole muffin tin with paper muffin cases.
2　In a large bowl, mix together the flour, baking powder, most of the grated cheese and a little salt and pepper.
3　In another bowl, whisk together the butter, milk, beaten eggs, mustard, parsley and spinach. Add to the flour mixture and mix well together.
4　Divide the mixture among the paper cases, and sprinkle the remaining grated cheese over. Cook in the oven for 12–15 minutes until the muffins are risen and golden brown.

preparation 15 minutes　cooking time 12–15 minutes

Makes 6

SPICED YOGURT MUFFINS

225g/8oz/2¼ cups plain (all-purpose) flour

2 tsp baking powder

½ tsp freshly grated nutmeg

½ tsp ground cinnamon

¼ tsp allspice

a pinch of salt

50g/2oz/¼ cup light muscovado (brown) sugar

225g/8oz/1 cup Greek yogurt

125ml/4fl oz/½ cup milk

1 medium (US large) egg

50g/2oz/4 tbsp butter, melted

1 Preheat the oven to 200°C/400°F/Gas 6. Line a 12-hole muffin tin with paper muffin cases.
2 Sift the flour, baking powder, nutmeg and salt into a bowl. Stir in the sugar.
3 In another bowl, blend the yogurt with the milk and beat in the egg and melted butter. Stir lightly into the flour mixture. Divide the mixture among the paper cases.
4 Bake in the oven for 15–20 minutes until the muffins are well risen and golden brown.
5 Cool the muffins on a wire rack.

preparation 15 minutes   cooking time 15–20 minutes plus cooling

Makes 12

WELSH CAKES

225g/8oz/2¼ cups plain (all-purpose) flour, plus extra to dust

1 tsp baking powder

½ tsp mixed spice

50g/2oz/4 tbsp butter

50g/2oz/4 tbsp lard (shortening)

6 tbsp caster (superfine) sugar

50g/2oz/⅓ cup currants

1 medium (US large) egg, beaten

splash of milk

1 Grease a griddle or heavy frying pan. Sift together the flour, baking powder and spice. Rub in the fats until the mixture resembles fine breadcrumbs. Add the sugar and currants.
2 Make a well in the centre, then stir in the beaten egg and milk to make a stiff paste.
3 Roll out on a lightly floured surface to 5mm/¼in thick. Cut into rounds with a 7.5cm/3in cutter.
4 Cook on the griddle over a medium heat for 3 minutes on each side or until golden brown. Cool on a wire rack.

preparation 10 minutes   cooking time 3 minutes per batch plus cooling

Makes 16

ROCK CAKES

125g/4oz/½ cup butter, plus extra to grease

225g/8oz/2¼ cups plain (all-purpose) flour

2 tsp baking powder

6 tbsp demerara (light brown) sugar plus extra to sprinkle

75g/3oz/½ cup mixed dried fruit

grated zest of ½ lemon

1 medium (US large) egg, beaten

milk to mix

1 Preheat the oven to 200°C/400°F/Gas 6. Butter two baking sheets.
2 Sift together the flour and baking powder. Rub in the butter until the mixture resembles fine breadcrumbs. Add the sugar, dried fruit and lemon zest and mix thoroughly.
3 Using a fork, mix to a moist but stiff dough with the beaten egg and a little milk.
4 Place rough heaps of the dough on the prepared baking sheets and sprinkle with sugar.
5 Bake in the oven for 20 minutes or until golden brown. Cool on a wire rack.

preparation 5 minutes   **cooking time** 20 minutes plus cooling

Makes 12

MADELEINES

125g/4oz/½ cup butter, melted and cooled until tepid

125g/4oz/1 cup plain (all-purpose) flour, plus extra to dust

3 medium (US large) eggs

125g/4oz/½ cup caster (superfine) sugar

finely grated zest and juice of 1 lemon

1 tsp baking powder

icing (confectioner's) sugar to dust

1 Brush two Madeleine trays with a little of the melted butter, then dust lightly with flour.
2 Beat the eggs, caster sugar and lemon zest together in a bowl, until pale and creamy. Sift in half the flour and the baking powder. Pour in half the melted butter and the lemon juice and gently fold in until evenly and thoroughly mixed. Repeat with the remaining flour and butter.
3 Cover the bowl and leave to stand for 20 minutes. Preheat the oven to 200°C/400°F/Gas 6.
4 Divide the mixture among the prepared Madeleine trays and bake in the oven for 10 minutes until well risen and golden. Remove from the tins and cool on a wire rack. Serve dusted with icing sugar.

preparation 20 minutes plus standing   **cooking time** 10 minutes plus cooling

Makes 24

ICED FAIRY CAKES

125g/4oz/1 cup self-raising (self-rising) flour, sifted

1 tsp baking powder

125g/4oz/½ cup caster (superfine) sugar

125g/4oz/½ cup butter, softened

2 medium (US large) eggs

1 tbsp milk

225g/8oz/1⅔ cups icing (confectioner's) sugar, sifted

food colourings (optional)

sprinkles or coloured sugar

1 Preheat the oven to 200°C/400°F/Gas 6. Put paper cases into 18 cups in two bun tins.

2 Put the flour, baking powder, caster sugar, butter, eggs and milk in a mixing bowl and beat until the mixture is pale and very soft. Divide the mixture among the paper cases.

3 Bake in the oven for 10–15 minutes until risen and golden brown. Cool on a wire rack.

4 Put the icing sugar in a bowl and blend in 2–3 tbsp warm water until the icing is quite stiff, but spreadable. Add a couple of drops of food colouring, if wished.

5 Spread over the tops of the cold cakes and decorate with sprinkles or coloured sugar.

preparation 20 minutes cooking time 10–15 minutes plus cooling and setting

Makes 18

VICTORIA SPONGE

175g/6oz/¾ cup butter, plus extra to grease

175g/6oz/¾ cup caster (superfine) sugar

3 medium (US large) eggs

175g/6oz/1½ cups self-raising (self-rising) flour, sifted

4 tbsp raspberry jam

icing (confectioner's) sugar to dust

1 Preheat the oven to 190°C/375°F/Gas 5. Butter two 18cm/7in sandwich tins and line the bases with parchment paper.

2 In a large bowl, beat the butter and caster sugar until pale and fluffy. Beat in the eggs, one at a time, with a spoonful of flour. Fold in the remaining flour with a metal spoon.

3 Divide the mixture between the prepared tins and level the surface. Bake in the centre of the oven for 20–25 minutes until the sponges are well risen and spring back when lightly pressed with a finger. Leave in the tins for 5 minutes.

4 Turn out, remove the lining paper and cool on a wire rack. Sandwich the two sponges together with raspberry jam and dust the top with icing sugar.

preparation 30 minutes cooking time 25 minutes plus cooling

Makes 10 slices

SPICED CARROT CAKE

250ml/9fl oz/1 cup sunflower oil, plus extra to grease

225g/8oz/1 cup light muscovado (brown) sugar

4 medium (US large) eggs

225g/8oz/2¼ cups self-raising (self-rising) flour

a pinch of salt

½ tsp each ground mixed spice, nutmeg and cinnamon

340g/12oz carrots, grated

For the frosting

50g/2oz/4 tbsp butter

225g/8oz/1½ cups cream cheese

25g/1oz/¼ cup icing (confectioner's) sugar

grated zest of 1 orange

1 Preheat the oven to 180°C/350°F/Gas 4. Butter two 18cm/7in sandwich tins and line the bases with parchment paper.
2 Beat the oil and muscovado sugar together until well mixed, then beat in the eggs, one at a time. Sift the flour, salt and spices over the top and fold in gently. Fold in the carrots.
3 Divide the mixture between the prepared tins and bake in the oven for 30–40 minutes until golden, well risen and a skewer inserted into the centre comes out clean. Leave in the tins for 10 minutes, then turn out and cool a wire rack.
4 To make the frosting, beat the butter and cream cheese until light and fluffy. Sift in the icing sugar, add the orange zest and beat until smooth.
5 Remove the lining paper from the cakes and spread one-third of the frosting over one cake. Sandwich together with the other cake. Spread the remaining frosting on top.

preparation 15 minutes   cooking time 40 minutes plus cooling

Makes 12 slices

COCONUT RASPBERRY BUNS

50g/2oz/¼ cup soft brown sugar

1 large (US extra-large) egg

125ml/4fl oz/½ cup reduced-fat coconut milk

50g/2oz desiccated coconut plus extra to sprinkle

125g/4oz plain (all-purpose) flour, sifted

1 tsp baking powder

150g/5oz/1 cup raspberries

icing (confectioner's) sugar to dust

1 Preheat the oven to 190°C/375°F/Gas 5.
2 Whisk the sugar and egg together until light and fluffy, then beat in the coconut milk.
3 Add the coconut, flour and baking powder and fold in gently but thoroughly. Stir in the vanilla extract and raspberries, distributing them evenly throughout the mixture.
4 Spoon the mixture into 8 paper cases placed in a muffin tin. Sprinkle the buns with a little coconut.
5 Bake in the oven for 15–20 minutes until the buns are well risen, golden brown and just firm to the touch.
6 Cool on a wire rack and dust lightly with icing sugar.

preparation 15 minutes   cooking time 15–20 minutes plus cooling

Makes 8

EASY FRUIT CAKE

125g/4oz/½ cup butter, plus
extra to grease
225g/8oz/2¼ cups self-raising
(self-rising) flour
2 tsp ground mixed spice
1 tsp baking powder
125g/4oz/½ cup soft brown
sugar
225g/8oz/1⅓ cups dried fruit
2 medium (US large) eggs
2 tbsp milk

1 Preheat the oven to 170°C/325°F/Gas 3. Butter an 18cm/7in round cake tin and line the base with parchment paper.
2 Sift the flour, spice and baking powder into a large bowl. Add the sugar and dried fruit.
3 Beat the eggs with the milk and beat into the cake mixture.
4 Put the mixture in the prepared tin and bake in the oven for 1¾ hours or until a fine skewer inserted in the centre comes out clean.
5 Turn out the cake and cool on a wire rack.

preparation 10 minutes **cooking time** 1 hour 45 minutes plus cooling

Makes 12 slices

TEABREAD

150ml/¼ pint/scant ⅔ cup hot
Earl Grey tea
175g/6oz/1 cup sultanas
(seedless white raisins)
175g/6oz/1 cup mixed ready-to-
eat dried apricots and prunes,
roughly chopped
a little vegetable oil
125g/4oz/½ cup dark brown
sugar
2 medium (US large) eggs
225g/8oz/2¼ cups plain
(all-purpose) flour
2 tsp baking powder
2 tsp ground mixed spice
butter to serve

1 Pour the hot tea into a bowl and add the sultanas, apricots and prunes. Set aside to soak for 30 minutes.
2 Preheat the oven to 190°C/375°F/Gas 5. Oil a 900g/2lb loaf tin and line the base with parchment paper.
3 Beat the sugar and eggs together in a large bowl until pale and fluffy. Add the flour, baking powder, mixed spice and the soaked fruit in the soaking liquid, then mix together well. Spoon into the prepared tin and level the surface.
4 Bake on the middle shelf of the oven for 45 minutes–1 hour. Set aside to cool in the tin. Serve sliced and buttered.

preparation 20 minutes plus soaking **cooking time** 1 hour plus cooling

Makes 12 slices

FRUITY GINGER TEABREAD

125g/4oz/¾ cup each dried apricots, pears and prunes
300ml/½ pint/1¼ cups fruit tea
butter to grease
4 tbsp chopped preserved stem ginger in syrup
225g/8oz/2¼ cups plain (all-purpose) flour
2 tsp baking powder
125g/4oz/½ cup dark muscovado (brown) sugar
2 medium (US large) eggs

1 Chop the dried apricots, pears and prunes and place in a large bowl. Cover with tea and set aside to soak for 2 hours.
2 Preheat the oven to 180°C/350°F/Gas 4. Butter a 900g/2lb loaf tin and line the base with parchment paper.
3 Mix the ginger, flour, baking powder and sugar into the soaked fruit. Beat the eggs and stir into the mixture.
4 Pour into the prepared tin and bake in the oven for 1 hour or until a skewer inserted into the centre comes out clean.
5 Cool the teabread in the tin for 10 minutes, then turn out on to a wire rack to cool.

preparation 15 minutes plus soaking   cooking time 1 hour plus cooling

Makes 12 slices

BANANA BREAD

butter to grease
175g/6oz/1½ cups plain (all-purpose) flour, sifted
2 tsp baking powder
a pinch of salt
175g/6oz/¾ cup light muscovado (brown) sugar
3 medium (US large) eggs
3 ripe large bananas, mashed
25g/1oz/2 tbsp butter, melted
150g/5oz/1¼ cups natural yogurt
1 tsp ground cinnamon
1 tsp ground nutmeg
½ tsp ground ginger

1 Preheat the oven to 170°C/325°F/Gas 3. Butter a 1.4kg/3lb loaf tin and line with parchment paper.
2 Sift the flour, baking powder and salt into a large bowl and mix together well.
3 In another bowl, beat the muscovado sugar and eggs until pale and fluffy. Stir in the bananas, melted butter, yogurt and ground spices. Stir in the flour mixture.
4 Spoon the mixture into the prepared tin and level the surface.
5 Bake in the oven for 1 hour or until a skewer inserted into the centre comes out clean. Cool in the tin on a wire rack.

preparation 20 minutes   cooking time 1 hour plus cooling

Makes 15 slices

BLUEBERRY TRAYBAKE

275g/10oz/1¼ cups butter, softened, plus extra to grease

275g/10oz/1¼ cups caster (superfine) sugar

5 medium (US large) eggs

275g/10oz/2¾ cups self-raising (self-rising) flour

125g/4oz/1 cup ground almonds

1 tsp baking powder

grated zest of 1 orange

juice of 2 oranges

6 tbsp milk

225g/8oz/2 cups blueberries

4 tbsp hazelnuts

150g/5oz/scant 1 cup icing (confectioner's) sugar

1 Preheat the oven to 190°C/375°F/Gas 5. Butter a 30 x 20cm/12 x 8in shallow tin. Line with parchment paper.
2 Beat the butter and caster sugar in a large bowl until fluffy. Beat in the eggs, one at a time. Sift in the flour and baking powder, then add the ground almonds, orange zest, the juice of 1 orange and the milk. Beat until light and fluffy.
3 Fold in the blueberries with a metal spoon, distributing them evenly throughout the mixture. Spoon into the prepared tin and sprinkle with the hazelnuts.
4 Bake for 40–45 minutes until well risen and springy to the touch. Cool in the tin for 5 minutes, then turn out on to a wire rack and set aside to cool.
5 Sift the icing sugar into a bowl, then gradually mix in the remaining orange juice, until smooth and runny. Drizzle over the cold cake and set aside for 30 minutes to set.

preparation 20 minutes cooking time 45 minutes plus cooling and setting *Makes 24 squares*

MADEIRA CAKE

175g/6oz/¾ cup butter, softened, plus extra to grease

175g/6oz/¾ cup caster (superfine) sugar

3 medium (US large) eggs

250g/8oz/2¼ cups self-raising (self-rising) flour

grated zest and juice of 1 lemon

2–3 tbsp milk

1 piece candied citron peel

1 Preheat the oven to 180°C/350°F/Gas 4. Butter and line a deep 18cm/7in round cake tin.
2 Cream the butter and sugar together in a bowl until pale and fluffy. Add the eggs, one at a time, beating well after each addition.
3 Sift the flour and fold into the mixture with a metal spoon. Stir in the lemon zest and juice and milk. Spoon the mixture into the prepared tin and level the surface.
4 Bake in the oven for 50 minutes or until a skewer inserted into the middle of the cake comes out clean. Turn out on to a wire rack to cool. Decorate the top with candied peel.

preparation 20 minutes cooking time 50 minutes plus cooling *Makes 12 slices*

MOIST ORANGE CAKE

oil to grease
2 oranges
3 medium (US large) eggs
225g/8oz/1 cup caster (superfine) sugar
300g/11oz/2¾cups ground almonds
1 tsp baking powder
icing (confectioner's) sugar to dust

1 Grease and line a 20cm/8in springform cake tin.
2 Put the oranges in a pan and cover with water. Bring to the boil, then reduce the heat, cover with a lid and simmer gently for 1 hour or until tender. Remove the oranges from the pan and set aside to cool. Cut in half and discard the pips. Blitz in a blender to a smooth purée.
3 Preheat the oven to 180°C/350°F/Gas 4.
4 Beat the eggs and caster sugar in a bowl until pale and frothy. Fold in the ground almonds, baking powder and orange purée. Pour into the prepared tin.
5 Bake in the oven for 40–50 minutes until a skewer inserted into the middle comes out clean. Cool in the tin, then peel away the lining paper and lightly dust with icing sugar.

preparation 30 minutes cooking time 1 hour 50 minutes plus cooling

Makes 12 slices

PLUM TRAYBAKE

225g/8oz/1 cup butter, softened, plus extra to grease
225g/8oz/1 cup caster (superfine) sugar
4 medium (US large) eggs
275g/10oz/2¾ cups self-raising (self-rising) flour, sifted
1 tsp baking powder
grated zest and juice of 1 orange
50g/2oz/½ cup ground almonds
2–3 tbsp milk to mix
18 plums, halved and stoned
50g/2oz/½ cup walnut halves
icing (confectioner's) sugar to dust

1 Preheat the oven to 180°C/350°F/Gas 4. Butter a 30 × 20cm/12 × 8in shallow tin and line the base with parchment paper.
2 Beat the butter and caster sugar until light and fluffy, then beat in the eggs, one at a time. Fold in the flour, baking powder, orange zest and juice and ground almonds. Slacken the mixture with a little milk.
3 Spoon the mixture into the prepared tin, level the surface and press the plums, cut-side up, into the mixture, spacing them out evenly. Tuck in the walnuts around the plums.
4 Bake in the oven for 30–40 minutes until well risen and golden brown and a skewer inserted into the middle comes out clean. Set aside to cool in the tin.
5 Dust with icing sugar and cut into squares.

preparation 20 minutes cooking time 30–40 minutes plus cooling

Makes 18 squares

BANANA CARAMEL CAKE

225g/8oz/1 cup butter, softened, plus extra to grease

225g/8oz/1 cup light soft brown sugar

4 medium (US large) eggs

2 ripe bananas, mashed

1 tsp vanilla extract

200g/7oz/1¾ cups self-raising (self-rising) flour

For the frosting

150g/5oz/⅔ cup butter, softened

250g/9oz/2 cups icing (confectioner's) sugar, sifted

3 tbsp dulce de leche

1 Preheat the oven to 180°C/350°F/Gas 4. Butter a 20cm/8in deep cake tin and line with parchment paper.

2 In a large bowl, beat together the butter and brown sugar until pale and fluffy. Gradually beat in the eggs, one at a time. Fold in the mashed bananas and vanilla extract.

3 With a metal spoon, fold in the flour. Spoon into the prepared tin and bake in the oven for 50–55 minutes until a skewer inserted into the middle comes out clean. Cool in the tin for 5 minutes, then turn out on to a wire rack and set aside to cool completely.

4 Meanwhile, make the frosting. Beat the butter, icing sugar and dulce de leche until smooth and creamy. Spread over the top and sides of the cold cake.

preparation 25 minutes   cooking time 55 minutes plus cooling

Makes 10 slices

BLACKBERRY AND APPLE CAKE

125g/4oz/½ cup butter, diced, plus extra to grease

225g/8oz/2¼ cups self-raising (self-rising) flour, sifted

175g/6oz/¾ cup granulated sugar

2 large (US extra-large) eggs, beaten

2 large sweet dessert apples, peeled, cored and sliced

150g/5oz fresh blackberries

1 Preheat the oven to 190°C/375°F/Gas 5. Butter a 20cm/8in cake tin and line the base with parchment paper.

2 Put the flour in a bowl and rub in the butter until the mixture resembles fine breadcrumbs. Add 150g/5oz/⅔ cup sugar and the beaten eggs. Mix together well.

3 Spread half the mixture over the base of the tin, then layer the apples and blackberries over the top. Sprinkle with the remaining sugar, then cover with the remaining mixture.

4 Bake in the oven for 45–55 minutes until risen and a skewer inserted into the middle comes out clean. Cool in the tin for 10 minutes, then turn out and cool on a wire rack.

preparation 20 minutes   cooking time 45–55 minutes plus cooling

Makes 8 slices

SPICED APPLE CAKE

175g/6oz/¾ cup butter, softened, plus extra to grease

150g/5oz/scant ⅔ cup caster (superfine) sugar plus extra for sprinkling

3 medium (US large) eggs

150g/5oz/1¼ cups plain (all-purpose) flour

1 tsp baking powder

2 tbsp milk

1 tsp ground cinnamon

4 sweet dessert apples, peeled, cored and cut into cubes

125g/4oz/1 cup chopped walnuts

1 Preheat the oven to 180°C/350°F/Gas 4. Butter a 20cm/8in cake tin and line with parchment paper.
2 Beat 150g/5oz/⅔ cup butter with the sugar, eggs, flour, baking powder and milk until pale and fluffy. Spoon into the prepared tin and bake in the oven for 10 minutes.
3 Meanwhile, heat the remaining butter in a frying pan. Add the cinnamon and apples and cook for 3 minutes. Remove from the heat and stir in the walnuts.
4 Sprinkle the apple mixture over the surface of the part-baked cake. Return to the oven and cook for 40–50 minutes until a skewer inserted into the middle comes out clean.
5 Cool in the tin for 5 minutes, then remove the cake and peel away the paper. Sprinkle with caster sugar.

preparation 10 minutes   cooking time 1 hour

Makes 8 slices

SUMMER FRUIT CAKE

200g/7oz/scant 1 cup butter, melted, plus extra to grease

225g/8oz/2¼ cups self-raising (self-rising) flour, sifted

100g/3½oz/scant ½ cup caster (superfine) sugar plus extra for sprinkling

4 medium (US large) eggs, beaten

125g/4oz/1 cup blueberries

2 large peaches, halved, stoned and sliced

cream or ice cream to serve

1 Preheat the oven to 190°C/375°F/Gas 5. Butter a 20cm/8in cake tin and base-line with parchment paper.
2 Put the flour and sugar in a large bowl. Make a well in the centre and mix in the melted butter and eggs.
3 Spread half the mixture over the bottom of the cake tin and add half the blueberries and peaches. Cover with the remaining cake mixture, then add the remaining blueberries and peaches, pressing them down into the mixture slightly.
4 Bake in the oven for 1–1¼ hours until risen and golden brown and a skewer inserted into the middle comes out clean. Leave in the tin to cool for 10 minutes.
5 Dust with caster sugar before serving with whipped cream or ice cream.

preparation 15 minutes   cooking time 1–1¼ hours plus cooling

Makes 8 slices

LEMON POLENTA CAKE

50g/2oz/4 tbsp butter, softened, plus extra to grease

2 lemons

250g/9oz/1 cup + 2 tbsp caster (superfine) sugar

200g/7oz/generous 1 cup instant polenta

50g/2oz/cup ½ ground almonds

1 tsp baking powder

3 medium (US large) eggs

3 tbsp milk

2 tbsp poppy seeds

1 lemon, thinly sliced

1 Preheat the oven to 180°C/350°F/Gas 4. Butter a 900g/2lb loaf tin and base-line with parchment paper.

2 Grate the zest of 1 lemon and blitz in a food processor with the butter, 200g/7oz/scant 1 cup sugar, the polenta, ground almonds, baking powder, eggs, milk and poppy seeds.

3 Spoon the mixture into the prepared tin and bake in the oven for 1 hour or until a skewer inserted into the middle comes out clean. Leave to cool in the tin for 10 minutes.

4 Squeeze the juice from the 2 lemons into a pan. Add the sliced lemon, remaining sugar and 150ml/¼ pint/scant ⅔ cup water. Bring to the boil, stirring, then reduce the heat and cook for 10 minutes or until syrupy. Pierce the cake with a skewer in several places, arrange the slices over the top and spoon the syrup over the cake.

preparation 10 minutes   cooking time 1 hour plus cooling

Makes 12 slices

LEMON SYRUP CAKE

175g/6oz/¾ cup butter, softened, plus extra to grease

175g/6oz/¾ cup caster (superfine) sugar

4 medium (US large) eggs, lightly beaten

3 lemons

125g/4oz/1 cup self-raising (self-rising) flour

50g/2oz/½ cup ground almonds

75g/3oz/⅓ cup golden granulated sugar

crushed sugar to decorate

1 Preheat the oven to 180°C/350°F/Gas 4. Butter a 900g/2lb loaf tin and line with parchment paper.

2 In a large bowl, beat together the butter and caster sugar until pale and fluffy. Beat in the eggs, one at a time, and then the grated zest of 2 lemons and the juice of ½ lemon.

3 Fold in the flour and ground almonds and spoon into the prepared tin. Bake in the oven for 40–50 minutes until a skewer inserted into the middle comes out clean. Cool in the tin for 10 minutes, then turn out on to a wire rack.

4 Meanwhile, put the granulated sugar in a pan with the juice of 2 lemons and the shredded zest of 1 lemon. Heat gently, stirring to dissolve the sugar. Spoon over the warm cake and set aside to cool.

preparation 20 minutes   cooking time 50 minutes plus cooling

Makes 10 slices

ORANGE DRIZZLE CAKE

175g/6oz/¾ cup butter, plus extra to grease

225g/8oz/1 cup caster (superfine) sugar

2 medium (US large) eggs, beaten

175g/6oz/1¾ cups plain (all-purpose) flour

2 tsp baking powder

125g/4oz/1 cup ground almonds

grated zest and juice of 1 large orange

juice of 2 oranges

1 Preheat the oven to 180°C/350°F/Gas 4. Butter a shallow 20cm/8in round tin and line the base with parchment paper.

2 Beat the butter and half the sugar until fluffy. Gradually beat in the eggs. Fold in the flour, baking powder and ground almonds. Stir in the zest and juice of 1 orange and spoon the mixture into the prepared tin.

3 Bake in the oven for 50–60 minutes or until risen, golden brown and a skewer inserted in the middle comes out clean. Cool in the tin for 10 minutes, then cool on a wire rack.

4 Put the remaining sugar and the juice of 2 oranges in a pan. Bring to the boil, stirring, and cook for 2 minutes or until syrupy. Remove from the heat and cool a little.

5 Prick the top of the cake several times with a thin skewer. Drizzle with the syrup and let it soak in before serving.

preparation 20 minutes
cooking time 50–60 minutes plus cooling plus soaking

Makes 10 slices

HERBY POTATO FARLS

oil to grease

340g/12oz potatoes, chopped

250g/9oz/2⅓ cups plain (all-purpose) flour, plus extra to dust

1 tsp bicarbonate of soda (baking soda)

a pinch each of salt and cayenne pepper

a handful of fresh parsley, roughly chopped

150g/5oz/1¼ cups natural yogurt

1 medium (US large) egg, beaten

1–2 tbsp milk

1 Preheat the oven to 220°C/425°F/Gas 7. Lightly brush a baking sheet with oil.

2 Cook the potatoes in a pan of lightly salted boiling water for 15 minutes until tender. Drain, then mash and leave to cool.

3 Sift the flour and bicarbonate of soda into the mashed potato, season with salt and cayenne pepper and mix well. Mix in the parsley, yogurt and egg to make a smooth, soft dough, adding some milk if it is too stiff.

4 Knead the dough on a lightly floured surface, then roll out to 2cm/¾in thick. Use a 5cm/2in round plain cutter to cut out circles. Place them on the prepared baking sheet. Lightly dust with a little flour, then bake in the oven for 12–15 minutes until well risen and golden brown. Serve warm, split and buttered.

preparation 1 hour   cooking time 12–15 minutes

Makes 16

WHOLEMEAL BREAD

675g/1½lb/6¾ cups strong
wholemeal bread flour plus
extra to dust

2 tsp salt

1 tsp caster (superfine) sugar

2 tsp easy-blend dried yeast

vegetable oil to grease

1 Put the wholemeal flour in a large bowl with the salt, sugar and yeast. Stir well and make a well in the centre, then add 450ml/¾ pint/1¾ cups warm water. Mix to a smooth, soft dough, adding more water if necessary.
2 Knead the dough for 10 minutes or until smooth, then shape into a ball and put in an oiled bowl. Cover and set aside in a warm place for 2 hours or until doubled in size.
3 Knock back the dough on a lightly floured surface and shape into a rectangle. Place in an oiled 900g/2lb loaf tin, cover and set aside to rise for 30 minutes.
4 Preheat the oven to 230°C/450°F/Gas 8.
5 Bake for 15 minutes, then reduce the oven temperature to 200°C/400°F/Gas 6 and bake for 15–20 minutes until risen and the loaf sounds hollow when tapped underneath. Leave in the tin for 10 minutes, then cool on a wire rack.

preparation 15 minutes plus rising cooking time 30–35 minutes plus cooling

Makes 16 slices

CORNBREAD

oil to grease

125g/4oz/1 cup + 2 tbsp plain
(all-purpose) flour

175g/6oz/1 cup cornmeal

2 tsp baking powder

1 tbsp soft brown sugar

½ tsp salt

300ml/½ pint/1¼ cups
buttermilk

2 large (US extra-large) eggs,
beaten

4 tbsp olive oil

1 Preheat the oven to 200°C/400°F/Gas 6. Oil a 20cm/8in square shallow baking tin.
2 Put the flour in a large bowl with the cornmeal, baking powder, sugar and salt. Make a well in the centre and pour in the buttermilk, beaten eggs and olive oil. Mix together.
3 Pour the mixture into the prepared tin and bake in the oven for 25–30 minutes until firm to the touch or a skewer inserted into the middle comes out clean.
4 Leave in the tin for 5 minutes, then turn out the cornbread and cut into triangles. Serve warm with butter.

Serves 8

preparation 5 minutes cooking time 25–30 minutes plus resting

OATMEAL SODA BREAD

25g/1oz/2 tbsp butter, plus extra to grease

275g/10oz/2¾ cups wholemeal bread flour

175g/6oz/2 cups coarse oatmeal

2 tsp cream of tartar

1 tsp salt

300ml/½ pint/1¼ cups buttermilk

1 Preheat the oven to 220°C/425°F/Gas 7. Butter and base-line a 900g/2lb loaf tin.

2 Mix together all the dry ingredients in a bowl. Rub in the butter, then add the buttermilk to make a soft dough. Place in the prepared tin.

3 Bake in the oven for 25 minutes or until golden brown and well risen. Turn out on to a wire rack and set aside to cool.

preparation 10 minutes   cooking time 25 minutes

Makes 10 slices

BREAD-MAKER OAT LOAF

1½ tsp easy-blend dried yeast

300g/11oz/3 cups strong white bread flour

75g/3oz/¾ cup strong whole wheat flour

125g/4oz/1 cup oatmeal

1 tsp salt

3 tbsp molasses

150g/5oz/1¼ cups natural yogurt

25g/1oz/2 tbsp butter, melted

1 Put all the ingredients in a bread-maker bucket with 200ml/7fl oz/¾ cup water, following the method specified in the manual.

2 Fit the bucket into the bread maker and set to the basic programme with a light crust. Press start.

3 Just before baking, brush the top of the dough with water.

4 After baking, remove the bucket from the machine, then turn out the bread on to a wire rack to cool.

preparation 10 minutes   cooking time as per machine plus cooling

Makes 1 loaf

OVEN SCONES

50g/2oz/4 tbsp butter, diced,
plus extra to grease

225g/8oz/2¼ cups self-raising
(self-rising) flour

a pinch of salt

1 tsp baking powder

150ml/¼ pint/scant ⅔ cup milk,
plus extra to glaze

whipped cream or butter and
jam to serve

1 Preheat the oven to 220°C/425°F/Gas 7. Butter a baking sheet.

2 Sift the flour, salt and baking powder into a bowl. Rub in the butter until the mixture resembles fine breadcrumbs. Stir in enough milk to make a soft dough.

3 Roll out the dough 2cm/¾in thick on a lightly floured surface. Cut out rounds with a 5cm/2in plain cutter.

4 Place the scones on the prepared baking sheet and brush the tops with milk. Bake in the oven for 10 minutes or until golden brown and well risen. Cool on a wire rack.

5 Serve warm, split and filled with cream, or butter and jam.

preparation 15 minutes   cooking time 10 minutes plus cooling

Makes 8

FRUIT SCONES

25g/1oz/2 tbsp butter, diced,
plus extra to grease

125g/4oz/1 cup self-raising
(self-rising) flour

½ tsp baking powder

1 tbsp caster (superfine) sugar

2 tbsp sultanas (seedless white
raisins)

5 tbsp milk

2 peaches, halved and stoned

icing (confectioner's) sugar
to dust

100g/3½oz/½ cup light soft
cheese

1 Preheat the oven to 220°C/425°F/Gas 7. Butter and lightly flour a baking sheet.

2 Sift the flour and baking powder into a bowl. Rub in the butter, then stir in the caster sugar and sultanas. Make a well in the centre and pour in the milk. Mix together to make a soft, but not sticky, dough.

3 Turn out on to a floured surface and knead lightly. Roll the dough out to 2cm/¾in thick. Cut into 4 rounds with a 5cm/2in cutter. Place on the baking tray and bake in the oven for 10 minutes or until golden brown and well risen. Transfer to a wire rack and allow to cool.

4 Cut the peach halves into thick slices and dust lightly with icing sugar. Grill (broil) for 2 minutes. Cut the scones in half and spread with cheese. Top with the peach slices and serve.

preparation 15 minutes   cooking time 10 minutes plus cooling

Serves 4

DROP SCONES

125g/4oz/1 cup + 2 tbsp
self-raising (self-rising) flour

1 tbsp caster (superfine) sugar

1 medium (US large) egg, beaten

150ml/¼ pint/scant ⅔ cup semi-
skimmed milk

sunflower oil to grease

butter or whipped cream
and jam to serve

1 Mix the flour and sugar together in a bowl. Make a well in the centre and mix in the egg and the milk.

2 Heat an oiled griddle or frying pan and cook in batches, dropping in spoonfuls of the batter. Cook for 2–3 minutes until bubbles appear on the surface of the scones and burst, then flip them over and cook the other side for 2–3 minutes until golden brown.

3 Put the cooked drop scones on a clean teatowel (dishtowel) and cover with another teatowel to keep them moist.

4 Serve warm with butter, or cream and jam.

preparation 10 minutes   **cooking time** 12–18 minutes

Makes 16

AMARETTI

225g/8oz/2 cups ground almonds

225g/8oz/1 cup caster (superfine) sugar

2 medium (US large) egg whites

½ tsp almond extract

a few drops of amaretto liqueur (optional)

1 Preheat the oven to 180°C/350°F/Gas 4. Line two baking sheets with rice paper.
2 Mix together the ground almonds and sugar. Beat in the egg whites, almond extract and amaretto (if using).
3 Using a teaspoon, drop small heaps of the mixture on to the paper, leaving plenty of room for the amaretti to spread out during cooking.
4 Bake in the oven for 15 minutes or until pale golden brown. Cool on a wire rack and remove the rice paper from around the amaretti before serving.

preparation 5 minutes   **cooking time** 15 minutes plus cooling

Makes 24

LEMON TUILE BISCUITS

100g/3½oz/7 tbsp butter, softened

100g/3½oz/⅔ cup icing (confectioner's) sugar, sifted

3 large (US extra-large) egg whites

100g/3½oz/1 cup plain (all-purpose) flour

grated zest of 1 large lemon

1 Beat the butter and sugar until fluffy. Beat in the egg whites, one at a time, then stir in the flour and lemon zest. Cover and leave to rest for 30 minutes.
2 Preheat the oven to 180°C/350°F/Gas 4. Line a baking sheet with parchment paper.
3 Put 3 teaspoonfuls of the mixture, spaced well apart, on the prepared baking sheet and spread out into 9cm/3½in circles.
4 Bake in the oven for 6 minutes or until starting to brown.
5 Remove from the oven and shape each warm biscuit over a rolling pin to curl it. Repeat with the remaining mixture. Set aside on a wire rack until cold.

preparation 10 minutes plus resting   **cooking time** 6 minutes per batch plus cooling

Makes 24

FRUIT AND NUT COOKIES

125g/4oz/½ cup butter, softened, plus extra to grease
150g/5oz/scant ⅔ cup caster (superfine) sugar
1 medium (US large) egg
150g/5oz/1¼ cups plain (all-purpose) flour, sifted
½ tsp baking powder
a pinch of salt
125g/4oz/½ cup peanut butter
175g/6oz/1 cup dried cranberries

1 Preheat the oven to 190°C/375°F/Gas 5. Butter two baking sheets.
2 In a food processor or food mixer, beat together the butter, sugar, egg, flour, baking powder, salt and peanut butter until well blended. Stir in the cranberries.
3 Drop heaped teaspoonfuls of the mixture, spaced well apart, on to the prepared baking sheets, leaving room for them to spread out during cooking.
4 Bake in the oven for 15 minutes or until the cookies are golden brown. Leave to cool slightly, then transfer to a wire rack and set aside until cold.

preparation 10 minutes   cooking time 15 minutes plus cooling

Makes 30

WALNUT COOKIES

225g/8oz/1 cup butter, softened, plus extra to grease
175g/6oz/¾ cup light muscovado (brown) sugar
2 medium (US large) eggs, beaten
225g/8oz/2 cups walnut halves
300g/11oz/3 cups self-raising (self-rising) flour, sifted
½ tsp baking powder
125g/4oz/⅔ cup raisins
2 tbsp maple syrup

1 Preheat the oven to 190°C/375°F/Gas 5. Butter four baking sheets.
2 Cream the butter and sugar until pale and fluffy. Gradually beat in the eggs until well combined.
3 Put 20 walnut halves aside and roughly chop the rest. Fold into the mixture with the flour, baking powder, raisins and maple syrup.
4 Roll the mixture into 20 balls and arrange them, spaced well apart, on the prepared baking sheets. Use a dampened palette knife to flatten them and top each with a walnut half.
5 Bake in the oven for 12–15 minutes until pale golden. Leave on the baking sheets for 5 minutes, then cool on a wire rack.

preparation 15 minutes   cooking time 12–15 minutes plus cooling

Makes 20

CHRISTMAS COOKIES

75g/3oz/6 tbsp butter, softened

100g/3½oz/7 tbsp caster (superfine) sugar

1 medium (US large) egg, beaten

grated zest of 1 orange

250g/9oz/2⅓ cups plain (all-purpose) flour, plus extra to dust

1 tsp baking powder

1 tsp each ground cinnamon, ginger and nutmeg

coloured ready-to-roll fondant icings, royal icing (see page 587), food colourings and edible decorations

1 Cream the butter and sugar together in a large bowl until smooth. Beat in the egg and orange zest. Sift the flour and baking powder into the bowl and mix in with the spices.
2 On a lightly floured surface, knead gently to a soft dough. Cover and chill in the refrigerator for 1 hour or until firm.
3 Preheat the oven to 180°C/350°F/Gas 4.
4 Roll out the dough until 5mm/¼in thick. Use Christmas cookie cutters to cut out shapes. Arrange them on two non-stick baking trays.
5 Bake in the oven for 10–15 minutes until pale golden and risen. Leave to harden on the baking sheets for 3 minutes, then transfer to a wire rack to cool.
6 When the cookies are cold, decorate with coloured fondant or royal icing and edible decorations.

preparation 25 minutes plus chilling   **cooking time** 10–15 minutes plus cooling

Makes 20

GINGER COOKIES

50g/2oz/4 tbsp butter, plus extra to grease

125g/4oz/½ cup chopped stem ginger in syrup

50g/2oz/¼ cup dark muscovado (brown) sugar

grated zest of 1 orange

juice of ½ orange

175g/6oz/1½ cups self-raising (self-rising) flour

1 Preheat the oven to 180°C/350°F/Gas 4. Lightly butter two large baking sheets.
2 Put the butter, ginger syrup, sugar, orange zest and juice in a pan and heat gently, stirring, until melted and blended.
3 Set aside to cool slightly, then sift in the flour. Mix until smooth. Place small spoonfuls of the mixture on the prepared baking sheets, spacing them well apart to allow room for the cookies to spread during cooking.
4 Bake in the oven for 12 minutes or until golden brown. Transfer to a wire rack to cool.

preparation 15 minutes   **cooking time** 12 minutes plus cooling

Makes 24

STICKY FLAPJACKS

340g/12oz/1½ cups butter, plus extra to grease

225g/8oz/1 cup caster (superfine) sugar

225g/8oz/¾ cup golden (corn) syrup

450g/1lb/4½ cups rolled oats

1 tbsp ground ginger

1 Preheat the oven to 180°C/350°F/Gas 4. Lightly butter a 28 x 18cm/11 x 7in shallow cake tin and base-line with parchment paper.

2 Put the butter, sugar and syrup in a large pan and heat gently until melted. Stir in the oats and ginger, then pour the mixture into the prepared tin and level the surface.

3 Bake in the oven for 30–35 minutes until golden brown. Set aside to cool in the tin for 15 minutes, then cut into 24 pieces with a sharp knife. Leave in the tin until cold.

preparation 10 minutes   cooking time 40 minutes plus cooling

Makes 24

FRUITY FLAPJACKS

200g/7oz/scant 1 cup butter, plus extra to grease
175g/6oz/¾ cup Demerara (light brown) sugar
4 tbsp golden (corn) syrup
400g/14oz/4 cups jumbo oats
100g/3½oz/½ cup raisins
4 tbsp chopped walnuts

1 Preheat the oven to 190°C/375°F/Gas 5. Butter a 20cm/8in square baking tin and line with parchment paper.
2 Melt the butter in a large pan and stir in the sugar and syrup. Heat gently until the sugar dissolves.
3 Off the heat, stir in the oats, raisins and nuts. Press the mixture into the prepared tin and bake in the oven for 17–20 minutes until lightly golden.
4 Cool in the tin before cutting into squares.

preparation 10 minutes cooking time 17 minutes plus cooling

Makes 12 squares

ALMOND MACAROONS

2 medium (US large) egg whites
200g/7oz/1¾ cups caster (superfine) sugar
200g/7oz/1¾ cups ground almonds
½ tsp almond extract
30 blanched almonds

1 Preheat the oven to 180°C/350°F/Gas 4. Line two baking sheets with parchment paper.
2 Beat the egg whites in a clean, grease-free bowl until they form stiff peaks. Gradually beat in the sugar, a little at a time, until thick and glossy. Stir in the ground almonds and almond extract.
3 Spoon teaspoonfuls of the mixture on to the prepared baking sheets, spacing them well apart. Press an almond into the middle of each one. Bake in the oven for 12–15 minutes until just golden and firm to the touch.
4 Leave on the baking sheets for 10 minutes, then transfer the macaroons to a wire rack and set aside until cold.

preparation 10 minutes cooking time 12–15 minutes plus cooling

Makes 30

DESSERTS

There are very few people who don't enjoy something sweet at the end of a meal, even if it's just some fresh fruit. We have a really diverse selection of desserts in this section, ranging from old-fashioned puddings and pies to creamy concoctions and crêpes. There's something for everyone.

Traditional puddings have a special place in our hearts, and we have seasonal fruit crumbles and cobblers as well as rib-sticking baked and steamed puddings for cold winter evenings. Many of the recipes take literally minutes to prepare and can then cook away in the oven while you get on with other things – baked apples and rice pudding are good examples.

For entertaining on warm evenings, choose from cheesecake, summer pudding, meringues, jellies and ice cream. Or, if you want to impress your guests, a real baked Alaska – hot on the outside with a frozen centre – or a flaky, mouthwatering strudel. And there are classic desserts from Italy (zabaglione and tiramisu) and France (clafoutis and tarte tatin) as well as festive sweets like trifle and syllabub.

Whether you're looking for a time-honoured family pudding or an elegant way to finish a special dinner, we have the recipes.

< *Raspberry and Lemon Curd Cheesecake (page 465)*

APPLE CRUMBLE

125g/4oz/1 cup + 2 tbsp plain (all-purpose) flour

50g/2oz/4 tbsp butter, diced

125g/4oz/½ cup caster (superfine) sugar

a good pinch of cinnamon

900g/2lb cooking (green) apples, peeled, cored and sliced

cream or ice cream to serve

1 Preheat the oven to 180°C/350°F/Gas 4.
2 Sift the flour into a bowl, add the butter and rub in with your fingertips until the mixture resembles fine breadcrumbs. Stir in half the sugar and the cinnamon.
3 Put half the apples in a large ovenproof dish and sprinkle with the rest of the sugar. Add the remaining apple slices, then spoon the crumble mixture over the top.
4 Bake in the oven for 40 minutes or until crisp and golden. Serve hot with cream or ice cream.

preparation 15 minutes cooking time 40 minutes

Serves 4

BLACKBERRY AND APPLE CRUMBLE

125g/4oz/1 cup + 2 tbsp plain (all-purpose) flour

125g/4oz/½ cup brown sugar

50g/2oz/¼ cup ground almonds

50g/2oz/4 tbsp butter, diced

cream or ice cream to serve

For the filling

1kg/2¼lb cooking (green) apples

50g/2oz/4 tbsp butter

50g/2oz/¼ cup caster (superfine) sugar

225g/8oz/2 cups blackberries

1 Preheat the oven to 190°C/375°F/Gas 5.
2 Sift the flour into a bowl and stir in the brown sugar and ground almonds. Rub in the butter with your fingertips until the mixture resembles fine breadcrumbs.
3 To make the filling, peel and core the apples and cut them into chunks. Melt the butter in a large frying pan. Add the apples and caster sugar and cook, stirring, over a high heat for 5 minutes or until tender. Mix in the blackberries.
4 Put the apples and blackberries in a large ovenproof dish. Spoon the crumble topping over and bake in the oven for 25 minutes or until bubbling and golden brown.
5 Serve warm with cream or ice cream.

preparation 45 minutes cooking time 25 minutes

Serves 6

BAKED APPLES

125g/4oz/⅔ cup sultanas (seedless white raisins)

4 tbsp muscovado (light brown) sugar

a pinch of ground cinnamon

6 large cooking (green) apples, cored

125ml/4fl oz/1 cup orange juice

15g/½oz/1 tbsp butter, diced

cream or Greek yogurt to serve

1 Preheat the oven to 190°C/375°F/Gas 5.
2 In a bowl, mix together the sultanas, half the sugar and the cinnamon.
3 With a small sharp knife, score around the middle of each apple to prevent it bursting during cooking. Fill each apple with the sultana mixture.
4 Put the apples in a roasting pan and sprinkle them with the remaining brown sugar and the orange juice. Dot with butter and bake in the oven for 15–20 minutes until softened.
5 Serve the apples hot with cream or Greek yogurt.

preparation 5 minutes cooking time 15–20 minutes

Serves 6

PLUM COBBLER

900g/2lb plums or greengages, halved and stoned

175g/6oz/¾ cup caster (superfine) sugar

1 tbsp flour

grated zest and juice of 1 orange

225g/8oz/2¼ cups self-raising (self-rising) flour

75g/3oz/6 tbsp chilled butter, diced

125ml/4fl oz/1 cup buttermilk

1 medium (US large) egg

cream, ice cream or custard to serve

1 Preheat the oven to 200°C/400°F/Gas 6.
2 Cut the plums or greengages into large chunks and place in a large ovenproof dish with 4 tbsp sugar and the flour. Add the orange zest and juice and stir lightly together.
3 Blitz the flour, butter and most of the sugar in a food processor until the mixture resembles fine breadcrumbs (or rub in the butter by hand). Beat the buttermilk and egg together and blitz briefly or mix to a soft dough.
4 Drop spoonfuls of the dough haphazardly over the fruit, leaving a little space between them. Sprinkle with the remaining sugar.
5 Bake in the oven for 40 minutes or until the plums are tender and the cobbler is golden.
6 Serve hot with cream, ice cream or custard.

preparation 25 minutes cooking time 40 minutes

Serves 6

AUTUMN FRUIT CRUMBLE

100g/3½oz/7 tbsp butter, diced, plus extra to grease

900g/2lb pears, peeled, cored and chopped

juice of 1 lemon

225g/8oz/1 cup caster (superfine) sugar

2 tsp ground ginger

225g/8oz/2¼ cups plain (all-purpose) flour

75g/3oz/½ cup chopped hazelnuts

cream or ice cream to serve

1 Preheat the oven to 200°C/400°F/Gas 6. Lightly butter a large shallow ovenproof dish

2 Gently toss the pears in the lemon juice in a bowl. Add 8 tbsp sugar and the ginger, then spoon into the prepared dish and level down the top.

3 Put the butter, flour and the remaining sugar in a food processor and blitz until the mixture resembles fine breadcrumbs (or rub in with your fingers). Stir in the hazelnuts and spoon the crumble topping over the fruit.

4 Bake in the oven for 35–40 minutes until the fruit is tender and the crumble is golden brown and bubbling.

5 Serve hot with cream or ice cream.

preparation 20 minutes   cooking time 35–40 minutes

Serves 6

SPICY POACHED PEARS

6 ripe dessert pears

225g/8oz/1 cup caster (superfine) sugar

1 bottle red wine

2 tbsp sloe gin

1 cinnamon stick, halved

2 cloves

finely grated zest of 1 orange

Greek yogurt or cream to serve

1 Peel the pears, leaving the stalks intact. Carefully cut out the calyx at the base of each one.

2 Heat the sugar, wine and sloe gin in a small pan, stirring until the sugar dissolves.

3 Bring to the boil and add the cinnamon stick, cloves and orange zest. Add the pears, then reduce the heat, cover the pan and simmer gently for 30 minutes or until tender.

4 Remove the pears and set aside. Uncover the pan and simmer until the liquid reduces and is syrupy.

5 Discard the spices and pour the syrup over the pears.

6 Serve warm or chilled with Greek yogurt or cream.

preparation 15 minutes   cooking time 50 minutes

Serves 6

EASY BAKED APRICOTS

12 apricots, halved and stoned
4 tbsp caster (superfine) sugar
2 tbsp amaretto liqueur
50g/2oz/4 tbsp butter
4 tbsp flaked almonds
crème fraîche to serve

1 Preheat the oven to 200°C/400°F/Gas 6.
2 Put the apricot halves, cut-side up, in an ovenproof dish. Sprinkle with sugar and drizzle with amaretto. Dot the apricots with butter and sprinkle the flaked almonds over the top.
3 Bake in the oven for 20 minutes until the apricots are tender and the juices are syrupy. Serve with crème fraîche.

preparation 5 minutes   cooking time 20 minutes

Serves 6

SUMMER FRUIT COMPOTE

3 peaches, halved and stoned
4 greengages, halved and stoned
125g/4oz/1 cup blueberries
50g/2oz/¼ cup vanilla sugar
grated zest and juice of 1 orange
225g/8oz/1⅓ cups strawberries
cream or Greek yogurt to serve

1 Preheat the oven to 180°C/350°F/Gas 4.
2 Cut the peaches into thick slices and place in a large shallow ovenproof dish with the greengages, blueberries, vanilla sugar and orange zest and juice.
3 Bake in the oven for 20 minutes until the fruit is tender.
4 Stir in the strawberries, then set aside to cool. Cover and chill in the refrigerator. Serve with cream or Greek yogurt.

preparation 10 minutes   cooking time 20 minutes plus cooling and chilling

Serves 4

ROASTED SUMMER FRUIT

4 ripe peaches or nectarines, halved and stoned

8 plums, halved and stoned

125ml/4fl oz/½ cup orange juice

125ml/4fl oz/½ cup sweet dessert wine

2 tbsp runny honey

125g/4oz/1 cup raspberries

2 tbsp icing (confectioner's) sugar

1 Preheat the oven to 200°C/400°F/Gas 6.
2 Arrange the peaches or nectarines and plums, cut-side up, in a roasting pan or shallow ovenproof dish. Pour the orange juice and wine over them and cook in the oven for 20–25 minutes.
3 Preheat the grill (broiler) to medium. Stir the raspberries into the roasted fruit and sprinkle with icing sugar.
4 Grill (broil) for 2 minutes and serve hot.

preparation 10 minutes **cooking time** 30 minutes

Serves 4

SPICED FRUIT KEBABS

1 small pineapple

2 bananas

1 mango

¼ tsp freshly grated nutmeg

1 tsp ground cinnamon

½ tsp ground ginger

1 tbsp runny honey

25g/1oz/2 tbsp butter, melted

For the maple cream

300ml/½ pint/1¼ cups double (heavy) cream

1 tbsp maple syrup

1 Put the cream and maple syrup in a bowl and whip lightly to form soft peaks. Cover and chill.
2 Peel the pineapple, cut into quarters, lengthways and remove the core. Cut into 2.5cm/1in cubes. Peel the bananas and cut into 1cm/½in thick slices. Peel the mango and cut the flesh into 2.5cm/1in cubes. Thread the fruit onto wooden skewers that have been soaked in water.
3 Put the nutmeg, cinnamon, ginger, honey and melted butter in a bowl and mix together. Brush over the kebabs.
4 Place the kebabs in a foil-lined grill (broiling) pan and cook under a hot grill (broiler) for 5–6 minutes, turning occasionally, until warmed through and golden brown. Serve with the maple cream.

preparation 15 minutes **cooking time** 5–6 minutes

Serves 4

SYRUP SPONGE PUDDING

175g/6oz/¾ cup butter plus extra to grease

3 tbsp golden (corn) syrup

175g/6oz/¾ cup caster (superfine) sugar

3 large (US extra-large) eggs

a few drops of vanilla extract

grated zest of 1 lemon

175g/6oz/1½ cups self-raising (self-rising) flour, sifted

a little milk to mix

custard to serve

1 Half-fill a steamer or large pan with water and place over a high heat. Butter a 900ml/1½ pint/3⅔ cups pudding basin and drizzle the syrup into the bottom.
2 Cream together the butter and sugar until pale and fluffy. Add the eggs, a little at a time, beating well after each addition. Stir in the vanilla extract and lemon zest.
3 With a metal spoon, fold in half the flour, then fold in the rest, with enough milk to give a dropping consistency.
4 Pour the mixture into the prepared basin, cover with buttered parchment paper or foil and secure with string.
5 Steam for 1½ hours. Turn out the pudding on to a plate and serve, cut into slices, with custard.

preparation 15 minutes cooking time 1½ hours

Serves 4

STICKY TOFFEE PUDDINGS

2 tbsp black treacle (molasses)

150g/5oz/⅔ cup butter, softened

125g/4oz/½ cup caster (superfine) sugar

2 large (US extra-large) eggs, beaten

125g/4oz/1 cup self-raising (self-rising) flour, sifted

25g/1oz/¼ cup walnuts

6 Medjool dates, stoned and chopped

cream or custard to serve

1 Preheat the oven to 180°C/350°F/Gas 4.
2 Beat the black treacle and 25g/1oz/2 tbsp butter until smooth. Divide the mixture among four 150ml/¼ pint/scant ⅔ cup timbales or ramekins and set aside.
3 Put the remaining butter and the sugar in a food processor and blitz (or use a hand-held electric whisk). Add the beaten eggs and flour and blitz briefly. Stir in the nuts and dates.
4 Spoon into the timbales or ramekins, covering the syrup mixture. Bake in the oven for 25–30 minutes until risen and golden brown.
5 Set aside to rest for 5 minutes, then unmould on to warmed plates. Serve hot with cream or custard.

preparation 20 minutes cooking time 25–30 minutes plus 5 minutes resting

Serves 4

BREAD AND BUTTER PUDDING

50g/2oz/4 tbsp butter, softened, plus extra to grease

340g/12oz white bread, cut into 1cm/½in slices

75g/3oz/½ cup raisins

3 medium (US large) eggs

450ml/¾ pint/1¾ cups milk

4 tbsp icing (confectioner's) sugar, plus extra to dust

1 Preheat the oven to 180°C/350°F/Gas 4. Lightly butter a large ovenproof dish.
2 Butter the bread, then cut each slice into quarters. Arrange the bread in the dish and sprinkle with the raisins.
3 Beat the eggs, milk and sugar together in a bowl. Pour the mixture over the bread and set aside to soak for 10 minutes.
4 Bake in the oven for 30–40 minutes until golden brown and the custard is set.
5 Dust with icing sugar and pop under a hot grill (broiler) for 2–3 minutes to brown the top..

preparation 10 minutes plus soaking cooking time 30–40 minutes

Serves 4

RICE PUDDING

15g/½oz/1 tbsp butter, plus extra to grease

125g/4oz/½ cup short-grain rice

1.2 litres/2 pints/5 cups milk

50g/2oz/¼ cup caster (superfine) sugar

1 cinnamon stick

freshly grated nutmeg to taste

1 Preheat the oven to 170°C/325°F/Gas 3. Lightly butter a large ovenproof dish.
2 Put the rice, milk, sugar and cinnamon stick in the dish and stir well. Grate the nutmeg over the top and dot with butter.
3 Bake in the middle of the oven for 1½ hours or until the top is golden brown and the rice is tender and creamy.

preparation 5 minutes cooking time 1½ hours

Serves 6

PANETTONE PUDDING

50g/2oz/4 tbsp butter, softened, plus extra to grease

500g/1lb 2oz panettone, sliced

3 medium (US large) eggs

150g/5oz/scant ⅔ cup caster (superfine) sugar

300ml/½ pint/1¼ cups milk

150ml/¼ pint/scant ⅔ cup double (heavy) cream

grated zest of 1 lemon

1 Preheat the oven to 170°C/325°F/Gas 3. Butter a large ovenproof dish.
2 Lightly butter the panettone slices. Cut them into pieces and arrange in the dish.
3 Beat the eggs and sugar in a large bowl, then beat in the milk, cream and lemon zest. Pour the mixture over the panettone and set aside to soak for 20 minutes.
4 Stand the dish in a roasting pan and pour enough hot water into the pan to come halfway up the sides of the dish.
5 Bake in the oven for 35–45 minutes until the custard is just set in the middle and golden brown.

preparation 20 minutes plus soaking   **cooking time** 35–45 minutes

Serves 6

ORANGE PAIN PERDU

2 large (US extra-large) eggs

150ml/¼ pint/scant ⅔ cup milk

finely grated zest of 1 orange

50g/2oz/4 tbsp butter

8 slices raisin bread

1 tbsp caster (superfine) sugar

maple syrup to drizzle

1 Beat the eggs, milk and orange zest together in a bowl.
2 Heat the butter in a large frying pan over a medium heat. Cut the slices of raisin bread in half diagonally and dip them into the egg mixture.
3 Add to the pan, a few at a time, and fry on both sides until golden brown. Keep warm while you cook the remainder.
4 Sprinkle with the sugar and serve immediately drizzled with maple syrup.

preparation 10 minutes   **cooking time** 15 minutes

Serves 4

QUEEN OF PUDDINGS

4 medium (US large) eggs

600ml/1 pint/2½ cups milk

125g/4oz/8 tbsp caster (superfine) sugar

grated zest of 1 lemon

125g/4oz/2 cups fresh white breadcrumbs

4 tbsp raspberry jam (jelly)

1 Separate three eggs and beat the egg yolks with the remaining whole egg. Heat the milk in a small pan and stir into the beaten eggs with 2 tbsp sugar, the lemon zest and breadcrumbs, stirring until the sugar dissolves.
2 Spread the jam in the bottom of a large ovenproof dish. Pour in the custard mixture and set aside for 30 minutes.
3 Preheat the oven to 150°C/300°F/Gas 2.
4 Bake in the oven for 1 hour or until the custard is set.
5 Whisk the egg whites until stiff. Fold in the remaining sugar and whisk until glossy. Pile on top of the custard and return to the oven for 15 minutes or until set and golden brown.

preparation 20 minutes plus standing **cooking time** about 1¼ hours

Serves 4

BAKED ALASKA

1 x 25cm/10in sponge cake, about 2.5cm/1in thick

7 tbsp cherry jam (jelly)

1.2 litres/2 pints/5 cups vanilla ice cream

4 large (US extra-large) egg whites

225g/8oz/1 cup caster (superfine) sugar

1 Place the sponge cake on an ovenproof plate and spread with the jam. Scoop the ice cream on top of the jam, leaving a 1cm/½in border around the edge, then cover and put in the freezer for at least 30 minutes.
2 Whisk the egg whites in a clean, grease-free bowl until stiff. Using a large spoon, fold in the sugar, 1 tbsp at a time, then whisk until very thick and glossy.
3 Spoon the meringue over the ice cream, taking it all the way round and down to cover the edge of the cake. Swirl the top and sides. Freeze for at least 1 hour or overnight.
4 Preheat the oven to 230°C/450°F/Gas 8.
5 Bake for 3–4 minutes until the meringue is just set and golden brown. Serve immediately.

preparation 30 minutes plus freezing **cooking time** 3–4 minutes

Serves 8

RASPBERRY RICE PUDDING

125g/4oz/½ cup short-grain rice
1.2 litres/2 pints/5 cups milk
grated zest of 1 orange
4 tbsp caster (superfine) sugar
200ml/7fl oz/¾ cup double
(heavy) cream, whipped
6 tbsp raspberry sauce

1 Put the rice in a pan with 600ml/1 pint/2½ cups cold water and bring to the boil. Reduce the heat and simmer gently until the liquid has evaporated.
2 Pour in the milk and bring to the boil, then reduce the heat and simmer for 45 minutes or until the rice is tender and creamy. Set aside to cool, then transfer to a bowl.
3 Fold the orange zest, sugar and whipped cream into the rice. Cover and chill in the refrigerator for 1 hour.
4 Divide among six glass dishes and top with raspberry sauce.

preparation 10 minutes plus chilling   **cooking time** 1 hour plus cooling

Serves 6

CREAMY CHILLED RISOTTO

900ml/1½ pints/3⅔ cups milk
75g/3oz/⅓ cup risotto rice
3 tbsp caster (superfine) sugar
200ml/7fl oz/¾ cup double
(heavy) cream
ground cinnamon to sprinkle
poached fruit to serve

1 Put the milk in a large pan and bring to the boil. Stir in the rice, reduce the heat and simmer gently for 40 minutes, stirring occasionally, until the rice is tender and most of the liquid has been absorbed.
2 Stir in the sugar and set aside to cool. Stir in the cream and pour into a bowl. Cover and chill in the refrigerator.
3 Just before serving, sprinkle with a little ground cinnamon. Serve with poached fruit, such as peaches or apricots.

preparation 5 minutes plus chilling   **cooking time** 40 minutes plus cooling

Serves 8

CHERRY CREPES

125g/4oz/1 cup + 2 tbsp plain (all-purpose) flour

1 egg + 1 egg yolk

1 tbsp sunflower oil, plus extra to fry

250ml/9fl oz/1 cup milk

For the lemon filling

75g/3oz/6 tbsp butter, softened

50g/2oz/¼ cup caster (superfine) sugar

grated zest of 1 lemon

For the cherry compote

pared rind of ½ lemon

75g/3oz/6 tbsp caster (superfine) sugar

450g/1lb cherries, pitted

1 To make the crêpes, sift the flour into a bowl and stir in the egg, egg yolk and oil. Gradually whisk in the milk, beating until smooth. Set aside for 15 minutes.

2 Meanwhile, cream all the lemon filling ingredients together in a bowl until light and fluffy.

3 To make the cherry compote, put the lemon rind, sugar and 175ml/6fl oz/¾ cup water in a pan and heat gently, stirring until the sugar dissolves. Boil for 3 minutes until syrupy. Add the cherries and cook for 5 minutes. Discard the lemon rind.

4 Pour a little oil into an 18cm/7in frying pan and place over a medium heat. When hot, pour 2–3 tbsp batter into the pan, tilting it to coat the bottom. Cook until browned on the underside, then flip the crêpe over and cook the other side. Slide out on to a large plate and cook the remaining crêpes in the same way.

5 Spread each crêpe thinly with lemon butter, then fold into four. Place half the crêpes in a large frying pan and set over a medium heat for 5 minutes, turning once, until hot. Repeat with the remaining crêpes. Reheat the cherry compote.

6 Serve the crêpes immediately with the compote.

preparation 20 minutes plus standing **cooking time** 15 minutes

Serves 6

CHERRY CLAFOUTIS

400g/14oz cherries, pitted

3 tbsp kirsch (optional)

125g/4oz/½ cup caster (superfine) sugar

2 large (US extra-large) eggs

100g/3½oz/scant cup plain (all-purpose) flour, sifted

150ml/¼ pint/scant ⅔ cup milk

a few drops of vanilla extract

25g/1oz/2 tbsp butter, melted, plus extra to grease

icing (confectioner's) sugar to dust

1 Put the cherries in a bowl with the kirsch (if using) and 1 tbsp sugar. Mix together, cover and set aside for 1 hour.

2 Meanwhile, beat the eggs with the rest of the sugar in a bowl. Beat in the flour and then the eggs and milk. Stir in the vanilla extract and the melted butter.

3 Preheat the oven to 180°C/350°F/Gas 4.

4 Lightly butter a shallow ovenproof dish and add the cherries. Pour the batter over them and bake in the oven for about 40 minutes until puffed up and golden and just set.

5 Serve warm, dusted with icing sugar.

preparation 20 minutes plus soaking **cooking time** about 1 hour

Serves 4

TRADITIONAL CREPES

125g/4oz/1 cup + 2 tbsp plain (all-purpose) flour

a pinch of salt

2 medium (US large) eggs

300ml/½ pint/1¼ cups milk

a little lard (shortening) to fry

caster (superfine) sugar and lemon juice to serve

1 Sift the flour and salt into a bowl and make a well in the centre. Beat in the eggs. Gradually beat in the milk, drawing in the flour from the sides, to make a smooth batter. Cover and set aside to stand for 20 minutes.

2 Heat a tiny knob of lard in an 18cm/7in heavy-based non-stick frying pan. Pour in just enough batter to thinly coat the bottom of the pan, tilting it. Cook over a medium-high heat for 1–2 minutes until set and golden brown underneath. Flip the crêpe over and cook the second side.

3 Slide the crêpe out of the pan on to a plate and keep hot. Cook the remaining crêpes in the same way, stacking them on top of each other with parchment paper in between.

4 Serve the crêpes, folded over or rolled up, sprinkled with sugar and lemon juice.

preparation 10 minutes plus standing **cooking time** about 15 minutes

Makes 8

WAFFLES

125g/4oz/1 cup + 2 tbsp self-raising (self-rising) flour

a pinch of salt

1 tbsp caster (superfine) sugar

1 medium (US large) egg, separated

25g/1oz/2 tbsp butter, melted

250ml/8fl oz/1 cup milk

maple syrup to serve

1 Heat the waffle iron according to the manufacturer's instructions.

2 Mix the flour, salt and sugar together in a bowl. Add the egg yolk, melted butter and milk and beat until you have a smooth coating batter.

3 Whisk the egg white in a clean, grease-free bowl until stiff. Fold gently into the batter with a metal spoon. Pour just enough batter into the iron to run over the surface.

4 Close the iron and cook for 2–3 minutes, turning the iron if using a non-electric type. The waffle is cooked when it is golden brown and crisp and easily removed from the iron. Cook the remainder in the same way.

5 Serve the waffles immediately with maple syrup.

preparation 5 minutes **cooking time** 16 minutes

Serves 4

CINNAMON CREPES

125g/4oz/1 cup + 2 tbsp plain (all-purpose) flour

½ tsp ground cinnamon

2 medium (US large) eggs

300ml/½ pint/1¼ cups milk

olive oil to fry

sugar and Greek yogurt to serve

1 Beat the flour, cinnamon, egg and milk together in a bowl to make a smooth batter. Set aside to stand for 20 minutes.
2 Heat a small heavy-based frying pan over a medium heat. When the pan is really hot, add a few drops of oil, then pour in a little batter and tilt the pan to coat the bottom evenly. Cook for 1–2 minutes until golden underneath, then flip over and cook the other side. Slide out of the pan and keep warm.
3 Repeat with the remaining batter, adding more oil if needed, to make six crêpes.
4 Serve sprinkled with sugar with a spoonful of yogurt.

preparation 5 minutes plus standing   cooking time 15–20 minutes

Serves 6

PAIN PERDU

225g/8oz mixed blueberries, strawberries, raspberries

125g/4oz/½ cup caster (superfine) sugar

icing (confectioner's) sugar to dust or maple syrup

For the French toast

2 medium (US large) eggs

150ml/¼ pint/scant ⅔ cup milk

2 tbsp caster (superfine) sugar

a pinch of ground cinnamon

4 x 1cm/½in slices day-old brioche loaf

butter to fry

1 Put the berries and caster sugar in a pan over a low heat, stirring gently until the sugar dissolves in the juice. Simmer for 2 minutes, then remove from the heat.
2 Beat together the eggs, milk, caster sugar and cinnamon in a shallow dish.
3 Cut the slices of brioche into triangles. Dip the slices into the egg mixture, turning them over to soak the other side.
4 Melt the butter in a frying pan over a low to medium heat. Add the brioche and cook for 4–5 minutes until golden brown on both sides.
5 Serve the immediately with the warm poached berries, dusted with icing sugar or drizzled with maple syrup.

preparation 10 minutes   cooking time 15 minutes

Serves 4

ORANGE PANNA COTTA

3 sheets of leaf gelatine

vegetable oil to grease

600ml/1 pint/2½ cups double (heavy) cream

125ml/4fl oz/½ cup milk

finely grated zest of 1 orange

150g/5oz/scant ⅔ cup caster (superfine) sugar

2 oranges

1 Put the gelatine sheets in a shallow dish, then cover with 600ml/1 pint/2½ cups cold water and set aside to soak for 5 minutes. Lightly oil six 150ml/¼ pint/scant ⅔ cup dariole moulds.

2 Put the cream, milk, orange zest and 100g/3½oz/7 tbsp sugar in a pan and bring to the boil, stirring to dissolve the sugar. Remove from the heat.

3 Lift the gelatine sheets out of the water and squeeze out any excess liquid. Add to the cream mixture and stir until dissolved. Pour into the dariole moulds. When cool, chill in the refrigerator for 4–6 hours.

4 Squeeze the juice from the oranges and strain into a pan. Add the remaining sugar and bring to the boil, then reduce the heat and simmer for 10 minutes. Set aside to cool.

5 Run a palette knife around the edge of each panna cotta and invert on to a serving plate. Serve with the orange sauce.

preparation 15 minutes **cooking time** 12 minutes plus chilling

Serves 6

EASY PEACH BRULEE

8 tsp mascarpone cheese

4 amaretti, crumbled

4 peaches, halved and stoned

2 tbsp brown sugar

1 Preheat the grill (broiler) to hot. Mix the mascarpone and the amaretti and use to fill the cavity of each peach half. Sprinkle with sugar.

2 Place the peaches on a grill (broiling) pan and pop under the hot grill for 5 minutes or until caramelized.

preparation 10 minutes **cooking time** 5 minutes

Serves 4

STRAWBERRY BRULEE

275g/10oz/2 cups strawberries, hulled and sliced

2 tsp icing (confectioner's) sugar

grated zest of 1 orange

400g/14oz/1⅔ cups Greek yogurt

4 tbsp demerara (light brown) sugar

1 Divide the strawberries among four ramekins and sprinkle with icing sugar.
2 Stir the orange zest into the yogurt and spread over the strawberries.
3 Preheat the grill (broiler) to high. Sprinkle the demerara sugar evenly over the yogurt to cover it completely.
4 Place the ramekins on the grill (broiling) pan and grill (broil) until the sugar caramelizes. Set aside to cool and then chill in the refrigerator before serving.

preparation 15 minutes cooking time 5 minutes plus cooling and chilling

Serves 4

CREME BRULEE

600ml/1 pint/2½ cups double (heavy) cream

1 vanilla pod (bean), split lengthways

5 large (US extra-large) egg yolks

50g/2oz/¼ cup caster (superfine) sugar

1 Put the cream and vanilla pod in a pan and bring slowly to the boil. Remove from the heat, cover and set aside for at least 30 minutes, then remove the vanilla pod.
2 Preheat the oven to 150°C/300°F/Gas 2. Put six ramekins in a roasting pan.
3 Beat the egg yolks with 1 tbsp caster sugar in a bowl. Gradually stir in the vanilla cream, then strain into a jug and pour into the ramekins. Pour enough warm water into the pan to come halfway up the sides of the ramekins.
4 Bake in the oven for 40–45 minutes until set. Cool, then chill in the refrigerator for at least 4 hours or overnight.
5 Sprinkle the remaining sugar over the custards to form a thin layer. Pop under a very hot grill (broiler) for 2–3 minutes until it caramelizes. Set aside to cool for 1 hour until the caramel is crisp and cold.

preparation 15 minutes plus infusing and chilling cooking time 40–45 minutes plus cooling

Serves 6

SYLLABUB

pared zest and juice of 1 lemon

125ml/4fl oz/½ cup medium dry white wine or sherry

2 tbsp brandy

50g/2oz/4 tbsp caster (superfine) sugar

300ml/½ pint/1¼ cups double (heavy) cream

freshly grated nutmeg to dust

1 Put the lemon zest and juice in a bowl with the wine or sherry and brandy. Leave to stand for several hours.
2 Strain the liquid into a large bowl and stir in the sugar.
3 Gradually add the cream, whipping between each addition, until it just holds its shape.
4 Divide the syllabub among four serving glasses. Chill in the refrigerator for 1 hour before serving dusted with nutmeg..

preparation 15 minutes plus cooling and chilling

Serves 4

ZABAGLIONE

8 medium (US large) egg yolks

125g/4oz/½ cup caster (superfine) sugar

225ml/9fl oz/1 cup Marsala

sponge fingers to serve

1 Put the egg yolks and sugar in a large heatproof bowl set over a pan of gently simmering water. Using a hand-held electric whisk, beat until pale and creamy.
2 Gradually pour in the Marsala and whisk for 10–15 minutes until the mixture is thick and foaming.
3 Remove from the heat and pour into warmed glasses. Serve immediately with sponge fingers.

preparation 5 minutes **cooking time** 20 minutes

Serves 4

FRUITY YOGURT POTS

1 x 200g/7oz can apricots in juice

1 ball preserved stem ginger in syrup, finely chopped, plus 2 tbsp syrup from the jar

juice of 1 orange

2 oranges, cut into segments

1 papaya, peeled, seeded and chopped

½ small pineapple, peeled, cored and chopped

2 tbsp orange curd

225g/8oz/1 cup Greek yogurt

1 Drain the apricot juice into a pan and stir in the ginger syrup. Add the chopped stem ginger and orange juice. Warm over a low heat, stirring gently. Bring to the boil, then reduce the heat and simmer for 2–3 minutes until thick and syrupy.
2 Chop the apricots and mix in a bowl with the oranges, papaya and pineapple. Pour the syrup over the fruit. Divide among four glasses or bowls.
3 Swirl the orange curd through the yogurt and spoon over the fruit. Chill in the refrigerator before serving.

preparation 15 minutes   cooking time 5 minutes plus chilling

Serves 4

LEMON POTS

150g/5oz/⅔ cup condensed milk

50ml/2fl oz/¼ cup double (heavy) cream

grated zest and juice of 1 lemon

6 strawberries, hulled and sliced

1 Put the condensed milk, cream and lemon zest and juice in a bowl and beat until thick and fluffy.
2 Divide the strawberries between two small ramekins. Spoon the lemon mixture over the top and chill in the refrigerator before serving.

preparation 10 minutes plus chilling

Serves 2

GOOSEBERRY FOOL

450g/1lb gooseberries, topped and tailed

125g/4oz/½ cup caster (superfine) sugar

1 tbsp elderflower cordial

250g/9oz/1 cup mascarpone

150ml/¼ pint/scant ⅔ cup thick Greek yogurt

1 Put the gooseberries, sugar, elderflower cordial and 1 tbsp water in a pan. Cook gently over a low heat, stirring occasionally, for 10 minutes or until the gooseberries are soft. Set aside to cool.

2 Blitz the fruit in a blender or food processor. Pass the purée through a sieve to remove the pips.

3 Gently stir the mascarpone into the gooseberry purée and fold in the yogurt.

4 Spoon into four glasses and chill in the refrigerator until ready to serve.

preparation 20 minutes plus chilling **cooking time** 10 minutes

Serves 4

SHERRY TRIFLE

8 trifle sponges

125g/4oz/½ cup cherry jam

125g/4oz macaroons, crushed

125ml/4fl oz/½ cup sherry

600ml/1 pint/2½ cups milk

½ vanilla pod (bean)

2 medium (US large) eggs plus 2 yolks

2 tbsp caster (superfine) sugar, plus extra to sprinkle

300ml/½ pint/1¼ cups double (heavy) cream

3 tbsp flaked almonds,

1 Spread the trifle sponges with jam and place in a shallow glass serving bowl with the macaroons. Pour over the sherry and set aside for 2 hours.

2 Put the milk and vanilla pod in a pan and bring to the boil. Remove from the heat, cover and infuse for 30 minutes then remove the vanilla pod.

3 Beat together the eggs, yolks and sugar and strain on to the milk. Cook gently over a low heat, stirring, until the custard thickens slightly. Pour the warm custard over the trifle and leave to cool and set firm.

4 Lightly whip the cream and spoon over the top of the trifle. Sprinkle with flaked almonds and serve.

preparation 20 minutes plus infusing and cooling **cooking time** 15 minutes

Serves 6

TIRAMISU

4 medium (US large) egg yolks
50g/2oz/4 tbsp caster (superfine)
sugar
250g/9oz/1 cup mascarpone
300ml/½ pint/1¼ cups double
(heavy) cream
3 tbsp coffee liqueur
1 x 200g/7oz pack savoiardi or
sponge fingers
450ml/¾ pint/1¾ cups warm
espresso coffee
chocolate shavings to serve

1 In a large bowl, beat the egg yolks and sugar together until pale and thick, then whisk in the mascarpone until smooth.
2 Whip the cream in another bowl to soft peaks, then fold into the mascarpone mixture with the coffee liqueur.
3 Take half of the sponge fingers and, one by one, dip them into the warm coffee, then arrange over the bottom of a large shallow glass serving dish. Spread a layer of mascarpone mixture over the top, then dip the remaining sponge fingers into the coffee and arrange on top. Cover with the remaining mascarpone.
4 Cover and chill in the refrigerator for 2 hours.
5 Sprinkle the top with shaved chocolate and serve.

preparation 20 minutes plus chilling

Serves 10

GREEK GRILLED FIGS

6 figs
40g/1½oz/3 tbsp butter
1 tsp ground cinnamon
icing (confectioner's) sugar
to dust

For the honey yogurt
200ml/7fl oz/¾ cup Greek yogurt
2 tbsp Greek runny honey

1 To make the honey yogurt, mix together the yogurt and half the honey in a bowl, then set aside.
2 Cut the figs in half. Gently heat the butter in a small pan until melted and stir in the cinnamon.
3 Preheat the grill (broiler). Brush the butter over the figs and dust with icing sugar. Place the figs under the hot grill and cook for 3–4 minutes, turning once, until warmed through and the sugar caramelizes.
4 Place two fig halves on each serving plate. Spoon the yogurt on top and drizzle with the remaining honey.

preparation 10 minutes   cooking time 5 minutes

Serves 6

SUMMER PUDDING

700g/1½lb/6 cups mixed berries, e.g. redcurrants, blackcurrants, strawberries and raspberries

125g/4oz/½ cup caster (superfine) sugar

3 tbsp crème de cassis

9 thick slices slightly stale white bread, crusts removed

crème fraîche to serve

1 Put the redcurrants and blackcurrants in a pan with the sugar and cassis. Set over a low heat and simmer gently for 4–5 minutes, stirring, until the sugar dissolves. Add the raspberries and cook for 2 minutes.
2 Meanwhile, line a 1 litre/1¾ pint/4 cup bowl with clingfilm (plastic wrap). Put the base of the bowl on a slice of bread and cut around it. Put the bread in the bottom of the bowl.
3 Line the sides with more slices of bread, slightly overlapping them to avoid any gaps. Spoon in the fruit – the juice will soak into the bread. Reserve a few spoonfuls of juice.
4 Cut the remaining bread to fit the top of the pudding neatly, using a sharp knife to trim any excess bread from around the edges. Wrap in clingfilm (plastic wrap), weigh down with a saucer and a can and chill in the refrigerator overnight.
5 Unwrap the outer clingfilm (plastic wrap) and upturn the pudding on to a plate. Remove the inner clingfilm (plastic wrap). Drizzle with the reserved juice and serve, cut into slices, with crème fraîche.

preparation 15 minutes plus overnight chilling   **cooking time** 10 minutes

Serves 8

ETON MESS

200g/7oz/¾ cup fromage frais, chilled

200g/7oz/¾ cup Greek yogurt, chilled

6 meringues, roughly crushed

450g/1lb/2½ cups strawberries, hulled and halved

1 Put the chilled fromage frais and yogurt in a large bowl and stir well until thoroughly mixed.
2 Add the meringues and halved strawberries.
3 Mix everything together gently and divide among six dishes. Serve immediately.

preparation 10 minutes

Serves 6

RASPBERRY AND LEMON CURD CHEESECAKE

75g/3oz/6 tbsp butter, plus extra to grease

250g/9oz digestive biscuits (graham crackers)

600g/1lb 5oz/2½ cups cream cheese

125g/4oz/½ cup caster (superfine) sugar

1 tbsp cornflour (cornstarch)

grated zest of 1 lemon

4 medium (US large) eggs

175ml/6fl oz/⅔ cup double (heavy) cream

3 tbsp lemon curd

150g/5oz/1 cup raspberries, plus extra to decorate

sifted icing (confectioner's) sugar to decorate

1 Preheat the oven to 180°C/350°F/Gas 4. Butter a 23cm/9in springform tin.
2 Crush the biscuits to fine crumbs in a food processor or put them in a plastic bag and crush with a rolling pin.
3 Melt the butter in a pan over a low heat and stir in the crumbs. Spoon into the prepared tin and press down evenly. Bake in the oven for 5 minutes.
4 Remove from the oven and set aside. Reduce the oven temperature to 150°C/300°F/Gas 2.
5 Put the cream cheese, caster sugar, cornflour and lemon zest in a food processor or large mixing bowl and beat until smooth. Beat in the eggs, one at a time, then gradually beat in the cream until smooth. In a small bowl, mix 3 tbsp of this mixture with the lemon curd and set aside.
6 Pour the remaining cream cheese mixture on to the biscuit base. Sprinkle with the raspberries, then drop small spoonfuls of the lemon curd mixture randomly among them.
7 Bake in the oven for 35–45 minutes until the cheesecake is turning golden around the edges and the centre is just set. Turn off the oven and open the door slightly. Leave the cheesecake to cool in the oven for 2 hours (it will crack as it cools). Chill in the refrigerator until cold and firm.
8 Loosen the edge of the cheesecake, remove from the tin and place on a serving plate. Decorate with the extra raspberries and dust with icing sugar.

preparation 25 minutes   **cooking time** 40–50 minutes plus cooling and chilling

Serves 8–10

MERINGUES

3 medium (US large) egg whites, at room temperature

175g/6oz/¾ cup caster (superfine) sugar

200ml/7fl oz/¾ cup double (heavy) cream, whipped

1 Preheat the oven to 110°C/225°F/Gas ¼. Line two baking sheets with parchment paper.
2 Put the egg whites in a clean, grease-free bowl and beat with an electric whisk until they form stiff peaks. Gradually add the sugar, a tablespoonful at a time, beating well after each addition. Beat until the meringue is very stiff and glossy.
3 Using two large spoons, shape the meringue into 12 rounds, spacing them well apart on the lined baking sheets.
4 Bake in the oven for 2–3 hours until the meringues are dried out but still pale. Carefully peel them off the paper and cool on a wire rack.
5 Sandwich the meringues together with cream and serve.

preparation 20 minutes   cooking time 2–3 hours plus cooling

Serves 6

TANGERINE JELLIES

5 gelatine leaves

1kg/2¼lb tangerines plus 2 extra tangerines, segmented

150g/5oz/scant ⅔ cup caster (superfine) sugar

1 Put the gelatine in a shallow bowl and cover with cold water. Set aside to soak for 5 minutes.
2 Meanwhile, zest two tangerines and put the zest in a large pan. Squeeze the juice from the zested and whole tangerines and add to the pan with the sugar.
3 Lift the gelatine out of the water and add to the pan. Heat gently, stirring, until the sugar dissolves. Strain into a large jug and make up to 1 litre/1¾ pints/4 cups with cold water.
4 Divide the tangerine segments between 8 dishes, pour over the liquid and chill for at least 5 hours. Remove from the refrigerator 5 minutes before serving to soften slightly.

preparation 10 minutes   cooking time about 3 minutes plus chilling

Makes 8

STRAWBERRY PROSECCO JELLIES

3 tsp powdered gelatine

675g/1½lb/4 cups strawberries, hulled and chopped

50g/2oz/4 tbsp caster (superfine) sugar

125ml/4fl oz/½ cup Prosecco

juice of 1 lemon

1 Pour 4 tbsp cold water into a small bowl and sprinkle the gelatine over the top. Stir until the powder is absorbed by the water. Set aside for 5 minutes.
2 Put two-thirds of the strawberries in a pan with the sugar, Prosecco and lemon juice. Cook gently for 5 minutes until the strawberries soften and the sugar dissolves.
3 Blitz in a blender or food processor until smooth, then press through a sieve back into the pan.
4 Add the gelatine and heat gently, stirring constantly for 1–2 minutes, until it dissolves. Remove from the heat and set aside to cool.
5 Stir the remaining strawberries into the jelly, then pour into eight individual silicone or metal dariole moulds set on a small tray. Chill in the refrigerator for 3–4 hours, until set, then turn out and serve immediately.

preparation 10 minutes plus setting   cooking time 6–7 minutes

Serves 8

KNICKERBOCKER GLORY

½ x 140g/4½oz pack lemon jelly (jello)

150g/5oz/1 cup raspberries plus extra to decorate

50g/2oz/4 tbsp caster (superfine) sugar

1 x 400g/14oz can peach slices in juice, drained and chopped

500ml/18fl oz/2¼ cups vanilla ice cream

150ml/¼ pint/scant ⅔ cup double (heavy) cream, whipped

6 tsp flaked (slivered) almonds

1 Make up the jelly as directed on the pack. When set, chop it roughly into pieces.
2 Blitz the raspberries and sugar in a blender to a purée.
3 Divide some of the peaches among six tall sundae glasses. Cover with a layer of jelly and a scoop of ice cream. Drizzle some raspberry purée over the top..
4 Continue layering in this way, finishing with a layer of whipped cream.
5 Decorate with raspberries and sprinkle with flaked almonds and serve immediately.

preparation 15 minutes plus chilling

Serves 6

LEMON SORBET

4 juicy lemons

125g/4oz/½ cup caster (superfine) sugar

2–3 tbsp limoncello

1 large (US extra-large) egg white

1 Finely pare the lemon zest, then squeeze the juice. Put the zest in a pan with the sugar and 350ml/12fl oz/1½ cups water and heat gently, stirring until the sugar dissolves. Increase the heat and boil for 10 minutes. Set aside to cool.
2 Stir the lemon juice and limoncello into the cooled sugar syrup. Cover and chill in the refrigerator for 30 minutes.
3 Strain the syrup through a fine sieve into a bowl. In a clean, dry bowl, beat the egg white until just frothy, then whisk into the lemon mixture.
4 Freeze in an ice-cream maker and follow the instructions. If you don't have one, pour into a shallow freezerproof container and freeze until almost frozen. Remove and mash well with a fork, then freeze until solid.
5 Transfer the sorbet to the refrigerator 30 minutes before serving to soften slightly.

preparation 10 minutes plus chilling and freezing   **cooking time** 15 minutes

Serves 4

STRAWBERRY ICE CREAM

500g/1lb 2oz frozen strawberries
grated zest of 1 orange
75g/3oz/⅔ cup icing (confectioner's) sugar
125ml/4fl oz/½ cup whipping cream

preparation 10 minutes

1 Put all the ingredients in a food processor and blitz until the mixture is smooth.
2 Serve immediately or spoon into a freezerproof container and freeze for up to one month. Allow the ice cream to soften a little at room temperature before serving.

Serves 6

PEAR AND CRANBERRY STRUDEL

75g/3oz/6 tbsp butter, melted,
plus extra to grease

125g/4oz/1 cup cranberries

550g/1¼lb pears, peeled, cored
and sliced

50g/2oz/¾ cup chopped walnuts

grated zest and juice of 1 lemon

2 tbsp caster (superfine) sugar

1 tbsp fresh white breadcrumbs

1 tsp ground cinnamon

7 sheets filo pastry

icing (confectioner's) sugar
to dust

1 Preheat the oven to 190°C/375°F/Gas 5. Butter a large
   baking sheet.
2 In a bowl, mix the cranberries with the pears, nuts and
   lemon juice. Stir in the lemon zest, 1 tbsp caster sugar,
   the breadcrumbs and cinnamon.
3 On a clean teatowel (dishtowel) put three sheets of filo
   pastry, overlapping each other by 2.5cm/1in to make a
   56 × 48cm/22 × 19in rectangle. Brush with melted butter,
   put three sheets on top and brush again.
4 Put the pear mixture on the pastry and roll up from a long
   edge. Place, seam-side down, on the prepared baking sheet.
   Cut the remaining filo pastry into strips, crumple and place
   on the strudel, then brush with melted butter. Sprinkle with
   the remaining caster sugar .
5 Bake in the oven for 40–45 minutes, covering with foil if it
   browns too quickly. Dust with icing sugar and serve.

preparation 20 minutes cooking time 40–45 minutes

Serves 8

APPLE PIE

1kg/2¼lb cooking (green)
apples, peeled, cored and sliced

50g/2oz/4 tbsp caster (superfine)
sugar plus extra to sprinkle

6 cloves

a good pinch of ground cinnamon

1 quantity sweet pastry
(see page 583)

flour to dust

cream to serve

1 Preheat the oven to 190°C/375°F/Gas 5.
2 Layer the apples and sugar in a large pie dish. Stud some of
   the apple slices with cloves and sprinkle with cinnamon.
3 Roll out the pastry on a lightly floured surface to a round
   2.5cm/1in larger than the pie dish. Cut off a strip the width
   of the rim of the dish. Dampen the rim of the dish and press
   on the strip. Dampen the pastry strip and cover with the
   pastry circle, pressing the edges together well. Crimp the
   edge by pressing down on it with a damp fork. Make a slit in
   the centre to allow steam to escape.
4 Bake in the oven for 35–40 minutes until lightly browned.
   Sprinkle with sugar before serving with cream.

preparation 20 minutes cooking time 35–40 minutes

Serves 6

TREACLE TART

1 quantity shortcrust pastry
(see page 582)

plain (all-purpose) flour to dust

675g/1½lb golden (corn) syrup

250g/9oz/4½ cups fresh white
breadcrumbs

grated zest and juice of 2 lemons

1 Preheat the oven to 200°C/400°F/Gas 6.
2 Roll out the pastry on a lightly floured surface and use to line
   a 25cm/10in deep, loose-based fluted tart tin. Prick the base
   with a fork and chill in the refrigerator for 30 minutes.
3 To make the filling, heat the syrup in a pan over a low heat.
   Remove from the heat and mix in the breadcrumbs and
   lemon zest and juice.
4 Pour the filling into the pastry case (pie crust) and bake for
   15 minutes, then reduce the heat to 180°C/350°F/Gas 4 and
   cook for 15 minutes until the filling is lightly set and golden.
   Serve warm.

preparation 25 minutes plus chilling   **cooking time** 30 minutes plus cooling

Serves 6

TARTE TATIN

1 quantity sweet pastry
(see page 583)
plain (all-purpose) flour to dust
cream or ice cream to serve

For the filling
200g/7oz/scant 1 cup caster
(superfine) sugar
125g/4oz/½ cup chilled butter
1.4kg/3lb dessert apples, e.g.
Granny Smiths, peeled and cored
juice of ½ lemon

1 To make the filling, sprinkle the sugar over the bottom of
   a 20cm/8in ovenproof frying pan. Cut the butter into small
   pieces and scatter over the sugar. Halve the apples and
   pack them in tightly, cut-side up, on top of the butter.
2 Cook over a low–medium heat for 30 minutes, making sure it
   doesn't bubble over or burn underneath, until the butter and
   sugar turn a dark golden brown. Remove from the heat and
   sprinkle with lemon juice. Set aside to cool.
3 Preheat the oven to 220°C/425°F/Gas 7.
4 Roll out the pastry on a floured surface to a round 2.5cm/1in
   larger than the pan. Prick several times with a fork. Lay it
   over the apples, tucking the edges down inside the pan.
5 Bake for 25–30 minutes until golden brown. Cool in the tin
   for 10 minutes, then upturn on to a serving plate.
6 Serve with cream or ice cream.

preparation 30 minutes plus chilling   **cooking time** about 1 hour plus cooling

Serves 6

SPICED PLUM PIE

250g/9oz ready-rolled sweet shortcrust pastry

flour to dust

900g/2lb plums or greengages, halved, stoned and quartered

2 green cardamom pods, split open, seeds removed and crushed

75g/3oz/6 tbsp caster (superfine) sugar, plus extra to sprinkle

milk to glaze

1 Preheat the oven to 220°C/425°F/Gas 7. Put a baking sheet in the oven to heat up.
2 Roll out the pastry on a lightly floured surface to a 30cm/12in circle. Place on a floured baking sheet. Pile the plums on to the pastry and sprinkle with cardamom seeds and sugar. Fold in the pastry edges and pleat together.
3 Brush the pastry with milk and sprinkle with sugar. Slide on to the preheated sheet and bake in the oven for 30 minutes or until golden brown and the plums are just tender.
4 Set aside to cool for 10 minutes, then loosen the pastry around the edges. Cool for another 20 minutes, then transfer to a serving plate. Sprinkle with sugar and serve.

preparation 15 minutes   cooking time 30 minutes plus cooling

Serves 6

BANOFFEE PIE

100g/3½oz/7 tbsp butter, melted, plus extra to grease

225g/8oz gingernut cookies, roughly broken

2 small bananas, peeled and sliced

8 tbsp dulce de leche

300ml/½ pint/1¼ cups double (heavy) cream, whipped

1 tbsp cocoa powder to dust

1 Butter the base and sides of a 23cm/9in loose-based tart tin or dish. Blitz the cookies in a food processor until they resemble breadcrumbs. Pour in the melted butter and pulse briefly to combine. Press the mixture into the prepared tin and level the surface. Chill in the refrigerator for 2 hours.
2 Arrange the banana slices over the biscuit base and spoon the dulce de leche on top. Spread the cream over the top. Dust with cocoa powder and serve.

preparation 15 minutes plus chilling   cooking time 2–3 minutes

Serves 12

QUICK APPLE TART

375g/13oz pack ready-rolled puff pastry

500g/1lb 2oz sweet dessert apples, cored, thinly sliced and tossed in the juice of 1 lemon

icing (confectioner's) sugar to dredge

cream to serve

1 Preheat the oven to 200°C/400°F/Gas 6.
2 Roll out the pastry on a 28 × 38cm/11 × 15in baking sheet. Score lightly around the edge, to create a 3cm/1¼in border.
3 Arrange the apple slices on top of the pastry, within the border. Turn the edge of the pastry halfway over, so that it reaches the edge of the apples, then press down and crimp the edge with your fingers. Dredge with icing sugar.
4 Bake in the oven for 20–25 minutes until the pastry is cooked and the sugar has caramelized. Serve warm with cream.

preparation 10 minutes   cooking time 25 minutes

Serves 8

EATING
LITE

If you're counting the calories and watching your waistline, you can still enjoy delicious meals with the low-fat recipes in the following pages. And they're not just salads – we have included healthy, slimming versions of some of your favourite dishes.

We have snacks, soups, light meals and main meals from around the world: Mexican enchiladas and fajitas; Chinese spring rolls; Thai crabcakes and curry; Hungarian goulash; Italian saltimbocca; and Indonesian laksa and nasi goreng. Alongside family favourites like chilli con carne and fish pie, there are low-calorie versions of classic pasta dishes, steak and sweet potato 'fries' and a seafood paella.

And we also have some delicious desserts – you'll be amazed at how few calories our traditional-style fruit crumble, muffins and pavlova contain. And for chocaholics, there's even a coffee-flavoured chocolate mousse. They are all good enough to serve at a dinner party or special occasion – your guests will never believe they are eating low-fat food!

Who says that you have to starve yourself or eat boring food when you're on a diet?

< Low-fat Chilli Beef (page 486)

SUMMER CHICKEN

1 small onion, finely chopped
1 garlic clove, crushed
spray oil
2 x 125g/4oz boneless, skinless chicken breasts
2 tbsp dry white vermouth
150ml/¼ pint/scant ⅔ cup hot chicken stock
75g/3oz/⅔ cup fresh shelled peas (or frozen)
2 tbsp half-fat crème fraîche
1 small bunch of fresh mint, finely chopped
salt and ground black pepper

1 Cook the onion and garlic for 2–3 minutes over a medium heat in a frying pan sprayed lightly with oil. Add the chicken breasts and cook for 4 minutes each side or until golden.
2 Pour in the vermouth and let it bubble a little, then add the hot stock and simmer over a low heat for 10 minutes, turning the chicken halfway through.
3 Add the peas and simmer gently for 5 minutes or until tender. If the chicken is cooked through, stir in the crème fraîche and chopped mint. Heat through gently and season to taste.
4 Serve the hot chicken in the sauce with seasonal green vegetables or baby carrots.

preparation 10 minutes   cooking time 35 minutes   calories 180 kcals

Serves 2

YOGURT SPICED CHICKEN

2 x 125g/4oz boneless, skinless chicken breasts
75g/3oz/6 tbsp low-fat natural yogurt
1 garlic clove, crushed
grated zest and juice of ½ lemon
½ tsp each ground cumin and ground coriander
340g/12oz sweet potatoes, peeled
spray oil
salt and ground black pepper
rocket (arugula) and cherry tomatoes to serve
balsamic vinegar to drizzle

1 Preheat the oven to 200°C/400°F/Gas 6.
2 Put the chicken in a bowl with the yogurt, garlic, lemon zest and juice and spices. Season with salt and pepper and mix well to coat the chicken. Set aside in a cool place.
3 Cut the sweet potatoes lengthways into wedges and arrange on a baking sheet. Spray lightly with oil and grind some black pepper over them. Bake in the oven for 20 minutes or until tender inside and crisp and golden outside.
4 Meanwhile, preheat the grill (broiler) and put the chicken breasts in a foil-lined grill (broiling) pan. Spoon the spicy yogurt over them.
5 Cook under the hot grill for 15–20 minutes, turning halfway through, until the chicken is thoroughly cooked.
6 Serve with the sweet potato wedges with a salad of rocket and cherry tomatoes sprinkled with balsamic vinegar.

preparation 10 minutes   cooking time 20 minutes   calories 310 kcals

Serves 2

CHICKEN ENCHILADAS

spray oil

175g/6oz skinless chicken breast fillets, cubed

½ green (bell) pepper, seeded and chopped

1 x 200g/7oz can red kidney beans, drained

250g/9oz ready-made enchilada sauce

2 x 30g/1oz soft tortilla wraps

25g/1oz/¼ cup grated reduced-fat Cheddar cheese

ground black pepper

1 Little Gem (Bibb) lettuce

6 cherry tomatoes, halved

2 tbsp tomato salsa

4 tbsp virtually fat-free fromage frais

1 Preheat the oven to 180°C/350°F/Gas 4.
2 Lightly spray a frying pan with oil and place over a medium heat. Add the chicken and green pepper to the hot pan and cook for 6–8 minutes until the chicken is cooked right through. Stir in the kidney beans and two-thirds of the enchilada sauce and heat through gently.
3 Divide the chicken and bean mixture between the tortillas. Roll up and place them, side by side and seam-side down, in a shallow ovenproof dish. Cover with the remaining sauce. Sprinkle with grated cheese and black pepper.
4 Bake in the oven for 15 minutes or until bubbling and golden. Serve immediately with lettuce, tomatoes, salsa and a dollop of fromage frais.

preparation 10 minutes   cooking time 25 minutes   calories 440 kcals

Serves 2

THAI LEMON CHICKEN

300g/11oz boneless, skinless chicken thighs

1 tbsp Thai curry spice seasoning

spray oil

2 garlic cloves, crushed

1 lemon, sliced

1 lemongrass stalk, crushed

150ml/¼ pint/scant ⅔ cup hot chicken stock

1 tbsp Thai fish sauce

200g/7oz/1¼ cups boiled rice

ground black pepper

2 tbsp chopped fresh coriander (cilantro)

1 Sprinkle the chicken thighs with the Thai curry seasoning.
2 Lightly spray a frying pan with oil and place over a medium heat. Add the chicken and cook for 6–8 minutes, turning occasionally, until well browned all over.
3 Add the garlic, sliced lemon and lemongrass and cook for 1 minute, then pour in the hot stock and Thai fish sauce. Cook over a low heat for 20 minutes or until the chicken is cooked.
4 Serve the chicken in the lemony sauce with boiled rice, sprinkled with black pepper and coriander.

preparation 4 minutes   cooking time 30 minutes   calories 450 kcals

Serves 2

GRIDDLED CHICKEN FAJITAS

300g/11oz chicken breast fillets, cut into chunky strips
1 tbsp fajita seasoning
spray oil
1 red (bell) pepper, seeded and sliced
1 red onion, thinly sliced
1 bunch of spring onions (scallions), halved
2 large flour tortillas
4 tbsp tomato salsa
4 tbsp low-fat guacamole
4 tbsp low-fat natural yogurt

1 Put the chicken strips in a shallow dish and toss together with the fajita seasoning. Spray a griddle with oil and place over a medium heat. Add the chicken and cook, turning occasionally, for 5 minutes or until golden brown and tender.
2 Add the red pepper and onion and cook for 5 minutes or until just tender and starting to char. Stir in the spring onions and cook for 2 minutes.
3 Meanwhile, warm the tortillas in a microwave on full power for 45 seconds, or wrap in foil and warm in a preheated oven at 180°C/350°F/Gas 4 for 10 minutes.
4 Arrange the griddled chicken and vegetables on the tortillas. Roll up or fold over and serve immediately with the salsa, guacamole and yogurt.

preparation 10 minutes cooking time 15 minutes calories 350 kcals

Serves 2

CHICKEN LAKSA

spray oil
1 onion, chopped
2 garlic cloves, crushed
1 tbsp chopped fresh root ginger
1 red chilli, seeded and chopped
1 lemongrass stalk, chopped
600ml/1 pint/2½ cups hot chicken stock
juice of 1 lime
100ml/3½fl oz/⅓ cup reduced-fat coconut milk
225g/8oz cooked skinless chicken breasts, cubed
125g/4oz bean sprouts
200g/7oz cooked egg noodles
4 spring onions (scallions), diced

1 Lightly spray a deep pan with oil and place over a high heat. Add the onion, garlic, ginger, chilli and lemongrass and stir-fry briskly for 2–3 minutes until the onion is tender.
2 Add the hot stock, lime juice and coconut milk. Reduce the heat and cook gently for 5 minutes, then add the cooked chicken and simmer for 5 minutes.
3 Stir in the bean sprouts and cooked noodles. Heat through gently for 5 minutes.
4 Ladle the laksa into four bowls and serve immediately, sprinkled with spring onions.

preparation 15 minutes cooking time 25 minutes calories 350 kcals

Serves 4

CHICKEN NASI GORENG

75g/3oz/⅓ cup basmati rice
spray oil
1 medium egg, beaten
1 yellow (bell) pepper, seeded and thinly sliced
1 red chilli, seeded and diced
1 tsp grated fresh root ginger
6 spring onions (scallions), sliced
200g/7oz chicken breast fillets, sliced
200g/7oz spring greens, shredded
1 tbsp soy sauce
2 tbsp low-fat natural yogurt

1 Boil or steam the rice according to the instructions on the pack.
2 Meanwhile, lightly spray a wok or deep frying pan with oil and place over a medium heat. Add the beaten egg to the hot pan, swirling it around to make an omelette. When set underneath, flip it over and cook the other side. Slide out on to a plate, roll up tightly and slice into ribbons. Set aside.
3 Add the yellow pepper, chilli, ginger, spring onions and chicken to the pan and stir-fry for 2 minutes. Add the spring greens and stir-fry briskly for 5 minutes, stirring in the cooked rice and soy sauce just before the end.
4 Divide between two shallow serving bowls and top with the omelette strips. Serve immediately with the yogurt.

preparation 15 minutes   cooking time 10 minutes   calories 400 kcals

Serves 2

CHICKEN SATAY

200g/7oz boneless, skinless chicken breasts
juice of 1 lime
1 garlic clove, crushed
1 tsp each ground coriander, cumin and turmeric
¼ cucumber, cut into matchstick strips

For the satay sauce
100ml/3½fl oz/⅓ cup reduced-fat coconut milk
1 tsp curry paste
2 tbsp reduced-fat peanut butter
squeeze of lemon juice

1 Place the chicken breasts between two sheets of clingfilm (plastic wrap) and beat with a rolling pin until thin. Cut each breast into 3 or 4 long strips, about 2.5cm/1in wide. Place in a shallow dish.
2 Mix the lime juice, garlic and spices to a paste and spoon over the chicken. Stir well, then cover and chill in the refrigerator for at least 1 hour.
3 Meanwhile, heat the coconut milk and curry paste in a small pan over a low heat for 3–4 minutes, stirring. Stir in the peanut butter and lemon juice and heat gently.
4 Remove the chicken from the spicy marinade and thread on to thin bamboo skewers that have been soaked in water.
5 Cook under a preheated hot grill (broiler) for 10 minutes, turning occasionally, or until the chicken is slightly charred and golden brown outside and thoroughly cooked inside.
6 Serve with the satay sauce and cucumber strips.

preparation 10 minutes plus chilling   cooking time 10 minutes   calories 220 kcals

Serves 2

TURKEY SALTIMBOCCA

4 x 75g/3oz turkey breast fillets

4 thin slices lean Parma ham, all visible fat removed

spray oil

150g/5oz thin green beans, trimmed

250g/9oz baby new potatoes

ground black pepper

fresh basil sprigs to garnish

1 lemon, halved

1. Place the turkey breast fillets between two sheets of parchment paper and beat them out flat with a rolling pin.
2. Grind a little black pepper over each turkey breast and wrap a slice of Parma ham around it.
3. Spray a non-stick frying pan lightly with oil and set over a medium heat. Add the turkey and cook for 6–8 minutes each side until cooked right through and golden brown.
4. Meanwhile, cook the green beans in a pan of boiling water until just tender. Drain well. Boil the potatoes in a separate pan until tender, then drain.
5. Serve the turkey breasts, garnished with basil, with the green beans and potatoes. Sprinkle with a little lemon juice.

preparation 10 minutes   **cooking time** 16 minutes   **calories** 300 kcals

Serves 2

POACHED CHICKEN AND NECTARINE SALAD

2 x 125g/4oz boneless, skinless chicken breasts

1 carrot, cut into matchstick strips

4 spring onions (scallions), chopped

2 nectarines, stoned and sliced

4 cherry tomatoes, quartered

100g/3½oz rocket (arugula)

1 tsp runny honey

1 tsp honey mustard

1 tbsp cider vinegar

1 tbsp soy sauce

2 tbsp oil-free vinaigrette

salt and ground black pepper

1. Half-fill a pan with water and bring to the boil. Add the chicken, reduce the heat, cover the pan and poach gently for 10–15 minutes until cooked through. Remove with a slotted spoon and set aside to cool.
2. Add the carrot strips to the hot water in the pan and cook for 5 minutes or until they are tender but still retain some crispness. Drain the carrots and refresh in cold water.
3. Mix together the spring onions, nectarines, tomatoes and rocket in a bowl. Blend the honey, mustard, vinegar, soy sauce and vinaigrette until thoroughly mixed and drizzle over the salad. Toss lightly and divide between two serving plates.
4. Slice the chicken and arrange on top of the salad with the carrots. Season and sprinkle the remaining dressing over.

preparation 15 minutes   **cooking time** 15–20 minutes   **calories** 200 kcals

Serves 2

RED THAI CHICKEN CURRY

spray oil
1 onion, chopped
2 garlic cloves, crushed
1 lemongrass stalk, finely sliced
1 tbsp red Thai curry paste
150g/5oz baby corn
250g/9oz chicken breast fillets, cut into large chunks
200ml/7fl oz/¾ cup reduced-fat coconut milk
2 tsp Thai fish sauce
175g/6oz mngetouts, trimmed
50g/2oz/¼ cup basmati rice
fresh coriander (cilantro) and lime wedgesto serve

1 Spray a frying pan lightly with oil and set over a low heat. Add the onion to the hot pan and cook for 5 minutes until tender and golden. Add the garlic and lemongrass and cook for 2–3 minutes.
2 Stir in the curry paste and cook for 1 minute, then add the chicken. Cook, turning frequently, for 2–3 minutes until golden. Pour in the coconut milk and Thai fish sauce and stir in the baby corn. Simmer for 10 minutes, then add the mangetouts and cook for 10 minutes until the chicken is thoroughly cooked and the sauce has reduced.
3 Meanwhile, cook the rice according to the instructions on the pack.
4 Serve the curry, garnished with coriander sprigs, with the rice and lime wedges.

preparation 10 minutes cooking time 30 minutes calories 370 kcals

Serves 2

SKINNY CAESAR SALAD

spray oil
200g/7oz chicken breast fillets
1 head cos (romaine) lettuce
2 tbsp salad croûtons
2 tbsp freshly grated Parmesan

For the Caesar dressing
2 tbsp oil-free vinaigrette
grated zest and juice of 1 lemon
1 large garlic clove, crushed
a few drops of Worcestershire sauce
1 small egg yolk
salt and ground black pepper

1 Lightly spray a ridged griddle pan with oil and place over a medium heat. Add the chicken and cook, turning occasionally, for 8–10 minutes until golden brown outside and thoroughly cooked inside.
2 To make the Caesar dressing, mix together the vinaigrette, lemon zest and juice, garlic and Worcestershire sauce. Beat in the egg yolk and season to taste with salt and pepper.
3 Tear the cos lettuce leaves into pieces and toss with the croûtons in the dressing. Divide the salad between two serving plates.
4 Cut the chicken into thin slices or cubes and scatter on top. Sprinkle with the Parmesan and serve.

preparation 15 minutes cooking time 6–8 minutes calories 310 kcals

Serves 2

AMERICAN ROAST BEEF HASH

spray oil
1 red onion, finely chopped
1 garlic clove, crushed
200g/7oz boiled potatoes, diced
250g/9oz lean roast beef, all visible fat removed, diced
2 medium eggs
2 tbsp chopped fresh parsley
salt and ground black pepper

1 Spray a deep frying pan lightly with oil and place over a low heat. Cook the onion for 5 minutes or until tender and golden. Stir in the garlic and diced potatoes and cook for 10 minutes, stirring occasionally, until crisp and golden.
2 Add the beef and season to taste with salt and pepper. Continue cooking and stirring occasionally until really hot.
3 Meanwhile, poach the eggs in a pan of barely simmering water, until the whites are cooked and set but the yolks are still runny. Remove carefully with a slotted spoon.
4 Serve the hot hash sprinkled with parsley with a poached egg on top.

preparation 10 minutes   cooking time 20 minutes   calories 325 kcals

Serves 2

LOW-FAT CHILLI BEEF

250g/9oz lean sirloin steak, all visible fat removed
2 red (bell) peppers
spray oil
1 hot red chilli, shredded
2 garlic cloves, crushed
1 tsp grated fresh root ginger
a pinch of five-spice powder
175g/6oz broccoli florets
175g/6oz mangetouts, trimmed
2 tbsp dark soy sauce
1 tsp hoisin sauce
225g/8oz cooked Chinese egg noodles (cooked weight)
ground black pepper

1 Cut the steak into thin strips and season with a generous grinding of pepper. Cut the red peppers in half, remove the seeds and ribs and cut the flesh into thin slices.
2 Lightly spray a wok or deep frying pan with oil and set over a medium heat. Add the strips of steak and stir-fry briskly for 1 minute or until seared on the outside.
3 Add the chilli, garlic, ginger, five-spice powder and red peppers. Stir-fry for 2 minutes. Add the broccoli and mangetouts and stir-fry for 3 minutes.
4 Add the soy sauce and hoisin sauce and cook for 2 minutes, then fold in the cooked egg noodles.
5 Divide between two serving plates and serve immediately.

preparation 10 minutes   cooking time 5–10 minutes   calories 300 kcals

Serves 2

CHICKEN TRAYBAKE

2 chicken drumsticks and
2 skinless chicken thighs

2 red onions, quartered

1 yellow and 1 red (bell) pepper,
seeded and cut into chunks

1 small squash, seeded and
quartered

1 lemon, cut into wedges

6 unpeeled garlic cloves

fresh thyme and rosemary sprigs

spray olive oil

juice of 1 lemon

salt and ground black pepper

1 Preheat the oven to 200°C/400°F/Gas 6.
2 Put the chicken, onions, yellow and red peppers, squash and lemon wedges in a non-stick roasting pan. Tuck in the unpeeled garlic cloves and herbs and spray with olive oil. Squeeze the lemon juice over the top and season with salt and pepper.
3 Bake in the oven for 45 minutes. Halfway through, turn the chicken and vegetables over in the pan juices.
4 When the chicken is cooked and the vegetables are tender, transfer them to two serving plates. Discard the herbs. Squeeze the garlic pulp out of their skins over the vegetables and serve.

preparation 5 minutes   **cooking time** 45 minutes   **calories** 250 kcals

Serves 2

STEAK AND 'FRIES'

340g/12oz sweet potatoes

spray olive oil

leaves stripped from a few
fresh rosemary sprigs

leaves stripped from a few
fresh thyme sprigs

a pinch of sea salt crystals

2 x 175g/6oz lean sirloin steaks,
all visible fat removed

ground black pepper

grilled mushrooms and cherry
tomatoes to serve

1 Preheat the oven to 200°C/400°F/Gas 6.
2 Peel the sweet potatoes and cut them lengthways into 'chips'. Place them in a roasting pan, spreading them out, and spray lightly with oil. Add the rosemary and thyme leaves and grind some black pepper over the top. Sprinkle lightly with the sea salt.
3 Cook in the oven for 20–30 minutes, turning occasionally, until tender inside and golden brown and crisp outside.
4 Lightly spray a non-stick ridged griddle pan with oil and place over a high heat. When it's really hot, add the steaks and cook for 2–3 minutes each side (rare); 4–5 minutes (medium); or 5–6 minutes (well done).
5 Serve the steaks with the 'fries' and some grilled mushrooms and cherry tomatoes.

preparation 10 minutes   **cooking time** 20–30 minutes   **calories** 350 kcals

Serves 2

SKINNY CHILLI

spray oil

1 onion, chopped

1 red (bell) pepper, seeded and chopped

2 garlic cloves, crushed

2 tsp chilli powder

250g/9oz/generous 1 cup minced (ground) beef (max. 5% fat)

1 x 200g/7oz can tomatoes

100ml/3½fl oz/⅓ cup beef stock

1 x 200g/7oz can red kidney beans, drained and rinsed

2 tbsp chopped fresh parsley

salt and ground black pepper

2 tbsp each tomato salsa, low-fat natural yogurt and guacamole

tortilla chips (optional) to serve

1 Lightly spray a large pan with oil and place over a low heat. Add the onion and red pepper and cook for 5 minutes, stirring occasionally, until tender.

2 Add the garlic and chilli powder and cook, stirring, for 1 minute. Stir in the minced beef and cook for 3–4 minutes, stirring, until browned all over.

3 Stir in the tomatoes and stock and bring to the boil. Reduce the heat and simmer gently for 15 minutes or until the sauce has reduced and thickened.

4 Season to taste with salt and pepper and stir in the kidney beans. Heat through gently and stir in the parsley.

5 Divide the chilli between two warm shallow bowls and serve immediately with the salsa, yogurt and guacamole. If you choose to serve it with tortilla chips, you will add approximately 100 kcals per 25g/1oz serving.

preparation 15 minutes   **cooking time** 30 minutes   **calories** 410 kcals

Serves 2

STEAK STROGANOV

spray oil

1 onion, thinly sliced

200g/7oz button mushrooms, thinly sliced

300g/11oz lean rump or sirloin steak, all visible fat removed

½ tsp crushed black peppercorns

½ tsp paprika

6 tbsp fat-free fromage frais

1 tsp wholegrain mustard

2 tbsp chopped fresh parsley

1 Lightly spray a large frying pan with oil and place over a low heat. Add the onion and cook for 5 minutes or until softened. Add the mushrooms and cook, stirring occasionally, for 3–4 minutes until tender and golden brown. Remove the onions and mushrooms and keep warm.

2 Cut the steak into thin strips. Place in a bowl and toss with the crushed peppercorns and paprika.

3 Add the steak to the pan and cook for 3–4 minutes until browned all over but pink and juicy inside. Reduce the heat and return the onion and mushrooms to the pan. Stir in the fromage frais and mustard. Heat through very gently.

4 Sprinkle with chopped parsley and serve with steamed green vegetables.

preparation 10 minutes   **cooking time** 15 minutes   **calories** 300 kcals

Serves 2

GOULASH SOUP

spray oil
1 small onion, chopped
1 carrot, chopped
1 yellow (bell) pepper, seeded and chopped
1 garlic clove, crushed
200g/7oz lean stewing steak, all visible fat removed, diced
1 tbsp paprika
½ tsp caraway seeds
450ml/¾ pint/1¾ cups hot beef stock
2 tomatoes, chopped
200g/7oz potatoes, cubed
salt and ground black pepper

1 Spray a large pan lightly with oil and place over a low heat. Add the onion, carrot, yellow pepper and garlic and cook for 5 minutes, stirring occasionally, until tender.
2 Stir in the diced steak and cook for 2–3 minutes, stirring, until browned all over. Stir in the paprika and caraway seeds and cook for 1 minute, then pour in the hot stock and bring to the boil. Reduce the heat and simmer the soup gently for 20 minutes.
3 Add the tomatoes and potatoes, season with salt and pepper and simmer for 25 minutes or until the beef is falling apart and the potato is cooked.
4 Ladle the hot soup into warmed bowls and serve.

preparation 10 minutes   cooking time 1 hour   calories 350 kcals

Serves 2

HUNGARIAN PORK GOULASH

250g/9oz lean pork leg or shoulder, all visible fat removed
1 tsp flour
spray oil
1 onion, thinly sliced
½ red and ½ green (bell) pepper, seeded and sliced
1 garlic clove, crushed
1 tbsp paprika
150ml/¼ pint/scant ⅔ cup hot chicken or vegetable stock
salt and ground black pepper
2 tbsp chopped fresh parsley
2 tbsp low-fat natural yogurt
200g/7oz/1¼ cups boiled rice

1 Cut the pork into bite-size cubes and dust lightly with flour.
2 Lightly spray a pan with oil and set over a medium heat. Add the pork and cook, stirring occasionally, until browned all over. Remove and set aside.
3 Add the onion, red and green peppers and garlic to the pan and cook gently for 5 minutes or until softened. Stir in the paprika and return the pork to the pan with the hot stock and salt and pepper. Bring to the boil.
4 Reduce the heat, cover the pan and simmer gently for 1¼–1½ hours until the pork is cooked. Check from time to time, adding more stock if needed.
5 Sprinkle with parsley and divide between two serving plates. Serve with a swirl of yogurt and the boiled rice.

preparation 10 minutes   cooking time 1½–1¾ hours   calories 380 kcals

Serves 2

SPANISH PORK AND BEANS

300g/11oz pork fillet (tenderloin)
½ tsp crushed chilli flakes
2 tbsp Spanish sherry vinegar
200g/7oz mushrooms, sliced
1 x 200g/7oz can haricot or cannellini beans, drained
3 garlic cloves, crushed
juice of 1 large orange
salt and ground black pepper
paprika to dust
2 tbsp chopped fresh parsley

1 Preheat the oven to 210°C/425°F/Gas 7.
2 Put the pork in an ovenproof dish or roasting pan and sprinkle with chilli flakes. Season with salt and pepper and pour the vinegar over the top.
3 Roast in the oven for 10 minutes. Turn the pork fillet over and add the mushrooms, beans, garlic and orange juice. Return to the oven and cook for 15 minutes or until the pork is thoroughly cooked.
4 Divide the beans and mushrooms and pan juices between two serving plates. Carve the pork thinly and arrange on top. Dust with paprika and serve sprinkled with parsley.

preparation 10 minutes   cooking time 25 minutes   calories 310 kcals

Serves 2

GAMMON AND POTATO STACKS

225g/8oz potatoes, cut into chunks
150g/5oz baby spinach leaves
1 tbsp half-fat crème fraîche
4 spring onions (scallions), finely chopped
spray oil
2 x 125g/4oz lean gammon steaks, all visible fat removed
2 medium eggs
salt and ground black pepper

1 Boil the potatoes in a pan of lightly salted water until cooked but not mushy. Drain well.
2 Put the spinach in a colander and pour boiling water over it. Press down with a saucer to squeeze out any liquid, then chop it finely.
3 Mash the potato with the crème fraîche and stir in the spinach and spring onions. Season with salt and pepper. Using your hands, shape into 2 round patties.
4 Lightly spray a non-stick frying pan with oil and cook the potato cakes over a low heat for 5 minutes each side, or until crisp and golden. Remove and keep warm.
5 Preheat the grill (broiler) to hot and grill (broil) the gammon steaks for 4–5 minutes each side until cooked.
6 Meanwhile, break the eggs into a pan of simmering water and cook until the whites are set but the yolks are still runny.
7 Serve each potato cake topped with gammon and an egg.

preparation 10 minutes   cooking time 30 minutes   calories 340 kcals

Serves 2

LOW-CAL BOLOGNESE

spray oil
1 onion, chopped
2 garlic cloves, crushed
1 large carrot, diced
1 celery stick, diced
225g/8oz/1 cup minced (ground) beef (max. 5% fat)
4 tbsp skimmed milk
300ml/½ pint/1¼ cups hot beef stock
1 x 200g/7oz can tomatoes
1 tbsp tomato paste
1 tsp chopped fresh thyme
100g/3½oz spaghetti
2 tsp freshly grated Parmesan
salt and ground black pepper

1 Spray a large pan lightly with oil and place over a low heat. Add the onion, garlic, carrot and celery and cook, stirring occasionally, for 5 minutes or until softened. Stir in the beef and cook for 3–4 minutes until browned all over.
2 Add the milk, turn up the heat and cook for a few minutes until slightly reduced. Add the hot stock, tomatoes, tomato paste and thyme. Bring to the boil, then reduce the heat and simmer gently for 1 hour or until reduced and richly coloured.
3 Meanwhile, cook the spaghetti according to the instructions on the pack. Drain well.
4 Season the Bolognese sauce with salt and pepper to taste. Toss with the spaghetti and serve sprinkled with Parmesan.

preparation 10 minutes cooking time 1 hour 15 minutes calories 450 kcals

Serves 2

ITALIAN STUFFED PORK FILLET

50g/2oz/⅓ cup reduced-fat soft cheese
1 garlic clove, crushed
4 ready-to-eat dried apricots, chopped
1 tbsp chopped fresh parsley
1 x 225g/8oz lean pork fillet (tenderloin)
2 thin slices lean Parma ham
salt and ground black pepper

1 Preheat the oven to 190°C/375°F/Gas 5.
2 In a bowl, mix together the soft cheese, garlic, apricots, parsley and seasoning to taste.
3 Make an incision lengthways down the centre of the pork fillet without cutting all the way through. Open up the fillet and flatten it out. Spoon the soft cheese filling along the middle of the pork and then fold over to enclose it. Remove any visible fat from the Parma ham and wrap the slices around the fillet. Place on a non-stick baking sheet.
4 Cook in the oven for 30 minutes or until the pork is thoroughly cooked and no longer pink.
5 Serve the pork cut into slices with green vegetables.

preparation 15 minutes cooking time 30 minutes calories 225 kcals

Serves 2

TAGLIATELLE CARBONARA

100g/3½oz tagliatelle

50g/2oz lean back bacon rashers (slices), all visible fat removed

2 medium eggs, beaten

2 tbsp half-fat crème fraîche

2 tbsp freshly grated Parmesan

2 tbsp chopped fresh parsley

salt and ground black pepper

salad to serve

1 Cook the pasta in a large pan of lightly salted boiling water according to the instructions on the pack. Drain well and return to the hot pan.
2 While the pasta is cooking, grill (broil) the bacon until crisp. Break roughly into pieces.
3 Add the bacon and beaten eggs to the hot pasta and stir gently over a low heat until the eggs start to scramble and set. Stir in the crème fraîche and half the grated cheese. Grind in some black pepper.
4 Serve immediately, sprinkled with the remaining Parmesan, with a crisp salad.

preparation 5 minutes cooking time 15 minutes calories 390 kcals

Serves 2

PRAWN, CHILLI AND ROCKET LINGUINE

100g/3½oz linguine

spray oil

2 garlic cloves

¼ tsp hot chilli flakes

juice of 1 lemon

75ml/3fl oz/5 tbsp white wine

200g/7oz peeled raw tiger prawns (shrimp)

25g/1oz rocket (arugula)

salt and ground black pepper

1 Cook the pasta in a large pan of lightly salted boiling water according to the instructions on the pack.
2 While the pasta is cooking, lightly spray a deep pan with oil and place over a low heat. Add the garlic and cook for 1 minute without browning.
3 Stir in the chilli flakes and then add the lemon juice and wine. Turn up the heat and let it bubble away for a few minutes to reduce slightly. Add the prawns and cook for 2–3 minutes, turning them occasionally, until pink all over.
4 Drain the pasta and stir into the prawn mixture with the rocket. Season to taste and serve immediately.

preparation 5 minutes cooking time 10–12 minutes calories 190 kcals

Serves 2

SCALLOP AND BACON SALAD

3 thin lean back bacon rashers (slices), all visible fat removed

6 large scallops

100g/3½oz rocket (arugula)

3 spring onions (scallions), diced

4 cherry tomatoes, halved

3 tbsp chopped fresh parsley

2 tbsp oil-free vinaigrette dressing

grated zest and juice of 1 lemon

salt and ground black pepper

fresh chives to garnish

1 With the blade of a knife, stretch out each bacon rasher and then cut in half. Wrap each piece of bacon around a scallop.

2 Cook under a preheated grill (broiler) for 5–6 minutes, turning occasionally, until the scallops are cooked but still tender and the bacon is crisp.

3 Meanwhile, mix together the rocket, onions, tomatoes and parsley. Blend the dressing with the lemon zest and juice and use to toss the salad.

4 Arrange a pile of salad on each serving plate and place the bacon-wrapped scallops on top. Season with salt and pepper and garnish with chives.

preparation 15 minutes   cooking time 5–6 minutes   calories 175 kcals

Serves 2

MUSSELS WITH PESTO

1kg/2¼lb mussels , scrubbed and beards removed

spray oil

1 onion, finely chopped

2 garlic cloves, crushed

1 x 400g/14oz can chopped tomatoes

100ml/3½fl oz/⅓ cup boiling water

50ml/2fl oz/¼ cup red wine

2 tbsp low-fat green pesto sauce

salt and ground black pepper

4 tbsp chopped fresh parsley

2 x 25g/1oz slices baguette

1 Discard any mussels that are open or cracked.

2 Lightly spray a large pan with oil and cook the onion and garlic over a low heat until softened. Add the tomatoes, boiling water and wine and bring to the boil. Cook vigorously for a few minutes and then tip in the mussels.

3 Cover the pan, reduce the heat and cook, shaking gently occasionally, for 5 minutes or until the mussels open. Remove them with a slotted spoon and keep warm. Throw away any that fail to open.

4 Add the pesto to the pan and bring back to the boil. Season to taste with salt and pepper.

5 Divide the mussels between two deep serving bowls and pour the sauce over them. Sprinkle with parsley and eat with the baguette slices to mop up the sauce.

preparation 15 minutes   cooking time 15 minutes   calories 340 kcals

Serves 2

THAI PRAWN CURRY

spray oil
1 tsp grated fresh root ginger
1 garlic clove, crushed
1 red chilli, finely chopped
2 kaffir lime leaves
100g/3½oz cherry tomatoes
100g/3½oz thin green beans
1 tbsp green Thai curry paste
100ml/3½fl oz/⅓ cup half-fat coconut milk
250g/9oz peeled raw tiger prawns (shrimp)
200g/7oz baby spinach leaves
75g/3oz/⅓ cup basmati rice
a few fresh coriander (cilantro) sprigs, chopped

1 Spray a non-stick frying pan lightly with oil and place over a medium heat. When hot, add the ginger, garlic and chilli and cook for 2 minutes without colouring.
2 Add the lime leaves, cherry tomatoes and beans and cook for 1 minute. Add the curry paste and coconut milk, then simmer gently for 8–10 minutes.
3 Stir in the prawns and spinach and cook for 3 minutes, stirring occasionally, until the prawns are pink all over. The spinach will wilt and turn bright green.
4 Meanwhile, cook the rice according to the instructions on the pack.
5 Serve the curry on a bed of rice, sprinkled with coriander.

preparation 10 minutes   cooking time 17 minutes   calories 350 kcals

Serves 4

THAI PRAWN SKEWERS

1 hot red chilli, finely chopped
1 tsp grated fresh root ginger
2 garlic cloves, crushed
1 tbsp Thai fish sauce
1 tbsp light soy sauce
juice of 1 lime
300g/11oz peeled raw tiger prawns (shrimp)
¼ small cucumber
1 yellow (bell) pepper
3 spring onions (scallions)
50g/2oz bean sprouts
sweet chilli sauce to serve

1 Preheat the grill (broiler) to hot. In a small bowl, mix together the chilli, ginger, garlic, fish sauce, soy sauce and lime juice.
2 Thread the prawns on to wooden skewers that have been soaked in water. Place in a foil-lined grill (broiling) pan and brush with some of the chilli and ginger mixture. Cook the prawns under the hot grill for 4–6 minutes, turning halfway through, until they turn pink and succulent.
3 Cut the cucumber into matchsticks. Remove the seeds, stalk and ribs from the yellow pepper and cut into thin slices. Chop the spring onions. Mix in a bowl with the bean sprouts and toss everything together in the remaining chilli and ginger mixture. Serve the hot prawn skewers with the salad and some sweet chilli sauce.

preparation 15 minutes   cooking time 4–6 minutes   calories 200 kcals

Serves 2

THAI CRABCAKES

300g/11oz fresh crabmeat
1 hot red chilli, seeded
3 spring onions (scallions), diced
2 garlic cloves, crushed
fresh coriander (cilantro) sprigs
1 tsp Thai fish sauce
2 tbsp low-calorie mayonnaise
juice of ½ small lime
25g/1oz/½ cup fresh white breadcrumbs
spray oil
lime wedges and herby lite mayonnaise to serve

1 Put the crabmeat, chilli, spring onions, garlic, coriander, Thai fish sauce, mayonnaise and lime juice in a blender or food processor. Blitz in short bursts until well combined and tip into a bowl.
2 Stir in the breadcrumbs, then cover the bowl and chill in the refrigerator for 20 minutes to firm the mixture.
3 Divide the mixture into 8 equal-sized portions and shape with your hands into small round patties.
4 Spray a non-stick frying pan lightly with oil and place over a medium heat. When hot, add the crabcakes and cook for 3–4 minutes each side until golden brown.
5 Serve them hot with lime wedges and 1 heaped tbsp each lite mayonnaise mixed with chopped herbs of your choice.

preparation 15 minutes plus chilling **cooking time** 6–8 minutes **calories** 280 kcals

Serves 2

MAJORCAN PAELLA

1 small red and 1 small yellow (bell) pepper
spray olive oil
1 onion, chopped
2 garlic cloves, crushed
125g/4oz/½ cup arborio rice
400ml/14fl oz/1¾ cups hot vegetable stock
a pinch of saffron
150g/5oz tomatoes, chopped
a pinch of chilli powder
250g/9oz mixed seafood, e.g. prawns (shrimp), mussels, squid
juice of 1 lemon
2 tbsp chopped fresh parsley
salt and ground black pepper

1 Cut the peppers in half and remove the stalks, ribs and seeds. Cut the flesh into thin strips.
2 Lightly spray a large deep frying pan or paella pan with oil and set over a low heat. Add the onion and garlic and cook for 5 minutes, stirring occasionally, until it starts to soften. Add the peppers and cook for 5 minutes or until tender.
3 Stir in the rice and cook for 1 minute before adding a little hot stock and the saffron. Bring to the boil, then reduce the heat to a bare simmer and add the tomatoes and chilli.
4 Cook gently, adding more stock as and when necessary, and stirring frequently, for 20 minutes. When all the liquid has been absorbed and the rice is tender, add the seafood. Season to taste with salt and pepper and cook for 10 minutes. If the rice starts to stick to the pan, add more stock.
5 Sprinkle the lemon juice and parsley over the paella, and serve immediately.

preparation 15 minutes **cooking time** 45 minutes **calories** 355 kcals

Serves 2

SALMON WITH LEMON OAT CRUST

25g/1oz/⅓ cup porridge oats

1 tbsp chopped fresh thyme, dill or parsley

1 tsp mixed seeds, e.g. sunflower, linseed

grated zest and juice of 1 lemon

1 small egg, beaten

2 x 100g/3½oz salmon fillets, skinned and boned

spray oil

225g/8oz baby carrots, trimmed

125g/4oz thin green beans

225g/8oz baby new potatoes

salt and ground black pepper

1 Preheat the oven to 200°C/400°F/Gas 6.
2 Mix together the porridge oats, herbs, seeds, lemon zest and seasoning. Stir in the beaten egg.
3 Arrange the salmon on a lightly oiled baking sheet and spoon the oat mixture over them, patting it down gently with your hands to make it stick to the fish. Spray lightly with oil.
4 Bake in the oven for 20 minutes or until the oat topping is crisp and golden and the salmon is thoroughly cooked.
5 While the salmon is cooking, boil or steam the carrots and beans and boil the new potatoes until tender.
6 Serve the salmon, sprinkled with lemon juice, with the carrots, beans and potatoes.

preparation 10 minutes cooking time 20 minutes calories 350 kcals

Serves 2

WARM TUNA SALAD

spray oil

75g/3oz baby asparagus

1 red (bell) pepper, seeded and sliced

8 cherry tomatoes, halved

a few fresh basil sprigs, torn

2 x 100g/3½oz tuna steaks

½ small ripe avocado

juice of ½ lemon

2 tbsp virtually fat-free fromage frais

1 tsp reduced-fat mayonnaise

salt and ground black pepper

200g/7oz boiled new potatoes

1 Spray a griddle pan lightly with oil and place over a medium heat. Add the baby asparagus and red pepper and cook for 2–3 minutes, turning the vegetables and pressing them on to the ridges with a spatula. Add the tomatoes and cook for 2 minutes to warm them through.
2 Put the cooked vegetables in a bowl with the basil. Toss gently, season to taste and set aside.
3 Add the tuna steaks to the hot griddle pan and cook for 3–4 minutes each side until cooked to your liking and attractively striped.
4 Meanwhile, peel and stone the avocado and mash the flesh. Beat in the lemon juice, fromage frais and mayonnaise.
5 Arrange the salad on 2 serving plates and top with the warm tuna and the avocado sauce. Serve with new potatoes.

preparation 10 minutes cooking time 12 minutes calories 340 kcals

Serves 2

SALMON AND BROCCOLI CRISP

200g/7oz broccoli florets

1 medium egg

150ml/¼ pint/scant ⅔ cup low-fat natural yogurt

1 tsp Dijon mustard

grated zest of 1 lemon

200g/7oz cooked salmon, skinned and boned

25g/1oz/½ cup fresh white breadcrumbs

2 tbsp grated reduced-fat Cheddar cheese

ground black pepper

1 Preheat the oven to 200°C/400°F/Gas 6.
2 Put the broccoli in a steamer or a colander set over a pan of simmering water. Cook for 5 minutes or until just tender but still a little crisp.
3 Beat the egg and whisk in the yogurt, mustard, some black pepper and lemon zest.
4 Cut the salmon into large flakes or chunks and place in an ovenproof dish with the broccoli. Pour the egg and yogurt mixture over the top and sprinkle with the breadcrumbs and grated Cheddar.
5 Cook in the oven for 20 minutes or until bubbling, crisp and golden. Serve piping hot with steamed green vegetables.

preparation 10 minutes   **cooking time** 25 minutes   **calories** 340 kcals

Serves 2

MONKFISH AND PARMA HAM BROCHETTES

250g/9oz monkfish (anglerfish) fillet, skinned and boned

6 wafer-thin slices Parma ham, all visible fat removed

4 cherry tomatoes

1 small red onion, cut into wedges

50g/2oz tagliatelle

75g/3oz/⅓ cup virtually fat-free fromage frais

1 tsp reduced-fat mayonnaise

1 tsp green pesto sauce

salt and ground black pepper

1 Cut the monkfish into six large chunks and wrap a slice of Parma ham around each one. Thread on to two skewers, alternating the fish with the cherry tomatoes and onion wedges. Sprinkle with black pepper.
2 Cook the pasta in a pan of lightly salted boiling water according to the instructions on the pack. Drain well.
3 Meanwhile, preheat the grill (broiler). Cook the brochettes under the hot grill for 10 minutes, turning occasionally, until the fish is cooked through.
4 Mix the fromage frais, mayonnaise and pesto in a small bowl and serve with the pasta and brochettes.

preparation 10 minutes   **cooking time** 10–12 minutes   **calories** 270 kcals

Serves 2

PORTUGUESE COD

2 x 175g/6oz cod fillets, skinned and boned
200g/7oz potatoes, cubed
2 tomatoes, halved
1 small onion, thinly sliced
1 yellow (bell) pepper, seeded and cut into chunks
1 tbsp capers
6 black olives, pitted
juice of ½ lemon
150ml/¼ pint/scant ⅔ cup fish stock
4 tbsp dry white wine
2 tbsp chopped fresh parsley
salt and ground black pepper

1 Preheat the oven to 200°C/400°F/Gas 6.
2 Place the cod, potatoes, tomatoes, onion and yellow pepper in a flameproof dish. Add the capers and olives and pour the lemon juice, fish stock and white wine over the top. Season with salt and pepper.
3 Cook in the oven for 20–25 minutes until the cod is cooked and the vegetables are tender. Remove the cod and potatoes to two serving plates and keep warm.
4 On the hob, boil up the pan juices for a few minutes until reduced. Stir in the parsley. Pour over the cod and potatoes and serve immediately with green beans.

preparation 10 minutes cooking time 25–30 minutes calories 300 kcals

Serves 2

FISH PIE

300g/11oz floury potatoes, cubed
250ml/8fl oz/1 cup skimmed milk
200g/7oz mixed fish, e.g. smoked haddock, cod, salmon fillets, prawns (shrimp)
spray oil
½ onion, chopped
1 leek, thinly sliced
1 tbsp plain (all-purpose) flour
2 tbsp chopped fresh parsley
ground black pepper

1 Preheat the oven to 200°C/400°F/Gas 6.
2 Cook the potatoes in a pan of boiling water until tender. Drain and mash with 4 tbsp skimmed milk, beating until smooth. Season with black pepper
3 Put the fish with the remaining milk in a pan and bring to the boil. Reduce the heat and simmer gently for 5 minutes. Strain the fish, reserving the milk.
4 Spray a clean pan lightly with oil and cook the onion and leek over a low heat for 10 minutes or until tender. Stir in the flour and cook for 1 minute, then add the reserved milk, a little at time, stirring until the sauce thickens. Add the cooked fish and parsley. Season with black pepper.
5 Spoon into an ovenproof dish and cover with the mashed potato. Rough up the surface with a fork and cook in the oven for 15 minutes or until crisp and golden brown.

preparation 15 minutes cooking time 35 minutes calories 370 kcals

Serves 2

PAN-SEARED COD

spray oil
1 red onion, chopped
2 garlic cloves, crushed
1 tbsp balsamic vinegar
250g/9oz vine-ripened cherry tomatoes, halved
1 x 200g/7oz can butter (lima) beans, drained
2 x 150g/5oz cod fillets, skinned
2 tsp lemon juice
2 tbsp chopped fresh parsley
salt and ground black pepper

1 Spray a frying pan lightly with oil and place over a low heat. Add the red onion and garlic and cook for 5 minutes, stirring occasionally, until tender.
2 Add the balsamic vinegar and cherry tomatoes and cook for 5 minutes. Add the beans and cook gently for 5 minutes. Season to taste with salt and pepper.
3 Meanwhile, spray a non-stick frying pan lightly with oil and place over a medium heat. Cook the cod for 8–10 minutes, turning halfway, until thoroughly cooked.
4 Arrange the tomato and bean mixture on two plates and place the cooked cod on top. Add a grinding of black pepper and a squeeze of lemon juice and sprinkle with parsley.

preparation 5 minutes   cooking time 15 minutes   calories 250 kcals

CRISPY SPRING ROLLS

spray oil
1 red (bell) pepper, seeded and thinly sliced
100g/3½oz carrots, cut into matchsticks
100g/3½oz spring greens, shredded
100g/3½oz bean sprouts
150g/5oz cooked peeled prawns (shrimp)
a few fresh coriander (cilantro) sprigs, chopped
2 tbsp dark soy sauce
6 x 15g/½oz sheets filo pastry
2 tbsp sweet chilli sauce to dip

1 Preheat the oven to 200°C/400°F/Gas 6.
2 Lightly spray a non-stick frying pan with oil and place over a medium heat. When hot, add the red pepper and carrots and stir-fry for 2 minutes. Add the spring greens, bean sprouts and prawns. Stir-fry for 2 minutes, then stir in the coriander and soy sauce.
3 Place the sheets of filo pastry on a board and spray each one lightly with oil. Divide the stir-fried mixture among them and fold over the sides to enclose the filling. Roll up to make secure parcels.
4 Place the spring rolls, seam-side down, on a lightly oiled baking sheet and cook in the oven for 12–15 minutes until crisp and golden brown.
5 Serve the spring rolls with the chilli sauce.

preparation 15 minutes   cooking time 20 minutes   calories 260 kcals

Serves 2

COD GOUJONS

300g/11oz cod fillets, skinned
flour to dust
2 egg whites
50g/2oz/1 cup fresh white breadcrumbs
spray oil

For the tartare sauce
150g/5oz/scant ⅔ cup virtually fat-free fromage frais
3 tbsp extra light mayonnaise
2 tbsp chopped capers
2 gherkins (cornichons), diced
2 spring onions (scallions), diced
a few fresh dill sprigs, chopped
a squeeze of lemon juice

1 To make the tartare sauce, mix all the ingredients together and check the flavour. Add a couple of drops of wine vinegar or some more lemon juice if needed. Cover and chill in the refrigerator until you're ready to serve.
2 Cut the cod into thick strips and dust them lightly with flour.
3 In a clean, dry bowl, whisk the egg whites until stiff. Dip the cod strips into the beaten egg white.
4 Spread the breadcrumbs out in a shallow dish and use to coat the cod. Place the goujons on a foil-lined grill (broiling) pan and spray lightly with oil.
5 Preheat the grill (broiler). When it's hot, cook the goujons for 4–5 minutes each side until golden brown and crisp outside and cooked through inside.
6 Serve the hot goujons with the tartare sauce.

preparation 15 minutes   cooking time 8–10 minutes   calories 400 kcals

Serves 2

GRIDDLED FISH WITH LENTILS

150g/5oz/scant 1 cup Puy lentils
400ml/14fl oz/1¾ cups hot vegetable stock
4 spring onions (scallions), diced
125g/4oz cherry tomatoes, halved
150g/5oz baby spinach leaves
1 tsp red wine vinegar
spray oil
2 x 150g/5oz white fish fillets
salt and ground black pepper
2 tbsp chopped fresh parsley

1 Put the lentils and hot stock in a pan and bring to the boil. Reduce the heat and simmer for 15–20 minutes until the lentils are tender. Drain well.
2 Return the lentils to the pan. Stir in the spring onions, tomatoes and spinach, then cover and place over a low heat for 2 minutes or until the spinach wilts. Season to taste and stir in the vinegar.
3 Meanwhile, lightly spray a griddle with oil and place over a medium heat. Add the fish fillets and cook for 4–5 minutes each side until the flesh is flaking and cooked.
4 Divide the lentils between two warm plates and place the fish on top.

preparation 5 minutes   cooking time 25 minutes   calories 380 kcals

Serves 2

CHICKPEA SOUP WITH HUMMUS

spray oil

1 large onion, chopped

2 garlic cloves, crushed

1 tsp coriander seeds, crushed

2 x 400g/14oz cans chickpeas (garbanzos), drained and rinsed

900ml/1½ pints/3⅔ cups boiling vegetable stock

1 tsp ground turmeric

½ tsp ground cumin

4 tsp 0% fat Greek yogurt

4 tsp low-fat hummus

a pinch of chilli powder

salt and ground black pepper

1 Lightly spray a large pan with oil and gently cook the onion and garlic until softened. Add the coriander seeds and cook for 1 minute.

2 Add most of the drained chickpeas, reserving a few for the garnish. Pour in the boiling stock and bring to the boil. Reduce the heat to a simmer and stir in the turmeric and cumin. Cook gently, uncovered, for 15–20 minutes.

3 Purée the soup in batches in a food processor or blender until thick and smooth. Pour into a clean pan and heat through gently, seasoning to taste.

4 Serve the soup in bowls. Swirl in the yogurt and hummus and sprinkle with chilli powder and the reserved chickpeas.

preparation 15 minutes   cooking time 30 minutes   calories 145 kcals

Serves 4

SPICY WINTER DHAL SOUP

spray oil

2 onions, finely chopped

3 carrots, diced

2 garlic cloves, crushed

2 tsp grated fresh root ginger

1 tsp black mustard seeds

½ tsp cumin seeds

1 green chilli, finely chopped

1 tsp ground turmeric

225g/8oz/1⅓ cups split red lentils

1.1l/2 pints/5 cups hot vegetable stock

1 x 400g/14oz can tomatoes

salt and ground black pepper

4 tsp low-fat natural yogurt

1 Lightly spray a large pan with oil and place over a low heat. When it is hot, add the onions, carrots, garlic and ginger and cook for 10 minutes, stirring occasionally, or until tender.

2 Stir in the mustard seeds and cumin seeds and cook for 1 minute. Stir in the chilli, turmeric and lentils and cook for 1 minute.

3 Add the hot stock and tomatoes, stir well and bring to the boil. Reduce the heat and simmer gently for 20 minutes until the lentils break down and thicken the soup. Season to taste with salt and pepper.

4 Ladle the soup into four serving bowls and swirl a spoonful of yogurt into each bowl.

preparation 10 minutes   cooking time 35 minutes   calories 270 kcals

Serves 4

SOUPE AU PISTOU

spray oil
1 onion, finely chopped
4 garlic cloves, crushed
2 celery sticks, diced
3 carrots, diced
2 medium potatoes, diced
340g/12oz tomatoes, peeled and diced
1.1l/2 pints/5 cups hot vegetable stock
3 courgettes (zucchini), diced
250g/9oz green beans, halved
2 tbsp green pesto sauce
salt and ground black pepper

1 Lightly spray a large pan with oil and cook the onion and garlic over a low heat, stirring occasionally. When they start to soften, add the celery, carrots and potatoes and cook for 10 minutes or until tender
2 Stir in the tomatoes and cook for 2–3 minutes before adding the hot stock. Bring to the boil, then reduce the heat and simmer gently for 15 minutes.
3 Add the courgettes and green beans and simmer gently for 15 minutes. Season to taste with salt and plenty of pepper.
4 Just before serving, stir the green pesto sauce into the soup.

Serves 6

preparation 15 minutes cooking time 50 minutes calories 120 kcals

BUTTERNUT SQUASH CHOWDER

1 large butternut squash
125g/4oz lean smoked bacon lardons
1 onion, finely chopped
2 garlic cloves, crushed
2 leeks, sliced
1 tbsp plain (all-purpose) flour
300ml/½ pint/1¼ cups hot vegetable stock
300ml/½ pint/1¼ cups semi-skimmed milk
3 ripe tomatoes, quartered
4 tbsp chopped fresh parsley
salt and ground black pepper

1 Peel the butternut squash and remove the seeds. Cut the flesh into bite-size cubes.
2 Dry-fry the bacon in a pan, stirring occasionally, until golden. Add the onion, garlic, leeks and squash and cook over a low heat for 5 minutes or until softened.
3 Stir in the flour and cook for 1 minute. Gradually stir in the hot stock and milk and then bring to the boil. Reduce the heat, add the tomatoes and simmer for 10–15 minutes.
4 Season to taste with salt and pepper and stir in the parsley. Serve the hot soup ladled into bowls.

Serves 6

preparation 10 minutes cooking time 25–30 minutes calories 80 kcals

ONION SOUP

spray oil
2 large onions, thinly sliced
2 bay leaves
2 tsp plain (all-purpose) flour
500ml/17fl oz/2¼ cups hot vegetable stock
75ml/2½fl oz/5 tbsp dry white wine
salt and ground black pepper

For the cheese croûtes
2 x 25g/1oz slices baguette
1 tsp Dijon mustard
2 tbsp grated reduced-fat Cheddar cheese

1 Lightly spray a large heavy-based pan with oil and place over a medium heat. Add the onions and bay leaves to the hot pan and cook very slowly for 15–20 minutes until the onions are really tender and starting to caramelize.
2 Stir in the flour and cook for 1 minute, then add the hot stock and wine. Increase the heat and bring to the boil. Season to taste with salt and pepper. Reduce the heat to a bare simmer and cook gently for 30 minutes.
3 Just before serving, preheat the grill (broiler). Toast the bread on one side only. Spread the untoasted sides with mustard and then sprinkle with grated Cheddar.
4 Divide the hot soup between two heatproof shallow bowls and float the croûtes, cheese-side up, on top. Pop the bowls under the grill for 2–3 minutes until the cheese melts. Serve immediately.

preparation 10 minutes cooking time 55 minutes calories 300 kcals

Serves 2

SQUASH AND LENTIL STEW

spray oil
1 onion, finely chopped
2 garlic cloves, crushed
2 celery sticks, chopped
1 tsp black mustard seeds
100g/3½oz/⅔ cup split red lentils
4 tomatoes, cut into chunks
500g/1lb 2oz butternut squash, peeled and cut into chunks
400ml/14fl oz/1¾ cups hot vegetable stock
salt and ground black pepper
a few fresh coriander (cilantro) sprigs, roughly chopped
4 tbsp low-fat natural yogurt

1 Spray a non-stick pan lightly with oil and place over a low heat. Add the onion, garlic and celery, and cook gently for 8–10 minutes until tender. Stir in the mustard seeds and cook for 1 minute.
2 Stir in the lentils and then add the tomatoes and butternut squash. Pour in the hot stock and bring to the boil, then reduce the heat and simmer gently for 20 minutes or until the squash is tender and the lentils have broken down and thickened the stew. Season to taste with salt and pepper.
3 Serve the stew, strewn with chopped coriander and topped with yogurt.

preparation 10 minutes cooking time 30 minutes calories 200 kcals

Serves 2

PESTO BEANBURGERS

1 x 400g/14oz can butter (lima) beans, rinsed and drained
1 small onion, finely chopped
1 garlic clove, crushed
1 red chilli, seeded and diced
1 tbsp red pesto sauce
a few fresh coriander (cilantro) sprigs
1 medium egg, beaten
25g/1oz/¼ cup grated reduced-fat Cheddar cheese
2 tbsp fat-free fromage frais
flour to dust
spray oil
2 tsp sweet chilli sauce
salt and ground black pepper

1 Put the beans in a food processor or blender with the onion, garlic, chilli, pesto, herbs, beaten egg, cheese and fromage frais. Add some seasoning and blitz to a stiff paste. For a rougher texture, you can mash the beans with a potato masher and then stir in the other ingredients. Chill in the refrigerator until ready to cook.
2 Divide the mixture into four portions and shape each one into a patty with your hands. Dust lightly with flour.
3 Lightly spray a large shallow frying pan with oil and place over a medium heat. When it's really hot, add the beanburgers and cook for 5 minutes each side until crisp and golden.
4 Serve immediately with some sweet chilli sauce.

preparation 15 minutes plus chilling   cooking time 10 minutes   calories 280 kcals

Serves 2

QUICK MEDITERRANEAN TART

8 x 15g/½oz sheets filo pastry
1 medium egg, beaten
2 tbsp green pesto
1 red onion, thinly sliced
1 courgette (zucchini), sliced
1 red (bell) pepper, seeded and thinly sliced
225g/8oz cherry tomatoes
50g/2oz reduced-fat Cheddar cheese, grated
salt and ground black pepper
3 tbsp chopped fresh parsley

1 Preheat the oven to 190°C/375°F/Gas 5.
2 Lightly spray a 20 x 30cm/8 x 12in non-stick shallow baking tin with oil. Brush a sheet of filo pastry with a little beaten egg and place in the tin with the edges hanging over the sides slightly. Repeat with the remaining sheets of pastry until the tin is lined.
3 Brush the pesto sauce over the pastry base. Scatter the vegetables over the top, season lightly and sprinkle with grated cheese.
4 Bake in the oven for 20 minutes or until the pastry is crisp and golden, the vegetables are tender and the cheese has melted. Sprinkle with parsley and cut into quarters to serve.

preparation 15 minutes   cooking time 20 minutes   calories 210 kcals

Serves 4

BEAN SOUP WITH CHEESE CROUTES

spray oil

2 leeks, thinly sliced

2 garlic cloves, crushed

300g/11oz potatoes, diced

500ml/18fl oz/2¼ cups hot vegetable stock

1 x 200g/7oz can butter (lima) beans, rinsed and drained

a few fresh parsley sprigs, finely chopped

4 x 15g/½oz slices baguette

4 tbsp grated half-fat Cheddar cheese

salt and ground black pepper

1 Lightly spray a large pan with oil and set over a low heat. When hot, add the leeks, garlic and potatoes and cook gently for 8–10 minutes until tender. Add the hot stock and bring to the boil. Reduce the heat, cover the pan and simmer for 15 minutes or until the potato is tender.

2 Blitz the soup to a purée in a blender (or use an electric hand blender). Return to the pan, add the beans, seasoning to taste and parsley and heat through gently.

3 Meanwhile, toast the baguette slices and cover them with the grated cheese. Pop them under a hot grill (broiler) until the cheese melts and bubbles.

4 Divide the soup between two deep soup bowls and put a cheese croûte in each one. Serve immediately.

preparation 10 minutes   cooking time 30 minutes   calories 345 kcals

Serves 2

PASTA WITH ROASTED CHERRY TOMATO SAUCE

spray oil

250g/9oz small cherry tomatoes

125g/4oz linguine or spaghetti (dry weight)

1 red bird's eye chilli, seeded and finely chopped

2 garlic cloves, crushed

grated zest and juice of ½ lemon

3 tbsp chopped fresh parsley

1 tsp freshly grated Parmesan

salt and ground black pepper

1 Preheat the oven to 200°C/400°F/Gas 6.

2 Lightly spray a roasting pan with oil and place the tomatoes in the pan. Roast in the oven for 10 minutes.

3 Meanwhile, cook the pasta in a large pan of lightly salted boiling water, according to the instructions on the pack. Drain well.

4 While the pasta is cooking, lightly spray a deep frying pan with oil and place over a low heat. Add the chilli and garlic and cook for 2 minutes.

5 Stir in the lemon zest and juice and parsley, then tip in the drained pasta and roasted tomatoes and toss gently together. Season with salt and pepper.

6 Divide between two plates and sprinkle with Parmesan.

preparation 5 minutes   cooking time 10 minutes   calories 240 kcals

Serves 2

HALLOUMI GREEK SALAD

1 small aubergine (eggplant)
1 small red (bell) pepper
spray oil
1 garlic clove, crushed
2 vine tomatoes, halved
1 x 200g/7oz can chickpeas (garbanzos), drained and rinsed
½ red onion, sliced very thinly
4 black olives, pitted
100g/3½oz lite halloumi cheese
1 tbsp oil-free vinaigrette
grated zest and juice of ½ lemon
2 tbsp chopped fresh mint
salt and ground black pepper

1 Cut the aubergine into cubes. Halve the red pepper, remove the stalk, ribs and seeds and cut the flesh into chunks.
2 Spray a ridged griddle pan lightly with oil. Place over a medium heat and cook the garlic, aubergine and red pepper for 10 minutes, turning occasionally, or until tender. Add the tomatoes and cook for 5 minutes.
3 Mix the chickpeas, red onion and olives together and divide between 2 plates. Top with the grilled vegetables.
4 Cut the halloumi into four slices and cook in the hot griddle pan for 2 minutes or until golden brown on both sides.
5 Blend the vinaigrette, lemon zest and juice and chopped herbs and drizzle over the salad. Arrange the warm halloumi slices on top and serve immediately.

preparation 10 minutes **cooking time** 17 minutes **calories** 270 kcals

Serves 2

SUMMER TORTILLA

spray oil
300g/11oz waxy potatoes, diced
2 garlic cloves, thinly sliced
1 red (bell) pepper
1 yellow (bell) pepper
4 large eggs
1 tbsp chopped fresh parsley
salt and ground black pepper

1 Preheat the grill (broiler). Spray a frying pan lightly with oil and place over a low to medium heat. Cook the potatoes and garlic gently until the potatoes are tender and golden.
2 Meanwhile, cook the peppers under the hot grill, turning occasionally, until the skins are charred. Peel away the skins and remove the seeds. Cut the pepper flesh into thin slices.
3 Beat the eggs, stir in the parsley and season with salt and pepper. Stir in the cooked potatoes and peppers.
4 Pour the egg mixture into the frying pan and place over a low heat. Cook gently for 15 minutes or until the tortilla is set around the sides and underneath.
5 Pop under a hot grill for 2–3 minutes until the top of the tortilla is set and golden brown. Serve cut into wedges.

preparation 15 minutes **cooking time** 30 minutes **calories** 290 kcals

Serves 2

VEGGIE CHEESE BAKE

1 cauliflower, cut into florets
1 head broccoli, cut into florets
2 tbsp grated half-fat Cheddar cheese
a pinch of cayenne pepper

For the cheese sauce
2 tbsp cornflour (cornstarch)
300ml/½ pint/1¼ cups skimmed milk
125g/4oz/½ cup virtually fat-free fromage frais
½ tsp mustard
40g/1½oz/⅓ cup grated half-fat Cheddar cheese

1 Cook the cauliflower and broccoli in a pan of lightly salted boiling water until just tender but not mushy. Drain well.
2 Meanwhile, blend the cornflour with a little of the skimmed milk. Heat the rest of the milk until it boils. Stir in the cornflour mixture and simmer gently, stirring with a wooden spoon, for 2–3 minutes until the sauce is thick and smooth. Remove from the heat and beat in the fromage frais, mustard and grated cheese.
3 Preheat the grill (broiler) to hot.
4 Put the broccoli and cauliflower in an ovenproof dish and pour the cheese sauce over the top. Sprinkle with grated cheese and dust lightly with cayenne.
5 Pop under the hot grill for 5 minutes or until bubbling and golden brown.

preparation 15 minutes cooking time 15 minutes calories 325 kcals

Serves 2

EGG AND PROSCIUTTO SALAD

2 large eggs
40g/1½oz thinly sliced lean Parma ham
1 tbsp oil-free vinaigrette
1 tbsp balsamic vinegar
1 tsp Dijon mustard
75g/3oz mixed salad leaves
¼ red onion, finely chopped
½ small avocado, peeled, stoned and diced
4 baby plum tomatoes, halved
10g/⅓oz Parmesan, shaved

1 Break the eggs into a pan of simmering water and poach gently until the whites are set but the yolks are still runny. Remove with a slotted spoon on to kitchen paper.
2 Meanwhile, remove any visible fat from the Parma ham and dry-fry in a non-stick frying pan for 2 minutes, turning halfway through, until crisp.
3 Blend the vinaigrette, balsamic and mustard together to make the dressing. Mix together the salad leaves, red onion, avocado and tomatoes and toss lightly in the dressing.
4 Divide the salad between two serving plates and top with the poached eggs and crisp Parma ham. Sprinkle with Parmesan shavings.

preparation 10 minutes cooking time 6–8 minutes calories 230 kcals

Serves 2

SKINNY FRUIT CRUMBLE

700g/1½lb cooking (green)
apples, peeled, cored and sliced

225g/8oz blackberries

artificial sweetener

125g/4oz/1 cup + 2 tbsp plain
(all-purpose) flour

50g/2oz/4 tbsp butter, softened

a pinch of ground cinnamon

25g/1oz/¼ cup icing
(confectioner's) sugar, sifted

1 Preheat the oven to 190°C/ 375°F/Gas 5.
2 Put the apples and blackberries in an ovenproof baking dish
   and sprinkle with artificial sweetener to taste.
3 Sift the flour into a large bowl. Cut the butter into tiny pieces
   and add to the flour. Rub in with your fingertips until the
   mixture resembles fine breadcrumbs. Stir in the cinnamon
   and icing sugar together with 1 tbsp cold water.
4 Spoon the crumble mixture over the fruit and smooth the
   top. Bake in the oven for 25–30 minutes until the crumble
   is cooked and golden brown and the fruit is tender.
5 Serve the crumble hot with low-fat yogurt (25 kcals per
   rounded tablespoon), or reduced-fat ice cream (45 kcals per
   level scoop).

preparation 15 minutes   cooking time 30 minutes   calories 190 kcals

Serves 6

PEACH FILO BASKETS

6 x 15g/½oz sheets filo pastry

1 small egg, beaten

50g/2oz/⅓ cup mascarpone

75g/3oz/⅓ cup 0% fat Greek
yogurt

4 ripe peaches, stoned and
chopped

icing (confectioner's) sugar
to dust

1 Preheat the oven to 200°C/400°F/Gas 6. Place four small
   ceramic ramekin dishes upside down on a baking sheet.
2 Cut each filo pastry sheet in half to form two squares, so
   you end up with 12 filo squares. Brush three squares lightly
   with beaten egg and place one of them over a ramekin dish,
   pressing it over the sides. Press two more squares down on
   top of it, at uneven angles. Repeat the process with the other
   three ramekins.
3 Bake in the oven for 8 minutes or until crisp and golden.
   Cool before removing the baskets from the ramekins.
4 Mix together the mascarpone and yogurt and stir in the
   peaches. Divide the mixture between the filo baskets and
   dust lightly with icing sugar before serving.

preparation 15 minutes   cooking time 8 minutes   calories 160 kcals

Serves 4

LOW-CAL CHOCOLATE ESPRESSO MOUSSE

2 medium eggs, separated

150g/5oz/⅔ cup virtually fat-free natural fromage frais

1 tbsp cocoa powder

2 tbsp strong espresso coffee

artificial sweetener to taste

2 tbsp hot water

½ sachet powdered gelatine

10g/⅓oz dark (semi-sweet) chocolate, grated

1 Put the egg yolks and fromage frais in a bowl. Sift in the cocoa powder and stir until smooth. Add the espresso coffee and sweeten to taste with artificial sweetener.

2 Pour the hot (not boiling) water into a separate bowl and sprinkle the gelatine over the top. Set aside for 5 minutes, stirring occasionally until dissolved. Leave to cool.

3 Whisk the egg whites in a clean, dry bowl until they stand in stiff peaks. Fold them gently into the chocolate mixture with a metal spoon. Gently stir in the dissolved gelatine, mixing it thoroughly, and spoon into two ramekins or glass dishes.

4 Chill in the refrigerator for 2 hours until set. Grate the chocolate over the top just before serving.

preparation 15 minutes plus cooling and chilling   **calories** 170 kcals

Serves 2

WINTER PAVLOVA

3 large egg whites

175g/6oz/¾ cup caster (superfine) sugar

1 tsp vinegar

1 tsp cornflour (cornstarch)

1 tsp ground cinnamon

300g/11oz/1¼ cups 0% fat Greek yogurt

seeds of 1 fresh pomegranate

1 tsp icing (confectioner's) sugar

1 Preheat the oven to 140°C/275°F/Gas 1. Line a large baking sheet with non-stick parchment paper and draw a 20cm/8in diameter circle on it.

2 Whisk the egg whites in a clean, dry bowl until they form stiff peaks. Beat in the caster sugar, a little at a time, until stiff and glossy. Whisk in the vinegar and cornflour.

3 Spoon the meringue on to the circle you have drawn, swirling it out to the edges and making a slight indent in the middle.

4 Cook in the oven for 1¼–1½ hours, then turn the oven off and leave the pavlova inside until it is completely cold.

5 Gently remove the backing paper from the pavlova base and place it on a serving plate. Stir the cinnamon into the yogurt and spoon over the pavlova. Sprinkle the pomegranate seeds over the top and dust with icing sugar.

preparation 20 minutes   **cooking time** 1¼–1½ hours plus cooling   **calories** 170 kcals

Serves 6

LOW-FAT TIRAMISU

4 tbsp very hot strong espresso coffee

1 tsp Tia Maria

6 sponge fingers

1 egg yolk

1 tbsp caster (superfine) sugar

175g/6oz/⅔ cup low-fat Quark soft cheese

2 drops vanilla extract

1 tsp cocoa powder

1 Pour the hot coffee and Tia Maria into a bowl. Quickly dip 3 sponge fingers into the hot coffee and put them into two sundae glasses.

2 Beat the egg yolk and sugar until thick, pale and creamy. Beat in the Quark and vanilla essence. Spoon half of this mixture over the coffee-soaked sponge fingers.

3 Dip the rest of the sponge fingers into the hot coffee and place on top of the Quark layer. Cover with the remaining Quark mixture and dust with cocoa powder. Chill in the refrigerator before serving.

preparation 15 minutes plus chilling   **calories** 205 kcals

Serves 2

RASPBERRY MUFFINS

250g/9oz/2½ cups plain (all-purpose) flour

2½ tsp baking powder

a pinch of salt

100g/3½oz/7 tbsp caster (superfine) sugar

200g/7oz/¾ cup low-fat natural yogurt

75g/3oz/6 tbsp melted butter

2 medium eggs, beaten

125g/4oz/scant 1 cup raspberries

1 Preheat the oven to 190°C/375°F/Gas 5.

2 Sift the flour and baking powder into a mixing bowl. Mix in the salt and sugar.

3 Blend the yogurt with the melted butter and beaten egg and stir into the dry ingredients until thoroughly mixed. Fold in the berries to distribute them evenly through the mixture.

4 Line a muffin pan with 12 paper cases and divide the mixture among them. Bake in the oven for 20 minutes or until well risen and golden. Cool on a wire rack.

preparation 15 minutes   **cooking time** 20 minutes plus cooling   **calories** 185 kcals

Makes 12

TOP 10 SALSAS

RED PEPPER SALSA

2 garlic cloves, crushed
4 ripe tomatoes, chopped
½ red onion, finely chopped
1 red (bell) pepper, seeded and diced
1 red chilli, diced
a few sprigs of fresh coriander (cilantro), chopped
juice of 1 lime

1 Mix together all the ingredients in a bowl.
   Cover and then chill in the refrigerator
   until required.

preparation 15 minutes

Serves 4

MANGO SALSA

1 large ripe mango, peeled, stoned and diced
3 ripe tomatoes, diced
4 spring onions (scallions), finely chopped
1 yellow (bell) pepper, seeded and diced
1 red chilli, seeded and diced
juice of 1 lime
salt and ground black pepper
4 tbsp chopped fresh coriander (cilantro)

1 Mix all the ingredients together in a bowl.
   Chill in the refrigerator until required.

preparation 15 minutes

Serves 4

EXOTIC FRUIT SALSA

2 roasted garlic cloves
1 mango, peeled, stoned and diced
1 papaya, peeled, seeded and diced
1 red onion, finely chopped
1 red or green chilli, seeded and diced
225g/8oz ripe tomatoes, chopped
1 x 200g/7oz can red kidney beans, drained and rinsed
juice of 2 limes
4 tbsp chopped fresh coriander (cilantro)

1 Crush the garlic with a fork and mix with
   the remaining ingredients. Cover and chill
   in the refrigerator for 30 minutes.

preparation 15 minutes

Serves 8

BALSAMIC SALSA

4 tbsp olive oil
1 small onion, finely chopped
3 red (bell) peppers, seeded and diced
2 red chillies, seeded and diced
2 tbsp balsamic vinegar
4 tbsp chopped fresh coriander (cilantro)

1 Heat the oil and cook the onion, peppers
   and chillies over a medium heat for
   5 minutes, stirring until softened.
2 Add the balsamic and coriander and
   transfer to a bowl. Set aside to cool.

preparation 10 minutes
cooking time 5 minutes

Serves 6

CHORIZO SALSA

125g/4oz chorizo, skinned and diced
1 red onion, finely chopped
1 red (bell) pepper, seeded and diced
4 ripe tomatoes, finely chopped
2 garlic cloves, crushed
juice of 1 lime

1 Cook the chorizo for 2–3 minutes, stirring, until the oil starts to run. Drain off the oil and mix with the remaining ingredients.

preparation 15 minutes
cooking time 2–3 minutes

Serves 4

HARISSA SALSA

4 large ripe tomatoes, diced
½ red onion, finely chopped
juice of 1 lime
a dash of harissa paste to taste
6 tbsp chopped fresh mint and coriander (cilantro)

1 Mix together all the ingredients in a bowl.

preparation 15 minutes

Serves 4

AVOCADO SALSA

1 ripe avocado, peeled, stoned and diced
2 large ripe tomatoes, chopped
½ red onion, diced
1 green chilli, seeded and chopped
juice of 1 lemon
4 tbsp chopped fresh coriander (cilantro)

1 Mix all the ingredients in a bowl, then cover and chill in the refrigerator until required.

preparation 15 minutes

Serves 4

LEMON SALSA

2 large lemons
1 red onion, diced
1 small bunch of fresh parsley or mint, chopped
3 tbsp olive oil
salt and ground black pepper

1 Peel the lemons, removing the white pith. Chop the flesh, discarding the pips, and mix in a bowl with the remaining ingredients.

preparation 15 minutes

Serves 6

MELON SALSA

1 small ripe Cantaloupe or Charentais melon
½ tsp mixed peppercorns, crushed
1 bunch spring onions (scallions), chopped
grated zest and juice of 1 lime
a few sprigs of fresh mint, chopped

1 Scoop out and discard the melon seeds. Dice the flesh and place in a bowl.
2 Add the remaining ingredients and mix well.

preparation 15 minutes

Serves 6

SPICY CORIANDER SALSA

1 red chilli, seeded and roughly chopped
grated zest and juice of 1 lime
1 small bunch of fresh coriander (cilantro)
125g/4oz/½ cup 0% fat Greek yogurt

1 Blitz all the ingredients in a blender. Spoon into a bowl and chill in the refrigerator.

preparation 5 minutes

Serves 4

FOOD FROM THE FREEZER

It's always a good idea to have a well-stocked freezer for when you're in a hurry and don't have time to cook. Just take out a portion, defrost in the microwave, reheat and, hey presto, a meal in minutes! In this section, you will discover a wide range of delicious recipes that you can cook ahead and freeze until required, including a vegetarian tart and fish cakes.

It's also great when you're planning a party or family gathering and can prepare the food at leisure over several weeks rather than having a stressful last-minute marathon session in the kitchen. We have soups, curries and even a risotto for these occasions, as well as delicious fruit tarts.

In addition, we've got some great home-baked cakes, cookies, muffins and bread that all freeze well and will taste just as good when thawed. If you keep these in your freezer, you always have something to serve to your unexpected guests when they drop by unannounced.

And, finally, a freezer is a boon when there's a glut of seasonal fruit and vegetables that need using up. Make them into soups, tarts or even a compote to serve on breakfast cereal or muesli.

< Plum Frangipane Tart (page 535)

VEGETABLE AND BARLEY SOUP

50g/2oz/4 tbsp butter
1 onion, finely chopped
1 leek, thinly sliced
3 carrots, cubed
½ small swede (rutabaga), cubed
1 parsnip, cubed
1.3 litres/2¼ pints/5½ cups hot vegetable stock
40g/1½oz/¼ cup pearl barley
salt and ground black pepper
3 tbsp chopped fresh parsley

1 Melt the butter in a pan over a low heat. Add the onion and the white leek slices (reserve the green slices) and cook gently for 5 minutes, stirring occasionally, until softened. Stir in the carrots, swede and parsnip, cover the pan and cook gently for 5 minutes.
2 Pour in the hot stock, add the barley and seasoning, and then bring to the boil. Reduce the heat, cover the pan and simmer for 1 hour until the barley is tender.
3 Add the green leek slices and cook for 5 minutes.
4 Check the seasoning. Cool and freeze, or sprinkle the hot soup with parsley, ladle into bowls and serve.

preparation 20 minutes   cooking time 1 hour 20 minutes

Serves 4

LENTIL AND SQUASH SOUP

1 tbsp sunflower oil
1 onion, finely chopped
4 tsp medium curry paste
1 tsp cumin seeds, crushed
2 garlic cloves, crushed
450g/1lb butternut squash, peeled, seeded and cubed
1 dessert apple, peeled, cored and cubed
1.2 litres/2 pints/5 cups hot vegetable stock
50g/2oz/⅓ cup red lentils
salt and ground black pepper
3 tbsp chopped fresh coriander (cilantro)

1 Heat the oil in a pan over a low heat. Add the onion and cook gently for 5 minutes or until softened. Stir in the curry paste, cumin seeds and garlic and cook for 1 minute, then stir in the cubed squash and apple.
2 Add the hot stock and lentils and season with salt and pepper. Bring to the boil, then cover the pan and simmer gently for 45–50 minutes until the lentils are soft.
3 Blitz half the soup to a purée in a blender, then taste and adjust the seasoning.
4 Cool and freeze, or stir in the coriander and reheat gently. Ladle into warmed bowls and serve.

preparation 20 minutes   cooking time 50–60 minutes

Serves 4

LETTUCE AND GARDEN HERB SOUP

50g/2oz/4 tbsp butter
1 onion, chopped
1 medium baking potato, cubed
1 litre/1¾ pints/4 cups hot vegetable stock
1 round lettuce, torn into pieces
50g/2oz fresh parsley, chives and/or basil, roughly chopped
salt and ground black pepper
croûtons to serve

1 Melt the butter in a pan over a low heat. Add the onion and cook gently for 5 minutes or until softened. Stir in the potato, then cover and cook for 10 minutes, stirring occasionally.
2 Pour in the hot stock and season with salt and pepper. Bring to the boil, then reduce the heat, cover and simmer for 10 minutes or until the potatoes are cooked.
3 Add the lettuce and herbs and cook for 1 minute or until the lettuce wilts. Blend, in batches, until smooth.
4 Cool and freeze, or reheat and serve the hot soup with a sprinkle of croûtons.

preparation 15 minutes   cooking time 25–30 minutes

Serves 4

LAMB ROGAN JOSH

1 tbsp sunflower oil
4 x 300g/11oz lamb shanks
2 onions, sliced
4 garlic cloves, crushed
1 tbsp grated fresh root ginger
1 cinnamon stick, halved
8 cardamom pods, crushed
4 tbsp medium-hot curry paste
2 tbsp plain (all-purpose) flour
2 tbsp tomato paste
2 tsp caster (superfine) sugar
500g/1lb 2oz tomatoes, chopped
600ml/1 pint/2½ cups lamb stock
salt and ground black pepper
boiled rice to serve

1 Preheat the oven to 180°C/350°F/Gas 4.
2 Heat the oil in a frying pan, add the lamb shanks and cook over a medium heat for 10 minutes, turning until browned all over. Transfer to an ovenproof casserole.
3 Add the onions to the pan and cook over a low heat for 5 minutes or until they start to turn golden. Stir in the garlic, ginger, cinnamon and cardamom. Mix in the curry paste and cook for 1 minute.
4 Mix in the flour, tomato paste and sugar, then stir in the tomatoes and stock. Season with salt and pepper, bring to the boil and pour over the lamb. Cover the dish and cook in the oven for 2 hours or until the lamb is tender.
5 Cool and freeze, or serve immediately with boiled rice.

preparation 15 minutes   cooking time 2¼ hours

Serves 4

TEOCHEW-STYLE CHICKEN

1 tbsp sunflower oil
900g/2lb chicken thighs
1 large onion, finely chopped
2 tsp cornflour (cornstarch)
pared rind and juice of 1 orange
2 garlic cloves, crushed
2 tsp grated fresh root ginger
3 star anise
300ml/½ pint/1¼ cups hot chicken stock
4 tbsp Chinese rice wine
1 tsp Sichuan peppercorns
3 tbsp soy sauce
boiled egg noodles to serve

1 Preheat the oven to 180°C/350°F/Gas 4. Heat the oil in a large frying pan and cook the chicken over a medium heat for 5 minutes or until browned all over. Using a slotted spoon, transfer to a casserole.
2 Add the onion to the pan and cook for 5 minutes, stirring, until just tender. Mix the cornflour with the orange juice in a small bowl until smooth.
3 Add the garlic, ginger and star anise to the pan, cook for 1 minute, then stir in the hot stock, wine and orange juice. Crush the peppercorns and add to the pan with the soy sauce and orange rind. Bring to the boil, then pour over the chicken.
4 Cover the casserole and cook in the oven for 1 hour until the chicken is cooked. Discard the orange rind.
5 Cool and freeze, or serve immediately with egg noodles.

preparation 15 minutes cooking time 1 hour 10 minutes

Serves 4

POT-ROASTED CHICKEN

1 red onion, cut into wedges
2 leeks, thickly sliced
2 celery sticks, sliced
2 carrots, sliced
4 tomatoes, peeled and chopped
1 x 1.4kg/3lb chicken
150ml/¼ pint/scant ⅔ cup apple juice
150ml/¼ pint/scant ⅔ cup cider
4 tbsp chopped fresh parsley
salt and ground black pepper
boiled rice to serve

1 Put the onion, leeks, celery, carrots and tomatoes in a large pan. Add the chicken, breast-side down, pushing it into the vegetables.
2 Pour the apple juice and cider over the top and cover the pan. Bring to the boil, then reduce the heat and simmer gently for 30 minutes.
3 Turn the chicken over, cover the pan and cook gently for 50 minutes or until it is thoroughly cooked. Season to taste.
4 Cool and freeze or remove the chicken, discard the skin and carve into slices. Arrange on serving plates with the vegetables and juices. Sprinkle with parsley and serve with boiled rice.

preparation 10 minutes cooking time 1 hour 20 minutes

Serves 4

THAI MONKFISH CURRY

1 onion, quartered
1 lemongrass stalk, sliced
2 tsp grated fresh root ginger
1 tbsp coconut oil
1 tbsp Thai green curry paste
1 x 400ml/14fl oz can coconut milk
150ml/¼ pint/scant ⅔ cup fish stock
grated zest and juice of 1 lime
2 tsp Thai fish sauce
450g/1lb monkfish (anglerfish) fillets, halved
basil leaves, rice noodles and stir-fried vegetables to serve

1 Put the onion, lemongrass and ginger in a food processor or blender and blitz until very finely chopped. Heat the oil in a large pan and cook the onion mixture over a low heat for 5 minutes, stirring, until softened but not coloured. Stir in the curry paste and cook for 30 seconds.
2 Stir in the coconut milk, stock, lime zest and juice and fish sauce. Bring just to the boil, reduce the heat, cover the pan and simmer gently for 5 minutes.
3 Add the monkfish in a single layer, push down into the liquid, cover and simmer gently for 8 minutes or until just cooked.
4 Using a slotted spoon, lift the fish out of the pan and slice thickly, then return to the pan and heat through gently.
5 Cool and freeze, or serve immediately in bowls over cooked rice noodles. Top with stir-fried vegetables and basil leaves.

preparation 15 minutes   cooking time 20 minutes

Serves 4

SALMON AND PEA RISOTTO

2 tbsp olive oil
1 onion, finely chopped
225g/8oz/1 cup arborio rice
grated zest of 1 lemon
175ml/6fl oz/¾ cup white wine
900ml/1½ pints/3⅔ cups hot fish stock
450g/1lb salmon fillet
250g/9oz asparagus, trimmed
4 tbsp crème fraîche
125g/4oz/1 cup frozen peas
salt and ground black pepper
4 tbsp freshly grated Parmesan

1 Heat the oil in a large frying pan over a low heat and cook the onion for 5 minutes, stirring occasionally, until softened.
2 Stir in the rice and lemon zest and cook for 1 minute or until the rice is glossy. Add the wine and 2 ladlefuls of hot stock, then arrange the salmon, cut into four pieces, on top. Cover and simmer for 10 minutes, adding stock as needed, or until the salmon is just cooked. Remove the salmon from the pan, discard the skin and bones and flake the flesh. Set aside.
3 Simmer the rice for 15 minutes, uncovered, adding more stock and stirring frequently, until it is soft and creamy.
4 Meanwhile, cook the asparagus in a pan of boiling water for 2 minutes. Drain well, then add to the pan with the crème fraîche and peas. Cook for 3 minutes. Season to taste.
5 Cool and freeze, or serve with the salmon in bowls, sprinkled with Parmesan.

preparation 15 minutes   cooking time 35 minutes

Serves 4

CHEESE-TOPPED FISH PIE

1 litre/1¾ pints/4 cups milk
225g/8oz smoked cod fillet
300g/11oz unsmoked cod fillet
675g/1½lb salmon fillet
250g/9oz peeled raw prawns (shrimp)
900g/2lb potatoes, thinly sliced
bunch of fresh parsley, chopped
125g/4oz/½ cup butter
125g/4oz/1 cup plain (all-purpose) flour
6 tbsp dry white wine
150ml/¼ pint/scant ⅔ cup fish stock
50g/2oz/½ cup grated Cheddar
salt and ground black pepper

1 Preheat the oven to 190°C/375°F/Gas 5.
2 Put the milk, cod and salmon in a pan and bring to the boil. Reduce the heat, cover and simmer gently for 5 minutes. Add the prawns and cook for 3–4 minutes until they are pink.
3 Meanwhile, cook the potato slices in a pan of boiling water for 4–5 minutes until just tender. Drain and leave to cool.
4 Lift the fish and prawns out of the pan, reserving the milk, and remove the skin and bones. Cut into large flakes and place in an ovenproof dish with the parsley.
5 Melt the butter in a pan, whisk in the flour and cook for 30 seconds. Gradually whisk in the milk, wine and stock and bring to the boil, whisking until thick and smooth. Pour just under two-thirds of the sauce over the fish in the dishes.
6 Arrange the potato on top, drizzle with the remaining sauce and sprinkle with cheese. Cool and freeze or cook in the oven for 30–35 minutes until golden. Serve with peas.

preparation 30 minutes   cooking time 45–50 minutes

Serves 8

MACKEREL FISH CAKES

500g/1lb 2oz potatoes, cubed
25g/1oz/2 tbsp butter
2 hard-boiled eggs, chopped
225g/8oz smoked mackerel fillets, skinned and flaked
4 spring onions (scallions), diced
a large handful of watercress, roughly chopped
2 medium eggs
75g/3oz/1½ cups fresh white breadcrumbs
olive oil to fry
crème fraîche flavoured with horseradish sauce to serve

1 Cook the potatoes in a pan of boiling water for 15 minutes or until tender. Drain and mash with the butter.
2 Stir in the chopped hardboiled eggs, fish, spring onions and watercress. Set aside to cool for 15 minutes.
3 Beat the eggs in a shallow dish and tip the breadcrumbs on to a plate. Divide the fish mixture into eight portions and shape into patties. Dip them in the beaten egg to coat both sides and then into the breadcrumbs. Coat all over and place on a non-stick baking sheet. Cover and chill in the refrigerator for 1 hour to firm up.
4 Heat 2 tbsp oil in a large frying pan over a medium heat and cook the fish cakes for 5 minutes on each side or until golden brown, crisp and piping hot. Cool and freeze, or serve with crème fraîche flavoured with horseradish sauce.

preparation 25 minutes plus cooling and chilling   cooking time 15 minutes

Makes 8

GOAT'S CHEESE AND ROASTED PEPPER TART

225g/8oz/2¼ cups plain (all-purpose) flour plus extra to dust

50g/2oz/4 tbsp butter, cubed, plus extra to grease

50g/2oz/4 tbsp white vegetable fat (shortening), cubed

For the filling

1 red, 1 yellow and 1 green (bell) pepper, quartered and seeded

1 tbsp olive oil

4 tsp green pesto sauce

4 tbsp freshly grated Parmesan

100g/3½oz goat's cheese, cubed

leaves from 2–3 fresh basil sprigs, roughly chopped, plus extra leaves to garnish

8 olives, pitted and halved

3 medium eggs

250ml/8fl oz/1 cup milk

salt and ground black pepper

1 Butter a 23cm/9in loose-bottomed fluted tart tin. Put the flour in a food processor with a pinch of salt and the fats and pulse to fine crumbs. Gradually mix in 3 tbsp cold water to make a smooth dough.

2 Knead on a lightly floured surface, then roll out thinly until a little larger than the tin. Lift the pastry over the rolling pin and use to line the tart tin. Trim the edge, prick the bottom with a fork and chill in the refrigerator for 30 minutes.

3 Preheat the oven to 190°C/375°F/Gas 5.

4 Put the tart tin on a baking sheet, fill with parchment paper and baking beans and bake in the oven for 10 minutes. Remove the paper and beans and cook for 5 minutes or until dry and crisp. Reduce the oven temperature to 180°C/350°F/Gas 4.

5 Put the peppers, skin-side up, in a single layer on a foil-lined grill (broiling) pan, brush with oil and add salt and pepper. Grill (broil) for 10 minutes or until softened. Leave to cool in the foil.

6 Peel the peppers and slice the flesh. Spread pesto over the base of the tart, arrange the peppers on top, then sprinkle the cheeses and basil leaves over, plus the olives.

7 Beat the eggs and milk with salt and pepper, pour into the pastry shell and bake in the oven for 30 minutes or until golden brown and set.

8 Set aside to cool for 10 minutes, then serve cut into wedges, garnished with basil. Or leave to cool completely, wrap in foil and freeze.

preparation 30 minutes plus chilling and cooling **cooking time** 45 minutes

Serves 4–6

FREEFORM FRUIT TARTS

340g/12oz red plums

225g/8oz raspberries

70g/2½oz/⅓ cup caster (superfine) sugar plus extra to sprinkle

1 tsp cornflour (cornstarch)

grated zest of 1 lemon

cream or custard to serve

For the sweet pastry (pie crust)

225g/8oz/2¼ cups plain (all-purpose) flour

50g/2oz/½ cup icing (confectioner's) sugar

150g/5oz/⅔ cup cold butter, diced plus extra to grease

3 egg yolks

1 tsp vanilla extract

beaten egg to brush

1 To make the pastry, put the flour in a large mixing bowl, add the icing sugar and butter and rub in the butter until it resembles fine breadcrumbs. Mix the egg yolks with the vanilla extract, add to the flour and mix to a smooth ball. Cover and chill in the refrigerator for 30 minutes.

2 Stone and slice the plums and mix with the raspberries, caster sugar, cornflour and lemon zest.

3 Preheat the oven to 180°C/350°F/Gas 4. Butter two baking sheets.

4 Divide the pastry into six pieces and roll out each one to a 15cm/6in diameter circle. Divide the fruit among the circles, leaving a border of 2.5cm/1in. Fold the pastry up and around the fruit, pleating it in soft folds and leaving the centre uncovered. Place the tarts on the prepared baking sheets. Brush the edges of the pastry with beaten egg and sprinkle with a little caster sugar. Bake in the oven for 20–25 minutes.

5 Leave on the baking sheets to cool for 10 minutes. Serve the warm tarts with cream or custard. Or cool, wrap in foil and freeze.

preparation 25 minutes plus chilling cooking time 20–25 minutes

Serves 6

RED FRUIT REFRESHER

2 tsp cornflour (cornstarch)

50g/2oz/¼ cup caster (superfine) sugar

300ml/½ pint/1¼ cups red grape juice

225g/8oz red plums, halved and stoned

150g/5oz blackberries

225g/8oz seedless red grapes, halved

1 Put the cornflour and sugar in a pan, then gradually mix in the red grape juice until smooth. Heat gently, stirring until the sugar dissolves.

2 Increase the heat and bring to the boil, stirring until thickened. Reduce the heat and add the plums, blackberries and grapes. Mix together.

3 Simmer for 2–3 minutes until just tender. Cool and serve or freeze.

preparation 10 minutes plus cooling cooking time 2–3 minutes

Serves 4

CHEAT'S SUMMER BERRY SORBET

500g/1lb 2oz frozen mixed
summer berries

6 tbsp blackcurrant cordial

4 tbsp caster (superfine) sugar

2 fresh mint sprigs

4 tbsp Greek yogurt with honey

1 Put the frozen mixed summer berries in a food processor with the undiluted blackcurrant cordial and sugar. Pulse in short bursts until the mixture is smooth and thick. Add the leaves from the mint sprigs and blitz again.

2 Spoon into glasses and stir through the honey-flavoured yogurt for a rippled effect.

3 Serve immediately while the fruits are still frozen, or return to the freezer.

preparation 10 minutes

Serves 4

PLUM FRANGIPANE TART

150g/5oz/⅔ cup butter, softened

150g/5oz/scant ⅔ cup caster (superfine) sugar

150g/5oz/1½ cups ground almonds

2 tbsp plain (all-purpose) flour

2 medium eggs, beaten

450g/1lb red plums, stoned and sliced

3 tbsp flaked almonds

2 tbsp icing (confectioner's) sugar

For the pastry (pie crust)

225g/8oz/2¼ cups plain (all-purpose) flour plus extra to dust

50g/2oz/¼ cup caster (superfine) sugar

125g/4oz/½ cup cold butter, diced

1 To make the pastry, put the flour, sugar and butter in a bowl and rub in the butter with your fingertips until it resembles fine breadcrumbs. Mix in 3 tbsp cold water to make a smooth dough.

2 Knead on a lightly floured surface, then roll out a little larger than a 28 x 18 x 4cm/11 x 7 x 1½in fluted loose-bottomed tart tin. Line the tin with the pastry, prick the base with a fork, then chill in the refrigerator for 20–30 minutes.

3 Preheat the oven to 190°C/375°F/Gas 5. Line the pastry shell with parchment paper and baking beans, then bake in the oven for 15 minutes. Remove the paper and beans and cook for 5 minutes or until crisp. Leave to cool. Reduce the oven temperature to 180°C/350°F/Gas 4.

4 Meanwhile, cream the butter and sugar until light and fluffy. Gradually beat in alternate spoonfuls of ground almonds and flour with the beaten eggs, until smooth. Spoon the mixture into the pastry shell and top with the plums and almonds.

5 Bake in the oven for 30–35 minutes until the frangipane is golden. Leave to cool for 20 minutes. Remove from the tin and cut into pieces. Freeze when cold.

6 Serve warm, dusted with sifted icing sugar.

preparation 30 minutes plus chilling   cooking time 50–55 minutes

Makes 12 pieces

CHEESE AND APPLE SCONES

sunflower oil to grease
1 cooking (green) apple, peeled, cored and cubed
2 tbsp cider vinegar
1 tbsp light brown sugar
1 tbsp wholegrain mustard
450g/1lb/4½ cups self-raising (self-rising) flour plus extra to dust
50g/2oz/4 tbsp butter, cubed
175g/6oz/1½ cups grated Cheddar cheese
2 medium eggs, beaten
6 tbsp milk
salt and ground black pepper

1. Preheat the oven to 200°C/400°F/Gas 6. Lightly oil a large baking sheet.
2. Cook the apple in the vinegar, sugar and mustard in a small pan over a medium heat for 5 minutes or until soft.
3. Put the flour, butter and seasoning in a bowl and rub in the butter until the mixture resembles fine breadcrumbs. Stir in the apple and two-thirds of the cheese. Add three-quarters of the beaten egg and enough milk to make a soft dough.
4. Put the dough on a lightly floured surface and cut in half. Roll out each piece to a circle about 2cm/¾in thick.
5. Place both dough rounds on the prepared baking sheet, then cut each one into 6 wedges and separate them slightly to allow space for rising in the oven. Brush the tops with the remaining egg and sprinkle with the remaining cheese.
6. Bake in the oven for 20 minutes or until golden brown and well risen. Serve warm or set aside to cool and then freeze.

preparation 25 minutes cooking time 20 minutes

Serves 12

PASSION FRUIT COMPOTE

2 lemongrass stalks, slit lengthways
125g/4oz/½ cup caster (superfine) sugar
1 large pineapple
grated zest and juice of 1 lime
2 passion fruit, halved

1. Bruise the lemongrass by pressing with the end of a rolling pin. Place in a pan with 600ml/1 pint/2½ cups water and the sugar. Heat gently, stirring occasionally, until the sugar dissolves. Increase the heat and simmer for 5 minutes. Set aside for 20 minutes for the syrup to cool.
2. Meanwhile, slice off the top and bottom of the pineapple. Remove the skin and slice the fruit into circles. Cut them in half and discard the central core.
3. Discard the lemongrass and add the lime zest and juice to the syrup. Scoop out the seeds from the passion fruit and stir into the syrup.
4. Put the pineapple in a glass serving dish and pour the syrup over. Set aside to cool completely and then serve or freeze.

preparation 15 minutes plus cooling cooking time 5 minutes plus cooling

Serves 4

BEETROOT DRIZZLE CAKE

3 medium eggs

150ml/¼ pint/scant ⅔ cup sunflower oil

175g/6oz/¾ cup light brown sugar

225g/8oz/2¼ cups self-raising (self-rising) flour

1 tsp baking powder

3 tsp ground ginger

grated zest and juice of 1 orange

175g/6oz cooked beetroot (beets), coarsely grated

2 tbsp chopped preserved ginger

2 tbsp sunflower seeds

150g/5oz/scant ¾ cup granulated sugar

1 Preheat the oven to 180°C/350°F/Gas 4. Line a 20 x 30cm/8 x 12in cake tin with parchment paper.
2 Beat the eggs, oil and brown sugar in a bowl. Sift in the flour, baking powder and ground ginger and beat well. Add the orange zest and beetroot and mix until smooth.
3 Pour into the prepared tin and sprinkle with the preserved ginger and seeds. Bake in the oven for 30–35 minutes until well risen and a skewer inserted into the centre comes out clean. Remove the cake from the tin, place on a wire rack and pierce the top in several places with a skewer.
4 Meanwhile, heat the granulated sugar and orange juice, stirring until the sugar dissolves. Spoon the syrup over the top of the hot cake and set aside to cool.
5 When cold, peel away the paper and cut the cake into small squares. Freeze or serve.

preparation 25 minutes cooking time 30–35 minutes plus cooling

Serves 12

BLUEBERRY CHOC MUFFINS

125ml/4fl oz/½ cup sunflower oil

150g/5oz/scant ⅔ cup natural yogurt

2 medium eggs, beaten

1 tsp vanilla extract

250g/9oz/2½ cups self-raising (self-rising) flour

1 tsp baking powder

125g/4oz/½ cup caster (superfine) sugar

125g/4oz/1 cup blueberries

125g/4oz white chocolate, roughly chopped

1 Preheat the oven to 190°C/375°F/Gas 5. Put twelve paper muffin cases into a 12-hole muffin pan.
2 With a fork, mix the oil, yogurt, eggs and vanilla extract in a bowl. Put the flour, baking powder and sugar in a large bowl. Add the wet ingredients to the dry ones and fork together until just mixed – the briefer the mixing the lighter the muffins will be.
3 Add the blueberries and chocolate and stir briefly, then spoon the mixture into the paper cases.
4 Bake in the oven for 15–20 minutes until well risen and golden brown. Cool and freeze, or serve warm.

preparation 15 minutes cooking time 15–20 minutes

Makes 12

TRIPLE CHOC COOKIES

250g/9oz/2½ cups plain (all-purpose) flour

125g/4oz/½ cup caster (superfine) sugar

175g/6oz/¾ cup butter, cubed

1 tsp vanilla extract

50g/2oz dark (semi-sweet) chocolate, roughly chopped

50g/2oz milk chocolate, roughly chopped

50g/2oz white chocolate, roughly chopped

1 Put the flour and sugar in a bowl, add the butter and rub in with your fingertips until it resembles fine breadcrumbs.
2 Stir in the vanilla and chocolates, mixing until the crumbs and chocolate stick together. Squeeze gently to make a ball.
3 Knead the dough lightly until smooth, then place on a piece of parchment paper and roll into a cylinder, 25cm/10in long and 5cm/2in diameter. Wrap the parchment around the dough and chill in the refrigerator for 30 minutes.
4 Unwrap and cut into 20 slices, about 1cm/½in thick.
5 Preheat the oven to 180°C/350°F/Gas 4. Arrange the slices on a non-stick baking sheet and bake in the oven for 12–15 minutes. Cool and serve or freeze.

preparation 20 minutes plus chilling **cooking time** 12–15 minutes plus cooling

Makes 20

FUDGE BROWNIES

100g/3½oz/¾ cup blanched hazelnuts

½ tsp coarse salt

250g/9oz dark (semi-sweet) chocolate, broken into pieces

175g/6oz/¾ cup butter

3 medium eggs, beaten

225g/8oz/1 cup light brown sugar

75g/3oz/¾ cup self-raising (self-rising) flour

1 tsp baking powder

100g/3½oz cream fudge, roughly chopped

1 Preheat the oven to 180°C/350°F/Gas 4. Line a 20 x 30cm/8 x 12in roasting pan with parchment paper.
2 Dry-roast the hazelnuts and salt in a small frying pan over a low heat until the nuts are golden. Chop roughly.
3 Melt the chocolate and butter in a large bowl set over a pan of gently simmering water for 5 minutes.
4 Whisk the eggs and sugar together until light and frothy, then gradually whisk in the melted chocolate mixture. Sift the flour and baking powder over the top and gently fold in with half the nuts. Pour the mixture into the prepared pan. Sprinkle with the remaining nuts and salt.
5 Bake in the oven for 25–30 minutes until well risen, the top has begun to crack and the centre is still slightly soft.
6 Sprinkle the fudge over the top, then put back in the oven for 2 minutes to soften. Leave the brownies to cool in the pan. When cool, lift out and peel away the paper.
7 Freeze or cut into small squares and serve.

preparation 25 minutes **cooking time** 25–30 minutes plus cooling

Makes 24

FARMHOUSE BREAD

sunflower oil to grease

1kg/2¼lb/8 cups strong white bread flour plus extra to dust

50g/2oz/4 tbsp butter, cubed

2 tbsp caster (superfine) sugar

2 tsp salt

2½ tsp easy-blend dried yeast

600ml/1 pint/2½ cups warm water

1 Oil two 900g/2lb loaf tins. Put the flour in a bowl and rub in the butter until it resembles breadcrumbs. Stir in the sugar, salt and yeast, then mix in the water to make a soft dough.
2 Knead on a floured surface for 5 minutes or until smooth and elastic. Return the dough to the bowl, cover loosely and leave in a warm place to rise for 45–60 minutes.
3 Knock the dough back with your fist, then knead again. Cut into two and shape into loaves. Press into the prepared tins and cover loosely with oiled clingfilm (plastic wrap). Leave to rise for 30–40 minutes until just above the top of the tin.
4 Preheat the oven to 220°C/425°F/Gas 7. Dust the loaves with flour and cook in the oven for 25 minutes or until golden brown and the bread sounds hollow when tapped. Turn out on to a wire rack to cool. Freeze when cold.

preparation 25 minutes plus rising cooking time 25–30 minutes

Makes 2 loaves

CORIANDER NAAN BREADS

500g/1lb 2oz/4 cups strong white bread flour plus extra to dust

a handful of fresh coriander (cilantro), roughly chopped

1 tsp salt

1 tsp cumin seeds

1 tsp caster (superfine) sugar

2 tsp easy-blend dried (active dry) yeast

50g/2oz/4 tbsp butter or ghee, melted

4 tbsp low-fat natural yogurt

250ml/8fl oz/1 cup warm water

ground black pepper

1 Put the flour, coriander and cumin in a large bowl. Season with pepper and stir in the sugar, yeast and salt.
2 Add the melted butter or ghee and the yogurt, then gradually mix in enough warm water to form a soft dough.
3 Knead the dough on a lightly floured surface for 5 minutes or until smooth and elastic. Place in the bowl, cover loosely with oiled clingfilm (plastic wrap) and leave in a warm place for 45–60 minutes until doubled in size.
4 Knock the dough back with your fist, then knead well. Cut into eight pieces, then roll out each piece to a rough oval. Place on two baking sheets, cover loosely and leave to rise for 10–15 minutes until puffy.
5 Cook under a hot grill (broiler) or on a hot, ungreased griddle pan for 3–5 minutes on each side until puffed and golden brown. Serve or freeze.

preparation 30 minutes plus rising cooking time 8–10 minutes

Makes 8

ICE POPS

Ice-pop moulds can be bought in cookshops, department stores and most large supermarkets. To serve, dip the mould into a bowl filled with hot water from the tap, count to three, then flex each mould slightly and ease the ice pop from it.

All recipes serve 6

ICED COFFEE LIQUEUR

1 Mix 250ml/8fl oz/1 cup strong fresh coffee with 2 tbsp soft brown sugar, 4 tbsp double (heavy) cream and 4 tbsp coffee cream liqueur. Cool, then pour into ice-pop moulds and freeze until firm.

LEMON LIME CRUSH

1 Pare the rind from 4 unwaxed lemons with a vegetable peeler. Put the pared rind in a pan with 450ml/¾ pint/1¾ cups water and 150g/5oz/scant ⅔ cup caster (superfine) sugar. Heat gently until the sugar dissolves, then boil for 5 minutes. Leave to cool. Strain into a jug, add the juice of 2 limes, then pour into ice-pop moulds, adding a sprig of mint to each one if liked. Freeze until firm.

BANANA CUSTARD

1 Mash or purée 2 large bananas with the juice of ½ lemon, then mix with 225g/8oz/1 cup custard. Pour into ice-pop moulds and freeze until firm.
2 Dip the moulds into hot water and remove the ice pops, then dip the tip of each one into 75g/3oz melted milk chocolate and sprinkle with multicoloured sugar sprinkles. Return to the freezer on a baking sheet lined with parchment paper until firm. Wrap individually in clingfilm (plastic wrap) and pack in a plastic container before refreezing until firm.

WATERMELON

1 Put 3 tbsp caster (superfine) sugar and 3 tbsp water in a pan and heat gently, stirring until the sugar dissolves. Bring to the boil and cook for 1 minute. Take off the heat and add the grated zest and juice of 1 lime. Purée 340g/12oz seeded and diced watermelon in a blender or food processor, stir into the syrup and leave to cool. Pour into ice-pop moulds and freeze until firm.

PEACH BELLINIS

1 Halve, stone and slice 4 large ripe peaches. Place in a pan with 2 tbsp caster (superfine) sugar and 2 tbsp water. Cover and simmer gently for 10 minutes or until the peaches are soft. Purée in a food processor or blender until smooth, then rub through a sieve. Stir in 250ml/8fl oz/1 cup Prosecco or other dry sparkling white wine. Pour into ice-pop moulds and freeze until firm.

STRAWBERRY YOGURT

1 Purée 250g/9oz/2 cups strawberries, then rub through a sieve, discarding the seeds. Mix with 125g/4oz/½ cup natural Greek yogurt and 1 tbsp runny honey. Pour into ice-pop moulds and freeze until firm.

TOP 10 SMOOTHIES

BERRY ORANGE

2 oranges, peeled
50g/2oz/½ cup cranberries
50g/2oz/½ cup raspberries
1 tsp runny honey (optional)

1 Chop the orange flesh and blitz in a blender with the cranberries and raspberries until smooth. Sweeten to taste with honey and pour into two glasses.

preparation 10 minutes   *Serves 2*

PEACH CRUSH

2 ripe peaches, stoned and chopped
250g/9oz pineapple, peeled and chopped
1 small, ripe banana, peeled

1 Put all the fruit in a blender and blitz until thick and smooth. Pour into two glasses.

preparation 10 minutes   *Serves 2*

SUMMER CRUSH

175g/6oz/1½ cups strawberries, hulled
150ml/¼ pint/scant ⅔ cup pressed apple juice

1 Put the strawberries on a tray and freeze for 40 minutes or until firm. Blitz in a blender with the juice until slushy. Pour into a glass.

preparation 5 minutes plus freezing   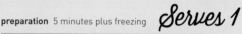 *Serves 1*

PAPAYA PASSION

½ medium papaya, peeled, seeded and chopped
juice of ½ lime
2 passion fruit

1 Blitz the papaya, lime juice and passion fruit seeds and pulp in a blender until smooth, then pour into a glass.

preparation 10 minutes   *Serves 1*

BLUE ORANGE

175g/6oz/1½ cups blueberries
2 medium oranges, peeled
1–2 tsp maple syrup

1 Chop the orange flesh, then blitz briefly in a blender with the blueberries. Taste and add maple syrup to sweeten. Pour over ice in a large glass.

preparation 10 minutes   *Serves 1*

BLACK BEAUTY

175g/6oz/1½ cups blackcurrants, stalks removed
150ml/¼ pint/scant ⅔ cup pressed apple juice
3 fresh mint sprigs
2 tsp runny honey

1 Put the blackcurrants in a blender with the
   apple juice and mint. Blitz until smooth, and
   sweeten with honey. Pour over ice cubes
   into two glasses.

preparation 10 minutes   *Serves 2*

PINK MANGO

1 pink grapefruit, peeled
300g/11oz mango, peeled and stoned
150ml/¼ pint/scant ⅔ cup pressed apple juice

1 Chop the grapefruit flesh, discarding any
   pips. Chop the mango flesh.
2 Blitz the grapefruit, mango apple juice in a
   blender until smooth. Pour into two glasses.

preparation 5 minutes   *Serves 2*

VEGGIE COMBO

375g/13oz cucumber, seeded and chopped
50g/2oz kale
150ml/¼ pint/scant ⅔ cup pressed carrot juice
ground black pepper

1 Put the cucumber, kale and carrot juice in a
   blender. Season with black pepper and blitz
   until smooth. Pour over ice in two glasses.

preparation 5 minutes   *Serves 2*

CARROT BLITZ

2 medium oranges, peeled
1cm/½in piece fresh root ginger, peeled
150ml/¼ pint/scant ⅔ cup orange juice
150ml/¼ pint/scant ⅔ cup pressed carrot juice

1 Chop the orange flesh roughly, discarding
   any pips. Chop the ginger.
2 Blitz the orange, ginger and apple and
   carrot juices in a blender until smooth.
   Divide between two glasses.

preparation 10 minutes   *Serves 2*

MEXICANA

1 small lemon, peeled
2 ripe pears, peeled, cored and chopped
1 small, ripe avocado, peeled and stoned
50g/2oz baby spinach leaves

1 Chop the lemon flesh, discarding any pips.
   Place in a blender with the chopped pear.
2 Chop the avocado roughly and add to the
   blender with the spinach. Blitz until smooth,
   then pour into a glass to serve.

preparation 5 minutes   *Serves 1*

GLUTEN FREE

If you're gluten intolerant, don't despair – we have exciting dishes for you, too. You can enjoy cooking pasta, cakes, pastries and bread with our delicious gluten-free recipes. They are not difficult to make; they taste far superior to store-bought alternatives; and all the ingredients are readily sourced from your local supermarket, deli or health food store.

Avoiding wheat and wheat products is easy if you follow our simple recipes. There are many alternatives to wheat flour – including rice flour and xanthan gum – and our cakes and bakes taste just as good as those made the conventional way. Be sure to use gluten-free baking powder and gluten-free oats – unless they are labeled as such, don't cook with them.

We've got an exciting array of savoury dishes from around the world, including Greek pastitsio, South African bobotie and pad Thai, as well as French spinach and salmon crêpes and a pasta bake made with spicy Spanish chorizo.

Among the baking recipes you'll find gluten-free versions of old favourites like carrot cake and cheese straws, as well as flat breads and an unusual seedy soda bread. And there are delicious raspberry drizzle cakes and some sweet muffins made with store-cupboard ingredients.

< Pad Thai (page 549)

CHICKEN PASTA BAKE

250g/9oz cherry tomatoes,
450g/1lb chicken breasts
1.2 litres/2 pints/5 cups gluten-free chicken stock
a large pinch of saffron
500g/1lb 2oz gluten-free pasta
3 garlic cloves, crushed
a handful of fresh basil leaves, torn, plus extra to garnish
250g/9oz gluten-free chorizo sausage, thickly sliced
50g/2oz/⅓ cup black olives
2 tbsp olive oil
salt and ground black pepper

1 Preheat the oven to 180°C/350°F/Gas 4.
2 Cut the cherry tomatoes in half. Skin the chicken breasts and cut the flesh into chunks.
3 Bring the stock to the boil in a pan, stir in the saffron and set aside to infuse for 5 minutes.
4 Put the pasta in a large casserole. Stir the garlic into the hot saffron stock and pour over the pasta. Add the basil and season with salt and pepper. Scatter the tomato halves, chicken, chorizo and olives over the top.
5 Drizzle with the oil, then cover and cook in the oven for 30 minutes. Stir well, then return to the oven, uncovered, for 20–30 minutes until the chicken is browned and cooked through and the top is golden.
6 Garnish with basil and serve in shallow bowls.

preparation 20 minutes   cooking time 1 hour

Serves 4

PASTITSIO

1 tbsp olive oil
450g/1lb minced (ground) lamb
1 onion, finely chopped
2 garlic cloves, crushed
1 aubergine (eggplant), diced
1 x 400g/14oz can tomatoes
200ml/7fl oz/¾ cup gluten-free lamb stock
250ml/8fl oz/1 cup red wine
340g/12oz gluten-free pasta
250g/9oz/1½ cups cream cheese
2 medium eggs, beaten
4 tbsp freshly grated Parmesan
salt and ground black pepper

1 Heat the oil in a pan over a low heat. Fry the lamb and onion for 5 minutes, stirring until the meat is browned. Mix in the garlic and aubergine and cook for 3–4 minutes.
2 Stir in the tomatoes, stock, wine and seasoning. Bring to the boil, then reduce the heat, cover the pan and simmer gently for 45 minutes.
3 Preheat the oven to 190°C/375°F/Gas 5. Cook the pasta according to the instructions on the pack. Drain well.
4 Add the cream cheese to the pasta pan and beat in the eggs. Season with salt and pepper. Gently stir in the pasta.
5 Spoon the meat mixture into a large ovenproof dish and spoon the pasta in an even layer over the top. Sprinkle with grated Parmesan and bake in the oven for 30–35 minutes until the topping is golden brown.

preparation 30 minutes   cooking time 1¼ hours

Serves 4

BOBOTIE

1 tbsp sunflower oil

450g/1lb minced (ground) beef

1 onion, finely chopped

2 garlic cloves, crushed

4 tsp medium-hot curry powder

1 tbsp apricot jam (jelly)

1 tbsp tomato paste

2 tbsp red wine vinegar

1 carrot, grated

1 small banana, peeled and diced

3 tbsp raisins

50g/2oz/⅓ cup red lentils

4 bay leaves

2 medium eggs

200ml/7fl oz/¾ cup milk

salt and ground black pepper

1 Preheat the oven to 180°C/350°F/Gas 4.
2 Heat the oil in a frying pan over a medium heat, and fry the beef and onion for 5 minutes, stirring until the beef is browned and the onion is just tender.
3 Stir in the garlic, curry powder, jam, tomato paste, vinegar, carrot, banana, raisins and lentils. Season and press into a large rectangular ovenproof dish and smooth the top.
4 Place the bay leaves on top. Beat the eggs and milk together with a little salt and pepper and pour over the bay leaves.
5 Bake in the oven for 40–45 minutes until the topping is set and golden and the meat is cooked. Check after 30 minutes and loosely cover the top with foil if it's browning too quickly.
6 Set aside to cool for 15 minutes, then serve cut into slices.

preparation 20 minutes **cooking time** 45–50 minutes plus cooling

Serves 4

SALMON CREPES

4 x 125g/4oz skinned salmon fillets

200g/7oz baby spinach leaves

2 tbsp sunflower oil

150g/5oz/⅔ cup crème fraîche

4 tbsp freshly grated Parmesan

salt and ground black pepper

For the crêpes

75g/3oz/¾ cup fine polenta

75g/3oz/¾ cup rice flour

a pinch of grated nutmeg

2 medium eggs

2 tbsp freshly grated Parmesan

200ml/7fl oz/¾ cup milk

1 Preheat the grill and line the grill rack with foil.
2 Lay the salmon on top. Season and grill for 10–12 minutes, turning once, until golden brown and cooked. Flake the salmon, discarding the skin and bones. Keep warm.
3 Cook the spinach with 1 tsp water in a covered pan over a low heat until it wilts. Drain well, pressing down with a plate.
4 Put half the spinach in a blender or food processor with the crêpe ingredients and blitz until smooth. Pour into a jug.
5 Heat a little oil in a frying pan over a medium heat. Pour in one-quarter of the crêpe batter, tilting the pan to swirl it evenly over the surface. Cook until golden brown underneath, then flip over and cook the other side. Slide out on to a plate and make three more crêpes in the same way.
6 Spoon the remaining spinach on to each crêpe and pile the salmon on top. Spoon the crème fraîche and Parmesan over. Roll up the crêpes and serve.

preparation 20 minutes **cooking time** 25 minutes

Serves 4

BEETROOT AND BEAN CHILLI

1 small dried chipotle chilli

2 red (bell) peppers

5 beetroot (beets)

1 tbsp sunflower oil

1 large onion, chopped

2 garlic cloves, crushed

1 tsp dark brown sugar

1 x 400g/14oz can black beans, drained and rinsed

1 x 400g/14oz can tomatoes

300ml/½ pint/1¼ cups gluten-free vegetable stock

salt and ground black pepper

Greek yogurt, gluten-free corn chips and grated cheese to serve

1 Soak the chilli in a bowl of boiling water for 5 minutes, then chop and set aside. Halve and seed the red peppers and cut into dice. Trim, peel and cube the beetroot.

2 Heat the oil in a large pan over a low heat and fry the onion for 5 minutes or until beginning to soften and turn golden. Add most of the red pepper with the beetroot, garlic and sugar.

3 Stir in the black beans, tomatoes, stock, chopped chilli and the soaking liquid. Season with salt and pepper. Bring to the boil, then reduce the heat, cover and simmer gently for 35–40 minutes, stirring occasionally, until the beetroot is just tender.

4 Spoon into four shallow bowls. Top the chilli with spoonfuls of yogurt, corn chips and grated cheese. Sprinkle the remaining red pepper over the top and serve.

preparation 20 minutes   cooking time 35–40 minutes

Serves 4

PAD THAI

250g/9oz flat rice noodles

2 carrots

4 spring onions (scallions)

2 tbsp sunflower oil

225g/8oz raw prawns (shrimp)

300g/11oz beansprouts

2 medium eggs

gluten-free Thai fish sauce

2 tsp light brown sugar

1 red chilli, seeded and diced

juice of 2 limes

4 tbsp chopped salted peanuts

a large handful of fresh coriander (cilantro) chopped, and cucumber strips to serve

1 Cook the noodles in boiling water for 5 minutes or according to the instructions on the pack. Drain well. Meanwhile, cut the carrots and spring onions into matchsticks.

2 Heat the oil in a wok or deep frying pan over a high heat, add the carrots and stir-fry for 2 minutes. Add the spring onions and stir-fry for 1 minute. Add the prawns and stir-fry for 2 minutes. Stir in the beansprouts and stir-fry briskly for 1–2 minutes.

3 Beat the eggs with 2–3 tbsp Thai fish sauce, the sugar, chilli and juice of 1 lime. Add the noodles to the wok together with the peanuts and egg mixture and stir-fry until the egg is just beginning to cook. Taste and add more fish sauce if needed.

4 Spoon into bowls and garnish with the coriander and cucumber. Squeeze the juice of the other lime over the top.

preparation 10 minutes plus soaking   cooking time 10 minutes

Serves 4

PECORINO CHEESE STRAWS

50g/2oz/½ cup fine polenta

75g/3oz/¾ cup rice flour plus extra to dust

75g/3oz/6 tbsp butter, diced

1 tsp gluten-free mustard powder

2 tsp chopped fresh thyme

75g/3oz/½ cup grated pecorino cheese

2 medium eggs

salt and ground black pepper

1 Preheat the oven to 180°C/350°F/Gas 4.
2 Put the polenta and flour in a bowl and rub in the butter until it resembles fine breadcrumbs. Stir in the mustard, salt and pepper, half the thyme and two-thirds of the cheese. In a bowl, beat one egg with a fork and add to the flour mixture. Beat the other egg and add enough to make a soft dough.
3 Roll out the dough between two sheets of parchment paper, lightly dusted with rice flour, to form a 25cm/10in square. Peel off the top piece of parchment, cut the dough in half, then cut each half into thin strips about 1cm/½in wide. Brush lightly with some of the remaining beaten egg.
4 Lift the paper on to a large baking sheet. Sprinkle with the remaining thyme and cheese and a little black pepper.
5 Bake in the oven for 10 minutes or until golden brown. Leave the cheese straws to cool on the paper. Store in an airtight plastic container for up to three days.

preparation 25 minutes   cooking time 10 minutes plus cooling

Makes 30

CHEDDAR GRIDDLE CAKES

1 tbsp olive oil plus extra to cook the cakes

125g/4oz leek, thinly sliced

50g/2oz/4 tbsp butter

125g/4oz/1 cup potato flour

125g/4oz/1 cup rice flour plus extra to dust

1 tsp gluten-free baking powder

125g/4oz/1 cup grated Cheddar cheese

1 medium egg, beaten

6–8 tbsp milk

salt and ground black pepper

1 Heat the oil in a frying pan over a low heat, add the leek and cook for 5 minutes or until softened. Take the pan off the heat, add the butter and stir until melted.
2 Put the flours and baking powder in a bowl and stir in the cheese and a little salt and pepper. Add the leek, butter and beaten egg. Stir in enough milk to make a soft dough.
3 Cut the dough in half and roll out on a floured surface to two 15cm/6in circles. Cut each one into four wedges.
4 Reheat the frying pan over a medium heat, add a little oil and cook the four potato cakes for 8 minutes, turning once or twice, until golden brown. Remove and wrap in a clean teatowel (dishtowel) to keep warm while you cook the remaining potato cakes in the same way. Serve hot.

preparation 15 minutes   cooking time 20 minutes

Makes 8

ORCHARD PUDDING

125g/4oz/½ cup butter, diced, plus extra to grease

2 pears

2 dessert apples

340g/12oz plums

150g/5oz/scant ⅔ cup caster (superfine) sugar

grated zest and juice of 1 lemon

75g/3oz/¾ cup rice flour

3 tbsp gluten-free cornflour (cornstarch)

1 tsp gluten-free baking powder

2 medium eggs

2 tbsp milk

1 Preheat the oven to 180°C/350°F/Gas 4. Butter a large deep baking dish.

2 Peel, core and slice the pears and apples. Stone the plums and cut into slices. Place the fruit in the baking dish and sprinkle with 3 tbsp sugar and the juice of ½ lemon. Bake in the oven, uncovered, for 15 minutes.

3 Meanwhile, mix the flours and baking powder together in a bowl. Cream the butter and remaining sugar until light and fluffy. Beat in the eggs, one at a time, then gradually mix in the flour. Add the milk, lemon zest and remaining lemon juice. Spoon it over the fruit and level the top.

4 Bake in the oven for 25 minutes or until the topping is golden and well risen. Serve warm.

preparation 40 minutes cooking time 40 minutes

Serves 6

GLUTEN-FREE WALNUT BREAD

sunflower oil to grease

450g/1lb/4½ cups gluten-free bread flour

1 tsp salt

2 tbsp light brown sugar

2 tsp easy-blend dried yeast

1 tsp white wine vinegar

6 tbsp olive oil

2 medium eggs

75g/3oz/scant ¾ cup walnut pieces

2 tbsp sunflower seeds

1 Lightly brush two 450g/1lb loaf tins with oil. Put the flour, salt, sugar and yeast in a large bowl. In a separate bowl, lightly beat together the vinegar, oil and eggs, then stir into the dry ingredients and mix in about 325ml/11fl oz/1½ cups warm water to make a smooth, thick mixture.

2 Stir in the walnuts, then divide the bread mixture between the prepared tins. Sprinkle with the sunflower seeds and loosely cover the tins with oiled clingfilm (plastic wrap) and leave in a warm place for 45–60 minutes until well risen.

3 Preheat the oven to 220°C/425°F/Gas 7. Remove the clingfilm (plastic wrap), put the tins on a baking sheet and cook in the oven for 30–40 minutes until well risen, golden brown and the bread sounds hollow when gently tapped. Turn out on to a wire rack to cool. Serve warm or cold.

preparation 15 minutes plus rising cooking time 30–40 minutes plus cooling

Makes 2 loaves

APRICOT MUFFINS

175g/6oz/1½ cups rice flour

75g/3oz/¾ cup tapioca flour

150g/5oz/scant ⅔ cup caster (superfine) sugar

2½ tsp gluten-free baking powder

½ tsp xanthan gum

50g/2oz/4 tbsp butter, melted

2 medium eggs

200g/7oz/¾ cup natural yogurt

1 tsp vanilla extract

125g/4oz/¾ cup ready-to-eat dried apricots, diced

2 tbsp dried goji berries

2 tbsp hulled sunflower seeds

1 Preheat the oven to 190°C/375°F/Gas 5. Line a 12-hole muffin tin with paper cases.

2 Mix the flours, sugar, baking powder and xanthan gum together in a large bowl. In a separate bowl, mix the butter, eggs, yogurt and vanilla extract together, then pour into the dry ingredients and fork together until only just mixed. Add the apricots and goji berries and stir briefly – the briefer the mixing, the lighter the muffins will be.

3 Spoon the mixture into the muffin cases and sprinkle with sunflower seeds. Bake in the oven for 15 minutes or until well risen, golden brown and the tops are firm when pressed with a fingertip. Cool for 10 minutes, then serve while still warm.

preparation 20 minutes   cooking time 15 minutes

Makes 12

SEEDY DATE SODA BREAD

sunflower oil to grease

50g/2oz/⅓ cup golden flaxseeds, ground

50g/2oz/½ cup hemp flour

125g/4oz/1 cup rice flour

1 tsp bicarbonate of soda (baking soda)

½ tsp salt

½ tsp xanthan gum

2 tbsp light brown sugar

3 tbsp sunflower seeds

3 tbsp pumpkin seeds

75g/3oz/½ cup chopped dates

300ml/½ pint/1¼ cups buttermilk

1 Preheat the oven to 200°C/400°F/Gas 6. Lightly grease an 18cm/7in round deep cake tin.

2 Put the ground flaxseeds in a mixing bowl, then sift in the hemp and rice flours, bicarbonate of soda, salt and xanthan gum. Stir in the sugar, 2 tbsp each of the sunflower and pumpkin seeds and the dates, then mix in the buttermilk with a fork to make a soft dropping consistency, adding a little water if needed.

3 Spoon into the prepared tin, level the surface and sprinkle with the remaining seeds, pressing the seeds into the top.

4 Bake in the oven for 35–40 minutes until well risen and golden brown and the bread sounds hollow when tapped. Turn out of the tin. Wrap in a clean tea towel (dishtowel) for a soft crust or leave unwrapped for a crisp crust. Serve the bread warm or cold, cut into slices.

preparation 20 minutes   cooking time 35–40 minutes

Makes 1 loaf

MINI CARROT CAKES

150ml/¼ pint/scant ⅔ cup sunflower oil

3 tbsp runny honey

3 medium eggs

115g/4oz/½ cup brown sugar

150g/5oz carrots, grated

2 pieces preserved ginger in syrup, drained and chopped

125g/4oz/¾ cup rice flour

50g/2oz/½ cup tapioca flour

2 tsp gluten-free baking powder

2 tsp ground ginger

200g/7oz/¾ cup mascarpone

50g/2oz/½ cup gluten-free icing (confectioner's) sugar

¼ tsp ground ginger

1 Preheat the oven to 180°C/350°F/Gas 4. Oil and line eight small loaf tins (10 x 5 x 3cm/4 x 2 x 1¼in) and place on a baking sheet.

2 Put the honey, eggs, brown sugar and oil in a bowl and whisk together until smooth. Stir in the carrots and ginger.

3 Sift the flours, baking powder and ground ginger over the carrot mixture and stir until smooth. Divide among the prepared loaf tins and bake in the oven for 20 minutes or until risen, the tops feel firm and a skewer inserted into the middle comes out clean. Turn out on to a wire rack to cool.

4 Beat the mascarpone with the icing sugar and ground ginger, then spread over the cakes. Store in a plastic container in the fridge for up to two days.

preparation 25 minutes   cooking time 20 minutes plus cooling

Makes 8

ORANGE SHORTBREAD

50g/2oz/½ cup gluten-free
cornflour (cornstarch)

125g/4oz/1 cup rice flour

75g/3oz/¾ cup ground almonds

75g/3oz/6 tbsp caster (superfine)
sugar, plus extra to sprinkle

175g/6oz/¾ cup butter, diced

grated zest of ½ orange

1 tbsp chopped fresh rosemary

1 Preheat the oven to 170°C/325°F/Gas 3.
2 Put the cornflour and rice flour in a bowl. Add the ground almonds and sugar, then rub in the butter with your fingertips until the mixture resembles breadcrumbs.
3 Add the orange zest and rosemary and stir until the mixture sticks together to form a ball. Tip into a 25cm/10in loose-bottomed tart tin and press down evenly. Mark the edge of the shortbread with the tines of a fork and prick the centre.
4 Bake in the oven for 30–35 minutes until the shortbread is pale golden. Cool in the tin for a few minutes, then mark into 12 wedges. Sprinkle with caster sugar and set aside to cool completely. Remove from the tin and cut into wedges. Store in an airtight tin for up to three days.

preparation 20 minutes   cooking time 30–35 minutes plus cooling

Makes 12 pieces

CHOCOLATE ALMOND COOKIES

75g/3oz/6 tbsp butter, diced

175g/6oz/¾ cup caster
(superfine) sugar

2 tbsp cocoa powder

6 tbsp rice flour

50g/2oz/½ cup tapioca flour

2 tsp gluten-free baking powder

1 medium egg

75g/3oz/¾ cup ground almonds

100g/3½oz gluten-free milk
chocolate, diced

25g/1oz/¼ cup flaked almonds

1 Preheat the oven to 190°C/375°F/Gas 5. Line two large baking sheets with parchment paper.
2 Cream the butter and sugar together in a bowl or food processor until light and fluffy. Sift the cocoa, flours and baking powder into the creamed mixture, then add the egg and beat until smooth.
3 Stir in the ground almonds and diced chocolate. Spoon into 24 mounds on the prepared baking sheets, leaving space for them to spread. Sprinkle with the flaked almonds and bake in the oven for 8–10 minutes until the tops are cracked.
4 Leave to cool on the paper. Lift off the paper and store in an airtight container for up to three days.

preparation 20 minutes   cooking time 10 minutes plus cooling

Makes 24

LEMON AND LIME TART

grated zest and juice of 2 lemons
grated zest and juice of 2 limes
225g/8oz/1 cup caster (superfine) sugar
150g/5oz/⅔ cup butter, diced
4 medium eggs
2 egg yolks
gluten-free icing (confectioner's) sugar to dust
blackberries and blueberries to serve

For the almond pastry
125g/4oz/1 cup rice flour plus extra to dust
50g/2oz/½ cup tapioca flour
½ tsp xanthan gum
50g/2oz/½ cup ground almonds
2 tbsp caster (superfine) sugar
125g/4oz/½ cup butter, diced
1 medium egg

1 To make the pastry, blitz the flours, xanthan gum, almonds, sugar and butter in a food processor. Add the egg and mix in about 1 tbsp cold water, if needed, to make a soft but not sticky dough. Squeeze into a ball.

2 Dust your fingers with rice flour and press the dough over the bottom and up the sides of a 25cm/10in loose-bottomed fluted tart tin, making a thin even layer. Prick the base with a fork. Chill in the refrigerator for 15–30 minutes.

3 Preheat the oven to 190°C/375°F/Gas 5. Line the pastry with parchment paper and baking beans and bake in the oven for 10 minutes. Carefully remove the paper and beans and return to the oven for 5–8 minutes until the bottom of the pastry is cooked through.

4 Meanwhile, make the filling: put the lemon and lime zest and juice in a pan with the caster sugar and butter. Cook over a low heat, stirring, until the butter has melted and the sugar dissolved. Set aside to cool for 10 minutes, then gradually stir in the eggs and egg yolks, until smooth.

5 Pour the filling into the pastry shell. Reduce the oven temperature to 140°C/275°F/Gas 1 and cook the tart for 30–40 minutes until the filling is set.

6 Remove from the oven and set aside to cool. When cold, carefully remove the tart from the tin and transfer to a serving plate. Dust with a little sifted icing sugar and scatter the berries over. Serve cut into slices.

preparation 35 minutes plus chilling   **cooking time** 40–50 minutes plus cooling

Serves 8

CINNAMON PANCAKES

6 tbsp fine polenta

5 tbsp tapioca flour

a large pinch of ground cinnamon

1 tsp bicarbonate of soda (baking soda)

1 medium egg

200g/7oz/¾ cup natural yogurt plus extra to serve

2 tbsp sunflower oil

ground cinnamon to serve

For the fruit compote

3 tbsp caster (superfine) sugar

2 tsp gluten-free cornflour (cornstarch)

juice of ½ lemon

225g/8oz/2 cups blueberries

1 To make the compote, put the sugar and cornflour in a small pan and stir in the lemon juice to a paste. Add the blueberries and cook over a low heat, stirring occasionally, until they soften and the juices thicken.
2 To make the pancakes, mix the polenta, tapioca flour, cinnamon and bicarbonate of soda together in a bowl. Add the egg, yogurt and 4 tbsp cold water and mix to a smooth, thick batter.
3 Pour a little oil into a large frying pan, wipe off the excess with kitchen paper, then heat the pan over a medium heat. Add 1 heaped tbsp of the pancake batter, leaving a little space in between. Cook until the underside is golden and bubbles are just beginning to appear on the surface.
4 Turn the pancakes over and cook the other side. Remove and wrap in a clean teatowel (dishtowel) to keep warm. Make the remaining pancakes in the same way.
5 Divide the pancakes among four warmed plates and drizzle with the warm compote. Serve with spoonfuls of yogurt and a dusting of cinnamon.

preparation 25 minutes **cooking time** 15 minutes

Serves 4

RASPBERRY DRIZZLE CAKES

175g/6oz/¾ cup butter, diced, plus extra to grease

175g/6oz/¾ cup caster (superfine) sugar

grated zest and juice of 2 lemons

3 medium eggs

175g/6oz/1½ cups gluten-free white self-raising (self-rising) flour

3 tbsp milk

125g/4oz/1 cup raspberries

150g/5oz/scant ⅔ cup granulated sugar

1 Preheat the oven to 180°C/350°F/Gas 4. Butter eight small rectangular cake tins (10 x 5 x 3cm/4 x 2 x 1¼in) and line the bottoms with a strip of parchment paper.
2 Cream the butter, caster sugar and lemon zest in a bowl until light and fluffy. Beat in the eggs, one at a time, then stir in the flour. Add the milk to make a soft, creamy mixture.
3 Divide among the prepared tins, then press the raspberries lightly into the top of the cakes. Bake in the oven for 20 minutes or until well risen, golden brown and a skewer inserted into the middle comes out clean. Set aside to cool.
4 Mix the granulated sugar with the lemon juice. Spoon a little over the hot cakes, then leave to cool completely for a sugary crust to develop.

preparation 25 minutes **cooking time** 18–20 minutes plus cooling

Makes 8

TRIPLE CHOCOLATE FINGERS

50g/2oz/4 tbsp butter

50g/2oz gluten-free milk chocolate, chopped

75g/3oz gluten-free plain (semi-sweet) chocolate, chopped

2 tbsp golden (corn) syrup

175g/6oz gluten-free digestive biscuits (graham crackers), broken into small pieces

100g/3½oz gluten-free white chocolate, chopped

3 tbsp dried cranberries, diced

3 tbsp pistachios, chopped

50g/2oz/⅓ cup diced dried apricots

1 Line a 20cm/8in square shallow tin with parchment paper.
2 Put the butter, milk and plain chocolate and syrup in a pan and heat very gently, stirring occasionally, until the butter and chocolate melt and the mixture is smooth. Remove from the heat and stir in the biscuits.
3 Put the mixture in the prepared tin and press down evenly, levelling the top. Chill in the refrigerator for 30 minutes.
4 Melt the white chocolate in a bowl over a pan of gently simmering water. Drizzle over the set biscuit layer. Sprinkle the cranberries, pistachios and apricots over the top, then chill in the refrigerator for 2 hours or until set.
5 To serve, lift out of the tin and peel away the paper. Cut into 3 bars, then cut each bar into 5 fingers. Store in the refrigerator for up to three days.

preparation 15 minutes plus chilling

Makes 15

TOP 10 BAKED POTATOES

CHEESE AND BACON

2 hot baked potatoes, halved
2 tbsp low-fat yogurt
15g/½oz/1 tbsp butter
2 spring onions (scallions), diced
3 grilled bacon rashers (slices), crumbled
50g/2oz/½ cup grated Cheddar cheese

1 Scoop out the potato flesh and mash with the yogurt and butter. Stir in the spring onions, bacon and cheese.
2 Spoon into the potato skins and pop under a hot grill for 2–3 minutes.

preparation 5 minutes plus baking
cooking time 2–3 minutes

COTTAGE CHEESE

1 grilled red (bell) pepper, skinned, seeded and diced
50g/2oz/⅓ cup cottage cheese
2 tbsp chopped fresh parsley
2 hot baked potatoes, halved
2 tbsp low-fat fromage frais
15g/½oz/1 tbsp butter

1 Mix together the grilled red pepper, cottage cheese and parsley.
2 Mash the potato flesh with the fromage frais and butter. Stir in the pepper mixture and spoon into the shells.

preparation 5 minutes
plus baking and grilling

Serves 2

MUSHROOM

125g/4oz button mushrooms, sliced
1 garlic clove, crushed
25g/1oz/2 tbsp butter
4 tbsp fat-free fromage frais
2 tbsp chopped fresh parsley
2 hot baked potatoes, halved

1 Fry the mushrooms and garlic in half the butter until golden. Mix with the fromage frais and parsley.
2 Mash the potato flesh with the rest of the butter. Spoon into the potato skins and top with the mushrooms.

preparation 5 minutes plus baking
cooking time 5 minutes

STIR-FRY

1 red or yellow (bell pepper), seeded and diced
4 spring onions (scallions), thinly sliced
1 red chilli, diced
1 tsp oil
a dash of soy sauce
2 hot baked potatoes, halved
15g/½oz/1 tbsp butter
2 tbsp chopped fresh coriander (cilantro)

1 Stir-fry the pepper, spring onions and chilli in the oil for 3 minutes. Add the soy sauce.
2 Mash the potato flesh with the butter and spoon into the shells. Top with the vegetables and coriander.

preparation 5 minutes plus baking
cooking time 3 minutes

Serves 2

HERBY TOMATO

2 hot baked potatoes, halved
2 tbsp natural fromage frais
50g/2oz sunblush tomatoes, chopped
3 tbsp chopped fresh chives

1 Mash the potato flesh with the fromage
   frais. Add the tomatoes and chives and
   spoon into the potato shells.

preparation 5 minutes plus baking

 Serves 2

LOW-FAT PRAWNS

2 hot baked potatoes, halved
4 tbsp low-fat fromage frais
1 tsp lite mayonnaise
175g/6oz peeled cooked prawns (shrimp)
a few fresh basil leaves, chopped

1 Mash the potato flesh with the fromage
   frais. Stir in the mayonnaise, prawns and
   basil. Spoon into the potato shells.

preparation 5 minutes plus baking

 Serves 2

TUNA MAYO

2 hot baked potatoes, halved
2 tbsp low-fat fromage frais
15g/½oz/1 tbsp butter
1 x 200g/7oz can tuna, drained
2 tbsp lite mayonnaise
2 tbsp chopped fresh parsley

1 Mash the potato flesh with the fromage frais
   and butter. Mix in the tuna, mayonnaise and
   parsley and spoon into the shells.

preparation 5 minutes plus baking

 Serves 2

BAKED BEANS

2 hot baked potatoes, halved
2 tbsp low-fat fromage frais
15g/½oz/1 tbsp butter
1 x 200g/7oz can baked beans

1 Mash the potato flesh with the fromage frais
   and butter and spoon back into the shells.
2 Heat the baked beans in a pan for
   3–4 minutes. Pile on top of the potatoes.

preparation 5 minutes plus baking
cooking time 3–4 minutes

 Serves 2

COLESLAW

2 hot baked potatoes, halved
2 tbsp low-fat fromage frais
15g/½oz/1 tbsp butter
4 tbsp coleslaw
4 tbsp grated Cheddar cheese

1 Mash the potato flesh with the fromage frais
   and butter. Spoon into the shells and top
   with the coleslaw and grated cheese.

preparation 5 minutes plus baking

Serves 2

ASIAN CHICKEN

150g/5oz boneless, skinless chicken breast
2 spring onions (scallions), diced
2 tbsp natural fromage frais
a dash of sweet chilli sauce
2 hot baked potatoes, halved

1 Grill the chicken breast for 15 minutes or
   until cooked through. Dice and mix with the
   spring onion, fromage frais and chilli sauce.
2 Pile on top of the baked potatoes.

preparation 5 minutes plus baking
cooking time 15 minutes

 Serves 2

BASIC RECIPES

This final section is dedicated to all the basic recipes you will need to make your life in the kitchen simpler. As well as all the old standbys – savoury stocks, gravy, shortcrust pastry and white sauce (béchamel) – there are some unusual recipes for a wide range of stuffings, embellished with herbs, spices and fruit, for chicken, goose and turkey.

The sauces featured include classic savoury ones, such as festive Cumberland and cranberry sauces, classic hollandaise and creamy mayonnaise, as well as aromatic pesto, rouille and salsa verde. There's even a recipe for homemade tomato ketchup. Among the sweet sauces you will find out how to make real custard, a quick chocolate sauce and fresh raspberry coulis, as well as crème pâtissière and Chantilly cream for special occasions.

For the adventurous pastry chef, we tell you how to make your own melting puff pastry or an easier flaky version, as well as choux pastry, suet crust and even gluten-free pie crust.

And, lastly, we have a range of icings and frostings to add the finishing touches to your cakes – from basic buttercream to glossy chocolate ganache.

< Pesto (page 574)

FISH STOCK

1kg/2¼lb fish bones and trimmings

2 carrots, chopped

1 onion, chopped

2 celery sticks, chopped

1 bouquet garni (see page 10)

6 white peppercorns and ½ tsp sea salt

1 Put the fish bones and trimmings, the vegetables, 900ml/1½ pints/3⅔ cups cold water, the bouquet garni, peppercorns and salt in a pan. Bring to the boil and skim the surface. Cover and simmer for 30 minutes.
2 Strain the stock through a fine sieve into a bowl. When cool, cover and keep in the refrigerator for up to 2 days.

Makes 900ml/1½ pints/3⅔ cups

preparation 10 minutes   cooking time 35 minutes

BONE STOCK

1kg/2¼lb meat bones, fresh or from cooked meat

2 onions, roughly chopped

2 celery sticks, roughly chopped

2 carrots, roughly chopped

1 tsp salt and 3 black peppercorns

1 bouquet garni

1 Chop the bones. Place them with the vegetables, salt, peppercorns, herbs and 2l/3½ pints/8¾ cups water in a pan. Bring to the boil and skim off any scum. Cover and simmer for 3 hours.
2 Strain and remove the fat when cold. Store in the refrigerator for up to three days.

Makes 1.1l/2 pints/5 cups

preparation 10 minutes   cooking time 3 hours

BEEF STOCK

1.6kg/3½lb mixed beef bones: shin, rib or sawn marrow bones

2 tbsp oil

3 streaky bacon rashers (slices), chopped

2 onions, roughly chopped

2 carrots, sliced

3 celery sticks, sliced

3 fresh thyme sprigs

2 bay leaves

½ tsp salt

½ tsp black peppercorns

1 Preheat the oven to 190°C/375°F/Gas 5. Put the bones in a roasting pan, drizzle with 1 tbsp oil and cook for 45 minutes or until browned.
2 Heat the remaining oil in a large pan over a low heat, add the bacon and onions and cook gently for 10 minutes or until the onions are tender and golden.
3 Add the carrots, celery, herbs, salt and pepper and browned bones with 2.8 litres/ 5 pints/12½ cups cold water, or enough to cover the bones by about 5cm/2in. Bring slowly to the boil over a low heat. Skim off any foamy scum with a slotted spoon, then partially cover the pan and simmer gently for 3 hours.
4 Strain through a fine sieve into a bowl. Set aside to cool, then skim off the fat. Store in the refrigerator for up to three days.

Makes 2.6l/4½ pints/11¼ cups

preparation 10 minutes   cooking time 4 hours

CHICKEN STOCK

1.6kg/3½lb raw chicken bones
2 onions, roughly chopped
1 large leek, roughly chopped
2 celery sticks, roughly chopped
1 bouquet garni
1 tsp black peppercorns and ½ tsp sea salt

1 Put the chicken bones in a large pan with
   the vegetables, 3l/5¼ pints/13 cups cold
   water, the bouquet garni, peppercorns and
   salt. Bring slowly to the boil and skim the
   surface. Partially cover the pan and simmer
   gently for 2 hours. Check the seasoning.
2 Strain through a fine sieve into a bowl and
   remove the fat. When cold, cover and keep
   in the refrigerator for up to three days.

Makes 1.1l/2 pints/5 cups

preparation 10 minutes   **cooking time** 2 hours

BASIC GRAVY

hot fat from the roast
300–450ml/½ –¾ pint/1¼–1¾ cups vegetable
water or stock

1 Pour the fat from a corner of the roasting
   pan, leaving the sediment behind. Put the
   pan on the hob over a medium heat and
   pour in the vegetable water, or chicken,
   vegetable or meat stock.
2 Stir well, scraping up the sediment, and boil
   until the gravy is a rich brown colour.

Makes 300ml/½ pint/1¼ cups

preparation 2 minutes   **cooking time** 2–3 minutes

VEGETABLE STOCK

2 onions, roughly chopped
3 celery sticks, roughly chopped
2 leeks, roughly chopped
3 carrots, roughly chopped
2 bay leaves
a few fresh thyme sprigs
1 small bunch of fresh parsley
10 black peppercorns
½ tsp sea salt

1 Put the onions, celery, leeks and carrots in
   a large pan. Add 1.7 litres/3 pints/7½ cups
   cold water, the herbs, peppercorns and
   salt. Bring slowly to the boil, then skim any
   foamy scum off the surface. Partially cover
   the pan and simmer for 30 minutes. Check
   the seasoning.
2 Strain the stock through a fine sieve into a
   bowl and leave to cool. Cover and keep in
   the refrigerator for up to three days.

Makes 1.1l/2 pints/5 cups

preparation 10 minutes   **cooking time** 35 minutes

MUSHROOM STUFFING

50g/2oz/4 tbsp butter

2 onions, finely chopped

450g/1lb mushrooms, roughly chopped

4 tbsp chopped fresh parsley

4 tbsp pinenuts (pignoli)

125g/4oz/2 cups fresh white breadcrumbs

1 large (US extra-large) egg, beaten

salt and ground black pepper

1 Melt the butter in a pan and cook the onions over a low heat for 7–10 minutes until soft and golden. Add the mushrooms and fry for 4–5 minutes until softened and the moisture has evaporated. Turn into a bowl. Mix in the parsley, pinenuts and breadcrumbs. Set aside to cool.
2 Add the beaten egg and mix well to bind the stuffing. Season with salt and pepper.
3 Use to stuff a 4.5kg/10lb turkey.

Serves 10

preparation 15 minutes
cooking time 15 minutes plus cooling

CHESTNUT STUFFING

450g/1lb fresh chestnuts

25g/1oz/2 tbsp butter

2 onions, finely chopped

1 apple, peeled, cored and chopped

340g/12oz/6 cups fresh white breadcrumbs

2 tbsp finely chopped fresh sage

salt and ground black pepper

1 Preheat the oven to 200°C/400°F/Gas 6.
2 Make a small incision in each chestnut. Bake in the oven for 10 minutes. Peel when cool, then simmer in a pan of salted water for 20 minutes. Drain and chop.
3 Meanwhile, melt the butter in a pan over a low heat and fry the onions until soft. Remove from the heat, stir in the chestnuts, apple, breadcrumbs, sage and seasoning. Set aside to cool.
4 When cold, use to stuff a 4.5kg/10lb turkey.

Serves 10

preparation 15 minutes
cooking time 30 minutes plus cooling

CRANBERRY STUFFING

225g/8oz/1 cup wild rice

225g/8oz streaky bacon, cut into strips

2 red onions, finely chopped

2 sticks celery, chopped

75g/3oz/½ cup dried cranberries

1 large (US extra-large) egg, beaten

salt and ground black pepper

Serves 10

preparation 5 minutes
cooking time 15 minutes plus cooling

1 Cook the rice according to the instructions on the pack. Drain and cool.
2 Meanwhile, cook the bacon in a pan until crisp and brown. Remove and cool. Add the onions and celery to the pan and cook in the bacon fat for 7–10 minutes until softened. Leave to cool.
3 Mix the cold rice, bacon and onions with the cranberries and bind with beaten egg. Season to taste. Use to stuff a 4.5kg/10lb turkey or goose.

HERB AND LEMON STUFFING

40g/1½oz/3 tbsp butter
1 onion, finely chopped
2 garlic cloves, crushed
125g/4oz/2 cups fresh white breadcrumbs
4 tbsp chopped fresh parsley
4 tbsp chopped fresh tarragon or thyme
finely grated zest and juice of 1 small lemon
1 medium (US large) egg yolk
salt and ground black pepper

1   Melt the butter in a small pan, add the onion and garlic and fry gently over a low heat for 7–10 minutes to soften. Tip into a bowl and set aside to cool.
2   Add the breadcrumbs, herbs, lemon zest and juice and bind with the egg yolk. Season with salt and pepper. Use to stuff a 1.4kg/3lb chicken.

Serves 4

preparation 10 minutes
cooking time 10 minutes plus cooling

SPICY SAUSAGE STUFFING

450g/1lb spicy Italian-style pork sausages
125g/4oz/½ cup butter
2 onions, finely chopped
3 sticks celery, chopped
4 tbsp chopped fresh parsley
salt and ground black pepper

1   Remove the skin from the sausages and then break up the sausagemeat in a bowl.
2   Melt the butter in a pan and fry the onions over a low heat for 7–10 minutes until soft and golden, then mix in the celery and parsley. Set aside to cool.
3   Mix the cold mixture into the sausagemeat and season with salt and pepper.
4   Use to stuff a 4.5kg/10lb turkey.

Serves 10

preparation 10 minutes
cooking time 10 minutes plus cooling

SAGE AND SAUSAGE STUFFING

1 tbsp oil
1 onion, finely chopped
2 garlic cloves, crushed
125g/4oz/½ cup pork sausagemeat
1 tbsp chopped fresh sage
salt and ground black pepper

1   Heat the oil in a pan and cook the onion and garlic over a low heat for 7–10 minutes until tender. Turn into a bowl and leave to cool.
2   Add the sausagemeat and sage to the cold onion mixture and season with salt and plenty of pepper.
3   Use to stuff a 1.4kg/3lb chicken.

Serves 4

preparation 10 minutes
cooking time 10 minutes, plus cooling

PORK AND APPLE STUFFING

2 tbsp olive oil

1 onion, finely chopped

1 parsnip, diced

2 apples, peeled, cored and cut into chunks

400g/14oz/1¾ cups pork sausagemeat

grated zest of and juice of 1 lemon

2 tbsp chopped fresh thyme

125g/4oz/2 cups fresh white breadcrumbs

2 large (US extra-large) eggs, beaten

salt and ground black pepper

1 Heat the oil in a pan and fry the onion and parsnip over a low heat for 7–10 minutes until soft.
2 Add the apples and cook for 2–3 minutes, then set aside to cool.
3 Add the sausagemeat, lemon zest, thyme, breadcrumbs and eggs. Season and stir until evenly mixed. Use to stuff a 4.5kg/10lb turkey.

Serves 10

preparation 10 minutes   **cooking time** 15 minutes

PORK AND CHESTNUT STUFFING

50g/2oz/4 tbsp butter

1 red onion, roughly chopped

4 celery sticks, roughly chopped

4 tbsp chopped fresh flat-leafed parsley

1 tbsp chopped fresh sage

175g/6oz white bread, diced

2 cooking (green) apples, peeled, cored and diced

6 ready-to-eat prunes, chopped

225g/8oz cooked, peeled (or vacuum-packed) chestnuts, roughly chopped

a good pinch of grated nutmeg

450g/1lb/2 cups pork sausagemeat

salt and ground black pepper

1 Melt the butter in a frying pan and gently fry the onion and celery for 10–12 minutes until soft and golden.
2 Tip into a bowl. Mix in the parsley, sage, bread, apples, prunes, chestnuts and nutmeg. Season and cool.
3 Stir in the sausagemeat and divide into walnut-sized pieces. Fry, in batches, until golden brown and cooked through.

Serves 8

preparation 15 minutes   **cooking time** 15–20 minutes

ROSEMARY AND LEMON STUFFING

50g/2oz/4 tbsp butter
1 onion, finely chopped
125g/4oz/2 cups fresh white breadcrumbs
1 tbsp chopped fresh rosemary leaves
grated zest and juice of 1 lemon
1 medium (US large) egg, beaten
salt and ground black pepper

1 Melt the butter in a pan and fry the onion
   over a low heat for 10 minutes or until soft
   and golden. Tip into a bowl and cool.
2 Add the breadcrumbs, rosemary leaves,
   lemon zest and juice and seasoning.
   Add the egg and stir to bind.
3 Use to stuff a 1.4kg/3lb chicken

Serves 4

preparation 10 minutes **cooking time** 10 minutes

ORANGE AND HERB STUFFING

50g/2oz/4 tbsp butter
1 large onion, finely chopped
2 garlic cloves, crushed
75g/3oz/1½ cups fresh white breadcrumbs
50g/2oz/½ cup pinenuts (pignoli), chopped
6 ready-to-eat dried apricots, chopped
grated zest and juice of 1 orange
2 tbsp each chopped fresh thyme and sage
1 medium (US large) egg yolk, beaten
salt and ground black pepper

1 Heat the butter in a pan and fry the onion
   and garlic over a low heat for 7–10 minutes
   until soft but not brown.
2 Put the remaining ingredients in a large
   bowl. Add the onion mixture and stir to bind,
   adding more orange juice if needed.
3 Use to stuff a 4.5kg/10lb turkey.

Serves 10

preparation 10 minutes **cooking time** 10 minutes

CLASSIC SOUP DUMPLINGS

125g/4oz/1 cup + 2 tbsp self-raising (self-rising
flour
50g/2oz/⅓ cup shredded suet
salt and ground black pepper

1 Mix the flour, suet and seasoning with some
   cold water to make an elastic dough.
2 Divide the dough into 16 portions and, with
   lightly floured hands, roll into small balls.
3 Add to soups or stews and simmer gently
   for 15–20 minutes.

Serves 4

preparation 10 minutes **cooking time** 15–20 minutes

BECHAMEL SAUCE

300ml/½ pint/1¼ cups milk

1 slice onion

8 whole black peppercorns

1 mace blade

1 bay leaf and a few parsley stalks

25g/1oz/2 tbsp butter

15g/½oz/2 tbsp plain (all-purpose) flour

freshly grated nutmeg

salt and ground black pepper

1 Put the milk, onion, peppercorns, mace and herbs in a pan. Bring almost to the boil, remove from the heat, then cover and leave to infuse for 20 minutes. Strain into a jug.
2 Melt the butter in a clean pan, stir in the flour and cook, stirring, for 1 minute until cooked but not coloured.
3 Remove from the heat and gradually whisk in the infused milk. Season with salt, pepper and nutmeg.
4 Return to the heat and cook, stirring constantly, until thickened and smooth. Simmer gently for 2 minutes.

Makes 300ml/½ pint/1¼ cups

preparation 5 minutes, plus infusing
cooking time 5 minutes

HOLLANDAISE SAUCE

3 tbsp white wine vinegar

6 black peppercorns

1 mace blade

1 slice onion

1 bay leaf

2 medium (US large) egg yolks

125g/4oz/½ cup unsalted butter, at room temperature, diced

2 tbsp single (light) cream

a dash of lemon juice to taste

salt and ground white pepper

1 Put the vinegar, peppercorns, mace, onion slice and bay leaf in a pan. Bring to the boil and reduce to 1 tbsp liquid. Set aside.
2 Put the egg yolks in a heatproof bowl with 15g/½oz/1 tbsp butter and a pinch of salt. Beat until well combined, then strain in the reduced vinegar.
3 Put the bowl over a pan of barely simmering water and whisk for 3–4 minutes until the mixture is pale and starting to thicken.
4 Beat in the remaining butter, one piece at a time, until the sauce starts to thicken and emulsify. Do not let it overheat or the eggs will scramble and split. Remove the pan from the heat.
5 Whisk in the cream and season to taste. Add a little lemon juice and serve.

Serves 6

preparation 20 minutes **cooking time** 8 minutes

BEARNAISE SAUCE

4 tbsp white wine vinegar

1 shallot, finely chopped

4 black peppercorns

a few fresh tarragon sprigs, chopped

2 medium (US large) egg yolks

75g/3oz/6 tbsp butter, at room temperature, diced

1 tbsp chopped fresh tarragon

salt and ground white pepper

1 Put the vinegar, shallot, peppercorns and tarragon sprigs in a pan. Bring to the boil and reduce to 1 tbsp. Cool, then strain.
2 Beat the egg yolks and reduced vinegar in a heatproof bowl. Put the bowl over a pan of barely simmering water and whisk for 3–4 minutes until pale and starting to thicken.
3 Beat in the butter, a piece at a time, until the mixture thickens and emulsifies. Do not allow it to overheat or the eggs will scramble and split. Remove from the heat.
4 Season to taste. Stir in the tarragon.

Serves 4

preparation 20 minutes cooking time 8–10 minutes

MUSHROOM SAUCE

50g/2oz/4 tbsp butter

1 onion, finely chopped

175g/6oz button or cup mushrooms, sliced

150g/5oz mixed wild mushrooms, sliced

1 garlic clove, crushed

150ml/¼ pint/scant ⅔ cup white wine

200ml/7fl oz/¾ cup crème fraîche or cream

4 tbsp chopped fresh parsley

salt and ground black pepper

1 Heat the oil in a pan and cook the onion over a low heat for 10 minutes. Add the mushrooms and garlic and cook over a high heat for 4–5 minutes until tender and all the moisture has evaporated.
2 Add the wine, bring to the boil and bubble away until reduced by half.
3 Add the crème fraîche and the seasoning. Bring to the boil and bubble away for 5 minutes or until slightly thickened. Stir in the parsley.

Serves 6

preparation 10 minutes cooking time 20 minutes

CUMBERLAND SAUCE

finely pared zest and juice of 1 orange

finely pared zest and juice of 1 lemon

4 tbsp redcurrant jelly

1 tsp Dijon mustard

1 tsp ground ginger

4 tbsp port

salt and ground black pepper

1 Cut the zests into fine julienne strips and place in a pan. Cover with cold water and simmer for 5 minutes, then drain.
2 Put the orange and lemon juices, drained zest, redcurrant jelly, mustard and ginger in a pan and heat gently, stirring, until the jelly dissolves. Simmer for 5 minutes, then stir in the port.
3 Set aside to cool. Season to taste with salt and pepper.

Serves 4

preparation 10 minutes
cooking time 10 minutes plus cooling

CRANBERRY SAUCE

2 tbsp olive oil

1 red onion, diced

grated zest and juice of 1 large orange

a pinch of ground cloves

1 tsp grated fresh root ginger

1 bay leaf

150g/5oz/⅔ cup light muscovado sugar

125ml/4fl oz/½ cup port

450g/1lb/4 cups cranberries

1 Heat the oil in a pan and cook the onion over a low heat for 5 minutes. Add the orange zest and juice, spices, bay leaf, sugar and the port. Simmer gently for 40 minutes.
2 Add the cranberries, bring back to the boil and simmer for 10–15 minutes until tender. Cool and chill in the refrigerator. Bring to room temperature before serving.

Serves 8

preparation 30 minutes
cooking time 1 hour plus chilling

FRENCH DRESSING

1 tsp Dijon mustard

a pinch of caster (superfine) sugar

2 tbsp white or red wine vinegar

6 tbsp olive oil

salt and ground black pepper

1 Whisk the mustard, sugar, vinegar and seasoning together in a bowl. Gradually whisk in the oil until the dressing amalgamates and thickens.

Makes 100ml/3½fl oz/⅓ cup

preparation 10 minutes

PESTO

a large bunch of fresh basil leaves

2 garlic cloves, peeled

50g/2oz/½ cup pinenuts (pignoli)

125ml/4fl oz/½ cup olive oil

50g/2oz/½ cup freshly grated Parmesan

a squeeze of lemon juice

salt and ground black pepper

1 Roughly tear the basil and place in a large mortar with the garlic, pinenuts and a little of the oil. Pound with a pestle to a paste. Or work in a food processor to a paste.
2 Gradually add the rest of the oil and season to taste. Transfer to a bowl.
3 Stir in the Parmesan and a squeeze of lemon juice.
4 Store in a screw-topped jar in the refrigerator for up to three days.

Serves 8

preparation 10 minutes

ROUILLE

1 large red pepper, grilled (broiled) and seeded

4 garlic cloves, crushed

1 red chilli, halved and seeded

125ml/4fl oz/1 cup olive oil

2 tbsp fresh white breadcrumbs

1 Blitz the red pepper in a food processor or blender with the garlic and chilli.
2 Gradually pour in the oil until combined. Stir in the breadcrumbs.

Serves 6

preparation 10 minutes

TOMATO SAUCE

1kg/2¼lb tomatoes, roughly chopped

2 tbsp olive oil

2 garlic cloves, crushed

grated zest of 1 lemon

2 tbsp torn fresh basil

a pinch of sugar

1 tbsp balsamic vinegar

salt and ground black pepper

1 Put the tomatoes in a pan with the oil, garlic, lemon zest and basil. Bring to the boil, then cover and simmer for 20 minutes.
2 Add salt and pepper to taste and the sugar. Simmer, uncovered, for 10 minutes or until reduced. Add the vinegar. If wished, pass through a sieve and reheat before serving.

Serves 4

preparation 10 minutes   **cooking time** 30 minutes

SALSA VERDE

a handful of fresh parsley

6 tbsp fresh white breadcrumbs

6 tbsp olive oil

2 tsp capers

2 gherkins (cornichons)

grated zest and juice of 1 lemon

a small bunch of fresh chives

salt and ground black pepper

1 Put all the ingredients, except the salt and pepper, in a blender or food processor and blitz until thoroughly combined.
2 Turn into a bowl and season to taste. Store in the refrigerator for up to five days.

Serves 4

preparation 5 minutes

SLOW-COOKED TOMATO SAUCE

3 tbsp olive oil

2 large onions, finely chopped

4 garlic cloves, crushed

1kg/2¼lb tomatoes, roughly chopped

500g/1lb 2oz/2 cups passata (strained tomatoes)

150ml/¼ pint/scant ⅔ cup red or white wine

a large handful of fresh basil sprigs

1 tsp caster (superfine) sugar

1 tbsp balsamic vinegar

salt and ground black pepper

1 Heat the oil in a large pan and cook the onions over a low heat for 10 minutes or until tender and golden. Add the garlic and tomatoes and cook for 5 minutes. Stir in the passata, wine, half the basil, the sugar and balsamic vinegar. Season to taste and bring to the boil, stirring. Cover and cook gently for 1 hour until thick.
2 Discard the basil sprigs. Finely chop the leaves of the remaining basil and stir into the sauce.

Makes 1.6l/2¾ pints/6¾ cups

preparation 10 minutes   **cooking time** 1 hour 15 minutes

MAYONNAISE

2 medium (US large) egg yolks, at room temperature

2 tsp lemon juice or white wine vinegar

1 tsp Dijon mustard

a pinch of sugar

300ml/½ pint/1¼ cups olive oil

salt and ground black pepper

1 Put all the ingredients except the oil and seasoning in a food processor. Pulse briefly until pale and creamy.
2 With the motor running, add the oil through the feed tube, in a steady stream, until the mayonnaise is thick. Thin, if needed, with a little hot water. Season to taste.
3 Store the mayonnaise in a screw-topped jar in the refrigerator for up to three days.

Makes 300ml/½ pint/1¼ cups

preparation 10 minutes

VANILLA CUSTARD

600ml/1 pint/2½ cups milk

1 tsp vanilla extract

6 large (US extra-large) egg yolks

2 tbsp caster (superfine) sugar

2 tbsp cornflour (cornstarch)

1 Put the milk and vanilla in a pan. Slowly bring to the boil. Remove from the heat.
2 Whisk the egg yolks, sugar and cornflour in a bowl and gradually whisk in the milk.
3 Rinse the pan and pour the mixture back in. Heat gently, whisking or stirring constantly, for 2–3 minutes until the custard thickens. Serve immediately.

Serves 8

preparation 10 minutes
cooking time 10 minutes

TOMATO KETCHUP

2.7kg/6lb ripe tomatoes, sliced

3 tbsp tomato paste

225g/8oz/1 cup sugar

300ml/½ pint/1¼ cups red wine vinegar

a few drops of Tabasco sauce

1 tsp celery salt

1 Cook the tomatoes in a pan over a very low heat for 45 minutes, stirring frequently, until they reduce to a pulp. Bring to the boil and cook rapidly until the pulp thickens.
2 Press the pulp through a nylon or stainless steel sieve, then return to the pan and stir in the remaining ingredients. Simmer gently until the mixture thickens.
3 Pour the ketchup into warm, sterilised bottles. Seal and label, and store in a cool, dark place for up to one year.

Makes 1.1l/2 pints/5 cups

preparation 30 minutes **cooking time** 1 hour

SABAYON CREAM

50g/2oz/4 tbsp golden caster (superfine) sugar
3 medium egg yolks
125ml/4fl oz/½ cup double (heavy) cream
grated zest and juice of 1 lemon

1 Stir the sugar and 125ml/4fl oz/½ cup water in a pan over a low heat until dissolved. Increase the heat and boil for 7–8 minutes until the syrup reaches 105°C/221°F on a sugar thermometer.
2 Whisk the egg yolks in a bowl and gradually whisk in the hot syrup in a thin stream. Beat until thick, mousse-like and cool.
3 Whisk the cream until it forms stiff peaks, then add the lemon zest and juice and whip again to form soft peaks. Fold into the mousse mixture. Cover and chill in the refrigerator. Whisk well before serving.

Serves 6

preparation 15 minutes
cooking time 10 minutes plus chilling

ANCHOVY SAUCE

15g/½oz/1 tbsp butter
15g/½oz/2 tbsp flour
150ml/¼ pint/scant ⅔ cup milk
150ml/¼ pint/scant ⅔ cup fish stock
2 tsp anchovy essence
a squeeze of lemon juice
salt and ground black pepper

1 Melt the butter in a pan, stir in the flour and cook gently for 1 minute, stirring. Remove from the heat and gradually stir in the milk and fish stock. Bring to the boil and cook over a medium heat, stirring all the time, until the sauce thickens.
2 Simmer gently for 2–3 minutes. Stir in the anchovy essence and lemon juice. Season to taste with salt and pepper.

Makes 300ml/½ pint/1¼ cups

preparation 5 minutes   **cooking time** 10 minutes

BUTTERSCOTCH SAUCE

50g/2oz/4 tbsp butter
75g/3oz/6 tbsp light muscovado (brown) sugar
50g/2oz/4 tbsp golden caster (superfine) sugar
150g/5oz/generous ⅓ cup golden (corn) syrup
125ml/4fl oz/½ cup double (heavy) cream
a few drops of vanilla extract

1 Put the butter, sugars and syrup in a pan over a low heat and stir occasionally until melted and smooth. Cook gently, stirring, for 5 minutes.
2 Off the heat, slowly stir in the cream. Add the vanilla extract and stir over a low heat for 1–2 minutes until smooth. Serve the sauce hot or cold.

Serves 8

preparation 5 minutes   **cooking time** 10 minutes

ORANGE/LEMON SAUCE

grated zest and juice of 2 large oranges or lemons

1 tbsp cornflour (cornstarch)

2 tbsp sugar

a knob of butter

1 medium egg yolk (optional)

1 Put the fruit zest and juice in a bowl and make up to 300ml/½ pint/1¼ cups with water. Blend the cornflour and sugar with a little of the liquid until smooth.
2 Heat the remaining liquid until boiling, then pour on to the blended mixture, stirring all the time. Return to the pan and bring to the boil, stirring until the sauce thickens. Stir in the butter.
3 Cool, then beat in the egg yolk, if using, and reheat, stirring, without boiling.

Serves 4

preparation 10 minutes
cooking time 15 minutes plus cooling

COFFEE SAUCE

5 tsp instant strong coffee powder

2 tsp cornflour (cornstarch)

1 x 175g/6oz can evaporated milk

2 tbsp soft light brown sugar

1 Mix the coffee powder and cornflour to a smooth paste with a little water, then make up to 150ml/¼ pint/scant ⅔ cup with more water.
2 Pour into a pan, add the evaporated milk and sugar and slowly bring to the boil, stirring. Simmer for 1 minute.

Serves 4

preparation 5 minutes   **cooking time** 3 minutes

CHOCOLATE SAUCE

125g/4oz plain (semisweet) chocolate (at least 70% cocoa solids), cut into pieces

2 tbsp light muscovado (brown) sugar

25g/1oz/2 tbsp unsalted butter

1 Put the chocolate in a small pan with the sugar and 150ml/¼ pint/scant ⅔ cup water. Stir over a low heat until the chocolate melts and the sugar dissolves, then bring to the boil, stirring.
2 Let it bubble for 1 minute, then remove from the heat and stir in the butter.

Serves 6

preparation 5 minutes   **cooking time** 5 minutes

RASPBERRY COULIS

225g/8oz raspberries
framboise eau de vie (optional)
icing (confectioner's) sugar to taste

1 Put the raspberries in a blender or food processor with the framboise eau de vie, if using. Blitz until puréed.
2 Press the purée through a fine sieve, until nothing is left but the pips.
3 Sweeten with sugar to taste and chill in the refrigerator until needed.

Serves 4

preparation 10 minutes plus chilling

CARAMEL SAUCE

50g/2oz/4 tbsp sugar
150ml/¼ pint/scant ⅔ cup double (heavy) cream

1 Melt the sugar in a small heavy-based pan over a low heat until liquid and golden. Increase the heat to medium and cook to a rich, dark caramel.
2 Immediately take the pan off the heat and pour in the cream in a slow steady stream, taking care, as the hot caramel will make the cream boil up in the pan.
3 Stir over a gentle heat until the caramel melts and the sauce is smooth. Serve hot or cold.

Serves 6

preparation 5 minutes   **cooking time** 10 minutes

CREME PATISSIERE

300ml/½ pint/1¼ cups milk
1 tsp vanilla extract
3 medium egg yolks, beaten
50g/2oz/4 tbsp golden caster (superfine) sugar
2 tbsp plain (all-purpose) flour
2 tbsp cornflour (cornstarch)

1 Put the milk and vanilla extract in a heavy-based pan and bring to the boil.
2 Meanwhile, whisk the egg yolks and sugar in a bowl until thick and creamy. Whisk in the flour and cornflour until smooth. Gradually whisk in the hot milk, then strain back into the pan.
3 Slowly bring to the boil, whisking constantly. Cook, stirring, for 2–3 minutes until thickened and smooth.
4 Pour into a bowl, cover the surface and set aside to cool.

Makes 450ml/¾ pint/1¾ cups

preparation 15 minutes
cooking time 5 minutes, plus cooling

BLACKBERRY SAUCE

125ml/4fl oz/½ cup red wine
125ml/4fl oz/½ cup water
3 tbsp caster (superfine) sugar
2 whole cloves
5cm/2in piece of cinnamon stick
1 tbsp cornflour (cornstarch)
225g/8oz/2 cups blackberries
2 tbsp cold water

1 Put the red wine, water, sugar, cloves and
   cinnamon stick in a pan and heat gently,
   stirring, until the sugar dissolves.
2 Blend the cornflour with 2 tbsp cold water
   and add to the pan with the blackberries.
   Cook over a medium heat for 4–5 minutes,
   stirring, until the blackberries soften and
   the sauce thickens. Discard the spices and
   serve warm or cold.

Serves 6

preparation 2 minutes   **cooking time** 5 minutes

BRANDY BUTTER

150g/5oz/⅔ cup unsalted butter, at room temp
150g/5oz/⅔ cup icing (confectioner's) sugar, sifted
3 tbsp brandy

1 Put the butter in a bowl and whisk to soften.
   Gradually whisk in the sugar, pouring in
   the brandy just before the final addition.
   Continue whisking until the mixture is pale
   and fluffy, then spoon into a serving dish.
2 Cover and chill in the refrigerator until
   needed. Remove 30 minutes before serving.

Serves 8

preparation 10 minutes, plus chilling

CHANTILLY CREAM

300ml/½ pint/1¼ cups double (heavy) cream
1 tbsp golden caster (superfine) sugar
finely grated zest of 1 orange (optional)

1 Whip the cream with the sugar until it
   forms soft peaks. Fold in half the grated
   orange zest, if using. Cover and chill in
   the refrigerator.
2 Serve sprinkled with the remaining orange
   zest, if using.

Serves 8

preparation 10 minutes, plus chilling

APRICOT SAUCE

200g/7oz/1¼ cups ready-to-eat dried apricots
250ml/8fl oz/1 cup water
2 tbsp caster (superfine) sugar
juice of 2 oranges

1 Put the apricots and water in a pan and
   bring to the boil. Cover and simmer gently
   for 10 minutes.
2 Blitz the apricots and liquid in a blender or
   food processor with the sugar and orange
   juice. Add a little water if needed to make a
   pouring consistency.

Serves 6

preparation 5 minutes **cooking time** 10 minutes

BLUEBERRY SAUCE

4 tsp cornflour (cornstarch)
4 tbsp caster (superfine) sugar
175ml/6fl oz/⅔ cup water
250g/9oz/2 cups blueberries

1 Put the cornflour and sugar in a pan
   and gradually mix in the water. Add the
   blueberries and bring to the boil.
2 Simmer gently over a low heat for
   3–4 minutes, stirring, until the blueberries
   start to soften and the sauce is a deep
   colour. Serve warm or cold.

Serves 6

preparation 5 minutes **cooking time** 10 minutes

MANGO AND LIME SAUCE

2 large mangoes, peeled, stoned and diced
4 tbsp water
4 tbsp caster (superfine) sugar
grated zest and juice of 2 limes

1 Put the mango, water, sugar, lime zest
   and juice in a pan. Cover and simmer
   gently for 5 minutes, then blitz in a blender
   or food processor until smooth. Serve warm
   or cold.

Serves 6

preparation 5 minutes **cooking time** 5 minutes

SHORTCRUST PASTRY

225g/8oz/2¼ cups plain (all-purpose) flour, plus extra to dust

a pinch of salt

125g/4oz/½ cup butter, diced

1 Sift the flour and salt into a bowl. Rub in the butter with your fingertips until the mixture resembles fine breadcrumbs.
2 Sprinkle 3–4 tbsp cold water evenly over the surface and stir with a round-bladed knife until the mixture sticks together. If it's too dry, add a little water. Form it into a ball.
3 Knead on a lightly floured surface but do not over-work. Wrap in clingfilm (plastic wrap) and rest in the refrigerator for 30 minutes before rolling out.

Makes 225g/8oz pastry

preparation 10 minutes plus chilling

SUET CRUST PASTRY

300g/11oz/3 cups self-raising (self-rising) flour

½ tsp salt

150g/5oz/¾ cup shredded suet

1 Sift the flour and salt into a bowl, add the shredded suet and stir to mix.
2 Using a round-bladed knife, mix in about 175ml/6fl oz/⅔ cup cold water to make a soft dough. If it's too dry, add more liquid.
3 Knead lightly until smooth. Use as required.

Makes 300g/11oz pastry

preparation 10 minutes

RICH SHORTCRUST PASTRY

225g/8oz/2¼ cups plain (all-purpose) flour plus extra to dust

a pinch of salt

175g/6oz/¾ cup butter, diced

2 tsp caster (superfine) sugar

1 large (US extra-large) egg, beaten

1 Put the flour and salt in a bowl and rub in the fat until the mixture resembles fine breadcrumbs. Stir in the sugar.
2 Stir in the egg with a round-bladed knife until the ingredients stick together.
3 Knead lightly for a few seconds to give a firm, smooth dough. Wrap in clingfilm (plastic wrap) and chill in the refrigerator for 30 minutes before rolling out.

Makes 225g/8oz pastry

preparation 10 minutes plus chilling

PUFF PASTRY

450g/1lb/4½ cups strong plain (bread) flour plus extra to dust

a pinch of salt

450g/1lb/2 cups butter, chilled

1 tbsp lemon juice

1 Sift the flour and salt into a bowl. Cut off 50g/2oz/4 tbsp butter and flatten the remaining large block with a rolling pin to a slab, about 2cm/¾in thick. Set aside.
2 Cut the smaller piece of butter into dice and rub into the flour, using your fingertips.
3 With a round-bladed knife, stir in the lemon juice and 300ml/½ pint/1¼ cups chilled water to make a soft elastic dough.
4 Turn out on to a lightly floured surface and quickly knead until smooth. Cut a cross through half the depth, then open out to form a star.
5 Roll out, keeping the centre four times as thick as the flaps. Put the slab of butter in the centre and fold the flaps over the top. Press down with a rolling pin and roll out to a rectangle, 40 × 20cm/16 × 8in.
6 Fold the bottom third up and the top third down, keeping the edges straight. Wrap in clingfilm (plastic wrap) and rest in the refrigerator for 30 minutes.
7 Put the pastry on a lightly floured surface with the folded edges to the sides. Repeat the rolling, folding, resting and turning sequence five times.
8 Shape as required, then chill again for 30 minutes before baking.

Makes 450g/1lb pastry

preparation 40 minutes plus chilling

SWEET PASTRY

225g/8oz/2¼ cups plain (all-purpose) flour plus extra to dust

a pinch of salt

125g/4oz/½ unsalted butter, at room temperature, diced

2 egg yolks

75g/3oz/6 tbsp caster (superfine) sugar

1 Sift the flour and salt into a mound on a clean surface. Make a well in the centre and add the butter, egg yolks and sugar.
2 Using your fingertips, work them together until well blended. Gradually work in all the flour to bind the mixture together.
3 Knead the dough on a lightly floured clean surface until smooth. Wrap in clingfilm (plastic wrap) and rest in the refrigerator for 30 minutes before rolling out.

Makes 225g/8oz pastry

preparation 10 minutes plus chilling

CHOUX PASTRY

65g/2½oz/⅔ cup strong plain (all-purpose) flour

a pinch of salt

50g/2oz/4 tbsp butter

2 large (US extra-large) eggs, lightly beaten

1 Sift the flour and salt onto a large sheet of parchment paper.
2 Put the butter and 150ml/¼ pint/scant ⅔ cup cold water in a pan over a low heat. When the butter melts, turn up the heat and bring to a rolling boil.
3 Take off the heat and tip in the flour. Beat well with a wooden spoon until the mixture is smooth and leaves the sides of the pan to form a ball. Cool for 1–2 minutes.
4 Gradually beat in the eggs to give a smooth dropping consistency. The pastry should be smooth and shiny.

Makes a 2-egg quantity

preparation 20 minutes   **cooking time** 3 minutes

FLAKY PASTRY

225g/8oz/2¼ cups plain (all-purpose) flour plus extra to dust

a pinch of salt

175g/6oz/¾ cup butter, chilled

1 tsp lemon juice

1 Sift the flour and salt into a bowl. Cut the butter into 2cm/¾in cubes and add to the flour. Mix to coat the butter with the flour.
2 Mix in 100ml/3½fl oz/⅓ cup chilled water and the lemon juice with a round-bladed knife, to make a soft elastic dough. If the pastry is too dry, add more water.
3 Turn out on to a lightly floured surface and knead the dough until smooth.
4 Roll out to a rectangle, 30 x 10cm/12 × 4in. Fold the bottom third up and the top third down, then give the pastry a quarter turn, so the folded edges are at the sides. Press the edges with a rolling pin to seal. Wrap in clingfilm (plastic wrap) and rest in the refrigerator for 15 minutes.
5 Place on a lightly floured surface with the folded edges to the sides. Repeat the rolling, folding and turning sequence four more times. Wrap in clingfilm (plastic wrap) and rest in the refrigerator for 30 minutes.
6 Roll out and shape as required, then chill again for 30 minutes before baking.

Makes 225g/8oz pastry

preparation 25 minutes plus chilling

PIZZA DOUGH

225g/8oz/2¼ cups strong plain (bread) flour plus extra to dust

½ tsp fine sea salt

½ tsp easy-blend dried yeast

1 tbsp olive oil plus extra to oil

1 Sift the flour and salt into a bowl and stir in the dried yeast. Make a well in the centre and gradually work in 150ml/¼ pint/scant ⅔ cup warm water and the oil to form a dough.
2 Turn the dough out on to a clean lightly floured surface and knead well for 8–10 minutes until smooth and elastic. (Alternatively, knead in a large food mixer fitted with a dough hook.)
3 Place in an oiled bowl and turn the dough to coat it with oil. Cover the bowl with clingfilm (plastic wrap) and leave to rise in a warm place for 1 hour or until doubled in size.
4 Knock back the dough and shape into 1 large or 2 small circles.

Makes 1 large or 2 small bases

preparation 5 minutes plus rising

GLUTEN-FREE PASTRY

175g/6oz/1½ cups rice flour

125g/4oz/1 cup tapioca flour

1 tsp xanthan gum

a pinch of salt

150g/5oz/⅔ cup unsalted butter, diced

2 medium (US large) eggs, beaten

1 Put the flours, xanthan gum and a little salt in a bowl and mix well. Add the butter and rub in with your fingertips until it resembles fine breadcrumbs. Gradually mix in about three-quarters of the beaten egg – enough to mix to a soft dough.
2 Knead the dough on a clean lightly floured surface until smooth. Rest in the refrigerator for 30 minutes before rolling out and using.

Makes 300g/11oz pastry

preparation 10 minutes plus chilling

COFFEE FUDGE FROSTING

50g/2oz/4 tbsp butter

125g/4oz/½ cup light muscovado (brown) sugar

2 tbsp milk

1 tbsp coffee granules

200g/7oz/1⅓ cups icing (confectioner's) sugar, sifted

1 Put the butter, muscovado sugar and milk in a pan. Dissolve the coffee in 2 tbsp boiling water and add to the pan. Heat gently, stirring, until the sugar dissolves. Bring to the boil and boil for 3 minutes.
2 Remove from the heat and gradually stir in the icing sugar. Beat with a wooden spoon for 1 minute or until smooth.
3 Use the frosting immediately, spreading it over a cake with a wet palette knife, or dilute with water for a smooth coating.
4 This is enough to cover the top and sides of a 20cm/8in cake.

Makes 400g/14oz

preparation 5 minutes cooking time 5 minutes

BUTTERCREAM

75g/3oz/6 tbsp unsalted butter, softened

175g/6oz/1 cup icing (confectioner's) sugar, sifted

a few drops of vanilla extract

1–2 tbsp milk

1 Put the butter in a bowl and beat with a wooden spoon until light and fluffy.
2 Gradually stir in the sugar, vanilla extract and milk. Beat until light and smooth.
3 This is enough to cover the top of a 20cm/8in cake.

Makes 250g/9oz

preparation 10 minutes

GLACE ICING

225g/8oz/1⅔ cups icing (confectioner's) sugar

a few drops of vanilla extract (optional)

a few drops of food colouring (optional)

1 Sift the icing sugar into a bowl. Add a few drops of vanilla extract, if wished.
2 Using a wooden spoon, gradually stir in 2–3 tbsp hot water until the mixture is the consistency of thick cream. Beat until smooth and thick enough to coat the back of the spoon. Add colouring, if wished, and use immediately.
3 This is enough to cover the top of a large cake or 18 cupcakes.

Makes 225g/8oz

preparation 5 minutes

AMERICAN FROSTING

1 large (US extra-large) egg white
225g/8oz/1 cup golden caster (superfine) sugar
a pinch of cream of tartar

1 Put the egg white in a clean, grease-free bowl and whisk until it forms stiff peaks.
2 Put the sugar, 4 tbsp water and the cream of tartar in a pan and heat gently, stirring, until the sugar dissolves. Bring to the boil and boil until the sugar syrup reaches 115°C/239°F on a sugar thermometer. Or drop a little into cold water – when it forms a soft ball that you can squash between your finger and thumb, it's ready.
3 Remove from the heat and when the bubbles subside, pour on to the egg white in a thin stream, whisking constantly, until thick and white. Set aside to cool slightly.
4 When it is almost cold, pour quickly over the cake and spread evenly with a palette knife.
5 This makes enough to cover the top and sides of a 20cm/8in cake.

Makes 225g/8oz

preparation 15 minutes   **cooking time** 5 minutes

ROYAL ICING

2 large (US extra-large) egg whites
2 tsp liquid glycerine
450g/1lb/3⅓ cups icing (confectioner's) sugar, sifted

1 Put the egg whites and glycerine in a bowl and stir just enough to break up the egg whites. Add a little of the sugar and mix gently with a wooden spoon to incorporate as little air as possible.
2 Add a little more sugar as the mixture gets lighter. Keep adding the sugar, stirring gently but thoroughly, until the mixture is stiff and stands in soft peaks.
3 Transfer to an airtight container, cover the surface with clingfilm (plastic wrap) to prevent it drying out, then seal. When required, stir the icing slowly.
4 This is enough to cover the top and sides of a 20cm/8in cake.

Makes 450g/1lb

preparation 15 minutes

VANILLA FROSTING

150g/5oz/1 cup icing (confectioner's) sugar, sifted
5 tsp vegetable oil
1 tbsp milk
a few drops of vanilla extract

1 Put the sugar in a bowl and beat in the oil, milk and vanilla extract until smooth.
2 This is enough to cover the top and sides of an 18cm/7in cake.

Makes 175g/6oz

preparation 5 minutes

ALMOND PASTE

225g/8oz/1¾ cups ground almonds
125g/4oz/½ cup golden caster (superfine) sugar
125g/4oz/¾ cup golden icing (confectioner's) sugar
1 large (US extra-large) egg
1 tsp lemon juice
1 tsp sherry
1–2 drops of vanilla extract

1 Mix together the ground almonds and sugars in a bowl. In a separate bowl, whisk the egg with the remaining ingredients and add to the dry mixture.
2 Stir well to mix, pounding gently to release some of the oil from the almonds. Knead until smooth, then cover until ready to use.
3 This is enough to cover the top and sides of an 18cm/7in cake.

Makes 450g/1lb

preparation 10 minutes

APRICOT GLAZE

450g/1lb/2 cups apricot jam (jelly)
4 tbsp water

1 Gently heat the jam and water in a pan, stirring occasionally, until melted. Boil hard for 1 minute, then strain through a sieve, rubbing through as much fruit as possible.
2 Pour the glaze into a clean, hot jar, then seal and cool. Store in the refrigerator for up to two months. You only need 3–4 tbsp apricot glaze for a 23cm/9in cake, so this quantity will glaze six to seven cakes.

Makes 450g/1lb

preparation 5 minutes   cooking time 2 minutes

CHOCOLATE GANACHE

225g/8oz white or plain (semisweet) chocolate (at least 70% cocoa solids), chopped into small pieces
250ml/8fl oz/1 cup double (heavy) cream

1 Put the chocolate in a heatproof bowl. Bring the cream to the boil in a small pan and pour on to the chocolate. Stir until the chocolate melts and the mixture is smooth. Set aside to cool for 5 minutes.
2 Whisk until it begins to hold its shape.
3 This is enough to cover an 18cm/7in cake.

Makes 225g/8oz

preparation 10 minutes
cooking time 1 minute plus cooling

TOP 10 SANDWICHES

BOURSIN LIGHT

4 slices wholemeal bread
50g/2oz Boursin Light cheese
a few crisp salad leaves
1 ripe tomato, thinly sliced
4 lean bacon rashers (slices)

1 Spread the bread with the Boursin. Add the
   salad leaves and tomato to 2 slices.
2 Grill the bacon until crisp and put on top of
   the tomato. Cover with the remaining slices
   and cut in half.

preparation 5 minutes
cooking time 5 minutes

Serves 2

BLT

4 lean bacon rashers (slices)
4 slices Granary bread
2 tbsp lite mayonnaise
a few crisp lettuce leaves
2 ripe tomatoes, thinly sliced

1 Grill the bacon rashers until crisp.
2 Spread 2 slices of bread with mayonnaise
   and add the lettuce and tomatoes. Top with
   the bacon and cover with the remaining
   bread slices. Cut in half.

preparation 5 minutes
cooking time 5 minutes

Serves 2

SPICY CHICKEN

2 tbsp mayonnaise
2 tsp mango chutney
2 tsp sultanas (golden raisins)
a good pinch of curry powder
75g/3oz cooked chicken, shredded
4 slices wholegrain bread

1 Mix the mayonnaise, mango chutney,
   sultanas and curry powder. Stir in
   the chicken.
2 Spread over 2 slices of bread and cover
   with the other slices. Cut in half.

preparation 10 minutes

Serves 2

GRILLED TOFU

2 slices marinated tofu
4 slices wholemeal bread
4 tbsp low-fat fromage frais
a few drops of sweet chilli sauce
a few rocket (arugula) leaves, shredded

1 Grill the tofu on a non-stick griddle pan
   until golden. Toast the bread on one side
   only.
2 Spread 2 slices on the untoasted side with
   fromage frais. Sprinkle with chilli sauce
   and add the tofu and rocket. Cover with the
   other slices of toast and cut in half.

preparation 5 minutes
cooking time 3–4 minutes

Serves 2

EGG AND CRESS

2 hard-boiled eggs, peeled and mashed
2 tbsp mayonnaise
4 slices white bread
1 small punnet mustard and cress

1 Mix the egg with the mayonnaise and
   spread over 2 slices of bread. Sprinkle
   with the mustard and cress and cover with
   the remaining bread. Cut into quarters.

preparation 5 minutes
plus boiling eggs

Serves 2

TUNA MAYO

1 x 200g/7oz can tuna in brine, drained
1 tbsp mayonnaise
4 slices wholemeal bread
a few thin slices of cucumber

1 Mash the tuna with the mayonnaise until
   combined. Spread over 2 slices of bread.
2 Arrange the cucumber on top and cover
   with the remaining slices. Cut in half.

preparation 5 minutes

Serves 2

TURKEY

2 tsp lite mayonnaise
4 slices wholegrain bread
a few sprigs of watercress
75g/3oz thinly sliced cooked turkey breast
2 tsp cranberry sauce

1 Spread the mayonnaise over 2 slices of
   bread. Add the watercress and turkey.
2 Spread the remaining slices with cranberry
   sauce and place on top. Cut in half.

preparation 5 minutes

Serves 2

MEXICAN

3 tbsp hot tomato salsa
1 baby avocado, peeled, stoned and diced
75g/3oz cooked chicken, shredded
4 slices wholegrain bread
2 tbsp low-fat fromage frais

1 Mix together the salsa, avocado and
   chicken. Spread over 2 slices of bread.
2 Spread the remaining slices with the
   fromage frais and sandwich together.
   Cut in half.

preparation 10 minutes

Serves 2

PRAWN MAYO

125g/4oz peeled cooked prawns (shrimp)
2 tbsp mayonnaise
grated zest of 1 lemon
2 tbsp chopped fresh coriander (cilantro)
4 slices wholemeal bread

1 Mix the prawns, mayonnaise, lemon zest and
   coriander. Spread over 2 slices of bread and
   top with the other 2 slices. Cut into quarters.

preparation 5 minutes

Serves 2

FRUITY

4 slices wholegrain bread
1 large banana, mashed
2 tsp mango chutney

1 Spread 2 slices of bread with the mashed
   banana. Spread the other 2 slices with
   mango chutney. Sandwich together and
   cut into quarters.

preparation 5 minutes

Serves 2

TOP 10 DRESSINGS

VINAIGRETTE

2 tbsp extra virgin olive oil
2 tbsp grapeseed oil
1 tbsp white wine vinegar
a pinch each of sugar and English mustard powder
salt and ground black pepper

1   Put the oils, vinegar, sugar and mustard in
a large screw-topped jar. Tighten the lid and
shake well. Season to taste.

preparation 5 minutes   *Serves 6*

FRUITY YOGURT

150g/5oz/scant ⅔ cup low-fat natural yogurt
grated zest and juice of ½ orange
salt and ground black pepper

1   Blend together the yogurt, orange zest and
juice. Season to taste with salt and pepper.

preparation 5 minutes   *Serves 8*

BALSAMIC

2 tbsp balsamic vinegar
4 tbsp extra virgin olive oil
salt and ground black pepper

1   Whisk the vinegar and oil in a bowl. Season
with salt and pepper to taste.

preparation 5 minutes   *Serves 6*

MUSTARD

1 tbsp wholegrain mustard
juice of ½ lemon
6 tbsp extra virgin olive oil
salt and ground black pepper

1   Whisk the mustard, lemon juice and oil in a
bowl. Season to taste with salt and pepper.

preparation 5 minutes   *Serves 8*

SWEET CHILLI

2 tbsp Thai fish sauce
juice of 1 lime
1 tbsp sweet chilli sauce

1   In a small bowl, whisk all the ingredients
together until well blended.

preparation 3 minutes   *Serves 4*

FRENCH

1 tsp Dijon mustard
a pinch of sugar
1 tbsp red or white wine vinegar
6 tbsp extra virgin olive oil
salt and ground black pepper

1 Whisk the mustard, sugar, vinegar and
   seasoning in a bowl. Gradually whisk in the
   oil until thoroughly combined.

preparation 5 minutes   *Serves 6*

MINTY YOGURT

150g/5oz/⅔ cup Greek yogurt
3–4 tbsp chopped fresh mint leaves
2 tbsp extra virgin olive oil
salt and ground black pepper

1 Mix the yogurt with the mint and oil. Season
   to taste and stir to combine.

preparation 5 minutes   *Serves 8*

BLUE CHEESE

50g/2oz blue cheese, crumbled
2 tbsp cider vinegar
6 tbsp walnut oil
squeeze of lemon juice
salt and ground black pepper

1 Blitz all the ingredients together in a
   blender until creamy and smooth.

preparation 5 minutes   *Serves 6*

CAESAR

1 medium (US large) egg
1 garlic clove
juice of ½ lemon
2 tsp Dijon mustard,
1 tsp balsamic vinegar
150ml/¼ pint/scant ⅔ cup sunflower oil
salt and ground black pepper

1 Blitz the egg, garlic, lemon juice, mustard
   and vinegar in a blender until smooth. With
   the motor running, gradually add the oil
   and blitz until smooth. Season with salt and
   pepper. Cover and chill for up to three days.

preparation 5 minutes   *Serves 6*

THAI

2 tbsp Thai fish sauce
1 tbsp light soy sauce
2 tbsp groundnut oil
juice of 1 lime
a pinch of caster sugar
2 tbsp chopped fresh mint

1 Mix together all the ingredients in a small
   bowl until well blended.

preparation 5 minutes   *Serves 4*

INDEX

A

almond macaroons 439
almond paste 588
amaretti 435
American roast beef hash 486
American-style pancakes 39
apple compote 121
apple crumble 442
apple pie 470
apricot glaze 588
apricot muffins 553
artichoke and mozzarella salad 166
asparagus and minty rice salad 300
asparagus and quail's egg salad 298
asparagus risotto 112
aubergine linguine 98
autumn fruit crumble 445
avocado BLT 34
avocado, clementine and chicory salad 302

B

bacon and anchovy Caesar salad 48
bacon and avocado salad 49
bacon, chilli and herb pasta 141
Bajan grilled steaks 350
baked Alaska 452
baked apples 444
baked beetroot 244
baked eggs and beans 107
baked eggs with mushrooms and spinach 32
baked stuffed pumpkin 287
balsamic-glazed scallops 275
banana bread 421
banana caramel cake 424
banoffee pie 475
barbecue banoffee 380
barbecued figs with honey 380
basil and lemon chicken 348
BBQ red onions 364
BBQ sausages with mustard dip 350
BBQ spare ribs 353
BBQ squash 363
bean cassoulet 186
bean hotpot 202
bean and salmon salad 269
bean soup with cheese croûtes 511

bean and sunblush tomato salad 304
bean burgers 118
beef
  American roast beef hash 486
  Bajan grilled steaks 350
  beef goulash 183
  beef jambalaya 77
  beef Madras curry 184
  beef and mustard hotpot 184
  beef pilaff 183
  beef Stroganov 75
  bobotie 548
  boeuf Bourguignon 180
  boeuf en croûte 264
  cheeseburgers 218
  chilli con carne 221
  chilli steak stir-fry 221
  classic lasagne 223
  Cornish pasties 225
  cottage pie 220
  gulaschsuppe 109
  horseradish beef salad 136
  koftas with raita 137
  low-cal Bolognese 493
  low-fat chilli beef 486
  meat loaf 220
  paprika beef stew 182
  pesto steak salad 137
  quick goulash 180
  quick steak and rocket sandwiches 34
  roast rib of beef 218
  sesame beef 75
  skinny chilli 488
  spaghetti Bolognese 223
  spicy beef mince 182
  spicy Bolognese 222
  steak and 'fries' 487
  steak au poivre 134
  steak Stroganov 488
  stir-fried beef and mushrooms 76
  stir-fried chilli beef 187
  stir-fried ginger beef 135
  sweet chilli beef stir-fry 222
  Swedish meatballs 76
  Szechuan beef 77
  Thai beef noodle salad 136
beetroot and bean chilli 549
beetroot drizzle cake 538
beetroot and red cabbage salad 251
berries with chocolate sauce 406
berry freeze 121
blackberry and apple cake 424
blackberry and apple

crumble 442
BLT bagels with hollandaise sauce 37
blue cheese and redcurrant salad 302
blueberry choc muffins 538
blueberry muffins 412
blueberry traybake 422
bobotie 548
boeuf Bourguignon 180
boeuf en croûte 264
borscht 9
bouillabaisse 194, 272
boulangère potatoes 240
braised chicory 291
braised lamb shanks 192
braised red cabbage 244
brandy butter 580
bread and butter pudding 450
bread-maker oat loaf 430
broccoli and blue cheese quiche 289
broccoli, garlic and goat's cheese soup 8
broccoli and goat's cheese soup 284
brownie and strawberry kebabs 381
brownies 390, 391, 539
bruschetta 318
Brussels sprouts with chestnuts 246
bubble and squeak 242
buffalo wings and avocado dip 64
buttercream 586
butternut squash chowder 507
butternut squash soup 23

C

Cajun chicken salad 348
Cajun fish tortillas 146
calf's liver with sage and balsamic 134
Camembert melt 285
caramelized carrots 297
Caribbean chicken 73
Caribbean chicken salad 133
carrot and coriander soup 13
cauliflower cheese 234
ceviche 274
Chantilly cream 580
chargrilled vegetables 360
Cheddar griddle cakes 550
cheese and apple scones 536
cheese and chilli quesadillas 160
cheeseburgers 218
cheesecake brownies 391

cheese and courgette soup 342
cheese-topped fish pie 530
cherry clafoutis 454
cherry crêpes 454
cherry tomato risotto 113
chestnut soup 26
chicken
  Asian chicken baked potatoes 565
  basil and lemon chicken 348
  buffalo wings and avocado dip 64
  Cajun chicken salad 348
  Caribbean chicken 73
  Caribbean chicken salad 133
  chicken and artichoke pie 62
  chicken avocado wrap 36
  chicken, bean and spinach curry 68
  chicken with beans and tomatoes 176
  chicken with black-eyed beans 129
  chicken brochettes 346
  chicken and bulgur soup 28
  chicken burgers 43
  chicken cacciatore 177
  chicken Caesar salad 44
  chicken casserole 174
  chicken and chicory salad 349
  chicken chow mein 214
  chicken consommé 258
  chicken crispbakes 64
  chicken crostini 315
  chicken enchiladas 479
  chicken fajitas 128
  chicken and ham pie 210
  chicken pasta bake 546
  chicken laksa 480
  chicken and leek cheesy pasta bake 71
  chicken and leek pie 211
  chicken with mango couscous 212
  chicken and mushroom pies 210
  chicken nasi goreng 482
  chicken noodle stir-fry 178
  chicken with oyster sauce and mushrooms 216
  chicken and papaya salsa 214
  chicken and peppers 212
  chicken pilau 65
  chicken in a pot 172
  chicken Provençale 178
  chicken quesadillas 217

chicken rarebit 211
chicken salad baskets 378
chicken satay 482
chicken satay bites 312
chicken and spinach curry 124
chicken Stroganov 260
chicken tagine 175
chicken tikka masala 215
chicken tikka pittas 127
chicken traybake 487
chicken and vegetable gratin 62
chicken and vegetable broth 25
chicken with wine and capers 261
chilli chicken goujons 314
cock-a-leekie soup 208
coconut chicken noodles 70
coq au vin 172
creamy chicken pasta 74
creamy chicken soup 27
easy chicken noodle stir-fry 70
fiery mango chicken 127
fried chicken 206
fruity chicken skewers 312
garlic chicken thighs 347
Greek roast chicken 256
griddled chicken with red pesto 213
griddledchilli chicken 216
grilled chicken with bulgur wheat 74
griddled chicken fajitas 480
grilled chicken Waldorf 129
grilled spicy chicken 128
honey-mustard chicken salad 46
Indonesian chicken 73
Italian stuffed chicken breasts 60
jerk chicken 124
lemon chicken 126
lemon roast chicken 213
Lebanese chicken 259
Malay peanut chicken 260
Mexican chicken salad 132
Moroccan chicken with chickpeas 66
orange tarragon chicken 72
oriental chicken wings 42
pesto roast chicken 206
piri-piri chicken pieces 42
poached chicken and nectarine salad 483

pot-roasted chicken 526
quick chicken and vegetable hotpot 179
red Thai chicken curry 484
roast chicken with fruit and couscous 174
roast chicken with herbs 256
roast chicken traybake 209
skinny Caesar salad 484
Spanish chicken 179
Spanish chorizo chicken 177
spiced chicken with beans 130
spiced chicken kebabs 347
spicy chicken broth 25
spicy chicken noodle soup 71
spicy chicken with quinoa 65
sticky buffalo wings 346
sticky chicken thighs 66
stuffed chicken thighs 60
summer chicken 478
tandoori chicken 68
tandoori chicken with carrot raita 215
tandoori chicken pittas 43
tarragon chicken 175
tarragon chicken burger 208
Teochew-style chicken 526
Tex-Mex wraps 314
Thai chicken curry 72
Thai chicken noodle soup 26
Thai green chicken curry 130
Thai lemon chicken 479
Thai red chicken curry 176
warm chicken liver salad 47
warm chicken salad 259
warm lentil and chicken salad 47
yogurt spiced chicken 478
chickpea and coriander cakes 40
chickpea soup with hummus 506
chickpea soup with pasta and pesto 102
chickpea and spinach pilaff 236
chickpeas with spinach 162
chicory, fennel and orange salad 300
chicory, ham and walnut salad 49
chilled asparagus soup 342

chilled beetroot and apple soup 343
chilled cucumber and mint soup 340
chilled tomato soup 341
chilled vichyssoise 341
chilli chicken goujons 314
chilli con carne 221
chilli crab noodles 143
chilli prawns 356
chilli steak stir-fry 221
chilli tofu stir-fry 160
choc chip biscotti 396
choc chip cookies 396
choca mocha mousse 400
chocolate almond cookies 556
chocolate almond refrigerator cake 394
chocolate berry smoothie 409
chocolate brioche pudding 399
chocolate cupcakes 393
chocolate fondants 400
chocolate fudge 404
chocolate ganache 588
chocolate marble 408
chocolate muffins 393
chocolate roulade 398
chocolate tart 402
chocolate truffles 404
Christmas cookies 437
cinnamon crêpes 457
cinnamon pancakes 560
citrus cod and broccoli 195
clams with chilli spaghetti 93
clementine jelly shots 325
coconut chicken noodles 70
coconut raspberry buns 419
cod and coconut pilau 85
cod fillets with cheese crust 82
cod goujons 504
cod with lentils and butternut squash 82
colcannon 243
coleslaw 248
coq au vin 172
coriander naan breads 540
corn with chilli butter 362
cornbread 429
Cornish pasties 225
cottage pie 220
courgette and bean soup 24
courgette and leek soup 14
crab croustades 322
crab salad 281
crabcakes with chilli mayo 278
cranberry cooler 327
cream of parsley soup 19

cream of watercress soup 22
creamed spinach 292
creamy celeriac soup 285
creamy celery soup 21
creamy chicken pasta 74
creamy chicken soup 27
creamy chilled risotto 453
creamy leeks 246
crème brulée 459
crème pâtissière 579
crispy duck 262
curried coconut rice 114
curried parsnip soup 15
curried smoked haddock salad 152
curried tofu burgers 108

D
desserts
  apple crumble 442
  apple pie 470
  autumn fruit crumble 445
  baked Alaska 452
  baked apples 444
  banoffee pie 475
  barbecue banoffee 380
  barbecued figs with honey 380
  berries with white chocolate sauce 406
  blackberry and apple crumble 442
  bread and butter pudding 450
  brownie and strawberry kebabs 381
  cheat's summer berry sorbet 535
  cherry clafoutis 454
  cherry crêpes 454
  choca mocha mousse 400
  chocolate brioche pudding 399
  chocolate fondants 400
  chocolate roulade 398
  chocolate tart 402
  cinnamon crêpes 457
  clementine jellies 467
  creamy chilled risotto 453
  crème brûlée 459
  easy baked apricots 446
  easy peach brûlée 458
  Eton mess 464
  freeform fruit tarts 534
  fruity yogurt pots 461
  gooseberry fool 462
  Greek grilled figs 463
  Knickerbocker glory 468
  lemon pots 461
  lemon sorbet 468
  low-cal chocolate espresso mousse 516
  low-fat tiramisu 517

mallow melts 403
meringues 466
mini chocolate puddings 399
orange pain perdu 451
orange panna cotta 458
orchard pudding 552
pain perdu 457
panettone pudding 451
passion fruit compote 536
peach filo baskets 514
pear and cranberry strudel 470
plum cobbler 444
plum frangipane tart 535
queen of puddings 452
quick apple tart 475
quick chocolate pots 403
raspberry and lemon curd cheesecake 465
raspberry rice pudding 453
red fruit refresher 534
rice pudding 450
roasted summer fruit 447
sherry trifle 462
skinny fruit crumble 514
spiced fruit kebabs 447
spiced plum pie 474
spicy poached pears 445
sticky toffee puddings 448
strawberry brûlée 459
strawberry ice cream 469
strawberry Prosecco jellies 467
summer fruit compote 446
summer pudding 464
syllabub 460
syrup sponge pudding 448
tarte tatin 473
tiramisu 463
traditional crêpes 456
treacle tart 472
waffles 456
warm plum toasts with mascarpone 381
winter pavlova 516
zabaglione 460
devils on horseback 310
dips 168–169
dressed crab 278
dressings 476–477
drinks 306–307, 324, 326–335, 382–385, 408–409
drop scones 434
duck and mango salad 46
dumplings 571

E
easy baked apricots 446
easy beef pasta bake 100
easy fried rice 164

easy fruit cake 420
easy peach brûlée 458
easy turkey curry 217
Eccles cakes 414
egg fu yung 199
egg nog 307
egg and prosciutto salad 513
eggs Benedict 31
eggs mayonnaise 31
eggs and mushrooms on toast 37
energy muesli 120
Eton mess 464

F
falafel pittas 45
farmhouse bread 540
fennel au gratin 296
feta and avocado salad 304
fettuccine carbonara 236
fiery mango chicken 127
fig and prosciutto salad 268
fish
  balsamic-glazed scallops 275
  bean and salmon salad 269
  bouillabaisse 193, 272
  Cajun fish tortillas 146
  ceviche 274
  cheese-topped fish pie 530
  chilli crab noodles 143
  chilli prawns 356
  citrus cod and broccoli 195
  clams with chilli spaghetti 93
  cod and coconut pilau 85
  cod fillets with cheese crust 82
  cod goujons 504
  cod with lentils and butternut squash 82
  crab croustades 322
  crab salad 281
  crabcakes with chilli mayo 278
  curried smoked haddock salad 152
  dressed crab 278
  fish goujons 320
  fish pie 502
  fresh oysters 323
  fresh tuna salad Niçoise 51
  fried Dover sole 280
  griddled fish with lentils 504
  griddled sardines and vegetables 354
  grilled sardines 283
  herring, potato and dill

salad 53
Kerala fish curry 84
lemon tuna kebabs 352
linguine alle vongole 94
lobster thermidor 276
mackerel fish cakes 530
Majorcan paella 498
melon and prawn salad 268
Mexican swordfish 352
monkfish and Parma ham brochettes 501
moules marinière 276
mussels with pesto 496
pan-seared cod 503
penne with creamy smoked salmon 154
pissaladière 354
poached salmon 322
Portuguese cod 502
potted prawn pâté 270
prawn, chilli and rocket linguine 494
prawn gumbo 196
prawn noodle salad 151
prawn and peanut noodles 90
prawn pilaff 88
prawn poppadoms 321
quick fish and chips 232
roasted salmon, pea and tomato salad 88
salade Niçoise 50
salmon and broccoli crisp 501
salmon and coconut curry 144
salmon crêpes 548
salmon laksa 282
salmon with lemon oat crust 500
salmon linguine 86
salmon and pea risotto 528
salmon pilau 196
salmon and potato salad 87
sardine and olive pasta 97
scallop and bacon salad 496
scallops with rocket pesto 275
scampi Provençale 277
scrambled eggs with smoked salmon 33
sea bass with orange sauce 281
seafood cocktail 272
seafood fritto misto 280
seafood gumbo 91
seafood kebabs 358
seafood paella 112
seafood and pasta salad 93

shellfish curry 277
smoked haddock chowder 10
smoked haddock kedgeree 232
smoked mackerel citrus salad 52
smoked mackerel and grapefruit salad 52
smoked mackerel pâté 271
smoked mackerel salad 51
smoked salmon blinis 318
smoked salmon pasta 86
smoked trout and tomato toasts 271
spaghetti with anchovies and tomatoes 94
Spanish fish casserole 195
Spanish fried squid 274
speedy fish soup 153
spicy kale and anchovy pasta 99
spicy lime prawns 356
spicy prawn noodle salad 153
spicy rollmop salad 151
stir-fried prawns 198
stir-fried salmon 85
stir-fried salmon and broccoli 148
stir-fried scallops 198
sweet chilli prawns 320
sweetcorn and cod chowder 92
taramasalata 169
teriyaki salmon 148
Thai crabcakes 498
Thai curried mussels 143
Thai green curry prawn salad 152
Thai green seafood curry 197
Thai monkfish curry 528
Thai prawn curry 497
Thai prawn skewers 497
Thai red fish curry 146
traditional kippers 154
trout with almonds 282
trout with apple and beetroot salad 270
tuna and feta salad 150
tuna melt pizza 149
tuna and sesame noodles 84
tuna steaks with pak choi 149
warm tuna salad 500
yellow bean noodles with prawns 90
Florentines 397
French onion soup 10

French toast 33
fried chicken 206
fried Dover sole 280
frostings 586–588
fruit crostini 120
fruit and nut cookies 436
fruit salad 121
fruit scones 432
fruity chicken skewers 312
fruity chickpea and barley salad 56
fruity ginger teabread 421
fruity flapjacks 439
fruity Parmesan salad 303
fruity yogurt pots 461

G
gammon and potato stacks 492
garlic chicken thighs 347
gazpacho 338
gift chocolates 406
ginger cookies 437
ginger pork with rice 81
glazed ham 266
gnocchi 103, 159
goat's cheese platter 372
goat's cheese and radicchio salad 301
goat's cheese and roasted pepper tart 532
goat's cheese and tomato tart 106
gooseberry fool 462
goulash 180, 183, 490
goulash soup 490
grated carrot and beetroot salad 250
gratin Dauphinois 294
gravy 569
Greek bean and feta salad 366
Greek grilled figs 463
Greek pasta salad 56
Greek roast chicken 256
green beans and almonds 289
green cabbage with crème fraîche 292
griddled chicken with red pesto 213
griddled chilli chicken 216
griddled fish with lentils 504
griddled lamb steaks 349
grilled chicken with bulgur wheat 74
grilled chicken Waldorf 129
grilled mushrooms 363
grilled sardines 283
grilled spicy chicken 128
grilled sweet potatoes 367
guacamole 169
gulaschsuppe 109

H
halloumi and avocado salad 54
halloumi Greek salad 512
halloumi stacks 40
homemade mixed beans on toast 36
herb and pasta soup 21
herby potato farls 428
herring, potato and dill salad 53
honey-glazed shallots 291
honey-mustard chicken salad 46
horiatiki 378
horseradish beef salad 136
hot-and-sour soup 24
hot-and-sour turkey soup 28
hummus 169
huevos rancheros 199
Hungarian pork goulash 490

I
ice cream 469
iced coffee 333
iced fairy cakes 418
iced red pepper soup 340
icings 586–588
ice pops 541
Indonesian chicken 73
insalata caprese 368
Irish stew 225
Italian stuffed chicken breasts 60
Italian stuffed pork fillet 493

J
jambalaya 117
jelly 467
jerk chicken 124
Jerusalem artichoke soup 15

K
Kerala fish curry 84
kickstart 120
kippers 154
knickerbocker glory 468
koftas with raita 137

L
lamb
  braised lamb shanks 192
  griddled lamb steaks 349
  Irish stew 225
  lamb and coconut curry 81
  lamb with fried potatoes 79
  lamb and lentil curry 190
  lamb pasanda 191
  lamb rogan josh 524
  Parmesan-crumbed lamb cutlets 79
  pastitsio 546
  roast lamb and pasta 78
  roast leg of lamb 224
  Scotch broth 41
  spring lamb and bean salad 102
  stifado 191
  Thai red lamb curry 190
Lancashire hotpot 224
lasagne 223
last-minute stir-fry 165
Lebanese chicken 259
leek and Gorgonzola risotto 110
leek and kale soup 17
leek and potato soup 12
lemon chicken 126
lemon and lime tart 558
lemon polenta cake 426
lemon pots 461
lemon roast chicken 213
lemon sorbet 468
lemon sugar muffins 412
lemon syrup cake 426
lemon tuile biscuits 435
lemon tuna kebabs 352
lentil and bacon soup 9
lentil bake 200
lentil chilli 117
lentil and coconut soup 25
lentil and halloumi bake 202
lentil and squash soup 522
lettuce and garden herb soup 524
lettuce soup 23
linguine alle vongole 94
liver and onions 226
liver Stroganov 192
lobster thermidor 276
low-cal Bolognese 493
low-fat chilli beef 486
low-cal chocolate espresso mousse 516

M
macaroni cheese 235
mackerel fish cakes 530
Madeira cake 422
madeleines 416
Majorcan paella 498
Malay peanut chicken 260
mallow melts 403
marinades 386–387
mayonnaise 576
meat loaf 329
melon and chorizo salad 269
melon and mango salad 370
melon, mint and crispy ham 266
melon and prawn salad 268
meringues 466

Mexican chicken salad 132
Mexican swordfish 352
minestrone with pesto 16
mini carrot cakes 554
mini chocolate puddings 399
mixed bean salad 57, 368
moist orange cake 423
monkfish and Parma ham brochettes 501
Moroccan carrot salad 377
Moroccan chicken with chickpeas 66
moules marinière 276
mozzarella bites 316
mozzarella mushrooms 41
mozzarella, prosciutto and rocket pizza 118
mushroom, bacon and leek risotto 111
mushroom frittata 106
mushroom and ham fusilli 139
mushroom and halloumi kebabs 167
mushroom and miso soup 20
mushroom spaghetti 156
mussels 144, 276, 286
mussels with pesto 496
mustardy potato salad 249

N
neeps and tatties 243
new potatoes with mint and petits pois 296
nutty white chocolate brownies 390
nutty yogurt 120

O
oatmeal soda bread 430
omelette 167
omelette Arnold Bennett 104
onion soup 508
orange drizzle cake 428
orange pain perdu 451
orange panna cotta 458
orange shortbread 556
orange tarragon chicken 72
orchard pudding 552
oriental chicken wings 42
osso buco 186
oven chips 241
oven-baked spinach rice 113
oven scones 432
oysters 323

P
pad Thai 144, 549
paella 112, 194, 498
pain perdu 451, 457

pan-seared cod 503
pancakes 39, 561
paneer curry 109
panettone pudding 451
paprika beef stew 182
Parma ham, rocket and Parmesan salad 48
Parmesan potato and sausage kebabs 351
prosciutto melone 311
Parmesan-crumbed lamb cutlets 79
Parmesan puffs 310
parsnip soup with spicy chorizo 12
party eggs Benedict 317
party rolls 316
passion fruit compote 536
pasta and avocado salad 159
pasta with courgettes 290
pasta with pesto, potatoes and beans 157
pasta with roasted cherry tomato sauce 511
pasta and salami salad 135
pasta shells with cheese and tomatoes 290
pasta shells with leeks and mushrooms 99
pasta shells with spinach and ricotta 100
pasta with spicy sausagemeat 141
pasta with tomatoes, courgettes and pesto 158
pastitsio 546
pastrami pasta vinaigrette 101
pastry 582–585
pâtés 270, 271
pavlova 516
pea and ham soup 228
pea, mint and ricotta pasta 157
pea and rocket salad 250
peach filo baskets 514
pear, blue cheese and walnut Caesar salad 54
pear and cranberry strudel 470
Pecorino cheese straws 550
Peking duck 262
penne with creamy smoked salmon 154
penne and tuna 97
peperonata 360
pesto 574
pesto beanburgers 510
pesto goat's cheese salad 298
pesto pepper croûtes 321
pesto risotto with mussels 286

pesto roast chicken 206
pesto steak salad 137
petits pois à la française 293
pink grapefruit and avocado salad 305
piperade 30
pissaladière 354
pizza 118, 149, 585
plum cobbler 444
plum frangipane tart 535
plum traybake 423
poached chicken and nectarine salad 483
poached salmon 322
pork
    BBQ spare ribs 353
    gammon and potato stacks 492
    ginger pork with rice 81
    Hungarian pork goulash 490
    Italian stuffed pork fillet 493
    pork with cheese and cider 187
    pork with black bean sauce 80
    pork and garlic risotto 80
    pork noodle soup 142
    pork with tapenade 351
    pork Wiener schnitzel 138
    pork vindaloo 188
    roast pork with apple sauce 229
    Spanish pork and beans 492
    spiced pork chops with apple mash 228
    stir-fried pork with mango 139
    stuffed pork tenderloins 226
    sweet-and-sour pork 138
porridge 120
Portobello burgers 166
Portuguese cod 502
pot-roasted chicken 526
potato and chickpea curry 115
potato croquettes 294
potato salad 370
potatoes 562, 565
potted prawn pâté 270
prawn, chilli and rocket linguine 494
prawn gumbo 196
prawn noodle salad 151
prawn and peanut noodles 90
prawn pilaff 88
prawn poppadoms 321
prosciutto melone 311

Q
queen of puddings 452
quesadillas 160, 217
quiche 235
quick apple tart 475
quick bouillabaisse 194
quick chocolate pots 403
quick croque 121
quick curry 165
quick fish and chips 232
quick goulash 180
quick Mediterranean tart 510

R
raspberry coulis 581
raspberry drizzle cakes 560
raspberry and lemon curd cheesecake 465
raspberry muffins 517
raspberry rice pudding 453
raspberry ripple 382
ratatouille 338
red cabbage 244, 245
red fruit refresher 534
red onion bouilangere potatoes 288
red Thai chicken curry 484
ricotta spinach noodles 156
risotto Milanese 110
roast chicken with fruit and couscous 174
roast chicken with herbs 256
roast chicken traybake 209
roast lamb with boulangère potatoes 288
roast lamb and pasta 78
roast leg of lamb 224
roast parsnips 242
roast pork with apple sauce 229
roast potatoes 241, 293
roast rib of beef 218
roasted peppers with balsamic salsa 371
roasted salmon, pea and tomato salad 88
roasted summer fruit 447
roasted tomato bulgur salad 362
roasted vegetable soup 343
roasted vegetables with mustard mayonnaise 374
rock cakes 416

S
Sachertorte 392
salad dressings 574, 592–593
salads
    artichoke and mozzarella salad 166
    asparagus and minty rice salad 300
    asparagus and quail's egg salad 298
    avocado, clementine and chicory salad 302
    bacon and anchovy Caesar salad 48
    Cajun chicken salad 348
    bacon and avocado salad 49
    bean and salmon salad 269
    bean and sunblush tomato salad 304
    beetroot and red cabbage salad 251
    blue cheese and redcurrant salad 302
    Caribbean chicken salad 133
    chicken Caesar salad 44
    chicken and chicory salad 349
    chicken salad baskets 378
    chicory, fennel and orange salad 300
    chicory, ham and walnut salad 49
    crab salad 281
    curried smoked haddock salad 152
    duck and mango salad 46
    egg and prosciutto salad 513
    feta and avocado salad 304
    fig and prosciutto salad 268
    fresh tuna salad Niçoise 51
    fruity chickpea and barley salad 56
    fruity Parmesan salad 303
    goat's cheese and radicchio salad 301
    grated carrot and beetroot salad 250
    Greek bean and feta salad 366
    Greek pasta salad 56
    grilled chicken Waldorf 129
    halloumi and avocado salad 54
    halloumi Greek salad 512
    healthy chicken salad 132
    herring, potato and dill salad 53
    honey-mustard chicken salad 46
    horiatiki 378
    horseradish beef salad 136
    insalata caprese 368